2012

the best campsites
in **Britain & Ireland**

over 600 independent reviews

alan rogers publishing

experts in camping for over 40 years

Compiled by: Alan Rogers Guides Ltd

Designed by: Vine Design Ltd

Additional photography: T Lambelin, www.lambelin.com
Maps created by Customised Mapping (01769 540044)
contain background data provided by GisDATA Ltd

Maps are © Alan Rogers Guides and GisDATA Ltd 2011

© Alan Rogers Guides Ltd 2011

Published by: Alan Rogers Guides Ltd,
Spelmonden Old Oast, Goudhurst, Kent TN17 1HE
www.alanrogers.com Tel: 01580 214000

British Library Cataloguing-in-Publication Data:
A catalogue record for this book is available
from the British Library.

ISBN 978-1-906215-77-4

Printed in Great Britain by Stephens & George Print Group

Contents

Alan Rogers - in search of 'the best'

Alan Rogers Guides were first published over 40 years ago. Since Alan Rogers published the first campsite guide that bore his name, the range has expanded and now covers 27 countries in six separate guides. No fewer than 20 of the campsites selected by Alan for the first guide are still featured in our 2012 editions.

There are well over 5,000 camping and caravanning parks in Britain and Ireland of varying quality: this guide contains impartially written reports on almost 600, including many of the very finest, each being individually inspected and selected. We aim to provide you with a selection of the best, rather than information on all – in short, a more selective, qualitative approach. New, improved maps and indexes are also included, designed to help you find the choice of campsite that's right for you.

We hope you enjoy some happy and safe travels – and some pleasurable 'armchair touring' in the meantime!

" ...the campsites included in this book have been chosen entirely on merit, and no payment of any sort is made by them for their inclusion."

Alan Rogers, 1968

How do we find the best?

The criteria we use when inspecting and selecting campsites are numerous, but the most important by far is the question of good quality. People want different things from their choice of site so we try to include a range of campsite 'styles' to cater for a wide variety of preferences: from those seeking a small peaceful park in the heart of the countryside, to visitors looking for an 'all singing, all dancing' park in a popular seaside resort. Those with more specific interests, such as sporting facilities, cultural events or historical attractions, are also catered for.

The size of the park, whether it's part of a chain or privately owned, makes no difference in terms of it being required to meet our exacting standards in respect of its quality and it being 'fit for purpose'. In other words, irrespective of the size of the park, or the number of facilities it offers, we consider and evaluate the welcome, the pitches, the sanitary facilities, the cleanliness, the general maintenance and even the location.

Expert opinions

We rely on our dedicated team of Site Assessors, all of whom are experienced campers, caravanners or motorcaravanners, to visit and recommend campsites. Each year they travel some 100,000 miles around Europe inspecting new campsites for the guide and re-inspecting the existing ones. Our thanks are due to them for their enthusiastic efforts, their diligence and integrity.

We also appreciate the feedback we receive from many of our readers and we always make a point of following up complaints, suggestions or recommendations for possible new campsites. Of course we get a few grumbles too – but it really is a few, and those we do receive usually relate to overcrowding or to poor maintenance during the peak school holiday period. Please bear in mind that, although we are interested to hear about any complaints, we have no contractual relationship with the campsites featured in our guides and are therefore not in a position to intervene in any dispute between a reader and a campsite.

Independent and honest

Whilst the content and scope of the Alan Rogers guides have expanded considerably since the early editions, our selection of campsites still employs exactly the same philosophy and criteria as defined by Alan Rogers in 1968.

'telling it how it is'

Firstly, and most importantly, our selection is based entirely on our own rigorous and independent inspection and selection process. Campsites cannot buy their way into our guides – indeed the extensive Site Report which is written by us, not by the site owner, is provided free of charge so we are free to say what we think and to provide an honest, 'warts and all' description. This is written in plain English and without the use of confusing icons or symbols.

Looking for the best

Highly respected by site owners and readers alike, there is no better guide when it comes to forming an independent view of a campsite's quality. When you need to be confident in your choice of campsite, you need the Alan Rogers Guide.

- Parks only included on merit
- Parks cannot pay to be included
- Independently inspected, rigorously assessed
- Impartial reviews
- Over 40 years of expertise

Written in plain English, our guides are exceptionally easy to use, but a few words of explanation regarding the layout and content may be helpful. For England we have used official tourist board regions and the counties within them. For Wales, Scotland and Ireland (North and South) we use the counties.

Index town

Park name
Postal address (including county) T: telephone number. E: email address
alanrogers.com web address (including Alan Rogers reference number)

A description of the park in which we try to give an idea of its general features – its size, its situation, its strengths and its weaknesses. This section should provide a picture of the park itself with reference to the facilities that are provided and if they impact on its appearance or character. We include details on pitch numbers, electricity (with amperage), hardstandings etc. in this section as pitch design, planning and terracing affect the park's overall appearance. Similarly, we include reference to pitches used for caravan holiday homes, chalets, and the like. Importantly at the end of this column we indicate if there are any restrictions, e.g. no tents, no children, naturist sites.

Facilities	Directions
Lists more specific information on the park's facilities and amenities and, where available, the dates when these facilities are open (if not for the whole season). Off site: here we give distances to various local amenities, for example, local shops, the nearest beach, plus our featured activities (bicycle hire, fishing, horse riding, boat launching). Where we have space we list suggestions for activities and local tourist attractions.	Separated from the main text in order that they may be read and assimilated more easily by a navigator en-route. Bear in mind that road improvement schemes can result in road numbers being altered. GPS: references are provided in decimal format. All latitudes are North. Longitudes are East unless preceeded by a minus sign e.g. 48.71695 is North, 0.31254 is East and -0.31254 is West.
Open: Park opening dates.	Charges 2012 (or a general guide)

Maps, campsite listings and indexes

For this 2012 guide we have changed the way in which we list our featured campsites and also the way in which we help you locate the parks within each region.

We now include a map immediately after our Introduction to that region. These maps show the towns near which one or more of our featured parks are located.

Within each regional section of the guide, we list these towns and the park(s) in that vicinity in alphabetical order.

You will certainly need more detailed maps for navigation, for example the Ordnance Survey road atlas. We provide G.P.S. coordinates for each park to assist you. Our three indexes will also help you to find a park by its reference number and name, by region and park name, or by the town where the park is situated.

Understanding the entries

Facilities

Toilet blocks

We assume that toilet blocks will be equipped with WCs, washbasins with hot and cold water and hot showers with dividers or curtains, and will have all necessary shelves, hooks, plugs and mirrors. We also assume that there will be an identified chemical toilet disposal point, and that the campsite will provide water and waste water drainage points and bin areas. If not the case, we comment. We do mention certain features that some readers find important: washbasins in cubicles, facilities for babies, facilities for those with disabilities and motorcaravan service points. Readers with disabilities are advised to contact the site of their choice to ensure that facilities are appropriate to their needs.

Shop

Basic or fully supplied, and opening dates.

Bars, restaurants, takeaway facilities and entertainment

We try hard to supply opening and closing dates (if other than the campsite opening dates) and to identify if there are discos or other entertainment.

Children's play areas

Fenced and with safety surface (e.g. sand, bark or pea-gravel).

Swimming pools

If particularly special, we cover in detail in our main campsite description but reference is always included under our Facilities listings. We will also indicate the existence of water slides, sunbathing areas and other features. Opening dates, charges and levels of supervision are provided where we have been notified.

Leisure facilities

For example, playing fields, bicycle hire, organised activities and entertainment.

Dogs

If dogs are not accepted or restrictions apply, we state it here. Check the quick reference list at the back of the guide.

Off site

This briefly covers leisure facilities, tourist attractions, restaurants etc. nearby.

Charges

These are the latest provided to us by the parks. In those cases where 2012 prices have not been provided to us by the parks, we try to give a general guide.

Opening dates

These are advised to us during the early autumn of the previous year – parks can, and sometimes do, alter these dates before the start of the following season, often for good reasons. If you intend to visit shortly after a published opening date, or shortly before the closing date, it is wise to check that it will actually be open at the time required. Similarly some parks operate a restricted service during the low season, only opening some of their facilities (e.g. swimming pools) during the main season; where we know about this, and have the relevant dates, we indicate it – again if you are at all doubtful it is wise to check.

Sometimes, campsite amenities may be dependant on there being enough customers on site to justify their opening and, for this reason, actual opening dates may vary from those indicated.

Special pitches

We note an ever increasing number of 'special' pitches under a variety of fancy names (for example, Executive, Panorama, Super). These provide a range of extra facilities such as waste water disposal, TV and phone connections, hardstanding, patios, etc. and they are often booked up well in advance. Readers interested in such pitches should contact the park concerned to check exactly what is provided. People with disabilities are also advised to telephone before turning up to ensure that facilities are appropriate to their particular needs.

You're on your way!

Whether you're an 'old hand' in terms of camping and caravanning or are contemplating your first trip, a regular reader of our Guides or a new 'convert', we wish you well in your travels and hope we have been able to help in some way.

We are, of course, also out and about ourselves, visiting parks, talking to owners and readers, and generally checking on standards and new developments.

Our Holiday Home section

326 Over recent years, more and more parks in Britain and Ireland have added high quality holiday home accommodation in the form of caravan holiday homes, chalets and lodges. In response to feedback from many of our readers, and to reflect this evolution in campsites, we have decided to introduce a separate section on caravan holiday homes and chalets (see page 326). If a park has decided to contribute to this section, it is indicated above our site report in the main body of the guide with a page reference where the full details are given. We feature parks offering some of the best accommodation available and have included full details of one or two accommodation types at these parks.

Please note however that many other campsites listed in this guide may also have a selection of accommodation for rent.

We wish all our readers thoroughly enjoyable Camping and Caravanning in 2012 – favoured by good weather of course!

The Alan Rogers Team

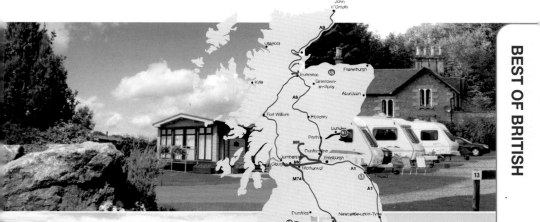

As the world's oldest club at 110 years old, The Camping and Caravanning Club is the perfect choice for a memorable holiday, however you choose to camp.

The Club boasts over half a million members, whilst offering over 4,000 places to camp across the UK and is proud to have over 100 award-winning Club Sites, giving both members and non-members the chance to experience the beauty of the great outdoors.

A selection of Club Sites offer a range of Self-Catering Holidays as an alternative to pitching. For those who fancy a break from it all; a family reunion; are looking for a spot of adventure with friends or simply want to share a romantic view or two, then this collection of properties is ready and waiting, offering stylish luxury to basic simplicity, all set in beautiful landscapes. The collection includes Luxury Lodges, Holiday Caravans, Safari Tents, Pods, Dens and Barns.

For more information on camping with the Club or to book a site call **+44 (0)24 7647 5426** or visit **www.thefriendlyclub.co.uk**

The **Camping** and **Caravanning Club**
The Friendly Club

Map locations:

INVEREWE GARDENS
DINGWALL — NAIRN
ROSEMARKIE — SPEYSIDE
TARLAND
ABERDEEN
GLENCOE
OBAN
SCONE — DUNDEE
MILARROCHY BAY
LUSS
EDINBURGH — DUNBAR
GLASGOW
LAUDER
KILMARNOCK
AYR — JEDBURGH — BEADNELL BAY
CULZEAN CASTLE — DUNSTAN HILL
MOFFAT
BELLINGHAM
DUMFRIES
NEWCASTLE
STRANRAER — CARLISLE — HALTWHISTLE
LARNE
BELFAST
DERWENTWATER — BARNARD CASTLE
KESWICK — TROUTBECK
DELAMONT COUNTRY PARK
ESKDALE — KENDAL
RAVENGLASS — WINDERMERE — SCARBOROUGH
DOUGLAS — SLINGSBY
BOROUGHBRIDGE — SHERIFF HUTTON
YORK
BLACKPOOL — CLITHEROE — LEEDS — HULL
SOUTHPORT — CHORLEY — HUDDERSFIELD — SCUNTHORPE
LIVERPOOL — MANCHESTER — CROWDEN
HOLYHEAD — DELAMERE FOREST — HAYFIELD — SHEFFIELD
LEEK — BAKEWELL — LINCOLN — MARLETHORPE
CHESTER — TEVERSAL — WOODHALL SPA
WREXHAM — STOKE — ASHBOURNE
LLANYSTUMDWY — BALA — OSWESTRY — ALTON, THE STAR — NOTTINGHAM — BOSTON
DERBY — SANDRINGHAM — WEST RUNTON
EBURY HILL — CANNOCK CHASE — CONKERS — PETERBOROUGH — NORWICH
WOLVERHAMPTON — KINGSBURY WATER PARK
ABERYSTWYTH — WOLVERLEY — BIRMINGHAM — THETFORD FOREST — KESSINGLAND
CLENT HILLS — HUNTINGDON
St NEOTS — CAMBRIDGE — IPSWICH
CARDIGAN BAY — RHANDIRMWYN — BLACKMORE — GULLIVER'S MILTON KEYNES — POLSTEAD
St DAVIDS — HEREFORD — WINCHCOMBE — CHIPPING NORTON — COLCHESTER
SWANSEA — OXFORD — THEOBALDS PARK — HERTFORD — KELVEDON HATCH
CARDIFF — BRISTOL — LONDON
DEVIZES — CHERTSEY — WALTON-ON-THAMES
WESTON SUPER MARE — CHEDDAR — BASINGSTOKE — HORSLEY — OLDBURY HILL — CANTERBURY
LYNTON — MINEHEAD — SALISBURY — CROWBOROUGH — FOLKESTONE
UMBERLEIGH — TAUNTON — CHICHESTER — GRAFFHAM
DARTMOOR BARLEY MEADOW — VERWOOD — SLINDON
BUDE — CHARMOUTH — MORETON — NORMAN'S BAY
EXETER — CORFE CASTLE — ADGESTONE
TREGURRIAN — TAVISTOCK — TORQUAY
St IVES — VERYAN — DARTMOUTH — SLAPTON SANDS
SENNEN COVE — CALIFORNIA CROSS

Countryside Discovery is a group of family-run camping and caravan parks in peaceful countryside locations, many in Areas of Outstanding Natural Beauty. Each park will have its own individual character, but all parks in Countryside Discovery share a common theme of tranquillity. How do we know that? Because each park is inspected before it can join Countryside Discovery. The park will be small, less than 150 pitches, away from busy roads and towns, and without the disturbance of noisy entertainment or discos, to ensure you enjoy a peaceful, tranquil holiday. Countryside Discovery Parks can be found throughout the UK.

In our own words

Parks in Countryside Discovery are in tune with the natural environment with rare birds, deer, badgers and otters visiting some parks, as well as a wide array of flora and fauna. The 'greenness' of an individual park may be recognised with many parks achieving a green award. If you are feeling energetic, some parks offer a range of activities including canoeing, abseiling, climbing or caving or you could enjoy the more traditional countryside pursuits of birdwatching, fishing or walking.

To ensure you enjoy a comfortable holiday, all parks in Countryside Discovery are inspected for quality under grading schemes run by VisitScotand, Visit Britain or the AA and they may also be a member of the British Holiday & Home Parks Association. It's not just touring

caravans and tents on Countryside Discovery parks. There is a wide range of accommodation available, including caravan holiday homes, chalets, lodges, cottages, timber tents and B&B. So you should be able to find a park that suits your needs.

COUNTRYSIDE DISCOVERY

www.countryside-discovery.co.uk
Telephone for a **FREE** directory – 0870 240 6085 (9am – 7pm)

SCOTLAND
1. Muasdale Holiday Park
2. Loch Ken Holiday Park
3. Linwater Caravan Park

NORTH OF ENGLAND
4. Holme Valley Camping & Caravan Park

WALES & THE MIDLANDS
5. Afon Lodge Caravan Park
6. Barcdy Touring Caravan & Camping Park
7. Plas Gwyn Caravan Park
8. Disserth Caravan & Camping Park
9. Lucksall Caravan and Camping Park

EAST of ENGLAND
10. Manor Farm Caravan Park
11. Meadowlands Lodge Park
12. Little Lakeland Caravan Park
13. Orchard Park Touring Caravan & Camping Park

SOUTH EAST ENGLAND
14. Tanner Farm Touring Camping & Caravanning Park

SOUTH WEST ENGLAND
15. Polruan Holidays Camping & Caravanning
16. Porthtowan Tourist Park
17. Silver Sands Holiday Park
18. Summer Valley Touring Park
19. Sun Haven Valley Country Holiday Park
20. Trevalgan Holiday Farm
21. Forest Glade Holiday Park
22. Galmpton Touring Park
23. Harford Bridge Holiday Park
24. Rowlands Wait Touring Park
25. Halse Farm Caravan & Camping Park
26. Westermill Farm
27. Summerlands Caravan Park
28. Riverside Holidays

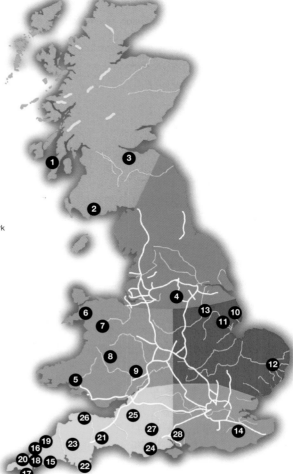

With a choice of 20 beautiful caravan and camping sites set among the woodlands of the Forestry Commission, you're sure to find your perfect pitch.

Whether it's a back to nature experience you're looking for or a range of on-site facilities, we have a site that will suit you down to the ground. Set up camp in the seclusion of the trees or on a heathland clearing; sleep under canvas in a leafy glade or by the shore of a loch or stream.

These sites make a great base for exploring the neighbourhood. From a walk in the woods to kayaking down the river and everything in between, you'll find a real choice of activities on site and in the local area.

Some of these sites have a dedicated Forest Ranger, who will share their Forest Experience with you, whether you'd like to observe the local wildlife or learn forest survival skills.

A Forest Holiday is about taking time to do the things you enjoy the most, whether that's discovering something new, getting active or simply relaxing in beautiful woodland surroundings. It's all about choice, and whatever you choose, Forest Holiday are the perfect place!

For more information about Forest Holidays or to book a site call **+44 (0)24 7642 3008** or visit **www.campingintheforest.co.uk**

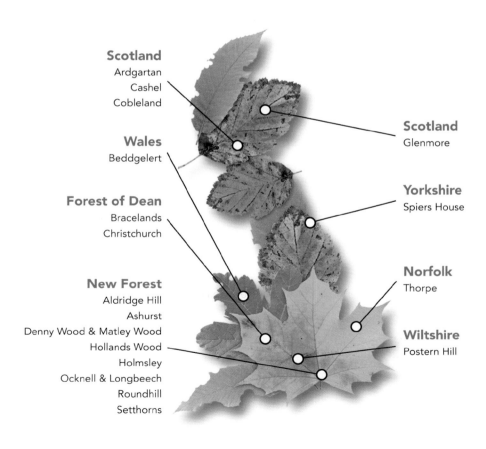

Scotland
Ardgartan
Cashel
Cobleland

Wales
Beddgelert

Forest of Dean
Bracelands
Christchurch

New Forest
Aldridge Hill
Ashurst
Denny Wood & Matley Wood
Hollands Wood
Holmsley
Ocknell & Longbeech
Roundhill
Setthorns

Scotland
Glenmore

Yorkshire
Spiers House

Norfolk
Thorpe

Wiltshire
Postern Hill

Park Resorts has a network of 24 award-winning seaside Holiday Parks that offer a wide range of touring and camping pitches. The Parks are all located close to the coast or in rolling countryside, some within easy walking distance of excellent Blue Flag beaches. There's a wide range of services and free activities, popular with families and couples alike. The majority of the Parks are located in England but there are also popular Parks in Scotland and Wales.

Park Resorts... in their own words

Choose the right Park for you

Each of our Parks is unique, with its own personality. Whether you're looking for a fun packed, active holiday or want to use the Park as a base to explore the local area, our Parks have something for everyone... the choice is yours.

You can enjoy all of these Park facilities for **FREE** during your stay:

- Super swimming pools
- Cool Kids' Clubs
- Entertainment to get your toes tapping and your hands clapping
- Sports & Water Resorts Programme for active kids and teens. Have a go at archery, Jet Racers, Surf Rescue & much more

Plus, we have a great choice of food and drink in the bars & restaurants

We've also negotiated some superb discounts and special offers at some of the top attractions and days out in the local areas around your chosen Park.

Creating Amazing Memories

Map locations: Glasgow, Edinburgh, Eyemouth, Sandylands, Newcastle, Sandy Bay, Crimdon Dene, Cayton Bay, Leeds, York, Skipsea Sands, Withernsea Sands, Liverpool, Manchester, Sunnydale, Sheffield, Southview, Manor Park, Ty Mawr, Nottingham, Leicester, Norwich, Braydon Water, Brynowen, Birmingham, Kessingland Beach, Naze Marine, Oxford, Waterside, Martello Beach, Highfield Grange, Cardiff, Bristol, London, Warden Springs, Southampton, Camber Sands, Thorness Bay, Nodes Point, Plymouth, Lower Hyde, Landguard

Making you feel right at home

Our friendly teams on the Parks will be there to welcome you at check-in and will be on hand to help you throughout your holiday. At each Holiday Park you will also find a friendly touring warden, to make your stay as enjoyable as possible.

We offer a wide selection of quality pitches from basic camping pitches to hard standing super pitches with TV connections. We also know how important facilities are to you, that's why we've invested thousands this season on your favourite Parks.

A great place to stay

The self-contained touring areas on our Holiday Parks offer a wide range of facilities to make your stay as enjoyable as possible:

- Touring warden
- Washbasins, WC's & hot showers
- Washing up area
- Fresh water collection & waste water disposal points
- Space to park your car
- Safe & secure environment
- Pets welcome
- Seasonal touring pitches

Check out our Parks and make your booking at **www.park-resorts.com/AR12**

The West Country is a diverse region of beautiful sandy beaches, steep craggy cliffs, desolate moors and rolling green hills. Home of clotted cream teas, it also boasts a range of historical and modern attractions, including the celebrated Eden Project.

THE SOUTH WEST COMPRISES: CORNWALL, DEVON, SOMERSET, BATH, BRISTOL, SOUTH GLOUCESTERSHIRE, WILTSHIRE AND WEST DORSET.

With its dramatic cliffs pounded by the Atlantic ocean, and beautiful coastline boasting warm waters, soft sandy beaches and small seaside towns, Cornwall is one of England's most popular holiday destinations. The coast is also a surfers' paradise, while inland the wild and rugged Bodmin Moors dominate the landscape. In Devon, the Dartmoor National Park has sweeping moorland and granite tors, where wild ponies roam freely. Much of the countryside is gentle, rolling, green fields, dotted with pretty thatched cottages. The coastline around Torbay is known as the English Riviera which, due to its temperate climate, allows palm trees to grow. Stretching across East Devon and West Dorset is the fossil-ridden Jurassic Coast, a World Heritage Site. West Dorset is also home to Lyme Regis and Weymouth, which comes alive in summer when regular entertainment, including a carnival and fireworks, is held along the seafront. Famous for its cider and cheese, Somerset is good walking country, with the Exmoor National Park, which also straddles Devon. Wiltshire's natural attractions include the Marlborough Downs, Savernake Forest and the River Avon. It also boasts one of the most famous prehistoric sites in the world, the ancient stone circles of Stonehenge.

Places of interest

Bath: World Heritage Site full of Roman and Georgian architecture, elegant streets such as the Circle and Royal Crescent, Roman baths.

Bristol: steeped in maritime history with the world's first great Ocean Liner; Brunel's Clifton Suspension bridge; a range of museums and art galleries.

Cornwall: seaside town of St Ives; Land's End; Eden Project; Penzance and St. Michael's Mount.

Devon: popular seaside resorts of Torquay, Paignton and Brixham; cities of Exeter and Plymouth.

Somerset: Weston-Super-Mare; Wells Cathedral; Glastonbury; Cheddar Gorge and Wookey Hole caves.

West Dorset: Dorchester, home of Thomas Hardy; Isle of Portland; Abbotsbury village, with swannery.

Wiltshire: Salisbury; Longleat stately home and safari park.

Did you know?

Chesil Beach is an 18-mile stretch of fortress-like walls of pebbles, formed 12,000 years ago.

There are numerous white horses carved into the landscape across the South West.

The Jurassic Coast is a Natural World Heritage Site stretching for 95 miles.

The black death entered England through the port of Weymouth in 1348.

Britain's oldest complete skeleton, Cheddar Man, was buried in Gough's Cave 9,000 years ago.

At 404 feet, Salisbury Cathedral has the tallest medieval spire in the world.

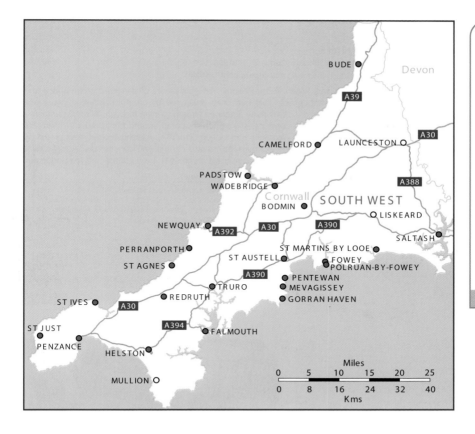

Bodmin

Mena Caravan & Camping Park

Lanivet, Bodmin PL30 5HW (Cornwall) T: 01208 831845. E: mena@campsitesincornwall.co.uk

alanrogers.com/UK0270

A family run park, tucked away in the Cornish countryside, yet close to the main routes, and open all year, a warm welcome awaits visitors. Set in 15 acres of secluded countryside with rural views, it is spacious and never crowded, offering only 25 level grass pitches on well drained, slightly sloping grass. There are 21 electricity connections (10A) and three hardstandings. Reception has facilities for hot drinks and keeps essentials, which is useful for walkers. The park is on the Land's End to John O'Groats route and gets walkers either at the beginning or end of their walk. The land includes a small fishing lake and a wooded area. Mena means 'hilltop' in the Cornish language, and the site is actually situated at the geographical centre of Cornwall, overlooked by Helman's Tor, one of the highest points on Bodmin Moor. With its position, visitors can choose between beaches on the north or south coast. Lanivet village has a shop and a pub serving meals. Children will love the chickens and two large Kune pigs.

Facilities

Four toilet and washbasin cabins are in an older wooden building. Two new showers and two toilets are behind the veranda building with laundry facilities. On the opposite side of the site is an en-suite facility for disabled visitors and a large games room with TV and a three-quarter size snooker table, and darts. Shop for basics (with gas). Hot drinks machine. Swings, etc. for children in the central grass area. Fishing lake (licence required). Two mobile homes for hire. Caravan storage. WiFi (charged). Dog kennel facilities. Off site: Riding 1.5 miles. Lanivet village with shop and pub 2 miles. Golf 3 miles. Bicycle hire 3 and 5 miles. Eden Project 4 miles. Nearest beach 8 miles.

Open: All year.

Directions

From the A30 Bodmin bypass, exit at the A30/A391 Innis Downs roundabout. Take the A389 north signed Lanivet and Bodmin. After 0.5 miles take first right (filter lane) and pass under the A30. Turn first left (Lostwithiel, Fowey) and in 0.25 miles turn right at top of hill (Celtic Cross on the left). Continue for 0.5 miles and take first right into lane and site is 100 yds. GPS: 50.430267, -4.757167

Charges guide

Per unit incl. 2 persons and electricity	£ 15.00 - £ 19.00
extra person	£ 4.00
child (3-16 yrs)	£ 1.00 - £ 2.50
dog	£ 1.00

For latest campsite news visit
alanrogers.com

Bodmin

Eden Valley Holiday Park

Lanlivery, Lostwithiel, Bodmin PL30 5BU (Cornwall) T: 01208 872277.
E: enquiries@edenvalleyholidaypark.co.uk **alanrogers.com/UK0280**

A pleasant, peaceful touring park, Eden Valley Holiday Park has plenty of sheltered green space and a natural, uncommercialised atmosphere. This has been enhanced by careful planting of trees and shrubs to form a series of linked paddocks with an unfenced stream running through. With 56 numbered touring pitches in total, each paddock contains 10-15 pitches spread around the perimeter. There are 20 hardstandings and 40 pitches have electricity connections (10/16A). Awning groundsheets must be lifted on alternate days. A separate field contains 35 private caravan holiday homes. A large, well equipped activity play area with adventure type equipment on grass is in one of the hedged paddocks.

Facilities

A smart log cabin toilet block is heated, with en-suite facilities. The more traditional block has individual cubicles. Unit for disabled visitors. Fully equipped laundry room. Motorcaravan service point. Gas supplies. Play area. TV room. Games room. Putting green. Torch useful. Off site: Riding nearby. Freshwater fishing 1.5 miles and sea fishing 3 miles. Golf 1.5 miles. Bicycle hire and beach 4 miles.

Open: Easter/1 April - 31 October.

Directions

Park approach road leads off A390 road 1.5 miles southwest of Lostwithiel. Follow white or brown camping signs. No other approach is advised. GPS: 50.40191, -4.69805

Charges guide

Per unit incl. 2 persons	
and electricity	£ 12.00 - £ 16.00
extra person	£ 2.00

No single sex groups (excl. bona fide organisations).

Bodmin

South Penquite Farm

South Penquite, Blisland, Bodmin PL30 4LH (Cornwall) T: 01208 850491. E: thefarm@bodminmoor.co.uk
alanrogers.com/UK0302

South Penquite offers real camping with no frills, set on a 200 hectare hill farm high on Bodmin Moor between the villages of Blisland and St Breward. The farm achieved organic status in 2001 and runs a flock of 300 ewes and a herd of 40 cattle and horses. The camping is small scale and intended to have a low impact on the surrounding environment. Fifty tents or simple motorcaravans (no caravans) can pitch around the edge of three walled fields, roughly cut in the midst of the moor. You can find shelter or a view. Four yurts – round Mongolian tents – are available to rent in one field, complete with wood burning stoves – quite original. Camp fires are permitted with wood available from the farmhouse.

Facilities

A smart new pine clad toilet block, with a separate provision of four family-sized showers, with solar heated rainwater. Washing machine and dryer. Small fridge and freezer. Home produced lamb, burgers and sausages available. LPG gas. Facilities for field studies and opportunities for educational groups and schools to learn about the local environment. Bushcraft days. Fishing (requires an EA rod licence and tokens available from the West Country Rivers Trust). Dogs are not accepted. Off site: Walking. Riding and cycling 1 mile. Pubs 1.5 and 2.5 miles. Sustrans Route 3 passes close by. North and south coasts within easy reach.

Open: 1 May - 1 November.

Directions

On the A30 over Bodmin Moor pass Jamaica Inn and sign for Colliford Lake and watch for St Breward sign (to right) at end of dual carriageway. Follow this narrow road for 2 miles ignoring any turns left or right. Ignore right turn to St Breward just before the South Penquite sign. Follow track over bridge beside ford through farm gate. Bear to left to camping fields. Walk back to book in at Farm House. GPS: 50.5445, -4.671833

Charges guide

Per person	£ 7.00
child (5-16 yrs)	£ 3.50

No credit cards.

For latest campsite news visit
alanrogers.com

Bodmin

Ruthern Valley Holidays

Ruthernbridge, Bodmin PL30 5LU (Cornwall) T: 01208 831395. E: camping@ruthernvalley.com

alanrogers.com/UK0306

This is a little gem of a site set in 8 acres of woodland, tucked away in a peaceful little valley not far from Bodmin. Run by Andrew and Nicola Johnson, the park was landscaped over 30 years ago with an amazing range of trees and shrubs and plenty of animal wildlife. There are 16 touring pitches informally spaced but numbered in the main, tree-lined field, six with 10A electricity, and a further 13 in smaller fields and alcove areas amongst the woods with a small stream meandering through.

Facilities

Small, fully equipped toilet block with solar heated water. Washing machines and dryer. Shop with basic provisions shared with reception (reduced hours in low season). Barbecue hire. Play area including five-a-side goal posts. Field with farm animals. Bicycle hire (delivered to site). Free WiFi. Dogs are not accepted. Off site: Fishing 2 miles. Nearest pub 3-4 miles. Riding, pony trekking and golf 4 miles. 10 miles to the coast.

Open: All year.

Directions

Approaching Bodmin from A30 or A38 turn right at first mini roundabout then anti-clockwise on inner ring road. Straight over double mini-roundabout, leaving Bodmin on A389/A391 towards St Austell. Ignore first Nanstallon - Ruthernbridge sign, after 1.5 miles, turn right. At Nanstallon village sign, turn left then filter left. Continue 1 mile into Ruthernbridge. Turn left before bridge. Site is on left in 300 yds. GPS: 50.46455, -4.8019

Charges guide

Per unit incl. 2 persons and electricity	£ 16.00 - £ 20.00
extra person (over 3 yrs)	£ 3.25 - £ 4.25

Bude

Wooda Farm Holiday Park

Poughill, Bude EX23 9HJ (Cornwall) T: 01288 352069. E: enquiries@wooda.co.uk

alanrogers.com/UK0380

Wooda Farm is spacious and well organised, with some nice touches. A quality, family run park, it is part of a working farm set within 40 acres, under two miles from the sandy, surfing beaches of Bude. In peaceful farmland with open spaces (and some up and down walking), there are marvellous views of sea and countryside. The 220 large touring pitches are spread over four meadows on level or gently sloping grass. There are 142 with electricity connections (16A), 83 hardstanding, hedged 'premier' pitches (all services) and five premier pitches with Sky TV, linked by tarmac roads. A 28 day field provides extra grass pitches for the peak season. Tractor and trailer rides, archery and clay pigeon shooting with tuition are provided according to season and demand, plus woodland and orchard walks and excellent coarse fishing. There are 55 caravan holiday homes for let. Member of the Best of British Group.

Facilities

Three well maintained toilet blocks, one heated, include a unit suitable for disabled campers, two baby rooms and five en-suite family bathrooms for hire. Two laundry rooms. Motorcaravan service point. Shop with off-licence. Courtyard bar/restaurant and takeaway. Play area. 9-hole fun golf course. Games room with TV. Tennis. Badminton. Fitness suite. Coarse fishing in 1.5-acre lake. Certain breeds of dog not accepted. Caravan storage. Internet access. WiFi. Off site: Local village inn five minutes walk.

Open: End March - end October.

Directions

Park is north of Bude at Poughill; turn off A39 on north side of Stratton on minor road for Coombe Valley, following camp signs at junctions. GPS: 50.84331, -4.51857

Charges guide

Per unit incl. 2 persons and electricity	£ 15.00 - £ 25.00
extra person	£ 4.00 - £ 6.00

Camping Cheques accepted.

LUXURY HOLIDAY HOMES - COTTAGES - SPORTS FACILITIES - FISHING - WI-FI - SANDY BEACHES

Wooda Farm Holiday Park

In the Countryside - Beside the Sea

www.wooda.co.uk   Bude - Cornwall - EX23 9HJ   Tel: 01288 352069

For latest campsite news visit

alanrogers.com

Bude

Widemouth Bay Caravan Park

Widemouth Bay, Bude EX23 0DF (Cornwall) T: 01288 361208

alanrogers.com/UK0373

Widemouth has a wonderful situation on the edge of Widemouth Bay amidst rural farmland. Covering 50 acres in total, a number of areas have mobile homes carefully fitted into the hillside. There are some 180 touring pitches on undulating meadowland at the top of the hill, with 16A electricity available and some level hardstandings. The views are magnificent. The sandy beach, just a 15 minute walk away, is very popular with bathers and surfers and the indoor heated swimming pool is a bonus. This is a big and lively park in season, very well catered for with a well stocked shop, a bar serving food and nightly entertainment for children and parents. Bude is some ten minutes away by car and Tintagel is close enough to visit if the tales of King Arthur, Merlin and the round table interest you; otherwise Port Isaac is the 'Port Wenn' of the Doc Martin TV series. A regular local bus service operates from outside the Manor Hotel, hourly in the low season and half hourly in the main season. In the main season you go to the touring field to book in with the wardens.

Facilities

Two traditional, fully equipped toilet blocks. Facilites for babies and an en-suite unit for visitors with disabilities. Launderette. Microwave. Shop, bar with food, and takeaway (limited hours). Indoor heated pool with lifeguard. Entertainment, quizzes, disco. Kids' club. Amusement arcade. Play area. Internet café/WiFi. Mini golf. Bus service. Mobile homes to rent. Off site: Tennis and riding nearby. Fishing and boat trips from Bude.

Open: 5 March - 31 October.

Directions

Using the A39 bypass Bude and after approx. 3 miles watch for right-hand turning for Widemouth Bay. Follow to beach and continue south alongside beach until road bends inland by the Manor Hotel. Lane to site on right. GPS: 50.78033, -4.5613

Charges guide

Per unit incl. 2 persons	
and electricity	£ 14.00 - £ 38.00
dog	£ 3.00

Camelford

Lakefield Caravan Park

Lower Pendavey Farm, Camelford PL32 9TX (Cornwall) T: 01840 213279.

E: enquiries@lakefieldcaravanpark.co.uk **alanrogers.com/UK0360**

Lakefield is a small, simple touring park on what was a working farm. Now the main focus is on the BHS approved equestrian centre. With only 40 pitches, it is no surprise that the owners, Maureen and Dennis Perring, know all the campers. The well spaced pitches backing onto hedges and with 24 electric hook-ups (16A) are in view of the small, fenced lake watched over by one of Cornwall's first wind farms. The whitewashed café/reception, converted from one of the old barns, is open all day between Easter and October offering traditional cream teas. Children will love the goats and 'Wabbit World'. With over 50 horses, from Shetlands to thoroughbreds, the riding school is very much part of the site, offering lessons and hacks with qualified supervision and instruction. You can even bring your own horse.

Facilities

Simple but adequate toilet block. Washing machine and dryer in the ladies' and a dishwashing sink and a laundry sink outside but under cover. Toilet for disabled visitors at riding centre. Tea room. Gas supplies (Calor). Torches may be useful. Off site: Golf 2 miles. Fishing (sea 4 miles, coarse 5 miles).

Open: 1 April - 30 September.

Directions

Follow B3266 north from Camelford. Park access is directly from this road on the left just before the turning for Tintagel, clearly signed. GPS: 50.635058, -4.687648

Charges guide

Per unit incl. 2 persons	
and electricity	£ 14.50 - £ 16.50
extra person (5 yrs and over)	£ 1.00
dog	free

For latest campsite news visit
alanrogers.com

Bude

Sandymouth Holiday Park

Sandymouth Bay, Bude EX23 9HW (Cornwall) T: 0844 272 9530. E: enquiries@sandymouthbay.co.uk

alanrogers.com/UK0375

Sandymouth is a popular family park with a good range of amenities. The beautifully maintained site is situated on the side of a valley with wonderful views but also a lot of up and down walking. Serviced pitches, 22 in all, with hardstanding are arranged either side of a tarmac roadway. A number of electric tenting pitches are to one side of a large, sloping open field where there are ten acres for camping. Pitches here are grassy and enjoy excellent views of Bude and Sandymouth. A good range of mobile homes, chalets and lodges are also available for rent. On-site amenities include an indoor pool, sauna and free membership of the Ocean Bar and Club. There is a great deal here for children – notably the Black Pearl Adventure Play area. There is a lively programme of nightly entertainment in peak season. Sandymouth beach is a 15 minute walk from the site with a National Trust car park and small café.

Facilities

Fully equipped toilet block. En-suite facilities for disabled visitors. Shop. Bar. Restaurant/snack bar. Takeaway. Ocean Bar and Club. Indoor swimming pool with slide. Sauna. Adventure playground. Soft ball area. Minigolf. Sports field. Activity and entertainment programme. Children's club. Amusement arcade. Fishing. WiFi (charged). Mobile homes, chalets and bungalows for rent. Off site: Summerleaze and Sandymouth beaches. Milky Way Adventure Park 13 miles. Clovelly 13 miles.

Open: 15 March - 26 November.

Directions

Approaching on the M5 motorway, leave at exit 27 and take the A361 and A39 towards Bideford and Bude. After passing through Kilkhampton turn right towards Stibb. Follow this road to Stibb and after the village turn left and the park is on the left. GPS: 50.866973, -4.53752

Charges guide

Per unit incl. 2 persons and electricity	£ 16.00 - £ 28.00

Falmouth

Pennance Mill Farm Chalet & Camping Park

Maenporth, Falmouth TR11 5HJ (Cornwall) T: 01326 317431. E: pennancemill@amserve.com

alanrogers.com/UK0450

Pennance Mill Farm has been in the hands of the Jewell family for three generations and is listed as a typical Cornish farmstead in an Area of Outstanding Natural Beauty. In the high season skittles, country games and barbecue evenings are organised, all in keeping with the relaxed and friendly atmosphere generated by the owners. The camping area is in four sheltered, south-facing and fairly level fields with views over the countryside and providing 75 pitches, all with 16A electricity and eight with hardstandings. Caravans are accepted but this is not a site for those who like neat manicured lawns.

Facilities

The two toilet blocks are fully equipped. Original block near the entrance is well kept with good hot water, washing machine, dryer, laundry and dishwashing sinks. The newer block in the top meadow is heated and includes dishwashing sinks. Small farm shop including some basic provisions. Gas supplies. Small play meadow with new play equipment. Off site: Tennis courts, golf course and pitch and putt within walking distance. Beach, watersports and indoor heated pool 2 miles. Riding 4 miles. Bar/restaurant/takeaway 5 miles. New Maritime Museum. Coastal footpath to the Helford River.

Open: Easter - November.

Directions

From Truro, follow signs for Falmouth on A39. At first roundabout pass Asda then turn right at next roundabout signed Industrial Estates (on Bickland Water Road), next roundabout signed Maenporth. Follow camping signs for 1.5 miles and continue down hill to site on your left as road bends right. GPS: 50.134983, -5.092667

Charges guide

Per unit incl. 2 persons and electricity	£ 23.00 - £ 26.00
extra person	£ 7.00 - £ 8.00

No credit cards.

For latest campsite news visit

alanrogers.com

Fowey

Penmarlam Caravan & Camping Park

Bodinnick-by-Fowey, Fowey PL23 1LZ (Cornwall) T: 01726 870088. E: info@penmarlampark.co.uk

alanrogers.com/UK0195

Penmarlam is situated high above the estuary opposite Fowey, close to the village of Bodinnick which is famous for being the home of Daphne du Maurier. The original field is level and sheltered with 29 pitches which are semi-divided by bushes. The newer field with 34 pitches has a slight slope, is divided with wild banks and enjoys good countryside views. Both fields have circular access roads. All pitches have 16A electricity and 14 also have water and drainage. The modern reception, shop and the toilet facilities are well situated between the two fields.

Facilities

The modern, colourful and heated toilet block is fully equipped including a baby and toddler room in the ladies' and a separate en-suite unit for disabled visitors, which doubles as a family room with baby changing. Laundry facilities. Well stocked, licensed shop with fresh fruit and vegetables. Coffee machine (available for reduced hours in low season). Video, DVD and book library. WiFi (charged). Off site: Fishing and boat launching 500 yds. Beach 1 mile. Riding 3 miles. Golf 6 miles. Car or passenger ferry for Fowey. Annual Daphne du Maurier Festival of Arts and Literature is held in Fowey (May). Fowey Regatta (mid August).

Open: 1 April - 31 October.

Directions

From the main A390 road at East Taphouse take B3359 towards Looe. After 5 miles fork right, signed Bodinnick and ferry. Site is signed on the right 1 mile past village of Lanteglos Highway, just before Bodinnick village. GPS: 50.34434, -4.62289

Charges guide

Per unit incl. 2 persons	
and electricity	£ 14.50 - £ 25.00
extra person	£ 4.00 - £ 8.00
child (3-15 yrs)	£ 2.00 - £ 3.00
dog	free

Fowey

Penhale Caravan & Camping Park

Fowey PL23 1JU (Cornwall) T: 01726 833425. E: info@penhale-fowey.co.uk

alanrogers.com/UK0285

Penhale is a traditional campsite on four and half acres of rolling farmland with magnificent views across the countryside to St Austell Bay. The Berryman family run an arable and beef farm alongside the campsite. The atmosphere here is relaxed and there is plenty of room in the touring fields. The fields do slope but a number of pitches have been levelled. In total, there are 56 pitches for all types of units, 41 with 16A electricity hook-ups. Ten holiday caravans occupy a separate field. It is possible to walk to Polkerris beach a mile away and Fowey is just a mile and a half.

Facilities

One fully equipped toilet block at the bottom of the touring fields. Laundry room. Games room. Reception at the farmhouse stocks basic necessities. WiFi. Off site: Garage with shop 600 yds. Sandy beach, pub and watersports centre at Polkerris beach 1 mile (windsurfing, sailing, paddle surf, kayak). Fishing and boat launching and shops and restaurants in Fowey 1.5 miles. Bicycle hire 5 miles. Three golf courses within 7 miles.

Open: Easter/1 April - 8 October.

Directions

From the A390 take B3269 for Fowey and 1 mile before town turn right at roundabout by petrol station on the A3082 St Austell road. Site is about 600 yds. on the left. GPS: 50.34309, -4.66848

Charges guide

Per unit incl. 2 persons	
and electricity	£ 14.25 - £ 21.00
extra person	£ 4.35 - £ 5.50
child (4-15 yrs)	£ 2.25
dog	£ 1.05 - £ 2.25

For latest campsite news visit

alanrogers.com

Gorran Haven
Sea View International

Boswinger, Gorran Haven, Saint Austell PL26 6LL (Cornwall) T: 01726 843425.
E: holidays@seaviewinternational.com **alanrogers.com/UK0150**

Sea View is an impressive, well cared for park, its quality reflected in the many awards it has won. Located at the gateway to the Roseland Peninsula on the South Coast of Cornwall with views of the sea and nearby Dodman Point, this park offers quality camping pitches, luxury self-catering lodges and caravan holiday homes. With over 200 touring pitches, all with electricity hook-ups and many being 'all service' with a choice of hardstanding or grass, there are pitches to suit all requirements. Available to hire are luxury two and three bedroom lodges and a variety of caravan holiday homes, many with sea views and some with decking to take advantage of this superb location. The park is full of colour with flowerbeds and flowering shrubs and has well manicured grass of exceptional quality. The area around the pool is particularly attractive with sunbathing areas on tiled terraces surrounded by flowers creating little private areas, all with magnificent views of the sea and the distant headland. Adjacent is a barbecue area with tables set out to take advantage of the view. A large recreation field provides plenty of play equipment as well as tennis, football and crazy golf. There is plenty to do and see in this area, from the gardens of Heligan and Trelissick, to Lanhydroc House and the seal sanctuary, not forgetting the safe beaches, one of which is only a half mile walk from the park. A member of the Best of British Group.

Facilities

Excellent toilet and shower blocks are well maintained and heated including facilities for disabled visitors and luxury bathroom suites on the family field. Fully equipped campers' kitchens. Well equipped laundry. Motorcaravan service point. Well stocked shop and off-licence. Café and takeaway with free WiFi. Heated outdoor swimming pool. Large play area. Tennis and badminton courts, pitch and putt (all free). Extensive dog walk area (certain breeds not accepted). Off site: Community bus picks up at the park. Fishing. Boat launching and riding 2 miles. Bicycle hire 5 miles. Golf 9 miles.

Open: 1 April - 31 October.

Directions

From St Austell take the B3273 towards Mevagissey for about 3 miles. At top of steep hill, turn right signed Lost Gardens of Heligan and Seaview International. Follow this road and brown signs to park. GPS: 50.2369, -4.820033

Charges guide

Per unit incl. 2 persons and electricity	£ 6.00 - £ 32.50
serviced pitch	£ 8.00 - £ 35.00
super pitch (fully incl.)	£ 10.00 - £ 56.00
extra person (over 5 yrs)	£ 3.00 - £ 5.00
dog (limited breeds and numbers)	£ 3.00

Helston
Silver Sands Holiday Park

Gwendreath, Ruan Minor, Helston TR12 7LZ (Cornwall) T: 01326 290631.
E: info@silversandsholidaypark.co.uk **alanrogers.com/UK0070**

Silver Sands is a small, peaceful 'away-from-it-all' park, under new ownership, in a remote part of the Lizard peninsula, the most southerly part of mainland Britain and an Area of Outstanding Natural Beauty. It is tucked away behind two other holiday home parks (possible noise in season). The park itself has 16 caravan holiday homes, along with 36 touring pitches of which 20 have 10A electrical hook-ups. The pitches are large, attractively situated and divided into individual bays by flowering shrubs and bushes. The adjoining tent field has similar pitches (7 with electricity) where the shrubs are growing (some pitches are slightly sloping). A member of the Countryside Discovery group.

Facilities

The fully equipped toilet block includes an en-suite room for disabled visitors, doubling as a family room. Some play equipment. An undeveloped three-acre field can be used for walking, kite flying, etc. Off site: Restaurant nearby, pub within walking distance. Fishing 1 mile. Boat launching 2 or 7 miles. Riding and bicycle hire 5 miles. Golf 6 miles.

Open: Easter - mid October.

Directions

From Helston take A3038 Lizard road. After Culdrose turn left on B3293 passing Goonhilly after 4 miles. At next crossroads turn right (Kennack Sands), continue for 1.5 miles then left to Gwendreath on single track road - site is 1 mile. GPS: 50.00900, -5.16900

Charges guide

Per unit incl. 2 persons, 2 children and electricity	£ 14.50 - £ 20.50
extra person	£ 3.20 - £ 4.30

Helston

Lower Polladras Touring Park

Carleen, Helston TR13 9NX (Cornwall) T: 01736 762220. E: lowerpolladras@btinternet.com

alanrogers.com/UK0475

Lower Polladras is a small, friendly park located north of Helston in beautiful rolling Cornish countryside. There are 44 touring pitches here as well as a number of mobile homes (for rent) and seasonal pitches. The site has a strong conservation interest and is actively working towards carbon neutral status. A two acre area adjoining the park accommodates play equipment for children and a sports area. The upper level here is reserved for 28-day camping in the peak season. A nature and dog walk has been developed around the perimeter and there are some excellent walks and cycle tracks in the surrounding countryside. The Eden Project is within easy reach and Helston is a delightful town. The Lizard peninsula is a stunning stretch of coastline leading to Lizard Point, the most southerly point of mainland Britain.

Facilities

Two traditional toilet blocks, both clean and light, with preset showers and hairdryer (20p). Baby changing area. Visitors with disabilities should check with site. Shop for basics. Playground. Sports area. Nature and dog walk. Tourist information. Mobile homes for rent. Off site: Helston (shops and restaurants). Golf and boat launching 3 miles. Fishing 4 miles. Riding 6 miles. Walking and cycling. Eden Project. Lizard Peninsula.

Open: 1 April - 2 January.

Directions

Take the A394 from Helston towards Penzance. On edge of Helston, turn right on to B3302, signed Camborne and Hayle. Take the second left to Carleen. Once in the village take the second right and follow signs to the park. GPS: 50.130156, -5.337199

Charges guide

Per unit incl. 2 persons	
and electricity	£ 14.00 - £ 20.00
extra person	£ 2.00 - £ 3.00
child (3-16 yrs)	£ 1.50 - £ 2.00

Lower Polladras Touring Park. Family Shower / Toilet / Baby changing area / Games Room. Sheltered level pitches / Luxury static caravans for hire. Seasonal Pitches and Caravan storage. NEW for 2011 Disabled shower and toilet. Quiet, rural and very friendly. Carleen - Helston - TR13 9NX Cornwall. Tel. 01736 762220 - www.lower-polladras.co.uk

Helston

Boscrege Caravan Park

Ashton, Helston TR13 9TG (Cornwall) T: 01736 762231. E: enquiries@caravanparkcornwall.com

alanrogers.com/UK0480

A pretty little site covering 12 acres and hidden deep in the countryside in an Area of Outstanding Natural Beauty, Boscrege will suit those who want a quiet peaceful base for their holiday. The main large touring field nestles at the foot of Tregonning Hill with its hill top cross, and has neatly cut grass with a gentle slope from the top. The pitches are generously spaced around the edge, backing on to hedging and leaving room in the centre for ball games. There are two small paddock areas with 26 caravan holiday homes and a field for touring units, providing a total of 51 pitches, 40 with 10A electricity.

Facilities

Traditional, fully equipped toilet block is showing its age but has been newly painted and includes a smaller basin for children (M/F). Washing machine, dryer and microwave. Two play areas for smaller children and central ball area. Amusement machines, pool table and TV room. Nature trail and dog walking area. Plans to include WiFi. Off site: Godolphin House and garden. Whole of the tip of Cornwall easily accessible – the Lizard, Land's End. Fishing 1 mile. Golf, riding and nearest beach (Praa Sands) 2 miles. Bicycle hire and boat launching 5 miles.

Open: Easter/1 April - 31 October.

Directions

From Helston take A394 (Penzance). At top of Sithney Common Hill turn right just before Jet garage onto B3302 (Hayle) road. Pass general stores and take next left (Carleen and Godolphin Cross). Carry on to Godolphin Cross and turn left at side of Godolphin Arms (Ashton). Go up hill bearing left at top until you see camp signs where road turns sharply left. Go straight over into lane to Boscrege. GPS: 50.12501, -5.36751

Charges guide

Per unit incl. 4 persons	
and electricity	£ 15.00 - £ 22.95

For latest campsite news visit
alanrogers.com

Helston

Franchis Holiday Park

Cury Cross Lanes, Mullion, Helston TR12 7AZ (Cornwall) T: 01326 240301. E: enquiries@franchis.co.uk

alanrogers.com/UK0485

A small rural site, Franchis is ideally situated for exploring the Lizard peninsula in an Area of Outstanding Natural Beauty. Mature trees edge the site's two fields (a total of 4 acres) that slope slightly, with 65 pitches arranged around the perimeters. There are 33 with 10A electricity. Natural woodland areas and a stream will keep children occupied. Continuing past the fields into a wooded area are 6 small bungalows and 6 mobile homes, some privately owned and some to rent. There is a small toilet block for each field and a small shop that opens morning and evening. Phil and Kate, the young couple who have owned the site for the last three years, will be pleased to welcome you and advise you in exploring the area. The Lizard is a unique area and well worth exploring with unspoilt coves and the Helford river. Goonhilly Earth station is just up the road and you pass by the extensive Culdrose Naval base on your way to the site. Helston is known for its famous 'Floral Dance', the origin of which is not certain, but for one day in May each year the inhabitants dress up and dance through the streets to celebrate.

Facilities

Two traditional small toilet blocks. Two washing machines and two driers. Freezer for ice blocks. Small shop (2/7-3/9). Small library. Play area. Dog exercise field. Tourist information. Mobile homes and chalets for rent. WiFi (charged). Off site: Riding, golf, beach, fishing and boat launching 2 miles. Sailing 4 miles. Helston 5 miles.

Open: Easter - 31 October.

Directions

From Helston take the A3083 road towards Mullion and the Lizard. Soon after passing through Curly Cross Lanes watch for site directly on the left. GPS: 50.039, -5.21843

Charges guide

Per unit incl. 2 persons	
and electricity	£ 13.00 - £ 18.00
extra person	£ 1.50 - £ 2.00
dog	£ 1.50 - £ 2.00

Mevagissey

Tregarton Park

Gorran, Mevagissey, Saint Austell PL26 6NF (Cornwall) T: 01726 843666. E: reception@tregarton.co.uk

alanrogers.com/UK0155

Run by the welcoming Hicks family, Tregarton Park itself dates back to the 16th century. It is little wonder that the listed buildings have created some problems in providing modern facilities, although the Hicks have done well with their conversions to create a pleasing environment. The 12-acre caravan park is made up of four meadows with wonderful rural views. The 125 pitches, all with 10A electricity hook-ups, some with hardstanding, are of a generous size with most separated by either hedges or fencing. All have been terraced as the park itself is quite hilly. Reception provides a well stocked shop, tourist information and a takeaway service offering freshly cooked food including a daily delivery of Cornish pasties. The large heated outdoor pool is surrounded by decked terraces, with tables and chairs where one can relax and watch the children – in fact, it is the focal point of the park.

Facilities

The fully equipped toilet block has been completely revamped and includes some excellent features. Facilities for disabled visitors. Laundry room. Well stocked shop with groceries and camping supplies, takeaway (all 28/5-24/9). Gas supplies. Heated swimming pool (28/5-2/9). Tourist information. Dog exercise meadow. Adventure playground. All weather tennis. WiFi. Max. 2 dogs. Off site: Bus stop at entrance. Heligan Gardens, Mevagissey and beaches all 2 miles. Bicycle hire 3 miles. Golf 5 miles. Eden Project 9 miles. Fishing trips available from Mevagissey and Gorran Haven.

Open: 1 April - 30 October.

Directions

Leave St Austell travelling south on the B3273 and pass through London Apprentice and Pentewen. Follow Tregarton Park's brown tourist signs by turning right at the crossroads at the top of the hill towards Heligan and Gorran Haven. Do not go into Mevagissey. GPS: 50.2588, -4.829417

Charges guide

Per unit incl. 2 persons,	
electricity and awning	£ 9.00 - £ 25.00
extra person (4 -17 yrs)	£ 3.00 - £ 18.00
dog (max. 2)	£ 1.00 - £ 3.00

Newquay

Newperran Holiday Park

Rejerrah, Newquay TR8 5QJ (Cornwall) T: 01872 572407. E: holidays@newperran.co.uk

alanrogers.com/UK0160

Newperran is a large, level park in rural Cornish countryside. Being on high ground, it is quite open but this also gives excellent views of the coast and surrounding countryside. The owners, Keith and Christine Brewer, have rebuilt the reception, shop and pub to a very high standard. The traditional layout of the park provides a number of flat, well drained meadows divided into over 370 individual pitches with 10/16A electricity. Some fields have larger and reservable spaces with more free space in the centre. There are now 77 fully serviced pitches, some with hardstanding and a TV point. Newperran is only 2.5 miles from Perranporth beach, but there is a free heated swimming pool with sunbathing area and paddling pool on the park. A state of the art entrance barrier is now in place operating on number plate recognition. Newly refurbished heated swimming pool and paddling pool. The pub or 'cottage inn' is a very comfortable area with a log burner for low season warmth and family entertainment such as quiz nights in high season. A new larger restaurant has been added, along with a games room and launderette. This is a well run park with plenty of space and activities for families with a few caravan holiday homes to rent.

Facilities

Toilet facilities comprise four clean blocks, two heated and all refurbished to a very high standard. Facilities include washbasins in cabins, family rooms, baby room, hairdressing room and a unit for disabled visitors. Laundry room. Well stocked self-service licensed shop. Licensed bar (mid May-Oct). Café (all season). New outdoor heated swimming pool with paddling pool (Whitsun-Sept). Adventure playground and separate toddlers' play area. Games room with TV. TV room. Off site: Goonhavern village within walking distance with pubs and post office. Fishing 1 mile. Riding and golf 2 miles. Beach 2.5 miles.

Open: 22 March - 31 October.

Directions

Turn off A3075 to west at camping sign 7 miles south of Newquay and just north of Goonhavern village. GPS: 50.350433, -5.101817

Charges guide

Per pitch incl. 2 persons and electricity	£ 14.80 - £ 23.00
extra person	£ 4.65 - £ 8.50
child (3-15 yrs)	£ 1.50 - £ 5.95

See advertisement on page 36

Newquay

Trevella Holiday Park

Crantock, Newquay TR8 5EW (Cornwall) T: 01637 830308. E: holidays@trevella.co.uk

alanrogers.com/UK0170

One of the best known and respected of Cornish parks with its colourful flowerbeds (a regular winner of a 'Newquay in Bloom' award), Trevella is also one of the first to fill up and has a longer season than most. Well organised, the pitches are in a number of adjoining meadows, most of which are on a slight slope. Of the 270 pitches for touring units (any type), some 200 can be reserved and these are marked, individual ones. Over 200 pitches have electricity (10A), with 59 serviced pitches (with hardstanding, electricity and TV hook-ups, water, waste water), some extra large with sewage drain as well. Trevella is essentially a quiet family touring park. Ready erected tents are available to hire. The accent is on orderliness and cleanliness with on-site evening activities limited, although Andy's Kitchen offers good home-cooked food. Access is free to two fishing lakes, (permits from reception); with some fishing instruction and wildlife talks for youngsters in season. There is a pleasant walk around the lakes, which are a haven for wildlife and a protected nature reserve. It is also possible to walk to Crantock beach but check the tides first.

Facilities

Three blocks provide good coverage with individual washbasins in private cabins, hairdressing room, baby rooms and large en-suite family rooms in one block. Laundry. Freezer pack service. Well stocked supermarket (Easter-Oct). Café (including breakfast) and takeaway. Heated outdoor pool. Games room. Separate TV room. Crazy golf. Large adventure playground. Play and sports area. Pets corner. Fishing. Caravan storage. WiFi (charged). Off site: Shuttle bus service to Newquay in high season. Nearest beach 0.5 miles on foot, 1 mile by car. Riding 1 mile. Pubs and restaurants at Crantock 1 mile. Newquay 2 miles. Golf 3 miles.

Open: Easter - 31 October.

Directions

To avoid Newquay leave the A30 or A392 at Indian Queens, straight over crossroads with the A39 and A3058, left at A3075 junction and first right at camp sign. GPS: 50.3973, -5.096133

Charges guide

Per person	£ 4.65 - £ 8.65
child (3-14 yrs)	£ 1.50 - £ 6.10
pitch incl. electricity	£ 6.00
service pitch	£ 10.30 - £ 14.50

Families and couples only.

See advertisement on page 36

For latest campsite news visit

alanrogers.com

Newquay

Treloy Touring Park

Newquay TR8 4JN (Cornwall) T: 01637 872063. E: treloy-tp@btconnect.com

alanrogers.com/UK0205

Just three miles from the wonderful beaches around Newquay, yet peacefully located away from the crowds, Treloy is a pretty park. Family owned and run, there are 197 pitches, many level, some slightly sloping, all with 16A electricity (new system) and 30 fully serviced. All are used for touring units and perhaps this contributes towards the relaxed family atmosphere. There are concrete hardstandings for caravans which are attractively interspersed with shrubs and form a pleasant landscape feature. Elsewhere hydrangea edge the roads around the more open pitches and the new trees have grown well. St Mawgan, the RAF air sea rescue base and Newquay's airport are nearby but there is little disturbance. There is an hourly bus service to Newquay from the park entrance which means the coast and beaches can be enjoyed without taking the car. On return to Treloy there is the Park Chef and the Surfrider's Bar for meals and drinks. If you do not fancy the beach there is a pool in the park. This is a real family site providing for all ages.

Facilities

Good overall provision including a smart new block at the top. Baby room with bath. En-suite facilities for disabled visitors (key). Laundry. Gas. Shop with all necessities. Bar (20/5-15/9). Pleasant café with a good reputation and including breakfast (20/5-1/9). Takeaway. Swimming pool (walled and gated). Good fenced play areas and field with goal posts. Nature trail. Family entertainment such as magic shows, bingo, folk and rock music. WiFi (charged). Off site: Golf 0.5 miles. Fishing 1 mile. Riding and boat launching 3 miles. Other beaches such as Watergate Bay, Mawgan Porth and Porth beach are a short car journey.

Open: 1 April - 30 September.

Directions

From A39 St Columb Major take the B3059 for Newquay. Park is signed after about 4 miles.
GPS: 50.432867, -5.0125

Charges guide

Per unit incl. 2 persons	
and electricity	£ 13.75 - £ 20.75
extra person	£ 4.00 - £ 7.25
child (3-14 yrs)	£ 3.00 - £ 4.25
dog	£ 1.00 - £ 2.50

See advertisement on page 37

Newquay

Hendra Holiday Park

Newquay TR8 4NY (Cornwall) T: 01637 875778. E: enquiries@hendra.co.uk

alanrogers.com/UK0210

Hendra is a long-established holiday park for all the family with a wide range of facilities and a comprehensive entertainment programme. There are comedians, show bands, cabaret, dancing, bingo, discos, plus a super pool complex. The 548 touring pitches are on well mown, mostly terraced grass fields with country views and mature trees, some more sheltered than others. There are 280 caravan holiday homes to rent in separate fields. With tarmac roads and lighting, 311 pitches have electricity (16A) and 28 pitches are fully serviced including water, electricity, light, sewer drainage, satellite TV connections and some innovative awning pads (dogs are not accepted on these pitches). The entrance and reception are very attractive with a mass of well tended flower beds which, along with the other facilities, form an attractive, village-like centre to the park. The 'star of the show' at Hendra is the Oasis complex consisting of an indoor fun pool with flumes, river rapids and beach. It is open to the public – really a mini water-park. The outdoor heated pool with grass sunbathing area is free to campers and activities are well catered for with a range of amenities. The park is only 1.5 miles from Newquay and its fabulous surfing beaches and a bus to the town passes the gate. Hendra welcomes families and couples. A member of the Best of British Group.

Facilities

Three modern fully equipped toilet blocks including facilities for babies and disabled visitors. Launderette. Motorcaravan services. Gas supplies. Well stocked shop. Various bars, restaurants and takeaway, open all season (limited hours in early season). Pizzeria (main season only). Outdoor swimming pool (25-5/31/8). Indoor pool complex (cost £2.95 per person or, if pre-booked, £14.60 for 7 tickets). Various play areas including one for soft play. Bicycle hire. WiFi (free). Minigolf. Bowling. Off site: Fishing and riding 1 mile. Beach 1.5 miles. Golf 2 miles.

Open: 30 March - end October.

Directions

Park is on left side of A392 Indian Queens - Newquay road at Newquay side of Quintrell Downs.
GPS: 50.402433, -5.04915

Charges guide

Per unit incl. 2 persons	
and electricity	£ 17.20 - £ 27.10
extra person	£ 5.05 - £ 9.15
child (3-14 yrs)	£ 1.50 - £ 6.05
dog	£ 4.10 - £ 5.00

Minimum charges apply at peak times.

See advertisement on page 34

For latest campsite news visit
alanrogers.com

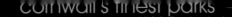

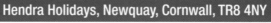

GLOBE VALE
HOLIDAY PARK

Globe Vale is a family run quiet countryside park situated close to the town of Redruth with easy access to A30. There are panoramic views across green fields to the coast; ten minutes drive to nearest beaches.

Campers/tourers; static caravans for hire, and also plots available if you wish to buy your own new static holiday home.

Facilities on site include fully serviced pitches, electric hook-ups, modern shower / toilet block, laundrette and chemical disposal. Licensed bar with games room. Evening meals served – open during peak periods. Children's play area and open spaces for ball games. Pets accepted on site for an extra charge. Caravan storage available.

FINEST MEMBER

AA	Globe Vale Holiday Park, Radnor, Redruth, Cornwall TR16 4BH
	Paul and Louise Owen - **t:** 01209 891183
	e: info@globevale.co.uk - **w:** www.globevale.co.uk

Caravan TOP 100 SITES 2011 FINALIST

NEWPERRAN
Holiday Park

Peaceful family holiday park, renowed for its spacious, flat perimeter pitching, with breathtaking open countryside and sea views.

Call for a Brochure
Tel: 0845 1668407
Local call rate

- luxury toilet blocks
- free showers
- family rooms
- disabled facilities
- new launderette
- premium all-service pitches
- shop/off licence
- entertainments
- new TV/Games Room
- the NEW Cottage Inn, restaurant & takeaway
- free WiFi access
- adventure playground
- toddlers play area
- swimming pool, paddling pool & sunbathing terraces
- caravan storage

Rejerrah, Newquay, Cornwall TR8 5QJ

www.newperran.co.uk

5 star park near to Newquay and Perranporth beaches

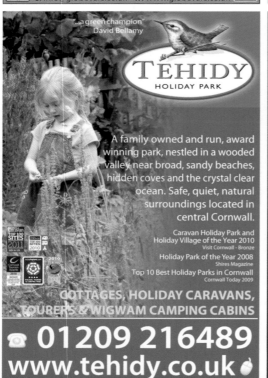

"...a green champion"
David Bellamy

TEHIDY
HOLIDAY PARK

A family owned and run, award winning park, nestled in a wooded valley near broad, sandy beaches, hidden coves and the crystal clear ocean. Safe, quiet, natural surroundings located in central Cornwall.

Caravan Holiday Park and Holiday Village of the Year 2010
Visit Cornwall - Bronze
Holiday Park of the Year 2008
Shires Magazine
Top 10 Best Holiday Parks in Cornwall
Cornwall Today 2009

COTTAGES, HOLIDAY CARAVANS, TOURERS & WIGWAM CAMPING CABINS

☎ **01209 216489**
www.tehidy.co.uk
✉ holiday@tehidy.co.uk

Tehidy Holiday Park, Harris Mill, Illogan, Redruth, Cornwall. TR16 4JQ

CARAVAN AND CAMPING PARK
Trevella Park
CRANTOCK   NEWQUAY   CORNWALL TR8 5EW

One of Cornwall's Finest Parks

* 5* award winning park set in beautiful landscaped parkland
* Superb touring facilities
* A range of well maintained/ spacious pitches
* Secure storage area for your caravan - leave your tourer with us for the season!
* 'Ready tents' - pitched and ready to use!
* Ideal base for Crantock and Newquay's beaches
* Perfect for walking, fishing, surfing and exploring the local area
* Heated outdoor swimming & paddling pools, fishings lakes, free fishing and nature reserve
* Play areas, TV & games room, cafe & takeaway and launderette
* Special rates available - quote 'Alan Rogers 2012'

For 2012
✓ 'Ready Tents' - pitched & ready for your arrival
✓ Leave your caravan and go home 'tow free'!

Follow us on Facebook

Tel: 0844 870 6031
Email: holidays@trevella.co.uk
www.trevella.co.uk

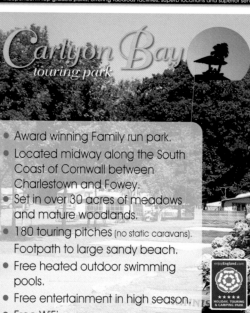
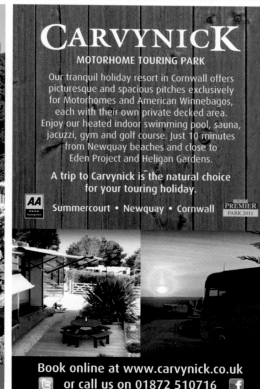

Newquay

Trevornick Holiday Park

Holywell Bay, Newquay TR8 5PW (Cornwall) T: 01637 830531. E: bookings@trevornick.co.uk

alanrogers.com/UK0220

Trevornick, once a working farm, is a modern, busy and well run family touring park providing a very wide range of amenities close to one of Cornwall's finest beaches. A modern reception with welcoming staff sets the tone for your holiday. The park is well managed with facilities and standards constantly monitored. It has grown to provide caravanners and campers (no holiday caravans but 56 very well equipped Eurotents) with some 550 large grass pitches (350 with 10A electricity and 55 fully serviced with electricity, water, drainage and TV connection with DVD channel) on five level fields and two terraced areas. There are few trees but some good views. Providing 'all singing, all dancing' facilities for fun packed family holidays, the farm buildings now provide the setting for the Farm Club. Recently refurbished, it provides much entertainment, from bingo and quizzes to shows, discos and cabaret. The Stables Grill also opens for breakfast and the Hungry Horse provides takeaway food. The rest of the development provides a pool complex, an 18-hole golf course with a small, quiet club house offering bar meals and lovely views out to sea, and three fishing lakes. Next door is the Holywell Bay Fun Park (reduced rates) and the sandy beach is five minutes by car or a downhill walk from the park. An innovative idea is the Hire Shop where it is possible rent anything you might have forgotten, from sheets, a fridge, a travel cot, to a camera or a wet suit to catch the famous Cornish surf!

Facilities

Five modern toilet blocks provide showers, two family bathrooms, baby bath, laundry facilities and provision for disabled visitors. Well stocked supermarket with bread made on site (from late May). Hire Shop. Bars (with TV), restaurant, cafe and takeaway. Entertainment (every night in season). Pool complex with heated outdoor pool, paddling pool, sunbathing decks, solarium, sauna and massage chair. Health and beauty salon. Super Fort Knox style adventure playground, crazy golf, Kiddies Club. Amusement arcade and bowling alley. Teenagers' room. 18-hole pitch and putt with golf pro shop. Bicycle hire. Coarse fishing with three lakes. Dogs are accepted in two fields only. Only limited facilities open at Easter and from 8 Sept. Off site: Riding within 2 miles. Bicycle hire and boat launching 4 miles.

Open: Easter; mid May - mid September.

Directions

From A3075 approach to Newquay - Perranporth road, turn towards Cubert and Holywell Bay. Continue through Cubert to park on the right. GPS: 50.384983, -5.128933

Charges guide

Per unit incl. 2 persons and electricity	£ 16.15 - £ 26.05
extra person	£ 5.45 - £ 10.20
child (3-14 yrs)	£ 1.45 - £ 7.20
dog	£ 4.10 - £ 5.10

Families and couples only.
Many special discounts.

See advertisement on page 35

Newquay

Porth Beach Tourist Park

Porth, Newquay TR7 3NH (Cornwall) T: 01637 876531. E: info@porthbeach.co.uk

alanrogers.com/UK0235

The park is just across the road from Porth Beach with its beautiful bay, sandy shoreline and rock pools. Situated in a small, rural valley with a gentle stream to one side you can enjoy the ducks and the wildlife. The 182 good sized grass pitches stretching up the valley in parallel lines accessed by tarmac roadways are level, marked by tram lines and back on to open fencing. Most have 16A electricity, there are also a few with hardstandings. A well equipped toilet block is to be found half way up, heated in cold weather and with air conditioning for warmer times. There is a shop near the entrance, a pub across the road, and a restaurant two doors up. Watergate Bay is just around the corner, and Newquay a couple of miles down the road, so if you are a surfer you will be in paradise. For walkers, Porth Headland and the South West Coastal path offer some outstanding views. Porth Beach is said to be the safest beach for swimming in the Newquay area. Altogether a super place for a family holiday.

Facilities

One modern, heated and fully equipped toilet block. Baby bath and facilities for disabled visitors. Launderette. Children's play area. Mobile homes to rent. Off site: Golf, riding and boat launching 1.5 miles.

Open: 5 March - 31 October.

Directions

From Newquay take the B3276 to Padstow. Site is about half a mile on right. GPS: 50.426071, -5.0534

Charges guide

Per unit incl. 2 persons and electricity	£ 15.00 - £ 29.00

See advertisement on page 35

For latest campsite news visit

alanrogers.com

Newquay

Trethiggey Touring Park

Quintrell Downs, Newquay TR8 4QR (Cornwall) T: 01637 877672. E: enquiries@trethiggey.co.uk

alanrogers.com/UK0530

Trethiggey is a garden-like park with a ten month season, set some three miles back from the busy Newquay beaches and night life, with an enjoyable, informal style. With natural areas including a small wildlife pond and fishing lakes to enjoy, conservation is high on the agenda. There are 157 pitches, 110 with 16A electricity, some with hardstanding and four with water and sewage connection. Some level pitches are formally arranged, with others more informal on gently sloping grass amidst 12 caravan holiday homes. A more open field provides extra pitches and room for tents. Facilities maintain the informal touch with reception alongside the Trethiggey Trading Post which provides basic supplies, an off-licence and a small library. The Mediterranean style bistro and café/bar is a real attraction, with an extensive menu in the main season. A barbecue bar is a nice touch in high season. Goats, chickens and geese are an added attraction for children. The relaxed atmosphere created by the two families who run the site makes this a different yet popular site.

Facilities

Two fully equipped, heated shower blocks, one in traditional style. En-suite facilities for families and disabled visitors. Baby bathroom. Motorcaravan service point. Laundry facilities and wetsuit wash. Games room at each toilet block with TV and amusement machines. Shop, (all season). Café, bar and takeaway (June-Sept). Adventure play area and recreation field. Coarse fishing. WiFi (charged). Off site: Riding 2 miles. Golf and bicycle hire 3 miles. All the delights of Newquay within 3 miles with nightly minibus service (book in shop). Pub within walking distance.

Open: 2 March - 2 January.

Directions

Site is a few hundred yards south of roundabout where A393 crosses the A3058 at Quintrell Downs (beside the A3058). GPS: 50.396833, -5.0283

Charges guide

Per unit incl. 2 persons	
and electricity	£ 15.90 - £ 22.70
extra person	£ 4.85 - £ 7.40
child (3-15 yrs)	£ 1.50 - £ 5.65
dog	£ 2.80 - £ 2.95

See advertisement on page 37

Newquay

Carvynick Motorhome Touring Park

Sumrnercourt, Newquay TR8 5AF (Cornwall) T: 01872 510716. E: info@carvynick.co.uk

alanrogers.com/UK0540

Carvynick is unique in having been specially created and developed for American motorhomes. As you approach, you catch a glimpse of large, colourful 'monsters' through the trees. The RVs are parked in fully serviced, landscaped bays which include sewerage connections. In the Paddock area there is also parking for the tow car, whilst in the Copse there are decking and patio areas. A newer area built on a section of the existing golf course has similar facilities and amazing views across to the sea at Newquay. The reception complex is impressive and boasts a heated indoor pool, a badminton court and a small fitness centre with sauna and solarium. A number of purpose built cottages provide extra accommodation overlooking the club's 5-hole, par 3 golf course. An extra luxury is an impressive bar and restaurant run by a highly rated Michelin chef. This is almost a resort in itself, attractively laid out and very well organised. For RV owners there are specialised workshops; a range of these vehicles is for sale, should you be tempted.

Facilities

Restaurant and bar, separate bar. Indoor heated pool and toddler pool with spectators' lounge. Sauna, solarium and fitness suite. Golf course (5 hole). Badminton court. Games room. Pool table. WiFi. Off site: North and south Cornwall coasts nearby. Eden Valley project 14 miles. St Ives and Tate Gallery within easy reach.

Open: All year.

Directions

From Bodmin on A30 continue until you pass a McDonalds and Jet service station on your right at Fraddon. Take the next exit, A3058, signposted Summercourt. Continue into village of Summercourt, turn right at traffic lights over A30 and take first turning left for site. GPS: 50.368736, -4.983035

Charges guide

Per motorhome incl. 4 persons, electricity, water and sewerage	£ 18.00 - £ 33.00
extra person	£ 3.00

See advertisement on page 37

For latest campsite news visit

alanrogers.com

Newquay

Monkey Tree Holiday Park

Rejerrah, Newquay TR8 5QR (Cornwall) T: 01872 572032. E: enquiries@monkeytreeholidaypark.co.uk

alanrogers.com/UK0165

Monkey Tree covers 56 acres and boasts an impressive entrance and smart reception. There are 600 pitches with 550 for touring units and 50 caravan holiday homes to rent in their own area. The pitches in the original part of the park benefit from mature hedging which offers a degree of privacy which the newer ones lack, but all have been planted with individual hedges. The pitches are of a good size and most have electricity (13/16A). Serviced pitches with hardstanding are being developed including some extra large pitches which include the use of private facilities in the toilet block.

Facilities

The original block (refurbished) supplements seven new modern blocks with heating and facilities for babies and disabled visitors. Private en-suite facilities for use with the super pitches. Laundry. Motorcaravan services. Shop. Club with entertainment, bar and restaurant (main season and B.Hs). Takeaway (high season). Outdoor pool and paddling pool (Whitsun-end Sept). Trampolines. Bouncy castles. Adventure play areas. Amusement arcade. Fishing lakes. Off site: Golf, riding and sailing 5 miles.

Open: All year.

Directions

Follow the A30 ignoring all signs for Newquay. At Carland Cross (windmills on right), straight over signed Perranporth. After 1 mile turn right at Boxheater Junction on B3285 (Perranporth and Goonhavern). Follow for 0.5 miles then turn right into Scotland Road for 1 mile to park on the left. GPS: 50.352218, -5.091659

Charges guide

Per person	£ 5.00 - £ 8.50
pitch incl. electricity	£ 5.00 - £ 5.50
incl. services	£ 12.50 - £ 18.75

Newquay

Sun Haven Valley Holiday Park

Mawgan Porth, Newquay TR8 4BQ (Cornwall) T: 01637 860373. E: sunhaven@sunhavenvalley.com

alanrogers.com/UK0215

An attractive, well maintained holiday park, Sun Haven Valley is on the edge of a small valley with views of the opposite hills. Owned and thoughtfully run by the Tavener family, it caters mainly for couples and families with children. On a gently sloping hillside, around 30 caravan holiday homes for rent border the top field with a central area of neatly cut grass left free for play. The lower field is edged by a small trout stream (unfenced) and provides over 100 level, grass touring pitches (in standard and large sizes), marked by tram lines and accessed by a circular road.

Facilities

One large, central toilet block and a smaller one in the far corner. Two en-suite family rooms double as facilities for disabled visitors. Laundry. Basic foodstuffs available in reception. Play area. TV room. Games room with amusement machines. WiFi (around reception, charged). Poor mobile phone reception. Max. 1 dog in high season. Off site: Pubs, restaurants and supermarket in village. Farm shop adjacent. Beach 0.75 miles. Fishing 100 yds.

Open: All year.

Directions

From B3276 at Mawgan Porth take narrow unclassed road up the Vale of Lanhorne for 1 mile. Site is on the left. GPS: 50.46203, -5.01385

Charges guide

Per unit incl. 2 adults and electricity	£ 16.00 - £ 30.00
child (5-13 yrs, first one free)	£ 1.00 - £ 3.50

Padstow

Mother Ivey's Bay Caravan Park

Trevose Head, Padstow PL28 8SL (Cornwall) T: 01841 520990. E: info@motheriveysbay.com

alanrogers.com/UK0425

Mother Ivey's is a well established family park located to the west of Padstow with good access to an excellent sandy beach and some superb coastal walks. The site has been owned by the Langmaid family for over 20 years. Pitches are mostly of a good size and most have electricity. A number of 'super' pitches are available with fine sea views, electricity, water and drainage. A large number of mobile homes are available for rent. On-site amenities include a well stocked shop and a children's adventure playground, but the emphasis is on peace and quiet, so there is no bar or restaurant.

Facilities

Adventure playground. Shop. Tourist information. Mobile homes and chalets for rent. Off site: Padstow (shops and restaurants). Riding. Fishing trips. Southwest coastal footpath.

Open: 26 March - 3 November.

See advertisement on page 34

Directions

Follow the A30 dual carriageway to Indian Queens. Follow signs firstly towards Wadebridge (A39), then Padstow (B3274). After 3 miles, turn left towards St Merryn. Follow signs to Trevose Golf Club and then Mother Ivey's Bay. GPS: 50.541334, -5.013923

Charges guide

Per unit incl. 6 persons and electricity	£ 18.00 - £ 42.00

For latest campsite news visit

alanrogers.com

Padstow

Padstow Touring Park

Padstow PL28 8LE (Cornwall) T: 01841 532061. E: mail@padstowtouringpark.co.uk

alanrogers.com/UK0430

Padstow Touring Park has wonderful views over the surrounding countryside and is owned and run by the Barnes family. They have worked hard to develop the site, and bushes and shrubs now break up the fields in smaller grass bays or levelled terraces. There are 150 pitches, of which 127 have water, waste water and 10A electricity and some have hardstanding. The site can accommodate up to 34 ft. motorhomes. Padstow itself is a mile away, either by footpath through fields or by bicycles on the road.

Facilities

Three toilet blocks, including one new with underfloor heating, en-suite shower rooms, facilities for disabled visitors and a family room. Exclusive washrooms for use with some pitches. Full laundry facilities. Reception/shop for gas, camping equipment and provisions. Play area. WiFi. Off site: Nearest beach is at Padstow, others are within 2 miles. Access to the Camel Trail cycle route. Riding and fishing 2 miles. Golf 5 miles.

Open: All year.

Directions

Park is situated on the main A389 road into Padstow, on the right about 1 mile before the town. If towing or in a motorhome avoid A389 between Wadebridge and St Issey; instead take B3274 which can take large units. GPS: 50.52705, -4.949183

Charges guide

Per unit incl. 2 persons and electricity	£ 14.00 - £ 22.00
extra person	£ 3.50 - £ 5.00

Pentewan

Pentewan Sands Holiday Park

Pentewan, Saint Austell PL26 6BT (Cornwall) T: 01726 843485. E: info@pentewan.co.uk

alanrogers.com/UK0250

Pentewan Sands is a popular, well managed family park with an ideal position right beside a wide sandy private beach. A busy, 32 acre holiday park with lots going on, there are 501 touring pitches, 401 with electricity, and 120 caravan holiday homes for hire. The good sized pitches are on level grass with nothing between them. They are marked and numbered by frontage stones, mostly in rows adjoining access roads. The area beside the Beach Club should now be rebuilt providing new indoor pools, both a lap pool and a fun pool, a gym, 'kid's zone' and a new bar and restaurant.

Facilities

Four main toilet blocks receive heavy use in peak season but are well maintained. Two bathrooms, a baby room and facilities for disabled visitors. Laundry room. Motorcaravan service point. Shop with off-licence, bistro, fast food, bars and bar meals (all Easter-mid Sept). Entertainment. Swimming pools (Whitsun-mid Sept). Playground. Games room. Tennis. Bicycle hire. Slipway and boat launching (Whitsun-mid Sept). Dogs are not accepted. WiFi around reception and bar. Off site: Bus stop 400 yds. Bicycle hire in village 0.5 miles. Riding and golf 2 miles.

Open: 1 April - 31 October.

Directions

From St Austell ring road take B3273 for Mevagissey. Park is 3.5 miles, where the road meets the sea. GPS: 50.288283, -4.78575

Charges guide

Per unit incl. 2 persons and electricity	£ 16.95 - £ 34.45
extra person	£ 2.80 - £ 5.30
child (3-15 yrs)	£ 1.60 - £ 4.15
Seafront pitch plus 10-20%.	

Penzance

Wayfarers Camping & Caravan Park

Relubbus Lane, Saint Hilary, Penzance TR20 9EF (Cornwall) T: 01736 763326. E: elaine@wayfarerspark.co.uk

alanrogers.com/UK0065

Wayfarers is a neat and tidy, garden-like park reserved for adults only, in rural Cornwall. Sheltered by perimeter trees and consisting of two finely mown fields interspersed by shrubs and palm-like trees, 30 places are available for caravans (up to 23 ft. single axle), motorcaravans (up to 22 ft) and tents, plus three holiday caravans available to rent. All have 16A electricity, with hardstanding available on 24. Should you enjoy walking you can follow the River Hayle down to St Erth.

Facilities

The modern toilet block is fully equipped. Ladies have a wash cubicle and there are two smart en-suite shower rooms (key system). Fully equipped laundry. Dishwashing sinks in the house. Shop stocks basics. No twin-axle caravans. Dogs are not accepted. Off site: Two pubs serving food in Goldsithney 1 mile. Fishing and riding 1 mile. Golf 1.5 miles. Beach 2 miles. Bicycle hire, sailing and boat launching 5 miles.

Open: 7 May - 25 September.

Directions

Following the A30 Penzance road take A394 Helston road after the St Ives turning. Follow for 1 mile then turn left on the B3280 and pass through Goldsithney village and site is 1 mile further on left. GPS: 50.133167, -5.416833

Charges guide

Per unit incl. 2 persons and electricity	£ 16.00 - £ 22.00
extra person	£ 6.00

Perranporth

Perran Sands Holiday Park

Perranporth TR6 0AQ (Cornwall) T: 01872 573551. E: nick.cook@bourne-leisure.co.uk

alanrogers.com/UK0135

An amazing site on grassy sand dunes, Perran Sands Holiday Park has over 1,100 pitches in total (350 for touring units), with numerous mobile homes are dotted amongst the dunes. It is a village in its own right, with all the facilities that you could need – shops, restaurants, bars, entertainment; a second entertainment area opens in high season. A magnificent sandy beach is just over the next dune, popular with surfers, but for something a little more relaxing there are indoor and outdoor heated pools on site, both with lifeguards. To get around the site, you will need the 'Perran Puffer' road train.

Facilities

Three basic toilet blocks (no electrical points) with two family rooms with facilites for babies and campers with disabilities. Launderette. Supermarket with bakery and off licence. Gift shop. Café/bar and grill with terrace. Fish and chips, Burger King, Papa John's takeaway pizza. Sports bar. Heated indoor fun pool with flume and heated outdoor pool (28/5-3/9). Multisports court. Mini 10-pin bowling. Amusement arcade. Pool tables. Surf school (equipment hire). Two family show/entertainment bars (one open outside July/Aug). Kids' club for all ages. Soft play area. Playland. Road train. Accommodation to hire. WiFi. Bus service. Off site: Fishing 2 miles. Newquay 8 miles. Eden Project 24 miles.

Open: 1 April - 31 October.

Directions

From Goonhaven take road for Perranporth. Site entrance on right before going down the hill. GPS: 50.359357, -5.143635

Charges guide

Per unit incl. 2 persons	
and electricity	£ 8.00 - £ 61.00
extra person	free - £ 2.00
dog	£ 3.00

Polruan-by-Fowey

Polruan Holidays Camping & Caravanning

Polruan-by-Fowey PL23 1QH (Cornwall) T: 01726 870263. E: polholiday@aol.com

alanrogers.com/UK0190

Polruan is a rural site in an elevated position on the opposite side of the river to Fowey, 200 metres from the coastal path. With 47 touring pitches and ten holiday caravans to let, this is a very pleasant little site. The holiday homes are arranged in a neat circle, with a central area for some touring units, including seven pitches with gravel hardstanding and electricity, one fully serviced. The remaining touring pitches are in an adjacent field with eight electricity hook-ups, which is part level for motorcaravans and part on a gentle slope for tents. There are marvellous sea views, but it could be a little exposed when the wind blows off the sea. A raised picnic area gives more views across the estuary to Fowey. This is a nice little park in a popular tourist area, within walking distance (downhill all the way, and vice versa!) of the village, where there are various hostelries and a passenger ferry to Fowey. A member of the Countryside Discovery group.

Facilities

The fully equipped, heated, sanitary block has modern, controllable showers, large enough for an adult and child. Laundry room and dishwashing sinks. Motorcaravan service facilities. Range of recycling bins. Reception (with a small terrace) doubles as a shop for everyday needs including fresh fruit and vegetables. Gas. Microwave. Hot drinks machine and freezer for ice packs. Tourist information and bus timetables (for Looe, etc). Sloping field area with swings for children. Max. 2 dogs. Off site: Coastal path 200 yds. Fishing 0.5 miles. Riding and bicycle hire 3 miles. Golf 10 miles.

Open: Easter - 1 October.

Directions

From main A390 at East Taphouse take B3359 towards Looe. After 5 miles fork right signed Bodinnick and ferry. Watch for signs for Polruan and site to left. Follow these carefully along narrow Cornish lanes to site on right just before village. GPS: 50.32759, -4.62515

Charges guide

Per unit incl. 2 persons	
and electricity	£ 14.00 - £ 22.00
extra person	£ 3.00 - £ 6.00
child (2-15 yrs)	£ 1.00 - £ 3.00
dog	£ 1.00 - £ 2.00

No credit cards.

Redruth
Globe Vale Holiday Park

Radnor, Redruth TR16 4BH (Cornwall) T: 01209 891183. E: info@globevale.co.uk

alanrogers.com/UK0114

A family run, well maintained, 13-acre site, in countryside where the tin mine chimneys are a stark reminder of the past. The Owen family have worked hard in the past few years to upgrade the site. A number of mobile homes are to be found in the first part of the site amidst a mix of trees and shrubs. A further neatly grassed and sheltered area has serviced pitches on hardstanding. Two large, open fields with wonderful countryside views and Cornish stone walls, have some 100 touring pitches around the edges with a central open space. Reception, in the centre of the site, is part of the Owen's home. A very pleasant bar open in peak periods has a popular patio area and serves food and takeaways. For children there is a super play area and large open spaces for running around. Altogether this makes a very good place to stay while visiting the tip of Cornwall. The beaches of St Agnes and Portreath are close and St Ives, Land's End, St Michael's Mount and the Lizard peninsula are all within close driving distance. The site is on the route of the coast-to-coast cycle route.

Facilities

Smart, well equipped Portacabin toilet facilities. Facilities for disabled campers, ramped access. Laundry room. Bar, restaurant, takeaway. Chidren's play area. Caravans to hire. Off site: Bicycle hire 2 miles. Beach 3 miles. 9-hole golf course, riding, boat launching, fishing, sailing all 5 miles.

Open: All year.

See advertisement on page 36

Directions

Heading west on A30 take Redruth/Porthtowan exit, then take Porthtowan exit at roundabout and follow site signs. GPS: 50.257212, -5.218644

Charges guide

Per unit incl. 2 persons and electricity	£ 12.00 - £ 22.00
extra person	£ 2.00
dog	£ 2.00

Redruth
Tehidy Holiday Park

Harris Mill, Illogan, Redruth TR16 4JQ (Cornwall) T: 01209 216489. E: holiday@tehidy.co.uk

alanrogers.com/UK0115

A traditional style, family park, Tehidy offers 30 touring pitches, 24 mobile homes to rent and 6 bungalows. Set on a wooded hillside with a stream at the bottom, there is direct access to a woodland walk alive with primroses and bluebells in springtime. The pitches are terraced where necessary and some are hedged, with others part fenced and with views across the countryside. All have 10A electricity and there are a few with hardstanding. The nearest beach is at Portreath which has a deep rock pool for swimming at low tide. The owners live on site and are constantly looking for ways to improve the site and to provide a peaceful and relaxing environment. Whilst the grass is neatly cut, the banks are left for nature to develop. There is a request bus stop outside the entrance for Truro, St Ives and Newquay. This is surfing country but you can also windsurf at St Stithian's reservoir. Tehidy Country Park (250 acres of woodland) is nearby, together with Tehidy Golf Club.

Facilities

Modern fully equipped toilet block. Laundry facilities. Reception with shop area. Games room and tourist information. Play area with small trampoline. Netball. Table tennis. Picnic tables. Woodland walk. Local takeaway delivery. Pub and restaurant within walking distance. WiFi. Dogs are not accepted. Off site: Golf and bicycle hire 1 mile. Beach and riding 2.5 miles. Sailing 4 miles.

Open: March - November.

Directions

Leave A30 at exit for Redruth, Porthtowan and Porthreath. Follow further signs for Porthreath and pick up signs to site. GPS: 50.244939, -5.252935

Charges guide

Per unit incl. 2 persons and electricity	£ 15.00 - £ 22.00
extra person	£ 2.00

See advertisement on page 36

For latest campsite news visit
alanrogers.com

Redruth

Lanyon Holiday Park

Loscombe Lane, Four Lanes, Redruth TR16 6LP (Cornwall) T: 01209 313474.
E: info@lanyonholidaypark.co.uk **alanrogers.com/UK0016**

Lanyon's location is a pleasant surprise after the somewhat grey landscape found in parts of the tip of Cornwall. Tucked away down a lane, the holiday caravans are attractively situated with hedged touring fields beyond. A neat tarmac road curves around to reception, the pub and an indoor swimming pool. There are 25 large hedged touring pitches around the edge of two level fields and room for around 40 tents in high season in a separate field. A large play area for children is overlooked by the roof top terrace of the bar. This is a pleasant destination for a family holiday with something for everyone.

Facilities

One traditional toilet block is attached to reception with heating. Two others are of Portacabin type but well maintained. Baby changing. Showers may be in short supply at peak times. Laundry room. Bar serving meals (22/5-5/9). Heated indoor pool (10x4 m. April-Oct). Games room. Play area and trampoline. Caravan Storage. WiFi (charged). Min. stay 5 nights in high season. Off site: Watersports at Stithians Lake 1 mile. Riding, fishing and bicycle hire 2 miles. Golf and beach 5 miles.

Open: Easter - 31 October.

Directions

From southwest side of Redruth take B3297 Helston road. After 1 mile enter Four Lanes village. Pass two shops then take second right into Loscombe Lane. Follow to park on right. GPS: 50.20292, -5.24554

Charges guide

Per unit incl. 2 persons and electricity	£ 12.00 - £ 22.00
extra person	£ 2.00 - £ 4.00

Saint Agnes

Beacon Cottage Farm Holidays

Beacon Drive, Saint Agnes TR5 0NU (Cornwall) T: 01872 552347. E: beaconcottagefarm@lineone.net
alanrogers.com/UK0125

Amazing views greet you as you arrive at Beacon Farm. The stark remains of Wheal Coates tin mine stand out against the cliffs and views over the sea stretch for 25 miles – as far as St Ives. A mixed beef and arable farm, Beacon has its own home bred herd of beef cows and calves. The buildings and the impressive stone walls are extremely well maintained. One large, sloping field and a smaller one enjoy sea views but can be less sheltered than the pitches in smaller paddocks which are sheltered by walls and trees. In all there are 70 pitches of varying size, 42 with 10A electricity.

Facilities

Good stone built toilet blocks are fully equipped and include a family room. Baby bath and changing mat. Laundry room. Motorcaravan station. Fresh supplies are kept in reception (papers, bread and eggs). Fish and chip van calls once a week. Play area with adventure type equipment. Dog exercise field. Min. 7 nights in school holidays. Off site: Fishing and beach 0.5 miles. Riding 1.5 miles. Bicycle hire 2 miles. Golf 3 miles.

Open: Easter/1 April - 30 September.

Directions

From the A30 travelling west take B3277 (signed St Agnes) at Chiverton roundabout. At roundabout approaching St Agnes, turn left for Chapel Porth and follow brown Beacon Cottage Farm signs. GPS: 50.30567, -5.2249

Charges guide

Per unit incl. 2 persons and electricity	£ 19.70 - £ 25.70
extra person	£ 3.20 - £ 4.70

Saint Austell

Heligan Park

Saint Ewe, Saint Austell PL26 6EL (Cornwall) T: 01726 843485. E: info@heliganpark.co.uk
alanrogers.com/UK0410

A peaceful, attractive park in a mature garden setting, Heligan Park complements its sister site, Pentewan Sands with its busy beach life and many activities. The mature trees and flowering shrubs here have been further landscaped to provide an attractive situation for a number of holiday homes (17 to rent). These face out over a part of the 'Lost Valley' of Heligan fame with the touring pitches below on sloping grass, some terraced and others in a more level situation (some with handstanding) amongst trees and shrubs. In all, there are 100 good sized touring pitches, 80 with 16A electricity.

Facilities

Fully equipped and well kept, the modern, heated toilet block includes a unisex room with bath and small size bath. Extra showers in separate block. Fully equipped laundry room. Small shop (Easter-14/09). Adventure playground. Off site: Beach/sailing 1.5 miles. Riding 2 miles. Golf 3.5 miles. Bicycle hire/boat launching. Lost Gardens of Heligan next door.

Open: Mid January - end November.

Directions

From the St Austell ring road take the B3273 for Mevagissey. After 3.5 miles, pass Pentewan Sands, continue up the hill and turn right following site signs. Park is on left just before reaching Heligan Gardens. GPS: 50.288833, -4.812083

Charges guide

Per unit incl. 2 persons and electricity	£ 11.35 - £ 26.45
extra person	£ 2.10 - £ 4.45

For latest campsite news visit
alanrogers.com

Saint Austell
Carlyon Bay Caravan & Camping Park

Bethesda, Carlyon Bay, Saint Austell PL25 3RE (Cornwall) T: 01726 812735. E: holidays@carlyonbay.net

alanrogers.com/UK0290

Tranquil open meadows edged by mature woodland, well cared for by the Taylor family who live on site, provide a beautiful holiday setting with the nearest beach five minutes walk from the top gate. The original farm buildings have been converted and added to, providing an attractive covered, central area with a certain individuality of design which is very pleasing. Pitches are in five spacious areas and allow for a family meadow and a dog free meadow (high season only). There are 115 marked pitches with electricity (10/16A), some with hardstanding and 8 have full services. All are on flat, terraced or gently sloping grass with flowers and flowering shrubs or edged with trees. The impressively tiled toilet blocks are of good quality and design. In addition to the attractive kidney shaped pool and paddling pool there is now a large rectangular pool (also heated) within a walled and paved area which is excellent for sunbathing. This forms part of the central area at the heart of the site and complete with tables and chairs it is the place to enjoy family entertainment in high season. There is also a pleasant family pub and Kidsworld for children within walking distance.

Facilities

Three individually designed, modern toilet blocks (one heated) provide a full range of comfortable facilities for all your needs. Fully equipped laundry room. Modern reception with little shop. Takeaway (May-mid Sept). Heated swimming and paddling pools (Whitsun-Sept). TV lounge. Crazy golf. Play areas (including adventure type). Eden Project tickets. Off site: Bus service on main road. Coastal footpath nearby. Buses to St Austell and Fowey from park entrance. Pub 1 mile. Sailing 2 miles. Eden Project 2 miles. Golf and riding 3 miles. Bicycle hire 4 miles. Boat launching 5 miles.

Open: Easter/1 April - end September.

See advertisement on page 37

Directions

From Plymouth direction on A390, pass Lostwithiel and 1 mile after village of St Blazey, turn left at roundabout beside Britannia Inn. After 400 yds. turn right on a concrete road and right again at site sign. GPS: 50.34085, -4.737217

Charges guide

Per unit incl. 2 persons	
and electricity	£ 15.00 - £ 28.00
incl. services	£ 18.00 - £ 31.00
extra person	£ 5.00 - £ 6.00
child (3-15 yrs)	£ 4.00 - £ 5.00
dog (max. 2)	£ 3.00

Motorcaravan less £1, hiker/tent less £2 per night. Camping Cheques accepted.

Saint Austell
Meadow Lakes

Hewas Water, Saint Austell PL26 7JG (Cornwall) T: 01726 882540. E: info@meadow-lakes.co.uk

alanrogers.com/UK0415

Meadow Lakes is a well equipped park set in 56 acres of rolling Cornish countryside of woodland and lakes and is a wonderful place for a family holiday. The level grassy or hardstanding touring pitches here are of a good size, most with electrical connections and views of the lakes or the surrounding rural countryside. The central farm buildings house all the amenities, including playbarn, games room and shop. Also available are the heated outdoor swimming pool, four coarse fishing lakes (each stocked with a different range of fish), pets corner (small animals and donkeys) and outdoor play area. Lodges, caravans and chalets are available to rent. A proportion of the site is given over to smart wooden lodges available to buy, and holiday caravans and small bungalows to rent or buy. In one corner there are two camping pods to rent. The park managers encourage a happy and friendly atmosphere.

Facilities

New sanitary building containing three en-suite units per sex. Launderette. Shop. Heated swimming pool (27/5-4/9). Indoor and outdoor play areas. Tennis court. Fishing (free, but rod licence needed). Play areas. Pets corner. WiFi (free). Off site: Golf (18 holes) 3 miles. Riding, bicycle hire and nearest beach 4 miles. Shipwreck rescue and heritage centre 5 miles. The Lost Gardens of Heligan 4 miles. Eden Project 8 miles.

Open: 19 March - 31 October.

Directions

Site is 4 miles west of St Austell. Take the A390 and then fork left to join the B3287 and the site is 1 mile further on the left. GPS: 50.30075, -4.85708

Charges guide

Per unit incl. 2 persons	
and electricity	£ 15.00 - £ 25.00
extra person	£ 5.00
child (3-12 yrs)	£ 3.50
dog (1st free)	£ 2.50

For latest campsite news visit
alanrogers.com

Saint Ives
Ayr Holiday Park

Higher Ayr, Saint Ives TR26 1EJ (Cornwall) T: 01736 795855. E: recept@ayrholidaypark.co.uk
alanrogers.com/UK0030

Ayr Holiday Park has an unparalleled position overlooking St Ives Bay and Porthmeor beach and is a popular, well cared for site. On first arrival it may seem to be all caravan holiday homes, but behind them is a series of naturally sloping fields with marvellous views providing a total of 90 pitches, of which 40 are for touring caravans and motorcaravans. These pitches are on grass, all with 16A electricity and several fully serviced with hardstanding. An extra field for tents is open in July and August.

Facilities

The excellent toilet block includes two family shower rooms and facilities for baby changing and disabled visitors. Wetsuit showers. Fully equipped laundry room. Motorcaravan point. Games room with TV, hot drinks and snack machines. Adventure play area. Max. 1 dog, contact site first. Bus calls. WiFi (charged). Off site: Spa shop nearby. Tate Gallery and beaches within walking distance. Leisure centre with indoor pool nearby. Golf 1 mile. Riding 2 miles. Sea and coarse fishing 2-3 miles.

Open: All year.

Directions

From A30 follow signs for St Ives for heavy vehicles (not town centre). After 2 miles join B3311 and then B3306 1 mile from St Ives (octagonal building on left). Heading for St Ives turn left at mini roundabout following camping signs through residential areas. Park entrance is 600 yds. at Ayr Terrace. GPS: 50.21261, -5.48928

Charges guide

| Per unit incl. 2 persons and electricity | £ 20.25 - £ 36.00 |
| extra person | £ 4.25 - £ 6.75 |

Saint Ives
Little Trevarrack Holiday Park

Laity Lane, Carbis Bay, Saint Ives TR26 3HW (Cornwall) T: 01736 797580. E: info@littletrevarrack.co.uk
alanrogers.com/UK0035

Little Trevarrack is a traditional Cornish park covering 20 acres, with wonderful views from the top of the site across St Ives bay towards Hayle and the surrounding countryside. It is owned by Neil, son of the owners of Polmanter Park, and Annette Osborne. There are 234 pitches, in five open fields (some with gentle slopes), 153 with 10A electricity and 15 with water and drain as well. Bushes and hedging provide individual pitches and give a continental appearance to the park.

Facilities

The large, central toilet block is well equipped. Baby room. Facilities for disabled visitors. Laundry. Heated swimming and paddling pools (27/5-12/9). Games room. Internet access and WiFi (charged). Play area. Play field. Wild flower field with paths for dog walking. Max. 2 dogs. No kites. Early and late arrivals area. Off site: Beach and fishing 1 mile (dogs are banned from the St Ives beaches in high season). Golf, riding 2 miles. Bicycle hire 4 miles.

Open: 1 April - 30 September.

Directions

Follow signs for St Ives and take A3074 to Carbis Bay. Site is signed on left opposite junction to Carbis Bay beach. Follow road for 150 yds, cross small crossroads and site is the second turn on the right. GPS: 50.187233, -5.470833

Charges guide

| Per unit incl. 2 persons and electricity | £ 17.00 - £ 28.25 |
| extra person | £ 4.00 - £ 7.50 |

Saint Ives
Polmanter Tourist Park

Halsetown, Saint Ives TR26 3LX (Cornwall) T: 01736 795640. E: reception@polmanter.com
alanrogers.com/UK0050

A popular and attractively developed park, Polmanter is located high up at the back of St Ives, with wonderful sea and country views. The Osborne family has worked hard to develop Polmanter as a complete family base. The 250 touring pitches are well spaced in several fields divided by established shrubs and hedges giving large, level, individual pitches with connecting tarmac roads. There are grass and hardstanding multi-serviced pitches with electricity, water, waste water and TV point, serviced pitches with 16A electricity and non-serviced tent pitches. A member of the Best of British group.

Facilities

Three modern toilet blocks can be heated and include en-suite family rooms. Facilities for disabled visitors. Baby room. Laundry. Motorcaravan service point. Shop. Bar with food and family area, takeaway (Whitsun-mid Sept). Heated swimming pool (Whitsun-mid Sept). Entertainment (peak season). Tennis. Putting. Play area. Sports field. Games room. WiFi (charged). Off site: Golf 1 mile. Fishing, riding and bicycle hire within 2 miles. Note: dogs are banned from the St Ives beaches in high season.

Open: 1 April - 31 October.

Directions

Take A3074 to St Ives from A30 and then first left at a mini roundabout taking 'Holiday Route' (B3311) to St Ives (Halsetown). At T-junction turn right (Halsetown), right again at the Halsetown Inn then first left. GPS: 50.196183, -5.491017

Charges guide

| Per unit incl. 2 persons and electricity | £ 17.50 - £ 30.00 |
| extra person | £ 4.00 - £ 8.00 |

Camping Cheques accepted.

For latest campsite news visit
alanrogers.com

Saint Ives

Trevalgan Touring Park

Saint Ives TR26 3BJ (Cornwall) T: 01736 792048. E: recept@trevalgantouringpark.co.uk

alanrogers.com/UK0040

Trevalgan is owned by the same family that owns Ayr Holiday Park. It is a quiet, traditional style of park, located on the cliffs 1.5 miles west of bustling Saint Ives. It is a truly rural location where you can enjoy spectacular views and an abundance of flora and fauna. There are 120 clearly marked pitches (88 with 16A electricity and some with water as well) in two level fields edged by Cornish stone walls – it could be a little exposed on a windy day. The park is very popular with walkers with direct access to the coastal path. A member of the Countryside Discovery group.

Facilities

A fully equipped toilet block includes a baby room and facilities for disabled visitors. Motorcaravan service point. Small shop (in reception). Mobile shop calls daily. Gas supplies. Games field, adventure play area. Purpose built games room with TV and coffee machine. Off site: Riding and golf within 2 miles. Fishing 3 miles. Bicycle hire 8 miles. Regular bus service to St Ives and back (June-mid Sept). As well as the coastal path, a path leads to St Ives across the fields (30-40 minutes).

Open: 1 May - 30 September.

Directions

Approach site down a narrow Cornish lane from the B3306 St Ives - Lands End road, following sign. GPS: 50.20769, -5.51882

Charges guide

Per unit incl. 2 persons	
and electricity	£ 18.25 - £ 28.25
extra person	£ 3.50 - £ 5.50
child (5-16 yrs)	£ 2.00 - £ 2.75
dog	£ 1.50 - £ 2.50

RAC AA

For a more rural experience

'A touring park just 2 miles from St.Ives town centre.
Beautiful scenery, new facilities, serviced pitches, summer bus service to town.
Ideal for families, walkers, cyclists - explore St.Ives and West Cornwall.'

www.trevalgantouringpark.co.uk   Telephone: 01736 792048

Saint Just

Roselands Caravan & Camping Park

Dowran, Saint Just, Penzance TR19 7RS (Cornwall) T: 01736 788571. E: info@roselands.co.uk

alanrogers.com/UK0025

Roselands is a small, family owned park situated on the Cornish moors overlooking the village of St Just and with marvellous views of the sea and countryside around Lands End. In all there are 14 holiday homes to let, 17 level grassy touring pitches (all with 16A electricity) and some provision for tents. The owner's home, providing a bar and conservatory, along with reception and a small shop, sits in the centre of the park. The conservatory acts as a community family room with games, Internet facility and tourist information with a play area outside and a games room nearby. This area is very popular with walkers and birdwatchers. Bicycles are available to hire. The park itself originated in 1972 in old clay pits – the area where most of the holiday homes are located was one of the pits and is consequently very sheltered. Subsequent owners have added to the house and the current owners, Craig and Kerry with their young family, do everything themselves.

Facilities

Small traditional toilet block, fully equipped and can be heated. Laundry facilities. Small shop mainly for basics and gas. Bar with bar food served in conservatory (all year). Conservatory with TV and Internet access. Play area. Games room. Bicycle hire. WiFi. Off site: Fishing and golf 1 mile. Riding, beach and surfing at Sennen Cove 2 miles. Boat launching 5 miles. Nearby Lands End and Cape Cornwall. Minack Outdoor Theatre.

Open: 1 January - 31 October.

Directions

Take the A3071 from Penzance for St Just. Follow for 5.5 miles then 0.5 miles before St Just turn left at sign for site. GPS: 50.11323, -5.658

Charges guide

Per unit incl. 2 persons	
and electricity	£ 12.50 - £ 18.50
extra person	£ 4.50
child (under 12 yrs)	£ 3.50
dog	£ 1.00

For latest campsite news visit
alanrogers.com

Saint Martins by Looe

Polborder House Caravan & Camping Park

Bucklawren Road, Saint Martins by Looe PL13 1QS (Cornwall) T: 01503 240265.
E: reception@polborderhouse.co.uk **alanrogers.com/UK0320**

Polborder House is a lovely site, open all year, which will appeal to those who prefer a quiet, well kept, small family site, to the larger ones with many on-site activities. With good countryside views, up to 36 touring units can be accommodated on well tended grass. Good sized pitches are marked with some hedging between pairs of pitches to give privacy and most have electrical connections (16A). There are several hardstandings and 17 serviced pitches. Five mobile homes are available to rent. The new owners, Amanda and Dale Byers, live on the park and make everyone very welcome.

Facilities	Directions
Fully equipped and heated sanitary block. Family room planned. Laundry room. En-suite toilet unit for disabled visitors. Shop for gas and basics, and some camping accessories. Play area. Tourist information. WiFi (charged). Off site: Restaurant 500 m. Fishing and golf within 2 miles. Diving school at Seaton 2 miles. Scuba centre and fishing trips Looe 2.5 miles. Riding 6 miles.	Park is less than half a mile south of the B3253. Turn off 2 miles east of Looe and follow signs to park at junctions; care is needed with narrow road. GPS: 50.377217, -4.4185

Open: All year.

Charges guide

Per unit incl. 2 persons and electricity	£ 15.00 - £ 24.50
extra person	£ 4.25 - £ 7.00

Saltash

Dolbeare Caravan & Camping Park

Saint Ives Road, Landrake, Saltash PL12 5AF (Cornwall) T: 01752 851332. E: reception@dolbeare.co.uk
alanrogers.com/UK0440

Dolbeare Park has a countryside setting. It is surrounded by trees and farmland and slopes slightly at the top. Connected by a gravel road, there are 60 hardstanding and gravel pitches, all with 16A electricity connections. A four acre camping paddock can also be used for rallies. For children there is a low level adventure play area and a separate area for games. Giant chess and Connect 4 games will entertain families. A small dog walk is provided at the top of the park. Reception has a good supply of tourist information and maps. A member of the Best of British Group.

Facilities	Directions
A modern sanitary block has underfloor heating, family rooms and a room for visitors with disabilities. Small drying room. Laundry. Motorcaravan services. Reception doubles as a small licensed shop for basics including takeaway food. Adventure play area. Giant chess and Connect 4. WiFi (charged). Barrier with card system (£10 deposit). Off site: Fishing 1 mile. Riding 3 miles. Golf 5 miles. Nearest beach 8 miles.	After crossing the Tamar Bridge into Cornwall, continue on A38 for 4 miles. In Landrake village turn right following signs and site is 0.75 miles on the right. GPS: 50.43064, -4.30551

Open: All year.

Charges 2012

Per unit incl. 2 persons and electricity	£ 16.50 - £ 23.00
extra person	£ 4.50

Truro

Chacewater Park

Cox Hill, Chacewater, Truro TR4 8LY (Cornwall) T: 01209 820762. E: enquiries@chacewaterpark.co.uk
alanrogers.com/UK0010

For those who want to be away from the hectic coastal resorts and take advantage of the peace and quiet of an adults only park, this will be an excellent, value-for-money choice. Chacewater has a pleasant rural situation and the site is run with care and attention by Richard Peterken and his daughters Debbie and Mandy. It provides 100 level touring pitches, all with electricity (10A) and 90 with hardstanding, in two large field areas (slight slope) edged with trees or in small bays formed by hedges. There are 29 serviced pitches (electricity, water, and drainage connections) and an area for dog owners.

Facilities	Directions
The main toilet block provides well equipped showers and two en-suite units. Laundry room. Second fully equipped block near reception providing roomy showers open direct to outside. Gas supplies. Icepack service. Library in reception. Only adults are accepted (over 30 yrs). Max. 1 dog, contact site first. Off site: Golf, riding and bicycle hire, all within 3 miles. Bus stop 100 yds. Cornish tramways/railway coast to coast trail to walk or cycle nearby.	From the A30 about 28 miles west of Bodmin take A3047 (Scorrier) and continue under bridge to roundabout then left towards St Day. Continue for 500 yards turning right at crossroads onto B3298 (St Day) and continue for 1 mile. Turn left at the crossroads and continue for 3/4 of a mile, then left at the crossroads with camping sign. Park is next right. GPS: 50.250802, -5.172557

Open: 1 May - 30 September.

Charges guide

Per unit incl. 2 persons and electricity	£ 15.00 - £ 18.00

Truro

Porthtowan Tourist Park

Mile Hill, Porthtowan, Truro TR4 8TY (Cornwall) T: 01209 890256. E: Admin@PorthtowanTouristPark.co.uk

alanrogers.com/UK0014

This delightful and sheltered park is set a mile back from the pretty seaside village of Porthtowan, a haven for surfers but enjoyed by families who can explore the rock pools and coves. The beach has Blue Flag status. In an Area of Outstanding Natural Beauty, tall chimney stacks, stark against the sky, remain a reminder of the tin mining for which this area of Cornwall was once renowned. This is now a peaceful spot with plenty of space on the park and tall trees surrounding the three camping fields. There are 80 pitches around the edges of the fields, on level grass and half with 10A electricity. There are a few hardstandings. The park is attractively laid out with tarmac roads and flowering shrubs. The facilities were spotless when we visited in high season. There is a recycling box for odds and ends left behind by holidaymakers but of potential use to future visitors. A large adventure type play area in the centre of the large top field is popular. There is a waiting list for seasonal pitches and caravan storage. The Coast to Coast Tramway trail passes within half a mile of the site. The Newquay - St Ives bus stops in the village.

Facilities

Modern fully equipped toilet block with two en-suite family rooms also suitable for disabled visitors. Shop in reception. Games room with tourist information. Adventure type play area. Fish and chip van calls Wednesday teatimes. Bicycle hire by arrangement. Off site: Riding 200 yds. Nearest beach 1 mile. Fishing and golf 8 miles.

Open: 1 April - 30 September.

Directions

From the A30 take exit for Redruth, Porthtowan and Portreath and follow signs for Porthtowan for 2 miles. At T-junction turn right up hill to park on the left just past a restaurant.
GPS: 50.27374, -5.23768

Charges guide

Per unit incl. 2 persons and electricity	£ 12.75 - £ 20.50
extra person	£ 4.00
child (3-16 yrs)	£ 2.50
dog	free - £ 1.00

A quiet family site with large level pitches on the outskirts of the village. Close to Blue Flag beach, Coastal Path and Cycle Trail, and central for touring Cornwall.

Mile Hill, Porthtowan, Truro, Cornwall. TR4 8TY
01209 890256
admin@porthtowantouristpark.co.uk
www.porthtowantouristpark.co.uk

Truro

Killiwerris Camping & Caravan Park

Penstraze, Chacewater, Truro TR4 8PF (Cornwall) T: 01872 561356. E: killiwerris@aol.com

alanrogers.com/UK0012

Tucked down a Cornish lane, Killiwerris is a rare find. It has been developed from a large garden and the field surrounding the house into a small and delightful touring park which provides 20 good sized pitches for caravans and motorcaravans. Of these, 16 are semi-separated either by low fencing or hedging, all with hardstanding in the front field with flowering shrubs sheltered by trees. The birds love it, as do adult humans – the park is adult only so it is very peaceful and now open all year. Three further pitches are found in the back field. Electricity (16A) is available for all the pitches with water points between two. The park is now owned by the Ashurst family and being centrally situated five miles from the city of Truro and four from the coastal village of St Agnes, this is an ideal base to explore the Cornish countryside.

Facilities

Excellent heated toilet block in a log cabin provides en-suite facilities to a very high standard. Separate provision for disabled visitors with ramped access. Separate laundry room. WiFi. Max. 2 dogs. Off site: Bus stop 8 minutes level walk. Chacewater village (shop, pub, etc) 1 mile. Riding 1.5 miles. Fishing and golf 2 miles. Bicycle hire 2-3 miles. Beach 4.5 miles.

Open: All year.

Directions

Using the A30 in the direction of Penzance, exit at Chiverton Cross roundabout (a large roundabout 28 miles west of Bodmin signed for Truro and St Agnes). Take third exit for Blackwater and in 500 yds turn left into Kea Down Road. Park is 1 mile on right. GPS: 50.2655, -5.155

Charges guide

Per unit incl. 2 persons, electricity and awning	£ 15.00 - £ 19.00
extra person	£ 4.00
dog (max. 2)	£ 0.50

No credit cards.

For latest campsite news visit
alanrogers.com

Truro

Silverbow Park

Goonhavern, Truro TR4 9NX (Cornwall) T: 01872 572347. E: silverbowhols@btconnect.com

alanrogers.com/UK0120

Silverbow has been developed by the Taylor family over many years and they are justifiably proud of their efforts. They believe Silverbow is a way of life and staying is an experience – they have certainly created a relaxed and tranquil atmosphere seeking to encourage couples and young families (teenagers are not accepted). Hard work, planting and landscaping has provided a beautiful environment set in 21 acres. There are 90 tourist pitches which are all of good size and include 69 'super' pitches in a newly developed area, with electricity, water and drainage, which are even larger. Many are on a slight slope with some attractive views. There are also 15 park-owned, high quality leisure homes. Much free space is not used for camping, including an excellent sports area with two grass and two all-weather tennis courts, as well as wild meadow and wooded areas ideal for walks. A natural area with ponds has been created to encourage wildlife (Silverbow was the first in Cornwall to gain the coveted '5-year Bellamy Gold' award for conservation). The park is 2.5 miles from the long sandy beach at Perranporth (30 minutes walk away from traffic) and 6 miles from Newquay.

Facilities

Two good toilet blocks include private cabins, four family shower/toilet rooms, two accessible by wheelchairs, and a bath on payment. Laundry room. Motorcaravan services. Free freezer service. Shop for basics (mid May-mid Sept). Covered, heated swimming pool and small paddling pool (mid May-mid Sept) gated and sheltered by high surrounding garden walls. Games room. Adventure playground. Play field. Tennis. Off site: Gliding, riding and fishing nearby. Concessionary green fees are available at Perranporth golf club. Pub within walking distance.

Open: 4 May - 28 September.

Directions

Entrance is directly off the main A3075 road 0.5 miles south of Goonhavern.
GPS: 50.336567, -5.120633

Charges guide

Per unit incl. 2 persons	£ 14.00 - £ 27.00
extra person under 50 yrs	£ 3.00 - £ 6.00
extra child (2-12 yrs)	
or adult over 50 yrs	£ 2.50 - £ 4.50
dog	free - £ 2.00

Children over 12 yrs with or without parents not accepted. Discounts available.

Truro

Trethem Mill Touring Park

Saint Just-in-Roseland, Saint Mawes, Truro TR2 5JF (Cornwall) T: 01872 580504. E: reception@trethem.com

alanrogers.com/UK0090

The Akeroyd family are proud of their park and work hard to keep it really well maintained and have been recognised for their commitment to high standards. They aim to attract couples and families who seek peace and tranquillity, and can manage without a bar and on-site entertainment. Trethem is a 'strictly touring' park with 84 pitches all with electricity, 60 with hardstanding and TV connections and 21 with water and waste water. All pitches are large, most on slightly sloping ground, some terraced, with the lower field more level and sheltered. All are individual or in bays, divided by hedging (some still growing) giving your own area. There is a comfortable and spacious feel as the park covers 11.5 acres, about half of which provides a dog and nature walk and recreation area. A member of the Best of British Group.

Facilities

The well equipped central toilet block is kept spotlessly clean and is heated in cooler weather. En-suite facilities for disabled visitors which can double as a family room. Baby room (under 4s). Reception/shop, only small but well stocked and licensed. Freezer for ice packs (free). Motorcaravan services. Well equipped adventure playground (closed at 21.00). Large field for ball games. Extra field for dog walking. WiFi throughout park (charged). Off site: Fishing 1.5 miles. Beach, sailing, boat launching and bicycle hire 2 miles. Golf 6 miles. Riding 8 miles.

Open: 30 March - 7 October.

Directions

From Tregony follow A3078 to St Mawes. About 2 miles after passing through Trewithian, watch for caravan and camping sign.
GPS: 50.19003, -5.00096

Charges guide

Per unit incl. 2 persons and electricity	£ 17.00 - £ 29.00
extra person	£ 5.00
child (3-14 yrs)	£ 4.00
dog	£ 1.00

For latest campsite news visit

alanrogers.com

Truro

Penrose Holiday Park

Halt Road, Goonhavern, nr. Perranporth, Truro TR4 9QF (Cornwall) T: 01872 573185.
E: info@penroseholidaypark.com **alanrogers.com/UK0140**

Penrose Holiday Park is owned and run by the Welch family and is situated on the edge of the village of Goonhavern. It is level and sheltered, with pitches spread over five fields with flower beds and bushes set amongst them. These colourful flowers and those at the entrance give the park a neat and well cared for feel. There are over 112 pitches with 10/16A electricity, many with hardstanding, water and drainage. Three new caravan holiday homes are for rent. A takeaway opens in peak season and other busy periods serving breakfast and evening meals. It is only a short walk to the village and its popular pub, and buses to Newquay stop in the village. The superb beach at Perranporth is just 2.5 miles away. Only couples and families are welcome.

Facilities

The fully equipped and refurbished toilet block is well maintained and includes four en-suite family rooms. Facilities for disabled visitors. Well equipped laundry. Gas supplies. Takeaway incl. breakfast and evening meals (high season). Playground. Dog field. Caravan storage. WiFi. Off site: Pub, bus stop, shop within two minutes walk. Fishing and riding 0.5 miles. Golf 1 mile.

Open: 1 April - 31 October.

Directions

Take the A30 from Exeter past Bodmin and Indian Queens. Just after a wind farm take the B3285 to Perranporth. Park is on the left as you enter Goonhavern village. GPS: 50.340133, -5.106567

Charges guide

Per unit incl. 2 persons and electricity	£ 14.00 - £ 25.00
incl. services	£ 16.00 - £ 30.00
extra person (5 yrs and over)	£ 3.50 - £ 4.25
dog	£ 1.00 - £ 2.00

Families and couples only.
Less 50p for over 60s if booked.

MOTORHOMES
TENTS
CARAVANS

PENR SE
HOLIDAY PARK

Goonhavern, (Nr. Perranporth,) Tr
TEL: 01872 573 185 - Web: www.pen

Truro

Carnon Downs Caravan & Camping Park

Carnon Downs, Truro TR3 6JJ (Cornwall) T: 01872 862283. E: info@carnon-downs-caravanpark.co.uk
alanrogers.com/UK0180

Carnon Downs is an excellent all year park run personally and enthusiastically by Simon Vallance, a very forward thinking owner. It has been thoughtfully laid out in a series of fields covering 20 acres so that all pitches back onto attractive hedging or areas of flowering shrubs and arranged to provide some pleasant bays or other, more open grass areas. Gravel roads connect the 150 pitches, most with electricity (10/16A) and over 70 with hardstanding. Of these 55 are serviced, with the newer ones being exceptionally large and surrounded by young shrubs. On arrival you will receive a warm welcome, a neatly presented layout plan of the park and a touring information pack. Affiliated to the Caravan Club.

Facilities

Two excellent modern, light and airy, heated blocks include en-suite units and dishwashing and facilities for the disabled. Another well maintained block, also heated, includes some washbasins in cubicles and showers (unisex). Three good family bath/shower rooms, one suitable for use by disabled visitors and families. Mother and toddler room, two baby sinks and full sized bath. Two laundries with freezers. Motorcaravan service point (ask at reception). Good adventure-type play area. Football field. Gas, newspapers and caravan accessories. General room with TV. Good dog walks. Caravan storage. Off site: Walks direct from site. Bus outside site for Truro/Falmouth. Pub/restaurant 100 yds across the road. Golf 1 mile. Riding and bicycle hire 2 miles. Fishing 5 miles.

Open: All year.

Directions

From Truro take A39 Falmouth road. After 3 miles, park entrance is directly off the Carnon Downs roundabout. GPS: 50.22529, -5.08012

Charges guide

Per unit incl. 2 persons and electricity	£ 19.00 - £ 27.50
extra person	£ 3.50
child (5-16 yrs)	£ 3.00
all-service hardstanding	£ 2.50

For latest campsite news visit
alanrogers.com

Truro

Cosawes Park

Perranarworthal, Truro TR3 7QS (Cornwall) T: 01872 863724. E: info@cosawes.com

alanrogers.com/UK0185

Cosawes is set in a beautiful wooded valley where there are woodland and river walks and the park offers a quiet and relaxing holiday. The Fraser family have owned the site for many years and the recent upgrading of the facilities is excellent, particularly for a site that is open all year. Cosawes now offers 25 large, serviced pitches on gravel hardstandings, each in its own fenced space. These are particularly popular with motorcaravan owners and very useful for twin-axle vans. This still leaves around 35 grass pitches which are slightly sloping, some with electricity. A separate large residential area is private and away from the touring section. The situation of the park makes it good for visiting both the north and south coasts. Falmouth with its maritime museum is well worth visiting, whilst the north coast is popular for its surfing beaches. Saint Ives, Lands End and the unique Lizard peninsula are all within easy reach.

Facilities

Modern new block beside the new serviced pitches provides 2 en-suite family rooms also good for disabled visitors. Toilets, laundry and dishwashing facilities are downstairs, upstairs are showers and washbasins in cubicles. Dog walking field. WiFi (charged). Walks from site. Off site: Two pubs within walking distance. Supermarket 3 miles. Sailing and boat launching 3-5 miles. Fishing, golf and bicycle hire 5 miles. Beach at Falmouth 7 miles.

Open: All year.

See advertisement on page 37

Directions

Site is midway between Truro and Falmouth. Approaching from Truro via A39, after village of Perranarworthal, the park is clearly signed on the right, and is 300 yds up the lane on the left. Use the second entrance. GPS: 50.197026, -5.128319

Charges guide

Per unit incl. 2 persons and electricity	£ 12.50 - £ 16.50
hardstanding, serviced pitch	£ 14.50 - £ 22.50
extra person	£ 3.00
child (5-16 yrs)	£ 2.00

Truro

Summer Valley Touring Park

Shortlanesend, Truro TR4 9DW (Cornwall) T: 01872 277878. E: res@summervalley.co.uk

alanrogers.com/UK0510

Summer Valley is a quiet and mature, but very pleasant, small rural park suitable for visiting both the north and south coast of Cornwall. South facing, the park consists of a large well kept grass area with reception and facilities to one side. A tarmac road circles this and mature trees edge the whole site providing shelter but still allowing rural views. Caravans go on the central area which slopes gently and is divided down the centre with more mature trees and shrubs. The pitches around the perimeter area are semi-divided by shrubs and used more for tents. There is provision for 60 units of all types, but only 50 are used, 45 with electricity connections (10/16A). A Countryside Discovery site.

Facilities

A good quality, solid toilet block is well maintained with ladies to the left and men to the right, plus unisex showers. Washbasins in cabins and one shower/toilet en-suite per sex. Laundry facilities. Campers' rest room with library. Reception/licensed shop (basics) with freezer pack service (reduced hours out of main season). Gas supplies. Small play area hidden in a corner but part of the central area is left for ball games. Off site: Village of Shortlanesend with post office and pub within walking distance. Fishing and bicycle hire 2.5 miles. Golf 3 miles. Riding 5 miles. Perranporth beach 6 miles (dogs are allowed away from the village end).

Open: 31 March - 31 October.

Directions

From Truro take B3284 north, signed Perranporth. Follow for 2.5 miles and site is signed on left just through the village of Shortlanesend. GPS: 50.29098, -5.08823

Charges guide

Per unit incl. 2 persons incl. electricity	£ 14.50 - £ 18.50
extra person	£ 3.00
child (3-16 yrs)	£ 2.00

For latest campsite news visit

alanrogers.com

Wadebridge

Saint Mabyn Holiday Park

Longstone Road, Saint Mabyn PL30 3BY (Cornwall) T: 01208 841677. E: info@stmabyn.co.uk

alanrogers.com/UK0230

The beaches of north Cornwall and the wilds of Bodmin Moor are all an easy drive from the site. The park has been extensively improved and is now carefully maintained by the Lloyd family and it provides a spacious and relaxed atmosphere. There are 110 level pitches, 90 with 16A electricity, on well drained and well mown grass with 50 hardstandings. There are caravan holiday homes and lodges to let. A nice, sheltered outdoor pool is an added attraction. However, there is no bar although the local village inn has a good reputation for food. The Camel Trail is only two miles, providing a means to cycle or walk all the way to Bodmin, Wadebridge or Padstow. Bodmin and Wadebridge are only five or six miles for supermarket shopping. It is also possible to telephone 'Cor Link' and they will arrange to transport you to the nearest bus route.

Facilities

The fully equipped modern toilet block includes an en-suite unit per sex. Laundry. Heated outdoor swimming pool and paddling pool (late May-early Sept), surrounded by a sheltered, paved and grass sunbathing areas. Good, fenced adventure play area. Play area for small children. Games room. Caravan storage. WiFi. Off site: Fishing, riding and golf 3 miles, bicycle hire 5 miles.

Open: Mid March - end October.

Directions

From Bodmin or Wadebridge on A389, take B3266 north signed Camelford. At village of Longstone turn left signed St Mabyn and brown camping sign. Site is 400 yds. on right. Ignore all other signs to St Mabyn. GPS: 50.5278, -4.745183

Charges guide

Per unit incl. 2 persons	
and electricity	£ 18.00 - £ 22.00
extra person	£ 5.00
child (3-13 yrs)	£ 2.50
dog	£ 1.50
Weekly rate available.	

Wadebridge

Trewince Farm Holiday Park

Saint Issey, Wadebridge PL27 7RL (Cornwall) T: 01208 812830

alanrogers.com/UK0500

A well established and popular park, Trewince Farm is four miles from Padstow and has been developed around a dairy farm with magnificent countryside views. Careful landscaping with flowering shrubs and bushes makes this an attractive setting. There are 35 caravan holiday homes discreetly terraced, some privately owned, some to let. Two touring areas on higher ground provide both hardstanding and level grass pitches with a sheltered tent area. Over half of the 120 touring pitches have electricity (10A) and 34 have water and drainage. The park's main feature is an excellent sheltered, walled and heated swimming pool with paddling pool, and paved sunbathing area. Farm rides and Cornish pasty suppers in the barn are organised in the high season.

Facilities

Two fully equipped, well maintained toilet blocks include washbasins in cabins, hair care rooms, dishwashing under cover and laundry rooms. Also children's room with bath (20p) and facilities for disabled visitors. Well stocked shop (all season) by reception. Fish and chip van calls twice weekly, a butcher once a week. Swimming pool. Play area. Games room. Crazy golf. Fishing lake and woodland walk. Off site: Pubs and restaurants in nearby village of St Issey. Riding 3 miles. Golf and bicycle hire 3.5 miles. Beach 4.5 miles. Camel Trail nearby (walking/cycling, goes to Padstow).

Open: 1 April - 31 October.

Directions

From Wadebridge follow A39 towards St Columb and pick up the A389 for Padstow. Site is signed on left in 2 miles. Follow for short distance to park entrance on right. GPS: 50.506604, -4.911692

Charges guide

Per unit incl. 2 persons	
and electricity	£ 12.50 - £ 17.50
extra person	£ 3.50 - £ 4.00
child (3-15 yrs)	£ 2.50 - £ 3.50
hardstanding, drainage	
and electricity	£ 13.50 - £ 18.50

For latest campsite news visit
alanrogers.com

Wadebridge
The Laurels Holiday Park

Padstow Road, Whitecross, Wadebridge PL27 7JQ (Cornwall) T: 01209 313474.
E: info@thelaurelsholidaypark.co.uk **alanrogers.com/UK0505**

This is a small park in a garden-like setting of which the managers are very proud. It is very well maintained and provides 32 level pitches with 16A electricity. Some have hardstanding and some are extra large. Neat hedging marks the pitches and the central area with shrubs and plants is kept clear for enjoyment. A good play area for children is well fenced from the A39 which could be the cause of some road noise. The Camel Trail for walking or cycling is close and follows the estuary from Wadebridge to Padstow. A bus stops outside the site.

Facilities

Well kept fully equipped toilet block. Laundry. Facilities for drying wetsuits. Freezer and communal fridge. Play area with trampoline. Off site: Shops 1 mile. Riding, bicycle hire, boat launching 3 miles. Beach 4 miles. Fishing 5 miles. Camel Trail (walking/cycling).

Open: Easter/1 April - 31 October.

Directions

The Park is half a mile from the Royal Cornwall Showground, at the junction between the A39 and A389 Padstow Road, at Whitecross, 2 miles from Wadebridge. GPS: 50.50827, -4.88192

Charges guide

Per unit incl. 2 persons and electricity	£ 12.00 - £ 22.00

Wadebridge
Tristram Camping Park

Polzeath, Wadebridge PL27 6UG (Cornwall) T: 01208 862215. E: info@tristramcampsite.co.uk
alanrogers.com/UK0525

Polzeath has one of the most spectacular surfing beaches in Cornwall and is just round the corner from the popular resorts of Rock and Padstow. The campsite is situated on the cliff just above the bay on sloping grass and a footpath leads to the beach. This is a popular and compact site for families so space can be tight. A few units up to 26 feet can be accommodated but most of the pitches take 20 foot units. In total there are 107 marked pitches with a smaller area for two-man tents. Two toilet blocks serve the site and 16A electricity is available over most of the site. The coastal path runs along the front of the site. A smart licensed Indian restaurant fronts the reception and toilet block, with a garden overlooking the beach and village.

Facilities

Two solid toilet blocks are fully equipped. 50p token required for showers. Washing machines and dryers. Restaurant. Surf hire (by day/hour). Off site: Shops in village (10 mins. walk). Two golf courses nearby. Foot ferry from Rock for the Camel Trail and Padstow (with Rick Stein's restaurants). Wadebridge 15 miles.

Open: March - October.

Directions

Follow directions to Polzeath from Wadebridge. Go downhill into village then keep left up hill. Site signed on right. Access by public parking barriers. GPS: 50.572947, -4.918816

Charges guide

Per unit incl. 4 persons and electricity	£ 30.00 - £ 40.00
Two-man tent	£ 20.00 - £ 25.00
extra person	£ 7.50 - £ 10.00
dog	£ 3.00

For latest campsite news visit
alanrogers.com

Hidden Valley
Touring & camping

This 5 star, family run park is set in a beautiful wooded valley, among rolling hills of stunning Devon countryside. Some of the country's most prestigious beaches are just 4 miles away, including Woolacombe and Putsborough Sands. Overlooking the gardens & stream is the licensed shop and a delightful coffee-shop - perfect after a forest walk!

- Luxury 5* facilities • Children's play parks • Coffee shop • Licensed shop
- Wi-Fi • Tourist information area • Dishwashing areas & launderettes
- Bus stop at entrance to site • Dog exercise field • Woodland walks

Ilfracombe's only **5 star** campsite!

Hidden Valley Park, West Down, Nr. Ilfracombe, North Devon EX34 8NU

01271 813 837 • info@hiddenvalleypark.com

www.hiddenvalleypark.com

Open all year!

Braunton

Lobb Fields Caravan & Camping Park

Saunton Road, Braunton EX33 1HG (Devon) T: 01271 812090. E: info@lobbfields.com

alanrogers.com/UK1140

Lobb Fields has two camping areas providing 180 pitches on sloping grass, with a few hardstandings. Twelve pitches are reserved for seasonal caravans, and 98 have 16A electricity hook-ups. A third field is open for campers for 28 days only in high season. The pitches are marked and grass roads lead to the amenities. As the two toilet blocks are at the very bottom or very top of the fields, some up and down walking is inevitable. Lobbs Fields may be close to many holiday activities, but it is also a peaceful retreat for those wanting a quiet holiday.

Facilities

Two elderly toilet blocks (one in each field). Two family/baby rooms. Laundry. Cleaning and maintenance can be variable. The lower block can be heated and has good facilities for disabled visitors. Hair dryers and irons available from reception. Takeaway. Play area. Surf shop. WiFi. Off site: Shops less than a mile. Fishing, golf, riding and bicycle hire 1 mile. Boat launching 1.5 miles.

Open: 29 March - 29 October.

Directions

Take A361 Barnstaple to Braunton road, then B3231 (signed Croyde) to Braunton. Park is 1 mile from Braunton on the right - take care through Braunton as roads are quite narrow and busy. GPS: 51.11165, -4.181233

Charges guide

Per unit incl. 2 persons	£ 9.00 - £ 27.00
extra person	£ 3.00 - £ 6.00

Brixham

Hillhead Caravan Club Site

Hillhead, Brixham TQ5 0HH (Devon) T: 01803 853204

alanrogers.com/UK0845

Hillhead is set in 22 acres of beautiful Devon countryside. Originally developed in the 1960s within what is now a coastal protection area two miles from Brixham, the park has benefited from a £3 million redevelopment. It comprises 239 pitches, all with electrical hook-ups (16A) and many with fine views. Amenities are to a uniformly high standard, notably the main complex based around an attractive courtyard, and housing a shop, bar, games room and Nico's restaurant, serving freshly-cooked meals using local produce, and a Sunday carvery.

Facilities

The two sanitary blocks are new and maintained to a high standard. Each block includes 3 private family bathrooms and facilities for disabled visitors. Laundry facilities. Motorcaravan service point. Shop. Bar and restaurant. Swimming pool (heated May-Sept) with children's pool adjacent. Play area. Skateboard ramp. Games room. TV. Entertainment in season. Games field. Dog walking area. WiFi (charged). Off site: Bus stop at site entrance. Nearest beach and coastal path 2 miles. Golf and riding 2 miles.

Open: March - January.

Directions

Site is well signed from the A379 Paignton - Dartmouth road and is located on the B3205 (Slappers Hill Road). Entrance is on the left after 400 yds. GPS: 50.369621, -3.544816

Charges guide

Per person	£ 5.40 - £ 10.00
child (5-16 yrs)	£ 1.85 - £ 4.60
pitch incl. electricity	£ 5.20 - £ 11.55

Brixham

Galmpton Park

Greenway Road, Galmpton, Brixham TQ5 0EP (Devon) T: 01803 842066. E: galmptontouringpark@hotmail.com **alanrogers.com/UK0850**

Within a few miles of lively Torbay, Galmpton Park lies peacefully just outside the village of Galmpton, overlooking the beautiful Dart estuary just upstream of Dartmouth and Kingswear. A family park, now under new ownership, with 120 pitches (60 marked for caravans) which are arranged on a grassy, terraced meadow with some hedging and all with a view of the river. Situated on the hillside, some parts have quite a slope, but there are flatter areas. There are 90 electrical connections (10A) and 23 pitches have water and drainage. There is a separate tent field. A member of the Countryside Discovery group.

Facilities

A central toilet block provides clean facilities including three washbasins in cabins, a bathroom for under 5's, a baby unit and hair care area. En-suite unit for disabled visitors. Laundry facilities. Reception/shop sells basics. Bread to order. Adventure play equipment. Max. 2 dogs (not accepted 16/7-30/8). Motorcaravans over 21 ft. are not accepted. Torches useful. Off site: Pub 5 minutes walk. Bus 15 minutes walk on main road. Golf 1 mile. Beach 2 miles. Fishing and bicycle hire 3 miles.

Open: Easter - 28 September.

Directions

Take A380 Paignton ring road towards Brixham until junction with the Paignton - Brixham coast road. Turn right towards Brixham, then second right into Manor Vale Road. Continue through the village, past the school and site is 500 yds. on the right. GPS: 50.391650, -3.568070

Charges guide

Per unit incl. 2 persons and electricity	£ 14.50 - £ 19.00
extra person	£ 3.50

For latest campsite news visit
alanrogers.com

Chudleigh

Holmans Wood Holiday Park

Harcombe Cross, Chudleigh TQ13 0DZ (Devon) T: 01626 853785. E: enquiries@holmanswood.co.uk

alanrogers.com/UK0940

Close to the main A38 Exeter - Plymouth road, with easy access, this attractive, neat park makes a sheltered base for touring south Devon and Dartmoor. The hedged park is arranged on well kept grass surrounding a shallow depression, the floor of which makes a safe play area for children. Many trees are growing and the park is decorated with flowers. In two main areas and accessed by tarmac roads, there are 116 level pitches (including a number of seasonal pitches) and 25 mobile homes in a private area. There are 100 pitches with electrical hook-ups and 70 with hardstanding, electricity, water and drainage.

Facilities

The single, good quality toilet block includes facilities for babies and disabled visitors. Laundry room. Play area. Caravan storage. Woodland and meadow walks. Dogs are not accepted. Off site: Bus stop outside gate. Pub/restaurant nearby in Chudleigh village. Spar shop 5 minutes walk. Sunday market at Exeter Racecourse 2 miles. Haldon Forest for walks 2 miles. Golf and riding 4 miles. Beach and Dartmoor 7 miles.

Open: Mid March - end October.

Directions

From Exeter on A38 Plymouth road, 0.5 miles after racecourse and just after a garage, take Chudleigh exit. Park is immediately on the left. From Plymouth turn off A38 for Chudleigh/Teign Valley, then right for Chudleigh. Continue through town and park is 1 mile. GPS: 50.61985, -3.582833

Charges guide

Per unit incl. 2 persons	£ 17.00 - £ 22.00
extra person	£ 2.50 - £ 3.50

Combe Martin

Newberry Valley Park

Woodlands, Combe Martin EX34 0AT (Devon) T: 01271 882334. E: relax@newberryvalleypark.co.uk

alanrogers.com/UK0685

Newberry Valley Park is set in a delightful semi-wooded valley that slopes down towards the rugged North Devon coast, close to the village of Combe Martin. Three wide terraces and several sheltered fields provide 110 good sized touring pitches with views to the hills. These vary from paved, fully serviced pitches with picnic tables to simple grass areas suitable for tents. Combe Martin bay has two beaches with rock pools and caves, and is only a five minute walk from the site down a small path. The site provides an atmosphere of peace and tranquillity, except perhaps at high season. The newly refurbished toilet block is centrally located and the reception area houses a small shop and tourist information. A lovely on-site lake provides fishing (licence available at reception). From the site the wild North Devon coast offers wonderful beaches and access to the South West Coastal Path.

Facilities

Central modern toilet block with all the usual facilities including those for disabled visitors, all with under-floor heating. Laundry with washing machines, driers and free iron. Children's play area. Fishing (licence available). Small shop (Apr-Sept) in reception. Motorcaravan service point. Off site: Beach 0.25 miles. Shops/restaurants in Combe Martin 0.5 miles. Golf 5 miles. Ilfracombe with boat trips to Lundy Island (bookable on-site) 5 miles. Riding 8 miles. Lynton and Lynmouth 10 miles.

Open: 1 April - 31 October.

Directions

From the A361 (exit 27 off the M5) at South Molton take the A399 to Combe Martin and Ilfracombe. Site is approx. 20 miles on this road, through Combe Martin. From Barnstaple take the A39 towards Lynton/Lynmouth. Follow signs to Combe Martin and Ilfracombe. Drive through Combe Martin towards Ilfracombe, climb the hill at the seaward end of town and site is on the left. GPS: 51.204191, -4.042599

Charges guide

Per unit incl. 2 persons and electricity	£ 15.00 - £ 36.00
extra person	£ 3.00 - £ 5.00

For latest campsite news visit

alanrogers.com

Crediton

Yeatheridge Farm Caravan Park

East Worlington, Crediton EX17 4TN (Devon) T: 01884 860330. E: yeatheridge@talk21.com

alanrogers.com/UK1060

Yeatheridge is a friendly, family park with riding, fishing lakes, and indoor pools. Based on a 200 acre farm, nine acres have been developed over many years into an attractive touring park. Around the site there are views of the local hills and Dartmoor away to the south, and Exmoor lies to the north. The touring area is very neat and tidy with a spacious feel as units are sited around the perimeter or back onto hedges, leaving open central areas. The 85 numbered pitches are flat, gently sloping or on terraces and are sufficiently large, 80 with electricity. Seasonal units take 25 pitches and there are four caravan holiday homes. You can explore three woodland walks ranging from 1 to 2.5 miles and the banks of the River Dalch. There are two deep coarse fishing lakes (bring your own rod), the top one offering family fishing and the lower one for serious fishing. Horse riding is available on site (best to bring your own hat) with hour-long and park rides available. The ponies and goats are also popular with adults and children alike. The owners, Geoff and Liz, are constantly upgrading the park (they recently opened a new reception and amenity building) and they try very hard to make everyone feel at home.

Facilities

Two toilet blocks provide family rooms, washbasins in cubicles, showers and facilities for babies. En-suite room for disabled visitors. Laundry. Motorcaravan service point. Shop. Bar, restaurant and snack bar (hours vary by season). Unsupervised indoor swimming pools, toddlers' pool and water slide (10.00-20.00). Fenced play area with fort for under 10s (parental supervision). Football field. TV room. Games room. Fishing. Riding. WiFi (charged).

Open: 15 March - 3 October.

Directions

Park is off the B3042 Witheridge - Chawleigh (not in East Worlington). From M5 exit 27 onto the A361 to Tiverton. Turn left onto A396 for 0.5 miles then right on B3137 almost to Witheridge, then left on B3042 for 3 miles to site, well signed down concrete roadway on left. GPS: 50.8887, -3.7501

Charges guide

Per unit incl. 2 persons	
and electricity	£ 11.00 - £ 19.50
extra person (over 4 yrs)	£ 3.00
dog (first two)	£ 2.00

Croyde

Ruda Holiday Park

Parkdean Holidays, Croyde Bay, Croyde EX33 1NY (Devon) T: 01271 890671.
E: rudatouring@parkdeanholidays.com **alanrogers.com/UK1150**

Ruda Holiday Park is a recent addition to Parkdean Holidays, now comprising 12 parks in Scotland, Wales and southwest England. Ruda is right beside a Blue Flag beach and provides 312 camping and touring pitches in two distinct areas. A large camping area divided into four sections is reserved for tent campers and small motorcaravans (there are some electricity hook-ups around the perimeter and it is served by two clean toilet blocks). Touring caravan and motorcaravan pitches, all with 16A connections, are in a separate field across the road and have direct access to the beach. Here, the toilet facilities are modern with coded entry to stop day visitors using them.

Facilities

Two blocks in the camping fields provide toilets, showers with preset controls, and communal washbasins. A separate bathroom with toilet has a door wide enough for wheelchairs, however there are no aids for visitors with disabilities. A third, modern building provides all facilities in the touring field. Laundry facilities. Bar, restaurant, snack bar and takeaway. Amusement arcade. Cascade Tropical pool. Adventure playground. Tennis court. Sports field. Fishing lake. Supermarket, boutique and hire centre. Surfing equipment for hire. Direct access to sheltered beach. Caravan holiday homes and lodges for hire. Dogs are not accepted. WiFi. Off site: Golf 3 miles. Bicycle hire 8 miles. Surfing. Lundy Island excursion.

Open: March - November.

Directions

From Barnstaple, take A361 signed Braunton and Ilfracombe. At Braunton, take sharp left (narrow road) towards Croyde (signed) and follow the road all the way to the beach. Entrance to Ruda is on the right. GPS: 51.135183, -4.2352

Charges guide

Per unit incl. 4 persons	£ 13.50 - £ 37.50
pitch with services	£ 17.50 - £ 41.50

Prices are for pitch and up to four persons; maximum of eight persons per pitch.

For latest campsite news visit
alanrogers.com

Cullompton

Forest Glade Holiday Park

Kentisbeare, Cullompton EX15 2DT (Devon) T: 01404 841381. E: enquiries@forest-glade.co.uk

alanrogers.com/UK1000

Forest Glade, owned and run by the Wellard family, is set in the Blackdown Hills (designated an Area of Outstanding Natural Beauty), deep in mid-Devon away from the hectic life on the coast. A sheltered site set amongst woodland with extensive walking opportunities, there are 80 level touring pitches, 62 of which have 10/16A electricity connections, two have full services and 39 have hardstanding. Touring caravans must book in advance and the easiest route for them will be explained then (phone bookings accepted). Although set in the country, the beaches of East Devon are a fairly easy drive away. There is a small heated, covered pool with a paddling pool, sauna and patio area outside, and a large games room (up a flight of steps, so not suitable for visitors with disabilities). There is also a soft play area. The surrounding 300 acres of forest makes this a nature and dog lover's paradise.

Facilities

There is one main toilet block, heated in cold weather, with some washbasins in cubicles. Separate suite for disabled visitors. Laundry facilities. Facilities for babies. Extra facilities of 'portacabin' style with toilets, washbasins and showers are at the swimming pool. Shop sells gas, bread and pastries. Takeaway (open evenings except Sunday). Microwave in campers' kitchen. Adventure play area. Heated swimming pool. Sauna (on payment). Games room. Tennis. Ball game area. WiFi throughout (charged). Caravan storage. Wildlife information. Off site: Fishing and riding 1.5 miles. Beach 17 miles.

Open: Mid March - end October.

Directions

Park (at the top of a steep hill) is 5.5 miles from the M5 exit 28. Take A373 for 3 miles, turning left at camp sign, just past thatched pub on right, towards Sheldon. Park is on left after 2.5 miles. This access is not suitable for touring caravans owing to a steep hill – phone the park for alternative route details. GPS: 50.857833, -3.277517

Charges 2012

Per unit incl. 2 persons and electricity	£ 15.00 - £ 21.00
extra person	£ 6.50
child (4-18 yrs)	£ 1.80 - £ 3.60

Dartmouth

Little Cotton Caravan Park

Dartmouth TQ6 0LB (Devon) T: 01803 832558. E: enquiries@littlecotton.co.uk

alanrogers.com/UK0835

This lovely, family run park on the outskirts of Dartmouth is ideally situated for exploring this attractive area of South Devon. Well tended and immaculate, the 7.5-acre park is open and grassy. On level and gently sloping ground, it is situated on a hilltop and has views across the other fields. There are 95 pitches, all with electricity (16A) and mostly level with some hardstanding available. The park is divided into four areas with one dedicated to rallies. A dog walking area is to one side. Barbecues are allowed off the ground. A path leads from the site to the bus stops.

Facilities

The modern, heated toilet block is centrally situated. It is very clean, light, airy and warm. Some washbasins are in cubicles. Free showers are preset. Excellent facilities for disabled visitors. Laundry facilities. Unisex baby room. Well stocked shop in reception. Bread and sandwiches to order. Freezer. WiFi (charged). Off site: Dartmouth Castle and the steam railway can be easily accessed by ferry. Beach, fishing and boat launching 2 miles. Golf 3 miles.

Open: 15 March - 31 October.

Directions

Park is on the outskirts of Dartmouth on the A3122 opposite Sainsburys. From Totnes take the A381 (Kingsbridge) and turn left at Halwell on the A3122. Site is on right just before entering Dartmouth. GPS: 50.345106, -3.607606

Charges guide

| Per unit incl. 2 persons and electricity | £ 15.50 - £ 21.00 |
| extra person | £ 2.25 - £ 3.25 |

For latest campsite news visit

alanrogers.com

Dartmouth

Woodlands Grove Caravan & Camping Park

Blackawton, Dartmouth, Totnes TQ9 7DQ (Devon) T: 01803 712598. E: holiday@woodlandsgrove.com

alanrogers.com/UK0840

Woodlands is a pleasant surprise – from the road you have no idea of just what is hidden away deep in the Devon countryside. To achieve this, there has been sympathetic development of farm and woodland to provide a leisure centre, which is open to the public and offers a range of activities and entertainment appealing to all ages. The camping and caravan site overlooks the woodland and the leisure park, taking 350 units on three sloping, grassy fields, the original terraced one maturing well. One of the others has been fully terraced to provide groups of four to eight flat, very spacious pitches (90% with 10A electricity and a shared water tap, drain and rubbish bin). The newest field has 120 pitches (with electricity) designed with a more open feel to provide space for larger groups or rallies. Children (and many energetic parents too!) will thoroughly enjoy a huge variety of imaginative adventure play equipment, amazing water coasters, toboggan runs, the new 'Sea Dragon Swing Ship', a white knuckle monster, the 'Avalanche' and much more, hidden amongst the trees. Those more peacefully inclined can follow woodland walks around the attractive ponds. The 'Empire of the Sea Dragon', an indoor play centre, provides marvellous wet weather facilities comprising five floors of play areas and amazing slides. With a two night stay, campers on the touring park are admitted free of charge to the leisure park. A popular touring park, early reservation is advisable. A member of the Best of British Group.

Facilities

Three modern, heated toilet blocks, include private bathrooms (coin-operated, 20p) and 16 family shower cubicles. Two laundry rooms. Freezer for ice packs. Baby facilities. The leisure park café provides good value meals and a takeaway service for campers. Café opening hours and camping shop (with gas and basic food supplies) vary according to season and demand. TV and games room. Dogs are accepted on the campsite but not in the leisure park (kennels available). Caravan storage. Off site: The charming town of Dartmouth and the South Hams beaches are nearby. Golf 0.5 miles. Riding 7 miles. Beach 6 miles. Fishing 9 miles.

Open: 30 March - 4 November.

Directions

From A38 at Buckfastleigh, take A384 to Totnes. Before the town centre turn right on A381 Kingsbridge road. After Halwell turn left at Totnes Cross garage, on A3122 to Dartmouth. Park is on right after 2.5 miles. GPS: 50.357898, -3.675001

Charges guide

Per unit incl. 2 persons and electricity	£ 16.50 - £ 23.00
extra person (over 2 yrs)	£ 7.75
awning or extra small pup tent	£ 3.50
large tent or trailer tent (120 sq.ft. plus) extra	£ 3.50
dog (contact site first)	£ 2.75

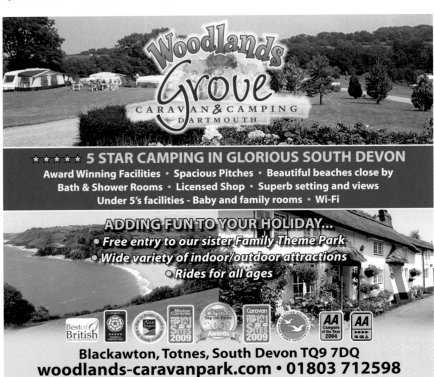

Dawlish

Cofton Country Holidays

Starcross, Dawlish EX6 8RP (Devon) T: 01626 890111. E: info@coftonholidays.co.uk

alanrogers.com/UK0970

A popular and efficient family run park, Cofton is 1.5 miles from a sandy beach at Dawlish Warren. It has space for 450 touring units on a variety of fields and meadows with beautiful country views. Although not individually marked, there is never a feeling of overcrowding. The smaller, more mature fields, including a pleasant old orchard for tents only, are well terraced. While there are terraces on most of the slopes of the larger, more open fields, there are still some quite steep gradients to climb. There are some 450 electrical connections (10A), 16 hardstandings and 14 super pitches. Self-catering accommodation on site includes holiday homes, cottages and apartments. A well designed, central complex overlooking the pool and decorated with flowers and hanging baskets houses reception, a shop and off-licence and a bar/lounge, the Cofton Swan, where bar meals are available (all Easter-end October). A family room and bar are on the first floor of this building and there is an outdoor terrace and some light entertainment in season. A new indoor swimming pool and bar complex should open in 2012. The adjacent supervised kidney-shaped heated pool with paddling pool, has lots of grassy space for sunbathing. Coarse fishing is available in five lakes on the park. The adjoining unspoilt woodland of 50 acres provides wonderful views across the Exe estuary and a woodland trail of two miles to Dawlish Warren.

Facilities

Six amenity blocks are well placed for all areas across the park. Facilities for disabled visitors and a few family bathrooms. Hair dryers. Two launderettes. Gas available. Ice pack hire service. Bar lounge serving bar snacks (31/3-26/10). TV. Shop (31/3-26/10). Fish and chip shop also serving breakfast (31/3-6/10). Swimming pool (overall length 100 ft. open Spr.B.H-mid Sept). Indoor pool for 2012. Games room. Adventure playground in the woods overlooking the pools and two other well equipped play areas. Coarse fishing (from £ 25 per rod for 7 days, discount for senior citizens outside July/Aug). Caravan storage. Seasonal pitches available. Off site: Woodland walks/pub 0.5 miles. Beach and boat launching 1.5 miles. Golf 3 miles. Riding 5 miles. Bicycle hire in Dawlish.

Open: All year.

Directions

Access to the park is off the A379 road 3 miles north of Dawlish, just after Cockwood Harbour village. GPS: 50.6126, -3.460467

Charges guide

Per unit incl. 2 persons and electricity	£ 14.50 - £ 29.00
hardstanding pitch	£ 18.00 - £ 32.00
serviced pitch	£ 21.50 - £ 36.00
extra person (over 2 yrs)	£ 2.75 - £ 5.00

Small discount for senior citizens outside peak season.

Camping Cheques accepted.

For latest campsite news visit

alanrogers.com

Dawlish

Lady's Mile Holiday Park

Exeter Road, Dawlish EX7 0LX (Devon) T: 01626 863411. E: info@ladysmile.co.uk

alanrogers.com/UK1010

Lady's Mile is a popular, large family touring park that caters well for children. It has extensive grassy fields (with some trees for shade), in addition to the main, landscaped camping area which is arranged in broad terraces. There are 486 good sized pitches, mostly marked by lines but with nothing between them, most with electricity (10A) and some with water and hardstanding. To one side of the park there are also some caravan holiday homes to let. It is a 20 minute walk to a good sandy beach at Dawlish Warren and 10 minutes to Dawlish beach, but the park also has a good sized outdoor swimming pool with a 200 ft. slide, plus a super heated indoor pool with 100 ft. flume and separate paddling pool.

Facilities

Four toilet blocks of various ages are of a good standard and well spaced with an additional shower block. Facilities for disabled visitors. Four family bathrooms (50p). Two launderettes. Supermarket. Fish and chip takeaway. Bars and entertainment. Restaurant and carvery. Café with pizzeria and snack bar. All these Easter-mid Sept. Indoor (Easter-Oct) and outdoor (May-Sept) pools. Adventure play area. New soft play area. Games room. WiFi throughout. Off site: Golf, riding and bicycle hire 1 mile.

Open: All year.

Directions

Park is 1 mile north of Dawlish with access off the A379 (Exeter - Teignmouth) road.
GPS: 50.59525, -3.459467

Charges guide

Per unit incl. 2 persons and electricity	£ 13.00 - £ 27.50
extra person over 2 yrs	£ 2.50 - £ 4.75
dog	£ 2.50 - £ 4.75

Dawlish

Golden Sands Holiday Park

Week Lane, Dawlish Warren EX7 0LZ (Devon) T: 01626 863099. E: goldensands@ParkHolidaysUK.com

alanrogers.com/UK1085

Dawlish is a deservedly popular South Devon resort. Golden Sands is one of three Park Holidays sites in this area. There is some up and down walking to access a good range of facilities. There are only 28 touring pitches at Golden Sands, most with 16A electricity. Accommodation is mainly provided in mobile homes and chalets for rent. Dawlish Warren can be accessed on foot and is home to an important nature reserve. The Warren is the main roost for the wildfowl and wading birds of the Exe estuary. This part of Devon is well known for the quality of its beaches.

Facilities

Basic toilet block with washbasins and preset showers. Facilities for disabled visitors (but quite hilly ground to access). Laundry facilities. Shop. Playground. Tourist information. Mobile homes and chalets for rent. WiFi throughout (charged). Off site: Beach within walking distance. Golf 1 mile. Riding 4 miles. Dawlish (shops and restaurants). Crealy Adventure Park. Dawlish Warren.

Open: 28 March - 31 October.

Directions

Leave the M5 at exit 30 and take the A379 to Dawlish. Drive through Starcross and continue on the A379 for about 2 miles. Golden Sands is signed to the left 1 mile before reaching Dawlish.
GPS: 50.596267, -3.456316

Charges guide

Per unit incl. 2 persons and electricity	£ 16.00 - £ 32.00

Dawlish

Peppermint Park

Warren Road, Dawlish Warren, Dawlish EX7 0PQ (Devon) T: 01626 863436. E: info@peppermintpark.co.uk

alanrogers.com/UK1090

Now part of the Park Holidays group, Peppermint Park is a green oasis in a popular holiday area. Extensive, green, sloping fields edged with mature trees have been partly terraced to give level pitches for caravans and some more informal areas that cater for tents. There are 90 holiday homes (many privately owned but some to rent) along with timber lodges to rent close to a small fishing lake. There are 75 touring pitches, 60 with 16A electricity, which are marked and numbered. Visitors staying at Peppermint Park can use all the facilities at nearby Dawlish Sands and Golden Sands.

Facilities

Two fully equipped sanitary blocks can be heated. Two units (WC, washbasin and shower) for disabled visitors. Baby room. Laundry facilities. Shop with gas. Adventure playground on a hill. Field for ball games. Small coarse fishing lake (£5 for adult day ticket). WiFi throughout. Off site: Golf at Dawlish Warren (18-hole links course), 9-hole course at Starcross. Riding and bicycle hire 2 miles. Sailing and boat launching 5 miles.

Open: 1 March - 31 October.

Directions

Leave the M5 at exit 30 and take A379 Dawlish road. Pass through Starcross (7 miles) then turn left to Dawlish Warren just before Dawlish. Continue for 1.5 miles down hill and park is on left in 300 yds.
GPS: 50.599367, -3.446967

Charges guide

Per unit incl. 2 persons and electricity	£ 8.00 - £ 27.00
extra person (2 yrs and over)	£ 2.00 - £ 4.00

For latest campsite news visit

alanrogers.com

Dawlish

Leadstone Camping

Warren Road, Dawlish Warren, Dawlish EX7 0NG (Devon) T: 01626 864411. E: info@leadstonecamping.co.uk

alanrogers.com/UK1095

Leadstone provides traditional camping at its best in a series of hedged grass fields, sloping in parts, in a natural, secluded bowl. In a designed Area of Outstanding Natural Beauty, the Blue Flag beach and sand dunes of Dawlish Warren are only a half mile walk. The area can get somewhat frenzied in peak holiday times but Leadstone provides a haven of peace and tranquillity. Owned by the same family since 1974, the Leadstone welcome is personal and the site totally relaxed. In all, there are 137 pitches, 102 with 16A electricity. A regular bus service passes the gate every 15 minutes. The toilet facilities are centrally situated but of the Portacabin variety. This is due to the site's situation on the seaward side of the Warren road where it is subject to Coastal Preservation regulations (it must be possible to move buildings within 24 hours). However, the provision is good under the circumstances, if somewhat short on toilets. Extra toilet pods are brought in for peak times. The site is only open for a short season but is popular and well run. Dawlish Warren is renowned for its good weather and average temperatures of over 70 degrees are not uncommon.

Facilities

Fully equipped, centrally located Portacabin style provision is well kept. Unisex showers (20p for 5-6 minutes). Washing machines (£3). Basic supplies and gas from reception. Play area with real tractor. WiFi (charged). Off site: Beach with shops, cafés, etc. at Dawlish Warren 0.5 miles. Golf 0.5 miles. Bicycle hire 2 miles. Riding 5 miles. Boat launching 7 miles.

Open: 10 June - 4 September.

Directions

From Exeter follow the A379 Teignmouth road (M5 exit 30). After Starcross watch for left turn to Dawlish Warren and site is on right after 0.5 miles. GPS: 50.59396, -3.45162

Charges guide

Per unit incl. 2 persons and electricity	£ 17.00 - £ 25.50
extra person	£ 6.75 - £ 9.00
child (3-13 yrs)	£ 2.75 - £ 3.25
dog	£ 2.50 - £ 3.25

Drewsteignton

Woodland Springs Touring Park

Venton, Drewsteignton EX6 6PG (Devon) T: 01647 231695. E: enquiries@woodlandsprings.co.uk

alanrogers.com/UK1250

Hidden away in a corner of the Dartmoor National Park, Woodlands Springs is a haven of peace and tranquillity. Set in a dip, it is sheltered by woodland with some views across the rural countryside. It provides 77 fairly level, grass pitches (44 with hardstanding) and 69 with electricity (10A), with a circular gravel access road and a central toilet block. There is a small shop and off licence; bread is baked daily. A large field provides good dog walking. The resident owners provide a warm welcome on this quiet park that only accepts adults. With 600 miles of public right-of-way on Dartmoor, there is plenty to keep walkers busy. Over 50 species of birds have been seen on the park over the last few years so it would also be a good base for bird watching.

Facilities

Award winning toilet block including full facilities for disabled campers. Shop (limited hours). Dog kennels for rent. Torches useful. WiFi (charged). Off site: Fishing 3 miles. Riding 5 miles. Golf 9 miles. Castle Drogo and the Mythic Gardens nearby.

Open: All year.

Directions

From M5 exit 31 follow the A30 towards Okehampton. After 15 miles at Whiddon Down junction turn on A382 Moretonhampstead road. Stay on A382 for 0.5 miles then left at roundabout. After 1 mile turn left at brown caravan sign, then left and park is 150 yds. down drive. GPS: 50.706417, -3.850667

Charges guide

Per unit incl. 2 persons and electricity	£ 18.00 - £ 21.00
extra person	£ 4.00

For latest campsite news visit

alanrogers.com

Exmouth

Devon Cliffs Holiday Park

Haven Holidays, Sandy Bay, Exmouth EX8 5BT (Devon) T: 01395 226226

alanrogers.com/UK1260

Haven Holiday's flagship park, Devon Cliffs at Exmouth, is a very large, vibrant holiday resort, complete with its own almost private sandy beach. There are over 1,600 caravan holiday homes here (400 for hire). They are arranged in avenues on the attractively landscaped, hilly site around a central complex full of top class amenities. Overlooking this complex is a small, modern touring area providing 43 very neat pitches for caravans and motorcaravans, a good toilet block and its own warden. Fully serviced (electricity, aerial point, water and drain), each pitch has areas of gravel, concrete and grass. Tents are accepted in high season on another area of the park with a second toilet block. Comprehensive and very lively, the excellent amenities include an indoor and outdoor, multi-level pool complex, a spa centre, sports facilities and coaching, evening entertainment programme, a huge noisy hall with amusements and games, and much more. For families with children who need entertainment, this park is ideal. There is a good supermarket and plenty of options for eating in or out. Sandy Bay has a safe, sandy beach with lifeguards in high season and at high tide is only accessible from the park. An hourly bus takes visitors to Exmouth and its resort facilities and larger sandy beach.

Facilities

Very neat and clean toilet facilities with open washbasins, preset showers and hairdryers. Excellent room for visitors with disabilities. Good family bathroom. Launderette. Shopping arcade. Sonny Jim's buffet and grill, two café bars, fish and chips, Burger King, pizzas, Starbucks Coffee. Two indoor 'show bars'. Indoor and outdoor pool complex (outdoor 22/5-31/8). Spa centre. Sports facilities. Amusements hall. Evening entertainment and clubs for children. Adventure play areas. Beach (lifeguards in high season). Tents accepted 24/7-4/9. Off site: Exmouth centre 2.5 miles with hourly bus. Bicycle hire 2.5 miles. Golf and riding 6 miles.

Open: 20 March - 2 November.

Directions

From the M5 take exit 30, then the A376 signed Exmouth. On the outskirts of the town (just after a garage), turn left at traffic lights following signs for Budleigh Salterton, Littleham, Sandy Bay and the park. GPS: 50.615645, -3.366387

Charges guide

Per unit incl. up to 4 persons and services	£ 17.00 - £ 46.50
extra person	£ 2.00 - £ 3.00

Exeter

Webbers Caravan & Camping Park

Castle Lane, Woodbury, Exeter EX5 1EA (Devon) T: 01395 232276. E: reception@webberspark.co.uk

alanrogers.com/UK1100

Set in a lovely location in East Devon, with beautiful views of the Maldon Hills, this family run park has developed over 20 years to one that can boast spacious, modern facilities, yet still retain its relaxed, rural atmosphere. The 115 marked, grass pitches are large, with the majority level and a few gently sloping. Some of the higher pitches have marvellous views across the Exe river valley. There are 100 electricity connections (10/16A). The park is surrounded by fields and visitors can watch the wildlife and grazing sheep from a fenced walk around the park perimeter. Within the park is a 'pets paddock' with a friendly donkey, sheep and goats. A member of the Countryside Discovery and Best of British groups.

Facilities

There are three modern toilet blocks, one is a light and airy building with four family shower rooms, a bathroom (£1) and a unit for disabled visitors (WC, shower and washbasin). Laundry facilities. Unusual in terms of number, are seven chemical disposal points, located at each water point (and adequately separated). Motorcaravan service point. Small shop at reception for essentials. Ice pack service. Gas supplies. Play area and games field. All year caravan storage. Off site: Woodbury village within walking distance with excellent pub/restaurant, post office, etc. Fishing and golf (Woodbury Park Golf Club) 1 mile. Riding 4 miles. Bicycle hire and boat launching 5 miles. Exeter 6 miles.

Open: 15 March - 29 October.

Directions

From M5 exit 30 take A3052 (Sidmouth) for 5 miles and turn right at Halfway Inn. From A30, Daisymount exit, take B3180 for 3 miles to Halfway Inn and go straight across at crossroads. All routes then follow B3180 (Budleigh Salterton/Exmouth). After 2 miles turn right into lane (signed Woodbury, golf and caravan parks). Follow downhill for 1 mile to park on left just before Woodbury village. GPS: 50.678083, -3.392017

Charges guide

Per unit incl. 2 persons and electricity	£ 13.00 - £ 18.00
extra person (over 3 yrs)	£ 3.50
pup tent	£ 2.00

Min. booking of 4 nights in high season.

For latest campsite news visit

alanrogers.com

Ilfracombe
Stowford Farm Meadows

Berry Down, Combe Martin, Ilfracombe EX34 0PW (Devon) T: 01271 882476. E: enquiries@stowford.co.uk
alanrogers.com/UK0690

Stowford Farm is a friendly, family park set in 500 acres of the rolling North Devon countryside, available for recreation and walking, yet within easy reach of five local beaches. The touring park and its facilities have been developed in the fields and farm buildings surrounding the attractive old farmhouse and provide a village like centre with a comfortable spacious feel. There are 710 pitches on five slightly sloping meadows separated by Devon hedges of beech and ash. The numbered and marked pitches, some with hardstanding, are accessed by hard roads, most have electricity (10/16A) and there are well placed water points. Stowford also provides plenty to keep the whole family occupied without leaving the park, including woodland walks and horse riding from the park's own stables. The Old Stable Bar offers entertainment in high season including barn dances, discos, karaoke and other musical evenings. There is also much for children to do, from the indoor heated pool and under-cover mini zoo (Petorama) where they can handle many sorts of animals (on payment), to the wide range of organised activities on offer. In low season some facilities may only open for limited hours. However, it is also a good base for exploring the North Devon coast and Exmoor. A new development of 40 very smart holiday lodges with wonderful views has been added to the park.

Facilities

Five identical toilet blocks, each looked after by resident wardens, are fully equipped and provide good, functional facilities, each block with laundry facilities. The newest block (in field 5) has under-floor heating and includes facilities for disabled visitors. Extra good facilities for disabled visitors and private family washrooms are beside reception. Well stocked shop (with holiday goods and gas). Good value takeaway with restaurant area. Bars and entertainment in season. Indoor pool (22x10 m; heated Easter-Oct) at a small charge. Riding. 18-hole pitch and putt. Crazy golf. 'Kiddies kar' track (all charged). Games room. Large play area. Games and activities organised in high season. WiFi. ATM. Woodland walks. Max. 2 dogs (in separate areas). Summer parking and winter caravan storage. Caravan centre with caravan sales, workshop, accessories and repair centre. Rallies accepted.
Off site: Fishing and boat launching 4 miles. Bicycle hire 10 miles.

Open: All year.

Directions

From Barnstaple take the A39 towards Lynton. After 1 mile turn left on B3230. Turn right at garage on A3123 and park is 1.5 miles on the right.
GPS: 51.174983, -4.05475

Charges guide

Per unit incl. 2 persons	
and electricity	£ 10.40 - £ 23.00
extra person	free - £ 4.50
child (5-12 yrs)	free - £ 4.50
dog	£ 1.60 - £ 2.60

Low and mid season discounts for over 50s.

Ilfracombe
Sandaway Beach Holiday Park

Combe Martin Bay, Berrynarbor, Ilfracombe EX34 9ST (Devon) T: 01271 866766
alanrogers.com/UK0695

Sandaway Beach is set in a commanding position on the beautiful North Devon coast and is close to the charming fishing village of Combe Martin. The town is on the western edge of Exmoor National Park and offers all facilities including sea fishing trips. The park has a touring area for 20 caravans or motorcaravans, 12 of which have electricity, water and drainage. There are also two fields for tents at the far end of the park with wonderful coastal views. The remainder of the pitches are for rented caravan holiday home accommodation. Families will enjoy exploring the wild coast with its small coves and rocky cliffs which are accessible from the park. The park is steep with terraced areas for the holiday homes.

Facilities

The single toilet block is downhill from the touring field and may pose access problems for disabled visitors. There are clean hot showers and two private cubicles. The tent areas have their own toilets. Shop. Bar, restaurant and takeaway. Lovely heated outdoor pool with views to the coast. Enclosed play area. Kids' club. Off site: Bus stop at the gate for visiting Combe Martin and Ilfracombe (4 miles). Boat launching and riding 2 miles. Golf 6 miles. Shops, restaurants, cafés, fishing at Combe Martin and Ilfracombe.

Open: 15 March - 1 November.

Directions

From A361 turn north at South Molton onto the A399 towards Ilfracombe and Combe Martin. Drive through Combe Martin and up steep hill towards Ilfracombe. Park is on the right side 1 mile out of town. Entrance is tight, especially from Combe Martin direction. GPS: 51.206393, -4.044642

Charges guide

Per unit incl. 2 persons	£ 24.00 - £ 45.00

See advertisement on page 26

For latest campsite news visit
alanrogers.com

escape to the
stowford
life

Stowford Farm Meadows is a family owned, award winning touring **caravan and camping site** close to Combe Martin, North Devon

Stowford Farm Meadows

COMBE MARTIN · NORTH DEVON · EX34 0PW

FACILITIES INCLUDE

Indoor Heated Swimming Pool • Horse Riding Centre • Mini Indoor Zoo • Woodland Walks • 18 Hole Fun Golf • Restaurants & Bars • Fun Packed Activities • Fantastic Family Entertainment

SPECIAL OFFERS
£49.50 low season
£69.50 mid season
for a weeks holiday including electric check our website for vouchers

Stowford also includes a **Caravan Sales Centre and Accessory Shop** as well as the opportunity to purchase your very own **luxury holiday lodge**.

To save your place or request a brochure call our Booking Hotline

01271 882476
Combe Martin North Devon EX34 0PW

Ilfracombe

Napps Touring Holiday Park

Old Coast Road, Berrynarbor, Ilfracombe EX34 9SW (Devon) T: 01271 882557. E: info@napps.fsnet.co.uk

alanrogers.com/UK1120

Set in an idyllic location in North Devon, this popular, family-run site offers peace and quiet. A path just outside the gates leads down to a private beach with safe bathing. There are 200 steps down to the beach so it is not suitable for wheelchair users. Combe Martin and Ilfracombe beaches are also close by. The 200 touring pitches (100 hardstandings), most with views of Watermouth Bay, are terraced and spacious, 95 have electricity, a water tap and waste point, and another 70 have a 16A hook-up.

Facilities	Directions
Two modern toilet blocks include open plan washbasins, showers and family wash cubicles. Laundry. Licensed shop. Bar with terrace and light entertainment during high season. Restaurant (open mornings and evenings). Takeaway. Heated outdoor pool with paddling pool. Tennis. Games room. Adventure play area. Off site: Beach and fishing 200 yds. Combe Martin and golf 1.5 miles. Ilfracombe 3.5 miles. Bicycle hire and riding 5 miles.	Leave M5 at exit 27, take A361 to South Molton and then A399 to Combe Martin. Site is 1.5 miles west of Combe Martin on the A399 (signed). GPS: 51.208517, -4.064083

Open: 1 March - 31 October.

Charges 2012

Per unit incl. 2 persons and electricity	£ 10.00 - £ 27.00
extra person (over 10 yrs)	£ 1.00 - £ 5.00

Ilfracombe

Hele Valley Holiday Park

Hele Bay, Ilfracombe EX34 9RD (Devon) T: 01271 862460. E: holidays@helevalley.co.uk

alanrogers.com/UK1145

Hele Valley is a well established park which has been in the same family for over 30 years. Located a mile from Ilfracombe in a wooded valley, it is only a few minutes walk from Hele Bay beach. Apart from the 80 attractively laid out caravan holiday homes (20 for rent), the park caters for tents, motorcaravans and smaller caravans only because of the difficult access. Some 50 pitches are set in two lush green fields surrounded by trees and hedges. Being in a valley, some of the pitches are terraced. Eight gravel pitches for motorcaravans have electricity and water and 50 for tents (12 large ones) have hook-ups.

Facilities	Directions
The modern, heated toilet block (access by key with deposit required) provides a mixture of open and enclosed washbasins and showers. Separate deluxe baby room. Unit for disabled visitors. Two good adventure play areas and a play field. Parents must keep children away from the steep-sided stream running the length of the park. WiFi (charged). Off site: Minimarket, pubs and cafés 5 minutes walk. Beach and golf 400 yards. Fishing, sea fishing, sailing, many shops in Ilfracombe 1 mile. Riding 4 miles. Bus service in main road.	From Ilfracombe, take A399 east (Combe Martin). With Ilfracombe swimming pool on the left, proceed down hill for a further 400 yds. At Hele Valley sign, sharp right turn (easier to approach from Combe Martin). Down steep road and on to T-junction (right-angled and narrow). Turn right to park. From Combe Martin follow A399 west for 8 miles, past golf course. Down hill then left at Hele Valley sign and as above. GPS: 51.205404, -4.101202

Open: 1 April - 31 October.

Charges guide

Per unit incl. 2 persons	£ 24.00 - £ 32.00
extra person	£ 4.00 - £ 6.00

Ilfracombe

Watermouth Cove Holiday Park

Ilfracombe EX34 9SJ (Devon) T: 01271 862504. E: info@watermouthcoveholidays.co.uk

alanrogers.com/UK1257

This park is set in a lovely position, being at the side of a stream as it flows into the harbour and sea at Watermouth Cove. It has its own private beach from where there are lovely views across the sea. Part of the park is arranged on the fairly level valley floor, whilst the tent area is on the side of the private headland with views of the coast from the higher ground. Electricity hook-ups (16A) are available. Children will enjoy fishing from the rocks and there is an adventure play area.

Facilities	Directions
New heated facilities are provided in Portacabin style units with decking and seating joining them together. Preset showers. Basic toilets and new showers on camping field. Laundry. Shop. Bar, restaurant and takeaway (weekends only in low season). Heated outdoor pool (26/5-30/9). Play area. Activities for children (high season). Beach access. Sea kayaks for hire. Fishing. Entertainment. WiFi (free). Off site: Golf 1.5 miles. Riding 3 miles.	From M5 exit 27 follow signs for Barnstaple A361. At South Molton roundabout turn right signed A399 and continue for 16 miles following signs to Combe Martin. Go through Combe Martin on A399. After 2 miles Watermouth Cove is signed on the right. GPS: 51.212484, -4.071298

Open: End March - end October.

Charges guide

Per unit incl. 2 persons	£ 18.00 - £ 38.50
extra person	£ 1.50 - £ 3.00

Kingsbridge

Karrageen Caravan & Camping Park

Bolberry, Malborough, Kingsbridge TQ7 3EN (Devon) T: 01548 561230. E: phil@karrageen.co.uk

alanrogers.com/UK0825

Karrageen is to be found in a wonderful area of Devon, near Kingsbridge and Salcombe, with a mixture of rolling countryside, hidden coves, cliff tops and sandy beaches. You can walk, sail, surf or just relax and enjoy the wonderful scenery. This is a small family park run personally by the Higgin family situated in the hamlet of Bolberry, one mile up the lane from Hope Cove. The main camping field slopes gently with either sea or rural views. It has been terraced with hedging to provide 70 grassy pitches with 54 electricity connections (10A). There are some 20 places specifically designed for touring caravans.

Facilities

Modern toilet block includes two curtained washbasins for privacy. Showers are metered (20p). En-suite provision for disabled visitors doubles as a family shower room. Parent and baby room. Laundry room. Shop. Fresh baguettes and croissants daily. Takeaway (evenings only, last orders 19.00). No play area as such but two open areas for ball games. Off site: Fishing, boat launching and beach 1 mile. Golf 3 miles. Salcombe, sailing Mecca and fishing port with sandy beaches 3.5 miles. Riding 6 miles. Kingsbridge, ancient market town, 6 miles.

Open: Easter - 29 September.

Directions

Travelling south from Exeter on the A38, take the A3121 (Ermington and Modbury). Follow signs to Kingsbridge and Salcombe. At Malborough, sharp right through village, following signs for Bolberry for 0.6 mile. Turn right to Bolberry, then after 0.9 miles park is on the right. Take care with single track lanes. GPS: 50.23929, -3.84004

Charges guide

Per unit incl. 2 adults, 2 children	£ 16.00 - £ 28.00
extra person	£ 3.00 - £ 5.00

No credit cards.

Kingsbridge

Higher Rew Caravan & Camping Park

Malborough, Kingsbridge TQ7 3BW (Devon) T: 01548 842681. E: enquiries@higherrew.co.uk

alanrogers.com/UK0826

The Squire family have developed this rural park over the last 50 years on their farm which is located about a mile up a single track lane from South Sands, near Salcombe. A large, sloping, open field has been terraced to provide 90 grass pitches, 60 of which have 16A electricity. South Sands is ideal for boating, sailing and windsurfing as well as providing safe bathing. The five miles of estuary which stretches between Salcombe and Kingsbridge is a local nature reserve famed for its unique marine habitats and its bird watching opportunities. The coastal path can be reached from the park.

Facilities

Good quality toilet facilities. Separate unisex showers (metered, 20p for 4 mins) with the laundry sinks. Tourist information. Reception with shop for basics (open main season). Play area. Tennis court. Skittle alley. Caravan storage. Hogroast on Thursdays at 6pm (high season). Fish and chip van calls at certain times. Off site: Beach, fishing and sailing 1 mile. Golf 4.5 miles. Riding 5 miles.

Open: Easter - October half term.

Directions

Park signed from Malborough. Follow signs to Soar for 1 mile. Turn left at Rew Cross, then first right for Higher Rew. Take care with single track roads. GPS: 50.230174, -3.805647

Charges guide

Per unit incl. 2 persons	£ 15.00 - £ 22.00
extra person	£ 3.00 - £ 4.00

No credit cards.

Lynton

Channel View Caravan & Camping Park

Manor Farm, Barbrook, Lynton EX35 6LD (Devon) T: 01598 753349. E: relax@channel-view.co.uk

alanrogers.com/UK0680

Channel View is a quiet, family run park situated in a sunny, south-facing position overlooking Lynton and Lynmouth. The gently sloping ground provides fairly level pitches which are mostly on hardstandings. The park is divided into two areas, an open area that is sheltered by bushes and trees, and one that is more exposed but enjoys panoramic views over the coast. Of the 75 touring pitches, 60 have electricity (16A) and the remainder are fully serviced. The grass is well cared for and there is site lighting, although a torch would be useful. There is a café on the site that also offers takeaways.

Facilities

The modern and very clean toilet and shower block is partly tiled. Showers are free (there are three steps down to the ladies' showers from the toilets). Baby changing/family washroom. Facilities for disabled visitors (Radar key). Laundry facilities. Café. Small shop. Play area. WiFi. Off site: Lynton and Lynmouth, Exmoor and the Doone Valley are nearby. Walks from the site. Riding and fishing 1 mile. Beach 2 miles. Golf 15 miles.

Open: 15 March - 15 November.

Directions

Take the A399 from Ilfracombe. Turn left on the A39 and continue past the turn for Lynton to site on the left after 2 miles. It is not advisable to approach from Lynton and Lynmouth. GPS: 51.21800, -3.82930

Charges guide

Per unit incl. 2 persons	£ 14.00 - £ 19.00
extra person	£ 3.00 - £ 4.00

For latest campsite news visit

alanrogers.com

Modbury

Moor View Touring Park

California Cross, Modbury PL21 0SG (Devon) T: 01548 821485. E: info@moorviewtouringpark.co.uk

alanrogers.com/UK0820

Moor View has a gently sloping position with terraced, individual, level pitches with marvellous views across to the Dartmoor Tors. This is a park in a lovely corner of Devon, run by the enthusiastic owners, Edward and Liz Corwood. A member of the Countryside Discovery group and an adults only park. It provides 68 pitches of varying size, connected by hardcore roads. All are on hardstanding with 10A electricity, water and drainage. A two acre field provides space for tents but with no electricity.

Facilities	Directions
Traditional style, heated and well maintained toilet facilities have access from a courtyard area, providing all necessary facilities including a laundry room and sink, and covered dishwashing sinks. Shop. Takeaway in season (to order, 18.30-20.30). TV room. WiFi. Off site: Local country pub is within walking distance. Small town of Modbury is 3 miles. Golf and bicycle hire 5 miles. Fishing 6 miles. Beach is 15 minutes away.	On the A38 from Exeter, pass exit for A385 (Totnes) and continue for 2 miles. Just past Woodpecker Inn leave A38 at Wrangaton Cross (Ermington, Modbury and Yealmpton). Turn left and over crossroads (Kitterford Cross) signed Modbury, Kingsbridge for 3 miles to California Cross. Leave garage on left on towards Modbury (B3207). Park is 0.5 miles on left. GPS: 50.363691, -3.817444
Open: All year.	

Charges guide

Per unit incl. 2 persons and electricity	£ 11.50 - £ 20.50
extra person	£ 4.00

Mortehoe

Warcombe Farm Camping Park

Station Road, Mortehoe EX34 7EJ (Devon) T: 01271 870690. E: info@warcombefarm.co.uk

alanrogers.com/UK0725

This park is set in a quiet position on a hill above Woolacombe. It is a large, fairly open site on gently sloping land. There are 260 level or fairly level pitches, some secluded, others extra large with hardstanding and electricity, and others fully serviced. Shrubs and trees help to divide some of the pitches. Two hardstanding pitches are designed to provide facilities and access for disabled campers. In total, 160 pitches have electricity hook ups (16A). The site has panoramic views across to the sea and at its centre has a fully fenced, lovely, well kept lake that is a haven for wildlife.

Facilities	Directions
Two modern toilet blocks are spotlessly clean, with preset showers. En-suite facilities in one block. Family bathrooms and facilities for disabled visitors (coded locks). Laundry facilities. Motorcaravan services. Shop. Takeaway (w/ends only in low season). Play area. Fishing. Torches useful. WiFi (charged). Off site: Footpaths and cycle trails. Riding and golf 1.5 miles. Beach 1.5 miles. Bicycle hire 4 miles.	From Barnstaple on A361 follow signs for Ilfracombe. At Mullacott Cross (10 miles from Barnstaple) turn left and follow B3343 (Woolacombe). After 1.8 miles turn right for Mortehoe. Park on right in 500 yards. GPS: 51.190441, -4.180639
Open: 15 March - 31 October.	

Charges guide

Per unit incl. 2 persons and electricity	£ 15.00 - £ 33.00
extra person	£ 4.00

Newton Abbot

Ross Park

Park Hill Farm, Ipplepen, Newton Abbot TQ12 5TT (Devon) T: 01803 812983.
E: enquiries@rossparkcaravanpark.co.uk alanrogers.com/UK0910

Mark and Helen Lowe are rightly proud of Ross Park and strive to provide quality facilities and maintain standards. A wide variety of shrubs form hedging for most of the pitches to provide your own special plot. Many pitches have wonderful views over the countryside and for those who prefer the more open style, one small area has been left unhedged. The park covers 31 acres but 21 acres are managed specifically as conservation areas providing a haven for wildlife. A member of the Best of British Group.

Facilities	Directions
Twelve well equipped, heated en-suite units, two with baby facilities, one suitable for disabled visitors. Laundry room. Motorcaravan services. Reception with licensed shop. Bar, snacks and restaurant (all Apr-end Oct, plus Christmas and New Year). New conservation and tourist information room. Games room. Recreation area. Croquet. Badminton. Volleyball. Playground. WiFi. Off site: Golf adjacent. Riding 1 mile. Fishing 3 miles. Beach 6 miles.	From A381 Newton Abbot - Totnes road, park is signed towards Woodland at Park Hill crossroads and Texaco filling station. GPS: 50.491940, -3.634240
Open: All year excl. January and February.	

Charges guide

Per unit incl. 2 persons and electricity	£ 14.00 - £ 27.20
extra person	£ 3.25 - £ 5.50
No credit cards.	

For latest campsite news visit

alanrogers.com

Newton Abbot

Dornafield

Two Mile Oak, Newton Abbot TQ12 6DD (Devon) T: 01803 812732. E: enquiries@dornafield.com

alanrogers.com/UK0880

The entrance to Dornafield leads into the charming old courtyard of a 14th-century farmhouse giving a mellow feeling that is complemented by the warm welcome from the Dewhirst family. Having booked in, continue down the lane (with a tree covered bank alive with wild flowers) to the Buttermeadow, a tranquil valley providing 75 individual pitches on flat grass, separated by grassy ridges and in some places, wild rose hedges. You pass the walled orchard, secluded and cosy for tents. Or take the road up the hill to Blackrock Copse with large luxury pitches with all facilities including a chemical disposal point and cleverly concealed TV connections. Electricity points are 10A. Whilst having been carefully designed, the environment remains natural. Both Buttermeadow and Blackrock have super, well maintained woodland adventure play areas and all pitches in these areas have gravel all-weather surfaces. The reception, shop, tourist information/ecology room have been sympathetically converted from farm outbuildings, with the games room from the old milking parlour, complete with stalls. Dornafield is a member of the Caravan Club's 'Affiliated site' scheme, with both members and non-members made welcome. The rural situation is delightful and, being away from the coast and without any evening activities, it is a haven for those seeking a quiet, restful holiday. A park that is well worth consideration and a member of the Best of British Group.

Facilities

Both modern toilet blocks are excellent and heated, with some washbasins in cubicles and comfortable roomy showers, but the new block up the hill could be said to be 'state of the art' with underfloor heating and a heat recovery system. Both blocks have facilities for disabled visitors and babies. Laundry rooms. Shop (13/3-2/1). Gas supplies. All-weather tennis court. 7 acres for dog walking. Games room. Play areas. WiFi. All year caravan storage. Half-mile walk to main road for bus stop. Off site: Local inn 0.5 miles. Golf 1 mile. Fishing 2.5 miles.

Open: 13 March - 2 January.

Directions

Park is northwest of A381 Newton Abbot - Totnes road. Leave A381 at Two Mile Oak Inn, opposite garage, and turn left at crossroads after about half a mile. Entrance is on the right.
GPS: 50.50032, -3.63717

Charges guide

Per unit incl. 2 persons and electricity	£ 15.00 - £ 31.00
extra person	£ 4.00 - £ 8.00
child (5-16 yrs)	£ 2.00 - £ 4.00

Newton Abbot

Woodville Caravan Park

Totnes Road, Ipplepen, Newton Abbot TQ12 5TN (Devon) T: 01803 812240. E: info@woodvillepark.co.uk

alanrogers.com/UK0915

A lovely little site exclusively for adults, Woodville is in a sheltered situation, attractively laid out with a wide variety of shrubs and trees. There are 26 pitches all with hardstanding and 16A electricity. They are accessed by a circular roadway which provides a central lawned area. A caravan storage area is to one side. This is a quiet site with few services, although the park is adjacent to a garden centre which also sells food and drinks. Dainton Park golf course is directly opposite and Ipplepen village is within walking distance and has three pubs. The owners live on the site and take a pride in their park.

Facilities

A fully equipped toilet block also provides a separate unit for visitors with disabilities. Washing machine and freezer. Vans selling fish and chips and eggs call weekly. Wooden chalet with tourist information doubles as reception (limited opening hours). Off site: Shop and golf course adjacent. Three pubs within walking distance. Bus service on main road. Riding 3 miles. Fishing 5 miles. Beach and boat launching 7 miles.

Open: 1 March - 2 January.

Directions

From Newton Abbot follow A381 Totnes road for about 3 miles. Site is on the right just after Fermoys Garden Centre. The site gate is kept closed.
GPS: 50.49505, -3.62965

Charges guide

Per unit incl. 2 persons and electricity	£ 13.90 - £ 18.50
extra person	£ 4.50 - £ 5.00
dog	£ 0.50

For latest campsite news visit
alanrogers.com

Newton Abbot

Parkers Farm Holiday Park

Higher Mead Farm, Ashburton, Newton Abbot TQ13 7LJ (Devon) T: 01364 654869.
E: parkersfarm@btconnect.com **alanrogers.com/UK0960**

Well situated with fine views towards Dartmoor, Parker's Farm is a modern touring site offering a unique chance to experience Devon country life at first hand, with pigs, sheep, goats, calves and rabbits to feed and touch. The 100 touring pitches are on broad terraces giving groups of flat pitches, all with good views across the valley (over the A38 which may give some road noise). Electricity (12A) is provided throughout and 11 pitches also have large hardstanding with TV and waste water connections. Trees and hedges have matured nicely on the terraces, with many more planted. Caravan holiday homes are available to hire. In addition the Parker family has added a family bar which provides entertainment during the main season (live singers, family bingo, children's entertainers) and a restaurant using locally sourced ingredients. Farm walks and tractor rides are tremendously popular and take place three evenings a week in high season, on request at other times. Parker's Farm provides a warm welcome; in the words of one camper, 'you come here and feel you belong'.

Facilities	Directions
Two modern, fully equipped toilet blocks also provide two family shower rooms. Baby bathroom. En-suite room for disabled visitors. Laundry. Shop (Easter-mid Oct). Restaurant, comfortable bar with family room (Easter, then Whitsun-mid Sept) and entertainment. Games room. Indoor play and TV area. Large outdoor play area. Trampolines. 6 acres of fields for dog walking. Caravan storage. Caravan holiday homes to hire. Rallies welcome. American motorhomes accepted by prior arrangement. Off site: Golf 4 miles. Riding and bicycle hire 5 miles. Coast 12 miles.	From Exeter on A38 turn left at Alston Cross signed Woodland Denbury. Site is 400 yds. GPS: 50.527646, -3.723459

Open: Easter - 31 October.

Charges 2012	
Per unit incl. 2 persons and electricity	£ 10.00 - £ 25.00
extra person	£ 3.00
child (3-15 yrs)	£ 2.00
dog	£ 1.50

PARKERS FARM
HOLIDAY PARK

01364 654869

Higher Mead Farm, Ashburton
Devon TQ13 7LJ
www.parkersfarmholidays.co.uk

AA

- Friendly family run park
- Views to Dartmoor
- Level terraced touring site
- Static caravans to let
- Children's paradise
- 12 miles to the coast
- Dogs very welcome
- Short breaks available

Newton Abbot

Lemonford Caravan Park

Bickington, Newton Abbot TQ12 6JR (Devon) T: 01626 821242. E: info@lemonford.co.uk

alanrogers.com/UK0980

Lemonford is a well run, neat and tidy site for all ages and families on the southern edge of the National Park, some three miles from both Ashburton and Newton Abbot. Personally run by the Ayres family, it is nicely landscaped with a mix of trees and shrubs and covers 7.5 acres. Although close to the main road, it is set in a sheltered, peaceful dip bordered by the pretty River Lemon. There are 87 touring pitches (around 40 used as seasonal pitches) on level grass and grouped in four areas with some new fully serviced pitches available. Most pitches have 10A electricity (some 16A), 76 have hardstanding. There are several holiday homes in the centre of the touring area and in separate areas at the back of the site, with some available to rent.

Facilities	Directions
Two modern toilet blocks. The newer one can be heated and provides some large private cabins, a ladies' bathroom (£1 payment) and a family bathroom with facilities for disabled visitors. Laundry facilities. Shop. Gas supplies. Freezer service. Play area. No commercial vehicles are accepted. Off site: Pub within walking distance. Golf 2 miles. Riding and bicycle hire 3 miles. Fishing 4 miles. Leisure pool in Newton Abbot.	Travelling from Exeter, turn off A38 Plymouth road at A382 (Drumbridges) exit signed Newton Abbot, Bovey Tracey, Mortonhampstead. At roundabout take third exit to Bickington. Continue for 3 miles and park is on left at the bottom of the hill. From Plymouth, take A383 (Goodstone) exit, cross the A38 and take first left to Bickington to site on right. GPS: 50.5391, -3.704

Open: All year.

Charges guide	
Per unit incl. 2 persons and electricity	£ 13.00 - £ 21.50
extra person (over 16 yrs)	£ 3.00
child (3-15 yrs)	£ 2.50
dog	£ 1.50

For latest campsite news visit
alanrogers.com

Okehampton

South Breazle Holidays

Bratton Clovelly, Okehampton EX20 4JS (Devon) T: 01837 871752. E: louise@southbreazleholidays.co.uk
alanrogers.com/UK0785

Tucked away down a half mile long Devon lane is a rather special campsite. Purpose built by Steve and Louise, who own and run South Breazle farm, the site is spacious with large pitches around the edge of a well mowed field, accessed by a circular roadway. Pitches are marked with young hedging and all named, e.g. Badgers's Den or Squirrel's Secret. Yes, you may spot a squirrel in the magnificent tall trees which edge the field but do not block the views across the rolling Devon countryside. In all there are 29 large pitches (180 sq.m), 23 with 16A electricity and water, and some with hardstanding.

Facilities

Comfortable toilet block, with facilities for children and disabled visitors. Washing machine and dryer. Shop for basics and local products. Fun fountain. Recycling. Games field. Walks from site. Free WiFi on every pitch. Barbecues off ground. No dogs allowed (working farm). Caravan storage. Seasonal pitches available.
Off site: Bicycle hire (can be delivered). Radford Lake 2 miles for fishing etc. Watersports centre 4 miles (far side of lake). Riding 10 miles. Golf 15 miles.

Open: 1 March - 31 October.

Directions

Exit A30 at Stowford Cross. Follow signs for Roadford Lake. At top of hill (1 mile) turn right. Signed Bratton Clovelly then take second left signed Germansweek. South Breazle Holidays signed first right and follow for 0.5 mile down lane to site. GPS: 50.70007, -4.20982

Charges 2012

Per unit incl. 2 persons, electricity and water	£ 14.00 - £ 22.00
extra person	£ 4.00 - £ 4.50

Paignton

Whitehill Country Park

Stoke Road, Paignton TQ4 7PF (Devon) T: 01803 782338. E: info@whitehill-park.co.uk
alanrogers.com/UK0860

Whitehill Country Park is beautifully situated in rolling Devon countryside, just 2.5 miles from the nearest beaches. Extending over 40 acres, a definite sense of space characterises this park and 10 acres of ancient woodland are available for walks and attract a great deal of wildlife. Whitehill is a friendly park with 320 large grassy pitches which are located in separate fields around the site. Most pitches have electrical connections (16A, 15 m. cable). Around 60 pitches are used for caravan holiday homes. A new upmarket development of wooden lodges are for private ownership and more may be added. The park was once a stud farm where shire horses were bred but now the stables and farm buildings are used for the wide range of park facilities. There is also an amusement barn and Hayloft bar (with satellite TV), a café and an extensive decking area for outside eating. A marvellous holiday venue for all the family.

Facilities

Good sanitary provision includes private, individual washing facilities for ladies and facilities for disabled visitors. Laundry facilities. Gas. Well stocked shop and bar. Café/takeaway (Easter, 1/6-9/6 and 14/6-16/9). Swimming and paddling pools (heated 21/5-1/9). Three play areas. Electronic games and amusement machines. Craft centre for children. Children's nature trail. Walking and cycle routes. WiFi throughout. Dogs are not accepted in the touring area from 2/6-11/6 and 21/7-3/9.
Off site: Bus stop at site entrance. Fishing and golf 2 miles. Paignton 2.5 miles. Beach 3 miles. Riding 4 miles.

Open: Easter - 29 September.

Directions

Turn left at The Parkers Arms off the A385 Paignton to Totnes road, signed Stoke Gabriel. Site is 1 mile along this road. GPS: 50.417867, -3.609

Charges guide

Per unit incl. 2 persons and electricity	£ 15.00 - £ 27.70
tent pitch incl. 2 persons	£ 13.10 - £ 24.10
extra person	£ 4.00
child (4-14 yrs)	£ 3.00
Camping Cheques accepted.	

Paignton

Beverley Park

Goodrington Road, Paignton TQ4 7JE (Devon) T: 01803 661978. E: info@beverley-holidays.co.uk

alanrogers.com/UK0870

Beverley Park is an amazing holiday centre catering for every need. It has been developed and run by the Jeavons family for over 50 years to very high standards. It is popular, busy and attractively landscaped with marvellous views over Torbay. The pools, a large dance hall, bars and entertainment, are all run in an efficient and orderly manner. The park has 190 caravan holiday homes and 23 lodges, mainly around the central complex. There are 179 touring pitches in the lower areas of the park, all reasonably sheltered, some with views across the bay and some on slightly sloping ground. All pitches can take awnings and 87 have 16A electricity (15 m. cable), 38 have hardstanding and 42 are fully serviced. Tents are accepted and a limited number of tent pitches have electrical connections. The park is open all year and reservations are essential for caravans in high season. Entertainment is organised at Easter and from early May in the Starlight Cabaret bar. There are indoor and outdoor pools, each one heated and supervised. The Oasis fitness centre provides a steam room, jacuzzi and an excellent fitness room. The park is in the heart of residential Torquay, with views across the bay to Brixham and the English Riviera, and sandy beaches less than a mile away. There is a regular local bus service to Paignton, Torbay and Brixham and minibus service to the beach and town. This popular park has lots to offer and is well maintained and run. A member of the Best of British Group.

Facilities

Good toilet blocks adjacent to the pitches, heated and well maintained, include roomy showers, some with washbasins en-suite. Baths on payment. Unit for disabled visitors. Facilities for babies. Laundry. Gas supplies. Motorcaravan service point. Large general shop (30/3-26/10). Restaurant, bars and takeaway (13/3-15/4, 4/5-28/9, and 20/10-26/10). Heated swimming pools, outdoor 22/5-4/9, indoor all year. Fitness centre. Tennis. Crazy golf. Playground. Nature trail. Amusement centre with pool, table tennis and amusement machines. Soft play area. WiFi throughout. Dogs are not accepted. Off site: Regular minibus service to Paignton (timetable at reception) and public services from outside the park. Fishing, bicycle hire, riding and golf all within 2 miles.

Open: All year.

Directions

Park is south of Paignton in Goodrington Road between A379 coast road and B3203 ring road and is well signed on both.
GPS: 50.413533, -3.568667

Charges guide

Per unit incl. 2 persons and electricity	£ 15.20 - £ 38.50
tent pitch incl. 2 persons	£ 13.00 - £ 29.30
extra person	£ 4.70
child	£ 3.50

Max. 6 persons per reservation.

Paignton

Widdicombe Farm Tourist Park

The Ring Road, Compton, Paignton TQ3 1ST (Devon) T: 01803 558325. E: info@widdicombefarm.co.uk

alanrogers.com/UK0900

Widdicombe Farm is an adults only park, just three miles from Torquay and with easy access from the A380, well situated for the Torbay area. There are 200 numbered pitches, 160 with electricity (10A) of which most have hardstanding and 48 are fully serviced. Situated on a hillside and surrounded by farmland, the pitches are on terraces with open views across the countryside. Many trees have been planted and there are tarmac access roads and steps linking the terraces. There may be some background traffic noise but it is not too intrusive. Touring areas are separated into sections for couples, tent campers, etc. The park has been owned and run for over 40 years by the Glynn family.

Facilities

Three older style toilet blocks are kept very clean (the men's has been refurbished). The original heated block near reception is fully equipped and includes facilities for disabled visitors, dishwashing area and laundry room. Shop. Restaurant (evening meals, breakfasts, cream teas and takeaway) and bar with singers or comedy acts (Easter, then Spring B.H-mid Sept). Certain breeds of dog are not accepted. Caravan storage. Minibus to the town can be booked if there are 6 persons. WiFi throughout (charged). Off site: Golf 1.5 miles. Fishing 2 miles. Bicycle hire, beach and boat launching 2.5 miles.

Open: 19 March - 29 October.

Directions

From Newton Abbot take A380 south for about 5 miles. On outskirts of Torquay turn right at roundabout onto ring road. Site is well signed off this road. GPS: 50.467081, -3.586797

Charges 2012

Per unit incl. 2 persons and electricity	£ 12.50 - £ 25.50
extra person	£ 3.60
dog	£ 1.50
Bargain breaks available.	

Plymouth

Riverside Caravan Park

Leigham Manor Drive, Marsh Mills, Plymouth PL6 8LL (Devon) T: 01752 344122.
E: office@riversidecaravanpark.com **alanrogers.com/UK0810**

As you leave the A38 for Plymouth and negotiate the Marsh Mills roundabout you can have no idea that there is a lush green touring park tucked away from the modern, out-of-town shopping units in a quiet green valley. Part of the park is being developed to provide a residential area alongside the river Plym which has therefore meant a reduction in the number of touring pitches. However, there are still some 200 spaces available for touring, 80 of which have electricity (10A) and many are on hardstanding. There are also a number of grass pitches for tents. Hidden behind a high, evergreen hedge are an attractive swimming pool and children's pool. A play area is nearby and a restaurant with a bar and games room provide welcome facilities and entertainment in high season. Over 30 years ago this park was a corn field but, with careful development by its owner, it now provides an oasis from which to explore Dartmoor, to enjoy the amazing views from Plymouth Hoe or even to overnight quietly before catching the ferry to France. The wooded valley sides give way to level grass where the trees and shrubs have matured to give a park-like feel. The River Plym runs down one side of the site but it is carefully fenced.

Facilities

Three modern, fully equipped toilet blocks include cubicles with toilets and washbasins. Laundry room. Motorcaravan service point. Gas supplies. Some basics are kept in reception (more in high season). Bar, restaurant and takeaway (B.Hs and high season) with family entertainment included. Heated swimming pool and children's pool (end May-12 Sept). Games room with TV. Play area. Dogs accepted (max. 2). Off site: Fishing possible in River Plym (licence required). Dry ski slope, supermarket and retail park within walking distance. Bus stop 10 minutes. Bicycle hire, sea fishing and boat launching 3.5 miles. Golf 5 miles. Riding 4 miles. Beach 10 miles.

Open: All year.

Directions

From the A38 Marsh Mills roundabout for Plymouth take the third exit. After a few yards turn left following caravan signs, then right alongside the River Plym to the park. GPS: 50.398167, -4.087333

Charges guide

Per unit incl. 2 persons and electricity	£ 14.00 - £ 24.00
tent pitch without electricity	£ 10.50 - £ 20.00
extra person	£ 5.00
child (0-16 yrs)	free - £ 2.50
dog	£ 2.50

Our family owned and run touring park offers an established, level parkland setting just 3 miles from Plymouth City Centre (including The Hoe and Barbican) and within easy reach of Dartmoor, Cornwall and the beautiful South Hams coastline. Local supermarket, pubs and park and ride are all within a 15min walk.

Facilities include:
♦ Laundry and ironing room with hair drying facilities
♦ Bar, restaurant, takeaway, games room and TV room (Easter and Summer only)
♦ Heated swimming pool (Summer only)

Riverside Caravan Park, Leigham Manor Drive, Plymouth, PL6 8LL
www.riversidecaravanpark.com office@riversidecaravanpark.com Telephone: (01752) 344 122

For latest campsite news visit
alanrogers.com

Salcombe

Bolberry House Farm Caravan & Camping

Bolberry, Malborough, Kingsbridge TQ7 3DY (Devon) T: 01548 561 251. E: enquiries@bolberryparks.co.uk

alanrogers.com/UK0824

Five generations have farmed the land at Bolberry and the present owner's grandfather started the campsite in the field on top of the hill; this main field enjoys marvellous views of the surrounding countryside and out to sea. There are breathtaking sunsets, and even shooting stars. This is a traditional campsite, which caters for all units in three fields connected by grass paths with some up and down walking – this is a small price to pay for the views! There are around 100 pitches (75 have 10A electricity) with extra allowed in the peak period, well spaced around the edges of fairly level fields with plenty of central space for children to play. There are a few static vans to let in a separate area. However, it is not just the situation which makes this site special, but the warm welcome from Fiona and Elaine who run it. There is no reception; the sisters meet all their visitors personally and provide them with comprehensive information and they are real ambassadors for this wonderful area - nothing is too much trouble for them. They believe they live in a magical place and want their visitors to share it - especially families, who can enjoy a bucket-and-spade holiday at Hope Cove, or couples enjoying a walking holiday. The coastal path is close by and many other walks can be enjoyed.

Facilities

Two dated toilet blocks fully equipped. Coin operated showers (20p). Laundry. Play area. Small van open in mornings sells basics. Fish and chip van (Sun). Hog roast (Weds. all main season). Four different takeaways will deliver to site. Hope Cove holiday weekend (entertainment, events, music etc) last weekend in August. Off site: Pubs, farmhouse teas all within walking distance. Coastal paths half a mile. Hope Cove with sandy beach 1 mile. Fishing 1 mile. Salcombe with its creeks for sailing and watersports and safe sandy beaches 3 miles.

Open: Easter - end September.

Directions

From Totnes follow A381 bypassing Kingsbridge via Chuchstow, following signs for Salcombe. At Malborough turn sharp right through village. Follow signs for Bolberry until you come to park on right. GPS: 50.238221, -3.831081

Charges guide

Per unit incl. 2 persons	£ 14.00 - £ 24.00
extra person	£ 3.00 - £ 4.00
electricity (10A)	£ 3.00
dog	free - £ 1.00

Bolberry House Farm
NR. SALCOMBE · SOUTH DEVON
Friendly, family run park in a very beautiful and unspoilt coastal area. An ideal base.
Tel: (01548) 561251
Email: enquiries@bolberryparks.co.uk
www.bolberryparks.co.uk

Sidmouth

Oakdown Touring & Holiday Caravan Park

Weston, Sidmouth EX10 0PT (Devon) T: 01297 680387. E: enquiries@oakdown.co.uk

alanrogers.com/UK1020

Oakdown is a very attractive, well planned park which has just celebrated its 60th birthday (2011). Run by the Franks family since 1972, the family and their team continue to work hard carrying out developments in keeping with the environment. The attention to detail is evident at this award-winning park as soon as you arrive. There are 100 level touring pitches arranged in landscaped bays, screened by a wide variety of trees and shrubs and linked by a circular road. All have electricity and hardstanding and many have water and drainage. An additional touring area near the golf course, Beech Grove, provides a further 50 large pitches with hedging and 16A electricity. A Best of British Group member.

Facilities

The original central toilet block has been completely renewed, is well maintained and heated and includes a private cabin for ladies. Two unisex family bathrooms double as units for disabled visitors. Laundry facilities. New facilities in Beech Grove include a room for families and disabled visitors, and a laundry area. Motorcaravan service point. New café/shop selling essentials and snacks (mid May-mid Sept). Internet room. TV room. Two adventure play areas and castle. Lake. Dew pond. No cycling, skate-boarding or kite flying is permitted. Off site: Golf adjacent. Swimming 1 mile. Beach 2 miles.

Open: 17 March - 7 November.

Directions

Turn south off the A3052 (Exeter-Lyme Regis) road between Sidford and Colyford, 2.5 miles east of the A375 junction and park is on left. GPS: 50.7056, -3.18063

Charges guide

Per unit incl. 2 persons and electricity (10/16A)	£ 15.20 - £ 22.00
with water and drainage	£ 20.50 - £ 27.50
extra person (5 yrs and over)	£ 3.00
dog	£ 2.30

For latest campsite news visit
alanrogers.com

Sidmouth

Salcombe Regis Camping & Caravan Park

Salcombe Regis, Sidmouth EX10 0JH (Devon) T: 01395 514303. E: contact@salcombe-regis.co.uk

alanrogers.com/UK1110

On the edge of Salcombe Regis village, 1.5 miles from Sidmouth and less than a mile from the sea. Salcombe Regis Park covers 16 acres of land. It is surrounded by farmland with views of the combe and the sea beyond. The focal point of the main camping area is a large 'village green' where the play area and pitch and putt are located. The reception and pitches are arranged around the green, all connected by a tarmac road. The 110 pitches are level and have their own water supply, with 98 electricity hook-ups (16A). A 25 minute walk across fields takes you to a small secluded beach, although the walk there is fairly steep – we are told there are 129 steps! There are many footpaths and coastal walks nearby, protected by the National Trust and with views of Sidmouth and Weston Mouth. Sidmouth town, originally a small fishing town but now a seaside resort, is host to the annual International Folk Festival, where for one week in summer the town is filled with folk artists from all over the world.

Facilities

The traditional style toilet block (to one side of the site and a longer walk for some) is kept spotlessly clean by the resident wardens and includes a bathroom for families and disabled visitors. Shop at reception selling basic supplies and local produce. Dishwashing area under cover. Laundry room with washing machines, dryers and ironing board. Motorcaravan service point. Play area. Pitch and putt. Caravan storage. Torches useful. WiFi (charged). Off site: Fishing, bicycle hire and golf 1.5 miles. Sidmouth and beach 1.5 miles. Riding 3 miles.

Open: Easter - 28 October.

Directions

Park is well signed on the A3052 Exeter - Lyme Regis road. From the east, take first left after Donkey Sanctuary. From the west proceed up the hill out of Sidford. Do not take first road signed Salcombe Regis, but take the next right at top of hill. Follow road round to site on left after golf range. GPS: 50.695717, -3.205367

Charges guide

Per unit incl. 2 persons and electricity	£ 16.50 - £ 23.00
dog	£ 1.50 - £ 1.90
extra person	£ 4.10
child (5-15 yrs)	£ 2.70

Salcombe Regis
CAMPING
& CARAVAN PARK
Sidmouth, Devon
EX10 0JH

Tranquil setting with excellent touring facilities Ideal base for exploring rural East Devon, Superb walking country
Within walking distance of the sea & famous Donkey Sanctuary
Ten Luxuriously equipped Rose Award leisure homes for hire. Situated ½ OFF main A3052 Exeter to Lyme Regis coast road. Spacious level sites with some views. Hardstanding with individual taps/soakaways, available for Tourers/Motor caravans at no extra cost. Heated amenity block.

Tel: (01395) 514303
Fax: (01395) 514313
www.salcombe-regis.co.uk
E-mail:
contact@salcombe-regis.co.uk
FREE colour brochure

South Molton

Riverside Caravan & Camping Park

Marsh Lane, North Molton Road, South Molton EX36 3HQ (Devon) T: 01769 579 269.
E: relax@exmoorriverside.co.uk **alanrogers.com/UK0745**

A very impressive purpose-built campsite beside the River Mole, set in 40 acres of meadow and woodland. All the 54 pitches at this park have hardstanding, 16A electricity connection, water, drainage and TV aerial socket. Neat grass, tarmac roads and growing trees and hedges contribute to the attractive, overall impression. The heated toilet block gleams and visitors will appreciate the hairdryers, hand-dryers and shaver points. The owners, Joy and Nicky Penfold, are not resting on their laurels and have developed fishing lakes with specimen carp down by the river and a play area on the opposite bank. A road runs alongside the site, so a little noise can be expected.

Facilities

Modern, fully equipped and heated toilet block accessed by code. Facilities for disabled visitors. Laundry room. Shop (limited hours in low season). Children's play area. Entertainment (B.Hs and high season). Fishing. Caravan storage. Swimming in river. Off site: Market town of South Molton with all facilities 1 mile. Riding 2 miles. Golf 5 miles. Boat launching and beach 12 miles.

Open: All year.

Directions

From M5 exit 27 take the North Devon Link road A361. Near South Molton watch for site sign (direction North Molton). GPS: 51.02918, -3.823467

Charges guide

Per unit incl. 2 persons and electricity	£ 14.00 - £ 25.00
extra person	£ 6.00
child (under 8 yrs)	free - £ 4.00
Camping Cheques accepted.	

For latest campsite news visit
alanrogers.com

Tavistock

Harford Bridge Holiday Park

Peter Tavy, Tavistock PL19 9LS (Devon) T: 01822 810349. E: enquiry@harfordbridge.co.uk

alanrogers.com/UK0790

Harford Bridge has an interesting history – originally the Wheal Union tin mine until 1850, then used as a farm campsite from 1930 and taken over by the Royal Engineers in 1939. It is now a quiet, rural, mature park inside the Dartmoor National Park. It is bounded by the River Tavy on one side and the lane from the main road to the village of Peter Tavy on the other, with Harford Bridge, a classic granite moorland bridge, at the corner. With 16.5 acres, the park provides 120 touring pitches well spaced on a level grassy meadow with some shade from mature trees and others recently planted; 52 pitches have electrical hook-ups (16A) and 11 have 'multi-services', 5 with hardstanding. Out of season or by booking in advance you may get one of the delightful spots bordering the river (these are without electricity). Some holiday caravans and chalets are neatly landscaped in their own area. At the entrance to the park a central grassy area is left free for games, which is also used by the town band, village fete, etc. While the river (unfenced) will inevitably mesmerise youngsters, a super central play area on a hilly tree knoll will claim them. In early summer there are chicks to watch, horses to make a fuss of and the park ducks are a feature. With its own and the local history, plus its situation, this is a super place to stay.

Facilities

The single toilet block has been modernised and is fully equipped and well kept, with free hot water and showers all year. Facilities for disabled visitors and babies. Good launderette and drying room. Freezer. Motorcaravan service point. Games room with table tennis and separate TV room. Play area. Tennis court (free). Two communal barbecue areas. Fly fishing (by licence, £3 p/day, £10 p/week). WiFi (charged). Off site: Bicycle hire, riding and golf, all within 2.5 miles. West Devon cycle way (Route 27). It is possible to cycle into Tavistock, which has a market twice monthly. Bus stop on main road.

Open: All year.

Directions

Two miles north of Tavistock, off A386 Tavistock - Okehampton road, take the road to Peter Tavy. GPS: 50.5713, -4.114

Charges guide

Per unit incl. 2 persons and electricity	£ 15.75 - £ 19.95
with full services	£ 17.50 - £ 21.70
extra person	£ 5.50
child (3-16 yrs)	£ 2.70

Tavistock

Woodovis Park

Woodovis House, Gulworthy, Tavistock PL19 8NY (Devon) T: 01822 832968. E: info@woodovis.com

alanrogers.com/UK0805

Woodovis Park is set in the grounds of Woodovis House, owned in the 19th century by a mine captain in the days when the valley had a thriving copper mining industry. It nestles in a sheltered wooded position covering 14 acres, by the edge of the Tamar Valley on the borders of Devon and Cornwall. John and Dorothy Lewis have been running Woodovis Park since 1999, helped by their very welcoming staff. There are 50 good sized pitches, all with 10A electricity. You have a choice of grass, all weather and 11 super pitches (with 16A, water, waste and tv hook-ups too). Split over two fields and landscaped in between are 35 caravan holiday homes, 24 for hire. A member of the Best of British Group.

Facilities

Fully equipped and heated toilet block. Bathroom (coin operated) is useful for disabled visitors or those with babies. Family cubicles. Toilet for disabled visitors at the pool. Laundry. Motorcaravan service point. Shop for basics with off licence doubles with reception. Indoor heated swimming pool (no swimming alone), spa and sauna. Games room with large size Connect 4. Fenced play area. Pétanque. Archery and 'water-walking' weekly during school holidays. WiFi. Off site: Pub with restaurant within walking distance. Walking and cycling trails. Fishing 3 miles. Golf, riding and boat launching 7 miles. Canoeing and tree walking 3 miles. Tavistock 4 miles.

Open: 23 March - 3 November.

Directions

From Tavistock follow A390 for Liskeard. After 3 miles turn right at Gulworthy roundabout signed Chipshop, Lamerton and Caravan Park. After 1 mile entrance is signed on left. GPS: 50.548867, -4.21585

Charges guide

Per person (over 5 yrs)	£ 7.50
pitch incl. electricity	£ 5.00 - £ 20.00
awning	£ 2.00

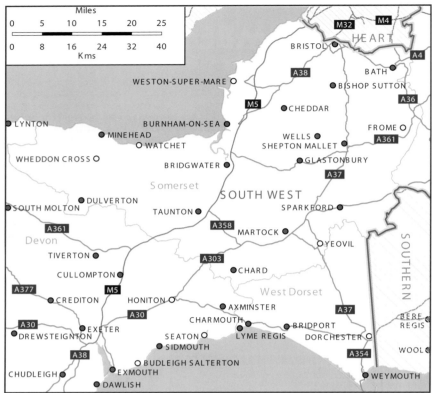

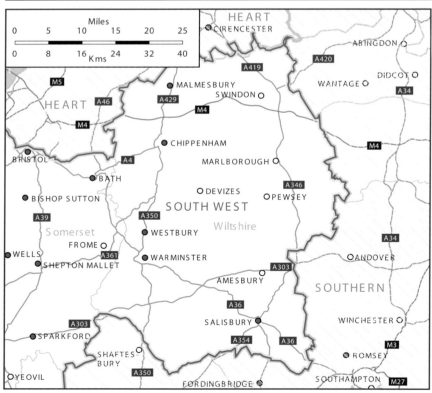

For latest campsite news visit
alanrogers.com

Bath

Newton Mill Holiday Park

Newton Road, Bath BA2 9JF (Somerset) T: 0844 272 9503. E: enquiries@newtonmillpark.co.uk

alanrogers.com/UK1460

In a peaceful valley three miles from the centre of the historic city of Bath and with direct access to the local cycle track network, Newton Mill is an excellent base from which to explore the city and the area. There are two meadows for tents and 90 caravan pitches (with 30 long stay) which are located at the other end of the valley. All of these have hardstandings, with 16A electricity and satellite TV hook-ups. This end of the park is closest to the main Bristol to London railway line, not visually obtrusive but occasional rail noise may be noticeable. The site has been created around an old mill, the bar and restaurant now occupying part of the original building, and there is a modern timber chalet-style reception building with a small, well stocked shop. The restaurant serves good value, speciality meals. The tent meadow is in an elevated position, or alternatively you may prefer the paddock, a small field alongside the stream which is a car free zone with a separate parking area.

Facilities

Two new heated toilet blocks provide excellent modern facilities with some washbasins in cubicles, hot showers, bathrooms (on payment), baby rooms and a good suite for disabled campers. Basic motorcaravan service point. Shop, bar, restaurant (open evenings and breakfasts are available at weekends Easter-Oct, daily in summer) with seating area. Play area. Boules court. Fishing. Off site: Bus service into Bath runs every ten minutes from Twerton village. Nearby Bristol and Bath Railway Path (a traffic-free cycle way) links to the West Bath Riverside Path, and the Kennet and Avon towpath.

Open: All year.

Directions

Site is 2 miles west of Bath city centre, about 1 mile southeast of the roundabout where the A4 meets the A39. From the north take M4 exit 19, turn on to M32 and almost immediately take A4174 (Avon ring road) for 7.5 miles to the A4. Turn left towards Bath and after 5 miles at second roundabout, take second exit signed Newton St Loe and pass The Globe public house. Site entrance is on the left after about 1 mile. GPS: 51.378133, -2.410817

Charges guide

Per unit incl. 2 persons
and electricity   £ 15.00 - £ 25.00

Bishop Sutton

Bath Chew Valley Caravan Park

Ham Lane, Bishop Sutton BS39 5TZ (Somerset) T: 01275 332127. E: enquiries@bathchewvalley.co.uk

alanrogers.com/UK1510

A small and secluded garden site for adults only, Chew Valley has been developed with much tender love and care by the Betton family and is now affiliated to the Caravan Club. Caravans are sited on neat lawns amongst colourful beds of flowers, and cars are tucked away on the nearby car park, providing a tranquil and restful atmosphere. Woodland is adjacent with an enclosed dog walking area. The warden will assist you in placing your caravan. There are neat hardstandings for all pitches and 27 spacious, fully serviced pitches, all with 16A electricity connections. A member of the Best of British Group.

Facilities

Heated toilet block. Separate en-suite units each with WC, basin and shower. One unit has facilities for disabled visitors. Laundry facilities. Use of freezer. Motorcaravan service point. Internet access and WiFi. Max. 2 dogs. Off site: Village 100 yds with useful general store, newsagent, two pubs and post office. Supermarkets within 15 minutes drive. Fishing 1 mile. Golf 5 miles. Riding 8 miles. Beach 15 miles.

Open: All year.

Directions

From the A37 or A38 take the A368 (which links them) to Bishop Sutton. Ham lane is opposite the Red Lion Public House. The park is 800 m. along Ham Lane on the left. GPS: 51.336583, -2.597183

Charges guide

Per unit incl. 2 persons
and electricity   £ 20.00 - £ 30.00

For latest campsite news visit

alanrogers.com

Bridgwater

Mill Farm Caravan & Camping Park

Fiddington, Bridgwater TA5 1JQ (Somerset) T: 01278 732286

alanrogers.com/UK1306

On the edge of the village of Fiddington, in a countryside location at the foot of the Quantock Hills, Mill Farm is just seven miles from Bridgwater and four miles from the sea. This is an extensive and popular family holiday site with three main fields, each taking 50-60 units with a toilet block, a playground and a plentiful supply of water points. Extra fields are opened for the peak season allowing a total capacity of 275 units, all with electricity (10A). The site has a large swimming pool complex with indoor and outdoor pools, free to campers. There is a licensed riding school, rowing boats on the little lake, and entertainment during high season and at weekends during mid-season. American motorhomes accepted, motorcyclists at the management's discretion. Mill Farm is a good family holiday base, very much children orientated with a wide range of activities to keep them happy.

Facilities

Three toilet blocks include facilities for disabled visitors (Radar key), one washbasin in cubicle for each sex, bathrooms (charged) and baby rooms. These blocks do come under pressure in peak seasons and a fourth is opened to cater for the 'overflow' fields. Launderette. Shop. Club room with bar, takeaway (weekends and peak seasons), games room and entertainment (high season). Heated indoor pool with whirlpool and paddling pool (Easter-early Nov) and outdoor pool with giant waterslide (15/5-31/9). Pony riding and trekking, canoe hire, and trampolining (charged). Boating lake. WiFi. Off site: Golf 3 miles. Beach and fishing 4 miles.

Open: All year.

Directions

From M5 exit 23 or 24, turn west and pass through Bridgwater and continue on the A39. After 6 miles turn right towards Fiddington. Continue through narrow lane with passing places for 1 mile to site entrance. Park where instructed on the long entry driveway and report to reception.
GPS: 51.16, -3.120517

Charges 2012

Per unit incl. 2 persons and electricity	£ 16.00 - £ 25.00
extra person	£ 3.00 - £ 4.00
dog	£ 2.00

Mill Farm Caravan and Camping Park
Fiddington, Bridgwater, Somerset

Swimming * Riding * Boating

Activity park with Lots for children, making the ideal family holiday.

HIRE: Trampolines, Pony rides, Canoes, Pool tables

FREE: Heated Swimming Pool and Large water slide Children's Boating Lake, Swings and Slides, Games room, Hot showers, WIFI

ALSO: Hot take-away and shop during high season.

* Club with Entertainment
* Meadow for Rallies
* Holiday Cottage's
* Caravan Storage

01278 732286   www.millfarm.biz

Bridport

Golden Cap Holiday Park

West Dorset Leisure Holidays, Seatown, Chideock, Bridport DT6 6JX (Dorset) T: 01308 422139.

E: holidays@wdlh.co.uk **alanrogers.com/UK1740**

Golden Cap, named after the adjacent high cliff which overlooks Lyme Bay, is only 150 m. from a shingle beach at Seatown and is surrounded by National Trust countryside and the Heritage Coastline. The park is arranged over several fields on the valley floor, sloping gently down towards the sea. It is in two main areas, each separated into fields with panoramic views and providing 108 touring pitches. All have electricity and 30 also have hardstanding with drainage and gravel awning area. An extra sloping tent area is used for peak season, although it is a five minute walk from here to the toilet blocks and shop.

Facilities

The modern toilet block is of good quality with spacious shower cubicles (some with toilet and washbasin). Facilities for disabled visitors. Baby room. Two further smaller blocks. Laundry room. Motorcaravan service point. Shop. Small play area. Coarse fishing lake (day tickets from shop). American motorhomes are not accepted. WiFi throughout (charged). Off site: Pub nearby. Beach 150 yds. Golf 2 miles. Bicycle hire 3 miles.

Open: 20 March - 8 November.

Directions

Turn off A35 road at Chideock, 3 miles west of Bridport, at sign to Seatown opposite church. Park is less than 1 mile down narrow lane.
GPS: 50.715333, -2.821667

Charges guide

Per unit incl. 2 persons and electricity	£ 15.10 - £ 25.00
extra person	£ 4.20 - £ 5.20
pitch with sea view	£ 21.90 - £ 32.50

Bridport

Freshwater Beach Holiday Park

Burton Bradstock, Bridport DT6 4PT (Dorset) T: 01308 897317. E: office@freshwaterbeach.co.uk

alanrogers.com/UK1780

Family run parks for families with direct access to their own private beach are rare in Britain and this one has the added advantage of being in beautiful coastal countryside in West Dorset. It also has an excellent new leisure centre that includes a gym, 10-pin bowling and an indoor pool. The park is next to the sea and a beach of fine pebbles, sheltered from the wind by pebble banks and has been run by the same family for the last 40 years. Approached by a fairly steep access road, the park itself is on level, open ground. The 500 plus touring pitches, 400 with 10A electricity, are on an open, undulating grass field connected by tarmac or hardcore roads. Caravan pitches (10x11 m) are marked and evenly spaced in lines. Some tent pitches are in the main field, with others well spaced on a terraced field. In separate areas there are 260 caravan holiday homes, with 60 for hire. This lively holiday park has an extensive range of facilities which include an outdoor pool, a good value licensed restaurant, a main bar and two further small bars with an evening entertainment programme in season. Daytime entertainment caters for all ages – don't miss the donkey derby! Footpaths lead to the thatched village of Burton Bradstock or West Bay. The overall impression is of a large, busy holiday park with a friendly reception and happy atmosphere. Units over 23' long can have extra free space during non-peak periods.

Facilities

Two toilet blocks serve the caravan fields and a third newer block is in the tent field. Facilities for disabled visitors (Radar key). Baby care room (key system). Launderette. Bars with entertainment and evening shows. Licensed restaurant (weekends only in late season; closed Mondays all season). Main bar and two smaller bars. Supermarket and takeaway. New leisure complex with indoor pool, water play area, gym and 10-pin bowling. Heated, supervised outdoor swimming and paddling pools (25/5-25/9) with lessons. Games room with TV, amusements and soft drinks bar. Activities for children. Two play areas. High season pony trekking. Internet café and WiFi (charged). Off site: Bus stop on main road. Golf course 0.5 miles. Fishing possible from Chesil Bank.

Open: 17 March - 12 November.

Directions

Park is immediately west of the village of Burton Bradstock, on the Weymouth - Bridport coast road (B3157). GPS: 50.70500, -2.73867

Charges guide

Per unit incl. up to 6 persons, car and awning	£ 14.00 - £ 40.00
extra person, car or boat	£ 2.00
electricity	£ 2.00
small tent incl. 2 persons walking or cycling	£ 5.00 - £ 17.00
dog	£ 2.50

Single sex groups not admitted.

TOURING HOLIDAY HOMES CAMPING

FreshwaterBeach HOLIDAY PARK

Private Beach
- **Family pools**
- **Children's Activities**
- **Great Entertainment***
- **Family Friendly Bars**
- **Restaurant**

All on Dorset's World Heritage Coast.

* Spring Bank Holiday to mid Sept.

PLUS... OUR NEW INDOOR LEISURE COMPLEX

JURASSIC FUN CENTRE

INCLUDING 10-PIN BOWLING, INDOOR SWIMMING POOLS & WATER SLIDES, HOT TUB, SAUNA, STEAM ROOM, GYM & RESTAURANTS.

Call 01308 897 317

freshwaterbeach.co.uk Burton Bradstock Dorset DT6 4PT Wi Fi

Bridport

Highlands End Holiday Park

West Dorset Leisure Holidays, Eype, Bridport DT6 6AR (Dorset) T: 01308 422139. E: holidays@wdlh.co.uk

alanrogers.com/UK1750

On slightly sloping ground with open views, both coastal and inland, Highlands End is quietly situated on the Dorset Heritage Coastline. A path in front of the park runs along the cliff top and then leads down to a shingle beach. It is a good quality park with 180 caravan holiday homes, mostly privately owned, and 195 touring pitches in two areas nearest to the sea – one has to travel through the holiday homes to reach them. The field for tents has 73 pitches, 10 with electricity and the field for touring is all electric with 45 pitches also having water, drainage and hardstanding. A member of the Best of British Group.

Facilities

Two quality toilet blocks with some washbasins in cubicles and showers are well maintained and can be heated. En-suite facilities for disabled visitors. Baby room. Laundry room. Motorcaravan service point. Shop. Bar and restaurant/takeaway (evenings and Sunday lunch). Tennis. Indoor pool (20x9 m), gym, sauna/steam room. Games room. 9-hole pitch and putt. Adventure play area. Field for ball games. WiFi throughout (charged). Off site: Beach 0.5 miles. Bicycle hire 2 miles.

Open: 20 March - 8 November.

Directions

Follow Bridport bypass on A35 around the town and park is signed to south (Eype turning), down narrow lane. There is a new exit road.
GPS: 50.725333, -2.777

Charges guide

Per unit incl. 2 persons	
and electricity	£ 15.10 - £ 25.00
all services and hardstanding	£ 17.45 - £ 27.35
extra person	£ 4.20 - £ 5.20

Bridport

Bingham Grange Touring & Camping Park

Melplash, Bridport DT6 3TT (Dorset) T: 01308 488234. E: enquiries@binghamgrange.co.uk

alanrogers.com/UK1770

Bingham Grange is an attractive, purpose built park for adults only with an excellent restaurant. In a pleasant, rural situation two miles from the market town of Bridport, there are views seaward towards West Bay and inland across Beaminster Downs and Pilsdon Hill. There are over 135 individually landscaped pitches, 118 with 10A electricity, and 83 with hardstanding, 26 serviced. Shrubs and trees are fully developed in the original field and have been planted in the newer field. Pitches here have been levelled and terraced and have super views. Some non-electric for tents.

Facilities

Well equipped toilet block, with underfloor heating. Separate room for disabled visitors and five luxury en-suite shower rooms. Laundry room with microwave and freezer. Reception with small shop. Popular bar/restaurant with good value upmarket menu. Gas available. WiFi (charged). Only adults (over 18 yrs) are accepted. Off site: Sea fishing and golf 3 miles. Bicycle hire 5 miles.

Open: March - end October.

Directions

At the roundabouts on the A35 road, on the east side of Bridport, follow signs for Beaminster on the A3066. After 2 miles watch for site on the left.
GPS: 50.765076, -2.740911

Charges guide

Per unit incl. 2 persons	
and electricity (10A)	£ 16.00 - £ 24.00
extra person	£ 5.00

Bristol

Baltic Wharf Caravan Club Site

Cumberland Road, Bristol BS1 6XG (Somerset) T: 01179 268030

alanrogers.com/UK1440

This excellent Caravan Club site in Bristol's redeveloped dockland, is well laid out and maintained to a high standard. It is screened from the road by a high wall with a boatyard on one side and residential apartments on the other, with access via a lockable gate to the Baltic Wharf dockside. The view across the dock towards Clifton village and Bristol is unique and you can even glimpse the suspension bridge. Accessed by a circular tarmac road, the 55 pitches are on stone chippings and are ideal for all year round use (steel pegs are sold at reception). All have electricity (16A) and TV aerial points.

Facilities

The toilet block provides good clean facilities including controllable showers and washbasins in cubicles (heated in winter). Good facilities for disabled visitors, plus toilets and showers for the walking disabled in the main block. Fully equipped laundry room. Motorcaravan service point. Dogs are welcome but there is no dog walk. Wardens live on the site. There is no space for trailers, boats, etc. and tents and units over 28 ft. are not accepted. Off site: Fishing and boating (permits from Harbour Master's office) 400 yards.

Open: All year.

Directions

From M5, J18, take A4 (Bristol West). Follow signs for Historic Harbour and SS Great Britain under Clifton Suspension Bridge and through Hotwells. Cross over Dock bridge and site is about 500 yds. on left. From the east follow signs for Historic Harbour and SS Great Britain. Site on right just to the west of SS Great Britain. Look out for the Caravan Club sign. GPS: 51.446533, -2.61425

Charges guide

Per person	£ 5.60 - £ 7.60
pitch incl. electricity (non-member)	£ 14.00 - £ 17.50

Cheddar

Bucklegrove Caravan & Camping Park

Wells Road, Rodney Stoke, Cheddar BS27 3UZ (Somerset) T: 01749 870261. E: info@bucklegrove.co.uk

alanrogers.com/UK1550

Bucklegrove is set right in the heart of Somerset on the southern slopes of the Mendip Hills and close to the tourist attractions of Cheddar Gorge, Wookey Hole and Wells. The 120 touring pitches, 90 of which have 10A electricity connections, are split between two fields joined by a woodland walk. The top slightly undulating field is more suitable for tents and caravans, while the lower field with some short hardstandings is a little more level and would be suitable for caravans and smaller motorcaravans (under 7 metres). The play area (for under 14s) has a safety surface and includes a multiplay unit, slide and spring riders. Campers also have a games room, a heated indoor swimming pool and separate children's pool. Adjoining the pool is a licensed bar with terrace providing simple bar menus and low-key entertainment mainly during high season or depending on the number of campers on site. A new development includes four privately-owned lodges.

Facilities

Two toilet blocks house all the usual amenities including some washbasins in cubicles and some spacious showers. The larger, heated block near reception also provides bathrooms (£1) with baby changing facilities, and a room for visitors with disabilities. Laundry rooms. Freezer for ice packs. Well stocked shop. Indoor swimming pool and paddling pool with terrace bar. Games room. Play area. Dogs are accepted in certain fields. WiFi (charged). Off site: Wookey Hole and riding 2 miles. Golf 3 miles. Wells Cathedral 4 miles. Fishing 5 miles. Cheddar 7 miles. Beach at Weston-Super-Mare 12 miles. A bus to Wells and Cheddar stops regularly at the park entrance.

Open: 1 March - 14 December.

Directions

Take A371 Wells to Cheddar road. Park is on right about 1 mile past Westbury village. Take care as the road between Wells and Cheddar is rather narrow through some of the villages.
GPS: 51.243317, -2.7323

Charges guide

Per unit incl. 2 persons and electricity	£ 15.00 - £ 27.00
extra person	£ 5.00
child (4-17 yrs)	£ 2.50 - £ 3.50
dog (max. 2)	£ 2.00 - £ 5.00

Bucklegrove Holiday Park

Online booking via our website: www.bucklegrove.co.uk
01749 870261

A perfect base to explore the West Country
Touring, Camping & Self-Catering
Heated Indoor Swimming Pool
Family Friendly Bar
Children's Play park
Shop & Laundry
Offering traditional & relaxing family holidays for over 60 years.

Chippenham

Piccadilly Caravan Park

Folly Lane West, Lacock, Chippenham SN15 2LP (Wiltshire) T: 01249 730260. E: piccadillylacock@aol.com

alanrogers.com/UK1660

Piccadilly Caravan Park is set in open countryside close to several attractions, notably Longleat, Bath, Salisbury Plain, Stourhead, and Lacock itself. You will receive a warm welcome from the owner at this small, quiet family owned park that is beautifully kept. Well kept shrubs, plants and trees have been landscaped to give the impression of three separate areas and create a very pleasant ambience. There are 47 well spaced, clearly marked pitches, 12 of which have hardstanding, and two good areas for tents. Electrical connections (10A) are available on 42 pitches. A bus service runs from Lacock village to Chippenham (free entry to the Chippenham museum and Heritage centre). Lacock Abbey was once the home of Henry Fox-Talbot, pioneer of photography, and there is now a museum in the village.

Facilities

The one toilet block is well maintained and equipped, should be adequate in size for peak periods and can be heated in cool weather. Laundry room with baby changing facilities. Ice pack service. Bark-based playground and a large, grass ball play area. Limited gas supplies. Papers can be ordered. Off site: Fishing 1 mile. Riding 4 miles. Golf 3 miles. Bicycle hire 6 miles.

Open: Easter/1 April - October.

Directions

Park is signed west off A350 Chippenham - Melksham road (turning to Gastard with caravan symbol) by Lacock village. 300 yds. to park.
GPS: 51.4138, -2.129683

Charges guide

Per unit incl. 2 persons and electricity	£ 18.00

No credit cards.

For latest campsite news visit
alanrogers.com

Chippenham
Plough Lane Caravan Site

Plough Lane, Kington Langley, Chippenham SN15 5PS (Wiltshire) T: 01249 750146.
E: enquiries@ploughlane.co.uk **alanrogers.com/UK1680**

Catering for adults only, this is a good example of a well designed, quality, modern touring site. The 50 pitches (all for touring units) are attractively laid out over four acres, access roads are gravel and the borders are stocked with well established shrubs and trees. The pitches are half grass, half hardstanding and all have electricity (16A), with 25 having full services. The site entrance has a barrier system for security. This site is an ideal base for visiting Bath and the Cotswolds, Avebury and Stonehenge, the Caen Hill locks at Devizes and Bristol.

Facilities

The sanitary building is heated, spacious, light and airy, and has all the usual facilities including some washbasins in cubicles, with a hairdressing area for ladies. Separate en-suite room for disabled visitors with ramp access. Dishwashing under cover. Fully equipped heated laundry with two further dishwashing sinks. Max. 2 dogs per unit, a gravel dog walking path is provided. This park is for adults only (over 18 yrs). Barrier card deposit. WiFi throughout. Off site: Supermarket, two public houses, and two garages (both with gas). Golf less than 1 mile.

Open: Easter - October.

Directions

From M4 junction 17 turn south on A350 for 2 miles, then left at traffic lights where site is signed. From Chippenham head north on A350 (towards M4), approaching traffic lights (signed for site and Kington Langley) you need the right hand lane.
GPS: 51.486367, -2.1257

Charges guide

Per unit incl. 2 persons and electricity	£ 20.50 - £ 22.50
extra person (max. 2 extra)	£ 5.00

No credit cards.

Dulverton
Exe Valley Caravan Site

Bridgetown, Dulverton TA22 9JR (Somerset) T: 01643 851432. E: paul@paulmatt.fsnet.co.uk
alanrogers.com/UK1590

Occupying a prime position in a wooded valley alongside the River Exe, within the National Park, Exe Valley Caravan Site is ideally situated for visiting the Doone Valley, Tarr Steps, Dulverton and many other beautiful venues in the area. This quiet, four acre adult only campsite is owned and managed by Paul and Christine Matthews. Set beside the River Exe, or the millstream, there are 50 large pitches (mostly grass but with some hardstandings at the top end), of which 41 have 10A electricity and TV hook-ups (cable provided on loan). Reception is now at the entrance. The owner's home is an old mill, complete with water wheel and grindstones that are in working order. Open for visits every Sunday at 10.00, CCTV has been installed so campers may watch the bat colony in the loft from a screen in the mill. A small shop run by a village co-operative stocks local produce and crafts. Fly fishing along the River Exe is possible from the site or at Wimbleball Reservoir just over four miles away. This part of Somerset is a haven for walking, cycling, pony trekking, or as a place to just sit and relax.

Facilities

The toilet block houses the usual facilities and an en-suite room for disabled visitors (short steep ramp to enter). Excellent laundry with domestic washing and drying machines, plus a microwave (free). Motorcaravan service point. Small shop. Bicycle hire. Gas supplies. Free fly fishing. WiFi. This is an adult-only park. Off site: Riding 4 miles. Golf 12 miles. Pub at Bridgetown. Winsford village has a general stores and tea rooms.

Open: 16 March - 15 October.

Directions

Bridgetown is roughly midway between Dunster and Tiverton on the A396. As you enter Bridgetown from Tiverton, look for site sign and turn left on minor road. Site is 100 yds. on the right.
GPS: 51.0882, -3.53875

Charges 2012

Per unit incl. 2 persons, electricity (10A) and TV hook-up	£ 13.00 - £ 19.00
extra person	£ 4.50
awning	£ 1.00
dog	£ 1.00

No credit cards.

EXE VALLEY CARAVAN SITE
Within Exmoor National Park
Tel: 01643 851432   www.exevalleycamping.co.uk

Glastonbury

The Old Oaks Touring Park

Wick Farm, Wick, Glastonbury BA6 8JS (Somerset) T: 01458 831437. E: info@theoldoaks.co.uk

alanrogers.com/UK1390

The Old Oaks, an adults only park, is tucked below and hidden from the Glastonbury Tor in a lovely secluded setting with views across to the Mendips. The grounds are immaculate with a great deal of attention to cleanliness. There are 100 large pitches in a series of paddocks, all with electricity and hardstanding and 30 are fully serviced. Mainly backing on to hedges, they are arranged in a circular development, interspersed with shrubs or terraced with fantastic views. There is a quiet orchard area for camping and six cabins provide a luxurious alternative to tents. A member of the Best of British Group.

Facilities	Directions
The heated toilet block is excellent. A second block will be ready for the 2012 season. Some washbasins are in cubicles. Two en-suite rooms and a bathroom (£1). Disabled visitors have two rooms. Laundry. Motorcaravan service facilities. Dog wash. Licensed shop. Pool table. Library room. Bicycle hire. Fishing. Painting holidays. Internet access. WiFi throughout (charged). Adults only (18 yrs and over). Off site: Riding 0.5 miles. Golf 6 miles.	Park is north off A361 Shepton Mallet - Glastonbury road, 2 miles from Glastonbury. Take narrow, unclassified road signed Wick for 1 mile and park is on the left. GPS: 51.152633, -2.6803

Open: 10 February - 12 November.

Charges 2012

Per unit incl. 2 persons	
and electricity (16A)	£ 16.00 - £ 26.50
with full services	£ 18.00 - £ 30.50
extra person	£ 8.00

Lyme Regis

Shrubbery Caravan & Camping Park

Rousdon, Lyme Regis DT7 3XW (Dorset) T: 01297 442227. E: info@shrubberypark.co.uk

alanrogers.com/UK1720

Three miles south of historic Lyme Regis in a good situation to explore the Jurassic Coast, this well cared for park has distant views of the surrounding countryside. There are 120 generous pitches, 20 with hardstanding and more than enough room to pitch for most units. On slightly sloping, neatly cut grass which undulates in places, they are accessed by tarmac roads and all have 10A electricity. The pitches back on to shrubs or the perimeter trees. A welcoming reception area stocks basic supplies and local provisions. This is a comfortable park where couples and families with young children are welcomed.

Facilities	Directions
Excellent heated toilet blocks, the newest (part of the reception building) with en-suite units, bathroom and laundry facilities. Two further blocks nearer the top of the park, fully equipped and well maintained. Facilities for disabled visitors. Simple shop at reception specialising in local produce. General store at adjacent fuel station. Play area. Crazy golf. Off site: Fishing 1 mile. Golf, beach and boat launching 3 miles. Riding 5 miles	From the A35 near Axminster follow the A358 towards Seaton. At T-junction turn left on A3052 signed Rousdon and Lyme Regis. Site entrance is on the left a few yards after Rousdon Garage. GPS: 50.71734, -2.99521

Open: 1 April - 31 October.

Charges guide

Per unit incl. 2 persons	
and electricity	£ 14.50 - £ 19.50
extra person	£ 3.75

Malmesbury

Burton Hill Caravan Park

Arches Lane, Malmesbury SN16 0EH (Wiltshire) T: 01666 826 880. E: audrey@burtonhill.co.uk

alanrogers.com/UK1665

The owners of this park, Audrey and Warren Hateley, tend it with pride. It is a flat, grassy site surrounded by hedges, with open views across farmland on the outskirts of historic Malmesbury. There are 28 numbered touring pitches each with 16A electricity, eight more for tents also with electricity and eight without hook-ups. It is a short walk (10-15 minutes) along the river bank to the town, its shops, Abbey House Gardens, Abbey and 15th century market place. Within easy travelling distance are the towns of Bath, Chippenham, Tetbury, Trowbridge and Bradford-on-Avon.

Facilities	Directions
Modern, well equipped and well maintained heated toilet block with free hot water. Separate well equipped facilities for disabled visitors. Washing machine. Off site: Malmesbury has a new sports centre and swimming pool. Golf 6 miles. The Cotswold Water Parks, Castle Combe Racecourse and village and Westonbirt Arboretum are all within easy reach.	From M4 exit 17 follow the A4129 towards Cirencester for 5 miles. At approach to Malmesbury at international caravan sign, turn left into Arches Lane, and follow signs. If you miss the turning carry on to roundabout, return and turn right into Arches Lane. GPS: 51.579083, -2.097321

Open: 1 April/Easter - 31 October.

Charges guide

Per unit incl. 2 persons and electricity	£ 18.50
extra person	£ 3.00 - £ 4.00
Credit cards accepted.	

99

Martock

Southfork Caravan Park

Parrett Works, Martock TA12 6AE (Somerset) T: 01935 825661. E: southforkcaravans@btconnect.com

alanrogers.com/UK1420

Don't be put off by the address, which is historic – this was once a 17th-century flax mill. Michael and Nancy Broadley now own and run this excellent, modern, well drained site just outside the lovely village of Martock. With 25 touring pitches on grass with a gravel access road (22 with 10A electrical hook-ups and two with water and waste water), it is an orderly, quiet park on two acres of flat, tree lined meadow near the River Parrett. All the expected facilities are close to the entrance and as the owners live on the premises, the park is open all year. Most things are available, including an NCC approved caravan repairs/servicing centre. Despite the rural setting, the A303 trunk road is just five minutes away. This area of south Somerset contains much of interest, including gardens, historic houses and sites, the Fleet Air Arm Museum, Haynes Motor Museum and Cricket St Thomas Wildlife Park. Information about access to many cycle routes and numerous walks, including the Parrett Trail, is available from reception.

Facilities

The heated well maintained toilet block is fully equipped and includes some washbasins in cabins and free hot showers. Laundry room with washing machine and dryer. Shop with local produce. Off-licence selling local cider and beer. Play area. Fishing permits from reception. Enclosed dog exercise area. Off site: Fishing (with licences) on the River Parrett a few yards from the park. Pubs with good food in South Petherton and Martock, less than 2 miles in each direction. Golf 5 miles. Bicycle hire 8 miles. Riding 10 miles.

Open: All year.

Directions

From A303 between Ilchester and Ilminster turn north at the roundabout signed for South Petherton. At T-junction in middle of village, turn right towards Martock. Park is at Parrett Works midway between the two villages (about 1.5 miles from South Petherton). GPS: 50.965367, -2.789817

Charges guide

Per unit incl. 2 persons and electricity	£ 14.00 - £ 19.00
extra person	£ 1.75
child (under 5 yrs)	free
dog	£ 1.00

Minehead

Westermill Farm

Exford, Minehead TA24 7NJ (Somerset) T: 01643 831238. E: info@westermill.com

alanrogers.com/UK1301

This superbly located farm campsite can be found nestling in a valley beside the River Exe. The working farm provides four meadows, all without electricity, and is ideal for 'back to basics' style touring. Uniquely, open fires are permitted in one field with logs being available to purchase. You can marvel at the wildlife, wander around the working farm and sample the farm's own produce in the shop, which also stocks basic provisions. Walking maps can be found at reception which is located in the old dairy. A converted farm building provides the only sanitary block with hot water provided by solar energy. Natural spring drinking water is also available. The Edwards Family are helpful and friendly and encourage you to explore their farm. The site also has six self-catering holidays cottages to let.

Facilities

The unheated toilet block houses the usual facilities including showers and washbasins and hot water is provided by solar energy. Laundry facilities. Farm shop (End May - early Sept). Gas supplies. Facility for freezer packs (20p). Fishing in the River Exe. The river is also used for bathing. Off site: Village 2.5 miles. Bicycle hire 6 miles. Riding 15 miles. Beach 15 miles.

Open: All year.

Directions

Leave Exford on Porlock Road with Post Office on right. At Y fork turn left down single track road. Farm is 2 miles on right. Do not use sat nav. GPS: 51.145631, -3.682158

Charges guide

Per person	£ 6.50
child	£ 3.50
car	£ 2.50
dog	£ 2.50
No credit cards.	

Minehead

Halse Farm Touring Caravan & Camping Park

Winsford, Minehead TA24 7JL (Somerset) T: 01643 851259. E: ar@halsefarm.co.uk

alanrogers.com/UK1360

A truly rural park with beautiful, moorland views, you may be lucky enough to glimpse red deer across the valley or be able to see ponies and foals grazing outside the main gate which is adjacent to the moor. Two open, neatly cut fields (level at the top) back onto traditional hedging and slope gently to the middle and bottom where wild flowers predominate. One field provides electricity points (10A) and is used for motorcaravans and caravans, the other is for tents. There is no reception – you leave your unit by the toilet block and walk down to the farm kitchen to book in. Mrs Brown has laminated maps available (at a small cost) detailing six walks, starting and finishing at the farm. Also available is a list of the wild birds, flowers, etc. to be found on the site. A member of the Countryside Discovery group.

Facilities	Directions
The central toilet block is heated, well equipped and maintained. It includes a toilet, washbasin and shower for visitors with disabilities, washing machine, dryer and iron, and tourist information. Gas is available at the farm. Play equipment. Off site: Winsford village 1 mile. Riding 2 miles. Tarr Steps and Barle Valley 3 miles. Fishing 4 miles. Bicycle hire 15 miles. **Open:** 16 March - 31 October.	Turn off A396 Tiverton - Minehead road for Winsford (site signed). In Winsford village turn left in front of the Royal Oak (not over ford) and keep on uphill for 1 mile (go slowly round the sharp bend at the bottom). Cross cattle grid onto moor and turn immediately left to farm. Caravans should avoid Dulverton - keep to the A396 from Bridgetown (signed). GPS: 51.097717, -3.579983

Charges guide

Per unit incl. 2 persons and electricity	£ 15.00 - £ 17.00
extra person	£ 6.00 - £ 7.00
child (5-16 yrs)	£ 1.50 - £ 2.00
dog	free

Minehead

Burrowhayes Farm Caravan & Camping Site

West Luccombe, Porlock, Minehead TA24 8HT (Somerset) T: 01643 862463. E: info@burrowhayes.co.uk

alanrogers.com/UK1370

This delightful park with riding stables on site, is on the edge of Exmoor. The stone packhorse bridge over Horner Water beside the farm entrance sets the tone of the park, which the Dascombe family have created over the last forty years having previously farmed the land. The farm buildings have been converted into riding stables with escorted rides available (from Easter). Touring and tent pitches are on a partly sloping field with marvellous views, or a flatter location in a clearing by the river, while 20 caravan holiday homes are in a separate area. Electrical hook-ups are available (16A), although some require long leads (25 m). Six new fully serviced pitches have been added. With walking, bird watching, plenty of wildlife to observe, pretty Exmoor villages and Lorna Doone country nearby there is much to do. Children can ride, play in the stream or explore the woods at the top of the site. Limited trout fishing is available in Horner Water (NT permit) alongside the park.

Facilities	Directions
The heated toilet block provides controllable hot showers, one washbasin cubicle for each sex, hairdressing and shaving areas, laundry room, unit for disabled visitors and babies, and an indoor dishwashing room. A second older block is opened in high season with extra WCs and washbasins. Motorcaravan service point. Well stocked shop doubles with reception (from 1/4). Riding stables. Dogs must be kept on a lead at all times and exercised off site. Off site: Beach and fishing 2 miles. Minehead and bicycle hire 5 miles. Golf 6 miles. Pub 20 minutes walk. **Open:** 15 March - 31 October.	From A39, 5 miles west of Minehead, take first left past Allerford to Horner and West Luccombe. Site is on right after 400 yds. GPS: 51.203533, -3.5778

Charges guide

Per unit incl. 2 persons and electricity	£ 14.50 - £ 18.50
extra person	£ 4.00 - £ 6.00
child (3-16 yrs)	£ 2.00 - £ 3.00
dog	free

Salisbury

Greenhill Farm Caravan & Camping Park

New Road, Landford, Salisbury SP5 2AZ (Wiltshire) T: 01794 324117. E: info@greenhillholidays.co.uk

alanrogers.com/UK1640

Located on the northern edge of the New Forest National Park, this site occupies 14 out of a total of 50 acres of beautiful forest owned by the family. It is an uncommercialised hideaway and has two distinctive areas: the adults only area, fenced, gated and set around two small lakes, one of which is reserved for coarse fishing; and the family area with a playground, views over the meadow, sightings of deer and a generally open aspect. There are 160 pitches in total, with 50 for tents in a separate hilltop meadow with views over the nearby forest and its own fishing lake.

Facilities	Directions
New toilet block nearing completion; in the interim, Portacabin style units of varying ages provide facilities. No dedicated facilities for disabled guests. Laundry facilities. Reception/shop. Takeaway (high season). Bicycle hire. Coarse fishing lakes. Torches useful. Off site: Bus stop by site entrance. Several pubs are nearby. Landford village 15 minutes walk. Golf 3 miles. Riding 4 miles.	From M27 exit 2 take A36 north towards Salisbury for about 6 miles. Pass through West Wellow and after passing a B.P. garage on left, take next left into New Road. Continue for 0.9 miles to site entrance on left. GPS: 50.96445, -1.62575

Open: All year.

Charges guide

Per unit incl. 2 persons and electricity	£ 17.00 - £ 24.00
extra person	£ 2.00 - £ 4.00

Salisbury

Coombe Touring Park

Coombe Nurseries Race Plain, Netherhampton, Salisbury SP2 8PN (Wiltshire) T: 01722 328451
E: enquiries@coombecaravanpark.co.uk **alanrogers.com/UK1650**

A true touring park with outstanding views over the Chalke Valley, Coombe is adjacent to Salisbury racecourse. There are 100 spacious pitches all on level, well mown grass, 46 with electricity hook-ups (10A). The 50 tent pitches are generally around the outer perimeter and there are 4 caravan holiday homes to rent. Many pitches are individual and sheltered by hedging. Reception also has a small shop, there are supermarkets in Salisbury (4.5 miles), and pubs in Netherhampton and Coombe Bissett (2 miles) both serving meals.

Facilities	Directions
A well built, modern, centrally heated sanitary unit, provides an ample supply of WCs, spacious pushbutton showers, washbasins in cubicles for the ladies, and a family room (with bath) has facilities for disabled campers, babies and toddlers. Laundry. Small shop (May-Sept). Gas available. Tourist information. Play area. Off site: Golf 400 yards. Riding and tennis 2.5 miles. Indoor pool, leisure centre and cinema 4.5 miles. Nearby attractions include the Wilton Shopping Village, Salisbury Cathedral, Stonehenge.	From A36 two miles west of Salisbury, turn south on A3094 towards Netherhampton and Harnham. After 0.5 miles on sharp left hand bend, turn right (Stratford Tony and racecourse). Continue to top of hill by racecourse entrance, and turn left on narrow lane behind racecourse for 700 yds. to site entrance. GPS: 51.05428, -1.86092

Open: 1 January - 20 December.

Charges guide

Per unit incl. 2 persons and electricity	£ 15.00
extra person	£ 3.50
No credit cards.	

Salisbury

Church Farm Caravan & Camping Park

Sixpenny Handley, Salisbury SP5 5ND (Wiltshire) T: 01725 553005. E: churchfarmcandcpark@yahoo.co.uk

alanrogers.com/UK1655

Sixpenny Handley is a Saxon hilltop village with St Mary's church dating back some 900 years; from the site you can hear the bells and the chimes of its clock. Church Farm, a stone's throw from the village centre, offers 35 partly-sheltered, level, spacious pitches including some hardstandings, all with 16A, arranged around the perimeter of two fields, plus a tent field. It is in an Area of Outstanding Natural Beauty and the views and walks are an absolute delight. There are many places to visit around this junction of Dorset, Hampshire and Wiltshire.

Facilities	Directions
New spacious multi-function building houses reception, a seasonal café/bar, and heated toilet facilities. Room for disabled visitors. Baby changing. Laundry facilities. Motorcaravan service point. Play area. Two holiday caravans for rent. Off site: Village with shops, a small supermarket and Post Office. The Roebuck Inn. Tennis. Golf 4 miles. Riding 5 miles. Fishing 10 miles.	To avoid village centre, 1 mile south of Handley Hill roundabout on A354 turn towards Sixpenny Handley, then right by school and site 300 yds. by the church. GPS: 50.955317, -2.006883

Open: All year.

Charges guide

Per unit incl. 2 persons and electricity	£ 15.50 - £ 16.75
extra person	£ 6.50 - £ 7.00

Shepton Mallet

Greenacres Camping

Barrow Lane, North Wootton, Shepton Mallet BA4 4HL (Somerset) T: 01749 890497.
E: stay@greenacres-camping.co.uk **alanrogers.com/UK1490**

Greenacres is a rural site in the Somerset countryside for tents, trailer tents and small motorcaravans only. Hidden away below the Mendips and almost at the start of the Levels, it is a simple green site – a true haven of peace and quiet. The grass is neatly trimmed over the 4.5 acres and hedged with mature trees, though there is a view of Glastonbury Tor in one direction and of Barrow Hill in the other. All of the 40 pitches are around the perimeter of the park, leaving a central area safe for children to play.

Facilities

The central wooden toilet block is simple but kept clean. Hot showers are accessed directly from the outside. Small shop. Van calls in high season with local produce. Play equipment, football, badminton net and play house. Park office (and bicycle hire), is across the lane. New cabin with fridges and freezers, library and tourist information. WiFi (charged). Dogs are not accepted. No electric barbecues. Off site: North Wootton (under 1 mile) with large pub/restaurant and a vineyard. Fishing and riding nearby.

Open: April - September.

Directions

From A39 Glastonbury - Wells road turn east at Brownes Garden Centre and follow camping signs. From A361 Glastonbury - Shepton Mallet road follow camp signs from Pilton or Steanbow. (Roads are narrow with few passing places). GPS: 51.172367, -2.641883

Charges guide

Per person	£ 8.00
child (2-14 yrs)	£ 3.00
electricity	£ 4.00

Shepton Mallet

Batcombe Vale Campsite

Batcombe Vale, Shepton Mallet BA4 6BW (Somerset) T: 01749 831207. E: gary.butler1@virgin.net
alanrogers.com/UK1540

Set in a secluded valley with fields gently rising around it, contented cows grazing with watchful buzzards cruising above and views across the distant hills, this is a very special place. Descending slowly down the steep, narrow drive you see the pitches, attractively set and terraced where necessary, in an oval with the lakes below. The grass is left natural around the 32 pitches (20 have 10A electricity) and paths are mown where needed. Trees and shrubs have been skillfully placed to enhance the natural environment providing a range of colours and shapes.

Facilities

The small rustic toilet block covered in honeysuckle meets all needs, including a freezer (ice packs only) and dishwashing sinks. Groundsheet awnings must be lifted daily. Fishing. Caravan storage. One dog per pitch is welcome (no dangerous breeds). Bed and breakfast available in Batcombe Vale House. Max. 1 dog (unless by prior arrangement). Off site: Bruton and Evercreech (for shops, etc.) 2 miles. Golf and leisure facilities 9 miles. Launderettes at Shepton and Frome.

Open: 1 April - end September.

Directions

Bruton is south of Shepton Mallet and Frome and north of Wincanton where the A359 intersects the B3081. Access to the site must be via Evercreech or Bruton (B3081), then follow the brown and white camping signs. Access drive is steep. GPS: 51.136467, -2.453167

Charges guide

Per unit incl. 2 persons and electricity	£ 20.50
extra person	£ 3.00 - £ 5.00

No commercial vehicles or motorcycle 'packs'. Family groups only. No credit cards.

Sparkford

Long Hazel Park

High Street, Sparkford, Yeovil BA22 7JH (Somerset) T: 01963 440002. E: longhazelpark@hotmail.com
alanrogers.com/UK1500

Pamela and Alan Walton are really enthusiastic about their small, beautifully kept, adults only park in the Somerset village of Sparkford, where they will make you most welcome. This level, landscaped park is surrounded by beech hedging, silver birches and many other trees and it has a relaxed, comfortable feel. It provides 50 touring pitches for all types of units (max. 12 m.) with electrical hook-ups (16A), 40 pitches with hardstanding, some extra long with grass lawns at the side, and the entrance has been widened for easier access. Part of the park is being developed with pine holiday lodges for private ownership or rent.

Facilities

The toilet block is clean, well equipped and heated. En-suite facilities for visitors with disabilities. Laundry facilities. Motorcaravan waste water discharge. Gas supplies. Details of cycle routes and walks at reception. Seasonal pitches available. Off site: Bus service, village inn 100 yds. Spar shop, Post Office and McDonalds 400 yards. Golf 5 miles. Riding and fishing 8 miles.

Open: All year.

Directions

At roundabout on A303 take road into village of Sparkford and park is signed on the left 100 yds. Before the inn. GPS: 51.0344, -2.568633

Charges guide

Per unit incl. 2 persons and electricity	£ 20.00 - £ 25.00
extra person	£ 4.00

For latest campsite news visit
alanrogers.com

Taunton
Cornish Farm Touring Park
Shoreditch, Taunton TA3 7BS (Somerset) T: 01823 327746. E: info@cornishfarm.com
alanrogers.com/UK1340

This neat little park, which opened for its first full season in 2006, is on level ground and conveniently located close to the M5 motorway. There are 49 pitches, all with 10A electricity, of which 25 are on gravel hardstanding. Most pitches are accessed from a gravel road (one-way) with plenty of fresh water taps, lighting and some picnic tables. A separate area for tents is close to the toilet block. Light power cables cross the site and there is some motorway noise. Maximum length for motorcaravans is 30ft, unless by prior arrangement. With its old apple trees this park makes a very pleasant stop-over. Off to the left are the barns that house the Van Bitz workshops producing security systems for motorcaravans. The centrally situated toilet block is maintained to a high standard and includes underfloor heating, designed by the owners who are campers and caravanners themselves. There are no other facilities on the park but a cycle path and a footpath will take you into Taunton. The park is also a good base from which to visit Cheddar Gorge, Wookey Hole, and Clarke's shopping village at Street.

Facilities

One central block has underfloor heating and you can listen to the local radio. Large dual purpose room for disabled visitors and small children. Dusk to dawn low energy lighting. Laundry room. Motorcaravan service point. Camping supplies for sale and plenty of tourist information available. On-site PC repair facility. WiFi. Off site: Village pub and shops are a short walk away. Level cycle/footpath into Taunton (2 miles) which has a castle, museum, and markets. Tesco Express 1 mile. Golf, fishing and bicycle hire 2 miles. Riding 4 miles.

Open: All year.

Directions

From M5 exit 25 follow signs for Taunton. At first set of lights turn left (Corfe B3170). Take third left into Ilminster Road. Right at roundabout, left at next roundabout and on to T-junction (B3170). Turn right then next left. Second left (Killams Ave) and cross motorway. Site is after bridge (second entrance) on left. GPS: 50.99200, -3.09257

Charges guide

Per unit incl. 2 persons	
and electricity	£ 14.00 - £ 18.00
extra person	£ 2.10 - £ 3.50

Luxury Camping in the Heart of Somerset
Cornish Farm Touring Park, Shoreditch, Taunton
TA3 7BS Tel: 01823327746 **www.cornishfarm.com**

"The best we've ever seen" - a frequent comment from happy customers about our facilities.
Level gravelled hard standings. Only two miles away from town centre. Follow Racecourse signs from M5 or town centre until you pick up Cornish Farm brown signs. Rallies welcome. Large well equipped fully tiled and heated family/disabled shower room. Book exchange. Laundry room. Washing-up area. Low energy dusk to dawn lights for your security and safety.

Taunton
Quantock Orchard Caravan Park
Crowcombe, Taunton TA4 4AW (Somerset) T: 01984 618618. E: member@flaxpool.freeserve.co.uk
alanrogers.com/UK1350

Quantock Orchard nestles at the foot of the Quantocks in quiet countryside, close to many of the attractions of the area. Attractively developed, mature apple trees, recently planted trees, shrubs and flower beds make a pleasant environment. A dovecote at the entrance adds interest. With access from fairly narrow gravel roads, there are 69 touring pitches, part separated by growing shrubs and hedging, of which 40 are for tents. Of various sizes, all touring pitches have 15A electricity hook-ups, 30 have hardstanding and eight are fully serviced. Levelling blocks may be required.

Facilities

Central, heated sanitary block is well maintained with showers, some washbasins in cubicles for ladies, excellent family bathroom and baby rooms. Laundry facilities. Facilities for disabled visitors (no shower). Drain for motorcaravans. Licensed shop. Mountain bike hire. Swimming pool (40x20 ft. May-Sept). Leisure suite. Games room. Sky TV. Play area. Holiday homes for hire. WiFi. Off site: Pubs serving meals 3 miles. Coast 5 miles.

Open: All year.

Directions

Park is west off A358 road (Taunton - Minehead), about 1 mile south of Crowcombe village. GPS: 51.1084, -3.22645

Charges guide

Per unit incl. 2 persons	
and electricity	£ 14.00 - £ 26.50
extra person	£ 6.00
child (3-15 yrs)	£ 4.00 - £ 5.00

For latest campsite news visit
alanrogers.com

Taunton

Lowtrow Cross Caravan Site

Upton, Wiveliscombe, Taunton TA4 2DB (Somerset) T: 01398 371199. E: info@lowtrowcross.co.uk

alanrogers.com/UK1355

Lowtrow Cross is a small adults only park situated just inside Exmoor National Park and is ideal for owners of well-behaved dogs. It is quietly located on a hillside giving lovely views north towards the Brendon Hills. There are 18 pitches, three occupied by caravan holiday homes (two for hire) and six seasonal, and all the remaining touring pitches are hardstanding with grass surround, with electricity (16A) and TV socket. An adjacent meadow with stunning views over the rolling countryside can be used for tents. Although there is no bar or restaurant on site there is Lowtrow Cross Inn at the gate with local cask beers and excellent food. Lowtrow Cross is well situated for walking, cycling, riding and fishing in the beautiful Exmoor countryside with its wide variety of wildlife. Close by Haddon Moor, with its own herd of ponies and buzzards overhead, overlooks Wimbleball Lake where one can enjoy a variety of water based activities and nature trails. Clatworthy Reservoir is also convenient for walking and fishing, but dogs are not permitted here. Not far away are Dunster Castle, Porlock and the West Somerset Steam railway. The area is well known for its cider and there is a museum of cider making at Taunton.

Facilities

Traditional heated, well equipped, toilet block but no facilities for disabled visitors. Excellent laundry room. Freezer and microwave. Small shop in reception selling basic foodstuffs; milk, bread, free range eggs, frozen meals, local produce, toiletries and Calor gas. Tourist information. Maps for sale and book exchange. Off site: Lowtrow Cross Inn at gate. Garage 750 m. Excellent fishing and boating 3 miles. Golf and riding 10 miles.

Open: March - October.

Directions

From M5 junction 25 follow signs for Minehead (A358) through Taunton, then 5 miles from Taunton turn west (left) on B3224 signed Raleigh Cross. Shortly after passing Raleigh Cross Inn turn south on B3190 signed Bampton. Site is on right in 4 miles just before Upton village. GPS: 51.053342, -3.419923

Charges guide

Per unit incl. 2 persons and electricity	£ 15.00 - £ 19.00
extra adult	£ 5.00
dog	free

Lowtrow Cross

Upton, Taunton TA4 2DB

A small, quiet, adults only site set in a secluded area close to Wimbleball Lake on the edge of Exmoor National Park

* Spotless facilities
* Electric/TV hook ups
* Hardstandings
* Laundry
* Microwave/Freezer
* Small shop
* Wi Fi/Payphone
* Tourist info
* Dogs Welcome free

Email: info@lowtrowcross.co.uk
www.lowtrowcross.co.uk

Tel: (01398) 371199

Taunton

Waterrow Touring Park

Wiveliscombe, Taunton TA4 2AZ (Somerset) T: 01984 623464. E: waterrowpark@yahoo.co.uk

alanrogers.com/UK1520

Beside the River Tone in a pretty part of South Somerset, Tony and Anne Taylor have enthusiastically developed Waterrow into a charming, landscaped touring park for adults only. Nestling in a little sheltered valley, it is very peaceful and possible for an overnight stop (just over 30 minutes from M5) or ideal as a base for exploring nearby Exmoor and the Brendon Hills. There are 48 touring pitches, most of which are on level hardstandings, including five with full services. All have electricity (16A), spring and mains water are available and TV aerial points have been installed (your own lead is required, sometimes quite long). A small area has been set aside for tent campers. A member of the Best of British Group.

Facilities

A modern, clean toilet unit is heated and provides WCs and washbasins, some in curtained cubicles. Heated shower block. Facilities for disabled visitors (key). Laundry facilities. Motorcaravan service point. Limited provisions in reception. Regular watercolour painting and drawing courses are run (May-Oct) at the in-house studio. Additional fly fishing holidays can be arranged at certain times. WiFi (charged). Caravan storage with 'store and stay' system. Site is not suitable for large American motorhomes. Max. 2 dogs. Luxury holiday home and cottage for hire. Off site: The Rock Inn is a short walk. Wiveliscombe 3 miles. Fishing 5 miles. Golf 7 miles. Bicycle hire 10 miles. Riding 12 miles.

Open: All year.

Directions

From M5 exit 25 take A358 (signed Minehead) round Taunton for 4 miles, then at Staplegrove onto the B3227 for 11.5 miles to Wiveliscombe where straight over at lights to Waterrow (still on B3227). Park is on left shortly after the Rock Inn. Do not use sat nav as it takes you on roads unsuitable for caravans. GPS: 51.0165, -3.352717

Charges guide

Per unit incl. 2 persons and electricity	£ 15.00 - £ 25.00
full services, plus	£ 5.00
extra person	£ 5.00
dog (max. 2)	£ 1.50

For latest campsite news visit
alanrogers.com

Warminster

Longleat Caravan Club Site

Warminster BA12 7NL (Wiltshire) T: 01985 844663

alanrogers.com/UK1690

What a magnificent situation in which to find a caravan park, amidst all the wonders of the Longleat Estate including the Elizabethan House, gardens designed by Capability Brown and the Safari Park. The site sits alongside the National Cycle Network no. 24 and is situated in ten acres of lightly wooded, level grassland within walking distance of the house and gardens. It is well managed by Caravan Club wardens. There are 165 generous pitches (139 with hardstanding and 26 on grass), all with 16A electricity connections. Tents are not accepted (except trailer tents).

Facilities

Two heated toilet blocks provide washbasins in cubicles, controllable showers and a vanity section with mirrors and hairdryers. Baby/toddler room, suite for disabled visitors, laundry and a family room with a DVD player. Two motorcaravan service points. Play area. Basic food items, papers can be ordered and gas is available. Paperback exchange library. Fish and chip van calls some evenings. WiFi. Off site: Longleat House. Frome 7 miles.

Open: March - November.

Directions

The main entrance to Longleat, which caravans must use, is signed from the A362 Frome - Warminster road near where it joins the A36 Warminster bypass. Turn into the estate and follow the Longleat House route through the toll booths for 2 miles then club signs for 1 mile. GPS: 51.1907, -2.278517

Charges guide

Per person	£ 5.60 - £ 7.60
pitch incl. electricity (non-member)	£ 13.40 - £ 17.50

Wells

Cheddar, Mendip Heights Camping & Caravanning Club Site

Priddy, Wells BA5 3BP (Somerset) T: 01749 870241. E: cheddar@campingandcaravanningclub.co.uk

alanrogers.com/UK1430

Mendip Heights, operated as a franchise in partnership with the Camping and Caravanning Club, is a well kept site half a mile from the village. There are tranquil views across the Mendip fields which are characterised by dry stone walling. It has a simple charm with field margins left natural to encourage wildlife and nest boxes in the trees edging the three fields which comprise the site. These provide space for 90 units on mostly slightly sloping short grass with 67 electric hook-ups (16A), 36 with hardstanding. Historic Priddy is the highest village in the Mendips and is famed for its annual Sheep Fair in August.

Facilities

The refurbished toilet block is heated. Two family rooms. Facilities for disabled visitors. Laundry facilities. Motorcaravan service point. The reception/licensed shop doubles as the village shop. Fresh bread and pastries are baked each morning (advisable to pre-order). Wendy house, swings and table tennis. Torches useful. WiFi (charged). Off site: Two pubs by the village green within walking distance (0.5 miles). Riding 2 miles. Bicycle hire and golf 5 miles. Fishing 6 miles.

Open: 15 March - 5 November.

Directions

From M5 exit 21 take A371 to Banwell. Turn left on A368, right on B3134 and right on B3135. After 2 miles, left at camp sign. From M4 westbound exit 18, A46 to Bath, then A4 (Bristol). A39 (Wells) and right at Green Ore traffic lights on B3135; after 5 miles, left at camp sign. GPS: 51.2636, -2.685383

Charges 2012

Per person	£ 7.95 - £ 11.70
pitch incl. electricity (non-member)	£ 10.85

Westbury

Brokerswood Country Park

Brokerswood, Westbury BA13 4EH (Wiltshire) T: 01373 822238. E: info@brokerswoodcountrypark.co.uk

alanrogers.com/UK1630

This countryside campsite is located in an 80-acre country park, with ancient broadleaf woodland, plenty of marked walks and a woodland railway. The campsite has 65 pitches arranged around an open meadow area, served by a circular gravel roadway, with low level site lighting. There are 26 hardstanding pitches, and 44 electric hook-ups (10A). Although fairly recently laid out, the site is maturing well. American RVs and other large units should use the coach entrance and they (and all other arrivals after 18.00) are asked to phone ahead so that arrangements can be made for the barrier.

Facilities

Two heated, timber clad buildings are at one end of the site. Some washbasins in cubicles, large, controllable hot showers. Family rooms (on payment). Suite for disabled visitors with alarm. Laundry facilities. Motorcaravan services. Reception/shop. Fully licensed café. Takeaway (peak times). Fishing. Cycling (not in Country Park). Ready erected tents for hire. Off site: Shops at Dilton Marsh and Westbury. Golf and Longleat House 6 miles.

Open: All year.

Directions

From Trowbridge take A361 south for 2 miles, turning left (east) at Southwick, and follow signs to Country Park. GPS: 51.270283, -2.231417

Charges guide

Per unit incl. 4 persons	£ 15.00 - £ 30.00
extra person (aged 1 or more)	£ 3.95

Beaconsfield

Highclere Farm Country Touring Park

Newbarn Lane, Seer Green, Beaconsfield HP9 2QZ (Buckinghamshire) T: 01494 874505.
E: highclerepark@aol.com **alanrogers.com/UK2750**

A magnificent sweeping drive provides the entrance to this peaceful park that backs onto fields and woodland. Originally developed around a working farm, the owners continue to keep chickens. There are 115 level pitches all with 10A electricity. Of these, 60 with gravel hardstanding are reserved for caravans and motorcaravans, the remainder being mainly used for tents. The atmosphere is friendly but informal, with reception doubling as a small shop supplying freshly laid eggs. At the top of the park is an open play area and a footpath leading to walks in the surrounding fields.

Facilities

The toilet and shower block is fully equipped and can be heated. Large showers (20p). Unit with toilet and washbasin for disabled visitors. Baby changing. Two new units (in former stables) provide extra large facilities including showers at 50p. Launderette. Fridge and freezer. Basic shop in reception. Play area. WiFi. Freeview and Sky connections. Off site: Pub serving food 0.25 miles. Golf 0.5 miles. Riding 2 miles. Bicycle hire 3 miles. Fishing 8 miles. Bekonscot Model Village. Milton's Cottage.

Open: All year excl. February.

Directions

From M40 exit 2 follow signs for Beaconsfield at first roundabout. Take A355 towards Amersham and after 1 mile turn right signed Seer Green and Jordans following signs to park. From the north on M25 take exit 18 to Little Chalfont, B44442 to Chalfont St Giles, go through village and park is 1.25 miles on the right. GPS: 51.625617, -0.590867

Charges guide

Per unit incl. 2 persons and electricity	£ 17.50 - £ 23.50
extra person	£ 1.00

Bembridge

Whitecliff Bay Holiday Park

Hillway, Whitecliff Bay, Bembridge PO35 5PL (Isle of Wight) T: 01983 872671. E: holiday@whitecliff-bay.com
alanrogers.com/UK2510

Whitecliff Bay is a very large complex divided by a road, with a holiday home and chalet park on the right-hand side (230 units), and a touring site on the left-hand side (429 pitches). The large touring site is on a sloping hillside with commanding views over the surrounding countryside. The pitches are spread over three fields, the top and second fields are terraced, but field three is quite level. Most of the pitches have electricity hook-ups (16A), and there are 42 gravel hardstandings, 12 in the top field, the remainder in lowest field. There are just 18 individual hedged multi-serviced pitches available, so book early if these appeal. On the opposite side of the lane, in the holiday home park, you will find the main entertainment and leisure facilities. Close to the outdoor pool a very steep path leads down to a sandy beach.

Facilities

Three sanitary units. Showers and a suite (with shower) for disabled campers. A second suite with a hip bath/shower and a baby/family room. Motorcaravan service point. Small shop with reception. Playground. At holiday home park: Launderette, hairdresser and second larger shop. The Culver Club. Snack bars. Swimming pool (Whitsun-end Aug). Indoor fun pool. Most facilities open Mar-Oct. WiFi. Fully equipped tents to rent. Entertainment and activities. Off site: Bus service from park entrance. Courtesy minibus to Bembridge and Sandown (weekends).

Open: 30 March - 1 November.

Directions

From the A3055 between Ryde and Sandown, turn east at Brading on B3395 for 2 miles passing the Airfield and Propeller Club, fork right (site signed). Follow signs to site, first entry on right is static area, touring entrance is on left immediately after. GPS: 50.67498, -1.09606

Charges guide

Per unit incl. up to 6 persons and electricity	£ 6.00 - £ 41.00
dog	£ 1.00 - £ 3.00

Bere Regis

Rowlands Wait Touring Park

Rye Hill, Bere Regis BH20 7LP (Dorset) T: 01929 472727. E: enquiries@rowlandswait.co.uk

alanrogers.com/UK2050

Rowlands Wait is in a designated Area of Outstanding Natural Beauty and part of the park is officially of Special Scientific Interest. The top of the park, edged by mature woods (full of bluebells in spring) is a haven for tents (and squirrels) with marvellous views and provides 30 areas in three descending fields. The rest of the park is a little more formal, and nearer to the central toilet block. Most pitches back on to hedging or trees and they are generally level. There are 71 pitches in total with 23 seasonal pitches. Many walks are possible from the park with information leaflets available from reception. It is also possible to walk into the village of Bere Regis. The owners Ivor and Stevie Cargill are keen to welcome nature lovers who enjoy bird watching, walking, and cycling. Sightings of various owls and two pairs of buzzards have been reported on the park. The park is a member of the Countryside Discovery group and is open in winter by arrangement. Rallies are welcome.

Facilities

The refurbished toilet block is fully equipped. New family room and facilities for disabled visitors. Laundry room. Recycling bins. Shop (reduced hours in low season) providing basic essentials and a freezer for ice packs. Play area. Games room. Bicycle hire arranged. Torch useful. Off site: Village (10 minute walk) with shops, two pubs, etc. plus a bus service for Dorchester and Poole. Golf 3 miles. Fishing 5 miles. Riding 9 miles.

Open: All year (31 October - 16 March by arrangement.)

Directions

Park is about 0.5 miles south of Bere Regis on the road to Wool. GPS: 50.743683, -2.22405

Charges guide

Per unit incl. 2 persons	£ 14.00 - £ 18.00
incl. electricity	£ 16.00 - £ 21.00
extra person	£ 3.50 - £ 5.00
child (3-16 yrs)	£ 2.00 - £ 3.25
dog	free - £ 2.50

Blandford Forum

The Inside Park Touring Caravan & Camping Park

Blandford Forum DT11 9AD (Dorset) T: 01258 453719. E: mail@theinsidepark.co.uk

alanrogers.com/UK2070

The Inside Park is set in the grounds of an 18th-century country house that burned down in 1941. Family owned and carefully managed alongside an arable farm, this is a must for those interested in local history or arboriculture and it is a haven for wildlife and birds. The nine acre camping field, a little distant, lies in a sheltered, gently sloping dry valley containing superb tree specimens – notably cedars, with walnuts in one part – and a dog graveyard dating back to the early 1700s under a large cedar of Lebanon. In total there are 125 spacious pitches, 90 with electricity (10A) and some in wooded glades. The six acres adjoining are the old pleasure gardens of the house. The reception/toilet block and games room block are respectively the coach house and stables of the old house. No vehicle access to the park is allowed after 22.30 (there is a separate late arrivals area and car park). Extensive, marked walks are provided through the farmland and a guide is available in the shop.

Facilities

The toilet block provides some washbasins in cubicles, comfortably sized showers and facilities for disabled visitors and babies. Laundry room. Shop with basics, gas and camping provisions. Spacious games room. Safe based adventure play area. Day kennelling facilities for dogs. Mountain bike course. Winter caravan storage. Off site: Blandford leisure and swimming centre (temporary membership possible) 2 miles. Fishing and riding 2 miles. Golf 3 miles. Beach 25 miles.

Open: Easter - 31 October.

Directions

Park is about 2 miles southwest of Blandford, signed from roundabout junction of A354 and A350 roads. GPS: 50.841333, -2.19515

Charges guide

Per unit incl. 2 persons and electricity	£ 18.13 - £ 22.20
extra person	£ 4.00 - £ 4.50
dog	£ 0.60 - £ 1.00

Bletchingdon

Greenhill Farm Caravan & Camping Park

Greenhill Farm, Station Road, Bletchingdon OX5 3BQ (Oxfordshire) T: 01869 351600.
E: info@greenhill-leisure-park.co.uk **alanrogers.com/UK2590**

On a working farm in a rural setting, this is a newly established site. The approach is a half mile gravel track down into the valley, past recently planted woodlands, fields and the farm. A tarmac path continues round the park giving access to 92 pitches, 80 with 16A electricity and 30 with hardstanding. Growing trees and hedges partition the site and screen the water stands. An adjacent field is available for rallies and there is a second smaller field for tents. There are now two fishing lakes (carp, roach, bream and tench). Many trees and hedges have been planted and as these mature the aspect will be less open giving more shade and walks through the woodland. This is a quiet, pleasant park with modern facilities, convenient for visiting local attractions including Blenheim Palace, Oxford and Stratford.

Facilities

Three toilet blocks, two of which have ramp access to facilities for disabled visitors and families. Separate laundry room. Shop selling own farm produce (April-Sept). Play area with assault course and football nets. Fishing lakes. Games room which can also be used for meetings. Pets are not accepted 1/10-1/3. Caravan storage. Off site: Boat launching and canal walks 1 mile. Golf 2 miles.

Open: All year.

Directions

From M40 exit 9 take A34 to Newbury and Oxford. After 5 miles turn left on B4027 signed Bletchingdon. After 2.5 miles park is on left just past the village. GPS: 51.85754, -1.29142

Charges guide

Per unit incl. 2 persons and electricity	£ 16.00 - £ 18.00
extra person	£ 3.00
dog (max. 2)	£ 3.00

Brockenhurst

Forest Holidays Hollands Wood

Forest Holidays, Lyndhurst Road, Brockenhurst SO43 7QH (Hampshire) T: 01590 622967.
E: info@forestholidays.co.uk **alanrogers.com/UK2310**

Forest Holidays is a partnership between the Forestry Commission and The Camping & Caravanning Club. This is a large, spacious 168 acre secluded site in a natural woodland setting (mainly oak). It is set in the heart of the New Forest, with an abundance of wildlife. The site is arranged informally with 600 level unmarked pitches but it is stipulated that there must be at least 20 feet between each unit. There are no electrical connections and traffic noise is possible from the A337 which runs alongside one boundary. Brockenhurst village is only half a mile away, where there are shops, trains and buses.

Facilities

Three refurbished toilet blocks provide all necessary requirements, including for disabled visitors and babies. Good laundry room. All these may be under pressure at peak times. Motorcaravan services. Freezer packs and charging of batteries (fee). Maps and guides. Barbecues allowed (off ground). Milk stocked. Night security. Barrier closed 22.30-07.00. Torches essential. Off site: Bicycle hire and riding 2 miles. Golf 3 miles.

Open: 26 March - 27 September.

Directions

Site entrance is on east side of A337 Lyndhurst - Lymington road, 0.5 miles north of Brockenhurst. GPS: 50.83655, -1.56952

Charges guide

Per unit incl. 2 persons	£ 10.00 - £ 26.50
extra person	£ 4.25 - £ 8.50
child	£ 2.24 - £ 4.25

Burford

Wysdom Touring Park

The Bungalow, Burford School, Burford OX18 4JG (Oxfordshire) T: 01993 823207
alanrogers.com/UK2620

You'll have to go a long way before you find anything else remotely like this site! The land is owned by Burford School and the site was created to raise money for the school (£50,000 raised in 2009/10). It really is like stepping into their own private garden. This adults only park is screened from the main school grounds by trees and provides 23 pitches (six seasonal), separated by hedges, all with electricity (16A) and their own tap. Tents are accepted for short stays by arrangement.

Facilities

The heated sanitary building is clean and well maintained with two unisex showers (payable by token) – there may be a queue at peak times. (Max. 2 dogs per pitch). Tennis courts. WiFi (charged). Tourist information is available in Burford. Off site: Burford is yards away with its famous hill full of antique shops, old coaching inns and quaint shops. Burford Golf Club is next door.

Open: All year (excl. February).

Directions

From roundabout on A40 at Burford, take A361 towards Lechdale on Thames. Park is a few yards on right signed Burford School. Once in drive watch for narrow entrance to site on right in about 100 yds. GPS: 51.801983, -1.639367

Charges guide

Per unit incl. 2 persons and electricity	£ 10.00 - £ 15.00

Christchurch

Grove Farm Meadow Holiday Park

Meadowbank Holidays, Stour Way, Christchurch BH23 2PQ (Dorset) T: 01202 483597.
E: enquiries@meadowbank-holidays.co.uk **alanrogers.com/UK2130**

Grove Farm Meadow is a quiet, traditional park with caravan holiday homes and a small provision for touring units. The grass flood bank which separates the River Stour from this park provides an attractive pathway. The river bank has been kept natural and is well populated by a range of water birds. It is popular with bird watchers and there is fishing in the river. There are just under 200 caravan holiday homes (75 for hire), sited in regular rows. For touring units there are 41 level pitches (21 fully serviced and with hardstanding), all clearly numbered with electricity (10A), backing on to fencing or hedging and accessed by tarmac roads. The New Forest is just 15 minutes by car.

Facilities

The new heated toilet block provides a bathroom for each sex (50p). Separate toilets, washbasins and showers. Facilities for disabled visitors with ramped access. Baby room. Laundry facilities. Well stocked shop. Games room. Adventure play area beside the river bank. Fishing (permits from reception). WiFi throughout. Dogs are not accepted. Tents are not accepted. Off site: Golf 0.5 miles. Large supermarket 1.5 miles. Beach and sailing 2 miles.

Open: 1 March - 31 October.

Directions

From A388 Ringwood - Bournemouth road take B3073 for Christchurch. Turn right at first roundabout and Stour Way is the third road on the right. GPS: 50.750336, -1.807938

Charges guide

Per unit incl. 2 persons and electricity	£ 10.00 - £ 31.00
extra person (over 5 yrs)	£ 1.00 - £ 2.00

Cowes

Thorness Bay Holiday Park

Thorness Bay, Cowes PO31 8NJ (Isle of Wight) T: 01983 523109. E: holiday.sales@park-resorts.com
alanrogers.com/UK2520

Spread over a large area of rural down and woodland that slopes down to Thorness Bay, this large site has around 500 holiday homes. The touring area has 122 pitches, most with 16A electricity, including 27 multi-serviced pitches on gravel hardstandings with electricity, water, drainage and TV points. These and some grass pitches are on terraces off tarmac roads. The remainder are on sloping open grassland divided by ranch style rails, or in an open tent area, and all have views of the surrounding countryside. The main activity centre is located in the holiday home area, a short walk from the touring site.

Facilities

The toilet block provides showers, WCs and washbasins. Suite for disabled visitors. Baby changing. Laundry facilities. No motorcaravan services. Shop. Indoor pool. Adventure playground. Multisport court. Children's club. Archery. Trampolines. WiFi (charged). Off site: The bay is easily accessed from the main entertainment complex. All the attractions of the island are within easy day-trip distances. Golf 4 miles.

Open: Easter - 29 October.

Directions

From East Cowes ferry follow signs to Newport. Follow A3054 (Yarmouth). Continue for 2.5 miles to crossroads, turn right (Thorness Bay). After about 2 miles, on sharp right hand bend turn left, site signed. GPS: 50.731133, -1.360467

Charges guide

Per unit incl. up to 6 persons and electricity	£ 12.00 - £ 39.00

Cowes

Waverley Park Holiday Centre

51 Old Road, East Cowes PO32 6AW (Isle of Wight) T: 01983 293452. E: sue@waverley-park.co.uk
alanrogers.com/UK2530

This pleasant, small park (45 pitches) is family owned and set in the grounds of an old country house which was once frequently visited by Dr Arnold, the subject of Tom Brown's Schooldays. Watch out for the brown squirrels! The owners have terraced the grass area for touring units and have created 31 large and level, well spaced, fully serviced hardstanding pitches all with impressive views over the Solent. The remaining 14 pitches on a sloping grass area are for caravans and tents – these have no electricity. At the bottom of the park, a gate leads onto the promenade and the pebble beach.

Facilities

One heated toilet block provides the usual facilities, including those for disabled visitors, with baby changing. Motorcaravan service point. Laundry facilities. Heated outdoor pool with sun terrace. Club with restaurant, bar and outdoor terrace, plus family entertainment (Easter-early Sept). Small playground. Games room. WiFi. Boats by prior arrangement. Off site: Tennis courts. East Cowes within walking distance. Fishing and golf 0.5 miles.

Open: All year.

Directions

Immediately after leaving Southampton - Cowes car ferry, take first left, then right into Old Road, and park entrance is 300 yds. on left. GPS: 50.76088, -1.28366

Charges guide

Per unit incl. 2 persons and electricity	£ 16.00 - £ 21.00
extra person	£ 6.50 - £ 9.00

For latest campsite news visit
alanrogers.com

Fordingbridge
Sandy Balls Holiday Centre

Godshill, Fordingbridge SP6 2JZ (Hampshire) T: 0845 270 2248. E: post@sandy-balls.co.uk
alanrogers.com/UK2290

Sandy Balls sits high above the sweep of the Avon river near Fordingbridge, amidst woodland which is protected as a nature reserve. It well deserves the entry it has maintained in these guides for over 30 years and continues to improve and develop. Very well run and open all year, the 120-acre park has many private holiday homes as well as 26 caravan holiday homes and 117 lodges for rent. The touring areas have 233 marked, hedged, serviced pitches for caravans and tents on part-hardstanding and part-grass, with 16A electricity and TV connections. In August there is an additional unmarked tent area. In winter only 50 pitches are available. A woodland leisure trail allows wild animals and birds to be observed in their natural surroundings and the attractions of the New Forest are close at hand. The heart of this holiday centre is the architecturally designed, multi-million pound 'village'. Its traffic-free piazza houses the bistro, pub, guest services bureau, gift shop, cycle shop, small supermarket and leisure club, all providing space to relax and meet friends. A member of the Best of British Group.

Facilities

Three heated toilet blocks have washbasins in cubicles. Portacabin style units for the tent field. Toilets for disabled visitors. Baby facilities. Excellent launderette. Motorcaravan service point. Entertainment programme (high season). Outdoor pool (25/5-1/9). Indoor pool (66x30 ft). Well equipped gym, jacuzzi, steam room, sauna. Games room. Adventure playground. Tents for rent. River fishing (permit). Riding stables. Bicycle hire. Archery. Dogs only allowed on certain fields. Off site: Golf 6 miles. Beach 20 miles.

Open: All year.

Directions

Park is well signed 1.5 miles east of Fordingbridge on the B3078. GPS: 50.930267, -1.7602

Charges guide

Per unit incl. 2 persons	
and electricity	£ 10.00 - £ 60.00
extra person	free - £ 5.00
child	free
dog	free - £ 4.00

Fordingbridge
Hill Cottage Farm Camping & Caravan Park

Sandleheath Road, Alderholt, Fordingbridge SP6 3EG (Hampshire) T: 01425 650513.
E: hillcottagefarmcaravansite@supanet.com **alanrogers.com/UK2360**

This established, modern site is set in 47 acres of beautiful countryside on the Dorset and Hampshire border. The 35 pitches, all on hardstandings with electric hook-ups (16A), water taps and drainage are arranged around a circular gravel roadway. Secluded and sheltered, they have views across the surrounding countryside. A field, also with electric hook-ups, alongside the camping area is used for tents and rallies, and has space for ball games and a small playground. Also on site there are two small lakes for coarse fishing, and there are many woodland walks in the area. Overall this site is more suitable for adults and younger children – it is not really designed for active teenagers.

Facilities

A large modern barn-style building provides excellent heated facilities. Laundry room. Facilities for disabled visitors and babies. Facilities for tent pitches. Games room with full size snooker table, two pool tables and darts board, plus a separate function room. Motorcaravan services. Shop. Playground. WiFi (free). Off site: Village centre with pub and store is a 20 minute woodland walk.

Open: 1 March - 30 November.

Directions

From Fordingbridge take B3078 west for 2 miles to Alderholt. On entering the village, at left hand bend, turn right towards Sandleheath (site signed) and site entrance is about 300 yds. on the left. GPS: 50.919017, -1.832783

Charges guide

Per unit incl. 2 persons	£ 20.00 - £ 25.00
extra person	£ 5.00

Freshwater

Heathfield Farm Camping

Heathfield Road, Freshwater PO40 9SH (Isle of Wight) T: 01983 407822. E: web@heathfieldcamping.co.uk

alanrogers.com/UK2500

Heathfield is a pleasant contrast to many of the other sites on the Isle of Wight, in that it is a 'no frills' sort of place, very popular with tenters, cyclists and small camper vans. Despite its name, it is no longer a working farm. A large, open meadow provides 60 large, level pitches, 50 with electricity (10A). Two small fenced areas provide traffic free zones for backpackers and cyclists' tents. There is no shop as you are only eight minutes walk from the centre of Freshwater. The site overlooks Colwell Bay and across the Solent towards Milford-on-Sea and Hurst Castle. A playing field for ball games also has a picnic table and a communal barbecue. There is a wild flower meadow with the perimeter mown for dog walking. It is ideal for visiting attractions on the western side of the island including Totland and Freshwater Bays, The Needles and Old Battery, Compton Down, and Mottistone Manor Garden. The Military road which runs from Freshwater Bay to St Catherine's Point gives spectacular coastal views.

Facilities

The main toilet unit is housed in a modern, ingeniously customised, Portacabin style unit including a baby changing facility. Showers have two pushbutton controls, one for pre-mixed hot water, the other for cold only. A second similar unit has WCs and washbasins in cubicles, plus facilities for disabled visitors. Laundry facilities. Motorcaravan service point. Gas supplies. Ice pack service. Playing field. Bicycle hire arranged. WiFi (charged). No commercial vehicles are accepted. Gate locked 22.30-07.00. Off site: Bus stop 200 m. Riding, beach and fishing 0.5 miles. Golf 1.25 miles.

Open: 1 May - 30 September.

Directions

From A3054 north of Totland and Colwell turn into Heathfield Road where site is signed. Site entrance is on right after a short distance. GPS: 50.68940, -1.52704

Charges guide

Per unit incl. 2 persons and electricity	£ 12.25 - £ 18.50
extra person	£ 4.75 - £ 5.50
child (3-15 yrs)	£ 2.00 - £ 3.50
dog	£ 2.00
Min. pitch fee July/Aug £17.	

Heathfield Farm Camping www.heathfieldcamping.co.uk

Heathfield Rd., Freshwater, **Isle of Wight** PO40 9SH

Proprietors Mike & Doreen Haslin   Tel: 01983 407822

- Peaceful family park
- Magnificient views
- Friendly resident wardens
- Touring & tents
- Close to beach, bus routes and local shops
- Two miles Yarmouth & The Needles

Located in the peaceful West Wight with easy access to spectacular coastal and download walks.

Hayling Island

Fishery Creek Caravan & Camping Park

100 Fishery Lane, Hayling Island PO11 9NR (Hampshire) T: 023 924 621654. E: camping@fisherycreek.co.uk

alanrogers.com/UK2221

Fishery Creek is set in a beautiful and quiet location adjoining a tidal creek of Chichester harbour. Of the 150 pitches, 50 are for touring and the remainder are seasonal. All have 16A electricity connections and are individually marked on level grass. From the park you can enjoy a paddle, a spot of fishing, or launch a small boat from the private slipway. Local shops, restaurants and pubs and a coastal path are all within easy access. Unfortunately, access is shared with the local household amenity tip which can cause congestion at weekends. The south coast has many interesting places to visit including nearby Portsmouth with its naval base and historic dockyard where you'll find the Marie Rose and Nelson's flagship, HMS Victory. The Spinnaker Tower is a striking, modern addition to the city, providing breathtaking coastal views.

Facilities

The toilet and shower facilities are housed in separate blocks and have both been recently refurbished. The shower block has underfloor heating. Toilet facility for disabled visitors. Excellent laundry room with TV and a seating area. Motorcaravan service point. Small shop for basics. Play areas. Fishing. Slipway to launch small boats. Off site: Golf and bicycle hire 2 miles. Riding 3 miles.

Open: 1 March - 31 October.

Directions

From A27, follow A3023 onto Hayling Island. At first roundabout turn left then follow brown signs to park. GPS: 50.784205, -0.958565

Charges guide

Per unit incl. 2 persons and electricity	£ 18.10 - £ 27.75
extra person	£ 3.75
child (4-14 yrs)	£ 3.10
dog	£ 2.65

For latest campsite news visit
alanrogers.com

Hamble

Riverside Holidays

Satchell Lane, Hamble, Southampton SO31 4HR (Hampshire) T: 023 8045 3220.
E: enquiries@riversideholidays.co.uk **alanrogers.com/UK2315**

What makes Riverside so special is its location close to the River Hamble, a Mecca for international yachtsman. The site is family-owned and covers five acres surrounded by trees and hedges; it has 123 pitches of which 77 are level for touring caravans and tents, with 53 electricity hook-ups (16A). The remaining pitches are used for lodges and residential and static caravans on slightly rising ground, but so well spaced and with plenty of grass they are not too obtrusive. A warden-run log cabin reception, with tourist information, including local bus and rail times, is at the entrance. Hamble village, one mile away, with its cobbled streets, pubs and restaurants, is famed the world over for its association with yachting. This is an ideal base for the Southampton Boat Show, Cowes Week and its very own Hamble Week Regatta. In the marina adjacent to the site, a mere two minutes walk, is Oyster Quay with a bar and restaurant overlooking hundreds of yachts worth millions.

Facilities

A brand new lodge contains the sanitary facilities, including family and baby changing rooms. The old Portacabin style unit has been kept for busy periods. Small laundry room alongside. All these facilities could be under pressure in high season. Bicycle hire. Caravan storage. Off site: Fishing, sea fishing, sailing, supermarket, buses and trains in village 1 mile. Riding 3 miles. Golf 4 miles. You can catch a small ferry across to Warsash on the other bank or take a boat up to the Upper Hamble Country Park. The New Forest, Winchester and Portsmouth are nearby.

Open: 1 March - 31 October.

Directions

From M27 exit 8 follow signs for Hamble. Take the B3397 with Tesco on the left, continue 1.9 miles through traffic lights until Hound roundabout. After 50 yds. turn left into Satchell Lane (signed Mercury Marina) and site is on left in 1 mile. GPS: 50.868835, -1.313586

Charges guide

Per unit incl. 2 persons and electricity	£ 15.00 - £ 32.00
extra person	£ 4.00
child (4-16 yrs)	£ 3.00

Camping Cheques accepted.

Henley-on-Thames

Swiss Farm International

Marlow Road, Henley-on-Thames RG9 2HY (Oxfordshire) T: 01491 573419.
E: enquiries@swissfarmcamping.co.uk **alanrogers.com/UK2572**

Nestling at the foot of the Chiltern Hills and just a short stroll from Henley-on-Thames, Swiss Farm is ideally located for those seeking either a relaxing or an active break. The site can offer quiet, communal style pitches or the more family orientated field type. Of the 187 pitches, 156 have 10A electricity, 62 are hardstandings and 31 are fully serviced with 16A electricity and a TV point. This park boasts a heated, supervised, outdoor pool, bar and patio barbecue. Reception includes a small shop selling basic provisions. There is a children's adventure style wooden play area.

Facilities

Two fully equipped toilet blocks. One private bathroom. Free showers. Facilities for the disabled. Baby changing. Launderette. Basic shop in reception for camping essentials. Bar. Supervised swimming pool. Play area. Patio barbecue. Coarse fishing. WiFi. Dogs welcome in low season only. Off site: Boat launching 0.5 miles. Bicycle hire 1 mile. Golf 2 miles.

Open: 1 March - 31 October.

Directions

From M4 exit 8/9 or M40 exit 4A, take A404, A4130 to Henley-on-Thames. Follow Henley-on-Thames signs and site is signed on left just before town. GPS: 51.54594, -0.90504

Charges guide

| Per unit incl. 2 persons and electricity | £ 15.00 - £ 24.00 |
| extra person | £ 4.50 - £ 5.00 |

Maidenhead

Hurley Riverside Park

Hurley, Maidenhead SL6 5NE (Berkshire) T: 01628 824493. E: info@hurleyriversidepark.co.uk

alanrogers.com/UK2700

On the banks of the Thames, not far from Henley-on-Thames, you will find the picturesque village of Hurley where some buildings date back to 1086. Just outside the village is Hurley Riverside Park providing facilities for holiday homes, touring units, tents and moorings for boats. The touring area is flat and separated into smaller fields. With the pitches arranged around the outside of each field and the centre left free, the park has a spacious feel. There are 138 touring pitches with 10A electricity including 14 fully serviced and some on long hardstandings. A camping field provides a further 50 pitches including some with electric hook-ups. A very popular park, there is also a large rally field. You can enjoy walks along the banks of the Thames or visit the various pubs and restaurants in the village for a good meal and a pint. A new nature trail has been installed along the length of the touring park and there are large riverside picnic grounds alongside the Thames. Nearby Windsor has its famous castle or for younger members of the family, Windsor is the home of Legoland. At Henley you can watch the regatta. Alternatively, you can just relax in the peaceful settings of the site.

Facilities

Three wooden toilet blocks (raised on legs) include a new unisex block with private bathrooms (shower, washbasin, toilet). The other blocks have been renovated and are well equipped. Separate shower and toilet facilities for disabled visitors at reception. Baby area. Launderette. Motorcaravan service point. Well stocked shop at reception. Fishing. WiFi. Temporary moorings. Nature trail, riverside picnic grounds, slipway and fishing in season. Accommodation to rent. American RVs accepted. Off site: Golf 5 miles. Riding 10 miles. Legoland at Windsor (discounted tickets).

Open: 1 March - 31 October.

Directions

From M4 exit 8/9 take A404M towards Wycombe. After 3 miles take A4130 (Henley). Go down steep hill (Hurley village signed on right) – ignore this turning and take next right (site signed from here). GPS: 51.5466, -0.8248

Charges guide

Per unit incl. 2 persons	£ 14.00 - £ 22.00
full services	£ 16.00 - £ 24.00
extra person	£ 3.00
child (5-17 yrs)	£ 1.50
dog	£ 2.00

Milford-on-Sea

Lytton Lawn Touring Park

Lymore Lane, Milford-on-Sea SO41 0TX (Hampshire) T: 01590 648331. E: holidays@shorefield.co.uk

alanrogers.com/UK2280

Lytton Lawn is the touring arm of Shorefield Country Park, a nearby holiday home park and leisure centre. Set in eight acres, it provides 135 marked pitches. These include 53 'premier' pitches (hardstanding, 16A electricity, pitch light, water and waste water outlet) in a grassy, hedged area – this section, with its heated toilet block, is open for a longer season. The rest of the pitches, all with electricity, are in the adjoining, but separate, gently sloping field, edged with mature trees and hedges and with a further toilet block. The large reception and well stocked shop make this a good, comfortable, self-sufficient site. Visitors to Lytton Lawn are entitled to use the comprehensive leisure facilities at Shorefield itself (2.5 miles away). These include a very attractive indoor pool, solarium, sauna and spa, fitness classes and treatments, all weather tennis courts, outdoor pools, restaurant facilities including a bistro (Easter-November), and entertainment and activity programmes. These are of a very good standard and are mostly free (some cost extra). These include the 'Reflections' day spa.

Facilities

Two modern toilet blocks are well fitted. Washing machine and dryer. Baby changing. Facilities for disabled visitors (Radar key). Motorcaravan service point. Shop (Feb-Dec). Small fenced play area and hedged field with goalposts. Tents for rent. Off site: Village pub 10 minutes walk. Sailing, windsurfing and boat launching 1.5 miles. Golf, riding, coarse fishing within 3 miles. The New Forest, Isle of Wight, Bournemouth, Southampton and the beach at Milford-on-Sea are nearby.

Open: All year excl. 3 January - 4 Feburary.

Directions

From M27 follow signs for Lyndhurst and Lymington on A337. Continue towards New Milton and Lytton Lawn is signed at Everton; Shorefield is signed at Downton. GPS: 50.73497, -1.61803

Charges guide

Per unit incl. 6 persons and electricity	£ 12.00 - £ 36.00
premier pitch	£ 14.50 - £ 39.50
dog	£ 1.50 - £ 3.00

See advertisement on page 131

Newbridge

The Orchards Holiday Caravan & Camping Park

Newbridge, Yarmouth PO41 0TS (Isle of Wight) T: 01983 531331. E: info@orchards-holiday-park.co.uk
alanrogers.com/UK2450

In a village situation in the quieter western part of the island, The Orchards Holiday Park, a park for all seasons, has panoramic views of rolling countryside and the Solent. The park's neat 11-acre touring area has 168 marked pitches for tents, caravans and motorcaravans, broken up by apple trees, mature hedges and fences. All pitches have electricity, 62 have hardstandings and 22 are 'all service' pitches, also with hardstanding. A meeting room is suitable for small rallies. A separate area contains 64 caravan holiday homes. The Orchards is a good base from which to explore the island and there are two beaches within five miles. The scenic harbour of Yarmouth is five minutes away, as are the attractions of Fort Victoria and Chessell Pottery, with birdwatching at Newtown Creek. Osbourne House is 20 minutes away. There are walking and cycling routes from the park with leaflets available from reception. The park is part of the Caravan Club's affiliated scheme. A member of the Best of British Group.

Facilities

An excellent new heated facilities centre provides 24 shower and washbasin cubicles, a family bathroom, 2 family shower rooms, fully accessible facilities, laundry and ironing area, walkers' drying room, baby changing room, vegetable preparation and indoor dishwashing area. Motorcaravan services. Shop. Gas supplies. Indoor heated pool (Feb-Dec). Outdoor heated pool (May-Sept). Licensed coffee shop. Takeaway (mid Mar-Sept). Play areas. Football pitch. Fitness equipment. TV and games rooms. WiFi (charged). Off site: Riding 1 mile. Beach 4 miles. Bicycle hire 5 miles. Golf 8 miles.

Open: All year excl. 3 January - mid February.

Directions

Park is in Newbridge village, signed south from B3054 (Yarmouth - Newport) road. GPS: 50.687967, -1.419967

Charges guide

Per unit incl. 2 persons and electricity	£ 16.50 - £ 32.00
extra person	£ 5.00 - £ 7.00
child	£ 2.00 - £ 4.50

No pitch fee for hikers or cyclists. Packages incl. ferry travel - ring park for best deal. Camping Cheques accepted.

Oxford

Diamond Farm Caravan & Camping Park

Islip Road, Bletchingdon, Oxford OX5 3DR (Oxfordshire) T: 01869 350909. E: warden@diamondpark.co.uk
alanrogers.com/UK2595

Diamond Farm is a spacious, family run site located 5 miles north of Oxford and within easy access of the Cotswolds and Chilterns. The attractive, 300 year old Cotswold stone farmhouse is at the heart of the site, along with a bar and games room. This is a small site with just 37 touring pitches. These are level and all equipped with 16A electricity. A number of hardstandings are also available. A separate field is used for tents (with some electrical connections). On-site amenities include a bar (with TV and full size snooker table), a well equipped children's play area and a heated swimming pool. For dog owners, the adjacent bridle path is ideal for walks. Diamond Farm is located around 800 yards from the A34 and is also within easy reach of the M40 (3 miles). Blenheim Palace and Bicester Shopping Village are nearby.

Facilities

Modern toilet block with family room and laundry area. Shop. Bar. Takeaway (weekends). Games room. Swimming pool (May-Sept). Play area. Tourist information. WiFi (free). Off site: Oxford city centre, Blenheim Palace and Bicester Shopping Village all 6 miles.

Open: All year.

Directions

Diamond Farm is on the B4027, 1 mile from the A34 (signed), and 3 miles south of exit 9 of the M40. GPS: 51.84897, -1.25518

Charges guide

Per unit incl. 2 persons	£ 14.00 - £ 18.00
extra person	£ 5.00

Poole

Pear Tree Holiday Park

Organford Road, Holton Heath, Poole BH16 6LA (Dorset) T: 0844 272 9504. E: enquiries@peartreepark.co.uk

alanrogers.com/UK2110

Pear Tree is a neat, landscaped and well cared for park welcoming families with young children and couples only. Set in 7.5 acres, with mature trees and views across to Wareham Forest, there are 155 pitches in total, of which 87 are for touring with hardstanding, electricity (10A), water and drainage. Only breathable groundsheets are permitted for awnings. The tent area is a tranquil, secluded spot with many mature trees. Reception, incorporating tourist information and a small shop supplying milk, bread, gas and other basics, is at the park entrance. The gates (with key) are closed at dusk, although latecomers are admitted. A separate playing field is at the top of the park for younger children. A bus service stops outside for Wareham (2.5 miles) and Poole (5 miles). There is a walk from the back of the park into Wareham Forest.

Facilities

The main heated toilet block (opened by key and recently refurbished) provides some washbasins in cubicles, baby changing unit (two new family rooms with Belfast sink baby bath and a wet room for disabled visitors. Laundry. Separate small block near the tent area. All is spotlessly clean. Shop (basics only). Play area with range of equipment. All year caravan storage. Off site: The Clay Pipe Inn 500 m. Bicycle hire 0.5 miles. Golf 2.5 miles. Riding 5 miles. Beach 9 miles.

Open: 1 March - 31 October.

Directions

From the A351 (Wareham - Poole) road, turn west at traffic lights in Holton Heath (signed Organford and Sandford Park). Park is on left after about 550 yds. past Sandford Park and the Clay Pipe Inn. GPS: 50.724033, -2.086967

Charges guide

Per unit incl. 2 persons and electricity	£ 18.00 - £ 28.00
extra person	£ 5.00 - £ 6.00
child (5-16 yrs)	£ 2.00

Poole

South Lytchett Manor Caravan & Camping Park

Dorset Road, Lytchett Minster, Poole BH16 6JB (Dorset) T: 01202 622577. E: info@southlytchettmanor.co.uk

alanrogers.com/UK2120

Joanne and David are rightly proud of what they have achieved at South Lytchett Manor and, along with their staff, try hard to meet all your needs to make you very welcome. It has an unusual situation on parkland either side of what was once one of the driveways to the manor itself with impressive gates at the entrance. The access to the manor (it is now a school) is now closed off but there is room for 150 pitches in meadows or bays by the roadway. All are level, of a good size, with TV connections and electricity. There are 48 with hardstanding and some also have water and waste water. They are neatly landscaped with rural views. There is provision for tents on meadowland to one side. A path leads to the Courtyard Centre with craft shop and café, and Lytchett Minster is within walking distance.

Facilities

Three modern, fully equipped toilet blocks with 4 en-suite family rooms and facilities for disabled visitors. Laundry. Motorcaravan service point. Well stocked shop with off licence and gas. Games room. Play area. Playing field. Woodland walk. Dog walk. Tourist information centre. Internet and WiFi. Bicycle hire. Off site: Shops, pubs, ATM 1 mile. Beach and sailing 2 miles. Golf, fishing and riding 3 miles. Ferry port 3 miles.

Open: 1 March - 2 January.

Directions

At the roundabout at the end of the dual carriageway on the A35 west of Poole turn north on B3067 to Lytchett Minster. Go through village and site is on the left half a mile past church, through big iron gates. GPS: 50.73959, -2.05542

Charges guide

Per unit incl. 2 persons and electricity	£ 16.00 - £ 30.00
extra person	£ 4.75 - £ 8.00

Poole

Beacon Hill Touring Park

Blandford Road North, Poole BH16 6AB (Dorset) T: 01202 631631. E: bookings@beaconhilltouringpark.co.uk

alanrogers.com/UK2180

Beacon Hill is located in a marvellous, natural environment of partly wooded heathland, with certain areas of designated habitation for protected species such as sand lizards and the Dartford Warbler, but there is also easy access to main routes. Wildlife ponds encourage dragonflies and other species, but fishing is also possible. Conservation is obviously important in such a special area but one can ramble at will over the 30 acres with the hilltop walk a must. Grassy open spaces provide 170 pitches, 151 with 10A electricity, on sandy grass which is sometimes uneven. Of these, 50 are for tents only and a few are seasonal. The undulating nature of the land and trees allows for discrete areas to be allocated for varying needs, for example young families near the play area, families with teenagers close to the bar/games room, those with dogs near the dog walking area, and young people further away. The park provides a wide range of facilities, including an open air swimming pool and a tennis court. It is well situated for beaches, Poole harbour and ferries for France and the Channel Isles.

Facilities

Two fully equipped toilet blocks include facilities for disabled guests. Laundry facilities. Well stocked shop at reception. Coffee bar and takeaway (main season). Bar (July/Aug, B.Hs, half-terms). Heated swimming pool (mid May-mid Sept). All weather tennis court (charged). Adventure play areas including a hideaway. Games room with pool tables and amusement machines. TV room. Internet (WiFi). Fishing (charges). Off site: Riding 2 miles. Bicycle hire, Poole harbour and ferries 3 miles. Brownsea Island, Studland beach with Sandbanks ferry and the Purbecks nearby.

Open: 17 March - end September.

Directions

Park is about 3 miles north of Poole. Take the A350 (towards Blandford) at roundabout where A350 joins A35. Park signed to the right (northeast) after about 400 yds. GPS: 50.74953, -2.03446

Charges guide

Per unit incl. 2 persons	
and electricity	£ 14.50 - £ 36.00
extra person	£ 3.75 - £ 6.75
child (3-15 yrs)	£ 2.75 - £ 3.25
dog	£ 1.00 - £ 2.00

Ringwood

Forest Edge Holiday Park

229 Ringwood Road, Saint Leonards, Ringwood BH242SD (Hampshire) T: 01590 648331.
E: holidays@shorefield.co.uk alanrogers.com/UK2285

This popular family park is part of the Shorefield Group. Offering 120 pitches for tents and touring holidays and 37 caravan holiday homes, it is complemented by the leisure facilities available at Oakdene Forest Park (which is no longer taking any touring units). There is easy access to the level, marked pitches, each with 16A electricity hook-ups. The cheerful, flowery reception and well stocked shop help create a friendly and relaxed atmosphere. Picnic tables are dotted about the park giving it a country feel. A short walk through Hurn Forest (less than a mile) leads to Oakdene and its new clubhouse and entertainment centre. Visitors at Forest Edge may use the bar, restaurant, large pools, games room and other free entertainment which is ideal for families not wishing to travel too far. The location of Forest Edge is ideal for visiting Bournemouth (beaches, shops and shows), the New Forest and all the attractions of Dorset.

Facilities

The toilet block provides clean but fairly standard facilities. Unit for disabled visitors. Baby area. These facilities may be under pressure in high season. Laundry in a separate room near the children's adventure play area. Gas supplies. Shop with off-licence. Heated outdoor swimming pool (Whitsun-Sept, weekends only plus school holidays). Football and netball court. Games room. Off site: Riding, fishing and golf 1 mile. Beach 7 miles.

Open: 4 February - 2 January.

Directions

Take the A31 westbound from Ringwood. After 3 miles and two roundabouts, turn left at the second roundabout into Boundary Lane (before reaching Oakdene). Site is signed. GPS: 50.82137, -1.84989

Charges guide

Per unit incl. 6 persons and electricity	£ 12.00 - £ 36.00
dog	£ 1.50 - £ 3.00

See advertisement on page 131

Ringwood

Red Shoot Camping Park

Linwood, Ringwood BH24 3QT (Hampshire) T: 01425 473789. E: enquiries@redshoot-campingpark.com
alanrogers.com/UK2350

Red Shoot is set on four acres of open, slightly sloping, level grass, in the heart of the New Forest. A simple, rural retreat with panoramic views of the surrounding countryside and forest, it is very popular in high season. There are 120 good sized pitches, 45 with electrical hook-ups (10A), served by a circular gravel road. There is no site lighting so a torch would be useful. The adjacent Red Shoot Inn (under separate ownership) serves hot or cold meals and brews its own real ales – Forest Gold and Tom's Tipple. There are ample opportunities for walking, cycling and naturalist pursuits in the area. Local attractions include watersports at the New Forest Water Park near Ringwood, a Doll Museum in Fordingbridge, cider making in Burley, and Breamore House just north of Fordingbridge. Nearby Ringwood has a market on Wednesday.

Facilities

The toilet and shower facilities have been upgraded to a high standard with underfloor heating, including a family shower room/baby bath and changing area. Well equipped laundry room. Good unit for disabled visitors. Very well stocked, licensed shop. Fenced adventure style playground. Off site: Fishing 5 miles. Riding 6 miles. Golf 7 miles. Beach 12 miles.

Open: 1 March - 31 October.

Directions

From A338 about 1.75 miles north of Ringwood, turn east (signed Linwood and Moyles Court). Follow signs, over a staggered crossroads, and continue straight on for another 1.75 miles to Red Shoot Inn. GPS: 50.883917, -1.7347

Charges guide

Per unit incl. 2 persons and electricity	£ 20.00 - £ 30.00
extra person	£ 8.00
child (3-15 yrs)	£ 4.00
dog	£ 1.00
Min. pitch charge £11.50.	

Ringwood

Shamba Holidays

Ringwood Road, Saint Leonards, Ringwood BH24 2SB (Hampshire) T: 01202 873302.
E: enquiries@shambaholidays.co.uk **alanrogers.com/UK2340**

Shamba is a family run, very modern park, although the aim remains to create a relaxed, pleasant atmosphere. There are 150 pitches, most of which are used for touring units, 45 are on a seasonal basis and three new fields have been opened for tents (no electricity) for three weeks in August. Surrounded by trees, the camping area is on flat, open grass with electricity (10/16A) available on all pitches. A Scandinavian style building forms the focal point and here you will find reception, a bar/restaurant, takeaway and a shop. The indoor swimming pool has walls and a roof which can be opened in good weather. The park's location is excellent for a short stopover but well worth a longer stay for a family holiday. Bournemouth with its shops and beaches is eight miles away, while the delights of the New Forest and Dorset are within easy reach.

Facilities

Sanitary facilities with underfloor heating include modern showers, washbasins and toilets and family changing rooms. Baby rooms with bath and facilities for disabled visitors. Launderette. Motorcaravan service point. Bar with meals and takeaway. Indoor swimming pool (12x6 m, heated) and children's pool. Large children's play area. Amusements room. Adjacent field for dog walking and football/sports pitch. Off site: Moors Valley Country Park and riding 1 mile. Golf 2 miles. Ringwood, fishing and bicycle hire 2.5 miles. Beach 8 miles.

Open: 1 March - 31 October.

Directions

Take the A31 westbound from Ringwood, after 3 miles, at second roundabout, turn back on yourself and after only 20 yds. turn left at the park sign.
GPS: 50.825067, -1.853117

Charges guide

Per unit incl. 2 persons	
and electricity	£ 20.00 - £ 30.00
extra person	£ 4.00
child (6-13 yrs)	£ 3.00
dog	£ 2.50

A minimum advance booking policy applies at peak periods. Camping Cheques accepted.

For latest campsite news visit
alanrogers.com

Riseley

Wellington Country Park

Riseley, Reading RG7 1SP (Berkshire) T: 01189 326444. E: info@wellington-country-park.co.uk

alanrogers.com/UK2690

Wellington Country Park is open to the general public on payment (entry for campers however, is included in your pitch fees) and many visit it for a day out. It contains children's play areas, slides, sand pits, nine-hole crazy golf, animal farm and petting barn, miniature railway (£1 extra), four nature trails to follow, a deer park and a host of play equipment to climb in and on. It is situated within a woodland which is part of a 350-acre park. There are 85 pitches, 15 non-electric for tents, 56 with electricity (6A) and 22 hardstandings. A few premium pitches offer slightly more privacy. It is a very pleasant setting and once the park closes at 18.00 all is much quieter. You should aim to arrive before 16.30 (low season) and 17.30 (high season) when the main reception centre closes. Access to the site is through a locked gate (key from reception on check-in). The design of the site with individual pitches and some small groups all within woodland clearings gives a very rustic and relaxed ambience. A warden lives on site.

Facilities

The central toilet block provides modern style facilities including washbasins in cubicles and well equipped showers with good dry areas. Ample laundry. Shop stocks basics. Calor gas exchange. Country Park with nature walks, deer field, crazy golf, play areas and miniature railway (£1 extra). Family events are held all year round. Torch useful. Off site: Local shops, bars and entertainment including swimming, cinema, ice-skating, all within a short drive. Major attractions such as Legoland, Thorpe Park, Windsor etc. all within easy reach.

Open: Early March - 11 November.

Directions

Park is signed at Riseley, off the A33 road between Reading and Basingstoke. From M4 take exit 11 and park is 4 miles south off the second roundabout (signed). From M3 use exit 8 and follow A33 for 7 miles towards Reading. Turn right at roundabout after the Wellington monument and park is at the next roundabout. GPS: 51.3592, -0.961167

Charges 2012

Per unit incl. 2 persons	£ 17.00 - £ 32.50
extra person	£ 6.00 - £ 8.50
child (3-15 yrs)	£ 5.50
dog	£ 3.00

Wellington Country Park

*is situated within beautiful woodlands on the Hampshire/
Berkshire border near Reading. Facilities include toilets, free
showers, electric shaving points, hair driers and laundry.
Campers enjoy 'FREE' access to all Park facilities.
Please see website for full details.*
www.wellington-country-park.co.uk
Email:- info@wellington-country-park.co.uk
Tel:- 01189 326444

Romsey

Hill Farm Caravan Park

Branches Lane, Sherfield English, Romsey SO51 6FH (Hampshire) T: 01794 340402. E: gjb@hillfarmpark.com

alanrogers.com/UK2380

This 11-acre rural park is ideal for those seeking a quiet base but one that is within easy reach of all the main tourist attractions of Hampshire and Dorset. There are 120 pitches, of which 30 for seasonal units are located in a separate area. The touring area is a large open field surrounded by trees and hedges. All pitches are well marked, numbered and mainly level. All have electric hook-ups (6/10A), 20 pitches are fully serviced and some are available with hardstanding. Adding to the attractiveness of the site is a pitch and putt golf course, set in a sizeable and well landscaped area. For anyone interested in roses, nearby Mottisfont Abbey (National Trust) has a unique collection of old fashioned varieties. The New Forest with Beaulieu Estate and National Motor Museum is just a short drive away. A trip to the Isle of Wight makes a good excursion – the ferry terminal is within a 30 minute drive.

Facilities

Two very clean, traditionally built toilet blocks include washbasins, open style and in cubicles, and controllable showers. Facilities for babies and disabled visitors. Motorcaravan service point. Shop in reception for gas supplies and basics. Bread and pasties are cooked on the premises. Tea rooms serving breakfast, lunch and afternoon tea (homemade cakes & desserts). Play area. Pitch and putt golf. Off site: Riding, golf and fishing 3 miles. Bicycle hire 15 miles. Bournemouth and Southampton for shopping, leisure and family entertainment nearby.

Open: 1 March - 31 October.

Directions

From Romsey, drive north on the A27 for 3.5 miles, turning right into Branches Lane and site is a further 0.5 miles on right. GPS: 51.00627, -1.57682

Charges guide

Per unit incl. 2 persons and electricity	£ 16.00 - £ 32.00
extra person	£ 7.00
child (4-16 yrs)	£ 2.50 - £ 6.00

Minimum booking requirement for B.Hs, July and August weekends.
No credit cards.

Ryde

Whitefield Forest Touring Park

Brading Road, Ryde PO33 1QL (Isle of Wight) T: 01983 617069. E: pat&louise@whitefieldforest.co.uk

alanrogers.com/UK2495

This family run park, opened in May 2007, has been sympathetically developed by the owners working closely with the Forestry Commission to maintain the natural beauty of the ancient woodland, Whitefield Forest. There is a mixture of well drained all-weather hardstanding and grass pitches (90 in total) all with 16A electricity hook-up. Varying in size (100-170 sq.m), the pitches are level and sheltered with some on terraces. They are all suitable for tents, caravans and motorcaravans. There is good access to the park and the pitches. Some slight road noise is audible from a few pitches. The park is suitable for families and pre-teen children who want a peaceful relaxing holiday.

Facilities

The excellent well appointed heated toilet block has private cubicles, hairdryers and razor points. Family shower rooms. Baby changing and facilities for visitors with disabilities. Laundry room. Motorcaravan service point. Paperback book exchange. Adventure type play area with bark surface for children over 5 yrs. WiFi (free). Electric barbecues not permitted. Suitable for American style motorhomes and twin-axle caravans.
Off site: Network of public footpaths from the site. Supermarket 600 yds. Golf 1 mile. Riding 3 miles. Beach, fishing and boat launching 3 miles. Bicycle hire 4 miles.

Open: 30 March - 1 October.

Directions

From Fishbourne and East Cowes follow A3054 to Ryde. Follow the A3055 to Brading. Site is 800 yds. on left (signed) after Tesco roundabout. From Yarmouth follow A3054 to Newport, then to Ryde. Follow the A3055 to Brading and as above. GPS: 50.70049, -1.14574

Charges guide

Per unit incl. 2 persons	
and electricity	£ 12.20 - £ 19.80
extra person	£ 6.20 - £ 9.90
child (3-15 yrs)	£ 2.50 - £ 5.00

Shanklin

Ninham Country Holidays

Ninham, Shanklin PO37 7PL (Isle of Wight) T: 01983 864243. E: office@ninham-holidays.co.uk

alanrogers.com/UK2465

Ninham is an attractive, well maintained park tucked in a wooded valley, but only ten minutes drive to the bustling resort of Shanklin with its long, sandy beaches and good shops and restaurants. Two touring areas, one open all season, have spacious grass and gravel pitches, some open and some separated by hedges, with water and electrical hook-ups. There are two (unfenced) lakes for carp fishing, and numerous cycle paths, which can be used to access local amenities. Children will enjoy the heated outdoor pool, and the games room offers pool, table tennis and other activities. The site will appeal in particular to walkers and cyclists, who can take full advantage of the beautiful countryside.

Facilities

Clean and well maintained toilet facilities are housed in two traditional buildings, and a Portacabin style unit for use in high season. No special facilities for visitors with disabilities. Space for baby changing. Laundry facilities. No shop, but supermarkets nearby. Small outdoor pool with toddler pool and terrace (end May-Sept). Games room. Play areas. Coarse fishing (charged). Bicycle hire. WiFi (free). Dogs welcome in one area. Accommodation to rent. Off site: Bus stop by entrance. Leisure centre nearby. Beach 2 miles. Golf 2 miles. Riding 4 miles.

Open: 30 April - 4 September.

Directions

From Newport/Cowes direction, pass the park entrance and continue 400 yds. to Morrison's roundabout. Filter off left onto private drive. From Ryde - Fishbourne (A3055), turn onto A3056 at lake. Entrance is 0.5 miles on left after Morrison's roundabout. Look for brown and white tourist signs to Ninham Farm. GPS: 50.640607, -1.192424

Charges guide

Per unit incl. 2 persons	
and electricity	£ 15.50 - £ 22.00
extra person	£ 5.00 - £ 7.50

For latest campsite news visit
alanrogers.com

Shanklin

Lower Hyde Holiday Park

Landguard Road, Shanklin PO37 7LL (Isle of Wight) T: 01983 866131. E: holiday.sales@park-resorts.com

alanrogers.com/UK2475

This site is located on the edge of Shanklin, within walking distance of shops and services and only 1.5 miles from the beach. Lower Hyde is a large holiday park complex with around 200 caravan holiday homes for rent and 114 privately owned. The separate touring area has 85 well spaced and numbered pitches, all with 16A electricity and 26 with full services (hardstanding, water, waste-water drain, electricity and TV hook-up). There is a further area for tents (no electricity). The touring area is in an elevated position with good views over the surrounding countryside. The pitches are large and flat, easily accessed, with tarmac roads and low-level lighting. Landscaping is good, with much wildlife and planting throughout.

Facilities

The toilet block has WCs, open washbasins, showers, a family shower room and two bathrooms. Separate baby room. Suite for disabled visitors. Launderette. Shop. Bar. Restaurant and takeaway. Indoor and outdoor pools. Adventure playground. Children's clubs. Entertainment. Multisport court. Soccer. Archery. Fencing. Tennis. ATM. WiFi (charged). Off site: Fishing and boat launching 1.5 miles. Golf 2.5 miles. Riding and bicycle hire 5 miles. Many Isle of Wight attractions within a few minutes drive.

Open: 2 April - 29 October.

Directions

From East Cowes ferry take A3021 for 2.5 miles to roundabout and turn right on A3054 to Newport. From Newport take A3020 towards Sandown and Shanklin. After 1.5 miles (at Blackwater) continue straight on joining A3056 to Sandown. Keep on this road passing supermarket on the left. Turn right into Whitecross Lane (signed Landguard Camping). Continue past Landguard, site is on right after 1 mile. GPS: 50.633317, -1.180983

Charges guide

Per unit incl. up to 6 persons and electricity	£ 12.00 - £ 39.00

Swanage

Swanage Coastal Park

Priestway, Swanage BH19 2RS (Dorset) T: 01590 648331. E: holidays@shorefield.co.uk

alanrogers.com/UK2000

From 2012 this park will no longer accept touring units. With views over Swanage Bay and the Purbeck hills, Swanage Coastal Park is now part of Shorefield Holidays who own other parks in the New Forest. It offers a quiet holiday on the hills above Swanage with its lovely sandy beach (it is quite a steep climb up from the town). Over 100 holiday caravans are terraced up the hillside, of which two-thirds are privately owned. The use of a large field for tents without electricity and temporary toilet facilities may be a possibility. Swanage is at the start of the Jurassic Coast World Heritage Site and there is direct access to the coastal paths and to Durlston Country Park and Castle.

Facilities

Play area. Membership of the health and fitness club at the next door park allows use of the indoor pool, gym, sauna, solarium, bar and restaurant as paying customers (open all year). It also has a shop (open B.Hs. and high season). Off site: Beach and town 1 mile. Bicycle hire, fishing and boat launching 1 mile. Golf 3 miles. 'Hop on hop off' bus allows you to explore the whole of the Jurassic Coast.

Open: 14 March - 30 October.

Directions

From A351 Wareham - Swanage road turn right just after 'Welcome to Swanage' sign into High Street then immediately right again into Bell Street. At the top turn left into Priests Road then first right up hill towards Priestway. GPS: 50.60605, -1.974983

Charges guide

Per pitch	£ 10.00 - £ 19.00
incl. electricity	£ 11.00 - £ 25.50

See advertisement on page 131

Swanage

Ulwell Cottage Caravan Park

Ulwell, Swanage BH19 3DG (Dorset) T: 01929 422823. E: enq@ulwellcottagepark.co.uk

alanrogers.com/UK2020

Nestling under the Purbeck Hills on the edge of Swanage, in the Dorset and East Devon Coast World Heritage Site, Ulwell Cottage is a family run holiday park with an indoor pool and a wide range of facilities. A good proportion of the park is taken by caravan holiday homes (140), but an attractive, undulating area accessed by tarmac roads is given over to 77 numbered touring pitches interspersed with trees and shrubs. All have electricity (16A), eight are fully serviced and 16 are available with hardstanding. The colourful entrance area is home to the Village Inn with a courtyard adjoining the heated, supervised indoor pool complex (both open all year and open to the public) and modern reception. The hill above the touring area, Nine Barrow Down, is a Site of Special Scientific Interest for butterflies and overlooks Round Down. It is possible to walk to Corfe Castle this way. With Brownsea Island, Studland Bay, Corfe village and the Swanage Railway close by, Ulwell Cottage makes a marvellous centre for holidays.

Facilities

The modern, cheerful toilet block at the top of the site is heated and includes a unit for disabled visitors. Laundry room and baby sinks. Well stocked shop with gas (Easter-mid Sept). Bar snacks and restaurant meals with family room. Takeaway (July/Aug). Indoor pool with lifeguard (times vary acc. to season). Playing fields and play areas. WiFi throughout (charged). Off site: Beach, fishing and golf 1 mile. Bicycle hire, sailing and riding 2 miles.

Open: 1 March - 7 January.

Directions

From A351 Wareham - Swanage road, turn onto B3351 Studland road just before Corfe Castle. Follow signs to right (southeast) for Swanage and drop down to Ulwell. Park is on right about 100 yds. after 40 mph. sign. GPS: 50.626460, -1.969403

Charges guide

Per unit incl. up to 6 persons	£ 28.00 - £ 44.00
full services incl. hardstanding	£ 27.00 - £ 47.00
extra tent, car or boat	£ 4.00

Discounted rates for two or three persons only.

For a brochure call:
01929 422823
website: www.ulwellcottagepark.co.uk
e-mail: enq@ulwellcottagepark.co.uk

Find a warm welcome at this family run park in the Isle of Purbeck, an area of outstanding natural beauty and breath taking World Heritage coastline. Nearby sandy beaches, coastal walks and golf.
- 77 Touring Pitches with hard standings, electric, water and drainage hook-ups and views of the surrounding hills
- Superb meals at the 'Village Inn' • Heated Indoor Pool • General Shop

---

Ventnor

Appuldurcombe Gardens Holiday Park

Wroxall, Ventnor PO38 3EP (Isle of Wight) T: 01983 852597. E: info@appuldurcombegardens.co.uk

alanrogers.com/UK2480

Originally part of the grounds of an historic house, this pretty family holiday park is situated in 14 acres of beautiful countryside in the valley of Stenbury Downs and St Martin's Downs, close to the sandy beaches at Sandown, Shanklin and Ventnor. The camping field is set in a grassy meadow through which a stream meanders, with a tranquil seating area close by. With hard access roads, there are 100 spacious marked pitches for touring units and tents, all with 14A electricity. There are 30 serviced pitches with hardstanding. The old walled orchard contains 40 good quality caravan holiday homes. There is also the access-friendly Orchard Lodge (all accommodation on one level with ramp access to outside), plus two self contained apartments. In an Area of Outstanding Natural Beauty, it is an ideal spot for birdwatching and horse riding.

Facilities

Two good toilet blocks are fully tiled with free hot water throughout. Facilities for visitors with disabilities (but not for children). Launderette. Motorcaravan services planned. Shop. Café. Bar and family entertainment room. All amenities open from Spring B.H. - early Sept. Outdoor swimming pool (8x18m) and toddlers' pool. Play area. Crazy golf. WiFi (charged). Off site: Fishing, golf, riding, bicycle hire, boat launching, beach, sailing, all within 2-3 miles.

Open: March - November.

Directions

Do not use sat nav instructions, road with restricted access nearby. From Newport take A3020 towards Shanklin and Ventnor. Travel through Blackwater, Rookley, Godshill and Sandford. At Whiteley Bank roundabout turn right towards Wroxall (B3320). Pass Donkey Sanctuary and turn right into Appuldurcombe Road. Park entrance (narrow road) is second on the right, 150 yds. along this road. Do not turn into Red Hill Lane.
GPS: 50.61891, -1.22657

Charges guide

Per unit incl. 2 persons	£ 14.50 - £ 25.00
extra person	£ 4.50 - £ 7.00

Wareham

Wareham Forest Tourist Park

North Trigon, Wareham BH20 7NZ (Dorset) T: 01929 551393. E: holiday@warehamforest.co.uk

alanrogers.com/UK2030

This peacefully located and spacious park, on the edge of Wareham Forest, has 200 pitches and is continually being upgraded by its enthusiastic owners, Tony and Sarah Birch. The focal point of the park is the modern reception and shop, located by the pools. Four main areas provide a wide choice of touring pitches from grass to hardstanding and luxury, all with 16A electricity. Tenters have their own choice of open field or pinewood. The site has provided direct access for walkers into the forest or the seven miles of the Sika cycle trail may be used. The lovely market town of Wareham is accessible by bike without having to use the roads. This park has an almost continental feel, with plenty of space. Even when it is busy, it is calm and peaceful in its forest setting. In low season you may be lucky enough to spot the herd of Sika deer which live in the forest. The park is well situated to explore the Dorset coast and Thomas Hardy country. A member of the Best of British Group.

Facilities

Two well maintained toilet blocks are of a good standard with some washbasins in cubicles, and several family bathrooms (one with baby bath). Main block recently completely refurbised and both blocks are centrally heated. Facilities for disabled visitors. Well equipped laundry rooms. Motorcaravan service point. Small licensed shop with gas. Swimming pool (60x20 ft), heated 20/5-15/9. Large adventure play area. Barrier closed 23.00-07.00. Resident wardens on site. Caravan storage. WiFi. Off site: Cycle trail and walking in the forest. Bicycle hire and golf 3 miles. Fishing 5 miles. Riding 8 miles.

Open: All year.

Directions

From A31 Bere Regis, follow A35 towards Poole for 0.5 miles and turn right where signed to Wareham. Drive for a further 1.5 miles. First park on the left as you enter forest. GPS: 50.721733, -2.156217

Charges guide

Per unit incl. 2 persons	
and electricity	£ 16.00 - £ 34.00
'superior' pitch fully serviced	£ 18.75 - £ 37.50
extra person	£ 3.00 - £ 5.50
child (5-15 yrs)	£ 2.00 - £ 3.90
dog	free - £ 1.50
Couples and families only.	

Wimborne

Wilksworth Farm Caravan Park

Cranborne Road, Wimborne BH21 4HW (Dorset) T: 01202 885467.
E: rayandwendy@wilksworthfarmcaravanpark.co.uk alanrogers.com/UK2060

Opened by the parents of the present owners, the careful and sympathetic development of Wilksworth continues with the aim of providing all the 'mod cons' yet remain in keeping with the environment. It is a spacious, quiet park, well suited for families with a heated outdoor pool which has been totally refurbished in a beautiful Spanish style. The rural situation is lovely, just outside Wimborne and around 12 miles from the beaches between Poole and Bournemouth. The park takes 65 caravans and 25 tents mainly on grass. All pitches have electricity, 10 also have water and drainage. There are 77 privately owned caravan holiday homes in a separate area. With a duck pond at the entrance, the park has been well planned on good quality ground with fairly level grass and some views. Facilities are in attractively converted farm buildings designed to be in keeping with the listed status of the other buildings. A heated swimming pool and a tennis court are on the far side of the touring area.

Facilities

The central, well equipped toilet block has underfloor heating, washbasins in cubicles, a family bathroom and a shower/bath for children with baby changing. Facilities for disabled visitors. Laundry room. Modern reception and shop (basics only, limited hours, Easter-30 Sept). Gas supplies. Freezer for ice packs. Attractive coffee shop serving simple meals with takeaway service (weekends and B.Hs. only outside the main season). Heated 40x20 ft. swimming pool (unsupervised, but walled and gated, May-Sept). Small paddling pool with slide. Adventure play area. BMX track. Golf practice net. Two tennis courts, one full and one short size. Games room. Winter caravan storage. Off site: Wimborne town centre (with its Minster) 1 mile. Golf, fishing and riding 3 miles. Kingston Lacy (NT) 3 miles. Beach 12 miles.

Open: Easter/1 April - 30 October.

Directions

Park is 1 mile north of Wimborne, west off the B3078 road to Cranborne. GPS: 50.8167, -1.9904

Charges guide

Per unit incl. 2 persons	
and electricity	£ 16.00 - £ 30.00
extra person	£ 4.00
child (3-15 yrs)	£ 3.00
full services	£ 2.00
dog	£ 2.00
No credit cards.	

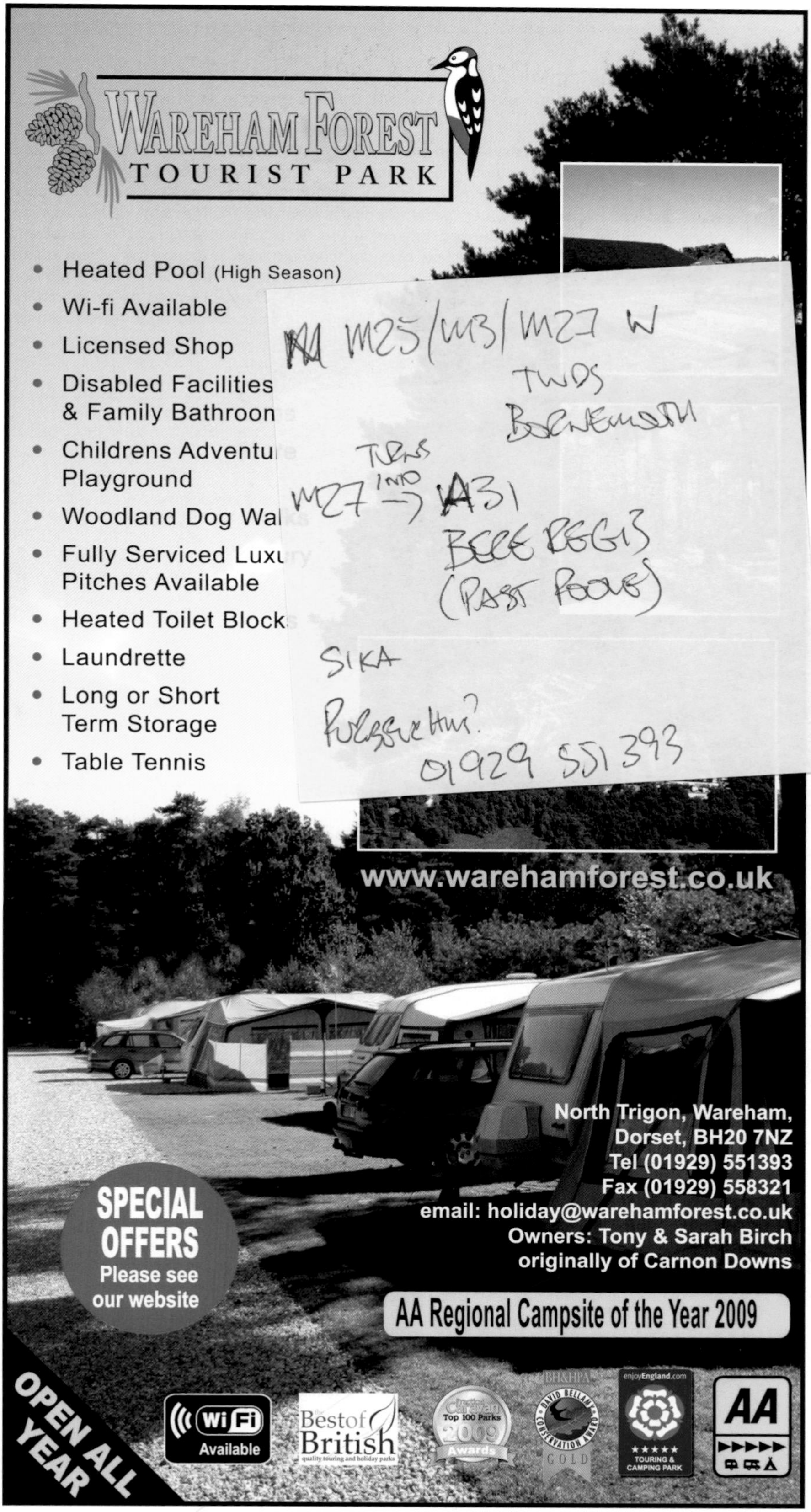
WAREHAM FOREST
TOURIST PARK
Heated Pool (High Season)
Wi-fi Available
Licensed Shop
Disabled Facilities & Family Bathroom
Childrens Adventure Playground
Woodland Dog Wal
Fully Serviced Luxu Pitches Available
Heated Toilet Block
Laundrette
Long or Short Term Storage
Table Tennis
M25/M3/M27 W
TWDS BOURNEMOUTH
M27 TURNS INTO A31
BERE REGIS
(PAST POOLE)
SIKA
01929 551393
www.warehamforest.co.uk
North Trigon, Wareham,
Dorset, BH20 7NZ
Tel (01929) 551393
Fax (01929) 558321
email: holiday@warehamforest.co.uk
Owners: Tony & Sarah Birch
originally of Carnon Downs
SPECIAL OFFERS
Please see our website
AA Regional Campsite of the Year 2009
OPEN ALL YEAR
WiFi Available
Best of British
Top 100 Parks 2009 Awards
David Bellamy Conservation Award GOLD
enjoyEngland.com
TOURING & CAMPING PARK
AA

Wimborne
Merley Court Touring Park
Merley, Wimborne BH21 3AA (Dorset) T: 01590 648331. E: holidays@shorefield.co.uk
alanrogers.com/UK2080

Merley Court is part of the Shorefield Group and all aspects of this well planned, attractively landscaped park are constantly maintained to the highest of standards. Tarmac roads connect 162 touring pitches, all of which have 16A electricity, on neat lawns or one of the many hardstandings. This provision includes 19 serviced pitches with water, waste disposal and satellite TV. The entire park is interspersed with a variety of shrubs, plants and the odd ornamental urn. Some attractive tent pitches are to be found in a small wooded valley. A well furnished club complex provides a lounge bar where meals are available. There is also a snack bar, takeaway, large games room with pool tables and a family room leading onto a spacious sheltered patio. This in turn leads to the paved walled swimming pool area. There are woodland walks (including dog walks) directly from the site connecting to the disused railway line where nature has returned with an abundance of wild flowers, which in turn leads to Delph woods with designated nature trails. A member of the Best of British Group.

Facilities

Three heated toilet blocks, two with showers, are of good quality. Separate facilities for disabled visitors and babies. Dishwashing and laundry facilities. Motorcaravan service point. Shop with caravan accessories and gas. Café and takeaway. Bar with food (limited hours in low and mid season). Outdoor pool (30x20 ft) with children's section (Whitsun-early Sept). Tennis and short tennis courts. Table tennis. Play area. Games room with pool tables. Tourist information. Barrier card £5 deposit. WiFi throughout (charged). Off site: Fishing, riding and golf all within 2 miles. Bicycle hire and Poole 5 miles. Bournemouth 8 miles. Tower Park leisure and entertainment centre nearby, Kingston Lacy House, Knoll Gardens, Brownsea Island and the Moors Valley Country Park are also close.

Open: All year excl. 3 January - 5 February.

Directions

Site clearly signed at the junction of A31 and A349 roads (roundabout) on the Wimborne bypass. GPS: 50.785733, -1.98525

Charges guide

Per unit incl. 6 persons	
and electricity	£ 14.50 - £ 38.50
all service pitch	£ 20.00 - £ 42.50
dog	£ 1.50 - £ 3.00

No extra pup tent as well as awning.

Wimborne
Woolsbridge Manor Farm Caravan Park
Three Legged Cross, Wimborne BH21 6RA (Dorset) T: 01202 826369. E: woolsbridge@btconnect.com
alanrogers.com/UK2150

Close to the Moors Valley Country Park, this friendly, family run site is within easy reach of the south coast, the resorts of Christchurch, Bournemouth and Poole, and the ancient market town of Wimborne Minster. Entry is restricted to couples and families. The seven acre camping meadow has 100 large level pitches (51 seasonal) all with electricity (16A) and arranged on either side of a central tarmac road. Reception has a well stocked shop and a good selection of tourist information. The site is part of a working beef cattle farm, so parents should be aware of moving farm machinery and tractors. A cycleway/footpath crosses the fields to the Country Park – very safe for children – where amenities include coarse fishing, golf, steam railway, bicycle hire, a tea room and a country shop.

Facilities

The neat, refurbished toilet block is well maintained and has ample facilities. Four newly built family rooms each with shower, WC, basin, handrails and ramped access provided for disabled visitors, babies and toddlers. Washing machine, dryer and ironing facilities. Shop. Gas. Playground. Fishing. American RVs accepted, advance booking appreciated. Torches useful. Caravan storage. Off site: Old Barn Farm inn and restaurant 400 m. Riding, golf and bicycle hire 0.5 miles. Boat launching and sailing 5 miles.

Open: 1 March - 31 October.

Directions

From Ringwood take A31 southwest to the large Ashley Heath roundabout (junction of A31 and A338 to Bournemouth). Take left hand slip road up to roundabout, avoiding underpass, and turn right (north) onto unclassified road signed for Three Legged Cross, Ashley Heath, Horton and Moors Valley Country Park. Follow signs to Country Park (2 miles), pass the park entrance on right, continue for another 400 yds to campsite entrance (well signed on right). GPS: 50.842982, -1.859982

Charges guide

Per unit incl. 2 persons	
and electricity	£ 17.50 - £ 24.50
extra person	£ 6.50 - £ 7.00
child (under 16 yrs)	£ 4.50 - £ 5.00
dog	£ 2.00

Witney

Lincoln Farm Park

High Street, Standlake, Witney OX29 7RH (Oxfordshire) T: 01865 300239. E: info@lincolnfarmpark.co.uk

alanrogers.com/UK2570

From its immaculately tended grounds and quality facilities, to the efficient and friendly staff, this park is a credit to its owner. Situated in a small, quiet village, it is well set back and screened by mature trees, with wide gravel roads, hedged enclosures, brick pathways and good lighting. All 90 numbered, level touring pitches are generously sized and have electrical connections (10/16A), 75 with gravel hardstanding and grass for awnings, and 22 are fully serviced (fresh and waste water, electricity and satellite TV). Gazebos or extra tents are not permitted on pitches. Although only a relatively small site its leisure facilities are quite outstanding. The indoor leisure centre boasts two heated pools plus a pool for toddlers, spa pools, saunas, steam room, sun bed and a fitness suite. Charges for all of these are made, and outside of the open sessions everything can be hired privately by the hour. Oxford and the Cotswolds are conveniently close. A member of the Best of British Group.

Facilities

Two heated toilet blocks are well maintained and exceptionally clean, with showers and washbasins in cubicles. A well equipped, separate unit for disabled visitors. Two family bathrooms (with baby bath and changing facilities). Laundry facilities, freezers, fridges and microwaves. Motorcaravan service point. Well stocked shop. Information kiosk. Outdoor chess/draughts, putting green and adventure play area. Indoor swimming pools. WiFi. Games room with pool, table football and electronic games machines. Off site: Bird hides 250 yds. Fishing (lake and river) 300 yds and 5 miles. Riding centre and water sports nearby. Golf 5 miles. Oxford 14 miles.

Open: 1 February - mid November.

Directions

Take A415 Witney - Abingdon road and turn into Standlake High Street by garage; park is 300 yds. on the right. GPS: 51.7232, -1.428783

Charges guide

Per unit incl. 2 persons	
and electricity	£ 16.95 - £ 27.95
extra person	£ 4.00
child (5-14 yrs)	£ 2.50
dog	£ 1.25

Low season offers.

Wool

Whitemead Caravan Park

East Burton Road, Wool BH20 6HG (Dorset) T: 01929 462241. E: whitemeadcp@aol.com

alanrogers.com/UK2090

The Church family continue to make improvements to this attractive little park which is within walking distance of the village of Wool, between Dorchester and Wareham. Very natural and with open views over the Frome Valley water meadows, it provides 95 numbered pitches on flat grass sloping gently north and is orchard-like in parts. The 76 touring pitches are well spaced, mostly backing onto hedges or fences and all have electrical connections (10A). All roads are now tarmac. There are no caravan holiday homes but 19 pitches are seasonal. There may be some rail noise but this is not intrusive at night. The park is 4.5 miles from the nearest beach at Lulworth and is handily placed for many attractions in this part of Dorset (railway station and main route bus stop is within 400 yards).

Facilities

The toilet block provides showers, private cubicles, a baby room, dishwashing and laundry sinks, washing machine and dryer. Shop (limited hours) with off-licence, gas supplies and information room/library. Games room with pool table and darts. Playground. Caravan storage. WiFi in games room. Off site: The Ship Inn 300 yards. Bicycle hire 2 miles. Riding, fishing and golf 3 miles.

Open: 15 March - 31 October.

Directions

Turn off main A352 on eastern edge of Wool, just north of level crossing, onto East Burton road. Site is 350 yds. on right. GPS: 50.68164, -2.22595

Charges guide

Per unit incl. 2 persons	
and electricity	£ 13.50 - £ 21.00
extra person (over 5 yrs)	£ 4.50
dog	£ 0.75 - £ 2.00

No credit cards.

For latest campsite news visit

alanrogers.com

Land of 1066, the South East is brimming with historical sights as castles, stately homes and cathedrals abound. It also boasts miles of footpaths and cycle routes through some of the best landscapes in England, passing chalk downland, wooded valleys and dramatic white-faced cliffs.

THE SOUTH EAST COMPRISES: EAST SUSSEX, WEST SUSSEX, SURREY AND KENT

The chalk countryside of golden downland in Sussex offers many opportunities for an active holiday, from walking and cycling to more adventurous pursuits such as rock climbing or ballooning. Once an ancient forest, much of the Weald is now taken up with farmland, but some areas still remain, including Ashdown Forest, a walkers' paradise with stunning views of the High Weald and South Downs. The many rivers of the county have cut their way through gaps in the chalk landscape, ending spectacularly in white cliffs on the coast. Here you will find the Regency resorts of Bognor Regis and Brighton with its Royal Pavilion, famous pier and quirky shops. Often referred to as the 'Garden of England', Kent is a richly fertile region flourishing with hop gardens, fruit orchards and flowers. It is also home to the world-renowned Canterbury Cathedral, several splendid castles, hidden towns, and quaint villages with oast houses. Surrey too boasts a rich heritage with numerous stately homes and National Trust sites plus large areas of ancient woodland. With a network of rivers, an enjoyable way to explore the beautiful countryside is by boat, stopping off at a riverside pub – or two!

Places of interest

East Sussex: Eastbourne; Bexhill; historical towns of Hastings and St. Leonards.

West Sussex: Chichester; Bognor Regis; Arundel, with castle; Littlehampton.

Surrey: Guildford castle and cathedral; Mole Valley; Royal Horticultural Society's gardens at Wisley; Chessington World of Adventures; Dorking, a renowned centre for antiques; Runnymede; Thorpe Park in Chertsey.

Kent: Leeds Castle and gardens, the oldest stately home in the country; Canterbury, a designated World Heritage Site; Dover, with museum and castle; traditional seaside resort of Folkstone; Hever Castle in Sevenoaks; market town of Maidstone; Isle of Thanet incorporating Margate, Broadstairs and Ramsgate.

Did you know?

Hastings is home to Britain's first Norman castle, built by William the Conqueror.

Some of England's finest writers have found inspiration from living in Sussex – Rudyard Kipling, Sir Arthur Conan Doyle and A.A. Milne.

Bexhill housed one of the country's first cinemas and was the first to permit 'risqué' mixed sea bathing.

The world famous McLaren F1 racing team has its base in Woking.

Runnymede takes its name from the meadow where the Magna Carta, the great charter of English liberties, was sealed by King John in 1215.

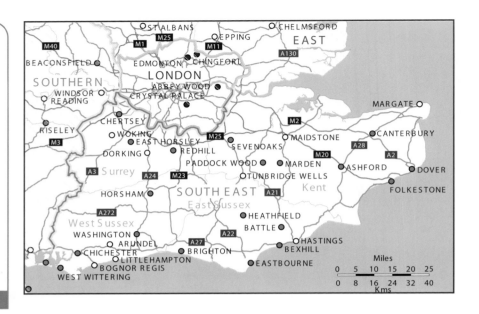

Ashford

Broadhembury Caravan & Camping Park

Steeds Lane, Kingsnorth, Ashford TN26 1NQ (Kent) T: 01233 620859. E: holidaypark@broadhembury.co.uk

alanrogers.com/UK3040

In quiet countryside just outside Ashford and within easy reach of London, Dover, Folkestone and the Kent coast, this sheltered park is attractively landscaped. There are areas for family camping with play areas and amenities designed with children in mind and separate quiet meadows just for adults with new luxury facilities. In total the park takes 65 touring units of any type. The well kept pitches are on level grass and backed by tall, neat hedges, with over 80 electricity connections (10/16A). In addition, five pitches are fully serviced and ten more have double hardstanding plus a grass area for an awning. The welcome is friendly at this popular park and it is often full in the main season. Reservation is advised for busy times. Thoughtfully considered amenities in the family area include a very good toilet block, well equipped campers' kitchen and provision for children of all ages. The new facilities in the couples area incorporate ecological consideratons with solar panels for heating and hot water, with rain water harvesting planned. LED lighting, low wattage hair and hand dryers and underfloor heating have all been used. Security arrangements are excellent, with coded entry through the gates and onto the park. A trip to France is easily possible with the International railway terminal at Ashford (Paris in two hours) – take your passport. A member of the Best of British Group.

Facilities

Well equipped toilet block for the family areas and new, ecologically considered block for the couples meadows, both kept very clean. Underfloor heating. Private cabins. High quality facilities for disabled visitors (can also be used as a family bathroom). Well equipped laundry room. Good campers' kitchen, fully enclosed with microwaves, fridge and freezer, all free of charge. Motorcaravan service point. Well stocked shop (bread and papers to order). Internet access. Pool room, games room with video games, table football and table tennis. Two play areas (one for children under 7 yrs) with wood-chip bases. Play field away from the touring area. Campers' herb garden. WiFi (charged). Dog exercise field – up to two dogs per pitch are accepted. Large units are accepted if pre-booked. Off site: Fishing 300 m. Golf 1 mile. Riding 2 miles. Beach 12 miles.

Open: All year.

Directions

From M20 exit 10 take A2070. After 2 miles follow sign for Kingsnorth. Turn left at second crossroads in Kingsnorth village. GPS: 51.10647, 0.86809

Charges guide

Per unit incl. 2 persons and electricity	£ 21.50 - £ 25.00
extra person	£ 5.50
child (5-16 yrs)	£ 2.00 - £ 3.50
tent incl. 2 persons	£ 18.00 - £ 22.50

Less 10% for bookings of 7 nights or more.

Battle

Crazy Lane Tourist Caravan Park

Crazy Lane, Sedlescombe, Battle TN33 0QT (East Sussex) T: 01424 870147. E: info@crazylane.co.uk

alanrogers.com/UK2960

This simple, neat two acre park has just 36 pitches arranged on grassy terraces, all with electricity (10A) and four with hardstanding. Many pitches are used by seasonal units so it may be best to phone to make sure space is available before travelling long distances. There is a sloping field towards the top of the site, popular with tent users. With easy access from the A21 (some background road noise), the park is set in the heart of 1066 country with its historical links. Other local attractions within easy reach include the pretty village of Sedlescombe, a steam railway, an organic vineyard and the seaside at Hastings. This is an ideal park for couples.

Facilities

New solar heated toilet facilities are unisex providing excellent private rooms, each with WC, shower and washbasin. Laundry facilities. Shop at reception. Caravan storage. Off site: Bus stop and pub in the village. Golf 0.5 miles. Riding 2 miles. Fishing 3.5 miles. The fascinating towns of Battle and Rye, plus Hastings (6.5 miles) with its beaches, markets and Heritage Shipwreck Centre.

Open: March - October.

Directions

From the A21, 6 miles north of Hastings, 100 yds. south of junction with B2244 (to Sedlescombe), turn right into Crazy Lane. Site is immediately on the right. GPS: 50.92453, 0.53495

Charges guide

Per unit incl. 2 persons and electricity	£ 17.00 - £ 21.00
extra person (over 8 yrs)	£ 2.00
dog	£ 1.50

No credit cards.

Crazy Lane Tourist Park

Whydown Farm, Crazy Lane, Sedlescombe Battle TN33 0QT East Sussex
Tel/Fax: +44 (0)1424 870147 • info@crazylane.co.uk

WELCOME!
Gill and Ron Morgan would like to welcome you to Crazy Lane Tourist Caravan Park. This family-run park is in a quiet, secluded, sun-trapped valley in the heart of '1066' country within easy reach of beach and historical sites.

Battle

Brakes Coppice Park

Forewood Lane, Crowhurst, Battle TN33 9AB (East Sussex) T: 01424 830322. E: brakesco@btinternet.com

alanrogers.com/UK2965

Brakes Coppice Park is a small and secluded site set in woodland just a mile away from historic Battle. Reached by an uneven, winding private track, it is signed to prevent visitors taking a wrong turn to the nearby farm of the same name. Ideal for tents, but welcoming any type of unit, the site has 30 grassy pitches, 21 with 6A electricity and TV aerial points, in a gently sloping field. An adjacent area of 15 small pitches has been set aside for adults only. A further area near a small fishing lake provides a few extra pitches. As well as fishing, visitors can enjoy walking in the surrounding woods. There is a wooden play area for younger children in the centre of the main field. The reception building at the site entrance also doubles as the shop and is stocked with basic essentials. Barbecues can be borrowed and a wealth of information about the attractions of 1066 Country can be found here.

Facilities

The single toilet block is simple but adequate. Facilities for disabled visitors. Laundry. Shop. Gas supplies. Fishing permits from reception. Off site: Pubs and shops in Crowhurst and Battle. Crowhurst station 10 minutes walk.

Open: 1 March - 31 October.

Directions

From Battle follow the A2100 towards Hastings for about 2 miles. Turn right on Telham Lane (signed Crowhurst). Continue into Foreword Lane and turn left on private track shortly after passing sign for Crowhurst village. GPS: 50.89065, 0.507083

Charges guide

Per unit incl. 2 persons	£ 12.00 - £ 14.00
incl. electricity	£ 14.00 - £ 16.00
extra person	£ 2.50
child (5-15 yrs)	£ 0.75
dog	£ 0.25

Booking is advisable.

For latest campsite news visit
alanrogers.com

Bexhill
Chestnut Meadow Camping & Caravan Park

Ninfield Road, Sidley, Bexhill-on-Sea TN39 5JG (East Sussex) T: 01424 892361.
E: info@chestnutmeadow.co.uk **alanrogers.com/UK2945**

In a peaceful country location near Bexhill, with Hastings and rural East Sussex to explore close by, a family, long used to camping themselves, have developed this into an attractive park. The well drained sheltered meadow is virtually surrounded by trees, with a glimpse of the sea. Flowers and shrubs enhance the entrance and buildings. The 75 large touring pitches (up to 150 sq.m) are marked by posts with numbered buckets which can be used for recycling. Seventy four have electricity (16A) and 22 have hardstanding beneath the grass, eight with their own water and drainage. They are well spaced, with the central area kept free for children to play and adults to gather and relax.

Facilities

Excellent new, heated sanitary building. Shop with local produce at reception. Bar, café (good value, serving breakfast through to evening meal) and takeaway (all high season and weekends). Launderette. Games hall with snooker, pool, table tennis, air hockey, table football. Large, new, fenced play area. WiFi. Off site: Golf and riding 1 mile. International fishing lakes 5 miles. Beach 3 miles. Drusillas Family Park 16 miles.

Open: Mid March - mid January.

Directions

The park is northwest of Bexhill on the A269 Ninfield Road between Sidley and Ninfield, with a 110 yd. entrance drive. GPS: 50.865412, 0.447312

Charges guide

Per unit incl. 2 persons and electricity	£ 22.00 - £ 28.00
extra person	£ 4.50

Bexhill
Kloofs Camping & Caravan Park

Sandhurst Lane, Whydown, Bexhill-on-Sea TN39 4RG (East Sussex) T: 01424 842839.
E: camping@kloofs.com **alanrogers.com/UK2955**

This peaceful, rural park is situated in a quiet country lane with countryside views yet within easy reach of several well known towns on the East Sussex coast. Set in three acres, Kloofs is owned and run by Terry and Helen Griggs who have taken great care in making this a most attractive and well maintained park. There are 50 level, generously sized touring pitches, divided into two areas. Most are on hardstanding, making them suitable for all-weather touring, and have 10/16A electricity, water and drainage. It is evident that considerable investment has ensured that visitors have a comfortable stay.

Facilities

One main, centrally heated toilet block has washbasins in cubicles and spacious hot showers. Large shower room for families and good en-suite facility for disabled visitors. Heated kitchen area. Washing machine, dryer, iron and board. Small shop in reception. Wooden adventure style play area, fenced. Small library. Off site: Footpath to village for pubs and other eating places 1.4 miles. Watersports, golf, riding and fishing all nearby. Beach 2 miles.

Open: All year.

Directions

From the north (Battle, Catsfield, Ninfield), take A269 and turn right into Pear Tree Lane, then right at crossroads. Sandhurst Lane is 300 yds. on the left and site is signed a short way down on the right. GPS: 50.8560, 0.4271

Charges 2012

Per unit incl. 2 persons, electricity and water	£ 25.00
extra person	£ 7.50

Brighton
Sheepcote Valley Caravan Club Site

East Brighton Park, Brighton BN2 5TS (East Sussex) T: 01273 626546
alanrogers.com/UK2930

Brighton is without doubt the South of England's most popular seaside resort and the Caravan Club's Sheepcote Valley Site is a first class base from which to enjoy the many and diverse attractions both in the town and this area of the south coast. A wide tarmac road winds its way through the site from reception, with gravel pitches on either side, leading to terraces with grass pitches on the lower slopes of the valley. The 169 pitches all have electricity (16A) and 86 have hardstanding.

Facilities

Two heated sanitary blocks include all washbasins in private cabins. Well equipped room for wheelchair users, another one for walking disabled and two baby and toddler wash rooms. Laundry facilities. Motorcaravan service point. Gas available. Milk and bread from reception. Play area with safety base. Off site: Brighton is 2 miles with a bus service from the entry road.

Open: All year.

Directions

From the M23/A23, join A27 (Lewes). Exit for B2123 (Falmer and Rottingdean). At roundabout turn left on B2123. Continue for 2 miles then turn right at traffic lights by Downs Hotel into Warren Ave. After 1 mile turn left into Wilson Ave, crossing racecourse. In 1.75 miles at foot of hill (just before lights) turn left and follow lane to site. GPS: 50.820975, -0.097799

Charges guide

Per person	£ 5.40 - £ 7.60
pitch incl. electricity (non-member)	£ 13.70 - £ 17.50

For latest campsite news visit
alanrogers.com

Canterbury
Yew Tree Park

Stone Street, Petham, Canterbury CT4 5PL (Kent) T: 01227 700306. E: info@yewtreepark.com

alanrogers.com/UK3060

Yew Tree Park is a small, quiet site located in the heart of the Kent countryside overlooking the Chartham Downs. Just five miles south of Canterbury and eight miles north of the M20, it is ideally placed either to explore the delights of the ancient city or the many attractions of eastern and coastal Kent. With some caravan holiday homes, the site also has 45 pitches for tourers and tents. The 20 pitches with electricity (10A) are marked on mainly level grass either side of the entrance road, the remainder unmarked on a rather attractive, sloping area, left natural with trees and bushes creating cosy little recesses in which to pitch. There are mobile homes and apartments to rent.

Facilities

Two sanitary blocks can be heated. Washbasins (H&C) and four showers (on payment). Toilet/shower room for families and disabled visitors. Laundry and dishwashing sinks, plus a washing machine, dryer and iron. Gas supplies. Outdoor heated pool (53x30 ft; June-Sept). Play area. WiFi (charged). Torches useful. Dogs are not accepted. Off site: Pub (serving food) 100 m.

Open: Easter - mid October.

Directions

From south, take exit 11 from M20. From Canterbury, on B2068 continue towards Folkestone. From either direction, turn into road beside Chequers Inn, turn left into park and follow road to reception. GPS: 51.2168, 1.058183

Charges guide

Per unit incl. 2 persons	£ 17.30 - £ 22.30
extra person	£ 4.00 - £ 5.00

Canterbury
Canterbury Camping & Caravanning Club Site

Bekesbourne Lane, Canterbury CT3 4AB (Kent) T: 01227 463216. E: canterbury.site@thefriendlyclub.co.uk

alanrogers.com/UK3070

Situated just off the A257 Sandwich road, about 1.5 miles from the centre of Canterbury, this site is an ideal base for exploring Canterbury and the north Kent coast, as well as being a good stopover to and from the Dover ferries, and the Folkestone Channel Tunnel terminal. There are 200 pitches, 109 with electric hook-ups (10/16A) and, except at the very height of the season, you are likely to find a pitch, although not necessarily with electricity. Most of the pitches are on well kept grass with hundreds of saplings planted, but there are also 72 pitches with hardstanding (more are planned).

Facilities

Two modern toilet blocks, the main one with a laundry room. Motorcaravan service point. Reception stocks a small range of essential foods, milk and gas. Excellent tourist information room. Play area with equipment on bark chippings. WiFi throughout (charged). Off site: Golf adjacent. Shop 0.5 miles. Bicycle hire 2 miles.

Open: All year.

Directions

From A2 take Canterbury exit and follow signs for Sandwich - A257. After passing Howe military barracks turn right into Bekesbourne Lane opposite golf course. Do not use sat nav due to narrow lanes. GPS: 51.2769, 1.113533

Charges 2012

Per person	£ 7.75 - £ 9.45
pitch (non-member)	£ 7.10

Chertsey
Chertsey Camping & Caravanning Club Site

Bridge Road, Chertsey KT16 8JX (Surrey) T: 01932 562405

alanrogers.com/UK2810

This long-established site (1926) is splendidly located on the banks of the River Thames, only a few minutes walk from the shops and amenities of Chertsey. A flagship site for the Club, it was totally redeveloped a few years ago at a cost of over £1 million. There are 200 pitches including 56 new serviced pitches with hardstanding and 16A electricity, and 15 super service pitches which have TV aerial points, water and waste drainage. The work included a new road system, heated toilet blocks with facilities for disabled visitors, recreation hall and much more.

Facilities

The well equipped toilet blocks can be heated and include washbasins in cabins and facilities for disabled visitors. Hairdryers. Laundry. Motorcaravan service point. Well stocked shop (08.00-11.00 and 16.00-18.00). Fish and chip van calls at weekends. Recreation hall. Play area on bark. Fishing (adults £1.70, NRA licence needed). Short dog walk areas. Caravan storage. Torches are necessary. WiFi (charged). Off site: Golf and bicycle hire 1 mile. Bus service in Chertsey 1.5 miles. Trains in Weybridge 3 miles.

Open: All year.

Directions

From M25 use junction 11. Turn left at roundabout on A317 towards Shepperton and continue to second set of traffic lights. Turn right then almost immediately left watching for green Club camp sign just before Chertsey bridge; the opening is narrow. GPS: 51.38986, -0.49008

Charges guide

Per person	£ 7.85 - £ 11.30
child (6-18 yrs)	£ 2.85 - £ 6.50
pitch (non-member)	£ 14.95 - £ 18.40

For latest campsite news visit
alanrogers.com

Chichester

Warner Farm Touring Park

Warner Lane, Selsey, Chichester PO20 9EL (West Sussex) T: 01243 604499. E: touring@bunnleisure.co.uk

alanrogers.com/UK2885

This site is a member of the Bunn Holiday Villages group, owners of several large holiday home parks which surround the pretty holiday town of Selsey. Warner Farm is a top quality touring park with 174 large grassy pitches and 47 on hardstanding, all with electrical connections. Pitches have a generally open aspect and there is a large area at the back of the site, the 'Camping Field', which offers an unmarked camping area, as well as providing picnic tables and barbecues. There are 42 serviced pitches with electricity, water and waste water. The site is modern and well maintained, and benefits from free access to the extensive leisure facilities on offer at the neighbouring holiday villages. These include the Oasis Pool and Leisure Complex with two indoor pools, a fun fair, a number of bars and restaurants and a lively 'top name' entertainment programme and kids' club. Surprisingly, the site retains a pleasant rural feel with plenty of space despite its proximity to the sea and the resort of Selsey.

Facilities

Modern toilet block with facilities for disabled visitors. Preset showers in large cubicles. Washing machines and dryers. Small shop. Takeaway. Play area. Multisport area. Communal barbecues, picnic area and dog walking area. Free shuttle bus to neighbouring parks. WiFi throughout (charged). Off site: Nearest beach 900 m. Oasis Pool and Leisure Complex, indoor pools, fun fair, bars, restaurants, entertainment and kids' club. Bicycle hire. Tennis.

Open: 1 March - 30 October.

Directions

Head for Chichester on the A27. At the Whyke roundabout join B2145 and follow signs to Selsey. Go across mini-roundabout, continue past entrance to Bunn Leisure. After next mini-roundabout take second right into School Lane, right into Paddock Lane, then first left into Warner Lane. Follow signs to park. GPS: 50.73815, -0.79913

Charges guide

Per unit incl. up to 4 persons and electricity	£ 21.00 - £ 37.00
extra person	£ 10.00

Chichester

Chichester Camping & Caravanning Club Site

345 Main Road, Southbourne PO10 8JH (West Sussex) T: 01243 373202

alanrogers.com/UK2320

This small, neat site is just to the west of Chichester and north of Bosham harbour. Formerly an orchard, it is rectangular in shape with 58 pitches on flat, well mown lawns on either side of gravel roads. All pitches have 16A electricity, 42 with level hardstanding. Although the A27 bypass takes most of the through traffic, the site is by the main A259 road so there may be some traffic noise in some parts (not busy at night). Opposite the park are orchards through which paths lead to the seashore. Arrival must be before 20.00 unless prior arrangements have been made with the site manager.

Facilities

The well designed, brick built toilet block is of first class quality. Fully tiled and heated in cool weather, with facilities for campers with disabilities (access by key). Washing machines and dryers. Gas supplies. WiFi (charged). No ball games permitted. Dogs can be walked in the lane opposite the entrance. Off site: Bicycle hire 1 mile. Fishing and golf 5 miles. Riding 6 miles. Chichester.

Open: 2 February - 19 November.

Directions

Park is on A259 Chichester - Havant road at Southbourne, 750 yds. west of Chichester Caravans. Coming from the west, it is 2.8 miles from the A27/A259 junction near Havant. GPS: 50.84498, -0.90299

Charges 2012

Per person	£ 7.85 - £ 11.70
child (6-18 yrs)	£ 2.85 - £ 6.75
pitch (non-member)	£ 7.10

Chichester

Chichester Lakeside Park

Vinnetrow Road, Chichester PO20 1QH (West Sussex) T: 0845 815 9775. E: lakeside@ParkHolidaysUK.com

alanrogers.com/UK2875

Located just outside the historic city of Chichester, this large site is a member of the Park Holidays group. Set amidst ten fishing lakes, it is within easy access of a sandy beach and the traditional resort of Bognor Regis. The 115 touring pitches with electricity (16A) are on three sides of a large, level and grassy field, the fourth side being used for seasonal units and storage. The central, unmarked space is for tents and caravans with no electric hook-ups and a large, fenced area provides space for sports and organised events for the whole park. The larger part of the park is occupied by 400 holiday caravans and the central entertainment area.

Facilities

Two, dated toilet blocks are likely to be under pressure at busy times. Facilities for disabled visitors. Shop. Dated bar and snack bar. Entertainment complex. Swimming pool. Fishing. Playing field. Children's club (high season). Tourist information. Mobile homes for rent. WiFi throughout (charged). Off site: Riding 2 miles. Golf 2.5 miles. Beach 3 miles. Nearby resort of Bognor Regis (good selection of cafés, restaurants and shops). Walking and cycle routes. Chichester (cathedral city).

Open: 1 March - 31 October.

Directions

The park is well signed on either side of a roundabout at the junction of the A27 and A259. Turning south on Vinnetrow Road, the park is 200 yards on the right. GPS: 50.823885, -0.75119

Charges guide

Per unit incl. 2 persons	
and electricity	£ 9.00 - £ 26.00
extra person	£ 2.00 - £ 4.00
child (under 2 yrs)	free
dog	£ 2.00 - £ 4.00

Dover

Hawthorn Farm Caravan & Camping Site

Martin Mill, Dover CT15 5LA (Kent) T: 01304 852658. E: info@keatfarm.co.uk

alanrogers.com/UK3100

Hawthorn Farm is a large, relaxed park near Dover. Set in 27 acres, it is an extensive park taking 226 touring units of any type on several large meadows which could accommodate far more, plus 160 privately owned caravan holiday homes in their own areas. Campers not requiring electricity choose their own spot, most staying near the toilet blocks, leaving the farthest fields to those liking solitude. There are 112 pitches with electricity (10/16A), 46 of which are large and separated by hedges, the remainder in glades on either side of tarmac roads. There are 15 new hardstandings available.

Facilities

Two heated toilet blocks are well equipped and of good quality. Facilities for disabled visitors. Baby room. Launderette. Motorcaravan services. Breakfast and other meals are served at the shop (all season). Gates close at 20.00 (22.00 in July/Aug), £10 deposit for card. Caravan storage. Off site: Martin Mill railway station 500 yds. Riding 0.5 miles. Golf 3 miles. Bicycle hire, fishing and boat launching 4 miles.

Open: 1 March - 31 October.

Directions

Park is north of the A258 road (Dover - Deal), with signs to park and Martin Mill where you turn off about 4 miles from Dover. GPS: 51.16855, 1.346333

Charges guide

Per unit incl. 2 persons	
and electricity	£ 16.50 - £ 20.50
unit over 7 metres with electricity	£ 21.00 - £ 26.00
extra person	£ 3.00
child (5-16 yrs)	£ 2.00
dog	£ 1.50

Less 10% for 4 nights booked
(and paid for on arrival).

For latest campsite news visit
alanrogers.com

East Horsley

Horsley Camping & Caravanning Club Site

Ockham Road North, East Horsley KT24 6PE (Surrey) T: 01483 283273

alanrogers.com/UK2820

London and all the sights are only 40 minutes away by train, yet Horsley is a delightful, quiet unspoilt site with a good duck and goose population on its part lily covered lake (unfenced). It provides 130 pitches, of which 73 have 10A electrical connections and 51 are on hardstandings. Seventeen pitches are around the bank of the lake, the rest further back in three hedged, grass fields with mostly level ground but with some slope in places. A new area has been developed in woodland. There is a range of mature trees and a woodland dog walk area (may be muddy).

Facilities

Two purpose built, heated toilet blocks with good design and fittings, with some washbasins in cabins, a Belfast sink and parent and child room with vanity style basin, toilet and wide surface area. Laundry room and new drying areas. Well designed facilities for disabled visitors. Small shop in reception. Play area. Recreation hall with table tennis. Fishing is possible from May (adult £6.10/children £3.10 per day, NRA licence required). WiFi (charged). Off site: Shops and the station are 1 mile. Pubs 1.5 - 2 miles. Golf 1.5 miles. Riding 2 miles.

Open: 1 April - 31 October.

Directions

From M25 junction 10, in the direction of Guildford, after 0.5 miles take first left B2039 to Ockham and East Horsley, continuing through Ockham towards East Horsley. After 2 miles start to watch for brown site sign (not easy to see) and site is on right in 2.5 miles. GPS: 51.28504, -0.44869

Charges guide

Per person	£ 7.65 - £ 10.15
child (6-18 yrs)	£ 2.65 - £ 2.85
pitch (non-member)	£ 14.75 - £ 17.25

Eastbourne

Fairfields Farm Caravan & Camping Park

Eastbourne Road, Westham, Pevensey BN24 5NG (East Sussex) T: 01323 763165.
E: enquiries@fairfieldsfarm.com **alanrogers.com/UK2915**

Part of a working, family-run farm, this is a simple peaceful park which is ideally located to enjoy the Sussex countryside and coast, just a short distance from Eastbourne. A single, rectangular meadow is split by a line of attractive silver birch trees and provides 66 large pitches, all but four with electricity connections. The farm and its rural landscape stretch towards the sea at Pevensey Bay and you can walk through the fields to the beach. Beyond the camping field there is a duck pond with grassy surrounds and picnic benches, pens with numerous small animals and pets and a pleasant walk to a fishing lake. Children are invited to feed the animals (with special food on sale). Within walking distance are the villages of Westham and Pevensey with a choice of pubs and restaurants, as well as Pevensey Castle which has a history spanning 16 centuries. Eastbourne has a promenade, beautiful beaches and a retail complex and cinema at the Sovereign Centre.

Facilities

The single, central toilet block is traditional in style and very clean. An adjacent building houses showers and toilets for disabled visitors. Laundry facilities. Farm shop. Small animals and pets. Fishing lake (licence required). WiFi (charged). Off site: Pubs, restaurants and fish and chip shop within walking distance. Beach 1.5 miles. Golf 4 miles. Eastbourne 5 miles.

Open: 1 April - 31 October.

Directions

From the roundabout junction of the A27 and A259 (Petrol station) take exit to Pevensey and the Castle. Go around the castle walls and into Westham village. At end of high street turn left (B2191), over level crossing and park is on left. GPS: 50.81358, 0.32448

Charges guide

Per unit incl. 2 persons	£ 17.00 - £ 18.50
incl. electricity	£ 20.50 - £ 22.00
extra person	£ 3.00
child (3-13 yrs)	£ 2.50
dog	£ 2.50

For latest campsite news visit
alanrogers.com

Eastbourne

Bay View Park

Old Martello Road, Pevensey Bay BN24 6DX (East Sussex) T: 01323 768688. E: holidays@bay-view.co.uk

alanrogers.com/UK2920

This friendly beachside park is located at the end of a private road right beside the beautiful Sussex coast and its pebble beach and the park's own brand new 9-hole golf course. Two separate areas of grass (some areas are a little uneven) are surrounded by low banks and hedges to give some shelter if it is windy. Careful use of wooden fencing adds to the attractiveness, whilst also keeping the rabbits off the flowers. The 94 touring pitches (80 sq.m, most with 16A electricity and some with hardstanding) are neatly marked and numbered. Several caravan holiday homes for hire are positioned at the back of the park. The golf course clubhouse provides tea, coffee and snacks. Visitors can enjoy all the attractions of Sussex, as well as swimming, fishing and windsurfing. This is an ideal park for a family beach holiday. A cycle path leads to Pevensey Bay and Eastbourne's new Sovereign Harbour marina with its shops, restaurants and cinema.

Facilities

Each area has toilet facilities, one a new, fully equipped block with private cubicles (shower, washbasin and WC) and facilities for babies and disabled visitors. Heated when required, both blocks are kept very clean. Fully equipped laundry room. Motorcaravan services. Well stocked shop. Golf (9-holes). Clubhouse for tea, coffee and snacks. Gas. Children's play area (10 yrs and under). Winter caravan storage. Off site: Sailing club. Sea fishing. Indoor swimming pool 1 mile. Bicycle hire (delivery to site) 1 mile. Riding 5 miles.

Open: 1 March - 31 October.

Directions

From the A27/A259 roundabout at Pevensey take A259 through Pevensey Bay. Park and golf course are signed after 1 mile (private access road) to the left, 2 miles east of Eastbourne. GPS: 50.79998, 0.33797

Charges guide

Per unit incl. 2 persons and electricity	£ 20.00 - £ 23.00
extra person	£ 3.00
child (5-16 yrs)	£ 2.00
dog	£ 1.00

Couples and families only.
No commercial vehicles, large vans or pick-ups.

BAY VIEW PARK
HOLIDAY HOMES, TOURING AND CAMPING

Tel:	01323 768688
Fax:	01323 769637
E-mail:	holidays@bay-view.co.uk
Web:	www.bay-view.co.uk

Award-winning caravan and camping park next to the beach on Eastbourne's sunshine coast

Folkestone

New Beach Holiday Park

Hythe Road, Dymchurch TN29 0JX (Kent) T: SiteTelephone. E: newbeach@parkholidaysuk.com

alanrogers.com/UK3085

New Beach Holiday Park is a member of the Park Holidays group. This is a popular family park located between Hythe and Dymchurch on Kent's south coast. This is a lively site in high season with a varied entertainment programme and a club for children (5-14 years). Evening entertainment is of a high standard and is organised on a nightly basis in peak season. Leisure facilities include a heated indoor swimming pool, an adventure playground and amusement arcade. There is a dining area and takeaway food facility. Off site, Dymchurch is a lively resort with a number of pubs and restaurants, as well as a station on the famous Romney, Hythe and Dymchurch steam railway. Inland, the mysterious Romney Marsh is an ideal place for cycling with miles of flat lanes and tracks.

Facilities

Shop. Bar. Restaurant. Indoor swimming pool. Adventure playground. Amusement arcade. Entertainment and activity programme (including children's club). Tourist information. Mobile homes and chalets for rent. Off site: Dymchurch (shops and restaurants). Port Lympne Wild Animal Park. Romney Marsh.

Open: 1 March - 31 October.

Directions

Leave the M20 at exit 11 (Canterbury). At roundabout take third exit onto the B2068 (signed Hastings, Hythe). At roundabout take second exit onto Ashford Road (A20). Entering Newingreen at T-junction turn left onto Hythe Road (A261, signed Hythe). Continue onto London Road (A261). Enter Hythe and at traffic lights continue onto Scanlons Bridge Road (A2008). Turn right onto Dymchurch Road (A259) and New Beach is on the right. GPS: 51.043687, 1.027458

Charges guide

Per unit incl. 2 persons and electricity	£ 9.00 - £ 24.00

For latest campsite news visit
alanrogers.com

Folkestone

Black Horse Farm Caravan Club Site

385 Canterbury Road, Densole, Folkestone CT18 7BG (Kent) T: 01303 892665

alanrogers.com/UK3090

This neat, tidy and attractive 6 acre park, owned by the Caravan Club, is situated amidst farming country in the village of Densole on the Downs just 4 miles north of Folkestone, 8 west of Dover and 11 south of Canterbury. Accessed directly from the A260, the tarmac entrance road leads past reception towards the top field which has gravel hardstanding pitches with a grass area for awnings (possibly some road noise), past hedging to the smaller middle area with 8 hardstandings, then to the large bottom field which has been redeveloped to give 140 large pitches (including 15 for tents and some extra large for large motorhomes), all with electricity (16A).

Facilities

Two carefully thought out and well constructed toilet blocks have washbasins in private cabins with curtains, good sized shower compartments, a baby room and facilities for disabled visitors, laundry and dishwashing facilities, all well heated in cool weather. Motorcaravan service point. Gas supplies. Play area. A fish and chip van calls on Thursdays (April-Sept). Caravan storage. Off site: Riding 1 mile. Golf and fishing 5 miles.

Open: All year.

Directions

Directly by the A260 Folkestone - Canterbury road, 2 miles north of junction with A20. Follow signs for Canterbury. GPS: 51.132617, 1.158483

Charges guide

Per person	£ 4.30 - £ 6.20
child (5-16 yrs)	£ 1.30 - £ 2.20
pitch incl. electricity (non-member)	£ 12.90 - £ 16.00

Folkestone

Little Satmar Holiday Park

Winehouse Lane, Capel-le-Ferne, Folkestone CT18 7JF (Kent) T: 01303 251188. E: info@keatfarm.co.uk

alanrogers.com/UK3095

Capel-le-Ferne is a relatively little known seaside town midway between Dover and Folkestone. Little Satmar is a quiet site a short walk from the delightful cliff top paths which run between these towns and which offer fine views across the English Channel. The site is a member of the Keat Farm group and is located about a mile from the village. There are 61 touring pitches, 51 of which have electricity (10A). The pitches generally have a sunny, open setting, a few with rather more shade. Privately owned mobile homes occupy 78 pitches between the entrance to the site and reception, but these are quite separate from the touring field.

Facilities

Two toilet blocks (one Portacabin style unit) are modern and kept very clean, and the main block has now been fitted with heating. Washing and drying machines. Shop (with gas). Play area. For more than 1 dog per unit, contact park. Off site: Bus at end of lane to Dover and Folkestone. Port Lympne Zoo, seafront funpark nearby.

Open: 1 March - 31 October.

Directions

Leave A20 Dover - Folkestone road at Capel-le-Ferne exit and follow signs to village. Site is clearly signed to right after about 0.75 miles. GPS: 51.101917, 1.222933

Charges guide

Per unit incl. 2 persons and electricity	£ 16.50 - £ 26.00
extra person	£ 3.00 - £ 3.50

Heathfield

Horam Manor Touring Park

Horam, Heathfield TN21 0YD (East Sussex) T: 01435 813662. E: camp@horam-manor.co.uk

alanrogers.com/UK2900

In the heart of the Sussex countryside, this rural touring park is part of (but under separate management from) Horam Manor which has a farm museum, nature trail and several fishing lakes. The 90 generously sized, numbered pitches, 54 with electricity, are on two open meadows. The area nearer reception has an undulating surface, the second field is flatter but slopes – levelling blocks are needed for motorcaravans. Both areas are ringed with a variety of mainly tall trees. The whole park, back from the main Eastbourne to Tunbridge Wells road, is a haven of peace and tranquillity.

Facilities

The well built toilet block (unheated) is fully equipped with some curtained cubicles. Family room (key from reception) with shower, washbasin, toilet and baby bath, suitable also for disabled visitors (not good for wheelchairs). Laundry. Gas supplies. Fenced play area (under 12 yrs). WiFi (charged). Off site: Horam Manor adjacent with café, fishing and riding. Shops and inns within walking distance. Tennis (small fee) 200 yds. Golf within 1 mile.

Open: 1 March - 31 October.

Directions

Horam is on the A267 between Tunbridge Wells and Eastbourne and entry to the park is signed at the recreation ground at southern edge of the village. GPS: 50.931783, 0.240167

Charges guide

Per unit incl. 2 adults, 2 children and electricity	£ 21.00 - £ 23.00
extra child	£ 2.50

For latest campsite news visit

alanrogers.com

Horsham

Honeybridge Park

Honeybridge Lane, Dial Post, Horsham RH13 8NX (West Sussex) T: 01403 710923.
E: enquiries@honeybridgepark.co.uk **alanrogers.com/UK2940**

This 15 acre park is situated amidst beautiful woodlands and countryside on the edge of the South Downs, within an Area of Outstanding Natural Beauty. Of the 150 pitches, 120 are for touring, some are on hardstandings and all have electricity (16A). The remaining pitches are occupied by holiday homes but these are in a separate area. Some pitches are hedged for privacy, others are on slightly sloping grass, well spaced and generously sized. A large wooden, adventure-style playground is provided for children away from the pitches, and simple family entertainment is organised on special occasions. A large games room provides darts, table tennis, pool, free use of many board games and a library. The tourist information centre is also here. This park is ideally situated for visiting the South Downs with its many attractive villages and the popular coastal resorts.

Facilities

Two modern toilet facilities (one new) are heated in cool weather and include spacious facilities for disabled visitors (Radar key). Laundry facilities. Motorcaravan service point. Licensed shop and café. Play area. Games room with library. Security barrier (card access) is locked 23.00-07.00. Caravan for hire. Off site: Bus 0.5 miles. Pub/restaurant in nearby Dial Post village. Old Barn Nurseries serves meals during the day. Fishing 1 mile. Riding 5 miles. Billingshurst and Horsham 8 miles. Golf and beach at Worthing 10 miles.

Open: All year.

Directions

Two miles south of the junction of A24 and A272 at Dial Post, turn east by Old Barn Nurseries. Follow signs to site (about 0.5 miles).
GPS: 50.94864, -0.35274

Charges guide

Per unit incl. 2 persons	
and electricity	£ 18.00 - £ 24.50
extra person	£ 3.25 - £ 6.50
child (5-14 yrs)	£ 2.50
dog	£ 1.35

Marden

Tanner Farm Touring Caravan & Camping Park

Goudhurst Road, Marden TN12 9ND (Kent) T: 01622 832399. E: enquiries@tannerfarmpark.co.uk
alanrogers.com/UK3030

Tanner Farm is a top class, quality park, developed as part of a family working farm in the heart of the Weald of Kent. It is surrounded by orchards, oast houses, lovely countryside and delightful small villages and the owners are much concerned with conserving the natural beauty of the environment. The park extends over 15 acres, most of which is level, and part gentle slope. The grass meadowland has been semi-landscaped by planting saplings, etc. which units back onto, as the owners do not wish to regiment pitches into rows. There are 100 pitches, all with 16A electricity, 38 with hardstanding, 25 with water tap and 12 with waste water point also.

Facilities

Two heated, well cared for sanitary units include some washbasins in private cubicles in both units. Facilities for disabled visitors. Bathroom (£1 token) and baby facilities in the newer block (closed Nov-Easter). Small launderette. Motorcaravan service point. Reception, shop and tourist information building (opening hours and stock limited in winter). Meeting/conference facilities. Gas supplies. WiFi in reception. Off site: Riding and golf within 6 miles. Many National Trust attractions in the area (Sissinghurst, Scotney Castle, Bodiam Castle).

Open: All year.

Directions

Park is 2.5 miles south of Marden on B2079 towards Goudhurst. GPS: 51.1471, 0.47482

Charges guide

Per person	£ 5.30 - £ 6.90
child (5-16 yrs)	£ 1.55 - £ 2.55
pitch incl. electricity (non-member)	£ 3.15 - £ 9.60
tent pitch	£ 1.65 - £ 6.60
Only one car per pitch permitted.	

For latest campsite news visit
alanrogers.com

Paddock Wood

The Hop Farm Touring & Camping Park

Maidstone Road, Paddock Wood TN12 6PY (Kent) T: 01622 870858. E: touring@thehopfarm.co.uk

alanrogers.com/UK3055

Set in 400 acres of the Garden of England, The Hop Farm is a popular family visitor attraction. There are plenty of activities to entertain children including adventure play areas (indoor and outdoor), a driving school, funfair rides, the Magic Factory and the Great Goblin Hunt. This is also the venue for many special events throughout the summer including music festivals, shows and other gatherings. To one side and overlooking all this activity and the attractive cluster of oasts is the touring park which provides over 300 grass and hardstanding pitches on flat, open fields. Electricity (16A) and water are available. There is also plenty more space for tents. The single toilet block is clean and provides simple facilities. It would be supplemented by portacabin units when events bring extra campers. Entry to the visitor attraction is half price for caravanners and campers and here are the Shires Restaurant and the Happy Hopper's café. This park would suit those looking to enjoy the visitor attraction or attend an event.

Facilities

Brick built toilet block with open washbasins, preset showers (with curtain) and toilets. Further Portacabin style units when the park is full for events. Small shop for essentials. Restaurant and café at the visitor attraction (half price entry for campers). Dogs accepted but not permitted inside the visitor attraction. Activities and entertainment at the visitor attraction. Off site: Shops, restaurants and golf courses nearby.

Open: 1 March - 31 October.

Directions

The Hop Farm is located on the A228 near Paddock Wood. Follow the brown tourist signs from junction 4 of M20 or junction 5 of M25 onto the A21 south. GPS: 51.200725, 0.39333

Charges guide

Per unit incl. 4 persons and electricity	£ 16.50 - £ 24.50
extra person (over 3 yrs)	£ 2.00
dog	£ 1.00

Redhill

Alderstead Heath Caravan Club Site

Dean Lane, Merstham, Redhill RH1 3AH (Surrey) T: 01737 644629

alanrogers.com/UK2800

Alderstead Heath is a surprisingly rural site given that it lies just 25 minutes from central London by train (from Coulsden, a London day ticket costs just £8.00). It is also well located for exploring the North Downs and is situated on the Pilgrim's Way. There are 150 touring pitches, all with 16A electrical connections. Most pitches are on well kept grass, but there are also 71 hardstandings. Given the proximity of the M25 and M23 motorways, there is a certain amount of background traffic noise in parts of the site, but this is not obtrusive. An attractive wooded area surrounds the site and concrete tracks there were laid during the war for tanks in preparation for the D-Day landings. Part of the site is used for seasonal pitches.

Facilities

Two well maintained toilet blocks, include a parent and toddler bathroom. The main block houses facilities for disabled visitors. Laundry facilities. Motorcaravan service point. Reception stocks a small range of essential foods, milk and gas. Two small play areas. Football field. Good tourist information room. WiFi throughout. Off site: Golf 2 miles. Fishing 3 miles.

Open: All year.

Directions

Leave M25 at junction 8 and join A217 signed Reigate. Fork left after 300 yds. (signed Merstham). After a further 2.5 miles turn left at T-junction and join A23. After 500 yds. turn right into Shepherd's Hill and after 1 mile turn left into Dean Lane. Site is on right after 175 yds. Do not allow sat nav to route via the M23/A23 (J7), where Dean Lane is very narrow. GPS: 51.283284, -0.138702

Charges guide

Per person	£ 4.60 - £ 6.20
child (5-16 yrs)	£ 1.30 - £ 2.20
pitch (non-member)	£ 13.15 - £ 16.00

Sevenoaks

Gate House Wood Touring Park

Ford Lane, Wrotham Heath, Sevenoaks TN15 7SD (Kent) T: 01732 843062.
E: contact@gatehousewoodtouringpark.com **alanrogers.com/UK3120**

This sheltered park has been created in a former quarry where all the pitches are on well drained grass. A spacious paved entrance with a new reception building and well stocked shop, leads on to the park itself. The 54 pitches are level and open with a few small trees, two brick built barbecue units, and 36 electric hook-ups (10A). A playground has swings, seesaw and a slide, all set on a safety base, and the entire site is enclosed by grassy banks on three sides, with a wild flower walk around the top.

Facilities

Comprehensive toilet facilities are well maintained, including a well equipped room which is designed for disabled visitors. The laundry and dishwashing room is at one end of the modern heated building. No dogs or other pets. Caravans/motorcaravans greater than 28 ft overall are not admitted. Commercial vehicles are not accepted. Off site: Within walking distance are three pubs and a good Cantonese restaurant. Golf 1 mile. Trains to London Victoria from Borough Green (2 miles). Riding 3 miles. Fishing 7 miles.

Open: 1 March - 31 October.

Directions

From M26 junction 2a, take A20 eastwards towards Wrotham Heath and Maidstone. Just past junction with A25, and opposite the Royal Oak pub, turn left into Ford Lane, and park is immediately on left. GPS: 51.300133, 0.345383

Charges guide

Per unit incl. 2 persons	£ 16.00 - £ 18.00
extra person	£ 4.00
child (5-12 yrs)	£ 2.50

No credit cards.

Washington

Washington Caravan & Camping Park

Old London Road, Washington RH20 4AJ (West Sussex) T: 01903 892869. E: washcamp@amserve.com
alanrogers.com/UK2950

Washington is a pleasant campsite to the north of Worthing with a bias towards tenting families and groups. It provides only 21 hardstanding pitches for caravans and motorcaravans, and a large gently sloping grassy field with enough space for 80 tents. There are 23 electric hook-ups (16A). There is some road noise from the A24. Local attractions (all with free admission, check opening times) include Highdown Chalk Gardens at Worthing, Nutbourne Vineyard near Pulborough, and Steyning Museum.

Facilities

A heated wooden chalet-style building houses the sanitary facilities including spacious shower rooms (20p) and indoor dishwashing and laundry facilities. No on-site shop but eggs, bread, butter and milk can be obtained from the reception office. Drinks machine and freezer. Off site: Bus stop 200 yds in village. Eating out options include the local pub and a nearby restaurant. Beach 9 miles.

Open: All year.

Directions

Site entrance is just east of the junction of A24 and A283 at Washington, 6 miles north of Worthing. GPS: 50.90875, -0.4056

Charges guide

Per unit incl. 2 persons	£ 21.00
extra person	£ 4.00 - £ 5.00
electricity on meter	£ 0.50
car	£ 5.00

West Wittering

Nunnington Farm Campsite

Rookwood Road, West Wittering PO20 8LZ (West Sussex) T: 01243 514013.
E: nunningtonfarm@hotmail.com **alanrogers.com/UK2895**

This no-frills, basic, family run farm site for touring units only can be found on the coast a mere seven miles from Chichester. There are 200 touring pitches, 110 with 15A electricity connections. The pitches are large, level and grassy, providing a comfortable feeling, even when the site is full. The safe, sandy beaches of The Witterings, only a mile away, make this an especially good venue for families in the holidays and a quieter one for off-season visitors. The easily accessible pets corner is an attraction for children of all ages. Visitors with tents are very welcome here and a second field is opened in busy periods, but with no electricity.

Facilities

Three rather dated but clean, central toilet blocks provide all facilities including showers in cubicles, open washbasins, baby bath, washing machines and ramped facilities for disabled visitors (key access). Motorcaravan service point. Gates closed 23.00-07.00. Off site: Local shops 300 yds. Bus service to Chichester every 30 minutes. Beach and boat mooring 1 mile. Bicycle hire 2 miles. Golf 3 miles.

Open: Easter - second week October.

Directions

From A27 at Chichester, take A286 signed The Witterings. Continue to roundabout. Take second exit on B2179 for West Wittering. Site is on left after 2 miles. GPS: 50.78377, -0.88588

Charges guide

Per unit incl. 2 persons and electricity	£ 22.00 - £ 25.00
extra person	£ 5.00

No credit cards.

The largest city in Europe, covering over 600 square miles, London is jam packed with hundreds of magnificent museums, impressive art galleries, historic buildings and monuments, beautiful parks, bustling shopping centres and markets; it really has something to offer everyone.

WE HAVE CHOSEN FOUR PARKS WHICH HAVE EASY ACCESS TO CENTRAL LONDON, INCLUDING ONE IN HERTFORDSHIRE

Despite its size, London is relatively easy to explore, largely thanks to the efficient underground service. Buses are also very useful and allow you to see the famous sights as you travel, in particular, the open-top tourist buses which ply the streets offer a good introduction to the city. Among London's many landmarks are the Tower of London, Trafalgar Square, Piccadilly Circus, Buckingham Palace, Big Ben and the Houses of Parliament, to name but a few! Running through the heart of London is the River Thames, dividing north and south; over the years many attractions, restaurants and chic bars have appeared along its banks. Being one of the most multicultural cities in the world, there is a huge choice of restaurants offering a diverse variety of cuisine; food markets are dotted all around the capital. Shopping is another major feature of the city, from the famous Harrods store and Harvey Nichols, to commercial Oxford Street and the street markets of Camden town and Portobello Road. If all the crowds become too much then head to one of London's beautiful parks such as St. James' Park next to Buckingham Palace, or Hyde Park, where you can take a boat trip along the Serpentine.

Places of interest

London Eye: world's highest observation wheel, reaching 443 feet. With 32 capsules, carrying 25 passengers in each, it offers breathtaking views.

Madame Tussaud's: huge collection of wax figures.

Tate Modern: contemporary art gallery housed in the converted Bankside Power Station.

Victoria & Albert Museum: decorative art and design from around the world.

Kew Gardens: beautiful botanical gardens, with over 40,000 varieties of plants.

London Dungeon: a grisly house of horrors.

Hampton Court Palace: one of the best palaces in Britain, with a maze.

British Museum: houses a treasure trove of objects from all over the globe.

Did you know?

One in eight of the UK population live in London and over 300 languages are spoken.

The London Underground dates back to 1863 when the first underground railway was opened from Paddington to Farringdon Street. Today, 150,000 people an hour enter the Tube network.

Founded in 1753, the British Museum is the oldest public museum in the world.

With 345 steps to the top, the Monument marks the start of the Great Fire of London.

London has over 21,000 licensed taxis.

At over 900 years old, the Tower of London has been a palace, prison, treasury, arsenal and even a zoo. It is now home to the Crown Jewels, which have been housed there since the 14th century.

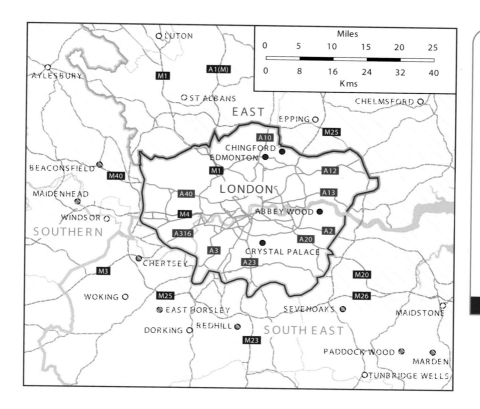

Abbey Wood

Abbey Wood Caravan Club Site

Federation Road, Abbey Wood, London SE2 0LS (London) T: 020 8311 7708

alanrogers.com/UK3260

Situated close to Abbey Wood, it is hard to believe that this park is in London and the wardens have made every effort to create an attractive environment. There are 120 level caravan pitches all with 16A electricity and TV aerial connections. Of these, 64 have hardstandings. A large tent area provides an additional 100 pitches. Many pitches benefit from shade by mature trees. A secure fence around the perimeter is linked to close circuit TV cameras for security and just outside is a late arrivals area with electric and toilets; also protected by cameras. This park attracts many UK and overseas visitors as it offers a very good base from which to visit central London. A train service runs every 15 minutes from Abbey Wood station (5 minutes walk) to either Charing Cross or Cannon Street.

Facilities

Three modern, fully equipped toilet blocks, two with underfloor heating, one designed to be open all year, include washbasins in cubicles, generous showers, baby/toddler washroom, laundry equipment and dishwashing sinks. Good private facilities for disabled visitors. Motorcaravan service point. Gas. Bread, milk and cold drinks from reception (high season). Play area. Good travel and information centre can provide tickets for travel and tourist attractions. Off site: Sports centre 1 mile. Golf 4 miles.

Open: All year.

Directions

From east on M2/A2 or from central London: on A2 (third exit) turn off at A221 into Danson Road (signed Bexleyheath, Welling and Sidcup). Follow sign Bexleyheath to Crook Log (A207 junction); at traffic lights turn right and immediately left into Brampton Road. In 1.5 miles at traffic lights turn left into Bostal Road (A206); in 0.75 miles at traffic lights turn right into Basildon Road (B213). In 300 yds. turn right into McLeod Road, in about 0.5 miles at roundabout turn right into Knee Hill; in 100 yds. turn right (second right) into Federation Road. Site on left in 50 yds. From M25, north, west or south approach: leave at junction 2 onto A2 (signed London), then as above.
GPS: 51.48693, 0.11757

Charges guide

Per person	£ 5.70 - £ 7.60
child (5-16 yrs)	£ 1.55 - £ 3.10
pitch incl. electricity (non-member)	£ 13.70 - £ 15.60
Tent campers apply to site.	

For latest campsite news visit
alanrogers.com

Chingford

Lee Valley Campsite

Sewardstone Road, Chingford, London E4 7RA (London) T: 020 8529 5689. E: scs@leevalleypark.org.uk

alanrogers.com/UK3250

This attractive site provides an excellent base from which to visit London, having both easy access to the M25 and excellent public transport links into the centre of London. Close to Epping Forest in the heart of the Lee Valley, this site is on a hillside overlooking the King George reservoir in a very pleasant and relaxed setting. Like its sister sites, it is understandably very popular with foreign tourers. With capacity for 200 units the site is mostly level, with several bush sheltered avenues and plenty of trees throughout providing shade. There are 20 pitches with tarmac hardstanding and 100 with electricity (10A). American motorhomes are not accepted. Just outside the gate is a bus stop (reception have full details of good value Travelcard schemes). The bus (no. 215) will take you to Walthamstow Central Underground station from where a frequent service runs to central London. Alternatively, you can park at South Woodford or Chingford stations and use the train for London visits. Staff are very helpful.

Facilities

Three blocks offer good facilities (one is heated in low season), all recently totally refurbished. Good en-suite room for disabled visitors. Baby changing area. Dishwashing. Laundry. Motorcaravan service point. Well stocked shop. Gas available. Playground. Off site: Fishing 500 yards. Shops within 2 miles. Riding 1 mile. 9-hole golf 1 mile, 18-hole golf 3 miles. Waltham Abbey 3 miles. River Lee Country Park and Epping Forest nearby.

Open: 1 April - 4 November.

Directions

From M25 take exit 26 on A112 to Chingford and site is on right in 3 miles. From A10 take A110 (Chingford). After passing between reservoirs, at next traffic lights turn left on A112. Site on left after 2 miles. GPS: 51.653983, -0.006517

Charges guide

Per unit incl. 2 persons	£ 24.90 - £ 38.20
child (under 16 yrs)	£ 2.50 - £ 5.50
electricity	£ 3.80

Min charge £8.60 per unit/night

Crystal Palace

Crystal Palace Caravan Club Site

Crystal Palace Parade, London SE19 1UF (London) T: 020 8778 7155

alanrogers.com/UK3270

The Caravan Club's site at Crystal Palace in south London provides easy access to the city centre and all its many attractions. The pitches are pleasantly arranged in terraces overlooking the ruins of the old Crystal Palace, its park and National Sports Centre. It is surprisingly quiet given its location (with the exception of police sirens and over-flying aircraft). In peak season advance booking is always necessary. Most pitches are on gravel hardstanding, so it is particularly useful for out of season stays. There are places for 126 caravans and motorcaravans, all with electricity (16A). Tents are placed on the site's well mown lawns near reception, where there are four additional electric points. The Crystal Palace park is extensive and provides open spaces for strolls or picnics and plenty of activities for children. The Sports Centre has two swimming pools, tennis and squash courts and gym facilities, with national events in a variety of sports to watch at certain times. An area at the site entrance is used for arrivals after 20.00.

Facilities

The main toilet block can be heated in cool weather with curtained washbasins for ladies. Another block provides basic unisex showers and toilets. Facilities for disabled visitors. Laundry room. Dishwashing sinks and rubbish bins. Motorcaravan service facilities. Gas available. Off site: Shops, pubs, etc. 400 yards. Many buses stop outside the site, including services to central London.

Open: All year.

Directions

On A205 South Circular road travelling east, pass Dulwich College and golf course on right, turn right at traffic lights. Within 400 yds, at traffic lights, turn right into Sydenham Hill. In 350 yds. at roundabout turn left. Site is 1 mile opposite mini-roundabouts. Travelling west on A205 South Circular, immediately after passing under Catford railway bridge, keep left onto A212 (Crystal Palace). After 2.75 miles, site is on left. GPS: 51.42587, -0.07379

Charges guide

Per person	£ 5.80 - £ 7.60
child (5-16 yrs)	£ 1.55 - £ 3.10
pitch incl. electricity (non-member)	£ 13.70 - £ 17.50

Tent campers apply to site.

Edmonton

Lee Valley Camping & Caravanning Park

Meridian Way, Edmonton, London N9 0AR (London) T: 020 8803 6900. E: leisurecentre@leevalleypark.org.uk

alanrogers.com/UK3230

Certainly one of the only sites in this guide with a multiplex cinema just outside the gate, you are greeted here by a very attractive entrance with flower displays. The site offers 140 spacious level pitches, with hardstandings and 100 with electricity hook-ups. The pitches are well laid out around a large field and there is a tent area just behind two grassy mounds. The grass and gardens are well trimmed and kept very tidy. The site also offers hook-up points for tents. The adjacent sports complex is being rebuilt and will be used for the 2012 Olympics. The cinema complex incorporates a pizza restaurant, and from here you can hop on a bus to Edmonton Green or Ponders End station from where there is a regular service into central London (journey time around 40 minutes). The friendly site managers have detailed information about the various Travel Card schemes available. Alternatively, historic Waltham Abbey, Epping Forest and the 1,000 acre River Lee Country Park are all within easy access. This is a popular site, very well looked after and kept clean and tidy by site managers, this is a peaceful stop within easy reach of the city.

Facilities

Two modern, heated toilet blocks include spacious showers and two large en-suite units for disabled visitors. Baby changing area. All facilities are accessed by combination locks. Dishwashing. Laundry. Motorcaravan service point. New barbecue area. Kitchen. Shop. Play area. Badminton. Off site: Cinema at entrance. Golf adjacent. Supermarket and fishing 0.5 miles. Riding 4 miles.

Open: All year excl. Christmas, Boxing Day and New Year's Day.

Directions

From M25 take exit 25. Follow signs for the city. At first set of traffic lights turn left (Freezywater). Continue on for about 6 miles. Follow signs for Lee Valley Leisure Complex. After roundabout (where A110 crosses), turn left at second set of traffic lights onto the complex. Follow site signs. GPS: 51.632383, -0.038383

Charges guide

Per unit incl. 2 persons	£ 24.90 - £ 38.20
extra person	£ 6.00 - £ 9.50
child (under 16 yrs)	£ 2.50 - £ 5.50
electricity	£ 3.80
Min. charge £ 9.60	

The East of England is a perfect mix of soft and gentle countryside, ancient cities, historical towns, and storybook villages. Its coastline is largely untouched and studded with nature reserves, ideal for birdwatching, while the traditional beach resorts offer old-fashioned seaside fun.

THIS REGION INCLUDES THE COUNTIES OF ESSEX, SUFFOLK, NORFOLK, CAMBRIDGESHIRE, HERTFORDSHIRE AND BEDFORDSHIRE

Bedfordshire and Hertfordshire are the smallest counties in the region, with peaceful canals, undulating countryside with chalk downs, and some of the greatest stately homes in the country. Essex is full of quaint villages with a smattering of old towns and traditional seasides resorts, including Colchester and Southend-on-Sea. The River Cam winds its way through Cambridgeshire; punting along the river in Cambridge is a good way to relax and take in the many famous university buildings that dominate the water-front along the 'Backs'. Further along the river is the ancient cathedral city of Ely, once an island before the Fen drainage. The flat Fenland has a network of rivers and canals, ideal for narrowboat trips, as are the Norfolk Broads. Norfolk itself is very flat, sparsely populated and tranquil, popular with walkers and cyclists, while the numerous nature reserves attract a variety of wildlife. It also has a beautiful coastline; the seaside towns of Great Yarmouth and Hunstanton are major draws. This unspoilt coastline stretches into Suffolk, 'Constable Country'. Full of space, with picturesque villages set amongst lush green countryside, dotted with timbered cottages and ruined abbeys, the county is home to Newmarket, the horse racing capital of the world.

Places of interest

Essex: Clacton-on-Sea; Walton-on-the-Naze, with nature reserve; Colchester, Epping; Chelmsford.

Suffolk: Ipswich; Felixstowe; Lowestoft; Bury St Edmonds; village of Clare with country park.

Norfolk: Norwich, seaside resort of Cromer; old fishing village of Sheringham, Sandringham Palace near King's Lynn; Banham Zoo.

Cambridgeshire: King's College and Chapel in Cambridge plus Fitzwilliam Museum; Peterborough; Imperial War Museum in Duxford; Huntingdon; Wildfowl & Wetland Trust near Wisbech.

Hertfordshire: St Albans; stately homes and gardens of Knebworth House and Hatfield House.

Bedfordshire: Bedford, Woburn with Abbey and safari park; Whipsnade Wild Animal Park; Shuttleworth Collection near Biggleswade.

Did you know?

Newmarket has been recognised as the Headquarters of Racing for over 300 years.

The highest point of the East of England is the Dunstable Downs at 244 metres.

Colchester is Britain's oldest recorded town with Europe's largest Norman Castle keep.

The artist John Constable was born in 1776 in the village of East Bergholt. Nearby Flatford Mill, was portrayed in his most famous scene, 'The Haywain'.

Peterhouse was the first Cambridge college, founded in 1284 by the Bishop of Ely.

Epping Forest was the haunt of the renowned highwayman, Dick Turpin.

Aldeburgh

Church Farm Holiday Park

Church Farm Road, Aldeburgh IP15 5DW (Suffolk) T: 01728 453433. E: aldeburgh@amberleisure.com
alanrogers.com/UK3350

This area of the Suffolk coast has always been a popular destination for visitors and Church Farm Holiday Park has an enviable location on the outskirts of Aldeburgh. The park includes a large area designated for caravan holiday homes as well as a separate touring area situated to the front of the park. The touring area provides 85 pitches for caravans and motorcaravans (tents and trailer tents are not accepted). Pitches are separated by attractive hedging that blends in well with the natural environment. Sixty two pitches have access to 16A electricity, as well as own water taps and a shared waste outlet (one between two pitches). The park lies opposite a shingle beach (to the south of Thorpeness) and is adjacent to a nature reserve, a haven for birds and other wildlife. The town of Aldeburgh is only 15 minutes walk away, where there are many pubs, restaurants and takeaways.

Facilities

The single toilet block has been fully upgraded with heating, free showers, toilets and washbasins (entry card with deposit). Access to the toilets and showers are via two steps, making it unsuitable for wheelchair users. However ambulant toilets are provided. Laundry room. Motorcaravan service point. Gas supplies. Off site: Bus service 0.5 - 1 mile. Shops, pubs, etc. 15 minutes walk. Beach 5 minutes walk. Fishing and bicycle hire 1 mile. Riding 6 miles.

Open: Easter - 31 October.

Directions

On arrival at Aldeburgh, site is signed at roundabout in the direction of Thorpeness. Where road meets seafront, site is on left. From town centre follow road along seafront to site on left at end of town.
GPS: 52.15827, 1.60330

Charges guide

Per pitch incl. all persons	£ 20.00 - £ 24.00
incl. services	£ 28.00 - £ 32.00

Cheques are not accepted.
Credit cards 2.5% surcharge.

For latest campsite news visit

alanrogers.com

Banham

Applewood Caravan & Camping Park

Banham Zoo, The Grove, Banham NR16 2HE (Norfolk) T: 01953 888370. E: caravanpark@banhamzoo.co.uk

alanrogers.com/UK3385

Applewood is a 13-acre touring park, adjacent to the famous Banham Zoo. One day's entrance fee gives unlimited access whilst on the campsite. Applewood has 200 pitches with 190 on level grass and ten on hardstanding; 120 have electric hook-ups (10A). The large central area has undelineated pitches for those who do not need electricity. Other pitches surrounding this area are in small groups separated by neat laurel hedges. There is a further area with pitches and a large field for rallies. Just four minutes walk from the park is a small supermarket, a pub/restaurant, a fish and chip shop and gift shops. At weekends, one of Norfolk's largest car boot sales is held in the arena area alongside the site. The zoo is an award winning attraction and home to almost a 1,000 amazing animals (open daily from 10am). Not far away the ancient market towns of Diss (Friday market) and Thetford are well worth a visit. Many of the scenes from the classic comedy, Dad's Army, were filmed around Thetford, which is the home to the Dad's Army museum.

Facilities

Two toilet blocks, one new and one refurbished provide clean and adequate facilities. Room for disabled visitors. Washing machine/dryer. Motorcaravan services. Gas supplies. Children's play area. Rally field and function room. Off site: Zoo adjacent. The Appleyard with shops and restaurant. Snetterton race circuit 3 miles. Diss 8 miles. Thetford and Norwich 15 miles.

Open: 10 February - 31 October.

Directions

Leave A11 at Attleborough, take B1077 south. Follow signs to New Buckenham and Banham Zoo. At T-junction with B1113 turn west. Continue through Banham. Park is on the left, entrance through Banham Zoo (not clearly signed). GPS: 52.44636, 1.02514

Charges guide

Per unit incl. electricity	£ 17.50 - £ 19.50

Bury Saint Edmunds

The Dell Caravan & Camping Park

Beyton Road, Thurston, Bury Saint Edmunds IP31 3RB (Suffolk) T: 01359 270121.
E: thedellcaravanpark@btinternet.com **alanrogers.com/UK3345**

Close to the A14 and surrounded by farmland, this small touring site, four miles east of Bury Saint Edmunds, provides a convenient base to explore the nearby town and surrounding villages or as a stopover point. The current owners have created 50 spacious pitches within the main touring area, divided into two sections – one of which is reserved for adults only. All pitches have 10A electricity. A separate field with a further 10 pitches situated under trees is available for contractors working locally, as well as any visitors who prefer shaded areas. The main touring field has some shade from well maintained hedges and the trees bordering the site. All pitches have access to the site's facilities. Food is available from local village pubs within two miles of the park. There is some noise from the nearby A14, especially to the south side of the park, but otherwise the site provides a quiet base for tourers to explore the area.

Facilities

Excellent and ample toilet and spacious shower facilities (free) are provided within a purpose built sanitary block. Ladies' toilets include a private bathroom and toilet. Family bathroom with bath, shower and baby changing facilities. Separate toilet/shower for disabled visitors. Laundry room. Motorcaravan service point. Off site: Bus service to Bury St Edmunds from outside park. Local pubs and restaurants in Thurston and neighbouring villages.

Open: All year.

Directions

From the A14 take exit for Thurston and Beyton, 4 miles east of Bury St Edmunds. Follow signs to Thurston. Park is on the left, shortly after arriving at Thurston and signed from Beyton. GPS: 52.24053, 0.82437

Charges guide

Per unit incl. 2 persons and electricity	£ 15.00 - £ 19.00
extra person	£ 3.00

For latest campsite news visit

alanrogers.com

Cambridge
Highfield Farm Touring Park

Long Road, Comberton, Cambridge CB23 7DG (Cambridgeshire) T: 01223 262308.
E: enquiries@highfieldfarmtouringpark.co.uk **alanrogers.com/UK3560**

Situated five miles from Cambridge, this eight-acre park is set in a delightfully quiet touring location yet close to major routes around Cambridge. The welcome is always warm from the friendly family owners. The facilities are of high quality and the grass and hedges are well cared for. Conifer hedges divide the site into five areas. There are also some shady glades for those who wish to retreat even further and one area is reserved for those without children. The pitches are fairly level and on grass with 60 numbered pitches for caravans and motorcaravans, and 60 for tents. All have 10A electricity and ten are on hardstanding. A good dog walk is provided, which can be extended to a pleasant 1.5 mile walk, with seats, around the farm perimeter. The site is a very good base for visiting the famous University town of Cambridge and a walking tour around the town exploring the colleges is highly recommended. The town can be accessed by car (park and ride recommended), by bus or by bike via a special cycle route. A member of the Best of British Group.

Facilities

Three heated toilet blocks provide more than adequate coverage and good facilities, all very clean and well maintained. Baby room but no dedicated provision for disabled visitors, although one block has extra wide doors and easy access. Laundry room. Small play area. Good shop. Motorcaravan service point. Excellent tourist information room. Gates closed midnight to 07.30.
Off site: Comberton village 0.5 miles. Golf 2 miles. Fishing 3.5 miles. Cambridge 5 miles. Duxford War Museum and National Trust properties.

Open: 30 March - 31 October.

Directions

From M11 exit 12, take A603 towards Sandy. After 0.5 miles turn right, B1046 to Comberton. Turn right just before village signed Madingley (also caravan sign). Site on right just north of village.
GPS: 52.194981, 0.031103

Charges guide

Per unit incl. 2 persons and electricity	£ 20.50 - £ 24.50
extra person	£ 4.00
child (5-16 yrs)	£ 2.50
dog	£ 1.00

No credit cards.

A warm welcome awaits you at our popular award winning park with its excellent facilities, set in peaceful farming countryside. It is close to the historic University City of Cambridge, the Imperial War Museum, Duxford and ideally suited for touring East Anglia.

Comberton, Cambridge CB23 7DG Tel/Fax: 01223 262308
www.highfieldfarmtouringpark.co.uk

Clacton-on-Sea

Homestead Lake Park

Thorpe Road, Weeley, Clacton-on-Sea CO16 9JN (Essex) T: 01255 833492.
E: lakepark@homesteadcaravans.co.uk **alanrogers.com/UK3300**

This well laid out, 25-acre park was opened in 2002. It is hidden from the road at the rear of Homestead Caravans' sales area and workshops in the countryside of the Tendring district, at Weeley near Clacton. It offers 50 fully serviced, hardstanding pitches on gently sloping ground overlooking a fishing lake and recently-built holiday lodge accommodation on the other side of the lake. Tents accepted for short stays only on a limited number of pitches. The park makes an ideal spot to stay either for fishing, for a relaxing weekend, or as a base for touring this part of Essex. A special area has been added to allow wheelchair users to fish. You could even arrange for your caravan to be serviced or repairs to be made while you stay. Homestead has a large accessories superstore and café, where breakfast is recommended.

Facilities

The toilet block offers clean and spacious facilities including an en-suite unit for disabled visitors. Baby changing facilities. Coffee shop/café and snack bar. Fishing lake. Woodland walks. Caravan sales, workshops and accessory shop. A large rally field is also available. Off site: The site is ideally situated for visiting the many attractions of this holiday area. The towns of Clacton-on-Sea, Frinton, Harwich and Brightlingsea are all within a 10-mile radius and the heart of 'Constable country', with Flatford Mill and Dedham, is a short drive away.

Open: 1 March - 31 October.

Directions

From Colchester take A120, then A133 signed Clacton. At roundabout, turn left on B1033 into Weeley and site and showrooms are on left just past council offices. GPS: 51.85989, 1.12021

Charges guide

Per unit incl. 2 persons	
and electricity	£ 15.50 - £ 22.50
extra person	£ 4.00
child (under 18 yrs)	£ 2.00
dog	£ 2.00

Colchester

Fen Farm Caravan & Camping Site

Moore Lane, East Mersea, Colchester CO5 8FE (Essex) T: 01206 383275. E: fenfarm@talk21.com
alanrogers.com/UK3290

Tents were first pitched at Fen Farm in 1923 and since then the park has 'grown rather than developed' – something of which owners Ralph and Wenda Lord and their family are proud. The 70 touring pitches are all unmarked, on level grass and within four fields that have a spacious feel to them. An area for 90 holiday homes is separate and screened from the touring area. All pitches have 10A electricity connections and three have hardstanding and are fully serviced. A limited number of seasonal pitches are available on the smaller field, with outstanding views and direct access to the beach. This is an attractive well laid out site with trees and two ponds. The site provides facilities for launching boats from the seashore and it is popular with water skiers and windsurfers. Jet skis are not allowed. There are also many opportunities for walking, either inland or along the beach.

Facilities

The toilet block in the main touring field includes a family room and shower/toilet for disabled visitors. Laundry room. Gas supplies. Two play areas. Caravan and boat storage. WiFi throughout (charged). Off site: Well stocked shop adjacent sells groceries, bread and milk. 'Pick your own' fruit farm and tea room. Shops, pubs, restaurants and banks in West Mersea. Pub within walking distance. Chinese and Indian takeaways will deliver to site.

Open: 19 March - 31 October.

Directions

From Colchester, take B1025 to Mersea Island. After crossing causeway, take left fork to East Mersea. Follow road for 2.75 miles to Dog and Pheasant pub. Site entrance is next right. NB. Access across the causeway onto Mersea Island is restricted at high tide. GPS: 51.78996, 0.98460

Charges guide

Per unit incl. up to 6 people	
and electricity	£ 18.00 - £ 25.00

Cromer

Woodhill Park

Cromer Road, East Runton, Cromer NR27 9PX (Norfolk) T: 01263 512242. E: info@woodhill-park.com

alanrogers.com/UK3500

Woodhill is a seaside site with good views and a traditional atmosphere. It is situated on the clifftop, in a large, gently sloping, open grassy field, with 300 marked touring pitches. Of these, 210 have electricity (16A), seven are fully serviced and many have wonderful views over the surrounding coastline and countryside. A small number of holiday homes are available with magnificent sea views. Although the site is fenced, there is access to the clifftop path which takes you to the beach. Locally, it is possible to take a boat trip to see the seals off Blakeney Point. Nearby attractions include the Shire Horse Centre at West Runton and the North Norfolk Steam Railway. Green technology plays a major role with solar panels added to one of the block roofs to heat the water. Access to nearby towns and resorts is available using the local bus stop outside the entrance, or by the tourist railway.

Facilities

Two modern toilet blocks with all necessary facilities including two family rooms with bath, showers, basin and WC, and four rooms with shower, basin and WC. Washing machine and dryer. Well stocked shop (19/3-31/10). Good, large adventure playground and plenty of space for ball games. Crazy golf. Giant chess and golf course adjacent to the site. Off site: Beach 0.5 miles. Fishing and shop 1 mile. Bicycle hire, golf and riding 2 miles. Bird Reserve at Cley. National Trust properties. North Norfolk Tourist Railway. Boat trips.

Open: 19 March - 31 October.

Directions

Site is beside the A149 coast road between East and West Runton. GPS: 52.93742, 1.26250

Charges guide

Per unit incl. 2 persons	
and electricity	£ 15.65 - £ 18.95
extra person	£ 2.60
child (4-16 yrs)	£ 1.05
dog	£ 2.15 - £ 3.75

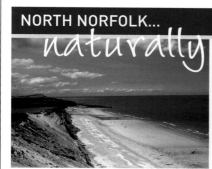

NORTH NORFOLK... naturally

Woodhill Park

Relax in your touring caravan or tent enjoying peace and tranquillity with magnificent views of the sea and surrounding North Norfolk countryside. Multi-service, electric pitches and amenity buildings available. Luxurious centrally heated holiday homes for hire.

Bookings or brochure **01263 512242** or online **www.woodhill-park.com** Cromer Road, East Runton, Cromer, Norfolk NR27 9PX

East Harling

The Dower House Touring Park

Thetford Forest, East Harling NR16 2SE (Norfolk) T: 01953 717314. E: info@dowerhouse.co.uk

alanrogers.com/UK3390

Set on 20 acres in the heart of Britain's largest forest on the Suffolk and Norfolk borders, The Dower House provides quiet woodland walks and cycle ways, with an abundance of wildlife. David and Karen Bushell continue to upgrade the facilities without compromising the park's natural features. There are 160 large pitches, 72 with electricity (10A). Most are reasonably level, although given the forest location there are a few tree roots. Six pitches for visitors with mobility problems are linked by a path to the main facilities. Torches are recommended as the site is unlit at night (ideal for stargazing!)

Facilities

Two toilet blocks, one with a baby room. A separate building houses the showers and a unit for disabled visitors. Dishwashing. Washing machine and dryer. Well stocked shop. Information room. Quiet rooms (no games machines). Heated outdoor swimming pool (31/5-1/9, under 15s must be with an adult). Paddling pool. Caravan storage. Torches necessary. Off site: Fishing nearby 1.5 miles. Riding 2 km. Bicycle hire 4 km. (bikes delivered to site). Snetterton motor racing circuit and Sunday market 2-3 miles. Walks and cycle rides in the forest.

Open: 25 March - 2 October.

Directions

From A11 (Thetford - Norwich) road, 7 miles east of Thetford, turn right on B1111 to East Harling. Turn right at church and in just under a mile turn right on unpaved road (site signed). Entrance in 0.8 miles. GPS: 52.42829, 0.89631

Charges guide

Per unit incl. 2 persons	£ 9.75 - £ 22.25
incl. electricity	£ 13.25 - £ 25.95
extra person	£ 5.00
child (4-15 yrs)	£ 2.00
No charge for awnings or dogs.	

Fakenham

The Old Brick Kilns Caravan & Camping Park

Little Barney Lane, Barney, Fakenham NR21 0NL (Norfolk) T: 01328 878305.
E: enquiries@old-brick-kilns.co.uk **alanrogers.com/UK3400**

This is an excellent, tranquil, family run park with a friendly, helpful atmosphere. The park's development on the site of old brick kilns has resulted in land on varying levels. This provides areas of level, well drained pitches with many on hardstanding. There are 65 pitches in total, all with electricity (16A) and 30 are fully serviced. A wide range of trees and shrubs provide shelter and are home for a variety of wildlife. There are garden areas, including a butterfly garden and a conservation pond. A comfortable bar area and restaurant open five days a week. A member of the Best of British Group.

Facilities

Very good heated toilet blocks provide very clean facilities. Baby room. Facilities for disabled guests (Radar key). Laundry room. Motorcaravan service point. Good shop with gas supplies. Bar/restaurant (5 days a week, April-Oct) and takeaway food (July/Aug). TV/games room. Giant chess. Library. Fenced play area. Fishing. WiFi (charged). B&B also available. Caravan storage. Off site: Golf 5 or 8 miles. Riding and bicycle hire 6 miles. Beach 7 miles.

Open: All year excl. 2 January - 14 March.

Directions

From Fakenham take A148 Cromer road north east. After 6 miles, at Thursford, fork right on B1354 signed Melton Constable. In 0.4 miles, turn right to Barney, and then first left along a narrow country lane with passing places, for 0.5 miles. GPS: 52.85804, 0.97583

Charges guide

Per unit incl. 2 persons	£ 16.00 - £ 22.00
extra person	£ 4.00

Great Yarmouth

Clippesby Hall

Clippesby, Great Yarmouth NR29 3BL (Norfolk) T: 01493 367800. E: holidays@clippesby.com
alanrogers.com/UK3485

Set in the heart of the Broads National Park this is a spacious, high quality site where you can be sure of a warm welcome from the Lindsay family, who have lived in the Hall for many years. Clippesby offers the choice of pitching amongst the shady woodland, on the gently sloping lawns of the hall with colourful mature trees and shrubs or in a new area, The Meadow, which offers fully serviced pitches with hardstanding. The 100 pitches are well spaced and clearly numbered (70 have 10A electricity). Children can roam at will in safety, and parents can relax and unwind at this beautiful park. Facilities include a sunken grass tennis court, a play area, a timber adventure playground, a football pitch and family golf with a seaside theme. There is also a small, heated simming pool with a separate paddling pool. The Muskett Arms with an attractive and comfortable family bar and a sheltered courtyard outside, provides fresh, home-cooked meals, music nights and other family entertainment. Susie's Coffee Shop has a good selection of food during the day. The Broads and Great Yarmouth are on the doorstep.

Facilities

Three timbered heated toilet blocks provide very clean, modern facilities. Some cabins with washbasin and WC. En-suite room for disabled visitors. Family room with baby changing. Laundry. Gas. Shop (Easter-end Oct). Café and family bar/restaurant (early May-end Oct). Pizza takeaway. Small swimming pool and paddling pool (end May-end Sept). Adventure play area. Football. Bicycle hire. Max. 1 dog per pitch. Dog walk. WiFi (free). Off site: Bus service 1.5 miles. Fishing 2 miles. Riding 3 miles. Beach 5 miles.

Open: All year.

Directions

From the A47 Norwich - Great Yarmouth road at Acle roundabout take exit for Filby (A1064). After 1.5 miles fork left on B1152 signed Potter Heigham. Take first left and park is 100 yds. on the right. GPS: 52.67283, 1.58299

Charges guide

Per unit incl. 2 persons and electricity	£ 14.75 - £ 33.75
extra person	£ 5.50
child	£ 2.75

Great Yarmouth

The Grange Touring Park

Ormesby St Margaret, Great Yarmouth NR29 3QG (Norfolk) T: 01493 730306. E: info@grangetouring.co.uk
alanrogers.com/UK3490

The appearance of this family touring site is that of a garden, with hanging baskets, flower beds, bluebells and daffodils under the trees in spring, all carefully tended by the resident wardens. There are 70 level pitches with electricity (16A), 13 with hardstanding, and ten pitches for tents, all arranged on well trimmed grass with tarmac access roads. Adjacent to the campsite is The Grange – a free house offering meals, beers and real ale, plus children's play equipment (open all year). The site owner also has a holiday campsite at Hemsby (four miles) with its own wide sandy beach, which guests at The Grange are welcome to use. The nearest beach is a mile away and local attractions include Caister Castle and Motor Museum and the Norfolk Rare Breed Centre. Great Yarmouth Centre with many attractions and The Broads are within 5 miles.

Facilities

A modern, heated toilet building is spacious and well maintained, housing all the usual facilities including free showers. Baby room in the ladies'. Laundry room with washing machine and dryer. Washing lines are provided at the rear of the building. Gas supplies. Internet café and WiFi (£3 per hour or per 24 hours if using own computer). Three family/disabled rooms and a motorcaravan service point have been added. Off site: Bus service 250 yds. Beach, shops and supermarket 1 mile. Riding 2 miles. Golf 3 miles. Fishing 4 miles. Great Yarmouth 5 minutes drive.

Open: Mid March - early October.

Directions

Site is just north of Great Yarmouth. Entrance is just south of the roundabout at the northern edge of the Caister bypass. GPS: 52.66812, 1.71097

Charges guide

Per unit incl. up to 4 persons and electricity	£ 15.00 - £ 21.50
extra person	£ 3.50
child (under 5 yrs)	free
dog	free - £ 3.50

THE GRANGE TOURING PARK Yarmouth Road, Ormesby St. Margaret, Great Yarmouth, Norfolk NR29 3QG **www.grangetouring.co.uk** info@grangetouring.co.uk **Tel: 01493 730306 - 01493 730023** **Fax: 01493 730188**	This level grassy park will accommodate seventy touring outfits and tents and adjoins the grounds of the Grange Free House. It is very conveniently situated as a touring centre for Great Yarmouth, the Norfolk Broads and the historic Cathedral City of Norwich. We are approximately one mile from the beach.	

Great Yarmouth

Rose Farm Touring Park

Stepshort, Belton, Great Yarmouth NR31 9JS (Norfolk) T: 01493 780896.
E: myhra@rosefarmtouringpark.fsnet.co.uk **alanrogers.com/UK3382**

Rose Farm, open all year, although close to Great Yarmouth is quietly situated offering campers space with peace and tranquillity. There are 145 reasonably level pitches, 20 are on hardstanding and the remainder on grass; 90 have electricity (16A). The park is split into three separate areas. The first is large and open, surrounded by fencing, the second area is long with pitches either side of the road and beyond this is an open area mainly for tents. A new toilet/shower block here offers top quality facilities, both blocks are immaculate with thoughtful decor.

Facilities

The two attractive blocks offer excellent facilities including 2 family rooms with shower, toilet and basin. Washing machine and dryer, iron and ironing board. Facilities for disabled visitors (pitching can be arranged in advance). Adventure playground. TV/information room. Dog walk. WiFi. Off site: Shops nearby. Bus stop. Sailing 2 miles. Fishing and golf 3 miles. Riding and bicycle hire 4 miles. Beach 5 miles.

Open: All year.

Directions

From Great Yarmouth and Gorleston take the A143 signed Beccles and Diss. At dual carriageway (Bradwell) turn right (signed Holiday Parks) to Burgh Castle. In 0.75 miles, take next right, site on right in 25 yds. GPS: 52.57136, 1.66876

Charges guide

Per unit incl. 2 persons and electricity	£ 16.00 - £ 20.00
tent with 2 persons	£ 12.00 - £ 17.00
extra person	£ 2.50 - £ 3.50
dog	free

Special offers available. No credit cards.

For latest campsite news visit
alanrogers.com

Great Yarmouth

Long Beach Caravan Park

Long Beach, Hemsby, Great Yarmouth NR29 4JD (Norfolk) T: 01493 730023. E: info@long-beach.co.uk

alanrogers.com/UK3492

This is a large caravan park alongside the sandy dunes bordering the sea. There are 270 reasonably level grassy pitches with 150 for touring, 90 with electricity (10-16A). About 30 touring pitches, open all season, are in the Long Beach site dotted amongst the static caravans close to all the main facilities. Most of the touring pitches are in the Hemsby Touring Park, a few hundred yards further inland and only open during school holidays. Here there are two large grassy fields with little shade and many of these pitches are a long way from the toilet block and other facilities. The beach and dunes extend for many miles along the coast offering plenty of opportunity for walking, beach activities and fun in the local amusement arcades. The nearby nature reserve is within walking distance. Not far away is the small seaside resort of Hemsby, the popular Great Yarmouth, the historic cathedral city of Norwich and the famous Norfolk Broads. There is a busy entertainment programme in July and August.

Facilities

Several small old but clean toilet blocks in main section plus one modern toilet block in the Hemsby section offering all necessary facilities. Shop, bar, restaurant, games room (open all season) in main section. Beach with miles of sand dunes. Play area. Sea fishing. WiFi (charge). Off site: Hemsby close by. Bicycle hire (800 yds). Great Yarmouth 5 miles, Norwich 18 miles.

Open: 14 March - 4 November.

Directions

Hemsby is 5 miles north of Great Yarmouth. Leave Great Yarmouth on the A149, bypass Caister and at Hemsby turn east towards beach and site. GPS: 52.7017, 1.7028

Charges guide

Per unit incl. 4 persons and electricity	£ 13.00 - £ 22.50
dog	£ 3.50

High season minimum stay 7 days (Sat-Sat).

LONG BEACH ESTATE COMPANY

Estate Office - Long Beach - Hemsby - GREAT YARMOUTH - NR29 4JD
Tel. 01493 - 73 00 23 - info@long-beach.co.uk - www.long-beach.co.uk

Harleston

Little Lakeland Caravan Park

Wortwell, Harleston IP20 0EL (Norfolk) T: 01986 788646. E: information@littlelakeland.co.uk

alanrogers.com/UK3480

This peaceful hideaway with its own fishing lake is tucked behind the houses and gardens that border the village main street. It is a traditional, mature little park with just 58 pitches. There are several caravan holiday homes and long stay units, but there should always be around 22 places with 10A electricity for touring units. The pitches are mostly individual ones separated by mature hedges and trees giving varying amounts of shade. Fishing in the attractive lake is free of charge and solely for the use of campers (bream, tench, roach, perch and carp). There are many local way-marked walks around Wortwell and nearby Harleston. Many interesting villages are close by with their weekly markets. A member of the Countryside Discovery Group.

Facilities

A modern, heated toilet block provides washbasins all in cubicles for ladies, and one for men. Fully equipped laundry. Separate en-suite room for disabled visitors also has facilities for baby changing. A further unit (also heated) by reception provides a shower, WC and basin per sex and is used mostly in the colder months. Reception stocks gas, newspapers and some basic essentials. Small play area. Library of paperback books in the summer house. Fishing (max. 4 rods per unit). WiFi (charged). Off site: Bus service on the main road 250 yds. Pub (with food) 500 yds. Golf and bicycle hire 4 miles. Riding 6 miles. Diss 12 miles. Beccles 13 miles.

Open: 15 March - 31 October.

Directions

Approaching from Diss, leave A143 at roundabout signed Wortwell. Continue to village, pass The Bell public house, a garage on the right, then turn right at first bungalow (Little Lakeland Lodge) watching carefully for signs. Site is down lane, 250 yds. on right. GPS: 52.41628, 1.35282

Charges 2012

Per unit incl. 2 persons and electricity	£ 18.00 - £ 21.00
extra person	£ 3.50
child (4-16 yrs)	£ 2.00

No credit cards.

For latest campsite news visit
alanrogers.com

Hunstanton

Searles Leisure Resort

South Beach Road, Hunstanton PE36 5BB (Norfolk) T: 01485 534211. E: bookings@searles.co.uk

alanrogers.com/UK3520

This is a high quality 'all-in' family holiday park on the North Norfolk coast offering everything for a great seaside family holiday. There is a beach within walking distance, a covered 'town plaza' including a sports bar, Chinese restaurant and American diner plus fish and chip bar, club house, pools, Country Club, golf course and driving range, fishing lakes and bowling greens; there should be something to entertain everyone. There are 823 pitches with 323 variable sized pitches for touring, 129 with 16A electricity. Some are on hardstanding and fully serviced with others on grass. There is an open area reserved for tents.

Facilities

Three large, modern, clean toilet blocks with washbasins and toilets in cubicles. Facilities for disabled visitors. Baby room. Launderette. Dishwashing facilities. Food hall. Restaurants, bars and cafés. Hair and beauty salon. Indoor and outdoor heated swimming pools. Gym. Tennis. Soft play area. Golf (9-hole course, driving range and putting course). Fishing lake. Bowling green. Bicycle, pedalo hire. WiFi. Off site: Nearest beach 400 yds. Hunstanton, attractive seaside resort with Sealife Sanctuary, water sports and boat trips 0.5 miles. Stately homes. Birdwatching at Snettisham and Titchewell. Sandringham.

Open: All year, excl. 25th Dec.

Directions

From King's Lynn take A149 north to Hunstanton. At first roundabout take B1161. After 0.3 miles cross roundabout (supermarket), site immediately on left. GPS: 52.93033, 0.48289

Charges guide

Per pitch	£ 15.00 - £ 39.00
fully serviced pitch	£ 17.00 - £ 53.00
dog	£ 3.00

Huntingdon

Wyton Lakes Holiday Park

Banks End, Wyton, Huntingdon PE28 2AA (Cambridgeshire) T: 01480 412715. E: loupeter@supanet.com

alanrogers.com/UK3555

Wyton Lakes is a family run, adults only park with four well stocked fishing lakes, very close to the River Great Ouse, between Huntingdon and St Ives. There are 80 level pitches of medium size with 60 for caravans and motorcaravans and 20 for tents. The tent pitches are on grass and have no electricity. The other pitches are mainly on hardstanding with gravel for awnings and all have electricity (16A) and a water tap. Most of the pitches border the lakes making fishing possible from the pitch. Well placed as a centre for touring, the park has easy access for large outfits. The old market towns of Huntingdon and St Ives are three miles away and the pretty village of Houghton with its old mill, pub and riverside walks is just one mile. Just across the road is a large garden centre complete with restaurant and coffee shop.

Facilities

Heated toilet block with all necessary facilities including those for campers with disabilities. Coarse lake and river fishing on payment (carp, bream, tench, perch, roach and rudd). Riverside walks. WiFi (charged). Off site: Garden centre, restaurant and coffee shop opposite entrance. Interesting old village of Houghton, pub, shop, National Trust mill, riverside walks, 1 mile. St Ives, Huntingdon, boat hire and golf 3 miles. Huntingdon Race Course 4 miles. Paxton Pits Nature Reserve. Hinchingbrooke Park.

Open: 1 April - 28 October.

Directions

From the A14 take exit 26 (St Ives). Take the A1096 north towards St Ives over four roundabouts. Turn left onto A1123, signed Huntingdon and site entrance is on the left in about 2 miles opposite garden centre. GPS: 52.33664, -0.13872

Charges guide

Per unit incl. 2 persons and electricity	£ 16.00
tent pitch incl. 2 adults	£ 13.00 - £ 15.00
extra adult	£ 2.00

Adults only (over 18 yrs). No credit cards.

For latest campsite news visit
alanrogers.com

Ipswich

Low House Touring Caravan Centre

Bucklesham Road, Foxhall, Ipswich IP10 0AU (Suffolk) T: 01473 659437. E: low.house@btinternet.com

alanrogers.com/UK3310

Set in a sheltered 3.5 acres, this site has 30 level, grass pitches and an abundance of shrubs and flowers. The park has been divided into two areas bordered by mature trees and the grounds are well maintained. There are many different varieties of trees with a tree walk leading round two sides of the park. All the pitches have electrical connections (10/16A) and they back onto trees that provide plenty of shade and the opportunity to observe a range of wildlife. A good bus service to Ipswich stops nearby. Low House lies between Felixstowe (8 miles) and Ipswich (4 miles) and would be a useful stopover for the Felixstowe port or Harwich.

Facilities

The older style, heated sanitary block is spotlessly clean with hot showers (50p). Motorcaravan service point. No on-site provisions but a supermarket is 2 miles (towards Ipswich). Frozen goods can be stored. Secure play area. Pet area with rabbit, hens and guinea fowl. Off site: Pub in Bucklesham village (1.5 miles) and other good pubs nearby. Golf 2 miles. Fishing 3 miles.

Open: All year.

Directions

Turn off A14 (was A45) Ipswich ring road (south) via slip road onto A1156 (signed Ipswich East). Follow road over bridge crossing over the A45 and almost immediately turn right (no sign). After 0.5 miles turn right again (signed Bucklesham) and site is on left after 400 yds. GPS: 52.03402, 1.24507

Charges guide

Per unit incl. 2 adults, 2 children and electricity	£ 14.00 - £ 20.00
extra person	£ 3.00
child (5-14 yrs)	£ 2.00
dog	free

No large commercial vehicles. No credit cards.

Ipswich

Westwood Park Caravan Park

Old Felixstowe Road, Bucklesham, Ipswich IP10 0BW (Suffolk) T: 01473 659637.
E: info@westwoodcaravanpark.co.uk **alanrogers.com/UK3335**

This park opened in Easter 2007 and has been developed on land previously owned by the neighbouring farm. The park is situated between Felixstowe and Ipswich and is within easy reach of the River Deben and Woodbridge. The 90 level grass and hardstanding pitches are of varying size to accommodate both small and large caravans, motorcaravans and tents. All pitches have 16A electricity. Families are welcome and a grass area has been fenced off for football and other games at the far end of the park. A dog walking area has been created screened by shrubs along two sides of the park and a nature area to encourage local wildlife is also being developed.

Facilities

A brand new, but traditionally built, toilet block in the centre of the park includes facilities for disabled visitors (£5 deposit for key). Laundry. Purpose built reception provides local information and sells a limited range of provisions e.g. milk. Recycling facilities planned. Grass play area for children. WiFi (charged). Off site: Free range eggs from a farm (short walk). Bus service to Ipswich nearby. Pubs serving meals in nearby Bucklesham and surrounding villages. Fishing 2 miles. Golf 3 miles. Beach 5 miles.

Open: All year excl. 16 January - 28 February.

Directions

Site is near Bucklesham. From the A12 (south) or A14(12) (north) take A14 towards Felixstowe. Continue for 5 miles and turn left signed Kirton, Bucklesham and Brightwell. Continue for about 1 mile: park is on the right, immediately after Tenth Road on the left. GPS: 52.02316, 1.28389

Charges guide

Per unit incl. 2 persons, 2 children and electricity	£ 18.00 - £ 20.00
extra person	£ 2.50

Ipswich

Orwell Meadows Leisure Park

Priory Lane, Ipswich IP10 0JS (Suffolk) T: 01473 726666. E: recept@orwellmeadows.co.uk

alanrogers.com/UK3315

This popular, family park is set on the edge of the Orwell Country Park near Ipswich with its many miles of walks and the famous Orwell Bridge with views of the Suffolk countryside. The park is run by David and Sally Miles and offers an ideal spot for a family holiday with an outdoor swimming pool and a good clubhouse with a bar, restaurant and a shop. Spacious pitches are around the edges of several separate meadows (surrounded on three sides by earth banks), all offering 16A electricity hook-ups.

Facilities

The modern toilet block includes clean and spacious free showers. It is kept to a very high standard. En-suite facilities for disabled visitors. Well stocked shop. Bar and restaurant. Outdoor pool. Play area. TV/family room. Max. two dogs per unit. Off site: Market town of Bury St Edmunds.

Open: March - January.

Directions

From A14 Ipswich bypass take Nacton/Ipswich exit (north of the A14) and follow signs for Orwell Country Park (narrow lane). Cross single track bridge over A14 to site entrance 20 yds. on left.
GPS: 52.02044, 1.19161

Charges guide

Per unit incl. 2 persons	£ 15.50 - £ 22.00
extra person	£ 4.00 - £ 6.00

Kings Lynn

The Garden Caravan Site

Barmer Hall, Syderstone, Kings Lynn PE31 8SR (Norfolk) T: 01485 578220. E: nlmason@tiscali.co.uk

alanrogers.com/UK3460

In the quiet Norfolk countryside, this imaginative touring park is a sun trap set in an enclosed walled garden. Sheltered from the winds by the high walls, visitors can relax in peace and tranquillity. Attractive mature trees, shrubs and climbers provide shade at various times of the day. The Mason family run the site in a relaxed way and the atmosphere is superb. There are 30 pitches, all with electricity (16A) and TV hook-up, but little shade. Some are slightly sloping and will require blocks. Reception is housed in a small kiosk (not always manned, so pitch yourself and pay later).

Facilities

The single toilet block (heated) has all the usual facilities including a toilet and washbasin for campers with disabilities. Dishwashing sinks, spin dryer and iron. No shop, but gas (not 'Camping Gaz'), ices, soft drinks and fresh, free range eggs are available. Off site: Bicycle hire 4 miles. Riding 6 miles. Golf 10 miles. Norfolk Lavender, Langham Glass and the Thursford collection of steam engines and mechanical organs.

Open: 1 March - 1 November.

Directions

About 6 miles west of Fakenham leave A148. Take B1454 signed Docking and Hunstanton. After 3 miles turn right to Barmer Hall (site signed). Road marked 'unsuitable for motor vehicles' but continue for 0.3 miles. Beyond Hall turn left to site.
GPS: 52.86414, 0.69116

Charges guide

Per unit incl. 2 persons	£ 17.50 - £ 19.50
extra person	£ 7.50 - £ 8.50
No credit cards.	

Lowestoft

Kessingland Beach Holiday Park

Kessingland, Lowestoft NR33 7RN (Suffolk) T: 01502 740636.
E: holidaysales.kessinglandbeach@park-resorts.com **alanrogers.com/UK3370**

Set near the most easterly point in the UK, this park offers all you need for that total family holiday experience – pool tables, an amusement arcade and indoor and outdoor swimming pools. If you so wish you need never leave Kessingland Beach until your holiday ends. There is evening entertainment, as well as a selection of bars and a restaurant. Although mainly a large park for static caravan holiday homes, there is a touring area to the west of the park with quite spacious pitching. Electricity hook-ups are available. The toilet block is older in style but has been refurbished.

Facilities

The toilet block has been refurbished, but access is unsuitable for wheelchairs. Laundry. Shop. Bars, restaurants, fish and chips. Entertainment complex. Indoor and outdoor swimming pools. All-weather sports court. Adventure play areas. Tennis courts. Amusements. WiFi (charged). Off site: Beach and sea fishing 200 yds. Bicycle hire 1 mile. Golf and riding 3 miles. Boat launching 5 miles.

Open: 20 March - 26 October.

Directions

From Lowestoft, north, on A12 ignore first turning to Kessingland village and continue along A12 to next roundabout. Take left turning on roundabout signed Kessingland Beach. From A12 south, turn right at roundabout signed Kessingland Beach. At beach take sharp right continuing along to park entrance.
GPS: 52.40715, 1.72470

Charges guide

Per caravan or motorcaravan incl. electricity	£ 6.00 - £ 40.00

For latest campsite news visit

alanrogers.com

Mundesley-on-Sea

Sandy Gulls Caravan Park

Cromer Road, Mundesley-on-Sea NR11 8DF (Norfolk) T: 01263 720513. E: info@sandygulls.co.uk

alanrogers.com/UK3410

This is an adults only park on the outskirts of Mundesley-on-Sea. One of the only clifftop parks with space for touring units on this coastline, there are panoramic views from most pitches. All 50 pitches (14 on hardstanding) have 10A electricity and TV aerial hook-ups. The unmarked pitches are arranged on an unshaded sloping meadow, so levelling blocks are advised. Primarily a caravan holiday home park, there are mobile homes to rent. The facilities are well maintained but some distance from the pitches. Access to the Blue Flag beach is via a large tarmac ramp. The village of Mundesley is only a mile away with a nine-hole golf course and a variety of shops and pubs. There is much to see and do in this area of Norfolk with a steam railway further along the coast. North Walsham is within easy reach and has a good range of shops and supermarkets.

Facilities	Directions
The heated toilet block is modern and spacious offering large shower rooms and open washbasins, all kept very clean. TV aerial hook-ups. WiFi (charged). Off site: Shops, pubs and restaurants nearby. Mundesley-on-Sea 1 mile. Tennis, boat launching, riding and golf nearby. National Trust. Tourist railway. Norfolk Broads.	Site is 1 mile north of Mundesley (4 miles south of Cromer) on the main coast road. GPS: 52.88457, 1.42074

Charges guide

Per unit incl. up to 4 persons and electricity	£ 13.00 - £ 24.00
dog	free

Open: March - November.

Nestling on the Mundesley cliffs, the area's only cliff top touring park, affording panoramic sea views. Norfolk Broads National Park is only a short drive away. The park offers easy access to clean, sandy, Blue Flag beaches. Mundesley has been voted one of the country's best kept seaside villages. Electric & TV hookups. This small, family-operated park has been owned and run for more than twenty five years by the current family.

SANDY GULLS CARAVAN PARK, CROMER ROAD, MUNDESLEY, NORFOLK, NR11 8DF

North Walsham

Two Mills Touring Park

Yarmouth Road, North Walsham NR28 9NA (Norfolk) T: 01692 405829. E: enquiries@twomills.co.uk

alanrogers.com/UK3420

Two Mills is a quiet, adults only site with a long season. Set in the bowl of a former quarry, the park is a real sun trap, both secluded and sheltered, with bird song to be heard at all times of the day. Neatly maintained with natural areas, varied trees, wild flowers and birds, the owners, Barbara and Ray Barnes, want to add their own touches to this popular park. Following the purchase of an adjacent field, there are now 81 average sized, level pitches for tourers, including 72 serviced pitches (patio, water and waste water drainage), and 48 on hardstanding. All have electricity (10/16A). This is a good centre from which to explore the north Norfolk coast, the Broads or for visiting Norwich. A footpath from the park joins the Weavers Way. A member of the Best of British Group.

Facilities	Directions
Two neat, clean central toilet blocks can be heated, including some washbasins in cabins and en-suite facilities for disabled visitors. Washing machine, dryer and spin dryer. Small shop at reception. TV room/library with tea and coffee facilities. WiFi (charged). Dogs are accepted by arrangement only. Off site: Hotel/pub 100 yds. North Walsham 20 minutes walk. Bicycle hire 1.5 miles. Fishing, golf and coast 5 miles.	From A149 Stalham - North Walsham road, watch for caravan sign 1.5 miles before North Walsham (also signed White Horse Common). The road runs parallel to the A149 and site is on right after 1.25 miles. From North Walsham take Old Yarmouth road past hospital, and park is on left after 1 mile. GPS: 52.80661, 1.41708

Open: 1 March - 31 December.

Charges guide

Per unit incl. 2 persons and electricity	£ 16.00 - £ 20.00
full service pitch	£ 17.50 - £ 22.00
extra person	£ 3.50
dog (by arrangement)	£ 0.75
Senior citizen discounts.	

Norwich

Little Haven Caravan & Camping Park

The Street, Erpingham, Norwich NR11 7QD (Norfolk) T: 01263 768959. E: patlhaven@tiscali.co.uk
alanrogers.com/UK3450

Within easy reach of the coast and the Broads, this is a very attractive, peaceful little site with good facilities. Only adults are accepted. There are 24 grassy pitches, all with electricity (16A) and five with hardstanding. They are arranged around a central lawn, beautiful flower beds and a decorative pergola with seating area; a credit to the owner, who does all the work herself. There is no shop, but two pubs serving food and traditional ales are within walking distance. An ideal base for cycling and walking (the Weavers Way footpath is within half a mile) or just relaxing.

Facilities

The well maintained toilet block is heated and includes spacious hot showers and a covered dishwashing and laundry area. Off site: Bus service on the main A140 road. Riding 1 mile. Fishing 3 miles. Bicycle hire 5 miles. Beach 6 miles. Golf 10 miles.

Open: 1 March - 31 October.

Directions

From A140 Norwich - Cromer road, 6 miles north of Aylsham, turn left signed Erpingham 1 mile, plus camping sign (narrow road). Site is 175 yds. on right. GPS: 52.84208, 1.27090

Charges guide

Per unit incl. 2 persons, electricity and awning	£ 13.00

No credit cards.

Norwich

Deer's Glade Caravan & Camping Park

White Post Road, Hanworth, Norwich NR11 7HN (Norfolk) T: 01263 768633. E: info@deersglade.co.uk
alanrogers.com/UK3455

In 2003, David and Heather Attew decided that they had an area that would make a superb setting for a caravan park and that they could give up farming. In early 2004 after much hard work, they opened this top quality park and it has since developed into a very popular site. Not far from the Norfolk Broads and close to the East Anglian coast, the park is open all year round. There are 125 level pitches (35 with hardstandings), all with 16A electricity and 100 with TV aerial points. New hedging between pitches is becoming established. Internet access is possible from all the pitches. Amenities are of a high standard and include two toilet blocks, a play area, small shop and a popular, well stocked fishing lake. As its name suggests, you would not be surprised to wake and see deer wandering on this park and in the surrounding woodland areas. If you do miss them, a short walk will take you to Gunton Park where deer are bred and wander in herds.

Facilities

Two spacious toilet blocks are of a very high standard and include vanity style washbasins for ladies, a room for disabled visitors and families, dishwashing room and a laundry. Motorcaravan service point. Licensed shop (all year). Play area. Fishing lake (charged). Bicycle hire. Caravan valet service. Dog kennels. Free minibus to local pub (Aug). WiFi (charged). Off site: Bus service under 1 mile. Pub 1.5 miles. Riding 2 miles. Small supermarket 3 miles. Beach and golf 5 miles. Blicking Hall. Felbrigg Hall. Market town of Yalsham. Cromer. Birdwatching. Poppy railway line (Sheringham to Holt).

Open: All year.

Directions

From Norwich take A140 towards Cromer and 5 miles beyond Aylsham turn right towards Suffield Green (White Post Road). Park is 0.5 miles on the right. GPS: 52.85781, 1.28765

Charges guide

Per unit incl. 2 persons and electricity	£ 11.50 - £ 15.50
extra person	£ 5.25 - £ 7.25
child (2-15 yrs)	£ 1.50 - £ 2.00
dog	£ 1.00

Family deals available.

For latest campsite news visit
alanrogers.com

Peterborough

Ferry Meadows Caravan Club Site

Ham Lane, Peterborough PE2 5UU (Cambridgeshire) T: 01733 233526. E: inquiries@caravanclub.co.uk

alanrogers.com/UK3580

Three miles from bustling Peterborough and close to the East of England Showground, the immaculate Ferry Meadows is an ideal family holiday site occupying 30 acres of the 500-acre Nene Country Park. Open all year the site provides 265 pitches (16A electricity) – 130 grass pitches on one side of the park, informally laid out in small groups and surrounded by a variety of mature trees, and 135 gravel hardstandings just across the road for caravans and motorcaravans. A very small area (no electricity) is reserved for up to six tents.

Facilities

Two modern, well appointed and heated toilet blocks, one with facilities for disabled visitors. Baby/toddler washroom. Laundry room. Motorcaravan service point. The office stocks basic provisions. Good play areas. TV socket and lead. WiFi (charged). Off site: Steam railway 500 yards. Bus service and pitch and putt 800 yards. Restaurants within 0.5 miles. Nearest shops 1 mile. Shops, cinema, lido and supermarkets in Peterborough 3 miles.

Open: All year.

Directions

Leave the A1 on A605, turn east, signed Showground, Peterborough. At fourth roundabout turn left, signed Ferry Meadows. Entrance is on the left just beyond railway. GPS: 52.56053, -0.30593

Charges guide

Per person	£ 5.10 - £ 6.90
pitch incl. electricity (non-member)	£ 13.10 - £ 16.60

Sheringham

Kelling Heath Holiday Park

Weybourne, Holt, Sheringham NR25 7HW (Norfolk) T: 01263 588181. E: info@kellingheath.co.uk

alanrogers.com/UK3430

Not many parks can boast their own railway station and Kelling Heath's own halt on the North Norfolk Steam Railway gives access to the beach at Sheringham. Set in 250 acres of woodland and heathland, this very spacious holiday park offers freedom and relaxation with 300 large, level, grass touring pitches, all with 16A electricity and six are fully serviced. Together with 384 caravan holiday homes (36 to let, the rest privately owned), they blend easily into the part-wooded, part-open heath. A wide range of facilities provides activities for all ages. 'The Forge' has an entertainment bar and a family room, with comprehensive entertainment all season. The leisure centre provides an indoor pool, spa pool, sauna, steam rooms and gym. An adventure playground with assault course is near. The central reception area is attractively paved to provide a village square with an open air bandstand where one can sit and enjoy the atmosphere. The park's natural environment allows for woodland walks, a nature trail and cycling trails, and a small lake for fishing (permit holders only).

Facilities

Three toilet blocks include facilities for disabled visitors, a baby room and dishwashing and laundry sinks. Well stocked shop. Gas. Bar, restaurant and takeaway. Indoor leisure centre with pool, gym, etc. with trained staff (daily/weekly membership). Outdoor pool (main season). Adventure play area. Tennis. Fishing. Bicycle hire. Entertainment. Special environmental Acorn activities for the family. WiFi (charged). Torches useful. Off site: The Norfolk coast, Felbrigg Hall, the Walsingham Shrine and the Norfolk Broads National Park are nearby.

Open: 10 February - 2 January.

Directions

On A148 road from Holt to Cromer, after High Kelling, turn left just before Bodham village (international sign) signed Weybourne. Follow road for about 1 mile to park. GPS: 52.92880, 1.14953

Charges guide

Per unit incl. electricity	£ 18.00 - £ 32.30
with full services	£ 23.45 - £ 39.00
dog (max. 2)	£ 3.10 - £ 5.15

Min. 7 day stay in high season. No single sex groups.

Pidley

Stroud Hill Park

Fen Road, Pidley PE28 3DE (Cambridgeshire) T: 01487 741333. E: stroudhillpark@btconnect.com

alanrogers.com/UK3575

Open all year round for adults only, Stroud Hill Park is a well designed, high quality park; a credit to its owners, David and Jayne Newman. The park has been landscaped to create a terraced effect and now incorporates a large fishing lake (well stocked with carp, tench, bream, rudd and roach) plus a superb tennis court. There are 60 large, slightly sloping pitches, fully serviced with electricity (16A), fresh water and drainage, 44 of which have hardstanding. Affiliated to the Caravan Club, non-members are equally welcome.

Facilities

Toilets and spacious en-suite shower facilities are in the main building. Well equipped room for disabled visitors. All spotlessly clean. Small, licensed shop stocks basic provisions, homemade cakes, local produce, gas and camping accessories. Attractive bar and superb café/restaurant. Fishing (£5 per day). All-weather tennis court. WiFi (charged). Off site: Golf course, 10-pin bowling and paintball adjacent to site. Riding 0.5 miles. Peterborough, Cambridge, Ely, Huntingdon and St Ives all within easy reach.

Open: All year.

Directions

Leave A1 near Huntingdon, take A14 east. Leave A14 at A141, signed March. In Warboys, at roundabout, turn right on B1040 signed Pidley. In Pidley turn left just beyond church, Fen Road. Site is about 1 mile on right. GPS: 52.38926, -0.03966

Charges guide

Per unit incl. 2 persons and full services	£ 23.00 - £ 26.50
extra person	£ 2.50
tent pitch	£ 17.00

Sheringham

Woodlands Caravan Park

Holt Road, Upper Sheringham NR26 8TU (Norfolk) T: 01263 823802.
E: enquiries@woodlandscaravanpark.co.uk **alanrogers.com/UK3435**

This pleasant caravan park is set in parkland in the beautiful surroundings of North Norfolk's protected heathland, next to Sheringham Park (National Trust). There are 225 sloping grass pitches with 216 having electricity (10A). They are in two main areas for caravans and motorcaravans (tents are not accepted). A major feature of this site is the superb new toilet block with electronically controlled showers. There are many lovely local walks including one to the beach (1.5 miles). The park is within easy reach of Holt, Cromer and Sheringham, with the major bird watching areas of Blakeney, Cley and Salthouse also within 30 minutes drive. There is a good bar on site offering entertainment at weekends and the excellent Pinewood Park Leisure Club is adjacent to the park. The Club has swimming pools, sauna, spa, gym and other fitness facilities at a discounted rate for those staying at Woodlands.

Facilities

One excellent new toilet block provides all the necessary facilities including those for disabled visitors, baby changing and laundry. Well stocked shop. Gas supplies. Lounge bar and family bar with musical entertainment most weekends. Barbecues. Play area (2 acres, fenced and gated). Pinewood Park Leisure Club with indoor pool, gym, sauna. etc (all year). Off site: Bicycle hire and fishing 1.5 miles. Norfolk coast, golf and riding 2 miles. Sailing 7 miles. Scenic railway. Stately homes.

Open: 20 March - 31 October.

Directions

From Cromer take the A148 towards Holt, pass signs for Sheringham Park and site is on right (camping sign) just before Bodham village. GPS: 52.92093, 1.17445

Charges guide

Per unit incl. electricity	£ 17.00 - £ 25.00
awning	£ 3.50

Swaffham

Breckland Meadows Touring Park

Lynn Road, Swaffham PE37 7PT (Norfolk) T: 01760 721246. E: info@brecklandmeadows.co.uk

alanrogers.com/UK3470

Open all year, this compact, adult only park offers peace and tranquillity yet is only ten minutes' walk from the historic market town of Swaffham. The site makes a good base to explore East Anglia and the local area with a wide range of diverse attractions. There are 40 average sized pitches, with hardstanding, 16A electricity and TV hook-ups. There are two main roads close to the park but well established hedges and trees help minimise any noise. A small shop sells basic supplies, ices and drinks, with a good library.

Facilities	Directions
The modern, well cared for toilet block provides all the usual facilities, including spacious showers and facilities for disabled visitors. Laundry room. Gas supplies. WiFi throughout (free). Off site: Swaffham with a range of shops, bars, restaurants, museums, Saturday market 0.5 miles. Bicycle hire 1 mile. Golf 2 miles. Riding 4 miles. Fishing 5 miles. Iceni village. Gooderstone Water Gardens.	Park is 0.5 miles west of Swaffham on Low Road (old A47). Entrance on right just beyond garage. GPS: 52.65115, 0.67687

Open: All year.

Charges guide

Per unit incl. 2 persons and electricity	£ 11.95 - £ 13.95
extra person	£ 3.00

No credit cards.

Wisbech

Parklands Caravan & Camping Park

Sutton Road, Four Gotes, Wisbech PE13 5PH (Cambridgeshire) T: 01945 420505.
E: enquiries@parklandsholidays.co.uk **alanrogers.com/UK3585**

A small, quiet, secluded family run site occupying five acres of level grassland on the borders of Cambridgeshire, Lincolnshire and Norfolk. The site is surrounded by tall conifers giving shelter from the wind. There are 58 good sized, level grass pitches, with 56 for touring and 45 have 10A electricity. The pitches are separated by low hedges and a few trees giving little shade but some will get some shade from the high conifer hedging surrounding the site. Access is easy for large outfits. There is a shop, small swimming pool, and a bar serving takeaway food to order. No charcoal barbecues.

Facilities	Directions
Small heated toilet block with good sized adjustable showers and facilities for disabled campers. Washing machine. Small swimming pool, corner spa, sunbathing area (all Apr-Sept). Shop with bread and newspapers to order. Bar/takeaway food/breakfast rolls (weekends only in low season). Games/TV room. Children's play area. Putting green. Evening music (weekends low season). WiFi (charged). Off site: Lake and river fishing nearby. Golf course with restaurant. Market town of Wisbech with shops, bars, restaurants.	Parklands is on A1101 between Wisbech and Long Sutton. From Wisbech go north to Four Gotes. Site is on right 800 yds. after entering village. GPS: 52.732953, 0.14698

Open: 15 March - 15 October.

Charges guide

Per unit incl. 2 persons and electricity	£ 14.60 - £ 18.80
extra person	£ 3.00 - £ 5.00
child	£ 2.00 - £ 3.00

Camping Cheques accepted.

Woodbridge

The Moon & Sixpence

Newbourne Road, Waldringfield, Woodbridge IP12 4PP (Suffolk) T: 01473 736650.
E: info@moonandsixpence.eu **alanrogers.com/UK3320**

This excellent site offers 60 large touring pitches that are positioned in the centre of an established and very spacious caravan holiday home park. The site is extremely well maintained and all the 60 touring pitches are equipped with 5A electricity, TV point, water tap and a drain. In the centre of the site, and easily accessible to all, is an unsupervised lake with a sandy beach. An area at one end of the lake is set aside for ten pitches for adults only, all with views of the lake. Quiet is essential from 9 pm to 8 am.

Facilities	Directions
Exceptionally well finished, centrally placed unisex sanitary block consists of 11 fully equipped private rooms containing a selection of WCs, washbasins, showers, baths and wet rooms. No specific facilities for disabled visitors but access to the block is via a ramp. Laundry facilities. Well stocked shop. Bar and restaurant (main season). TV room. Two adventure play areas. Dog walk trails. Lake with beach. Tennis. Golf. WiFi (charged). Off site: Boat launching and fishing 2 miles. Bicycle hire and riding 5 miles.	From the A12 (Ipswich - Lowestoft) turn right at roundabout, towards Waldringfield and follow signs to site. After one and a half miles, turn left at Waldringfield Golf Club to site, .three quarters of a mile on the left. GPS: 52.06252, 1.29858

Open: 1 April - 31 October.

Charges guide

Per person (over 2 yrs) incl. unit and services	£ 9.00 - £ 16.00
dog	£ 1.00

Min. charges apply. Max. length 6.5 m.

For latest campsite news visit
alanrogers.com

Woodbridge

Run Cottage Touring Park

Alderton Road, Hollesey, Woodbridge IP12 3RQ (Suffolk) T: 01394 411309. E: contact@run-cottage.co.uk

alanrogers.com/UK3322

This very attractive 20-pitch site in the heart of unspoilt Suffolk countryside offers an opportunity to explore many of the local attractions on Suffolk's Heritage Coast. Facilities on the site are limited but certainly adequate and the resident owners, Michele and Andy Stebbens are always available to ensure that you have an enjoyable stay. The site is open all year round and all pitches have 10A electricity, with six on hardstanding. This is a popular site and advance booking is strongly recommended. Local attractions include Sutton Hoo, Orford Castle and Framlingham Castle. The market town of Woodbridge is only 6 miles away. Within a short drive are the pretty coastal towns of Southwold, Dunwich, Orford and Aldeborough.

Facilities

New, well finished sanitary block with free hot water is easily accessed and is well equipped. Reception contains a comprehensive selection of tourist leaflets and details of local attractions. Off site: Excellent pubs and restaurants within 1 mile. Riding and Suffolk Punch Horse Trust 1 mile. Beach, fishing and bicycle hire 1.5 miles. Golf 5 miles.

Open: All year.

Directions

From A12 (Ipswich - Lowestoft) turn right at roundabout at Melton onto A1152 (Bawdsey, Orford). In 1.5 miles, at roundabout, turn right onto B1083 (Bawdsey, Hollesley). Within 0.75 miles take left fork to Hollesley. At Duck Corner cross road, turn right and continue through village to site on the left, 100 yds. past Red Brick Bridge. Note: Do not follow sat nav directions.
GPS: 52.04503, 1.42683

Charges guide

Per unit incl. 2 persons and electricity	£ 16.00
extra person (over 3 yrs)	£ 3.50
dog (max. 2)	free

Close to the town of Woodbridge we are a small family run touring park with 20 pitches. Set in a 2.5 acre parkland setting with a large pond and views over open farmland, we offer peace and tranquillity. A place to escape the hustle and bustle of today's busy lifestyle.

Run Cottage Touring Park, Alderton Road, Hollesey, Woodbridge, Suffolk. IP12 3RQ
Tel: 01394 411 309
Website:http://www.run-cottage.co.uk
Email: contact@run-cottage.co.uk

- All electric hook ups
- Six all weather caravan pitches
- Open all year
- Two acre dog exercise area
- Toilet & shower block
- Chemical disposal point
- Tourist information area
- 1.5 miles from shingle beach
- Village shop & pub within easy walking distance

Woodbridge

Moat Barn Touring Caravan Park

Dallinghoo Road, Bredfield, Woodbridge IP13 6BD (Suffolk) T: 01473 737520

alanrogers.com/UK3330

Mike Allen opened this small touring park in April 2000 on the Suffolk Heritage Cycle Route, and also the Hull - Harwich National Cycle Route. The main touring area is bordered by established hedging and incorporates a circular roadway. The park currently provides 34 level grass pitches, all with electricity (10A). The park is popular with both walkers and cyclists and provides a tranquil environment to explore nearby Woodbridge and surrounding areas. The park has limited provision for large units (e.g. American motorhomes). There are no facilities for children.

Facilities

The well equipped sanitary block can be heated. A separate unit houses a dishwashing sink. Motorcaravan service point. Bicycle hire. WiFi. Off site: Nearby pub serving food. Public footpath.

Open: 1 March - 15 January.

Directions

Park is midway between Woodbridge and Wickham Market. From A12 take turning signed Bredfield (left from south, right from north). At village pump in Bredfield turn right and follow road past public house and church. Continue through S-bends and, after 200 yds, site entrance is on left, just after farm buildings. GPS: 52.13510, 1.31710

Charges guide

Per unit incl. 2 persons and electricity	£ 15.00

For latest campsite news visit
alanrogers.com

Spanning central England, from the ancient borders of Wales in the west across to Lincolnshire on the east coast, the Heart of England is rich in glorious rolling countryside, magnificent castles, fine stately houses and beautiful gardens.

THE REGION COMPRISES LINCOLNSHIRE, RUTLAND, NORTHAMPTONSHIRE, NOTTINGHAMSHIRE, WEST MIDLANDS, DERBYSHIRE, STAFFORDSHIRE, LEICESTERSHIRE, WARWICKSHIRE, HEREFORDSHIRE, WORCESTERSHIRE, GLOUCESTERSHIRE & SHROPSHIRE

The charming and diverse countryside of the Heart of England includes: the Lincolnshire Wolds, with the dramatic open landscape of the Fens; the ragged crags, dales and moorland of the Peak District National Park in Derbyshire and Staffordshire; the heathered hilltops of Shropshire; the famous Sherwood Forest, in the heart of Nottinghamshire; and the miles of lush green countryside of Herefordshire, dotted with black and white timber houses. Rutland Water is a mecca for watersports and the whole region offers superb opportunities for walking, cycling and more daring activities such as rock climbing and caving. The Cotswolds to the west of the region is the largest Area of Outstanding Natural Beauty in England and Wales. Here you will find many traditional English villages, with charming country pubs and cottage gardens. Other significant features of the region are the rivers and canals. Passing pretty towns and villages, a large canal network threads its way through the area, weaving through the Lincolnshire Fens, past the waterside bars and restaurants of Birmingham and along to estuaries of the rivers of Severn and Avon.

Places of interest

Lincolnshire: Belvoir Castle near Grantham.

Rutland: market towns of Oakham and Uppingham.

Northamptonshire: Silverstone; Althorp House.

Nottinghamshire: Nottingham Castle.

West Midlands: Birmingham; Cadbury World.

Derbyshire: Bakewell; Buxton; Chatsworth House.

Staffordshire: Alton Towers; Stoke-on-Trent.

Leicestershire: Snibston Discovery Park; Twycross Zoo.

Warwickshire: Warwick Castle; Stratford-upon-Avon.

Herefordshire: Hereford Cathedral.

Worcestershire: West Midland Safari Park.

Gloucestershire: Sudeley Castle; Cheltenham.

Shropshire: Shrewsbury and Whitchurch.

Did you know?

Herefordshire is one of the largest apple cider producers in the world.

The World Toe Wrestling Championship, held every June in Wetton, is a registered international sport.

The hollow trunk of the 'Mighty Tree' in Sherwood Forest is reputedly where Robin Hood and his Merry Men hid from the Sheriff of Nottingham.

Quite different from the more familiar tart, the Bakewell pudding was first created in the 1860s.

Rutland is the smallest county in Britain, measuring just 16 miles by 16 miles.

The Peak District contains over 50 reservoirs, including Ladybower, where the bouncing bomb used in World War II was tested.

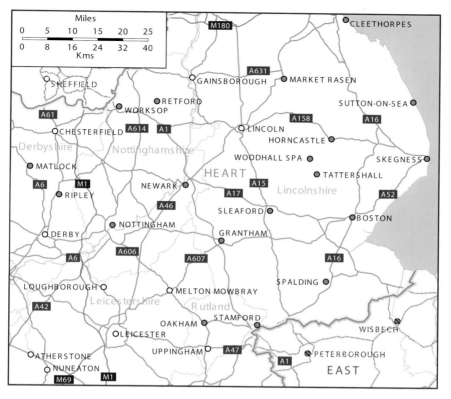

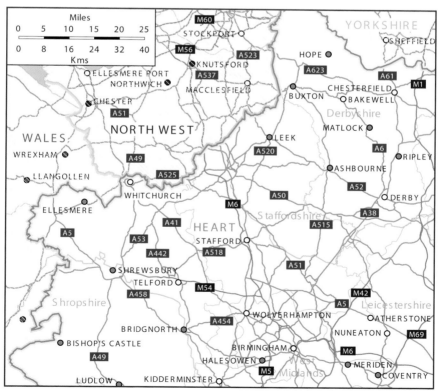

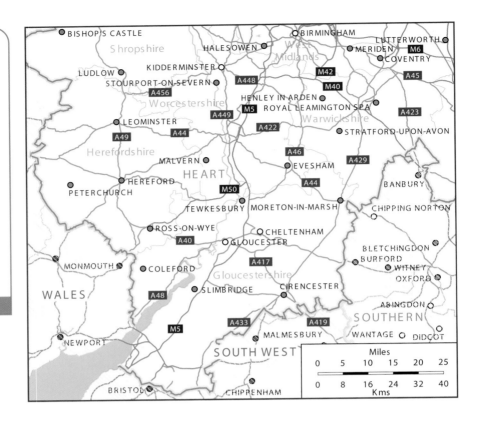

Ashbourne

Peak Gateway Leisure Club

Osmaston, Ashbourne DE6 1NA (Derbyshire) T: 01335 344643. E: info@peakgateway.com

alanrogers.com/UK3854

The motto of this park is 'more than just a campsite', and it lives up to that. This is a place that caters for all ages and interests, with children at its heart. A former WWII RAF flying school, the buildings centred around the officers' mess have been sensitively converted to their present functions. The owner and the manager are enthusiastically adding activities, entertainment and attractions to the park and refurbishment of some parts is well underway. There are 30 touring pitches (with 10 on grass), all with 10A electricity and a further 40 well-spaced pitches for tents. Privately owned caravan holiday homes occupy a further 42 pitches. The park is busy at weekends and a second shower block should now be complete. A camping and geocaching shop is on site.

Facilities

High standard heated toilet blocks with free showers and hairdryers. Laundry room. Rooms for families and disabled visitors. Further toilet block for the tent field, also with dishwashing facilities. Two bars with family room, breakfast café, takeaway and bar meals. Dance hall. Small shop. Games room and TV. Buggy racing (150cc) at weekends. Disco every Saturday. Varied entertainment programme all season especially B.Hs, Halloween, etc (bookings required). WiFi in some areas (charged). Only 1 dog per pitch is permitted. Off site: Leisure centre in town (Saturday shuttle bus provided). Golf and bicycle hire 1 mile. Riding 2 miles. Fishing 4 miles.

Open: All year.

Directions

The entrance is off the A52 one mile southeast of Ashbourne. From Ashbourne southern bypass turn right 300 yards after roundabout. From Derby on the A52, about 1 mile after the turn to Osmaston village. turn left. Site is clearly signed.
GPS: 53.003151, -1.721273

Charges guide

Per unit incl. 2 persons	
and electricity	£ 20.00 - £ 25.00
child (6-17 yrs)	£ 2.00
small dog (max. 1)	£ 3.00

Ashbourne

Rivendale Caravan & Leisure Park

Buxton Road, Alsop-en-le-Dale, Ashbourne DE6 1QU (Derbyshire) T: 01335 310311.
E: enquiries@rivendalecaravanpark.co.uk **alanrogers.com/UK3850**

This unusual park has been developed in the bowl of a hill quarry which was last worked over 50 years ago. The steep quarry walls shelter three sides with marvellous views over the Peak National Park countryside to the south. Near the entrance to the park is a renovated stone building which houses reception, shop, bar and a café/restaurant. Nearby are 136 level and landscaped pitches, mostly of a generous size with 16A electricity and a mix of hardstanding and grass. In two separate fields and a copse there is provision for 50 tents and that area includes a fishing lake. All the touring pitches are within easy reach of the central stone-built toilet block which is in keeping with the environment and provided with underfloor heating. A new lodge-type heated toilet block is at the entrance to the tent fields. For rent on the park are B&B rooms, camping pods, lodges and yurts. The park takes up about 11 acres and a further 26 acres belong to the owners, with certain parts suitable for walking – a must to appreciate the Derbyshire countryside with its dry stone walls, wild flowers and a little more of the quarry history. The park is situated almost on the Tissington Trail for walking or off-road cycling and links with the High Peak and Monsal Dale Trail. Other spectacular walks and cycle rides run along the Manifold, Wye and Dove valleys.

Facilities

Good toilet facilities include some washbasins in cubicles for ladies, and an excellent en-suite room for disabled visitors. Laundry room. Glass and paper recycling bins. Shop (all essentials). Bar (evenings) and café with home-made and local food (open mornings, lunch and evenings, both with limited opening in low season). Packed lunches from reception. Special events monthly and games in main season. Hot tubs for hire, delivered to your pitch. Electric bikes for hire. WiFi in some areas (charged). For rent on the park are B&B rooms, camping pods, lodges and yurts. Off site: Riding 5 miles. Sailing and boat launching 8 miles. Golf 10 miles. Alton Towers 35 minutes drive.

Open: All year excl. 9 January - 2 February.

Directions

Park is 7 miles north of Ashbourne on the A515 to Buxton, on the eastern side of the road. It is well signed between the turnings east to Alsop Moor and Matlock (A5012), but take care as this is a very fast section of the A515. GPS: 53.106383, -1.760567

Charges guide

Per unit incl. 2 persons and electricity	£ 18.50 - £ 23.00
extra person	£ 2.50
child (4-15 yrs)	£ 2.00
dog	£ 2.00

Camping Cheques accepted.

Ashbourne

Callow Top Holiday Park

Buxton Road, Sandybrook, Ashbourne DE6 2AQ (Derbyshire) T: 01335 344020. E: enquiries@callowtop.co.uk
alanrogers.com/UK3855

Situated just north of the market town of Ashbourne, Callow Top nestles within an elevated country setting. The park's location makes it well placed to allow visitors to explore the picturesque villages, bustling market towns and the many attractions of the Peak District. It is ideal for both walking and cycling holidays. Spread over seven separate areas at the top of a hill, there are 200 flat pitches of which 100 are for touring units. Those on hardstanding have 10A electricity, the grass pitches have no power supply. Water points tend to be rather scarce. Some of the pitches are rather small and on these, cars are parked away from the pitch.

Facilities

Three heated toilet blocks (only one open in low season) provide unisex showers (20p). Toilet for disabled visitors. Laundry room. Motorcaravan service point. Calor gas. Shop. Inn/restaurant. Snack bar and takeaway. Heated swimming and paddling pools (May-Sept). Bicycle hire. Games room. Play area. Entertainment (w/ends and high season). Fishing. WiFi in some areas (charged). Winter caravan storage. Off site: Ashbourne (supermarket etc) 1 mile. Golf 1 miles. Riding 3 miles. Alton Towers 10 miles.

Open: 15 March - 6 November.

Directions

At Sandybrook, 0.5 miles north of Ashbourne, turn west off the A515 (Ashbourne - Buxton) into site road which becomes steep. Site is signed. GPS: 53.02693, -1.74646

Charges guide

Per unit incl. 2 persons	£ 17.00 - £ 22.00
incl. hardstanding and electricity	£ 20.50 - £ 28.00
extra person	£ 2.50
child (4-16 yrs)	£ 1.50

For latest campsite news visit
alanrogers.com

Ashbourne

Woodland Caravan Park

Snelston Hall, Ashbourne DE6 2ET (Derbyshire) T: 01335 346 120

alanrogers.com/UK3860

Set in woodland within the privately-owned grounds of Snelston Hall, this site presents a charming, tranquil haven for those seeking a leafy retreat. The 900-acre estate has walks on private and public footpaths. The 52 pitches, constructed from local limestone are level, each with electric hook-up. Expect to see shafts of light falling on irregularly arranged pitches allowing a sense of privacy within the tall trees that give the site its name. These trees help screen out low level traffic noise, which is much reduced at night. Modern, clean, toilet blocks are tastefully coloured to blend with the surroundings.

Facilities	Directions
One modern, clean, toilet block (key) with room for visitors with disabilities. Water is within easy reach of each pitch. Laundry. Kitchen area with microwave. Area for dog walking (breeds restricted). Access to large private estate. Motorcaravan services. Off site: Darley Motorcycle Circuit 1 mile. Ashbourne 4 miles. Tissington Trail with bicycle hire 5 miles. Peak District National Park 6 miles.	Leave A50 at Sudbury and take A515 signposted Ashbourne. Continue for about 7 miles. Just before Darley Moor Motorcycle Circuit (on your right) turn left (signposted Snelston and Woodland Caravan Park) and turn almost immediately right into Woodland Park. GPS: 52.98102, -1.7531

Open: 22 March - 30 September.

Charges guide

Per unit incl. 2 persons	£ 14.00 - £ 23.00
extra person	£ 2.00

Bishop's Castle

The Green Caravan Park

Wentnor, Bishop's Castle SY9 5EF (Shropshire) T: 01588 650605. E: karen@greencaravanpark.co.uk

alanrogers.com/UK4440

Remotely situated in a pleasant valley, in a designated Area of Outstanding Natural Beauty, and sandwiched between the Stiperstones and The Long Mynd, the Green would make an ideal base for some serious walking; a footpath to the Stiperstones passes through the site. The 15-acre site is delightful, and divided into several fields. There are 160 pitches, taking 41 seasonal units, and around 20 holiday homes, with approximately 140 pitches for tourists (41 with 16A electric hook-ups). The main field has some hardstandings. The East Onny is a small, shallow river which runs through the site, much enjoyed by the youngsters, who can spend many hours catching minnows.

Facilities	Directions
One main sanitary block, rather austere in appearance, built into the side of a large barn. However it provides adequate and plentiful facilities with spacious hot showers (coin operated) and laundry facilities, but there is no dedicated unit for disabled campers. Small shop in new reception building. Playground. Off site: Four pubs within 3 miles, one next door. Fishing 3 miles. Riding 4 miles.	From Shrewsbury take A49. Right turn at Marsh Brook. At T-junction turn right onto A489 for 5 miles. Turn right at brown campsite sign. Site is just after The Inn on the Green. GPS: 52.53375, -2.91375

Open: Easter - 31 October.

Charges guide

Per unit incl. 2 persons	£ 14.50 - £ 16.00
extra person	£ 3.50

Boston

Long Acres Touring Park

Station Road, Old Leake, Boston PE22 9RF (Lincolnshire) T: 01205 871555.
E: enquiries@longacres-caravanpark.co.uk **alanrogers.com/UK3695**

An attractive, adults-only site on the Lincolnshire Fens north of Boston, yet only six miles from the coastline of the Wash, Long Acres is a purpose-built site opened in 2008 and attractively laid out to take maximum advantage of the great variety of trees and shrubs. Ranged on either side of the site's single road, the 40 pitches, all with electric hook-ups (10A), are on hardstandings separated by well-tended grass to cater for tents and awnings. The beaches and attractions of Skegness are just 17 miles to the northeast, while Gibraltar Point, Snipe Dales, Freiston Shore and Frampton Marshes are nearby.

Facilities	Directions
A single well equipped central toilet block provides preset showers, open-style washbasins with hairdryers, dishwashing sinks, a small freezer for ice packs, and an en-suite unit for disabled visitors. Motorcaravan service point. Reception has tourist information and a small library. Area available for small rallies. Boules pitch. WiFi (charged). Off site: Fishing 1 mile. Golf 7 miles. Bicycle hire 10 miles. Riding 12 miles. Beach (Skegness) 17 miles.	The site is best approached from the A16 Boston - Louth road. At Sibsey turn east on B1184 towards Old Leake. At T-junction turn left and in 1.7 miles turn right along Common Side Road to site on left in half a mile. GPS: 53.057487, 0.063732

Open: 1 March - 31 October.

Charges guide

Per unit incl. 2 persons and electricity	£ 15.00 - £ 18.00

For latest campsite news visit

alanrogers.com

Bridgnorth

Stanmore Hall Touring Park

Stourbridge Road, Bridgnorth WV15 6DT (Shropshire) T: 01746 761761. E: stanmore@morris-leisure.co.uk

alanrogers.com/UK4400

This attractive park is situated in the former grounds of Stanmore Hall, where the huge lily pond, fine mature trees and beautifully manicured lawns give a mark of quality. There are 135 generously sized pitches, 130 with 16A electricity including 30 hardstanding super pitches with TV connections. Also available are 23 standard pitches, but most are on grass. Some pitches are reserved for adult only use (over 18 years). Access and internal roads are tarmac; site lighting is adequate and reassuring. The park is a member of the Caravan Club's 'managed under contract' scheme but non-members are also very welcome. A size restriction of 30 ft. exists for motorcaravans.

Facilities

The upgraded, centrally-heated sanitary block provides washbasins in cubicles and a room for disabled guests and baby care. Full laundry facilities. Motorcaravan service points. A well equipped shop stocking camping and caravan accessories. A TV booster system is available. Play area. WiFi (charged). Off site: Fishing at Bridgnorth 1.5 miles. Golf and riding 2 miles.

Open: All year.

Directions

Site is 1.5 miles from Bridgnorth on the A458 (signed Stourbridge). If using sat nav approach from Bridgnorth only. GPS: 52.52715, -2.378617

Charges guide

Per unit incl. 2 persons and electricity	£ 22.60 - £ 25.30

Buxton

Lime Tree Holiday Park

Dukes Drive, Buxton SK17 9RP (Derbyshire) T: 01298 22988. E: info@limetreeparkbuxton.com

alanrogers.com/UK3840

Lime Tree is in a convenient, edge of town location that makes a very good base for touring the Peak District. The site has three widely spaced main areas, touring pitches on two levels with a toilet block on the upper level, a caravan holiday home area which has the reception shop and games room, and above and a short distance away a large, mainly sloping field area for tents. The toilet block for tents and the play area are above reception. Touring pitches (65) are mainly on hardstandings with electricity supply. With good views, the park is situated next to a thickly wooded, limestone gorge and a magnificent old railway viaduct provides a dramatic backdrop. This is an excellent dog walk.

Facilities

A modern toilet building includes some washbasins in cubicles, controllable showers, baby room and family room with facilities for disabled visitors. The refitted original unit serves the tent area. Laundry room with washing machine and dryer. Shop. Basic play area. Games/TV room. WiFi. Off site: Pub serving food just around the corner. Swimming, riding and golf 1 mile. Fishing, bicycle hire, sailing and boat launching 5 miles. Alton Towers 22 miles.

Open: 1 March - 31 October.

Directions

Park is on outskirts of Buxton. From town, just after hospital bear sharp left into Dukes Drive, go under railway viaduct and site is on the right. From south watch out for sharp turn right at foot of hill. GPS: 53.250230, -1.896673

Charges guide

Per unit incl. 2 persons and electricity	£ 21.00
extra person	£ 6.00
child (5-15 yrs)	£ 3.00

Buxton

Clover Fields Touring Caravan Park

1 Heath View, Harpur Hill, Buxton SK17 9PU (Derbyshire) T: 01298 78731. E: cloverfields@tiscali.co.uk

alanrogers.com/UK3845

The Redferns are more than happy to welcome you to their family owned, adults only park (over 18 yrs). It is located on the outskirts of the spa town of Buxton within easy reach of the Peak District National Park. You will be able to relax here in the 'away from it all' atmosphere. There are just 25 pitches with 20 more planned, serviced by a first rate toilet block. The pitches are divided by low hedges, part hardstanding and part grass, all with 16A electricity, a water tap and a concealed dustbin. There is a little noise from the adjacent road. Recently added is a newly constructed and stocked fishing pond.

Facilities

A clean, modern toilet and shower block with facilities for disabled visitors. Laundry room. Motorcaravan service point. Gas supplies. Small shop selling essentials. Newspapers and milk delivered to your pitch. Plant sales. Barbecues provided by reception. Small library. Fishing. Resident animals and birds. Torches recommended. Off site: Supermarket and fish and chip shop in Buxton. Golf 3 miles. Riding 5 miles. Bicycle hire 6 miles.

Open: All year.

Directions

From Buxton, at Harpur Hill just to southeast, turn right off the A515 onto the B5053. Turn immediately right towards Harpur Hill. Site entrance is 0.5 miles on the left (easily missed) at the start of the 40 mph limit. GPS: 53.23066, -1.8878

Charges guide

Per unit incl. 2 persons and electricity	£ 16.00 - £ 18.00
No credit cards.	

For latest campsite news visit

alanrogers.com

Cirencester
Hoburne Cotswold

Broadway Lane, South Cerney, Cirencester GL7 5UQ (Gloucestershire) T: 01285 860216.
E: enquiries@hoburne.co.uk **alanrogers.com/UK4100**

Since this park is adjacent to the Cotswold Water Park, visitors will have easy access to the varied watersports available. On the park itself there is a lake with pedaloes for hire. The wide range of other amenities includes outdoor and indoor heated swimming pools and an impressive, large indoor leisure complex. There are 189 well marked touring pitches for any type of unit, all with hardstanding (only fairly level) and a grass surround for awning or tent. Pitches are of a good size but with nothing between them, and very litle shade; all have electricity (10A, some need long leads). Part of the Hoburne Group.

Facilities	Directions
Four small toilet blocks are clean and well maintained with preset showers and heating. Baby changing facilities. Basic facilities for disabled visitors. Launderette. Supermarket. Indoor leisure complex including pool. Outdoor pool (mid May-early Sept). Clubhouse with bar, food and entertainment and free WiFi. Events weekends during season. Football pitch. Tennis. Adventure playground. Crazy golf. Fishing lake. Animals are not accepted. Off site: Swindon and Cheltenham.	Three miles southeast of Cirencester on A419, turn west towards Cotswold Water Park at new roundabout on bypass onto B4696 signposted South Cerney. Continue past Water Park for approximately 1.5 miles. Road leading to campsite is on the right, Take second right and follow signs. GPS: 51.66018, -1.91910

Open: March - October.

Charges guide

Per unit incl. max. 6 persons and electricity	£ 15.45 - £ 36.85

Cleethorpes
Thorpe Park Holiday Centre

Humberston, Cleethorpes DN35 0PW (Lincolnshire) T: 01472 813395
alanrogers.com/UK3655

Thorpe Park is a Haven Holiday Park at Cleethorpes on the north Lincolnshire coast. The touring site, although part of one of the largest caravan parks in Europe, is neat and compact. There are 69 landscaped 'Euro pitches' with brick-built hardstandings, electricity, water and drainage, and a further 55 in an open area, most with electricity available. There is direct access to the beach from one corner of the site and the park's main entertainment complex is a short walk away. A shuttle train will take you to more distant parts of the park, including a nine-hole golf course.

Facilities	Directions
Two modern toilet blocks, the main one with pushbutton showers in well fitted cubicles, open style washbasins, family room and facilities for disabled visitors. The newer, smaller block has fairly basic facilities. Motorcaravan services. Supermarket. Fish and chips. Launderette. Bicycle and buggy hire. Entertainment complex. Heated indoor pool and outdoor flumes. Play area. Crazy golf. Climbing wall. Roller rink. 9-hole golf courses.	From M180 take A180 to Grimsby, turn south on A16 towards Louth, then east on A1098 to Humberston and follow signs for Pleasure Island and Holiday Parks. Park is to right at roundabout. GPS: 53.5347, 0.00412

Open: Easter - 2 November.

Charges guide

Per unit incl. up to 4 persons	£ 10.00 - £ 86.00
extra person	£ 2.00 - £ 3.00

Coleford
Forest Holidays Christchurch

Bracelands Drive, Christchurch, Coleford GL16 7NN (Gloucestershire) T: 01594 837258.
E: fod.site@forestholidays.co.uk **alanrogers.com/UK4160**

Set high above the Wye Valley, a partnership between the Forestry Commission and the Camping and Caravanning Club, Forest Holidays makes a perfect family holiday destination. With 280 unmarked pitches (240 for touring), this 20-acre site occupies an open grassy area in the heart of the Forest of Dean. There are seven hardstandings and 102 pitches with electrical hook-ups (10A). The new reception block includes a shop, caféteria and ranger station. A viewing gallery overlooks the site and the Forest Rangers will hold tutorial events including 'Young Explorers' and 'Forest Survival'.

Facilities	Directions
Two fairly modern sanitary units with spacious, well equipped showers, some vanity style basins with dividers. The central block has a laundry and dishwashing room. Units for disabled visitors and baby changing in both blocks. Adventure playground on bark. No specified dog walk, but trails and footpaths surround the site. Limited television and mobile reception. Off site: Fishing and swimming 1 mile. Coleford 1.5 miles. Golf 2 miles.	From Monmouth take A4136 east for 5 miles turning north at crossroads at Pike House Inn and site is on the left after 0.5 miles. From centre of Coleford take road towards Monmouth, turning right to Symonds Yat and Berry Hill (site signed). GPS: 51.813333, -2.62735

Open: All year.

Charges guide

Per unit incl. 2 persons and electricity	£ 13.00 - £ 20.00

Coventry

Hollyfast Caravan Park

Wall Hill Road, Allesley, Coventry CV5 9EL (Warwickshire) T: 024 7633 6411.
E: sales@hollyfastcaravanpark.co.uk **alanrogers.com/UK4075**

Hollyfast is situated in beautiful countryside on the outskirts of Coventry, part of the park being set within a lovely woodland area giving peace and tranquillity all year round. Located on the Birmingham side of Coventry, this means a short drive into the centre of Coventry and a fifteen minute drive to Birmingham's National Exhibition Centre. You will receive a friendly welcome and be directed to a very clean and well spaced site with 40 pitches of varying sizes with 16A electricity connections. You may be asked to park your car on a nearby car park. A new toilet block provides very clean facilities, along with a games room. Rallies are welcome and a club house is provided with a stage, television and kitchen areas for groups. Under the same ownership, a motorcaravan sales centre with caravan and motorhome storage and LPG.

Facilities

The modern toilet block provides simple clean facilities with good sized showers (3 per sex) and open washbasins. Toilet and shower for disabled campers. Shop. Club house for rallies. Large outdoor ranch style children's play centre and indoor games room. Deposit for barrier (£25). Off site: The local area has shops, three pubs (hot and cold food), a golf course and a riding centre. Bus stop 1 mile for Coventry. British Road Transport museum. Birmingham, Stratford upon Avon, Leamington Spa and Warwick are within driving distance.

Open: All year.

Directions

From M1/M45 (or the M40/A46, or M69/A46) take A45 towards Birmingham. Turn right on A4114 and follow brown and white caravan signs. After turning by the White Lion pub, site is 0.5 miles on the left. From the north take M6 north of Birmingham or the M1 north (Nottingham) follow M42 to NEC, A45 towards Coventry and onto A4114 and as above.
GPS: 52.44588, -1.55572

Charges guide

Per unit incl. 2 persons	
and electricity	£ 17.50 - £ 20.00
extra person	£ 3.00
child (5-15 yrs)	£ 2.00
dog	£ 1.00

Ellesmere

Fernwood Caravan Park

Lyneal, Ellesmere SY12 0QF (Shropshire) T: 01948 710221. E: enquiries@fernwoodpark.co.uk
alanrogers.com/UK4380

Fernwood is set in an area known as the Shropshire Lake District – the mere at Ellesmere is the largest of nine meres – and the picturesque Shropshire Union Canal is only a few minutes' walk. The landscaped park is tranquil and presented to a very high standard, the natural vegetation blending harmoniously with trees and shrubs. In addition to 164 caravan holiday homes, with one unit for hire, there are 30 touring pitches (caravans, motorcaravans and trailer tents only) in several well cut, grassy enclosures (including 30 seasonal long stays). Some are in light woodland, others in more open, but still relatively sheltered situations. All pitches have electricity (10A) and six also have water and drainage. One area is set aside for units with adults only. Siting is carried out by the management and there is always generous spacing, even when the site is full.

Facilities

The small toilet block for tourers has background heating for cooler days and includes some washbasins in cabins and facilities for disabled campers. Basic motorcaravan services. Dishwashing facilities in laundry room, also additional sanitary facilities for ladies and men. Shop doubles as reception (from 1/4-30/10, hours vary). Coarse fishing lake. Forty acres of woodland for walking. Grassy play area for children. Off site: Shrewsbury, Oswestry and Chester are all within easy travelling distance.

Open: 1 March - 30 November.

Directions

Park is just northeast of Lyneal village, signed southwest off the B5063 Ellesmere - Wem road, 1.5 miles from junction of the B5063 with the A495.
GPS: 52.899167, -2.816017

Charges guide

Per unit incl. 2 persons	
and electricity	£ 22.00 - £ 26.00
multi-service pitch	£ 25.50 - £ 29.50

One night free for every 7 booked in advance.

Evesham

Ranch Caravan Park

Honeybourne, Evesham WR11 7PR (Worcestershire) T: 01386 830744. E: enquiries@ranch.co.uk

alanrogers.com/UK4180

This quiet, attractive caravan park set in the Vale of Evesham covers an area of 50 acres of flat, partly undulating, hedged meadows. The park lies between Bidford-on-Avon and Broadway and is only half an hour's drive from Stratford. The park takes 120 touring units – caravans, motorcaravans and trailer tents, but not other tents. The spacious pitches are not marked but the staff help to position units. All have electrical connections (10A) and there are 21 hardstandings including eight fully serviced pitches (electricity, TV, water and drainage). There are 193 caravan holiday homes in their own section. The Vale of Evesham is often overshadowed by its next door neighbour, the Cotswolds. It is, however, populated by some of the prettiest vilages in the area and it is well worth exploring in its own right. Hidcote Manor Gardens, Broadway Tower, the Fleece Inn at Bretforton are all within a short drive. The riverside town of Evesham is an attractive market town some six miles to the west, and well worth a visit.

Facilities

Two very well appointed, modern sanitary blocks with free hot showers and heating, one of which includes facilities for disabled visitors, plus baby changing area. Laundry facilities. Motorcaravan service point. Shop. Clubhouse (weekends only in early and late season) offering wide range of good value meals with entertainment arranged throughout the season. Heated pool (55x30 ft; Spr. B.H. - mid Sept). Gym and sauna (charged). Games room with TV. Playground. WiFi. Off site: Riding and bicycle hire 2 miles. Fishing 4 miles. Golf 6 miles.

Open: 1 March - 30 November.

Directions

From A46 Evesham take B4035 towards Chipping Campden. After Badsey and Bretforton before Weston Subedge pass over the old railway bridge, turn left at the crossroads to Honeybourne. Park is through village on left before station. GPS: 52.09722, -1.83124

Charges 2012

Per unit incl. 2 persons and electricity	£ 23.00 - £ 27.00
incl. water and drainage	£ 26.50 - £ 30.50
extra person (over 5 yrs)	free - £ 4.50
dog	free - £ 2.50
Tents are not accepted.	

Grantham

Woodland Waters

Willoughby Road, Ancaster, Grantham NG32 3RT (Lincolnshire) T: 01400 230888.
E: info@woodlandwaters.co.uk **alanrogers.com/UK3765**

This attractive holiday park occupies 70 acres of woodland, gently-sloping grassland and lakes, with the caravan park itself occupying about 20 acres. There are 120 pitches although only 60 are regularly used (all with 10A electricity and water taps nearby). There is a rally field of 20 pitches with hook-ups, plus areas for camping and for those not requiring electricity. The land slopes gently down to the 14-acre lake and the pitches nearer the water are more level, although probably not suitable for those with younger children since there is no fencing. Reception is housed in a neat modern building at the park entrance. The welcome is warm, fishing tickets are sold and tourist information is available. The pleasant bar and restaurant (open to the public) occupy a chalet-style building near the lake; the menu seemed varied and reasonably priced. There are four fishing lakes (plus a junior pool). Some aircraft noise is possible.

Facilities

A single, modern, heated toilet block is well maintained and kept clean. Open style washbasins and free showers (controllable for ladies, pushbutton for men). Facilities for disabled visitors. A second block provides extra facilities when the additional camping areas are fully occupied. Laundry room with washing machine, tumble dryer and iron, but no sinks. Motorcaravan service point. Bar and restaurant with takeaway (all year). Play area. Four fishing lakes. Chalets to rent. WiFi. Off site: Limited bus service from near entrance. Shop and trains in village 1 mile. Golf 3 miles. Riding 6 miles.

Open: All year.

Directions

The park entrance is off the A153 Grantham - Sleaford road, 600 yds. west of the junction with the B6403 High Dyke road (Ermine Street). GPS: 52.98053, -0.54698

Charges guide

Per unit incl. 4 persons and electricity	£ 17.50 - £ 19.50
extra person	£ 2.00
child	£ 1.00
dog	£ 2.00
2.5% surcharge on credit card payments.	

Grantham

Wagtail Country Park

Cliff Lane, Marston, Grantham NG32 2HU (Lincolnshire) T: 07814 481088. E: info@wagtailcountrypark.co.uk

alanrogers.com/UK3775

There has been a small campsite here for many years, but the new owner has transformed the appearance of the original camping area alongside an attractive little fishing lake and is in the process of creating a new, larger lake with additional pitches and facilities. There are currently just 11 pitches all with electricity, on gravel hardstanding and separated by raised flower beds or timber beams. A new development will offer a further 20 pitches, including a couple on grass and ten fully serviced with water and drainage. There will also be five privately owned wooden chalets.

Facilities

Two small heated buildings provide spacious controllable showers and open-style washbasins. A new heated toilet block with full facilities is planned including a unit for disabled visitors and laundry facilities. Motorcaravan service point. Security barriers plus overnight pitch for late arrivals. Calor gas. Secure caravan storage. Fishing (£3 per person). No special provision for children and lake not fenced. Off site: Shopping Outlet and Garden Centre 3 miles. Belton House and golf 5 miles. Grantham 6 miles. Riding 7 miles. Belvoir Castle 12 miles. Newark 14 miles. Sailing at Rutland Water 25 miles. Coast 40 miles.

Open: All year.

Directions

Site is off the A1 between Grantham and Newark. Turn east towards Marston at filling station 1.2 miles north of Gonerby Services, Grantham and 8 miles south of Newark. In 500 yards turn right into Green Lane towards Barkston, then right again in 0.75 miles into Cliff Lane where park is signed and is on the left in 0.5 miles after entrance to Wagtail Fisheries. GPS: 52.961229, -0.667269

Charges guide

Per unit incl. 2 persons and electricity	£ 15.00
extra person	£ 1.00

No credit cards.

Halesowen

Clent Hills Camping & Caravanning Club Site

Fieldhouse Lane, Romsley, Halesowen B62 0NH (West Midlands) T: 01562 710015

alanrogers.com/UK4040

Conveniently close to Birmingham and only a couple of miles or so off the M5/M42 intersection, this site is a real surprise in terms of being quiet and peaceful and very pretty with panoramic views. The site has partially sloping ground, but site staff are happy to assist where required. Direct from the site there is wheelchair access to the top of Clint Hills. The 95 pitches are all of a good size, 73 with electrical connections (16A) and 28 with hardstanding. The modern reception building with tourist information, arrivals area and car parking area is at the entrance. This is an attractive site, very usefully situated.

Facilities

The central sanitary toilet block can be heated and provides the latest facilities, including washbasins in cabins, hairdryers, child and parent room and a wet room for disabled campers. It was spotless when last visited. Washing machine, dryer and ironing facilities. Small play area with rubber safety surface. Gas supplies. Caravan storage. WiFi (charged). Off site: Riding and fishing 1 mile.

Open: 29 March - 3 November.

Directions

From M5 junction 4 take A491, branch right to Romsley on B4551 and watch for site signs in Romsley village by shops. Site is on left. GPS: 52.41469, -2.06814

Charges guide

Per person	£ 5.90 - £ 9.05
child (6-18 yrs)	£ 2.65 - £ 2.85
non-member pitch fee	£ 7.10

Henley-in-Arden

Island Meadow Caravan Park

The Mill House, Aston Cantlow, Henley-in-Arden B95 6JP (Warwickshire) T: 01789 488273. E: holiday@islandmeadowcaravanpark.co.uk **alanrogers.com/UK4090**

This peaceful, traditional, family run site is in a rural location, surrounded by the River Alne and its mill race. A good base for walking, cycling and bird watching, it has 80 pitches in total, with 56 holiday homes (four for rent) located around the perimeter. The 24 touring pitches are on the spacious, central grassy area of the site, all have 10A electric hook-ups. Only environmentally friendly groundsheets are permitted. Note: The site is on an island with obvious hazards for small children. There is an excellent playground in the village centre (five minutes walk via footpath across Mill Meadow).

Facilities

Two sanitary units, both heated. The original with WCs and washbasins for men, and the more modern unit for women, with a separate access shower unit for the men. Suite for disabled visitors. Laundry. The millpond and its weir offer good coarse fishing. Off site: The village has its own 'club' (campers welcome) and local pub. Golf 3 miles. Riding 4.5 miles. Bicycle hire 6 miles.

Open: 1 March - 31 October.

Directions

From A46 (Stratford - Alcester) follow signs for Mary Arden's House. At Wilmcote follow signs to Aston Cantlow and site. GPS: 52.23549, -1.80265

Charges guide

Per unit incl. 2 persons and electricity	£ 20.00
extra person	£ 2.00

No credit cards.

For latest campsite news visit

alanrogers.com

Hereford

Lucksall Caravan & Camping Park

Mordiford, Hereford HR1 4LP (Herefordshire) T: 01432 870213. E: karen@lucksallpark.co.uk

alanrogers.com/UK4310

Set in 17 acres and bounded on one side by the River Wye, and over 90 acres of woodland on the other, Lucksall has 120 large, well spaced and level touring pitches, all with 16A electricity and 65 with hardstanding. The river is open to the site with lifebelts and safety messages in evidence. Canoes are available for hire or bring your own (launching facilities); fishing permits may be obtained from reception. A large, fenced playground and a large grassy area for games are provided. A well stocked shop selling a variety of goods is in reception (a mini market is within 1.5 miles) and a café is planned. A member of the Countryside Discovery group.

Facilities

Three centrally heated toilet blocks provide top of the range facilities, a separate unit with ramped entrance for disabled campers. Laundry room. Dishwashing area. Family room. WiFi. Only breathable groundsheets are permitted. Off site: Golf 5 miles. Bicycle hire 9 miles. Sustrans cycle route nearby.

Open: 1 March - 30 November.

Directions

Between Mordiford and Fownhope, 5 miles south east of Hereford on B4224, the park is well signed. GPS: 52.02302, -2.63052

Charges guide

Per unit incl. 2 persons	£ 17.00 - £ 24.00
extra person (over 17 yrs)	£ 3.50
small 3-man tent	£ 14.00 - £ 22.00

Hope

Laneside Caravan Park

Station Road, Hope Valley, Hope S33 6RR (Derbyshire) T: 01433 620215. E: laneside@lineone.net

alanrogers.com/UK3807

Laneside Caravan Park is in a beautiful location facing Win Hill, Lose Hill, and the high gritstone hills of The Dark Peak, while the gentler rolling hills of The White Peak are to the south. The park is on the floor of Hope Valley with the River Noe running alongside. There are 160 marked level pitches, 95 on grass and 30 on hardstanding are for touring, while 35 are seasonal; 110 have 16A electric hook-ups. The two toilet blocks have recently been refurbished. The site welcomes families (although there is no swimming pool on site) and quiet couples, and does not accept single-sex groups and unaccompanied teenagers.

Facilities

Two heated toilet blocks with family/disabled showers. Covered dishwashing facility. Laundry room with baby changing. Motorcaravan toilet service point. Site shop with basics. Gas exchange and basic camping spares. Information room. Dog walk. Payphone. Picnic benches. Large riverside recreation area with picnic benches and boules courts. Security barriers and CCTV. WiFi. Off site: Shops, pub and restaurant in Hope. Golf 2 miles. Bicycle hire 4 miles. Chatsworth 15 mins.

Open: Mid March to early November.

Directions

From the east via A619/A623, at Tideswell crossroads (Anchor pub), turn right onto B6049 signed Castleton and Bradwell. Turn left at T-junction with A6187 opposite The Travellers' Rest. Follow signs towards Hope. 500m after Travellers' Rest, just before Hope, look for sign on right directing you left into the park. GPS: 53.345159, -1.735706

Charges guide

Per unit incl. 2 persons	£ 14.50 - £ 19.75
extra person (over 5 yrs)	£ 2.75

Horncastle

Ashby Park

West Ashby, Horncastle LN9 5PP (Lincolnshire) T: 01507 527966. E: ashbyparklakes@btconnect.com

alanrogers.com/UK3680

Ashby Park is a pleasant, well run site located in 70 acres of former gravel pits that now provide seven attractive fishing lakes. There is a series of clearings occupied by privately owned caravan holiday homes, seasonal caravans and 70 touring pitches. Most are on grass, but some have hardstanding. All have access to electricity (16A) and 25 pitches also have hardstanding, water tap and drainage. Lakeside pitches will no doubt appeal to anglers, whereas families with young children will probably prefer to be further away from the lakes, as they are unfenced. One field caters for dog owners.

Facilities

Three toilet blocks are well maintained with open style washbasins and controllable showers; metered hot water (20p). Good en-suite facilities for disabled visitors. Laundry room. Limited dishwashing (a long walk from lakeside pitches). Motorcaravan service point. Gas supplies. Fishing (day ticket £6). WiFi. Off site: Golf 0.5 miles. Shops and restaurants in Horncastle 2.5 miles. Riding 5 miles. Sailing 12 miles. Seaside beaches 20 miles.

Open: 1 March - 30 November.

Directions

Site is 2.6 miles north of Horncastle and is signed to the east from the A158 and to the west from the A153 Sleaford - Louth road. Follow signs to site, turning north in half a mile. GPS: 53.233293, -0.122426

Charges guide

Per unit incl. 2 persons and electricity	£ 19.00
extra person	£ 4.00
No non-electric pitches.	

For latest campsite news visit

alanrogers.com

Leek

Glencote Caravan Park

Station Road, Cheddleton, Leek ST13 7EE (Staffordshire) T: 01538 360745. E: canistay@glencote.co.uk

alanrogers.com/UK3970

Nestled in the Churnet Valley, three miles south of the market town of Leek, a pleasant stay awaits you at this, well-managed, family run park of six acres. Each of the 74 level touring pitches, accessed via tarmac roads, has grass and a paved hardstanding, electrical connections (16A) and a dedicated water supply. Pretty flowerbeds, trees and varied wildlife make a very pleasant environment. Alongside a fenced coarse fishing pool is a grass play area and this whole corner is enclosed by banks with an abundance of attractive shrubs and flowers.

Facilities	Directions
The clean, heated toilet block includes a private cabin for ladies, a combined shower and toilet for disabled visitors, a small laundry room, two dishwashing sinks and one vegetable preparation sink under cover. Gas supplies. Max. 2 dogs per unit. WiFi (charged). Information centre and small library. Off site: Small supermarket and post office in Cheddleton 0.5 miles. Several inns, including the canalside Boat Inn, within walking distance. Golf 4 miles.	Park is signed off A520 Leek - Stone road, 3.5 miles south of Leek on northern edge of Cheddleton Village. GPS: 53.06994, -2.02901

Open: 1 February - end December.

Charges guide

Per unit incl. 2 persons and electricity	£ 22.00
extra person	£ 5.00
child (5-16 yrs)	£ 2.50

Leominster

Townsend Touring & Caravan Park

Townsend Farm, Pembridge, Leominster HR6 9HB (Herefordshire) T: 01544 388527.
E: info@townsend-farm.co.uk   **alanrogers.com/UK4345**

This is a modern, family run campsite hidden in a natural dip next to a working farm, but within a short walk of Pembridge. It has tarmac roads, good site lighting, well spaced pitches and a drive-over motorcaravan service point. There is plenty of open space and a small fishing lake with ducks (completely unfenced). There are 60 pitches in total, 23 with gravel hardstanding, the remainder on grass, and all have access to electricity hook-up (16A), water and drainage. Reception is at the farm shop by the entrance, stocking a wide variety of goods. New for 2010 were three standard and one jumbo sized pods for rent. A member of the Best of British Group.

Facilities	Directions
A modern, heated building surrounded by wide decking has ramps giving easy access for wheelchairs to all facilities including the dishwashing area, laundry room and chemical disposal point. Inside are spacious controllable showers, some washbasins in cubicles, a suite for disabled guests, family bathroom and baby changing facilities. Off site: Riding and bicycle hire 0.5 miles. Kington 5 miles, Leominster and golf 7 miles.	Site is beside the A44, 7 miles west of Leominster. Site is just inside the 30 mph. speed limit on the eastern edge of Pembridge village. GPS: 52.21792, -2.88845

Open: 1 March - 15 January.

Charges guide

Per unit incl. 2 persons, electricity, water and drainage	£ 17.00 - £ 26.00
extra person	£ 5.00

Ludlow

Westbrook Park

Little Hereford, Ludlow SY8 4AU (Shropshire) T: 01584 711280. E: info@bestparks.co.uk

alanrogers.com/UK4390

A beautifully kept, traditional, quiet touring campsite in a working cider apple orchard, Westbrook Park is bordered on one side by the River Teme and is within walking distance of the village and pub. There are 60 level pitches with 16A electric hook-ups, gravel or concrete/gravel all-weather hardstandings with water and waste water drainage. Some pitches have semi-shade, others have none. All the pitches at Westbrook have recently been upgraded. The new spacious, hardstanding pitches, with new and improved electricity supply, TV aerial, water and waste water have been very well received.

Facilities	Directions
A modern, timber-clad, heated toilet block provides spacious hot showers (coin-operated), washbasins in curtained cubicles, a basic laundry room and dishwashing sinks. Full facilities for disabled visitors (WC and basin). Gas supplies. Playground. Fishing (£4 per day). Riverside walks. No gazebos. No cycling. Only well-behaved dogs accepted. Off site: The Temeside Inn (no credit cards but has ATM). Golf 3 miles. Riding and bicycle hire 5 miles.	From A49 midway between Ludlow and Leominster, turn east at Woofferton on A456 (Tenbury Wells, Kidderminster). After 2 miles turn right just before river bridge and Temeside Inn. Turn left after 150 yds. Park is on left. Access roads are narrow. GPS: 52.307377, -2.665815

Open: 1 March - 30 November.

Charges guide

Per unit incl. 2 persons	£ 18.00 - £ 25.00
extra person	£ 4.00

For latest campsite news visit

alanrogers.com

Lutterworth

Stanford Hall Caravan Park

Stanford Road, Swinford, Lutterworth LE17 6DH (Leicestershire) T: 01788 860387.
E: stanfordpark@yahoo.co.uk **alanrogers.com/UK3890**

This picturesque and tranquil site is ideally situated for an overnight stop where you are guaranteed a warm welcome and a pleasant stay. Formerly a Caravan Club site, it is set in the rural grounds of the Stanford Hall Estate, just a mile from the M1. There are 123 pitches (30 of which are seasonal), 80 on grass and 43 on hardstanding, all with 16A electricity. There are no shower or toilet facilities on the park, so your unit must be self contained. The site experiences high levels of repeat bookings so you are advised to contact them in advance of busy weekends to avoid being disappointed. Dogs are welcome but must be kept on a lead on the main site. A designated dog walk has been established through part of the estate woodland. Visitors staying on site (for two nights or more) receive free admission to the grounds of Stanford Hall during normal opening times, except on certain event days. There is a small charge for admission to the house.

Facilities

There are no toilets or shower facilities on site which means each unit must be totally self-contained. Tents are not accepted. A small shop sells basics. Newspapers can be ordered daily. Motorcaravan services. Picnic tables. Information room. Off site: Supermarkets and banks in Lutterworth. Warwick Castle 25 miles. NEC, Birmingham 30 miles. Stratford Upon Avon 35 miles. Silverstone, Rockingham and Mallory Park Race Circuits and Althorpe are all within easy reach. Good location for walking and fishing. Jurassic Walk and the Grand Union Canal nearby.

Open: All year.

Directions

From the north on M1 and from M6 leave at exit 19 and at roundabout take first exit, signed Swinford, and follow signs for Stanford Hall. Site is on the left on Stanford Road. From east on A14, at the junction with M1 roundabout, take exit to Swinford. From south on the M1, leave at exit 18 onto A428, A5 north and then follow signs for Stanford Hall. GPS: 52.406493, -1.149361

Charges guide

Per unit incl. 2 adults, 2 children and electricity	£ 14.00
extra person	£ 1.50
dog	free

STANFORD HALL CARAVAN PARK
- This picturesque and tranquil site is set in the rural Grounds of the Stanford Hall Estate
- Open all year
- Great location for Walkers, Twitchers and Fishing with Jurassic Walk and the Grand Union Canal close by
- Call Charlotte or Eddie on 01788 860387 or e-mail us at stanfordpark@yahoo.co.uk

Malvern

Kingsgreen Caravan Park

Kingsgreen, Berrow, Malvern WR13 6AQ (Worcestershire) T: 01531 650272
alanrogers.com/UK4190

An attractive, welcoming and well kept site with views of the Malvern Hills, Kingsgreen is in a lovely rural location. An ideal site for adults who like the quiet life, there are no amusements for children. The surrounding countryside is ideal for walking or cycling, and the small, fenced fishing lakes on the site are well stocked (£4 per day). There are 45 level, grass and gravel pitches, all with electricity (13A), plus an additional area for tents. Some old orchard trees provide a little shade in parts. The site is seven miles from the market town of Ledbury with its half-timbered buildings. A barrier is closed at all times.

Facilities

Modern heated toilet facilities (key on deposit) provide hot showers (25p token from reception) and a separate unit for disabled visitors (WC and washbasin). No baby changing facilities. Laundry room with coin-operated washing machine and dryer. Gas. Fishing.
Off site: Nearest shop and pub 1.5 miles. Riding 3 miles. Golf 5 miles.

Open: 1 March - 31 October.

Directions

From M50 exit 2, take A417 towards Gloucester, then first left, where site is signed, also signed the Malverns, back over the motorway. Site is 2 miles from the M50. GPS: 52.00211, -2.33929

Charges guide

Per unit incl. 2 persons and electricity	£ 15.00 - £ 17.50
extra person (over 2 yrs)	£ 1.50
dog	£ 1.50
No credit cards.	

For latest campsite news visit
alanrogers.com

Market Rasen

Walesby Woodlands Caravan Park

Walesby, Market Rasen LN8 3UN (Lincolnshire) T: 01673 843285. E: walesbywoodlands@talk21.com

alanrogers.com/UK3660

Surrounded by mature Forestry Commission woodland, this small family run, no frills touring park is mainly very peaceful (if the wind is in a certain direction trains may be heard in the distance). The owners, Paul and Christine Burrows will make you very welcome. There are 60 well spaced pitches, 52 with 10A electricity, marked out in a single, mainly flat, grassy field divided by a central gravel road and with a double row of trees providing useful visual screening. About a mile away is the small town of Market Rasen, but further afield and within easy driving distance, are Lincoln, the east coast including Skegness and, of course, the Lincolnshire Wolds. The Viking Way passes through Walesby and there are many other shorter walks in the forest and surrounding area.

Facilities

The single, heated toilet block (£5 deposit charged for the key) is spacious and ample for the site. Pushbutton showers and open style washbasins. Toilet facilities for disabled visitors. Laundry room. Some basic supplies kept in reception. Coffee shop open at busy weekends. Battery charging. Gas supplies. Bicycle hire. No kite flying (overhead wires). Winter caravan storage. Off site: Golf 1.5 miles. Shops, supermarkets, pubs and restaurants 1-2 miles. Riding and racecourse 2 miles. Fishing 3 miles. Lincoln 17 miles. Beach (at Cleethorpes) 20 miles.

Open: 1 March - 31 October, plus Christmas and New Year.

Directions

Market Rasen is on the A46, 17 miles northeast of Lincoln. Park is just over a mile northeast of the town. Take the B1203 towards Tealby, then turn left about half a mile along Walesby Road. Site is on the left and is signed from all the main approach roads to town. GPS: 53.40135, -0.321

Charges guide

Per unit incl. 2 persons and electricity	£ 16.00 - £ 18.00
extra person	£ 2.00
child (under 12 yrs)	£ 1.50

Matlock

Lickpenny Touring Park

Lickpenny Lane, Tansley, Matlock DE4 5GF (Derbyshire) T: 01629 583040. E: lickpenny@btinternet.com

alanrogers.com/UK3815

This spacious caravan park on a hill above Matlock has 122 terraced pitches, all on hardstandings and with electricity (16A). Most have good countryside views. There are 100 touring pitches, 27 of which are fully serviced and 22 are seasonal. Tents are not accepted. There are rows of mature trees and pitches are large and separated by shrubs and bushes. The enthusiastic owners have taken full advantage of the fact that this was previously a market garden. High standards have been maintained and some facilities improved. Recreational grassy areas and attractive flower borders are well tended, whilst the top corner of the park has been kept as woodland.

Facilities

Two well equipped, heated toilet blocks include free preset showers and some washbasins in cubicles. Good facilities for disabled visitors. Family room with small bath, toilet and washbasin. Bathroom for children. Laundry room with washing machines, dryers, irons and ironing boards. Motorcaravan service point. Play area. Security barrier with keypad access at all times. Tents are not accepted. Off site: Bus service from end of the road. Woodland walk to garden centre with restaurant serving snacks and lunches (200 yards). Riding 1 mile. Fishing 3 miles. Golf 4 miles. Bicycle hire 6 miles.

Open: All year.

Directions

Matlock is 18 miles west of M1 exit 28. From motorway, follow signs for Matlock on A38, A61 and A615. After 5 miles on A615 turn north on Lickpenny Lane to site (signed). From Matlock take A615; after Tansley fork left on B6014 (Clay Cross) and turn right at top of hill after Garden Centre. GPS: 53.134787, 1.491190

Charges guide

Per unit incl. 2 persons and electricity	£ 15.00 - £ 22.00
extra person	£ 5.00
child (4-15 yrs)	£ 2.50
dog	free

For latest campsite news visit

alanrogers.com

Meriden

Somers Wood Caravan Park

Somers Road, Meriden CV7 7PL (Warwickshire) T: 01676 522978. E: enquiries@somerswood.co.uk

alanrogers.com/UK4070

Somers Wood is a quiet, peaceful park, attractively situated amongst pine trees. This is a very pleasant park which only accepts adults and does not take tents. It is especially useful for those visiting the various shows at the NEC when it can get very busy. From the reception building at the entrance, an oval gravel road provides access to 48 pitches, all on hardstanding and with 10A electricity hook-ups. Areas of woodland, carpeted with flowers in summer, surround the site and partition it into small intimate areas that create a rural feel. Log buildings blend comfortably into the surroundings providing reception, the owners' home, separate sanitary facilities and tourist information. There are also wooden tables and chairs. The site is beside an 18-hole golf course and a fishing lake, both of which may be used by visitors and next to a bridle path which can be used to exercise dogs. A member of the Best of British Group.

Facilities	Directions
The central, heated, completely refurbished sanitary block is fully equipped, with facilities for disabled visitors. Shower cubicles are especially large. Two dishwashing sinks on the veranda area. Laundry service at reception. WiFi on payment. Off site: Local shops and restaurant less than 1 mile and visitors also welcome to use the bar and restaurant at the golf club next door.	From M42 exit 6 (NEC) take A45 towards Coventry. Keep in left lane down to roundabout and exit on A452 (signed Leamington/Meriden), then turn left into Hampton Lane at the next roundabout. Site is signed with golf and fishing centres on the left. GPS: 52.43930, -1.66947

Open: All year.

Charges guide

Per unit incl. 2 persons and electricity	£ 20.00 - £ 23.00
extra person	£ 3.00
dog	free - £ 1.00

Special offers for some weeks.

Moreton-in-Marsh

Moreton-in-Marsh Caravan Club Site

Bourton Road, Moreton-in-Marsh GL56 0BT (Gloucestershire) T: 01608 650519

alanrogers.com/UK4130

This excellent, busy but rural site is attractively located within mature woodland in the heart of the Cotswolds and offers what one would hope for from a camping holiday. Within easy walking distance (250 yards) of the interesting market town of Moreton-in-Marsh, there is ample choice for food and pubs. The town's main street is part of the Roman Fosse Way. The site has 183 pitches, all with 16A electricity and TV sockets, 173 with hardstanding. A size limit of 8.2 metres for motorcaravans and caravans exists. Milk and ice cream are available from reception. Family recreation facilities include crazy golf, 5-a-side football, volleyball, boules and an adventure climbing frame.

Facilities	Directions
The two main toilet blocks have been renovated and offer excellent facilities. A separate toilet block exists with disabled toilet and baby room containing a small toilet and bath with seat for children. Large laundry. Play area. Crazy golf. Volleyball. Boules. WiFi (charged). No kite flying (power cables). Off site: Shops, pubs and restaurants 400 yds. Golf 11 miles. Nearby are the Cotswold Falconry Centre, Hidcote Manor Gardens, Snowshill Manor and the Rollright Stones. Broadway Tower is under 10 miles away with panoramic views over the surrounding countryside.	From Evesham on A44, site on left after Bourton-on-the-Hill village, 150 yds. before town sign. From Moreton-in-Marsh take A44 towards Evesham and site is on right, 150 yds. past the Wellington museum. GPS: 51.988857, -1.710278

Open: All year.

Charges guide

Per person	£ 5.40 - £ 7.60
child (5-16 yrs)	£ 1.50 - £ 3.10
pitch incl. electricity (non-member)	£ 13.20 - £ 17.50

Newark
Smeaton's Lakes Touring Caravan & Fishing Park

Great North Road, South Muskham, Newark-on-Trent NG23 6ED (Nottinghamshire) T: 01636 605088.
E: lesley@smeatonslakes.co.uk **alanrogers.com/UK3940**

This 82-acre site is really ideal for anglers, with four fishing lakes (coarse, carp and pike) and river fishing on the Trent. There are 130 pitches of which 100 have electricity connections (16A). Non-anglers might choose this park if visiting antique fairs or events at nearby Newark Showground, or Newark town (1 mile) with its castle, air museum and various weekly markets. During your stay, you might visit Southwell Minster, Sherwood Forest, Clumber Park, Lincoln with its castle and cathedral or Nottingham with its castle, caves and shopping centres.

Facilities

Two toilet blocks (with keypad access) are heated and include a good unit for disabled visitors, but no laundry room. Laundry and dishwashing sinks are outside. Small shop with gas, soft drinks, dairy produce, etc. Newspapers can be ordered. On-site concessions for lake and river fishing. Entry barrier with key access. Security cameras and night-time height barrier (about 6 ft). Off site: Bus stop. Riding and boat launching 2 miles.

Open: All year.

Directions

From south on A1, take A46 west (signed Newark, then Leicester), turn north on A6065/A616 towards South Muskham. Pass through village and continue on A616 to site on the left.
GPS: 53.0936, -0.820667

Charges guide

Per unit incl. 2 persons and electricity	£ 16.00 - £ 20.00

Newark
Milestone Caravan Park

Great North Road, Cromwell, Newark NG23 6JE (Nottinghamshire) T: 01636 821244.
E: enquiries@milestonepark.co.uk **alanrogers.com/UK3945**

Situated just off the A1 north of Newark, Milestone has a good deal more to offer than simply a stopover option. Its 102 good-sized, level touring pitches all have electricity (16A) and nearby water points. Grass pitches are available, but most are all-weather in a variety of locations. Six are outside the barrier for those in transit (although key access is always available), then comes a pleasantly landscaped area and finally terraces overlooking an attractive fishing lake. An embankment built to muffle traffic noise provides a pleasant grassed walk with views across an adjoining lake and the surrounding countryside.

Facilities

Two heated toilet blocks provide pushbutton showers and open-style washbasins. Excellent en-suite facilities for disabled visitors. Laundry facilities. Motorcaravan service points. Comprehensive tourist information, guides and children's quiz sheets on the site's wildlife. No play area. Fishing (charged). Off site: Large fishing lake adjacent. Village has shop, small brewery and buses to Newark. Riding and boat launching 3 miles. Golf 5 miles.

Open: All year.

Directions

From the south on A1, 3.7 miles after A46 junction, take slip road to Cromwell and site is on the left after the village. From the north on A1, 9 miles after Markham Moor junction, take slip road for Cromwell, turn right over bridge and right again to site.
GPS: 53.14985, -0.80693

Charges guide

Per unit incl. 2 persons and electricity	£ 15.90 - £ 22.40

Newark
Orchard Park

Marnham Road, Tuxford, Newark NG22 0PY (Nottinghamshire) T: 01777 870228.
E: info@orchardcaravanpark.co.uk **alanrogers.com/UK3950**

This well established family run touring and caravan park has been created in an old fruit orchard in a quiet location, yet is very convenient for the A1. It has a friendly feel, with just 77 pitches, all with electricity (10A), 34 with hardstanding and about 30 occupied by seasonal units. There is also a spacious camping field with good views. Reception is at the owner's house with a nearby cabin with information on attractions including Sundown Adventureland, Laxton Medieval village and Victorian Times, Rufford Abbey, Clumber Park, Sherwood Forest and the Robin Hood Centre.

Facilities

The heated toilet block has pushbutton showers, open style washbasins and a well equipped room for disabled visitors. Laundry with washing machines, dryer and dishwashing sinks, free spin dryer, iron and freezer for ice-packs. Small shop with basics and gas. Picnic area. Excellent children's adventure trail and nature walk. Apples, pears and blackberries can be picked in season. WiFi available on most of site (charged). Off site: Pub 0.5 miles, shops 1 mile. Riding 3 miles. Fishing 4 miles.

Open: March - October.

Directions

The Park lies to the east of the A1. Leave at signs for Tuxford and turn east on A6075 towards Lincoln (A57), continue through village and turn south towards Marnham for 0.5 miles. Site is on right 0.5 miles after railway bridge (well signed).
GPS: 53.2296, -0.8695

Charges guide

Per unit incl. 2 persons and electricity	£ 17.00 - £ 19.00
extra person	£ 4.00

For latest campsite news visit
alanrogers.com

Nottingham

Thornton's Holt Camping Park

Stragglethorpe, Radcliffe-on-Trent, Nottingham NG12 2JZ (Nottinghamshire) T: 0115 9332125.
E: camping@thorntons-holt.co.uk **alanrogers.com/UK3935**

Thornton's Holt is an attractively laid out, great family camping park at Stragglethorpe, a scattered rural hamlet 3.5 miles southeast of the city of Nottingham. The 155 spacious pitches are arranged in four separate areas, including one with an orchard setting. With a mixture of grass and gravel hardstanding, most have access to 10A electricity. The owners encourage a friendly farm-type atmosphere with free range chickens, ducks and guinea fowl wandering around the park. You may also encounter Eric, Spike and Pickle the resident horses, as well as dogs and a cat. Amenities include a heated indoor swimming pool (charged) and a large play area for children.

Facilities

The single toilet block is dated and unheated but due to be replaced in 2012. Open washbasins, showers on payment (20p). Basic facilities for disabled visitors. Laundry. Small shop (1/4-31/10). Heated indoor pool (1/4-31/10). Play area. Bungalow to rent. Caravan storage. Off site: Pub/restaurant adjacent. Supermarket 1 mile. Golf 0.5 miles. Cotgrave Country Park 0.5 miles.

Open: All year.

Directions

From A46, join A52 westbound. Pass Radcliffe-on-Trent and after 1.5 miles turn left at traffic lights (white house) into Stragglethorpe Road signed Cotgrave and Cropwell Bishop. Site is on left just after railway bridge. GPS: 52.932024, -1.053404

Charges guide

Per unit incl. 2 persons and electricity	£ 15.50 - £ 20.00

Oakham

Rutland Caravan & Camping Park

Park Lane, Greetham, Oakham LE15 7FN (Rutland) T: 01572 813520.
E: info@rutlandcaravanandcamping.co.uk **alanrogers.com/UK3903**

First opened in 2002, this family-run site is situated in the heart of England's smallest county – Rutland. The family continue to invest in the site which is currently rather open. The 256 pitches have limited shade and are not fenced. There are four separate pitching areas, one reserved for adults and another for families, with two for tents. Hardstanding is provided on 66 pitches, 10A electricity on 156 pitches and full services on 10 pitches. There may be some noise from nearby RAF Cottesmore. The site is beside the village of Greetham (with a footpath from the site).

Facilities

Two modern heated toilet blocks. Private bathroom. Baby changing facility. Facilities for disabled visitors. Laundry. Motorcaravan services. Small shop (essentials only). Gas and camping gas. Play area. Picnic tables. Five-a-side football pitch. Security barrier (£10 deposit for card). WiFi (charged). Off site: Fishing, riding and bicycle hire 3 miles. Golf 4 mile. Rutland Water 4 miles. Oakham 5 miles.

Open: All year.

Directions

From the A1 turn off on the B668 towards Greetham Village. Turn right at crossroads before the village and take second left. From Oakham, take B668 through Greetham. Turn left at crossroads at end of village, then second left. GPS: 52.72402, -0.63288

Charges guide

Per unit incl. 2 persons and electricity	£ 15.90 - £ 22.40

Oakham

Greendale Farm Caravan & Camping Park

Pickwell Lane, Whissendine, Oakham LE15 7LB (Rutland) T: 01664 474516. E: enq@rutlandgreendale.co.uk
alanrogers.com/UK3904

This is a delightful little adults only park set in rolling countryside, ideal for those seeking peace and tranquillity. It is very eco-friendly and extremely well appointed for such a small site. There are only 13 pitches, all with 10 or 16A electricity, so it is worth checking availability! Reception, the shop and the toilet facilities are housed in a modern building adjoining the owners' house. The shop is well stocked with essentials and local produce. Cooked breakfasts are available on Sundays. It also has one of the best presented and most comprehensive information displays we have seen on any campsite. New flower beds and wild flower planting add to the appeal of the site. No arrivals before 13.30.

Facilities

Each of the two rooms of the toilet block has a power shower, WCs and two washbasins. All is beautifully clean. Laundry facilities. Small open-air swimming pool (6x3 m; June-Sept; £1 charge), solar heated, with summer house. Two bicycles for hire. WiFi (charged). Off site: Village with bus service 0.5 miles. Supermarket in Oakham and riding 4 miles. Fishing 3 miles. Golf 8 miles. Sailing, walking, cycling, birdwatching and fishing at Rutland Water 8 miles. Barnsdale Garden 8 miles.

Open: 15 April - 30 September.

Directions

Oakham is 20 miles east of Leicester. Approach park from A606, NOT through the village. From Oakham ignore first turning to Whissendine, continue 2 miles and turn right at campsite sign. From Melton ignore first two turnings to Whissendine; turn left 0.6 mile after Rutland sign. Park is on right in 0.6 mile. GPS: 52.711833, -0.788617

Charges guide

Per unit incl. two adults	£ 18.00 - £ 23.00

For latest campsite news visit
alanrogers.com

Peterchurch

Poston Mill Caravan Park

Peterchurch HR2 0SF (Herefordshire) T: 01981 550225. E: info@poston-mill.co.uk

alanrogers.com/UK4300

Set in pleasant undulating farmland in the heart of the Golden Valley, Poston Mill Park is a mile from the delightful village of Peterchurch. It is an ideal location for relaxation or exploring. There are currently 43 touring pitches set on level grass or hardstanding with mature trees around the perimeter of the park. All pitches are fully serviced with electricity (16A), water and TV connections (leads for hire), and new in 2010, an area set aside for tents. An attractive walk along one side of the park, edging the River Dore (fishing available), follows the line of the old Golden Valley railway. Adjoining the park is The Mill licensed restaurant (takeaways available) and a general store selling a range of produce and newspapers.

Facilities	Directions
One central sanitary block with a smaller, refurbished block near the holiday home area which includes private cubicles. Both include units for disabled guests. Laundry rooms. Motorcaravan service point. Play area. Pitch and putt. Tennis, pétanque and croquet. Golf driving range. Games room. Winter caravan storage. WiFi (charged).	Park is 1 mile southeast of Peterchurch on B4348 road. GPS: 52.02832, -2.9388

Open: All year.

Charges guide

Per unit incl. 2 persons and electricity	£ 18.00 - £ 25.00

Retford

Trentfield Farm Camping & Caravanning

Church Laneham, Retford DN22 0NJ (Nottinghamshire) T: 01777 228651. E: post@trentfield.co.uk

alanrogers.com/UK3955

A small, friendly, professionally run park, the owners of Trentfield Farm work on the policy of old-fashioned camping and caravanning with all the new amenities and mod-cons! Located in north Nottinghamshire, Trentfield Farm is set between historic Lincoln, Newark, Worksop and Gainsborough, immediately on the banks of the River Trent. It is just within the idyllic hamlet of Church Laneham, an old estate village of the Bishop of York which is steeped in history. The campsite is level and free draining with 70 grass pitches, 16A electricity hook-ups and nearby taps. There is private river frontage with free coarse fishing. Three excellent golf courses are also only a short drive away.

Facilities	Directions
The heated toilet block has push-button showers and open style washbasins. Family shower room. No facilities for disabled visitors. Laundry with washing machines, dryer and free spin dryer, iron and freezer for ice-packs. Small 24 hour vending machine with basics. No play area. WiFi in most areas (free). Off site: Sundown Adventureland, Lincoln City and Cathedral, Sherwood Forest and Clumber park, Pureland Japanese Garden. Tennis 1 mile. Riding 1 mile.	From A1/A57 roundabout at Markham Moor follow A57 towards Lincoln for 6 miles. Take second turning into Laneham and go 1.5 miles through village towards river and ferry. Continue through Church Laneham, past Ferry Boat Inn on left and river on right. Go past Manor House Residential Park, up small rise, park is 300 yds. on right. GPS: 53.287685, -0.777497

Open: Easter - 31 October.

Charges guide

Per unit incl. 2 persons and electricity	£ 18.50

Ripley

Golden Valley Caravan & Camping Park

Coach Road, Golden Valley, Ripley DE55 4ES (Derbyshire) T: 01773 513881.
E: enquiries@goldenvalleycaravanpark.co.uk **alanrogers.com/UK3865**

Golden Valley Caravan & Camping Park is located in the beautiful hamlet of Golden Valley alongside the Cromford Canal in the Amber Valley area of the Peak District. The site is situated within 26 acres of historic woodland which was once a thriving industrial centre for coal, iron foundries and canal workers on the adjacent canal. This secluded woodland site has just 40 pitches on grass or hardstanding for motorcaravans and caravans. There are 24 with independent water supply, electrical connection and mains drainage. There are also two wooded areas for tents and a communal barbecue area.

Facilities	Directions
A centrally positioned, heated utility block provides free showers and toilets, facilities for disabled visitors, a laundry room, heated jacuzzi, an indoor playroom and a gym. Bar and café (July/Aug and weekends). Fishing pond. Woodland walks. Play area. Tourist information. Off site: Midland Railway Centre. Denby Pottery. Derby 7 miles. Nottingham 15 miles. Walking and cycling in the Peak District National Park. Golf 1 mile. Riding 2 miles.	Leave M1 at exit 26, follow signs for Matlock and Ripley (A610). At Codnor, turn right at traffic lights then first right onto the Alfreton Road. After 2 miles turn left before passing the Newlands Inn to join Coach Road. Site entrance is on the left. GPS: 53.05669, -1.37267

Open: All year.

Charges guide

Per unit incl. 2 persons	£ 15.00 - £ 30.00

(185)

Ross-on-Wye

Doward Park Camp Site

Great Doward, Symonds Yat West, Ross-on-Wye HR9 6BP (Herefordshire) T: 01600 890438.
E: enquiries@dowardpark.co.uk **alanrogers.com/UK4360**

The site, which was created around 1997 in a disused quarry, has matured into a very pleasant, peaceful little site, partially terraced, and in a sheltered location. The access roads and the physical proportions of the site make it suitable only for tents, trailer tents and campervans. This site is popular with couples, nature lovers, walkers and those with young families, but has nothing for teenagers. There is a children's play area in Bluebell Wood (unsupervised) at the top of the site with a rope swing and a Timber Trak. Of the 25 pitches for touring (11 with 16A electricity), three are hardstanding for motorcaravans up to 23 feet in length, the remainder are on grass. Five hardstandings are used for seasonal units.

Facilities

A neat central building provides the usual facilities including refurbished hot showers. No designated area for disabled visitors, but toilet facilities have wide access. Dishwashing sinks and a freezer for ice packs. Small shop selling basic supplies. Service washing and drying facilities available. Torches are advisable. Bicycle hire. Off site: Variety of inns at both Symonds Yat West and East all offering meals. Fishing 1 mile. Shops and services in Monmouth 4 miles. Golf 4 miles. Bicycle hire 10 miles.

Open: 15 March - 31 October.

Directions

From A40 between Ross-on-Wye and Monmouth, turn for Symonds Yat West, and follow signs for Doward Park and Biblins. Turn into narrow lane for about 1 mile and site is on right, on sharp left hand bend. GPS: 51.838517, -2.657

Charges guide

Per unit incl. 2 persons	
and electricity	£ 16.00 - £ 20.00
extra person	£ 3.00
child (4-15 yrs)	£ 2.50
dog	£ 1.00

Ross-on-Wye

Broadmeadow Caravan & Camping Park

Broadmeadows, Ross-on-Wye HR9 7BW (Herefordshire) T: 01989 768076. E: broadm4811@aol.com
alanrogers.com/UK4320

Ross-on-Wye town centre is within easy walking distance of this modern, spacious park, complete with open views and its own fishing lake. The approach to the site is unusual, passing through an industrial estate, but eventually you will arrive at a well laid out and pleasant site with facilities of the highest quality. There are 150 large pitches on a mixture of hardstanding and level, open grass; the site is especially good for tents. Each set of four pitches has a service post with water, drain, electricity points (16A) and lighting. There may be some traffic noise from the A40 relief road. Seasonal pitches are now available. The market town of Ross-on-Wye is centrally placed for touring Herefordshire, the Wye Valley and the Forest of Dean. The town has many facilities such as an indoor swimming pool, putting greens and tennis courts, and lots of good places to eat and drink. Shopping is excellent with a general market held on Thursdays and Saturdays with a farmers' market on the first Friday of each month.

Facilities

Two fully equipped, modern sanitary blocks with baby rooms, family bathrooms each with WC, basin and bath, and a comprehensive unit for disabled visitors. Dishwashing room and laundry at each block. Basic motorcaravan service point. Entrance barrier and keypad exit system. Small part-fenced playground. Fenced fishing lake (coarse fishing £7.50 per rod per day – fishing licence not available at reception). Off site: Supermarket 200 yds. Bicycle hire in town. Golf 3 miles. Riding 8 miles.

Open: Easter/1 April - 30 September.

Directions

From A40 relief road turn into Ross at roundabout, take first right into industrial estate, then right in 0.5 miles before supermarket, where site is signed. GPS: 51.91657, -2.57489

Charges guide

Per unit incl. 2 persons	
and electricity	£ 22.25 - £ 24.75
extra person	£ 5.00
child (2-9 yrs)	£ 3.00
dog	£ 1.75

Royal Leamington Spa

Harbury Fields Farm Touring Caravan Park

Middle Road, Harbury CV33 9JN (Warwickshire) T: 01926 612457. E: rdavis@harburyfields.co.uk

alanrogers.com/UK4065

This is a delightful, family-run caravan park surrounded by a 222-acre working sheep farm. Peaceful and quiet, it is set in the unspoilt 'Shakespeare countryside'. Located well away from main roads, it is just a mile from the lively village of Harbury, an ancient prehistoric settlement on a hill near the Fosse Way Roman Road in Warwickshire. There are only 34 spacious pitches (31 on hardstanding, 3 on grass), all with 16A electricity and 8 with full services. Tents are not accepted. The surrounding area has several old quarries that were historically used to extract lyas, a form of limestone used in the manufacture of cement. These are now predominantly used for recreation and make for unique family excursions.

Facilities

Two heated toilet blocks have walk in shower cubicles with washbasin. Separate cubicles with WCs for men and similar for women. Toilet facilities for families and disabled visitors. Washing machine and dryer. Motorcaravan service point. No shop. Off site: Village with pubs, shops, post office and small supermarket. Bus service at end of drive. Fishing and golf 4 miles. Leamington Spa 4 miles. Warwick Castle 6 miles. Stratford upon Avon 11 miles.

Open: 2 January - 21 December.

Directions

From south M40, take exit 12 and turn left. After 0.5 miles turn right, then in 3 miles at second roundabout turn right (4th exit) onto B4455 Fosse Way (signed Harbury). After 2 miles turn right signed Harbury and site is 420 yds.
GPS: 52.23985, -1.48689

Charges guide

Per unit incl. 2 persons	£ 15.50 - £ 22.40
extra person	£ 2.50

Shrewsbury

Beaconsfield Farm Caravan Park

Battlefield, Shrewsbury SY4 4AA (Shropshire) T: 01939 210370. E: mail@beaconsfield-farm.co.uk

alanrogers.com/UK4410

Just north of the historic market town, a drive of half a mile through open fields lead to this purpose-designed park for adults only (over 21 years). It is neatly laid out in a rural situation, with a well stocked trout fishing lake and a small coarse pool forming the main feature. The ground has been levelled and grassed to provide 80 well-spaced pitches, all have 10A electricity connections, of which 50 are super hardstanding pitches. Two further areas accommodate 49 caravan holiday homes. The park is well lit with a circular tarmac access road, beyond a security barrier. A large timber chalet-style building provides reception and a coffee shop. A member of the Best of British Group.

Facilities

Heated toilet facilities (£2.50 key deposit) are of excellent quality, with preset showers and hairdryers. Excellent unit for disabled visitors. Laundry facilities. Motorcaravan services. Restaurant. Indoor heated swimming pool (£3 per person, incl. steam room). Small library. Security barrier and CCTV. WiFi. Only two dogs per unit are accepted. Car hire available. Luxury lodges and static caravans for hire. Off site: Bicycle hire and golf 2 miles.

Open: All year.

Directions

Site is north of Shrewsbury off A49 Whitchurch road. In the village of Hadnall, turn right opposite the New Inn at camping sign towards Astley and park entrance is 400 yds. on right. Continue down 800 yds. narrow access road with passing places.
GPS: 52.770917, -2.704817

Charges guide

Per unit incl. 2 persons and electricity	£ 18.00 - £ 22.00

Shrewsbury

Oxon Hall Touring Park

Welshpool Road, Shrewsbury SY3 5FB (Shropshire) T: 01743 340868. E: oxon@morris-leisure.co.uk

alanrogers.com/UK4430

Oxon Hall is a purpose-built park, well situated for visiting Shrewsbury. Under the same ownership as Stanmore Hall (no. 4400) the site has been developed to a very high standard with mature trees and shrubs providing some shade and shelter. Of the 120 pitches only 105 are in use for tourers, all of which have electric hook-ups (16A), 65 are full service pitches (fresh and waste water facilities, TV hook-up), the others being either grass or with hardstanding. An area is set aside as an adults only section. Some pitches for RV-style units have 32A electric hook-ups. A member of the Best of British Group.

Facilities

Toilet facilities are first rate with washbasins in cubicles, ample showers, baby room, facilities for disabled visitors, dishwashing room and laundry, all at the entrance in a centrally heated building, also housing reception and shop – perhaps a hike from some pitches. Motorcaravan service point. Dog walk on site (max. 2). Deposit for toilet block key £5. Off site: Supermarket and pub nearby.

Open: All year.

Directions

From junction of A5 and A458, west of Shrewsbury, follow signs for Oxon 'park and ride'. Park is signed just 0.5 miles from junction.
GPS: 52.71540, -2.804917

Charges guide

Per person	£ 6.30 - £ 6.70
standard grass pitch	£ 9.00 - £ 10.90

For latest campsite news visit

alanrogers.com

Skegness

Skegness Sands Touring Site

Winthorpe Avenue, Skegness PE25 1QZ (Lincolnshire) T: 01754 761484. E: info@skegness-sands.com

alanrogers.com/UK3730

This very well organised touring site is part of a much larger caravan holiday home park, but has its own entrance. It is a modern, well appointed site adjacent to the promenade and beach. There are 85 pitches, all level and with electricity (16A); 45 are grass and 37 on gravel hardstandings, four of which are fully serviced. Site lighting is good throughout and there are regular security patrols. The gate to the promenade is kept locked at all times, campers getting a key. The site is a Caravan Club Affiliated Site; members and non-members are all made welcome.

Facilities

The good quality, heated toilet block includes washbasins in cubicles, three family shower rooms with WC and washbasin and a well equipped room for disabled campers. Laundry room. Gas supplies. Hairdressing salon. Indoor heated swimming pool (Spr. B.H-30 Sept; charged). Small modern playground. Off site: Well stocked shop/post office 500 m. Pubs, fast food outlets and a supermarket within easy walking distance. Fishing 1 mile. Golf 2 miles. Bicycle hire 2.5 miles. Riding 5 miles.

Open: All year.

Directions

Site is off A52 Boston - Skegness - Mablethorpe road, 1.75 miles north of Skegness town. Turn east opposite Garden City pub into Winthorpe Avenue, site entrance is on the left at far end of road. New arrivals please contact site if unable to arrive before 17.00. GPS: 53.1668, 0.3495

Charges guide

| Per unit incl. 2 persons and electricity | £ 17.30 - £ 23.70 |
| extra person | £ 5.70 - £ 7.35 |

Sleaford

Low Farm Touring & Camping Park

Spring Lane, Folkingham, Sleaford NG34 0SJ (Lincolnshire) T: 01529 497322. E: lowfarmpark@sky.com

alanrogers.com/UK3770

This quiet, secluded park is a lovely spot to relax or to use as a base for touring the Lincolnshire countryside. Jane and Nigel Stevens work hard to make this site a pleasant place to stay and have a well laid out park offering good quality facilities which are kept clean and tidy. The site offers 36 pitches (some occupied by seasonal vans) with electric hook-ups (10A) and a field for tents and small rallies. Some hardstandings are available. The site is on the edge of the village of Folkingham with a pub (serving food) and a couple of small shops.

Facilities

Central, well maintained toilet block with controllable free showers and open style washbasins. Washing machine. Reception is at the owners' house and a tourist information room with toilets is adjacent. Large field where children can play (sometimes used by tenters). Off site: Fishing 2 miles. Golf and riding 7 miles. Shops and supermarkets in Bourne (9 miles) and Sleaford 10 miles. Lincoln 26 miles. Sailing 30 miles.

Open: Easter - mid October.

Directions

Folkingham is 26 miles south of Lincoln on A15 to Peterborough, 2 miles south of junction with A52. Park is on southern edge of village; at foot of hill at campsite sign, turn west, site is at end of lane. GPS: 52.88685, -0.411167

Charges guide

| Per unit incl. 2 persons | £ 12.50 - £ 16.50 |

No credit cards.

Spalding

Foreman's Bridge Caravan Park

Sutton Saint James, Spalding PE12 0HU (Lincolnshire) T: 01945 440346. E: foremansbridge@btconnect.com

alanrogers.com/UK3750

Foreman's Bridge is a compact park occupying a large, level and grassy meadow surrounded by trees and high hedges which give it a very secluded feel. The park has 42 level pitches, of which 24 are now occupied by caravan holiday homes (7 for rent). The remainder are touring pitches, all with electricity (16A) and gravel hardstanding. Up to half of these are occupied on a seasonal basis. The park could be a useful base from which to explore the Fens and to visit Spalding, famous for its annual flower festival held at the beginning of May. At times there can be noise from military aircraft.

Facilities

The modern, brick-built toilet unit is spacious and kept clean, providing really large individual shower rooms with seats and washbasins (showers on payment). Laundry room. Gas. Fishing possible in the river running past the entrance. Bicycle hire. Two cottages to rent. Winter caravan storage. Off site: Small shop in village 1 mile. Golf 3 miles. Riding 8 miles. Coast 12 miles (The Wash); nearest beach 32 miles.

Open: 1 March - 15 January.

Directions

Sutton St James is 26 miles northeast of Peterborough. From A17 Spalding - Kings Lynn road turn south on B1390 at Long Sutton towards Sutton St James for about 2 miles. Site entrance is on the left immediately after the bridge. GPS: 52.75785, 0.088

Charges guide

| Per unit incl. 2 persons and electricity | £ 14.00 |

No credit cards.

For latest campsite news visit

alanrogers.com

Slimbridge

Tudor Caravan & Camping Park

Shepherds Patch, Slimbridge GL2 7BP (Gloucestershire) T: 01453 890483. E: info@tudorcaravanpark.co.uk

alanrogers.com/UK4170

This attractive, peaceful campsite is adjacent to the Gloucester - Sharpness Canal. Located behind the Tudor Arms public house, a gate clearly identifies the entrance and reception is up a short path on the left. There are many trees and hedges, particularly surrounding the site, so the canal is not visible. Attractively laid out on two separate fields, there are 75 pitches, all with electric hook-ups (16A), and 50 with hardstanding. The old orchard is for long stay or adults only units, with gravel hardstandings, and the more open grassy meadow for family touring units. There is also a rally field beyond the meadow. The adjacent pub has a restaurant and bar (2009 CAMRA award winner) and just across the road, beside the canal, is a café and shop where boats and bicycles can be hired. This is a delightful, peaceful park with plenty to offer: walking, fishing and boating, not to mention ornithology as the Wildfowl and Wetlands Centre founded by Sir Peter Scott at Slimbridge is only 800 yards away.

Facilities

The toilet building (can be heated in winter) is located to one side of the orchard and provides all the usual facilities including pushbutton hot showers. A second, high quality shower block with underfloor heating provides large shower cubicles, private washing cubicles, baby changing room and facilities for disabled visitors. Laundry. Gas available. Some site lighting but a torch would be useful. Gate locked 22.30-07.00. WiFi (charged). No charcoal barbecues. Off site: Meals at the Tudor Arms pub. Shop and café in boatyard opposite the site (Easter-Sept), also serves breakfasts. Fishing adjacent. Towpath walks. Berkeley Castle, Frampton and Stroud.

Open: All year.

Directions

From A38 by the junction with A4135 (Dursley), turn west, signed WWT Wetlands Centre Slimbridge. Continue for 1.5 miles turning left into car park of the Tudor Arms. Site entrance is at rear of car park. GPS: 51.735533, -2.395817

Charges guide

Per unit incl. 2 persons and electricity	£ 15.00 - £ 20.00
extra person	£ 3.00
child (under 12 yrs)	£ 1.50
No credit cards.	

Welcome to TUDOR CARAVAN PARK
Shepherds Patch, Slimbridge, Gloucestershire, GL2 7BP

• Open All Year
• Separate Adults Only Area
• Beside Gloucester-Sharpness Canal
• Award-winning Pub & Restaurant adjacent

Tel: (01453) 890483 Email: info@tudorcaravanpark.co.uk
Web: www.tudorcaravanpark.com

Quiet country site set in the beautiful Severn Vale, along the Cotswolds Edge – a short walk to world famous Slimbridge Wetlands Centre
Ideal base for touring the Cotswolds, visiting Bristol, Gloucester, Forest of Dean. Walking on the Severn Way alongside or the Cotswold Way, 4 miles away.

Stamford

Tallington Lakes Camping & Caravanning

Barholm Road, Tallington, Stamford PE9 4RJ (Lincolnshire) T: 01778 347000. E: info@tallington.com

alanrogers.com/UK3760

This well maintained and attractive 160-acre site surrounds over 200 acres of clean, spring fed water that provides many watersport activities including water-skiing, jet-skiing, sailing, windsurfing, canoeing, pedaloes and angling, along with a pro shop for watersports. In addition there is a 120 m. high, floodlit dry ski slope and a 15 m. tower for climbing and abseiling. Of the 338 pitches, 88 are in a separate area for touring and 46 have 10A electricity. They are level, in groups, separated by some hedging and are either on grass or hardstanding. Some mature trees give a little shade.

Facilities

The heated sanitary unit has facilities for babies, small children and campers with disabilities. Additional WCs and showers (also used by the water skiers). Laundry and dishwashing facilities. Motorcaravan service point. Bar and restaurant. Swimming and paddling pools (charged). Climbing wall. Go-karting. Watersports. Fishing. Dry-ski slope, snowboard centre and tennis. Small, well fenced, adventure style playground. Off site: Bus stop 1 mile. Stamford, golf, riding and bicycle hire 5 miles. Peterborough 11 miles. Stamford Museum, Burghley House, Sacrewell Farm and Country Centre and the Nene Valley Railway.

Open: All year.

Directions

From A16, midway between Stamford and Market Deeping, just east of the railway crossing at Tallington, turn north into Barholm Road. Site entrance is on the right in 0.3 miles (site is signed). GPS: 52.67007, -0.37940

Charges guide

Per unit incl. 2 persons and electricity	£ 20.00 - £ 30.00
extra person	£ 5.00
dog (max. 2)	£ 3.00

For latest campsite news visit
alanrogers.com

Stourport-on-Severn

Lickhill Manor Caravan Park

Lower Lickhill Road, Stourport-on-Severn DY13 8RL (Worcestershire) T: 01299 871041.
E: excellent@lickhillmanor.co.uk **alanrogers.com/UK4210**

Lickhill Manor is a well managed touring and holiday site within easy walking distance of the town centre, which is accessed by a footpath along the River Severn. Opportunities exist for fishing and boating. The site is open for tourers all year and there are 120 touring pitches all with hook-ups (10A), 57 with hardstanding and some with water and waste water. A large, 14-acre rally field with 68 hook-ups is available for tourers. An attractive site with 124 holiday homes, which are well screened from the touring areas, so not visually intrusive. There are two excellent play areas for children and a dog exercise field within the park. The site is well laid out, populated with native trees and shrubs and wildlife ponds.

Facilities

An additional sanitary building serves the touring pitches and complements the older unit at the far end of the park. This heated building provides good, modern facilities including a well equipped suite for disabled guests which doubles as a family room and baby changing. Drive-over motorcaravan service point. Gas supplies. Fishing permits are available from site shop. Off site: Stourport shops and pub 10 minutes walk. Riding 1 mile. Bicycle hire 3 miles.

Open: All year.

Directions

From A451 in Stourport take B4195 towards Bewdley. After 1 mile turn left at crossroads (traffic lights), into Lickhill Road North where site is signed. GPS: 52.343404, -2.299088

Charges guide

Per unit incl. 4 persons and electricity	£ 17.50 - £ 23.50
extra person (over 2 yrs)	£ 2.50

Stratford-Upon-Avon

Riverside Caravan Park

Tiddington Road, Tiddington, Stratford-Upon-Avon CV37 7AB (Warwickshire) T: 01789 292312.
E: info@riversidestratfordcaravans.co.uk **alanrogers.com/UK4080**

On the bank of the River Avon, this spacious site has about 225 pitches in total, and about 100 privately owned mobile homes. The 100 touring pitches (no tents) are on level grass, all with electric hook-ups (10A). There is a small shop and café on site, which serves breakfasts and takeaways in addition to stocking a good selection of basic supplies. A clubhouse that incorporates a bar, playground, games room and TV room is on the adjacent Rayford Park which is under the same management. There is a possible flood risk during periods of inclement weather. A river taxi runs to Stratford from the site. The site also now offers camping snugs for rent.

Facilities

The heated main toilet unit has been re-fitted and is bright and comfortable. Spacious preset showers, some washbasins in cubicles, with a child-size toilet and shower in the ladies. Facilities for disabled visitors. Separate toilet block for the snugs. Dishwashing and laundry facilities. Slipway and fishing on site. River launch to Stratford. Gas supplies. No commercial vehicles. Off site: Buses 50 yds. River cruises 100 yds. Historic Stratford 2 miles.

Open: 1 April - 31 October.

Directions

From Stratford take B4086 towards Wellesbourne. Site entrance is on left, after one mile, just before Tiddington village (ignore entrance to Rayford Park C.P.). GPS: 52.20023, -1.68213

Charges guide

Per unit incl. 2 persons and electricity	£ 17.00 - £ 25.00
extra person	£ 2.50

Sutton-on-Sea

Cherry Tree Site

Huttoft Road, Sutton-on-Sea LN12 2RU (Lincolnshire) T: 01507 441626. E: info@cherrytreesite.co.uk
alanrogers.com/UK3650

This is a delightful, tranquil, adult only site and is a fine example of a small, good value touring park. It is a 15-minute walk from a Blue Flag beach and a short drive from some of the attractive villages of the Lincolnshire Wolds. A very warm welcome awaits from Geoff and Margaret Murray whose attention to detail is evident everywhere. The site is level, the grass is neatly trimmed and well drained, and screening is provided by lines of evergreen hedging. There are 40 good sized touring pitches, all with 10A electricity and hardstanding (no tents) and ten with water and waste water drainage.

Facilities

The clean, brick-built toilet block was recently extended and refurbished to a high standard. Controllable hot showers, hairdryers. En-suite unit for disabled visitors (Radar key). Combined dishwashing and laundry room with washing machine, spin dryer and tumble dryer. Neat reception and separate tourist information cabin. Gas. Off site: Riding adjacent. Shop and pub 0.6 miles. Beach, tennis, bowls and fishing 1.5 miles. Golf 2 miles.

Open: 4 March - 29 October.

Directions

Sutton-on-Sea is 15 miles north of Skegness and 40 miles east of Lincoln. The site is 1.5 miles south of the town on A52 coast road, with the entrance leading off a lay-by on the east. GPS: 53.29292, 0.28439

Charges guide

Per unit incl. 2 persons	£ 17.00 - £ 21.00
extra person	£ 3.50

For latest campsite news visit
alanrogers.com

Tattershall

Tattershall Lakes Country Park

57 Sleaford Road, Tattershall LN4 4JG (Lincolnshire) T: 01526 348800. E: info@tattershall-lakes.com

alanrogers.com/UK3685

This extensive park with seven lakes of varying sizes is well kept, offers great opportunities for enthusiasts of watersports and fishing and is only a few hundred yards from the pleasant village of Tattershall. The touring fields are flat and rather featureless but with views across the main lake. There are 269 pitches, numbered but with no hedges or markings to separate them; 180 have electrical connections (16A) and 50 also have an individual tap and drainage, plus hardstanding. Fifty lodges and static caravans of varying styles are available for rent and a further 300 are privately owned. The lakeside clubhouse includes a coffee shop serving a variety of meals and snacks, a comfortable bar downstairs where the evening discos and other entertainment take place and, upstairs, another bar overlooking the lake. This houses electronic games, darts and TV, with a spacious and comfortable lounge with satellite TV, and a games room equipped with a full-size snooker table and two pool tables. A large pub and eatery is close to the park entrance and the nearby village has a number of small shops and pubs.

Facilities

Toilet block with preset showers and open-style washbasins. Facility for disabled visitors. Dishwashing sinks. Washing machines and dryers. A Portacabin with basic en-suite units (shower, toilet, washbasin). Well stocked shop, Coffee shop serving food. Two bars. TV and games rooms. Water-skiing and jet-ski lakes. Four fishing lakes. Golf course. Archery. Cycle and pedalo hire. Activity and entertainment programme. New indoor swimming pool and spa complex, complete with lake view hot tubs. Off site: Shops, pubs, restaurants 1 mile. Woodhall Spa 5 miles. Riding 15 miles. Beach 25 miles.

Open: 1 April - 31 October.

Directions

Tattershall is 22 miles southeast of Lincoln on the A153 Sleaford/Horncastle road, 14 miles northeast of Sleaford. Park is on the western edge of the village between the River Witham and Tattershall Castle. GPS: 53.095794, -0.196799

Charges guide

Per unit incl. 6 persons and electricity	£ 4.00 - £ 30.00
dog	£ 5.00

Tewkesbury

Winchcombe Camping & Caravanning Club Site

Brooklands Farm, Alderton, Tewkesbury GL20 8NX (Gloucestershire) T: 01242 620259

alanrogers.com/UK4140

This is a popular, quiet site in a rural location, close to the Cotswold attractions. Some pitches surround a small coarse fishing lake, with others in a recently developed area of maturing bushes and shrubs with open views over the surrounding countryside. In total there are 80 pitches, 60 with electric hook-ups (16A) and 52 with gravel hardstanding. The reception building flanks a small gravel car park and late arrivals area approached from a tarmac drive. A number of lodges, an extended camping area and a new toilet block have been recently added.

Facilities

The main heated sanitary unit is kept very clean and tidy to an extremely high standard by the wardens. To the rear of the site is a small Portacabin style sanitary unit (also heated). Well equipped unit for disabled visitors. Laundry facilities. Gas supplies. Large recreation room. Small outdoor play area. WiFi throughout (charged). Fishing (on payment). Lodges to rent. Off site: Golf 7 miles.

Open: 12 March - 15 January.

Directions

From M5 exit 9, take A46 Evesham road for 3 miles to Toddington roundabout, then the B4077 towards Stow-on-the-Wold for a further 3 miles to the site entrance. Ignore signs for Alderton village. GPS: 51.9904, -1.990683

Charges 2012

Per person	£ 7.75 - £ 9.45
non-member pitch fee incl. electricity	£ 10.65

For latest campsite news visit
alanrogers.com

Tewkesbury

Croft Farm Water & Leisure Park

Bredon's Hardwick, Tewkesbury GL20 7EE (Gloucestershire) T: 01684 772321.
E: enquiries@croftfarmleisure.co.uk alanrogers.com/UK4150

Croft Farm is an AALA licensed Watersports Centre with Royal Yachting Association approved tuition available for windsurfing, sailing, kayaking and canoeing. The lakeside campsite has around 96 level pitches, with electric hook-ups (10A), but there are many seasonal units, leaving around 36 pitches for touring, plus some tent pitches. There are 36 gravel hardstandings with very little shade or shelter. Gym and Tonic is a fully equipped gymnasium with qualified instructors, sunbed and sauna. Sports massage, aromatherapy and beauty treatments are available by appointment. Activity holidays for families and groups are organised. Campers can use their own non-powered boats on the lake with reduced launching fees and there is river fishing. There are plans to include a launch ramp onto the river. Climb Bredon Hill (2 miles) for a panoramic view of the Severn and Avon Valleys. Places of interest include Bredon Barn, pottery and church, and the historic town of Tewkesbury with its Abbey, theatre and indoor swimming pool.

Facilities

A recently modernised building has excellent facilities with spacious hot showers, plus some dishwashing sinks. A heated unit in the main building is always open and best for cooler months; this provides further WCs, washbasins and showers, laundry and facilities for disabled visitors. Gas. Café/bar (Fri-Sun low season, daily at other times). Takeaway. Gym. Playground. River fishing. Barrier and toilet block key (£5 deposit). Fenced dog exercise area. WiFi in the clubhouse (free to visitors spending £5 or over). Off site: Pub opposite. Tewkesbury 1.5 miles. Golf 3 miles. Riding 8 miles.

Open: 1 March - 14 November.

Directions

Bredon's Hardwick is midway between Tewkesbury and Bredon on B4080. From M5 exit 9 take A438 (Tewkesbury), at first lights turn right into Shannon Way. Turn right at next lights, into Northway Lane, cross motorway bridge. Turn left into housing estate and cross second bridge. At T-junction turn right on B4080, site is on left opposite Cross Keys Inn. GPS: 52.015967, -2.130267

Charges guide

Per unit incl. 2 persons,	
electricity and awning	£ 16.00
extra person (over 3 yrs)	£ 4.00
dog	£ 1.00

Discount 10% for 8 nights or more (excl. July, August and B.Hs). Weekends min. 2 nights stay. B.Hs min. 3 nights.

Woodhall Spa

Bainland Country Park

Horncastle Road, Woodhall Spa LN10 6UX (Lincolnshire) T: 01526 352903. E: bookings@bainland.co.uk
alanrogers.com/UK3690

A family park with many amenities, Bainland has 170 spacious, level pitches in hedged bays (120 touring pitches) grouped in circles and islands and linked by curving roads. There are 51 fully serviced pitches with hardstanding, honeycombed for awning, individual water, drainage and chemical disposal, 16A electricity and TV aerial hook-ups. The remainder of the pitches are either on gravel hardstanding or level grass, all with 10A electricity. The friendly reception is housed in a pleasant Swiss-style building together with the heated indoor pool and jacuzzi, a bistro and spacious bar area.

Facilities

Three modern, well equipped, heated toilet blocks include a baby room, unisex en-suite shower rooms, family bathroom, fully equipped unit for disabled visitors. Laundry room. Motorcaravan service points. Licensed shop (Feb-Dec). Bistro and bar. Indoor pool (no unaccompanied under 16s). Adventure playground. Trampolines. Crazy golf. Croquet. Games room. Soft play area. Floodlit tennis dome. Par 3, 18-hole golf. Bowls. Leisure activities, including the pool, are individually booked and paid for at reception. Some entertainment in high season. WiFi (free). Off site: Fishing and boat launching 3 miles. Sailing 5 miles. Tattershall Castle 5 miles. Bicycle hire 6 miles.

Open: All year (in winter, super pitches only).

Directions

Woodhall Spa is 18 miles southeast of Lincoln. Entrance to park is off B1191 Horncastle road 1.5 miles northeast of village centre, clearly signed. GPS: 53.158617, -0.183517

Charges guide

Per unit incl. 2 persons	
and electricity	£ 15.00 - £ 32.00
serviced pitch, plus	£ 1.00 - £ 7.00
extra person	£ 2.00 - £ 5.00
child (5-12 yrs)	£ 2.00 - £ 3.00

Special rate for firework display (min. 2 nights, 4/5 Nov). Discounts for senior citizens.

Woodhall Spa

Glen Lodge Touring Park

Glen Lodge, Edlington Moor, Woodhall Spa LN10 6UL (Lincolnshire) T: 01526 353523

alanrogers.com/UK3692

This quiet, attractive and spacious site is ideal for couples and families who enjoy the rural lifestyle, yet it is only just over a mile from the thriving village of Woodhall Spa which retains much of its old-fashioned charm. All 35 pitches have hardstanding and 10A electricity hook-ups (one or two appeared to need long leads) and are served by shingle roads with some street lighting. The grass and flowerbeds are obviously tended by someone who enjoys gardening. In fact, the whole park has a much-loved feel. Behind the pitches, on one side of the park, is an attractive lawned area with trees and shrubs, whilst on the other side is a field where ball games are permitted. Woodhall Spa has two modern supermarkets and a good range of traditional shops, as well as tearooms, restaurants and pubs. There is also a delightful, old-style cinema called the Kinema in the Woods. Places to visit in the area include the Battle of Britain Memorial Flight, Tattershall Castle, Horncastle with its antiques centre and the city of Lincoln. Skegness is only 26 miles away.

Facilities

The modern heated toilet block (key-pad access) is kept spotlessly clean with controllable showers, vanity style washbasins and piped music. En-suite facilities for disabled visitors. Washing machine and dryer.
Off site: Pub serving good food 0.5 miles. Open-air pool, tennis and bowls 1 mile. Shops in village 1.5 miles. Golf and fishing 2 miles. Tattershall Castle 5 miles. Riding and Horncastle 6 miles.

Open: 1 March - 30 November.

Directions

Woodhall Spa is 18 miles southeast of Lincoln. From mini-roundabout in village turn northeast towards Bardney on B1190 (Stixwould Road) past Petwood Hotel. In just over 1 mile at sharp left bend, turn right. Site is 300 yds. on left. GPS: 53.166233, -0.22

Charges guide

Per unit incl. 2 persons and electricity	£ 15.00 - £ 15.50
extra person (over 4 yrs)	£ 3.00
dog	free

No credit cards.
Discount for over 65s Monday - Thursday.

Worksop

Riverside Caravan Park

Central Avenue, Worksop S80 1ER (Nottinghamshire) T: 01909 474118

alanrogers.com/UK3920

A town centre touring park, adjacent to the Worksop cricket ground, this excellent site is attractive and surprisingly peaceful. Riverside is within easy walking distance of the town centre pedestrian precinct and shops, and the Chesterfield Canal runs close to its northern side offering delightful towpath walks and fishing (children would need to be watched). For those who cannot resist the thwack of leather on willow, this site is ideal. Of the 60 marked level pitches, ten are seasonal and 43 are for touring, mainly on gravel hardstanding, seven are on grass and some are separated by trees and low rails, and all have electric hook-ups (10A).

Facilities

The single sanitary unit near reception can be heated and has all the usual facilities, although showers are on payment (£1 coin). No laundry. Motorcaravan service point. Off site: Fishing 0.5 miles. Several golf courses 1 mile. Bicycle hire 4 miles. Squash and flat or crown green bowling nearby. Campers are made very welcome at the cricket ground clubhouse. One of Worksop's most interesting buildings, the medieval Priory Gatehouse, is open free of charge. Market days are Wednesday, Friday and Saturday.

Open: All year.

Directions

Worksop is 7 miles west of the M1 at junction 30 and 4 miles east of the A1. Easiest approach is from A57/A60 roundabout west of the town – third roundabout from the A1. Turn east (at Little Chef) on B6024 towards town centre. Site is well signed. Turn left into Cricket Ground taking care at sharp left turn after bridge. Site entrance is to the left of clubhouse. GPS: 53.30600, -1.12867

Charges guide

Per unit incl. 2 persons, awning and electricity	£ 16.00 - £ 18.00

For latest campsite news visit
alanrogers.com

A beautiful and varied region of rolling hills and undulating moors, Yorkshire has a historic past with a wealth of new attractions. Its landscape has inspired famous authors and been the setting for some of Britain's best-loved television programmes.

THE REGION IS DIVIDED INTO NORTH, SOUTH, EAST AND WEST YORKSHIRE

The major attractions of this region are the parks: the Yorkshire Dales National Park comprises 680 square miles of unspoilt countryside with high fells, winding rivers, ancient castles and outstanding views of the surrounding landscapes; the Peak District is noted for its rocky peaks and limestone plateaux; while the North York Moors National Park has miles of open, heather-covered moorland and pretty villages in its valleys. These areas are ideal places for walking, cycling, horse riding and climbing. Or if you prefer to relax and take in the scenery, the North Yorkshire Moors Railway, starting at Pickering, is one of the many steam railways in the region. On the coast, traditional family resorts like Scarborough, Bridlington and Cleethorpes offer the holidaymaker a wide range of activities. Also by the sea is Kingston-upon-Hull, a maritime city with powerful links to Britain's proud seafaring tradition, and the picturesque fishing port of Whitby, once home to Captain James Cook. Elsewhere in the region are the vibrant cities of York, with its wealth of ancient sites including the Minster, Leeds and Sheffield, plus the busy market town of Doncaster.

Places of interest

North: Harrogate; Wensleydale Creamery in Hawes; Jorvik Viking Centre in York; Lightwater Valley Theme Park, near Ripon; Castle Howard near York; Flamingo Land Theme Park and Zoo in Malton; Skipton Castle.

South: Hatfield Waterpark near Doncaster; Tropical Butterfly House and Wildlife Centre in Anston; Sheffield Ski Village, Europe's biggest artificial ski resort; Magna science adventure centre in Rotherham.

East: Bempton Cliffs RSPB Nature Reserve near Bridlington, England's largest seabird colony; market town of Beverley; Captain Cook Museum in Whitby; Scarborough Millennium.

West: Bolling Hall in Bradford; Royal Armouries Museum in Leeds; 'Brontë Country' and village of Haworth; Pontefract.

Did you know?

The comedy series, Last of the Summer Wine, was filmed in the Pennine town of Holmfirth and its surrounding countryside.

York is the oldest city in Yorkshire, founded in AD71. The Minster is the largest Gothic cathedral in Northern Europe.

Pontefract has been growing liquorice since medieval times. It is believed that Pontefract cakes were made by the monks for medicinal purposes.

The Tan Hill Inn is the highest pub in England at 528 metres above sea level.

Dick Turpin, the notorious 17th-century highwayman, lived in Pontefract.

Rudston is said to be the oldest inhabited village in England, named after the Rood Stone, a mysterious 4,000-year-old monolith.

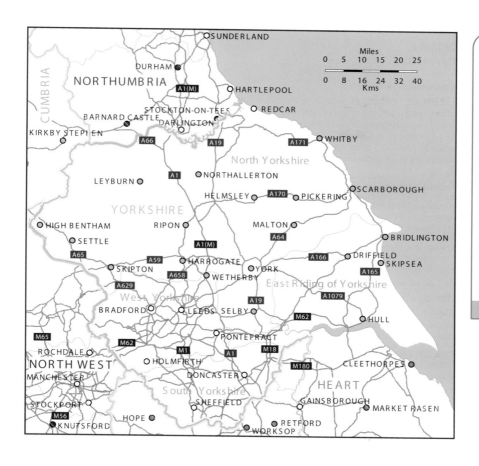

Bridlington
South Cliff Caravan Park

Wilsthorpe, Bridlington YO15 3QN (East Yorkshire) T: 01262 671051. E: southcliff@eastriding.gov.uk
alanrogers.com/UK4498

This traditional style caravan park is part of a large complex owned and operated by the East Riding of Yorkshire Council. There are 193 touring pitches, each with an electricity post (16A); 20 are for tents, the remainder have hardstanding surrounded by grass or, in a few cases, extended to the road. They are in rows across the field, so access for larger units can be tricky when the site is full. Direct access to the seafront is through the vast caravan holiday home park and from there a land train runs a mile along the shore to Bridlington.

Facilities

Two toilet blocks (one traditional, one new) provide pushbutton showers, open washbasins (a few in cubicles for ladies). Excellent en-suite units for disabled visitors. Three bathrooms with washbasins and baby changing facilities. No motorcaravan service point. Franchised facilities include a launderette, a well stocked shop (1/3-8/10), a fish and chip shop, and a leisure complex (bar, restaurant, clubroom, games room), entertainment evenings in high season and monthly themed weekends (outside August). Ten mobile homes for rent. WiFi (charged). Dogs are not accepted (except assistance dogs). No large motorhomes. Off site: Golf 0.5 m. Beach (by car), riding, sailing and boat launching 1 mile. Shops, pubs and restaurants within 2 miles. Fishing 2 miles.

Open: 1 March - 30 November.

Directions

Bridlington is 40 miles east of York via the A166/A614. From M62 exit 37, take A614 to Bridlington and turn south on re-routed A165 towards Hull. At roundabout south of town, turn north on newly-renumbered A1038; site is signed to right at next roundabout. From the Humber Bridge take A63 towards Hull; east of city follow signs to join A165 to Bridlington, then take A1038 as above. GPS: 54.0641, -0.2132

Charges guide

Per unit incl. up to 5 persons	£ 18.00 - £ 25.00

Discounts in low season and mid seasons.

Driffield

Thorpe Hall Caravan & Camping Site

Rudston, Driffield YO25 4JE (East Yorkshire) T: 01262 420393. E: caravansite@thorpehall.co.uk

alanrogers.com/UK4510

Just outside the village of Rudston, in the grounds of Thorpe Hall, this pleasant small touring park is six miles from the sea at Bridlington. Enthusiastically managed by Jayne Chatterton, it is set on flat grass, largely enclosed by the old kitchen garden wall. The 78 large pitches have electrical hook-ups (16A) and TV connections. A separate field accommodates 14 tents. There are no caravan holiday homes or seasonal pitches. Tourist information leaflets on a range of local walks are provided and Sir Ian MacDonald takes visitors on walks around the estate.

Facilities

The solid, central toilet block was refurbished in 2011 and can be heated. Some washbasins in cabins. Bathroom for disabled visitors and families. Laundry room. Small shop. Games room. TV room. Large games field. Coarse fishing lake (charged). WiFi (charged). Off site: Footpath to the village with a pub serving bar food and restaurant meals, a garage and a twice-weekly bus to Bridlington. Riding 2 miles. Beach 4.5 miles.

Open: 1 March - 31 October.

Directions

Site is by the B1253 road, 4.5 miles from Bridlington, on east side of Rudston.
GPS: 54.093817, -0.3125

Charges guide

Per unit incl. 2 adults, 3 children and electricity	£ 15.50 - £ 30.50
tent pitch incl. 2 persons	£ 11.00 - £ 26.00
extra person	£ 3.00

Harrogate

Ripley Caravan Park

Ripley, Harrogate HG3 3AU (North Yorkshire) T: 01423 770050. E: ripleycaravanpark@talk21.com

alanrogers.com/UK4630

Peter and Valerie House are the friendly, resident owners of Ripley Park, a 25-acre grassed caravan park with an indoor heated pool. It accommodates 100 touring units, all with access to electricity, on fairly level grass which undulates in parts. Connected by a circular gravel road, the pitches are marked or spaced (allowing the grass to recover). There are 20 hardstandings. The owners have planted 2,000 trees and these are developing well to provide individual areas and shelter. A pond with ducks provides an attractive feature. In addition, 100 caravan holiday homes occupy a separate area. The park is situated at the gateway to the Yorkshire Dales National Park.

Facilities

The toilet block can be heated and includes some washbasins in cubicles, individual washing facilities, baby bath and a separate unit for disabled visitors. Laundry. Motorcaravan service point. Shop with gas (limited hours in low seasons). Games/TV room. Nursery playroom. Adventure play equipment and football area. Heated indoor pool (£1 per person) and sauna. Caravan storage. Off site: Bus service 150 yds. Riding and golf 3 miles.

Open: Easter - 31 October.

Directions

About 4 miles north of Harrogate, park access is 150 yds. down the B6165 Knaresborough road from its roundabout junction with the A61.
GPS: 54.0369, -1.558833

Charges guide

Per unit incl. 2 persons and electricity	£ 15.50 - £ 18.50
extra person	£ 4.00 - £ 5.00

Harrogate

Rudding Holiday Park

Follifoot, Harrogate HG3 1JH (North Yorkshire) T: 01423 870439. E: holiday-park@ruddingpark.com

alanrogers.com/UK4710

The extensive part wooded, part open grounds of Rudding Park are very attractive, peaceful and well laid out. One touring area is sloping but terraces provide level pitches. All 95 touring pitches have electricity (10/16A), 15 have hardstandings with water and a drain and a small number of super pitches are available for touring units. Further pitches are let on a seasonal basis and caravan holiday homes and chalets are in separate areas. On the outer edge of the park is The Deer House, a family pub serving bar meals, with limited opening outside the high season weeks. A heated outdoor swimming pool (charged), a ball play area and a play park for children are near the pub.

Facilities

Two heated toilet blocks with some washbasins in private cubicles, baby room and bathroom. Laundry rooms. Facilities for disabled visitors. Motorcaravan service point. Shop (6/3-7/11; limited hours). Gas. Restaurant and bar. Heated outdoor swimming pools (25/5-30/8), supervised (extra charge). Adventure playground. Football. Golf. Games room. WiFi (charged). Off site: Buses to Harrogate and Knaresborough. Riding 1 mile.

Open: 4 March - 30 January.

Directions

From junction of A658 and A661 (roundabout), 3 miles southeast of Harrogate take A658 (Leeds). After 0.5 miles turn sharp right onto a road that passes the golf course, holiday park and hotel.
GPS: 53.97307, -1.49720

Charges guide

Per unit incl. 4 persons and electricity	£ 19.00 - £ 37.00
extra person	£ 5.50 - £ 10.50

Helmsley

Golden Square Caravan & Camping Park

Oswaldkirk, Helmsley, York YO62 5YQ (North Yorkshire) T: 01439 788269.
E: reception@goldensquarecaravanpark.com **alanrogers.com/UK4560**

Golden Square is a popular, high quality, family owned touring park. Mr. and Mrs. Armstrong are local farmers who have worked hard to turn an old quarry into an exceptionally attractive caravan park with a number of separate level bays that have superb views over the North York Moors. The 90 touring pitches are not individually separated but they do have markers set into the ground and mainly back on to grass banks. In very dry weather the ground can be hard so steel pegs would be needed (even in wet weather the park is well drained). All pitches have electricity (10A), 24 have drainage and six are deluxe pitches (with waste water drainage, sewerage, electricity, water and TV aerial connection).

Facilities

Two heated toilet blocks have been refurbished and have some washbasins in private cubicles. Showers are free. Bathroom (£1) also houses baby facilities. Facilities for disabled visitors. Laundry. Motorcaravan service point. Tourist information room also houses a microwave. Shop. Two excellent play areas. Games field and a barn with games. Bicycle hire. Caravan storage. CCTV. Off site: Golf 3 miles. Fishing and riding 5 miles. Outdoor pool at Helmsley, sports centre at Ampleforth with indoor pool.

Open: 1 March - 31 October.

Directions

From York take B1363 to Helmsley. At Oswaldkirk Bank Top turn left on B1257 to Helmsley. Take second left signed Ampleforth and caravan route to site. GPS: 54.209333, -1.073783

Charges guide

| Per unit incl. 2 persons and electricity | £ 16.00 - £ 23.00 |
| extra person | £ 3.50 |

No credit cards.

Helmsley

Foxholme Touring Caravan & Camping Park

Harome, Helmsley YO62 5JG (North Yorkshire) T: 01439 771904
alanrogers.com/UK4580

Foxholme is an adults only park suiting those who want a quiet holiday disturbed only by birdsong and passing deer. There are 30 touring pitches set either in an open, slightly sloping field, or between trees on grass. Both areas are attactive and well tended. A further 30 seasonal pitches are arranged amongst the trees. All the pitches have electricity (6A, a few need long leads) and six have hardstanding. Some picnic tables are provided. The site is managed by an on-site warden, with limited reception opening times. Very basic provisions are kept. Wildlife abounds and poppies and other wild flowers enhance this tranquil site. The park is in quiet countryside and would be a good base for touring, being within striking distance of the moors, the coast and York. There are no on-site activities. A torch would be useful.

Facilities

The toilet block is an older style building and is clean but basic and showing signs of its age. Some private cubicles. Laundry facilities and dishwashing area. Two further small blocks provide WCs only in other parts of the park. Basic motorcaravan service point. Caravan storage. Off site: The nearest shops are at Helmsley and Kirkbymoorside, both about 4 miles away, where there is also bicycle hire. Riding and golf 4 miles.

Open: Easter - 31 October.

Directions

Turn south off A170 between Beadlam and Nawton at sign to Ryedale School, then 1 mile to park on left (passing another park on right). From east ignore first camping sign at turning before Nawton. From west turn right 400 yds. east of Helmsley, signed Harome, turn left at church, go through village and follow camping signs. Sat nav postcode: YO62 7SD. GPS: 54.23745, -0.990333

Charges guide

| Per unit incl. 2 persons and electricity | £ 20.00 - £ 25.00 |

No credit cards.

For latest campsite news visit
alanrogers.com

High Bentham

Riverside Caravan Park

High Bentham, Lancaster LA2 7FJ (North Yorkshire) T: 01524 261272. E: info@riversidecaravanpark.co.uk

alanrogers.com/UK4715

The pretty, tree-lined approach to Riverside leads into an attractive park, owned by the Marshall family for over 40 years. Nestling in beautiful countryside, alongside the River Wenning, the park has easy access to the Yorkshire Dales and the Lake District. There are 49 marked, level grass touring pitches with 16A electricity and TV hook-ups. In addition there are 12 super pitches on tarmac. An area has been developed for 50 seasonal pitches on gravel. Located away from the touring area are 206 privately owned holiday homes. Tents are not accepted. The smart reception building includes a small shop selling caravan accessories. A member of the Best of British Group.

Facilities

The modern toilet block with underfloor heating is centrally situated. Washbasin cubicles. Unisex showers in a separate area. Toilet and shower room for disabled visitors (radar key). A new family shower/bathroom (charged). Motorcaravan services. Caravan storage. Outdoor play area for younger children, large field for ball games. Family games room. The river can be used for fishing (permit from reception) swimming, and small boats. WiFi (charged). Off site: Golf and riding nearby.

Open: All year excl. 15-28 December.

Directions

Leave the M6 at exit 34, and head east on the A683 towards Kirkby Lonsdale. After about 5 miles take B6480 signed to High Bentham. From the east, take A65 after Settle the site is signposted at B6480, turn left. At the Black Bull Hotel follow the caravan signs. The park entrance is on the right after crossing the river bridge. GPS: 54.11311, -2.51066

Charges guide

Per unit incl. 2 persons and electricity	£ 19.25 - £ 25.00
extra person	£ 4.50
child (2-15 yrs)	£ 2.50
dog	£ 1.50

Min. charge per night £ 15.90.
Less 10% for bookings over 7 nights.

Leyburn

Constable Burton Hall Caravan Park

Constable Burton Hall, Leyburn DL8 5LJ (North Yorkshire) T: 01677 450428.
E: caravanpark@constableburton.com **alanrogers.com/UK4690**

This tranquil park is in beautiful Wensleydale and the emphasis is on peace and quiet, the wardens working to provide a relaxing environment. Being in the grounds of the Hall, it has a spacious, park-like feel to it. On part level, and some a little uneven, well maintained grass, the 120 pitches (40 for touring units) are of a good size and all have electrical connections (10A). There are no pitches for tents. There is no shop on site but nearby Leyburn will provide all your needs. Opposite the park entrance is the Wyvill Arms for bar meals. Ball games are not permitted on site and there is no play area. The gardens of the Hall are open to the public, with a collection of maples and terraced gardens developed by Mrs Vida Burton. The park is ideally placed for visiting the Northern Dales.

Facilities

Two toilet blocks built of local stone and blending in with the local surroundings, have been refurbished recently, are well tiled, kept immaculately clean, and can be heated. Facilities for disabled visitors. Baby room. The former deer barn has been adapted for use as a laundry room and extra washrooms with basins for both men and women. Information leaflets and a few books for visitors can also be found here. Gas supplies. Gates closed 22.00-08.00. Off site: Irregular bus service from site gate. Fishing and golf within 5 miles.

Open: Late March - 31 October.

Directions

Park is by the A684 between Bedale and Leyburn, 0.5 miles from the village of Constable Burton on the Leyburn side. GPS: 54.3125, -1.754167

Charges 2012

Per unit incl. 2 persons and electricity	£ 18.00 - £ 23.00
extra person	£ 5.00
child (5-16 yrs)	£ 3.00
dog	free

No commercial vehicles.

Constable Burton Hall Caravan Park
01677 450428
caravanpark@constableburton.com

This tranquil park is set in the beautiful grounds of the historic Constable Burton Hall, Wensleydale off the A684

Constable Burton Hall Caravan Park, Leyburn, North Yorkshire, DL8 5LJ

Hull
Burton Constable Holiday Park & Arboretum

The Old Lodges, Sproatley, Hull HU11 4LN (East Yorkshire) T: 01964 562508. E: info@burtonconstable.co.uk
alanrogers.com/UK4500

The approach to this Holiday Park is set in the grounds of the stately home of Burton Constable, and is most impressive – one of the gatehouses acts as reception and tourist information room. The original 300-acre park which was landscaped by Capability Brown in the 18th century and the 90-acre holiday complex, with its well trimmed grass and hedges, has a spacious feel. Much of the park is devoted to holiday homes, but there is a separate touring area on grass, overlooking two sizeable lakes. The 160 pitches all have 10A electricity, there is a separate field for tents and a large hardstanding area for six motorcaravans. Privately owned caravan holiday homes are quite separate and do not intrude.

Facilities

Two heated toilet blocks – one older and small with unisex showers, the central newer block including a laundry room with baby changing. Well equipped room for disabled visitors (Radar key). Shop in the mobile home area. Bar with family room and tables outside overlooking the lakes. Adventure play area. Fishing. Arboretum. Off site: Sproatley with pubs, a shop and the occasional bus 1 mile. Riding 3 miles. Hull 7 miles. Golf and beach 8 miles. Beverley 15 miles. Bridlington 25 miles. York 50 miles.

Open: 1 March - 31 October.

Directions

Sproatley is 7 miles northeast of Hull. From south via the M62 or Humber Bridge, take A63 into Hull, then follow signs to join the A165 Bridlington. On eastern outskirts of Hull turn east on B1238 signed Aldborough. At Sproatley, site is signed to left. From the north and Beverley, take A1035 towards Hornsea. At roundabout with A165 (Hull - Bridlington) follow signs to Burton Constable for about 8 miles. Pass the Hall to Sproatley, then follow caravan signs. GPS: 53.80265, -0.199

Charges guide

Per unit incl. 2 persons and electricity	£ 16.00 - £ 28.00
extra person	£ 2.00

Malton
Wolds Way Caravan Park

West Farm, West Knapton, Malton YO17 8JE (North Yorkshire) T: 01944 728463. E: info@ryedalesbest.co.uk
alanrogers.com/UK4545

Opened in 2004, this park is located along the top of the Yorkshire Wolds with super panoramic views across the Vale of Pickering to the North Yorks Moors. The one and a half mile tarmac and gravel track from the road to the park is well worth while to reach this peaceful location set amongst glorious countryside. There are 80 level pitches (50 for touring units), most with 16A electricity and some with water points. There are 34 pitches with hardstanding. Seating areas, picnic benches and barbecues are provided on the park. There are many footpaths and cycle ways in the area. As well as the obvious attractions of walking the Wolds Way national trail, the park is well placed for visiting all the local attractions which include Scarborough, Bridlington, Sledmere House and Scampston Hall.

Facilities

A brand new toilet block is very well appointed and heated. Family bathrooms. Laundry facilities. Very large heated room with sinks, microwave, fridge/freezers, hot drinks machine, TV and tourist information. Room for disabled visitors. Reception also provides a small shop selling basic supplies. Play area and football field for children and many places to walk dogs. Caravan storage. A well equipped chalet for up to five people is available to rent. Off site: Bus stop 1 mile. Fishing 3 miles. Golf and riding 5 miles. Beach 15 miles.

Open: 1 March - 31 October.

Directions

Park entrance is on the south side of the A64 York - Scarborough road, just past the B1258 turn off and it is well signed. GPS: 54.16615, -0.654033

Charges guide

Per unit incl. 2 persons and electricity	£ 14.50 - £ 21.00
extra person (over 15 yrs)	£ 4.00
child (8-15 yrs)	£ 1.50
awning	£ 2.00
dog	free

For latest campsite news visit
alanrogers.com

Northallerton
Otterington Park

Station Farm, South Otterington, Northallerton DL7 9JB (North Yorkshire) T: 01609 780656.
E: info@otteringtonpark.com **alanrogers.com/UK4765**

This family-owned, five-acre park is located on a former farm. Between Thirsk and Northallerton, in the Vale of York, it is ideally placed for visiting the Yorkshire moors and dales, along with local market towns, theme parks and stately homes. Predominantly, it is a flat grass site with gravel hardstanding for 40 touring pitches, and a separate paddock for a further 28 pitches, all with 16A electricity. Privately owned chalets and static caravans are located in an adjoining park, separated from the tourers by an old, well established, tall hedge. A family park, there is a playground and grassy play areas for children.

Facilities

One purpose built, clean block in a heated building. Unisex en-suite style shower rooms with free showers. Facilities for disabled visitors. Family bathroom with a baby area. Laundry. Drinks/snacks vending machines in reception. Play area. Off site: Fishing 250 yds. Local bus service to Thirsk and Northallerton run every 2 hours from park entrance (not Sun). Several local country pubs serving meals within 1 mile. Large supermarkets 4 miles. Riding 5 miles. Golf 3 miles.

Open: 1 March - 31 October.

Directions

From A1M join A684 for Leeming Bar and Morton-on-Swale. At roundabout bear right on A167 signed South Otterington and Topcliffe. At South Otterington crossroads (pub) turn left signed Thornton-le-Moor to park in 500 yds. GPS: 54.28771, -1.42046

Charges guide

Per unit incl. 4 persons
and electricity £ 18.00 - £ 22.00

Northallerton
Cote Ghyll Caravan & Camping Park

Osmotherley, Northallerton DL6 3AH (North Yorkshire) T: 01609 883425. E: hills@coteghyll.com
alanrogers.com/UK4775

This attractive, family run park is set in a secluded valley, with the higher pitches terraced and the lower ones on a level grassy area either side of the small Cod Beck stream. Of the 80 pitches, 50 are for touring units, all with 10A electricity hook-ups, 12 with full services and hardstanding, plus three larger, super pitches. A further 18 pitches are used for caravan holiday homes and 30 are reserved for seasonal units. A simple site with a tranquil setting, Cote Ghyll is highly suited for lovers of peace and quiet, for bird watching or for more energetic hobbies such as cycling and walking.

Facilities

Two well-equipped, heated toilet blocks, one new, provide free power showers, vanity style washbasins and hairdryers. Bathroom and facilities for babies and disabled visitors. Laundry room with washing machine, dryer, iron and board. Drying room. Reception provides a small shop for essentials. Gas supplies. Two play areas. WiFi throughout (charged). Caravan storage. Off site: Shop and pubs 10 minutes walk. Fishing 1 mile. Mount Grace Priory 4 miles. Swimming pool and leisure centre 6 miles.

Open: 1 March - 31 October.

Directions

Osmotherley is east of the A19. Leave the A19 at A684 exit signed Northallerton and Osmotherley. Go to Osmotherley and site is at the northern end of the village, well signed. GPS: 54.37643, -1.29166

Charges guide

Per unit incl. 2 persons
and electricity £ 19.00 - £ 24.00
incl. full services plus £ 5.00
extra person £ 3.00

Pickering
Overbrook Caravan Park

Maltongate, Thornton-le-Dale, Pickering YO18 7SE (North Yorkshire) T: 01751 474417.
E: enquiry@overbrookcaravanpark.co.uk **alanrogers.com/UK4534**

Situated on the edge of the very pretty village of Thornton-le-Dale, this most attractive, well cared for, adults only site has been developed on a disused railway station. The station building now provides holiday cottages and the caravan park toilet facilities. The site is level with 50 pitches (20 for tourers, the remainder used for seasonal units) arranged either side of a tarmac access road and backed by trees. All are on hardstanding and all have electricity connections (16A). Some pitches are quite small. Neither children nor tents are accepted at this adults only park. The owners will do all they can to assist you during your stay. A half mile, level walk brings you to the village.

Facilities

The toilet and shower facilities are situated in the old station house. Laundry facilities. Gas supplies. Only adults are accepted (no children). No tents accepted. Off site: Village with bus stop, shops, pubs, fish and chips 800 yds. Bicycle hire 800 yds. Fishing 3 miles. Golf and riding 5 miles. Beach 25 miles.

Open: 1 March - 10 January.

Directions

Thornton-le-Dale is on the A170 Pickering - Scarborough road. In the village follow sign for Malton and park is 800 yds. on the left (follow the stream on the left). GPS: 54.228533, -0.7229

Charges guide

Per unit incl. 2 persons
and electricity £ 15.50 - £ 22.00
No credit cards.

FLOWER OF MAY

Magical Family Holidays

Discover the Beauty Surrounding Yorkshires Finest Holiday Parks

01723 584311

01765 602964

01751 417272

01347 810829

A choice of Holiday Parks situated at the Coast, on the Moors and in the Countryside of North Yorkshire.

Our well maintained Parks are superbly located within easy reach of North Yorkshires stunning landscapes and well known attractions.

Please send for our colour brochure –
**Flower of May,
Lebberston Cliff,
Scarborough, YO11 3NU.**

01723 584311

or e-mail us:
info@flowerofmay.com

Relax, Explore and Enjoy!

www.flowerofmay.com

Scarborough

Jasmine Park

Cross Lane, Snainton, Scarborough YO13 9BE (North Yorkshire) T: 01723 859240.
E: enquiries@jasminepark.co.uk **alanrogers.com/UK4740**

Jasmine is a very attractive, quiet and well manicured park with owners who go to much trouble to produce many plants to decorate a very colourful entrance. Set in the Vale of Pickering, the park is level, well drained and protected by a coniferous hedge. Of the 126 pitches 71 are for touring units, 21 on grass, with electricity connections (10/16A) for all caravans and some tents. A field is provided for games. Much tourist information is provided in a log cabin and the owners are only too happy to advise. This is an award-winning, peaceful park for a restful holiday.

Facilities	Directions
The heated toilet block has been refurbished and is kept very clean. Large room for families and disabled visitors contains a bath, shower, WC and washbasin (access by code). Laundry room. Motorcaravan service point. Shop sells essentials and gas. Dogs are welcome but there is no dog walk. Caravan storage. WiFi (charged). New play area. Off site: Bus in village 0.5 miles. Riding, golf driving range and 9-hole course 2 miles. Bicycle hire 5 miles.	Snainton is on the A170 Pickering - Scarborough road and park is signed at eastern end of the village. Turn down Barker's Lane and at small crossroads turn left and the park is 230 yds. on the left. GPS: 54.218583, -0.575567

Open: 1 March - 31 October.

Charges guide

Per unit incl. 4 persons and electricity	£ 18.00 - £ 30.00

Scarborough

Lebberston Touring Park

Filey Road, Lebberston, Scarborough YO11 3PE (North Yorkshire) T: 01723 585723.
E: info@lebberstontouring.co.uk **alanrogers.com/UK4780**

Lebberston Touring Park is a quiet, spacious touring site and is highly suitable for anyone seeking a quiet relaxing break, such as mature couples or young families (although tents are not accepted). There is no play area or games room, the only concession to children being a large central area with goal posts, so teenagers may get bored. The park itself has a very spacious feel – it is gently sloping and south facing and the views are superb. There are 125 numbered pitches with 75 for touring units. All have 10A (some 16A) electricity and 25 are on hardstanding. The circular access road is tarmac, the grass is well manicured and the entrance is a mass of flowers.

Facilities	Directions
Recently upgraded toilet blocks are of high quality and kept very clean. Large shower cubicles and washbasins in cubicles with curtains. Both blocks have dishwashing sinks and one has a family bathroom (20p). Good room for disabled visitors (Radar). Laundry. Reception sells a few supplies, plus papers, ice cream and gas. Only breathable groundsheets are permitted. WiFi (charged). Off site: Hourly bus and local pub 5 minutes walk. Parking details and discs for Scarborough given to new arrivals.	From A64 Malton - Scarborough road turn right at roundabout (McDonald's) signed B1261 Filey. Go through Cayton, Killerby and in 4.5 miles site is signed on left. If you miss the turning to the park, continue to roundabout and turn around. GPS: 54.22650, -0.34709

Open: 1 March - 31 October.

Charges guide

Per unit incl. 2 persons and electricity	£ 15.00 - £ 26.00

Settle

Knight Stainforth Hall Caravan & Camping Park

Little Stainforth, Settle BD24 0DP (North Yorkshire) T: 01729 822200. E: info@knightstainforth.co.uk
alanrogers.com/UK4720

In a very attractive setting, this park is located in the heart of the Yorkshire Dales, the whole area a paradise for hill-walking, fishing and pot-holing and has outstanding scenery. The camping area is on slightly sloping grass, sheltered by mature woodland. There are 100 touring pitches, 50 with electricity (16A) and ten with hardstanding, and a separate area contains 66 privately owned caravan holiday homes. A gate leads from the bottom of the camping field giving access to the river bank where the Ribble bubbles over small waterfalls and rocks and whirls around deep pools where campers swim in warm weather. This area is not fenced and children should be supervised.

Facilities	Directions
A modern, heated amenity block provides toilets and showers and includes some washbasins in cubicles. Facilities for disabled visitors and baby changing. Laundry facilities. Motorcaravan service point. Small shop. Games/TV room. Play area with safety base. Fishing. Security barrier. Deposit for key to toilet block and barrier £10. WiFi. Off site: Bicycle hire and golf 3 miles.	From Settle, drive west towards Giggleswick. Ignore turning marked Stainforth and Horton, after 200 yds. turn right into Stackhouse Lane (signed Knight Stainforth). After 2 miles turn right at crossroads. GPS: 54.10025, -2.284833

Open: 1 March - 31 October.

Charges guide

Per unit incl. 2 persons	£ 16.00 - £ 19.00
incl. electricity	£ 19.00 - £ 22.00

Skipsea

Skipsea Sands Holiday Park

Mill Lane, Skipsea YO25 8TZ (East Yorkshire) T: 0871 664 9812. E: skipsea.sands@park-resorts.com

alanrogers.com/UK4496

This well established holiday park is now owned by Park Resorts and is primarily dedicated to caravan holiday homes, of which there are 625 privately owned and 70 to rent. There is however a pleasantly laid out touring park occupying its own corner of the site and bordered by an attractive duck pond and a large playing area (both well fenced). The 91 marked, level pitches (some occupied by seasonal caravans) are separated by hedges and all have electricity (16A); some also have water, drainage and sewerage connections. The leisure facilities are outstanding and a full daily programme of activities and entertainment is offered for children and adults.

Facilities

Two refurbished, heated toilet blocks have pushbutton showers, open washbasins and en-suite facilities for disabled visitors. Motorcaravan service point. Washing machines and dryers. Well stocked shop. Bar, coffee shop and restaurant with takeaway. Leisure centre with heated indoor swimming pool. Fitness centre. Games 'kingdom'. Fishing pond (charged). WiFi (charged). Off site: Buses from park gate. Village with shops, pub, restaurant 1 mile.

Open: 1 March - 31 October.

Directions

Skipsea is 20 miles northeast of Hull. From Humber Bridge or from M62, take A63 to Hull, east of city follow signs to join A165 towards Bridlington. After 18 miles, turn east on B1249 to Skipsea. In village, turn right then left to site. GPS: 53.98957, -0.20716

Charges guide

Per unit incl. all services	£ 6.00 - £ 30.00
tent pitch	£ 5.00 - £ 25.00

Skipton

Wood Nook Caravan Park

Skirethorns, Threshfield, Skipton BD23 5NU (North Yorkshire) T: 01756 752412. E: enquiries@woodnook.net

alanrogers.com/UK4670

Wood Nook is a family-run park in the heart of Wharfedale, part of the Yorkshire Dales National Park. The access road is narrow for a short distance, so care should be taken. The site includes six acres of woodland with quite rare flora and fauna. Reception is in the farmhouse, as is the small shop. The gently sloping fields have gravel roads and provide 48 touring pitches with gravel hardstanding. All have electricity (10A) and nearby water and chemical disposal points. There is also room for 24 tents and there are some caravan holiday homes to let. This is a peaceful base or exploring the Yorkshire Dales.

Facilities

Converted farm buildings provide dated but clean sanitary facilities. Washbasins in cubicles for ladies. Roomy showers (coin operated). Laundry facilities. Motorcaravan service points. Licensed shop for basics and gifts (from Easter). Gas. Small play area. American motorhomes by prior arrangement. WiFi (charged). Off site: Fishing and bicycle hire 2 miles. Riding 3 miles. Golf 9 miles. Leisure centre.

Open: 1 March - 31 October.

Directions

Threshfield is 9 miles north of Skipton on the B6265. Continue through village onto B6160, after garage turn left (Skirethorns Lane). Follow signs for 600 yds, keeping left up narrow lane, then right up track for 300 yds. The last 900 yds. is single track – on arrival phone to check it is clear. GPS: 54.07267, -2.04199

Charges guide

Per person	£ 3.00
serviced pitch	£ 13.00

Skipton

Howgill Lodge Caravan & Camping Park

Barden, Skipton BD23 6DJ (North Yorkshire) T: 01756 720655. E: info@howgill-lodge.co.uk

alanrogers.com/UK4750

Howgill Lodge is a traditional family park set in the heart of the Yorkshire Dales. Arranged on a sloping hillside, the terraced pitches have fantastic views. It is a small park catering for the needs of walkers, tourers and people who like to just relax. The whole area is a haven for both experienced walkers or the casual rambler, without having to move your car. All the pitches at the upper part of the park are on hardstanding and have electricity connections (10A), the lower ones are mainly on grass (40 in total). Picnic tables and chairs are provided. There are four mobile homes available to rent

Facilities

Heated toilet facilities are at the entrance, close to reception, with dishwashing sinks outside, under cover. Showers are large and adjustable (on payment). Laundry room with four unisex showers also here. Two small WC blocks are lower down the site for tent campers. Shop. No play area. Fishing licences are available from reception. Off site: Bus service within walking distance (3 per day). Fishing 1 mile. Bolton Abbey 3 miles. Golf, riding and bicycle hire 7 miles. Skipton 8 miles.

Open: 1 April - 31 October.

Directions

Turn off A59 Skipton - Harrogate road at roundabout onto B6160 Bolton Abbey road. Three miles past Bolton Abbey at Barden Towers, bear right signed Appletreewick and Pateley Bridge onto narrow road for 1.25 miles (passing places). Park is signed on right at phone box. GPS: 54.025767, -1.909833

Charges guide

Per unit incl. 2 persons and electricity	£ 18.00 - £ 22.00

For latest campsite news visit
alanrogers.com

Wetherby

Maustin Caravan Park

Kearby with Netherby, Wetherby LS22 4BZ (North Yorkshire) T: 01132 886234. E: judith@maustin.co.uk

alanrogers.com/UK4755

A tranquil site for couples only, this manicured park is set within the North Yorkshire National Park. It offers 25 well-spaced pitches sited on grass, all with peaceful, scenic views of the surrounding area. Caravan holiday homes are in a separate area. A bowling club on the site offers membership to all visitors and competitions are held throughout the season. Relax in the comfortable lounge or in the tasteful bar and restaurant area. A covered terrace overlooks the bowling green. There is an information building providing books, DVDs, videos and games, which you may borrow free of charge.

Facilities	Directions
One heated, well-equipped toilet block has good showers, free hairdryers and roomy toilet and washing cubicles. Excellent facility for disabled visitors. Laundry room. Kitchen area with freezer. Milk, newspapers, etc. to order at weekends. Bowling club with lounge, bar, restaurant and takeaway (weekends from March). Internet facilities. WiFi throughout (charged). Off site: Fishing 2 miles. Riding 3 miles. Golf 4 miles.	From A1 south follow Harewood House signs through Collingham to join A61 (Harrogate). At lights turn right over River Wharfe, right for Kirkby Overblow, after 0.5 miles right to Kearby and park is 1.5 miles on the right. GPS: 53.917464, -1.497488

Open: All year excl. February.

Charges guide

Per unit incl. 2 persons	£ 17.50
incl. services	£ 20.00
extra person	£ 2.50

Whitby

Sandfield House Farm Caravan Park

Sandsend Road, Whitby YO21 3SR (North Yorkshire) T: 01947 602660. E: info@sandfieldhousefarm.co.uk

alanrogers.com/UK4528

Although it is set on a hill in undulating countryside on the low cliffs near Whitby, this park provides 200 level pitches, all with electricity. There are 60 pitches for touring caravans, all on hardstanding, and these are mainly set to the front of the park giving wonderful views over the golf course and the sea. Tents are not accepted here. Whitby is only a mile away and a quarter of a mile walk down a gently sloping track from the park brings you to a two mile long sandy beach. From here it is a gentle stroll along the new promenade to Whitby harbour.

Facilities	Directions
Two toilet blocks (one older, one new and very good) have free hot showers. Laundry room with washing machines, dryers and iron. No facilities for disabled visitors. Tents are not accepted. Off site: Hourly bus service to town centre. Golf 200 yds. Fishing 400 yds. Shops and boat launching 800 yds. Railway station 1 mile.	From Whitby follow signs for Sandsend on A174. The park is on the landward side of the road, opposite the golf course and well signed. GPS: 54.491717, -0.642767

Open: 1 March - 31 October.

Charges guide

Per unit incl. up to 4 persons	£ 17.00 - £ 20.00
extra person	£ 2.00
No credit cards.	

Whitby

Middlewood Farm Holiday Park

Middlewood Lane, Fylingthorpe, Robin Hood's Bay YO22 4UF (North Yorkshire) T: 01947 880414. E: info@middlewoodfarm.com **alanrogers.com/UK4532**

Middlewood Farm is a level park, surrounded by hills and with views of the sea from some of the pitches. A short walk through the farm fields and wild flower conservation areas leads to the picturesque old fishing village of Robin Hood's Bay and the sea. The park has 30 touring pitches for caravans and motorcaravans with 10A electricity, 17 with hardstanding and the remainder on grass. There is space for around 130 tents in two areas with 23 electricity connections (10A) available and 30 caravan holiday homes to rent. A good beach is only ten minutes walk through the fields.

Facilities	Directions
Two splendid toilet blocks have clean facilities and are modern, heated and tiled with free showers and private cabins. Fully equipped laundry room including iron and board. Facilities for babies and disabled visitors. Play area with bark base set amongst the tents. WiFi (charged). Off site: Sandy beach with fishing 0.5 miles (10 minutes walk). Boat launching 2 miles. Golf 7 miles. Shop and public transport in village 5 minutes walk.	From the A171 Scarborough - Whitby road turn right signed Robin Hood's Bay and Fylingthorpe (signed). Just past 30 mph sign bear right and after 100 yds. turn right into Middlewood Lane (signed). GPS: 54.43012, -0.54670

Open: Easter - early November.

Charges guide

Per unit incl. 2 persons and electricity	£ 15.00 - £ 25.00
extra person	£ 3.00

For latest campsite news visit

alanrogers.com

York

Moorside Caravan Park

Lords Moor Lane, Strensall, York YO32 5XJ (North Yorkshire) T: 01904 491208

alanrogers.com/UK4610

Strensall is only a few miles from York, one of England's most attractive cities and Moorside Caravan Park will provide a peaceful haven after a day's sightseeing. Children (under 16) are not accepted at this park. It will impress you with its pretty fishing lake, many flowers and the tranquillity (except for the odd passing daytime train). There are 53 marked touring pitches on neat well trimmed grass, most with electricity (6/10A) and 22 with paved hardstanding. The whole park is very well maintained making it a very pleasant environment. The small lake is well stocked for coarse fishing and the pitches bordering the lake are the most popular. York golf course is almost opposite the site entrance.

Facilities

The purpose built toilet block can be heated and houses immaculately kept facilities with washbasins in cubicles for ladies. Separate, recently constructed facility for disabled visitors. Fully equipped laundry room. Tourist information and books to borrow. Coarse fishing (£3 per day). Caravan storage. Off site: Strensall village with shops and pubs is less than a mile. Golf 0.5 miles. Riding 3 miles.

Open: March - end October.

Directions

From A1237 York outer ring road follow signs for Earswick and Strensall. At Strensall follow Flaxton road. The park entrance is on the left past signs to Strensall village and York Golf Club.
GPS: 54.042733, -1.011683

Charges guide

Per unit incl. 2 persons and electricity	£ 13.00 - £ 16.50
dog	£ 1.00

No credit cards.

York

Alders Caravan Park

Home Farm, Alne, York YO61 1RY (North Yorkshire) T: 01347 838722. E: enquiries@homefarmalne.co.uk

alanrogers.com/UK4638

The Alders is located in the village of Alne, nine miles from the centre of York. Carefully developed and managed on a working farm in historic parkland, the drive from reception around the village cricket ground to the pitches gives a real feeling of space. The extra large pitches are arranged in small bays designed to give privacy, and separate the 28 touring pitches from the seasonal units, storage and the camping pods. Service tracks throughout allow site maintenance without compromising privacy. Woodland walks and a water meadow with wild flowers enhance the wonderful peace and tranquillity marred only by the occasional light aircraft. The village centre is only a short stroll away.

Facilities

The first rate toilet blocks are heated with family sized shower rooms, one also has a bath (£1 charge for baths). The newer block includes en-suite bathrooms with bath or shower, laundry and dishwashing facilities. Provision for disabled visitors. Shop (all season). Gas is sold at reception. Only 2 dogs accepted per pitch.
Off site: Floodlit tennis courts in the village. Fishing 2 miles. Golf 3 miles. Riding and bicycle hire 4 miles.

Open: 1 March - 31 October.

Directions

From the north on the A19: after leaving Easingwold bypass take next right turn signed Alne. From the south (A19), 5 miles north of Shipton turn left at sign for Alne. In 1.5 miles at T-junction turn left and in about 0.5 miles, site is signed in the centre of the village. GPS: 54.08185, -1.24105

Charges guide

Per unit incl. 2 persons, 2 children and electricity	£ 17.00
extra person	£ 5.00
child (under 5 yrs)	free
dog (max. 2)	free

For latest campsite news visit

alanrogers.com

York

Goose Wood Caravan Park

Carr Lane, Sutton-on-the-Forest, York YO61 1ET (North Yorkshire) T: 01347 810829.
E: enquiries@goosewood.co.uk **alanrogers.com/UK4640**

Now part of the Flower of May group, Goose Wood has a natural woodland setting. It provides a quiet, relaxed atmosphere from which to explore York itself or the surrounding Yorkshire Dales, Wolds and Moors. The park has a well kept air and a rural atmosphere, with 100 well spaced and marked pitches, all with metered 10A electricity on hardstanding (five also have water and drainage). For children, there is a first rate adventure playground in the trees at one side of the park and for adults, a small coarse fishing lake and attractive, natural woodland for walking. The park is popular with families in high season when it can be busy at weekends. A Park and Ride scheme for York operates from nearby all year, six days a week or there is a local bus every two hours. The park is just over a mile from Sutton village. There are chalets and lodges for rent in a separate area from the touring pitches.

Facilities

Tiled and heated, the modern toilet block is spacious and well maintained. An additional unit provides shower rooms, WC and washbasins in cubicles and extra dishwashing sinks. Full facilities for disabled visitors. Laundry room. Motorcaravan service point. Well-stocked shop (with gas). Fishing lake. Large adventure playground. Games room. Outdoor table tennis. Dogs (max. two per pitch), to be exercised in nearby woodland. WiFi throughout (charged). Off site: Riding and golf 3 miles. Bicycle hire 6 miles. York 6 miles.

Open: March - 2 January.

See advertisement on page 205

Directions

Park is 6 miles north of York; from the A1237 outer ring-road take the B1363 for Sutton-on-the-Forest and Stillington, taking the first right after the Haxby and Wigginton junction and follow park signs. N.B. Do not use postcode for sat navs; use latlong or Carr Lane. GPS: 54.0591, -1.0861

Charges guide

Per unit incl. 4 persons (electricity metered)	£ 15.00 - £ 21.00
extra person	£ 3.00
dog	£ 1.00

York

South Lea Caravan Park

The Balk, Pocklington, York YO42 2NX (North Yorkshire) T: 01759 303467. E: info@south-lea.co.uk
alanrogers.com/UK4655

South Lea is situated just off the A1079 road near the delightful market town of Pocklington, about 12 miles from York. A well presented open park with 72 pitches set in 15 acres of flat grassland. Some are hardstanding and all have electricity (16A). The park is divided in to areas by shrubs and hedges, each named after a type of tree. Some areas are in the early stages of planting. The site is ideally positioned for touring the many places of interest in the surrounding area and is within reach of the coast. Entry to the site is by a barrier card. There is a public telephone box on site, and a large dog walking area.

Facilities

One toilet block (can be heated) with free showers and hairdryers. There are no facilities for campers with disabilities at present, but these are being planned. Dog showers. Calor Gas supplies. Off site: Pocklington nearby with shops and restaurants, a comprehensive leisure centre and pool. Local airfield for gliders, lessons and pleasure flight. Bus stop at site entrance.

Open: 1 March - 31 October.

Directions

Travelling from the west on the A1079 ignore the first turn off to Pocklington. Stay on the A1079 until you see the signs for the campsite. The turning will be on the left and the site is a short distance down this road on the left. GPS: 53.914298, -0.773592

Charges guide

Per unit incl. 2 persons and electricity	£ 14.00 - £ 18.00
extra person	£ 2.00
child (3-15 yrs)	£ 1.00
No credit cards.	

The North West region boasts a wealth of industrial heritage with undiscovered countryside, the vibrant cities of Manchester and Liverpool, the seaside resorts of Blackpool and Morecambe, plus miles of glorious coastline, home to a wide variety of bird species.

THIS REGION INCLUDES: CHESHIRE, LANCASHIRE, MERSEYSIDE, GREATER MANCHESTER AND THE HIGH PEAKS OF DERBYSHIRE

The miles of beautiful, North West countryside offers endless opportunities for recreation. For the more active, the peaceful plains of Cheshire are a walkers' haven with endless trails to choose from. Lancashire is also good walking country, with way-marked paths passing through the outstanding Forest of Bowland, which affords marvellous views over the Lake District in Cumbria and the Yorkshire Dales.

Birdwatchers are catered for too, with the coast offering some of the best birdspotting activity in the country, most notably along the Sefton coast and around the Wirral Peninsula. The region's cities have their own charm. Manchester, with its fabulous shopping centres and vibrant nightlife, boasts a rich Victorian heritage; the maritime city of Liverpool has more museums and galleries than any other UK city outside London; Lancaster features fine Georgian buildings and an imposing Norman castle; while Chester is renowned for its medieval architecture and shopping galleries. And offering good, old-fashioned seaside fun is Blackpool. England's most popular seaside resort is packed full of lively entertainment and attractions, such as the white knuckle rides at the pleasure beach, amusement games on the pier and the observation decks in the famous Tower.

Places of interest

Cheshire: Tatton Park in Knutsford; Chester Cathedral and Zoo; Cheshire Military Museum; Lyme Park stately home in Macclesfield; Beeston Castle; Boat Museum at Ellesmere Port.

Lancashire: Williamson Park, castle and leisure park in Lancaster; Camelot Theme Park; Museum of Football in Preston; Morecambe Bay; Hoghton Tower and National Museum of Football in Preston.

Merseyside: Liverpool Football Club Museum and Tour Centre; The Beatles Story Museum; Speke Hall garden and estate; The Wirral Country Park; Williamson Tunnels Heritage Centre.

Greater Manchester: Imperial War Museum North; Manchester United Football Club Museum; The Lowry; Corgi Heritage Centre in Rochdale; Stockport air-raid shelter.

Did you know?

The first public gallery to open in England was in Liverpool in 1877.

Lancaster Castle is infamous as host to the Pendle witch trials of 1612.

The first passenger railway station was built in Manchester.

Hoghton Tower is where King James I knighted a loin of beef in 1617 – hence the name Sirloin.

To date 300 bird species have been recorded within the boundaries of Sefton.

Chester has the most complete set of city walls in Britain.

Opened in 1894, the Blackpool Tower was copied from the Eiffel Tower; the height to the top of the flagpole is 518 feet 9 inches.

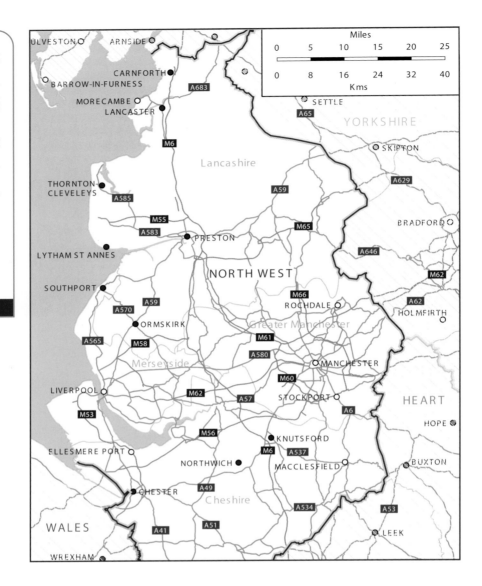

Carnforth

Silverdale Caravan Park

Middlebarrow Plain, Cove Road, Silverdale LA5 0SH (Lancashire) T: 01524 701508.
E: caravan@holgates.co.uk **alanrogers.com/UK5350**

This attractive, very high quality park is in an outstanding craggy, part-wooded, hillside location with fine views over Morecambe Bay. It takes 80 touring units, with 339 privately owned caravan holiday homes and 14 to rent, located in woodland away from the touring pitches. With just five grassy pitches for tents (steel pegs required), the remaining large touring pitches are on gravel hardstandings, all with electricity (16A), free TV connection, individual drainage and water points. The main complex with reception and the entrance barrier, provides a well stocked supermarket, lounge bar, restaurant with good value meals and a terrace with views over the bay. There is also an indoor leisure centre. Children have a choice of two adventure playgrounds and plenty of space for ball games. Also on site is a small but challenging pitch and putt course. Everything is completed to the highest standards.

Facilities

Two modern, heated toilet buildings are fully equipped with top quality fittings and include some private cubicles with WC and washbasin. Excellent provision for disabled visitors with a reserved pitch and parking bay adjacent. Launderette. Shop. Gas supplies. Bar and restaurant. Indoor pool (17x17 m, with lifeguard) with spa pool, steam room and sauna. Well equipped gym (charged). Playgrounds. Games room. Pitch and putt course (£2 per person). Facilities are limited mid week in January and early February. Off site: Riding, cycling, golf and fishing all within 4 miles. Morecambe and Lancaster 12 miles. Kendal 15 miles. RSPB nature reserve at Leighton Moss.

Open: All year excl. 6 November - 21 December.

Directions

From traffic lights in centre of Carnforth take road to Silverdale under low bridge. After 1 mile turn left signed Silverdale and after 2.5 miles over level crossing, carry on and turn right at T-junction. Follow Holgates sign from here watching for left then right forks (narrow roads). GPS: 54.176603, -2.836034

Charges guide

Per unit incl. 2 adults and all services	£ 31.00
extra person	£ 8.00
extra child (2-17 yrs)	£ 3.00
awning or pup tent	£ 2.00 - £ 3.50

Minimum stays apply for all B.H. weekends.

AA Campsite of the Year 2011
Winner for England & Overall

Discover an ever-changing landscape

Discover the very best of British holidays in one of our award winning holiday parks and cottages. Situated in the unspoilt Cumbria Lancashire borders, nestled between the Coast and Lake District Mountains.

Holgates
Make the discovery

For all enquiries contact Holgates Caravan Parks
Tel: **01524 701508** or Email: info@holgates.co.uk
Website: www.holgates.co.uk

Carnforth

Bay View Holiday Park

A6 Main Road, Bolton Le Sands, Carnforth LA5 8ES (Lancashire) T: 01524 732854.
E: info@holgatesleisureparks.co.uk **alanrogers.com/UK5270**

Bay View has been developed by the Holgate family into an excellent addition to their group. Situated on the north Lancashire coast, the park is an ideal base for exploring the Lake District, North Yorkshire and the Forest of Bowland. The park is divided into several grassy fields and many of the pitches have stunning views over Morecambe Bay, while others look towards the Lakeland Fells. It is a very open park with little shade. Of the 72 touring pitches, all have 6-15A electricity and are fully serviced. There are also 110 pitches for caravan holiday homes.

Facilities

Three toilet blocks with facilities for disabled visitors. Good laundry. Motorcaravan service point. Shop. An excellent new bar/restaurant with a pool room and children's games room. Playground for younger children. Large field for ball games. Farm park (visitors can view the animals). WiFi (charged). Off site: Fishing 200 yds. Golf and riding 3 miles. Canal cruises on Lancaster Canal. Leighton Moss RSPB nature reserve. Good shopping in nearby Lancaster.

Open: 1 March - 31 October.

Directions

From M6 exit 35 take A601M to roundabout and follow signs to Morecambe. Continue through Carnforth and after mini-roundabout look for site sign (at main entrance) in 500 yds. on the right. GPS will take you to rear entrance, which is less accessible. GPS: 54.11602, -2.78791

Charges guide

Per unit with 2 persons, and electricity	£ 20.00 - £ 23.00

For latest campsite news visit
alanrogers.com

Carnforth

Old Hall Caravan Park

Capernwray, Carnforth LA6 1AD (Lancashire) T: 01524 733276. E: info@oldhallcaravanpark.co.uk

alanrogers.com/UK5271

In a woodland clearing, just five minutes drive from junction 35 of the M6, Old Hall Caravan Park is a gem. Approached along a tree-lined road, this secluded park offers peace and tranquillity. There are 38 touring pitches which are accessed from a circular roadway, all on marked and level hardstandings and with 16A electricity, water and drainage (shared between two pitches). TV hook-ups are available (free). Tents are not accepted. There are 220 privately owned holiday homes which are quite separate from the touring pitches. A narrow river runs through the park.

Facilities	Directions
The central sanitary block (combination lock) is very clean and is heated during cooler months. Vanity style washbasins and large controllable showers. Separate unit for disabled visitors doubles as a family room. Laundry facilities. Gas supplies. WiFi. Off site: Canal fishing 300 yds. Over Kellet 2 miles. Carnforth 3 miles. Historic Lancaster and the seaside town of Morecambe (15 minutes drive). Grange-over-Sands (30 minutes drive).	From M6 exit 35 take link road signed Over Kellet. Turn left on B6254. At Over Kellet village green turn left signed Capernwray and follow for 1.5 miles. Park is on the right at the end of a 0.5 mile drive. GPS: 54.13958, -2.71357

Charges guide

Per unit incl. electricity	£ 20.00

Open: 1 March - 10 January.

Chester

Manor Wood Country Caravan Park

Coddington, Chester CH3 9EN (Cheshire) T: 01829 782990. E: info@manorwoodcaravans.co.uk

alanrogers.com/UK5220

Arranged on well maintained grass, on farmland with views towards the Welsh hills, this family owned and orientated site has a small swimming pool for use in the summer months. There are 50 level touring pitches with 16A electricity, accessed via tarmac roads. 39 have hardstandings and 30 have water and drainage. The footpaths and bridle paths from the park will appeal to those with an interest in nature, walking and cycling. Pools on the site allow a range of activities from serious fishing to pond dipping. Chester and its zoo are nearby and the seaside can be reached in an hour.

Facilities	Directions
Heated sanitary unit with showers and washbasins in cubicles. Disabled/family room. Laundry. Covered dishwashing sinks. Basics can be purchased. Small swimming pool (heated May-Sept), adventure play area (6-14 yrs). Games room. Tennis court. Security barrier with unrestricted card access. WiFi. Welly walk (2 dogs per pitch) and welly washing. Gas available. Fishing £5.00 per rod. Separate, central car parking for a number of pitches. Off site: Restaurant within 1 mile. Golf courses 1.5 and 2 miles. Riding 8 miles. Bicycle hire, Chester 10 miles.	From A41 Whitchurch - Chester Road, take A534 towards Wrexham, pass Carden Park Hotel and turn opposite Cock o'Barton. After a short distance through Barton the road narrows, bear left and continue for 500 yds. to find the site on the left. Do not rely on sat nav. GPS: 53.087471, -2.829731

Charges guide

Per unit incl. 2 persons and electricity	£ 13.50 - £ 24.00
extra person	£ 3.00

Open: All year.

Knutsford

Royal Vale Caravan Park

London Road, Allostock, Knutsford WA16 9JD (Cheshire) T: 01565 722355. E: canistay@royalvale.co.uk

alanrogers.com/UK5245

This brand new, family run site for adults only is located in countryside close to Knutsford, with Tatton Park and other attractions nearby. Expect a relaxed stay on 52 all weather pitches each with water, electricity and drainage and attractively arranged around a fully appointed, heated, modern central sanitary unit. There are a further ten grass pitches for tents. Access to the level, gravel and solid hardstandings is via compacted gravel roadways, landscaped on grass with mature and developing hedges and trees. The River Peover borders the park and a pleasant walk takes you along the valley to Lower Peover. The town of Knutsford is nearby, the model for Cranford in the Elizabeth Gaskell novels.

Facilities	Directions
The modern sanitary units include automatic lighting and the eco theme sees low level site lighting and reed beds servicing waste water. Facilities for disabled visitors include separate wet room and a toilet in each of the sanitary units. Laundry. WiFi (charged). Gas available. Off site: Golf 3 miles. Knutsford 3 miles. Tatton Park 6 miles. Little Moreton Hall. Jodrell Bank 6 miles.	From south on M6 take exit 18 and follow A50 north towards Holmes Chapel for 4 miles. At Allostock continue 1.2 miles, passing an Alfa Romeo garage on the right and turning left into the park at the old Drover's Arms Pub. GPS: 53.25170, -2.36984

Charges guide

Per unit incl. 2 persons and electricity	£ 22.00
extra adult	£ 5.00

Open: All year excl. 8 January - 6 February.

For latest campsite news visit

alanrogers.com

With spectacular lakes, undulating fells, impressive mountains and lush green valleys, Cumbria is ideal for those who wish to get away from it all and unwind in peaceful, natural surroundings, or for the more active who want to participate in a range of outdoor pursuits.

Cumbria is best known for the beautiful Lake District National Park, with the picturesque valleys and lakes of Windermere, Ullswater and Derwentwater, each with its own distinctive character. Windermere offers no shortage of watersports, whereas Ullswater mainly attracts peaceful sailing boats. While the Lake District is well known, there are also many quiet, undiscovered areas in the region including the wild, rugged moors of the north Pennines and the beautiful Eden Valley, an ideal place for a casual stroll along the riverside footpaths. The western lakes and fells offer more tranquillity. Here the fells drop down to a long and spectacular coastline, with many undiscovered corners from Ennerdale and Eskdale to the sandstone cliffs of St. Bees Head, now part of a designated Heritage Coast. The Lake District peninsulas along the southern coast of Cumbria also display beautiful scenery and are home to a cluster of ancient ruins such as Furness Abbey and the medieval castle built by monks on Piel Island. Rich in heritage, the historic city of Carlisle, which was sited on the Roman-built Hadrian's wall, boasts an impressive castle, Cumbria's only cathedral, a superb Victorian covered market and an array of speciality shops.

Places of interest

Barrow-in-Furness: South Lakes Wild Animal Park; Dalton Castle; Furness Abbey; Piel Island.

Carlisle: 11th-century castle; Birdoswald Roman fort; Lanercost Priory.

Ravenglass: Muncaster Castle, a historic haunted castle and headquarters of the World Owl Trust.

Ulverston: the world's only Laurel and Hardy museum.

Kendal: historic riverside town situated between the Lakes and Dales, famous for its mint cake and castle ruins.

Lake Derwentwater: lakeside theatre open all year hosting plays, music, dance, comedy and film.

Windermere: Steamboat Centre, a collection of Windermere's nautical heritage with boats on display; World of Beatrix Potter.

Grasmere: Dove Cottage and Wordsworth Museum.

Did you know?

Cumbria has the steepest road in England, called the Hardknott Pass.

The Lake District was the inspiration for many poets, writers and artists, including William Wordsworth, Beatrix Potter and John Ruskin.

Ulverston is the birthplace of Quakerism and pole vaulting.

Bassenthwaite is the only real lake in the Lake District! All the others are either meres, (Windermere) or waters (Derwentwater, Coniston Water and Ullswater).

Stretching 73 miles, Hadrian's Wall was built by Romans in the second century.

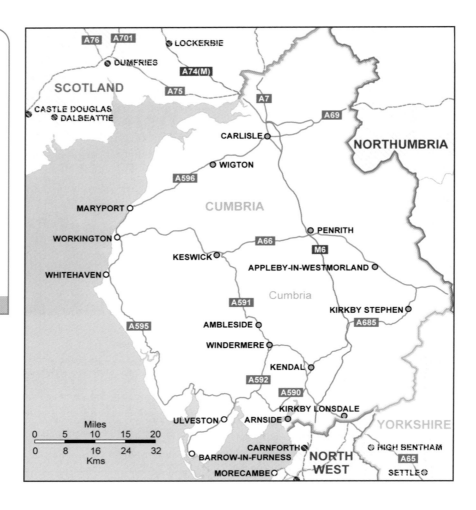

Ambleside

Skelwith Fold Caravan Park

Ambleside LA22 0HX (Cumbria) T: 01539 432277. E: info@skelwith.com

alanrogers.com/UK5520

Skelwith Fold has been developed in the extensive grounds of a country estate taking advantage of the wealth of mature trees and shrubs. The 300 privately owned caravan holiday homes and 150 touring pitches are absorbed into this unspoilt natural environment, sharing it with red squirrels and other wildlife in several discrete areas branching off the central, mile long main driveway. Touring pitches (no tents) are on gravel hardstanding and metal pegs will be necessary for awnings. Electricity hook-ups (10A) and basic amenities are available in all areas.

Facilities

Eight toilet blocks, well situated to serve all areas, have the usual facilities including laundry, drying and ironing rooms. Some blocks have facilities for disabled visitors. Well stocked, licensed shop. Motorcaravan service point. Battery charging, gas and caravan spares and accessories. Adventure play area. Family recreation area with picnic tables and goal posts in the Lower Glade. Off site: Pubs within walking distance. Fishing 200 m. Ambleside village 2.5 miles. Riding and sailing 3 miles.

Open: 1 March - 15 November.

Directions

From Ambleside take the A593 towards Coniston. Pass through Clappergate and on the far outskirts watch for the B5286 to Hawkshead on the left. Park is clearly signed 1 mile down this road on the right. Do not use sat nav to find this park – this will bring you to a locked gate! GPS: 54.41715, -2.995283

Charges guide

Per pitch	£ 19.50 - £ 25.00
incl. electricity	£ 22.50 - £ 28.00
awning	£ 3.00

For latest campsite news visit

alanrogers.com

Appleby-in-Westmorland

Wild Rose Park

Ormside, Appleby-in-Westmorland CA16 6EJ (Cumbria) T: 01768 351077. E: reception@wildrose.co.uk

alanrogers.com/UK5570

Set in the Eden Valley within easy reach of the Lake District and the Yorkshire Dales, Wild Rose is a well known park. The entrance is inviting with its well mown grass, trim borders and colourful flower displays. It is immediately apparent that this is a much loved park, and this is reflected throughout the site in the care and attention to detail. There are 226 touring pitches all with electricity, however 105 also provide water and waste water, plus the site boasts on-site wardens to ensure that everything is always neat and tidy. Wild Rose deserves its excellent reputation, which the owners strive to maintain and improve. There are five distinct areas on the park providing a variety of pitches and services. Hazel Heights and Egglestone Tiers provide fully serviced super pitches, Braithwaite Fold and the Chesters have pitches with electricity and shared water points. The grass area of Donkey's Nest provides pitches with shared electricity and water. There are five wooden teepees and ten Holiday Home units to rent providing all year round luxurious camping. Nothing is overlooked here, from recycling bins, electric buggies to reduce noise, 'sac-o-mat' special bags and bins in the dog walk to cycle racks placed around the park.

Facilities

Three toilet blocks (two heated) of excellent quality and kept spotlessly clean. Most washbasins are in cubicles. Facilities for babies and disabled visitors. Fully equipped laundry. Motorcaravan service point. Well stocked shop incl. gas (1/4-1/11). Licensed restaurant with takeaway (weekends only in low season). Outdoor pool (late May-Sept; 10.00-18.00). Indoor playroom for under fives. Games room. TV room. Cinema room. Tennis. Bicycle hire. Off site: Fishing 2 miles. Golf and riding 3 miles.

Open: All year.

Directions

Park is signed south off B6260 road 1.5 miles southwest of Appleby. Follow signs to park, in the direction of Ormside. GPS: 54.54893, -2.46422

Charges guide

Per unit incl. 2 persons and electricity	£ 17.00 - £ 27.50
'super pitch' incl. mains services and awning	£ 19.00 - £ 29.50

Eden's caravanning paradise

Nestling in magnificent Eden - very close to the Lake District and the Pennines, Wild Rose Park is a multi-award winning park set in beautiful tranquil surroundings. This superb park includes over 220 designated camping and touring pitches, holiday hire now available, mini market, restaurant, laundrette, adventure playgrounds, outdoor pools, TV and Games Rooms... paradise!

Call or write for a FREE brochure:
Ormside, Appleby, Cumbria, CA16 6EJ.
017683 51077 reception@wildrose.co.uk

www.wildrose.co.uk

Arnside

Hollins Farm Caravan & Camp Site

Far Arnside, Arnside LA5 0SL (Cumbria) T: 01524 701508. E: Info@hollinsfarm.co.uk

alanrogers.com/UK5595

Hollins Farm has been considerably improved since being taken over by the Holgate family just a year ago, without losing its appeal as a simple farm site. In a superb location overlooking Morecambe Bay, the park consists of several fields divided by trees. Of the 100 pitches, there are 40 for touring all with electricity (16A), water and TV connections, although large units may have difficulty negotiating the narrow country lanes. This is very popular walking country and leaflets may be obtained from reception. Visitors here are able to use the excellent facilities at the nearby Holgate Leisure Centre (charged).

Facilities

Smart new Portacabins house the toilets and showers, including facilities for disabled visitors. This site also now boasts fridge hire as well as caravan storage plus from 1/3-31/10 a site shop. In addition to this is a children's playground and TV room. Off site: Leighton Moss RSPB Nature reserve. Cross Bay walks. Golf 2 miles. Fishing 9 miles. Market town of Kendal 12 miles.

Open: 14 March - 31 October.

Directions

From exit 35 of the M6 take the A601(M) and at first roundabout take second exit A6 North. In 2.5 miles take left turn (Yealand Redmayne), then follow site signs for Holgates Caravan Park through Silverdale. Hollins Farm is about 0.5 miles beyond Holgates. GPS: 54.18077, -2.84352

Charges guide

Per unit incl. 2 adults and services	£ 13.00 - £ 31.00

For latest campsite news visit

alanrogers.com

Carlisle

Green Acres Caravan Park

High Knells, Houghton, Carlisle CA6 4JW (Cumbria) T: 01228 675418. E: info@caravanpark-cumbria.com

alanrogers.com/UK5640

Green Acres is a small, family run, adults only park. Situated in beautiful, rural surroundings, yet only two miles from junction 44 of the M6, it is perfect for an overnight stop or a longer stay to enjoy Cumbria, Hadrian's Wall and the delights of Carlisle city (four miles away). The Browns have developed Green Acres into an attractive, well maintained and level touring park. There are 30 numbered pitches, all on large hardstandings, arranged in a semicircle, with electricity connections (10A) and four serviced pitches (16A). Divided by a long beech hedge is a large camping field, including on one side 12 new hardstanding super pitches for seasonal letting.

Facilities

Small, clean toilet block with open style washbasins and coin-operated showers (50p/10 mins). Two bathrooms with toilet, shower and washbasin are under construction. No facilities for disabled visitors. Laundry room in farm building. Car wash area. Caravan storage. Off site: Shop. Golf 3 miles. Fishing 8 miles. Bicycle hire 10 miles.

Open: 1 April - end October.

Directions

Leave M6 at junction 44 and take A689 east for 1 mile. Turn left towards Scaleby (site signed) and site is 1 mile on left. GPS: 54.94505, -2.90728

Charges guide

Per unit incl. 2 persons and electricity	£ 14.00 - £ 18.00
extra person	£ 3.00

Kendal

Waters Edge Caravan Park

Crooklands, Kendal LA7 7NN (Cumbria) T: 015395 67708. E: info@watersedgecaravanpark.co.uk

alanrogers.com/UK5645

Close to the M6 motorway, Waters Edge makes an ideal stopover. However, it is also well worth a longer stay, being centrally situated for visiting the Lake District and the Yorkshire Dales. Surrounded by farmland, the park is long and narrow with one road running down the centre and the pitches on either side. There are 26 level touring pitches, all with hardstanding. These are open and a little on the small side. At each end of the park there are six privately-owned caravan holiday homes. There is a play area for children, but parents of young children would need to be vigilant here as there are well signed but unfenced fast flowing streams at both sides of the park.

Facilities

Centrally located heated toilet block, although a little dated, is spotlessly clean with showers and washbasins in cubicles. Facilities for disabled visitors. Laundry. No motorcaravan service point. Shop for basics. Bar with TV. Off site: Restaurant 300 yds. Riding 3 km. Golf 8 km. Canal and boat trips. Kendal 15 minutes drive.

Open: March - November.

Directions

From M6 exit 36 take the A65 (east) signed Kirkby Lonsdale for 300 yds. At next roundabout take first exit signed Crooklands and Endmoor. Park entrance is about 1 mile on the right at Crooklands Motor Co. GPS: 54.24697, -2.7162

Charges guide

Per unit incl. electricity	£ 15.80 - £ 22.90

Kendal

Ashes Exclusively Adult Caravan Park

New Hutton, Kendal LA8 0AS (Cumbria) T: 01539 731833. E: info@ashescaravanpark.co.uk

alanrogers.com/UK5650

The Ashes is a small, friendly, adult only park in an extremely peaceful setting in the rolling Cumbrian countryside, yet less than three miles from the M6, and only slightly further from Kendal. Thus it is not only a convenient night stop, but also a useful base from which to explore the Lake District and the Yorkshire Dales. A very tidy park, the central grass area is attractively planted with shrubs and bushes and there is an open vista (with little shade). There are 25 hardstanding gravel pitches, all with electrical connections (10A). These are neatly placed around the perimeter with an oval access road. The whole area slopes gently down from the entrance, with some pitches fairly level and others with a little more slope (levelling system for caravans on all pitches). No tents are accepted other than trailer tents.

Facilities

A small, purpose built stone building with a slate roof houses two unisex, shower rooms (underfloor heating) and the washing and toilet facilities. New facilities for disabled visitors. Laundry service. No shop. New electronic barrier. TV signal booster. WiFi. Off site: Mr and Mrs Mason have prepared an information sheet with details of shopping, eating and many other local venues. Fishing 2 miles. Golf and riding 3 miles. Bicycle hire and Kendal 4 miles.

Open: 1 March - 5 November.

Directions

From M6 junction 37 follow the A684 towards Kendal for 2 miles. Just past a white cottage turn sharp left at crossroads signed New Hutton. Site is on right in 0.75 miles at a left bend. Only approach and depart using this road. GPS: 54.313133, -2.675

Charges guide

Per unit incl. 2 persons and electricity	£ 16.00 - £ 18.00
extra person (over 18s only)	£ 4.50

For latest campsite news visit
alanrogers.com

Keswick

Castlerigg Hall Caravan & Camping Park

Keswick CA12 4TE (Cumbria) T: 01768 774499. E: info@castlerigg.co.uk

alanrogers.com/UK5660

This well laid out park was started in the late 1950s by the Jackson family, who over the years have developed and improved the site whilst maintaining its character. Good use has been made of the traditional stone buildings to house the reception and shop, whilst another building houses a modern amenity block along with a really excellent campers' kitchen. Tarmac roads wend their way around the site to the separate tent area of 110 pitches. Gently sloping with some shelter, these pitches have fine views across Keswick, Derwentwater and the western Fells. The 45 caravan pitches tend to be on terraces, again overlooking the lake. Each terrace has a maximum of eight pitches, all on hardstanding and with 10A electricity and nearly all with a water tap and grey water drain. Places to visit include Keswick (about 20 minutes walk), Derwentwater, Ullswater, Penrith, Carlisle, Hadrian's Wall, Rhegad (the village in the hill) and, quite close to the site, Castlerigg stone circle, believed to be some 4,000 years old, and of course as much walking as you might want. The Jacksons are committed to conservation.

Facilities

The main toilet block is beautifully fitted out, fully tiled and heated, with showers, vanity style washbasins (2 in cabins) and haircare areas. Unit for disabled visitors (key). Baby area. Fully equipped laundry and dishwashing area. Games room and campers' kitchen complete with microwave, toasters, kettle and hot plates. Two other toilet blocks are newly decorated and clean. Reception houses tourist information and a well stocked shop (with gas). WiFi. Off site: Hotel/pub for meals adjacent to site. Fishing, golf, riding, and bicycle hire 1.5 miles.

Open: 15 March - 1 November.

Directions

From Penrith take A66 towards Keswick and Cockermouth. Leave at first sign for Keswick (A591) and follow to junction (A5271). Turn left on A591 signed Windermere and after 1 mile, take small road on right signed Castlerigg and Rakefoot. Park entrance is on right after 400 yds. GPS: 54.5931, -3.112583

Charges guide

Per unit incl. 2 persons and electricity	£ 18.50 - £ 23.50
extra person (over 4 yrs)	£ 2.80 - £ 3.30

Castlerigg Hall Caravan and Camping Park
the Park with the View. . .
in the heart of the Lakes
Keswick, Cumbria CA12 4TE - English Lake District
Tel: +44 (0)17687 74499   www.castlerigg.co.uk   E-mail: info@castlerigg.co.uk

Kirkby Stephen

Pennine View Caravan & Camping Park

Station Road, Kirkby Stephen CA17 4SZ (Cumbria) T: 01768 371717

alanrogers.com/UK5600

Suitable for night halts or longer breaks to visit the Lake District or the Yorkshire Dales, Pennine View is a super small park, well managed and well maintained. With a very attractive rockery at the entrance, the whole site is very neat and tidy. Level, numbered pitches with gravel hardstanding are arranged around the perimeter with grass pitches in the centre. The pitches are of a good size (some being especially large) and all are supplied with electricity hook-ups (16A). Pennine View was opened in 1990 and is built on reclaimed land from a former railway goods yard. One end of the park adjoins the River Eden. There are trout but a licence is needed for fishing.

Facilities

Built of local stone, the modern toilet block is accessed by a digital keypad and includes individual wash cubicles and deep sink for a baby bath. Both ladies and men have large en-suite units for disabled visitors. Well equipped laundry room. Gas available. Play area. Off site: Nearby hotel offers bar meals. Bicycle hire 300 m. Kirkby Stephen 1 mile (on the Settle-Carlisle railway line). Golf 4 miles.

Open: 1 March - 31 October.

Directions

Park is on the A685 on the southerly outskirts of Kirkby Stephen (just under 1 mile from the town centre). Turn left at small site sign opposite the Croglin Castle hotel. Site is 50 yds. on right. GPS: 54.461667, -2.353367

Charges guide

Per person	£ 5.10 - £ 5.50
pitch	£ 5.00 - £ 6.00

For latest campsite news visit
alanrogers.com

Kirkby Lonsdale
Woodclose Caravan Park
Kirkby Lonsdale LA6 2SE (Cumbria) T: 01524 271597. E: info@woodclosepark.com
alanrogers.com/UK5605

Woodclose is an established, nine-acre park situated in the Lune Valley and just one mile from the market town of Kirkby Lonsdale, this park offers a peaceful and secluded setting catering for walkers, tourers and people who just want to relax. Access to the park is narrow, so care should be taken. The whole park has a very well cared for appearance with well mown grass, flowering tubs and neat hedges. Screened by a hedge and placed around the perimeter are several seasonal pitches with touring units being placed in the centre. In the camping area, there are a number of 'wigwam' pods with all facilities for luxury camping, one being at ground level for disabled access. These pitches are numbered and mostly level, some on hardstanding, some on grass, with 16A electricity and digital TV hook-ups. More seasonal pitches and holiday homes are on the lower part of the park, again most attractively terraced with stone walling and paths. Reception is part of the well stocked shop selling local produce and fresh bread; an information room is adjoining with tables and chairs and Internet access (£1 per half an hour).

Facilities

Two toilet blocks, the main one central to the touring area. These facilities are all unisex in large, heated, individual rooms with toilets, washbasin and toilet or washbasin and shower, all well equipped and very clean. Laundry. The second block has all unisex cubicles. Facilities for disabled visitors. Shop. Small adventure play area. Bicycle hire. Internet access. American style motorhomes accepted (limited space). Gates locked 24.00-07.30, warden and telephone on site for emergencies. Off site: Golf 1 mile. Fishing 7 miles. Beach 20 miles.

Open: 1 March - 1 November.

Directions

From M6 exit 36 take A65 to Kirkby Lonsdale. Site is off the A65 in 6 miles from the motorway. GPS: 54.19835, -2.585017

Charges guide

Per unit incl. 2 persons	
and electricity	£ 12.00 - £ 22.00
tent incl. 2 persons	£ 13.00 - £ 16.75
extra person	£ 4.00
child (6-16 yrs)	£ 2.25
awning	£ 2.00

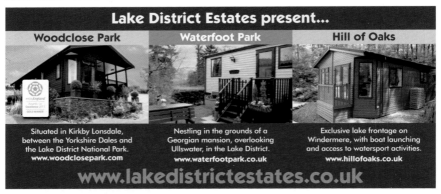

Penrith
Sykeside Camping Park
Brotherswater, Patterdale, Penrith CA11 0NZ (Cumbria) T: 01768 482239. E: info@sykeside.co.uk
alanrogers.com/UK5560

This small touring park is located in a really beautiful, quiet spot in the northern Lakes area (it is just 400 yards from Brotherswater). With views up the Dovedale valley, the park has 100 pitches in the valley floor, mainly for tents. There are 19 for motorcaravans on hardstanding, 16 of which have electricity (10A). Pitches are not marked and campers arrange themselves to best enjoy the superb views. The stone-built building, an original barn, near the entrance houses all the facilities. These include the recently extended and refurbished Barn End bar where meals are served.

Facilities

The toilet block includes hot showers and has been refurbished, with a chemical disposal point added. Small launderette and dishwashing room. Self-service shop with camping equipment, gas and an ice-pack service, doubles as reception. Cosy, licensed bar and restaurant (daily in summer, weekends only in winter). Bunkhouse accommodation for 30 persons in various groupings. Fishing nearby. Off site: Bicycle hire 3 miles. Good sailing on Ullswater 4 miles. Riding 8 miles. Golf 10 miles.

Open: All year.

Directions

From junction 40 of M6 take the A66 towards Keswick. At first roundabout take A592 and follow signs for Ullswater and Glenridding, continue to Brotherswater and Sykeside is on the right of the A592. The entrance is just behind the Brotherswater Inn. GPS: 54.4985, -2.9255

Charges guide

Per unit incl. 2 persons	£ 12.50 - £ 23.50
and electricity	£ 17.50 - £ 25.00

Penrith

Westmorland Caravan Park

Tebay, Orton, Penrith CA10 3SB (Cumbria) T: 01539 711322. E: caravans@westmorland.com

alanrogers.com/UK5590

For caravans, motorcaravans and trailer tents only, this is the ideal stopover for anyone heading either north or south, near the M6 motorway, but far enough away for the traffic noise not to be too disturbing. There are 80 level pitches on gravel, divided into bays of about six or seven units (25 are for touring units). All touring pitches have electricity (16A). The bays are backed by grassy banks alive with rabbits and birds – a long list in the office describes the large variety of birds to be seen on the site. There is good site lighting and a late arrivals area.

Facilities

The heated toilet block is basic but kept very clean and includes washbasins and showers. Bathroom for disabled visitors with ramped access. Family room. Laundry. Reception sells gas. Dog walk. Off site: Shops and restaurants five minutes walk away at the motorway service area. Fishing 2 miles. Golf 17 miles. Within 30 minutes drive are the market towns of Appleby, Penrith and Kendal. Boat rides on Ullswater.

Open: 5 March - 12 November.

Directions

From the M6, exit for Tebay Services (site signed) just north of junction 38. Site is accessible from the services travelling north or south.
GPS: 54.4477, -2.606467

Charges guide

Per unit incl. 4 persons and electricity	£ 18.50 - £ 21.50
child	free
awning	£ 2.50
dog	free

Special rates for 3, 5 or 7 days.
Discount on café meals and farm shop.

Penrith

Waterfoot Caravan Park

Pooley Bridge, Penrith CA11 0JF (Cumbria) T: 01768 486302. E: enquiries@waterfootpark.co.uk

alanrogers.com/UK5610

Waterfoot is a quiet family park for caravans and motorcaravans only. It is set in 22 acres of partially wooded land, developed in the fifties from a private estate. The 146 private caravan holiday homes are quite separate from the 34 touring pitches. Lake Ullswater is only about 400 yards away and a half mile stroll through bluebell woods brings you to the village of Pooley Bridge. Waterfoot's touring pitches are arranged very informally in a large clearing. Most are level, there are some hardstandings and all have 10A electricity. The park no longer accepts American RVs. There is a bar in a large, imposing mansion; in the past a family home then a golf hotel. Public footpaths lead straight from the park. The regular lake steamer service calls at Pooley Bridge, the Ullswater yacht club is only ten minutes drive and the market town of Penrith is five miles. The historic house and gardens of Dalemain are a short walk.

Facilities

The heated toilet block includes washbasins and preset showers in cubicles. New facilities for disabled visitors. Large, light and airy dishwashing room and fully equipped laundry. Small shop selling basics, gas and newspapers. Bar with strictly enforced, separate family room open weekend evenings in low season and every evening in high season. Large fenced field with play equipment to suit all ages and goal posts for football and a new play park. Off site: Fishing 0.5 miles. Riding 1.5 miles. Golf 5 miles. Pooley Bridge has a post office/general store, hotels and restaurants.

Open: 1 March - 14 November.

Directions

Do not use GPS here - it directs outfits the wrong way, finishing up on farm tracks. Please use the following directions. From M6 junction 40, take A66 signed Keswick. After 0.5 miles at roundabout take A592 signed Ullswater and site is on right after 4 miles. GPS: 54.614017, -2.83115

Charges guide

Per unit incl. all persons and electricity	£ 18.50 - £ 29.50

Pay for 7 nights in one payment and receive 1 night free.
See advertisement on page 224.

For latest campsite news visit
alanrogers.com

Penrith

Cove Camping Park

Ullswater, Watermillock, Penrith CA11 0LS (Cumbria) T: 01768 486549. E: info@cove-park.co.uk

alanrogers.com/UK5620

Cove Camping is a delightful small site, some of the 50 pitches having great views over Lake Ullswater. A separate area behind the camping field holds 39 privately owned caravan holiday homes. The grass is well trimmed, there are ramps to keep speeds down to 5 mph. and the site is well lit. At the top of the park are 17 level pitches with 10A electric hook-ups and hardstanding suitable for touring caravans and motorcaravans. The rest of the park is quite sloping. Rubbish bins are hidden behind wooden fencing, as are recycling bins. The park is well situated for walking, boating, fishing and pony trekking activities. The road up from the A592 is narrow, but a self imposed one way system is generally adhered to and the warden will advise on a different way to leave the site.

Facilities

The tiled toilet block is immaculate and heated in cooler months, providing adjustable showers, some washbasins in cabins and, for ladies, a hairdressing area with stool and a baby changing unit. Foyer containing a freezer (free), and tourist information. Laundry with washing machine, dryer and an iron. Gas supplies. Small, grass play area. Off site: Shop nearby. Fishing 1.5 miles. Riding 3 miles. Golf 6 mile. Bicycle hire 7 miles (will deliver).

Open: March - 31 October.

Directions

We would advise using directions rather than GPS. From A66 Penrith - Keswick road, take A592 south, signed Ullswater. Turn right at Brackenrigg Inn (site signed) and follow road uphill for about 1.5 miles to park on left. Larger units, telephone the park for advice about an alternative route as road is narrow. GPS: 54.604283, -2.881883

Charges guide

Per unit incl. 2 persons and electricity	£ 20.00 - £ 27.00
tent incl. 2 persons	£ 14.00 - £ 25.00
child (5-17 yrs)	£ 2.00
dog	free

Credit cards accepted.

A small and quiet caravan and camping park in The Lake District. Pure tranquility and escapism. We are easy to find only 7 miles from junction 40 on the M6, yet in the very heart of the Northern Lakes overlooking Ullswater.

www.cove-park.co.uk
01768 486549

Cove Park "The Peaceful Park"

Penrith

Lowther Holiday Park

Eamont Bridge, Penrith CA10 2JB (Cumbria) T: 01768 863631. E: alan@lowther-holidaypark.co.uk

alanrogers.com/UK5625

Sitting on the banks of the River Lowther this holiday park occupies 50 acres of rural, wooded parkland, home to the rare red squirrel. There are 400 caravan holiday homes and lodges around the park, together with 70 touring pitches. A proportion of these are taken by seasonal lets. Marked and numbered, on mostly level ground between mature trees, all have 10A electricity and hardstanding. A separate elevated grass area is available for tents. There is a small touring office with 24 hour security adjacent to the holiday home sales office. Here too is a well stocked, licensed shop also selling some caravan accessories. The Squirrel Inn is open all season and serves restaurant meals and takeaways.

Facilities

Two toilet blocks are central to the touring areas (key entry). Very clean, they provide large, preset showers. Fully equipped bathroom with baby changing. Drive through motorcaravan service. Well equipped laundry. Full facilities for disabled visitors (Radar key). Licensed shop. Squirrel Inn with restaurant, terrace and games room. Play areas. Fly fishing on river (permit from office). Activity weekends. Live entertainment and children's parties. Max. two dogs per unit. Off site: Golf, riding and bicycle hire 2 miles. Market town of Penrith 3 miles. Boat launching 4 miles.

Open: 7 March - 13 November.

Directions

From M6 exit 40 take A66 towards Scotch Corner for 1 mile. At roundabout take A6 south for 1 mile towards Shap. Lowther is on the right as you pass through village of Eamont Bridge. GPS: 54.647667, -2.737017

Charges guide

Per unit incl. 6 persons and electricity	£ 23.00 - £ 30.00

Penrith
The Quiet Site Caravan & Camping Park

Watermillock, Penrith CA11 0LS (Cumbria) T: 07768 727016. E: info@thequietsite.co.uk

alanrogers.com/UK5630

The Quiet Site is a secluded, family run park, operating as a carbon neutral company. It is situated on a hillside in the National Park with views over the fells and just 1.5 miles from Lake Ullswater. There are 100 unmarked touring pitches, most with hardstanding and 60 with electricity. All have been terraced to provide level surfaces. The camping area is undulating. In a separate part of the park, screened by mature trees, are 23 privately-owned caravan holiday homes. There are two cottages to rent and recent additions are timber built 'camping pods' as an alternative to bringing your own tent.

Facilities
The toilet block provides preset showers and open style washbasins. Three bathrooms and two private shower rooms. Bathroom with facilities for disabled visitors. Baby area. Laundry facilities. Motorcaravan services. Well stocked shop at reception. Gas supplies. Bar (weekends only in low season). TV and games room. Excellent adventure play area. Caravan storage. WiFi. American motorhomes would find access very difficult. Off site: Fishing 1.5 miles. Riding and bicycle hire 3 miles..

Open: All year.

Directions
From M6, exit 40, take A66 (Keswick) for 1 mile, then A592 signed Ullswater for 4 miles. Turn right at Lake junction, still on A592 signed Windermere. After 1 mile turn right (at Brackenrigg Inn) and follow for 1.5 miles to site on right (large units should phone for an alternative route). GPS: 54.604683, -2.882783

Charges guide
Per unit incl. 2 persons, £ 16.00 - £ 30.00
Camping Cheques accepted.

Penrith
Ullswater Caravan, Camping & Marine Park

Watermillock, Penrith CA11 0LR (Cumbria) T: 017684 86666. E: info@uccmp.co.uk

alanrogers.com/UK5635

Located within the Lake District National Park, Ullswater Caravan Park is centrally situated for touring the many attractions of this glorious area. It has 220 pitches, 58 for touring units, the rest used for holiday homes. All have 10A electricity, 50 also have water and drains. Some are situated very close to the bar and are also overlooked by mobile homes with little privacy. At the far end of the park other pitches are in a more wooded area. In between is a large grassy space for tents. There are occasional glimpses of the lake through the trees. Attractive self-catering holiday cottages are for rent.

Facilities
Two toilet blocks, both recently refurbished, have facilities for babies and disabled visitors. Laundry. Recently refurbished reception and shop with off-licence. Bar and games room open 20.00 at busy times. Well equipped playground for younger children. WiFi. Off site: Walks in the hills above the park. Steamer rides on the lake from Pooley Bridge 2 miles.

Open: 1 March - 14 November.

Directions
From M6 exit 40 take A66 west (Keswick). At first roundabout (Rheged) take second exit (Ullswater) on A592. At T-junction turn right and after Brackenrigg Inn, carry on downhill to telephone box on right, and sign for church. Turn right here and up to entrance on right in 800 yds. GPS: 54.5978, -2.87482

Charges guide
Per unit incl. 2 persons £ 17.00 - £ 26.00

Penrith
Flusco Wood Touring Caravan Park

Flusco, Penrith CA11 0JB (Cumbria) T: 01768 480020. E: info@fluscowoodtouringpark.co.uk

alanrogers.com/UK5670

Flusco Wood Caravan Park is still being developed but everything is to a very high standard. Set amongst woodland with the 12 touring pitches in bays, this park will meet the needs of those requiring a quiet holiday (with plenty of walks from the site) and also those travelling up or down the M6 looking for a quiet night's rest. All pitches are on hardstanding, with an area near reception with hardstandings for motorcaravans. Recent additions here include new log cabins (privately owned), with more planned. The area abounds with wildlife including deer and red squirrels, as well as many breeds of birds (we watched a woodpecker taking food from a bird feeder). Member of the Countryside Discovery group.

Facilities
A log cabin style building has clean, heated facilities with preset showers and vanity style washbasins. En-suite shower rooms for families and disabled visitors. Dishwashing sinks under cover. Laundry, drying room and boot washing sink. Reception/shop with basic supplies, gas and daily newspapers. Play equipment on bark. Grass area for ball games. Off site: Pub and P.O. store 2 miles. Fishing, bicycle hire and golf 4 miles. Riding 5 miles.

Open: Easter/1 April - 29 October.

Directions
From junction 40 of M6 take A66 west towards Keswick. Go straight on at first roundabout, then after 2.5 miles take right turn at top of hill (caravan sign). After 0.5 miles road turns right up hill (narrow), site is on left at the top. Site is 4 miles from M6. GPS: 54.655408, -2.841346

Charges guide
Per unit incl. 2 persons £ 17.50 - £ 20.50

For latest campsite news visit
alanrogers.com

Wigton

Stanwix Park Holiday Centre

Greenrow, Silloth CA7 4HH (Cumbria) T: 01697 332666. E: enquiries@stanwix.com

alanrogers.com/UK5505

Stanwix Park is a family run holiday park with absolutely everything anyone could want for a memorable holiday all year round. The park has 111 caravan holiday homes and chalets for rent, together with 212 which are privately owned. These are mostly located around the central complex. In addition at either end of the park, there are 121 fully serviced (10A electricity) pitches for touring units and tents, some on grass, some with hardstanding. A warm welcome awaits in the main reception, with lots of local and tourist information. Motorcaravans over 8 m. accepted by prior arrangement.

Facilities

The two clean heated sanitary blocks have been refurbished to a high standard. Large en-suite bathrooms, showers, vanity style washbasins and a unit in each for disabled visitors. Dishwashing. Kitchen. Laundry. Well stocked shop (6/3-15/11). Restaurant with takeaway. Bars (adults only and family) with evening entertainment (6/3-15/11). TV and snooker room. Indoor leisure centre. Outdoor swimming pool (31/5-1/9). Ten-pin bowling. Amusement arcade. Soft play area. Minigolf. Tennis. Bicycle hire. Off site: Beach 1 mile. Bus 1 mile in Silloth.

Open: All year.

Directions

From south, take exit 41 from M6 and follow B5305 through Wigton to Silloth. From north on A74/M6 take exit 44 and the A595 and A596 to Wigton. On entering Silloth, turn left following signs for park. Entrance is on the right. GPS: 54.8614, -3.388333

Charges guide

Per person	£ 4.00 - £ 4.80
child (under 5 yrs)	£ 2.60 - £ 3.10
pitch	£ 12.40 - £ 15.70
dog (max. 2)	£ 3.00

Wigton

Hylton Caravan Park

Silloth, Wigton CA7 4AY (Cumbria) T: 01697 332666. E: ericstanwix@stanwix.com

alanrogers.com/UK5506

Hylton Caravan Park is owned and managed by the Stanwix family and although it is only a short walk away from the livelier Stanwix Park, it is a peaceful haven for people who prefer the 'quiet life'. The only activity is an adventure park for children which is not visible from the touring area. Divided by a circular road, the 170 privately owned caravan holiday homes are visible but not intrusive. There are 90 open plan, mostly level touring and tent pitches, all fully serviced and with 10A electricity. There is no shop on site as the town and Stanwix Park are both within walking distance.

Facilities

A high quality toilet block is superbly fitted out and includes toilets, showers, vanity style washbasins, extra large bathrooms and a separate cubicle for disabled visitors. Dishwashing under cover. Fully equipped laundry. Gas sales. Max. 2 dogs per pitch. Off site: Bus stop 1 mile. Entertainment and amenities at Stanwix Park. Silloth golf course. Bowling. Windsurfing, boat launching and fishing 1 mile. Riding 7 miles.

Open: 1 March - 15 November.

Directions

On entering Silloth, turn left following signs to Hylton Caravan Park. GPS: 54.868333, -3.39835

Charges guide

Per person	£ 4.00 - £ 4.80
child (under 5 yrs)	£ 2.60 - £ 3.10
pitch	£ 10.00 - £ 12.50

Wigton

The Larches Caravan Park

Mealsgate, Wigton CA7 1LQ (Cumbria) T: 01697 371379. E: thelarches@hotmail.co.uk

alanrogers.com/UK5510

Mealsgate and The Larches lie on the Carlisle - Cockermouth road, a little way from the hectic centre of the Lake District, yet with easy access to it (and good views towards it) and to other attractions nearby. This quiet, family run, adults only park takes 45 touring units of any type, 42 of which have electricity (10A), water and drainage. Touring pitches are in separate grassy areas with tall, mature trees, shrubs and plenty of wildlife. Some are sloping and irregular, others on marked hardstandings. There are currently few privately owned holiday homes and there are plans to extend this area of the park.

Facilities

Toilet facilities are clean and provide en-suite facilities for both sexes. Separate unit for disabled visitors can be heated. Campers' kitchen with microwave (free). Laundry room. Small shop selling mainly camping accessories, gas and off-licence. Small indoor heated pool (June-Aug) Wildlife pond. Caravan storage. Off site: Riding 1.5 miles. Golf 3.5 miles. Bicycle hire 7 miles. Fishing 8 miles.

Open: 1 March - 31 October.

Directions

Park entrance is south off A595 (Carlisle - Cockermouth road) just southwest of Mealsgate. GPS: 54.763267, -3.2358

Charges guide

Per unit incl. 2 persons and electricity	£ 18.00 - £ 20.90
extra person	£ 4.00 - £ 5.00
No credit cards.	

Windermere

Hill of Oaks Caravan Park

Tower Wood, Windermere LA12 8NR (Cumbria) T: 01539 531578. E: enquiries@hillofoaks.co.uk

alanrogers.com/UK5615

This park on the banks of Lake Windermere lives up to its name, Hill of Oaks. Set on a hillside in mature woodland, the park offers families a safe natural environment with nature walks through the managed ancient woodlands, as well as six jetties for boat launching and access to watersport activities (jet skis are not allowed). The road into the park passing the farmhouse is long, winding and narrow, so long outfits should ring ahead for a different access, reception being about half a mile from the entrance. Although the park is situated on Lake Windermere the touring pitches nestle within the trees, not actually by the lake. All 43 have electricity (16A), digital TV hook-up and hardstanding. Most are large enough to take a car and boat and three large super pitches also have water and a drain. Tents are not accepted at Hill of Oaks. The entrance barrier is open from 08.00 till dusk with a security code being provided for exit. There is a new reception and shop selling basics, with a tourist information room adjacent on the lakeside in wooden chalet-type buildings with an abundance of hanging baskets and flowers. Privately owned caravan holiday homes have been built into the hillside on terraces and are quite unobtrusive, screened by hedges and trees.

Facilities

The central tiled toilet block, recently refurbished, is very clean and heated. Vanity style washbasins, controllable showers and free hairdryers. Baby changing areas. Fully equipped laundry. Unit for disabled visitors (combination lock). Motorcaravan service point. Shop for basics. Two fenced play areas, one for toddlers and an adventure type for over fives. Picnic areas and nature trails. Fishing (licence required). WiFi (charged). Off site: Fell Foot Park and Gardens 1 mile, with rowing boat hire and ferry rides to Lakeside and Ambleside. Aquarium of the Lakes at Newby Bridge 3.5 miles. Golf 4 miles. Riding and bicycle hire 6 miles.

Open: 1 March - 14 November.

Directions

From M6 exit 36 head west on A590 towards Barrow and Newby Bridge. Follow A590 to roundabout signed Bowness and turn right on A592 for about 3 miles. Site is signed on left. GPS: 54.30755, -2.9454

Charges guide

Per pitch	£ 27.00 - £ 32.00
awning	£ 3.50
boat	£ 5.00 - £ 10.50

See advertisement on page 224

Windermere

Park Cliffe Camping & Caravan Estate

Birks Road, Windermere LA23 3PG (Cumbria) T: 01539 531344. E: info@parkcliffe.co.uk

alanrogers.com/UK5545

This beautiful park is situated in the heart of the Lake District National Park and is well managed and maintained, with welcoming staff. The 60 touring pitches are open and unshaded, on gravel hardstanding, with electricity (10A), water and drainage. There are some seasonal units and three mobile homes available for hire. Tucked away in a valley are privately owned mobile homes. Two areas have been set aside for tents, one of which has electric hook-ups (steel pegs required). There is no automatic barrier, but the gates are closed to both campers and caravanners 23.00-07.30, with a warden on site for emergencies. A member of the Best of British Group.

Facilities

Two blocks of toilets and showers are heated and very clean. Full facilities for disabled visitors and excellent baby room. Four private bathrooms are available for hire (min 3 days), and one by the hour (with refundable deposit). Laundry. Motorcaravan service point. Bar, restaurant and takeaway. Small well stocked shop. Games room. Large outdoor adventure play area is set secluded to one side of the tourers, not fenced as a public footpath runs through to Moor How. Off site: Fellfoot Country Park with (sail)boat launching, walking, climbing, cycling and many other activities possible. Cruises on the lake. Many visitor attractions.

Open: 1 March - 11 November.

Directions

From M6 exit 36 take A590 to Newby Bridge. Turn right on A592 for 3.6 miles and turn right. Site is signed shortly on the right. Caravans and trailers must approach Park Cliffe from the direction of Newby Bridge on the A592. The park does not advise the use of sat nav to reach it. GPS: 54.312517, -2.9375

Charges guide

Per unit incl. 2 persons and electricity	£ 25.00 - £ 29.00
extra person	£ 5.00
child (5-17 yrs)	£ 2.50
dog	£ 2.00

For latest campsite news visit

alanrogers.com

The most northerly region of England, Northumbria is steeped in history, full of ancient forts and fairytale castles. The great outdoors offers limitless walking with plenty of trails stretching across moorlands and beaches, encompassing views of the beautiful scenery.

THE REGION COMPRISES: NORTHUMBERLAND, DURHAM, TYNE AND WEAR, AND TEESIDE

The 400 square mile Northumberland National Park is one of the most peaceful and remote places in England. With endless walks across moorlands and hills, it stretches south from the Cheviot Hills, through the Simonside Hills, to the crags of Whin Sill, where it engulfs a section of the historic Hadrian's Wall, built by the Romans to mark the northern limit of their empire. The Pennine Way was the country's first official long-distance path and is still the longest. At 268 miles, it stretches from the Peak National Park to the border. The coastline is not to be forgotten, with mile upon mile of deserted, sandy beaches, with resorts that still have an old fashioned feel to them, such as Whitley Bay, South Shields and Seaton Carew. The majestic castles of Bamburgh, and Dunstanburgh can be seen for miles along the Northumberland coast. Surrounded on three sides by the river Wear, the small, historic city of Durham is dominated by England's greatest Norman cathedral. With cobbled medieval streets and restricted car access, it is a popular place with visitors. Further north is the bustling city of Newcastle. Home to an array of cosmopolitan restaurants and bars, music venues, and fabulous architecture, it also boasts a lively nightlife.

Places of interest

Northumberland: Bamburgh Castle; Alnwick Castle and gardens; Berwick-upon-Tweed; bird reserve on Farne Islands, home to large colony of grey seals; Hauxley Nature Reserve; Dunstanburgh Castle; Corbridge Roman sites at Hadrian's Wall.

Durham: Durham Castle and Cathedral; Barnard Castle, a ruined castle overlooking the River Tees; Diggerland at Langley Park; Harperley POW Camp.

Tyne and Wear: New Metroland, Europe's only indoor theme park within a large shopping complex; Newcastle with Life Science Centre, Discovery Museum and Castle Keep; Whitley Bay.

Teeside: Kirkleatham Owl Centre; Darlington Railway Centre and Museum; Guisborough Hall; Hartlepool Historic Quay and HMS Trinacomalee; Butterfly World in Stockton-on-Tees.

Did you know?

Alnwick Castle was used as the setting for Hogwarts in the Harry Potter films.

Stretching from Wallsend to Bowness-on-Solway, Hadrian's Wall is 81 miles long; it is possible to walk the entire length.

Born in Northumbria in 1825, George Stephenson was the first person to design the steam engine that ran on wheels.

In the past 300 years Berwick has changed hands between the Scottish and the English no less than 13 times.

The Angel of The North is made up of 200 tonnes of steel and rises 20 metres from the ground.

Built in 1817, HMS Trinacomalee is the oldest ship afloat in the UK.

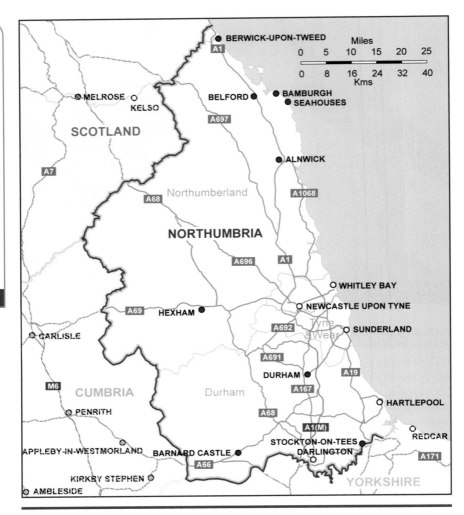

Alnwick

Dunstan Hill Camping & Caravanning Club Site

Dunstan Hill, Dunstan, Alnwick NE66 3TQ (Northumberland) T: 01665 576310

alanrogers.com/UK5770

Off a quiet lane between Embleton and Craster this is a rural site with a tree belt to shelter it from the north wind and access to the beach by a level footpath through the fields, across the golf course and past the ruins of Dunstanburgh Castle. This is just over a mile by car. With gravel access roads, the peaceful site has 150 level, well spaced pitches, 80 with 16A electricity. Reception is manned by very helpful managers and there is an area for outside parking and late arrivals at the entrance. This is a wonderful area to visit, with its unspoilt beaches and the whole area is steeped in history.

Facilities

Two very clean and well maintained toilet blocks have some washbasins in cubicles, hairdryers (20p) and a washroom for children with deep sinks. Fully equipped facility for disabled visitors in one block, a laundry in the other. Small shop for gas and basics. Bread and milk can be ordered and a mobile shop and the paper man visit. Fish and chip van on Fridays. Tourist information room. Small play area. Torches are useful. WiFi (charged). Off site: Buses pass the site entrance (request stop) and there are good eating places near including Craster (world famous fish restaurant). Beach, fishing and golf 1.5 miles. Riding 8 miles. Bicycle hire 10 miles.

Open: 29 March - 5 November.

Directions

From A1 just north of Alnwick take B1340 or B6347 (further north) for Embleton. Site is signed in Embleton village. Avoid signs to Dunstanburgh Castle and follow those for Craster. Site is (south) on the left after about 0.5 miles.
GPS: 55.4855, -1.6291

Charges 2012

Per person	£ 7.75 - £ 9.45
child (6-18 yrs)	£ 2.70 - £ 2.95
non-member pitch fee	£ 7.10

Bamburgh

Waren Caravan & Camping Park

Waren Mill, Bamburgh NE70 7EE (Northumberland) T: 01668 214366. E: waren@meadowhead.co.uk

alanrogers.com/UK5750

Developed from 100 acres of undulating, privately owned heath and woodland, Waren Park is a large, spacious family site with marvellous views over Northumberland's golden beaches and the sea. A large section of caravan holiday homes is separate from a self-contained four acre touring area. Enclosed by sheltering banks, this provides 150 reasonably level pitches, 100 with electrical connections (16A). Wooden wigwams are also available. As well as the spacious grounds to wander in, there is much to see nearby from historic castles and the Farne Islands to the Cheviot Hills and miles and miles of sandy beaches. There is a dog walk along the top of the embankment with views along the coast. The well spaced pitches, with a play area in the middle, provide an open and uncrowded feel to this quiet site.

Facilities

The older toilet facilities have been refurbished to a high standard and include four family en-suite shower rooms, a family bathroom and facilities for disabled visitors. A newer block situated in a separate static holiday home section also provides good facilities. Laundry room. Dishwashing sinks. Motorcaravan service point. Licensed shop. Bar with terrace serving bar meals (all season). Gaming machine room with pool table. Patio area. Children's play park and playing fields. Splash pool (June-Sept). WiFi. Off site: Beach 500 yds. excellent for birdwatching, unsuitable for bathing. Safe beach 4 miles (Bamburgh). Golf and bicycle hire 2 miles. Riding 5 miles.

Open: 14 March - 31 October.

Directions

Follow B1342 from the A1 to Waren Mill towards Bamburgh. After Budle Bay turn right and follow signs. GPS: 55.60045, -1.75487

Charges guide

Per unit incl. 2 persons	
and electricity	£ 17.50 - £ 22.50
extra person (over 5 yrs)	£ 5.00
1-man tent (no car)	£ 9.75 - £ 12.50
dog	£ 3.00

Less 10% for bookings of 7 days or over.

Barnard Castle

Doe Park Touring Caravan Park

Cotherstone, Barnard Castle DL12 9UQ (Co. Durham) T: 01833 650302. E: info@doepark.co.uk

alanrogers.com/UK5710

The Lamb family will make you very welcome and personally take you to your pitch at Doe Park. The camping fields have a lovely open aspect with wonderful views and the 70 pitches are spacious with well mown grass, all with 10A electricity, over 50 with hardstanding. This is Hannah Hauxwell country and the Dales, less frequented than other upland areas, provide wonderful walking country; indeed part of the Pennine Way runs near this peaceful site. The park's reception is a new wooden cabin at the entrance to the pitch area and is well stocked with tourist information guides.

Facilities

With toilet facilities at the farmhouse, two well kept blocks are closer to the pitches. Built in local stone, these are fully tiled with the newest one heated. Washbasins in cabins and adjustable showers. Well appointed unisex unit for disabled visitors. Small laundry. Eggs and milk are available from the farmhouse, plus gas supplies and battery charging. No play area but a large grass area in front of some of the pitches can be used for ball games. River fishing on site. Dogs and pets are accepted by arrangement only. Off site: Riding 2 miles. Reservoirs (sailing, waterskiing and fishing) 3 miles. Bicycle hire, golf and local leisure centre with pool 4 miles.

Open: 1 March - 31 October.

Directions

Follow B6277 from Barnard Castle in direction of Middleton in Teesdale. The farm is signed on the left just after Cotherstone village (there is no need to go into Barnard Castle). GPS: 54.578217, -1.99235

Charges 2012

Per unit incl. 2 persons	
and electricity	£ 15.00 - £ 19.00
family rate (2 adults, 2 children and awning)	£ 18.50 - £ 22.00
extra person (over 6 yrs)	£ 1.50

No credit cards.

For latest campsite news visit

alanrogers.com

Barnard Castle

Barnard Castle Camping & Caravanning Club Site

Dockenflatts Lane, Lartington, Barnard Castle DL12 9DG (Co. Durham) T: 01833 630228

alanrogers.com/UK5720

Welcoming non-members and tents, the Camping and Caravanning Club site at Barnard Castle was opened in 1996. There are 90 flat pitches, most on grass but including 25 hardstanding pitches (gravel base with room for both car and caravan and space for an awning on grass). There are 65 electrical hook-ups (16A). One side of the site is bordered by mature trees and there is an attractive woodland dog walking area leading to a riverside footpath which takes you into Barnard Castle. There are many footpaths and walks in the area and numerous local attractions.

Facilities

The good quality, centrally located toilet facilities can be heated and are spotlessly clean. Washbasins in cubicles, and free, controllable showers are roomy. Baby room. Fully equipped unisex unit for disabled visitors. Laundry and outside lines. Small shop in reception. Motorcaravan service point. Gas supplies. Central play area with safety base. Caravan storage. WiFi (charged). Off site: Riding 200 m. Golf 2.5 miles. Fishing 4 miles. Bus at end of lane.

Open: 30 March - 30 October.

Directions

Follow B6277 from Barnard Castle (towards Middleton in Teesdale) for 1 mile to Lartington. Turn left at club sign into narrow lane with passing places to site entrance on left (there is no need to go into Barnard Castle). GPS: 54.546883, -1.962583

Charges 2012

Per person	£ 5.95 - £ 9.35
child (6-18 yrs)	£ 2.70 - £ 2.95
non-member pitch fee	£ 7.10

Belford

South Meadows Caravan Park

South Meadows, Belford NE70 7DP (Northumberland) T: 01668 213326. E: g.mcl@btinternet.com

alanrogers.com/UK5755

South Meadows is set in the north Northumberland countryside, within walking distance of the village of Belford with its market cross and old coaching inn. Covering six acres of level grass, there are 150 hardstanding pitches, most with electricity (13A), water and TV aerial point. At present 60 pitches are available for touring units. A further area accommodates 50 tents. The manager is environmentally aware and encourages recycling. Determined that visitors have a relaxing holiday, he will site your caravan using his own towing equipment. There is an area especially for disabled visitors with wider paths and safety features including a 24 hour telephone directly to the manager's home on site.

Facilities

The fully tiled toilet block is excellent, heated in cool weather, with washbasins in cabins and roomy showers. Family shower rooms. An additional Portacabin block is open for the summer months. Hairdryers. Full facilities for disabled visitors. Laundry plus a baby unit. Kitchen area. Coffee shop (weekends, incl. Sunday roast) and takeaway (daily until 16.00). Play area. Caravan storage and servicing. Off site: Village with pub and shops 0.5 miles.

Open: All year.

Directions

Turn off A1 about 15 miles from Alnwick to Belford village and park is signed at the southern end. GPS: 55.590967, -1.822583

Charges guide

Per unit incl. 2 persons and electricity	£ 18.00 - £ 24.00
tent per adult	£ 12.00 - £ 15.00
No credit cards.	

Berwick-upon-Tweed

Ord House Country Park

East Ord, Berwick-upon-Tweed TD15 2NS (Northumberland) T: 01289 305288. E: enquiries@ordhouse.co.uk

alanrogers.com/UK5800

Ord House is a 40-acre park for 260 privately-owned holiday homes and 74 touring caravan and tent pitches. The park has a very well cared for appearance throughout, with well mown grass and colourful arrays of flowering bushes. Ord House itself, an 18th-century mansion, has been tastefully converted to provide a bar, lounge bar and family room. The touring pitches, 67 with electricity (16A), are in small sections, from the secluded, walled orchard to the more open areas nearer the toilet blocks. There are 39 hardstanding pitches, each with electricity, water and drainage, 12 are in the walled garden separated by shrubs and camomile lawns. A member of the Best of British Group.

Facilities

The main, modern toilet building is of excellent quality and cleanliness, very well maintained and can be heated. Two good large family bathrooms. Two rooms for disabled visitors. Laundry. Motorcaravan service point. Gas supplies. Bar, bar food and family room. Crazy golf. Draughts. Play area. Commercial vehicles are not accepted. Dogs are only accepted by prior arrangement. WiFi (free). Off site: Post office stores 50 yds.

Open: All year.

Directions

From A1 Berwick bypass take East Ord exit and follow signs. GPS: 55.75416, -2.03348

Charges guide

Per unit incl. up to 4 persons and electricity	£ 17.50 - £ 28.00
extra person (over 5 yrs)	£ 2.50
tent pitch	£ 12.50 - £ 23.00
dog	free - £ 1.50

Durham
Strawberry Hill Caravan Park

Running Waters, Old Cassop, Durham DH6 4QA (Co. Durham) T: 01913 723457. E: info@strawberryhf.co.uk

alanrogers.com/UK5700

This park is owned and managed by Howard and Elizabeth who are experienced caravanners. They have terraced their site to offer panoramic views over the fields and woodland from all the pitches. The park is licensed to accommodate more units but the owners prefer to offer space to visitors by providing generous pitches on either grass or hardstanding. There are 50 touring pitches (with 16A electric hook-ups), including ten on hardstanding, plus a separate terrace for tents. At present the new landscaping on the park offers limited shade. Nature corridors and the surrounding countryside make this a haven for nature lovers and visitors are encouraged to enjoy the tranquillity of the area.

Facilities

The single toilet block can be heated and is kept very clean. Free showers. Laundry. Facilities for disabled visitors incorporating a baby care area. Small but well stocked shop in reception. Gas. Off site: Buses (Durham – Hartlepool) from entrance. Country pub with meals 1 mile. Large hypermarket 3 miles. Riding 5 miles. Park and ride (07.00-19.00) into Durham city centre operates nearby.

Open: 1 March - 30 December.

Directions

From A1M exit 61 follow signs for Peterlee. At next roundabout take first left (A688). Straight on at next roundabout then right at the next (A181). Park is approx. 2 miles on the left as you go up a hill on a dual carriageway. GPS: 54.75326, -1.47809

Charges guide

Per unit incl. 2 persons and electricity (meter)	£ 15.60 - £ 17.85
extra person	£ 5.00

Durham
Grange Caravan Club Site

Meadow Lane, Durham DH1 1TL (Co. Durham) T: 01913 844778

alanrogers.com/UK5705

Fully refurbished and landscaped, this park offers 76 flat spacious pitches suitable for all units. Easy access to the A1M and the A690 make it an ideal stopover for those travelling north or south or for visiting the historic cathedral city of Durham, Beamish museum or Gateshead Metro centre. A coppice of mature trees and newly planted shrubs mask road noise and make an attractive dog walking area. The park has been redesigned with attention to detail in all areas offering pockets of privacy and a central area with picnic tables and benches. A purpose built central block offers spacious, heated, modern and clean facilities.

Facilities

The single toilet block is a heated building with free showers, hairdryers, and private cubicles. Laundry and food preparation area. Separate baby area and facilities for disabled visitors (key access). Shop in reception with basic supplies; bread, milk and newspapers to order. Gas. Secure caravan storage. WiFi (charged). Off site: Large supermarket 2 miles. Park and ride (07.00-19.00) into Durham city centre 800 yds. Local bus service.

Open: All year.

Directions

From A1M exit 62 turn left for Durham (A690). After 20 yds. turn right (across dual carriageway A690) – safer for large units, and continue along A690 to next exit (2 miles) and return on A690 left hand turn (signed just before A1M). GPS: 54.79545, -1.53065

Charges guide

Per person	£ 5.10 - £ 6.90
pitch incl. electricity (non-member)	£ 13.10 - £ 14.90

Hexham
Fallowfield Dene Caravan & Camping Park

Acomb, Hexham NE46 4RP (Northumberland) T: 01434 603553. E: info@fallowfielddene.co.uk

alanrogers.com/UK5810

Although only 2.5 miles from Hexham, Fallowfield Dene Caravan Park is very secluded, situated in mature woodland at the end of a no-through road. Set in woodland glades (formerly a Victorian lead mine), each with a Roman name (Hadrian's Wall is close), are 118 seasonal pitches and 32 touring pitches, all with 16A electricity. A further ten tent pitches have been added, suitable for smaller tents, and a barbecue area with views of woods and fields. The park entrance, with new reception and shop, is neat, tidy and colourful. There is no play area, but the surrounding woods are a paradise for children.

Facilities

Brick built toilet blocks are central and heated in cool weather. Well tiled and kept very clean, there are washbasins in cabins and free hairdryers. Fully equipped room for disabled visitors. Laundry and dishwashing sinks. Baby bath. Motorcaravan service point. Shop for basics, including gas. Barrier card £5 deposit. WiFi. Off site: Good restaurant five minutes walk. Supermarkets at Hexham and Corbridge. Fishing and riding 3 miles. Golf 5 miles.

Open: 14 March - 1 November.

Directions

From A69 Newcastle - Carlisle road, take A6079 north (Bellingham and Rothbury). At Acomb, site is signed to right. Follow site signs for about 1.5 miles. Turn left down single track road with passing places. GPS: 55.00166, -2.09470

Charges guide

Per unit incl. 2 persons	£ 16.00 - £ 17.00
extra person	£ 3.00

For latest campsite news visit

alanrogers.com

Seahouses

Seafield Caravan Park

Seahouses NE68 7SP (Northumberland) T: 01665 720628. E: info@seafieldpark.co.uk

alanrogers.com/UK5745

The park is situated just across the road from the sea and rock pools. The site has caravans to rent and pitches for 18 tourers (no tents). All the pitches have concrete bases, water, waste, sewerage and electricity (20A), but none has a sea view. A number of small gates give immediate access to Seahouses with its excellent range of shops and eating places. The large site is attractive with landscaped gardens, pools and a stream among the caravans and tourers. The private mobile homes are set apart from those available to rent. The fee includes free access to the Ocean Club facilities.

Facilities

The single toilet block is housed in an old building but is of the highest standard with a family bathroom, controllable showers with door and ample changing space. The block has heating, hairdryers (charged) and the latest hand dryers. There is a well equipped baby room. The laundry has four sinks, three for dishwashing and one for clothes. All facilities are accessed by a code. Snack bar/takeaway. Swimming pool, children's pool, spa, steam room, sauna, fitness suite and coffee shop in adjacent Ocean Club. Children's play area. WiFi throughout. Off site: Immediate access to the town of Seahouses with all amenities, local transport, and various trips available from the harbour. A good beach at Bamburgh just along the coast.

Open: All year (excl. 10/1-8/2).

Directions

On entering Seahouses from the south take the road to Bamburgh and the site is on your left just past the road down to the harbour.
GPS: 55.583162, -1.657171

Charges guide

Per unit incl. 2 persons and electricity	£ 25.00 - £ 48.00
extra person	£ 8.00
child (2-15 yrs)	£ 5.00

Stockton-on-Tees

White Water Caravan Club Park

Tees Barrage, Stockton-on-Tees TS18 2QW (Teeside) T: 01642 634880

alanrogers.com/UK5740

Being part of the multi-million pound development at the Tees Barrage, this pleasantly landscaped club site caters for all tastes, especially watersports enthusiasts. The Tees Barrage has transformed 11 miles of the Tees, providing clean, non-tidal water for many activities. The site itself provides 115 pitches, hedged with bushes, all with 16A electricity connections, and includes 21 fully serviced pitches set within bays and hedges (fresh water and waste disposal). The site is well lit, with a security barrier. The adjoining White-Water Course (Britain's largest purpose-built canoe course) provides facilities for both advanced and beginner canoeists, and hosts major national and international events. There are walks through the adjacent nature reserve wetlands (home to a variety of birds) and along the riverside.

Facilities

The central, heated toilet block of high quality includes washbasins in cubicles, baby changing facilities and a well appointed unit for disabled visitors. Laundry room. Motorcaravan service point. Play area on fine gravel. Heated family room with TV and pool table for wet weather. Off site: Supermarket 6 minutes. Hotel near the entrance. Retail and leisure park, just across barrage bridge, with 14-screen cinema, 10-pin bowling, shops and fast food outlets. Fishing and bicycle hire 2 miles. Golf and riding 3 miles. North York Moors and the Hartlepool Historic Quay within 40 minutes drive.

Open: All year.

Directions

From A1(M) take A66 for Darlington and follow until you pick up signs for Teeside Retail Park and the Tees Barrage. Cross railway bridge and the Barrage bridge, then first right to site on left in 400 yds.
GPS: 54.567869, -1.286039

Charges guide

Per person	£ 3.90 - £ 5.85
child (5-16 yrs)	£ 1.30 - £ 2.05
pitch incl. electricity (non-member)	£ 12.70 - £ 15.00
Tent campers apply to site.	

For latest campsite news visit
alanrogers.com

Land of ancient myths and Celtic legends, Wales is a small and compact country boasting a diverse landscape, from lakes and mountains, rivers and valleys to beautiful coastlines and rolling wooded countryside. It offers superb opportunities for an active holiday.

Wales' biggest asset is undoubtedly its countryside, home to three National Parks that make up almost a quarter of the country's total area. Snowdonia National Park in the north combines dramatic mountain scenery with glacial valleys, lakes and streams, while in the south the Brecon Beacons boast mountains, moorlands, forests and wooded gorges with deep caves. The surrounding area of the Wye Valley on the borders with England is a designated Area of Outstanding Natural Beauty; as are the Gower Peninsula, the Lleyn Peninsula, the Anglesey Coast and the Clwydian Range. The endless miles of largely unspoilt and beautiful Pembrokeshire coastline in the west have some of the finest long beaches in Europe, with pretty little bays plus the lively traditional seaside resorts of Tenby and Whitesand. Further inland is the secluded and pretty Gwaun Valley. The capital of Wales, Cardiff, has many attractions, including its newly developed waterfront, the Millennium Stadium. Castles can be seen all over Wales, ranging from tiny stone keeps to huge medieval fortresses; some of the best preserved are Caernarfon, Conwy and Harlech, all built by Edward I.

Places of interest

North: Isle of Anglesey; Victorian School of 3Rs and Motor Museum at Llangollen; Victorian seaside resort of Llandudno; Colwyn Bay; Caernarfon Castle; Snowdon Mountain Railway at Llanberis.

West: Oakwood Park, Wales' only theme park; the National Botanic Gardens at Aberglasney; Dolaucothi Goldmines; historic, stone-walled Aberaeron.

Mid: Brecon Beacons National Park; the lakes of the Elan Valley; entertaining events all summer at Llanwrtyd Wells; the Centre for Alternative Technology near Machynlleth.

South: Merthyr Tydfil, the Iron Capital of the World; Caerphilly's truly massive medieval castle; Cardiff, capital of Wales; the Wye Valley and the Vale of Usk of the Welsh borderlands with Tintern Abbey.

Did you know?

The origins of the Red Dragon flag may date back to the Roman period, when the dragon was used by military cohorts.

St. David's in Pembrokeshire is Britain's smallest city by virtue of its cathedral to the patron saint of Wales.

There are many sites in Wales linked to the legend of King Arthur: Castell Dinas Brân, near Llangollen, is reputed to be the resting place of the Holy Grail.

At 1,085 metres, Mount Snowdon is the highest mountain in England and Wales.

'The Dam Busters' was filmed on location in the Elan Valley.

The Welsh language is one of Europe's oldest languages and shares its roots with Breton, Gaelic and Cornish.

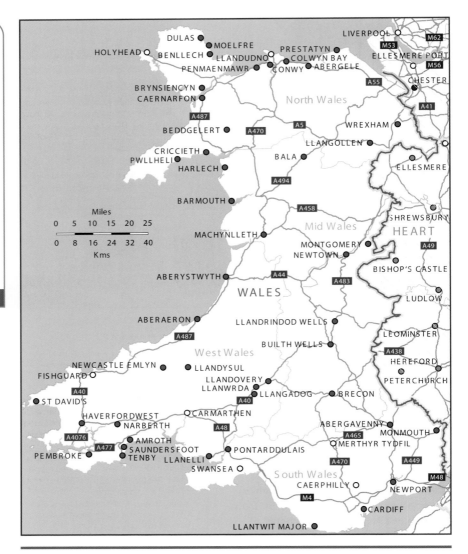

Aberaeron

Aeron Coast Caravan Park

North Road, Aberaeron SA46 0JF (Ceredigion) T: 01545 570349. E: enquiries@aeroncoast.co.uk

alanrogers.com/UK6280

Aeron Coast is a family holiday park with a wide range of recreational facilities, on the west coast of Wales. Although it has a high proportion of caravan holiday homes (200 privately owned), touring units of all types are provided for in two fields separated from the beach and sea by a high bank (although the best beach is on the south side of this traditional fishing village). Pitches are on level grass with all units regularly and well spaced in lines in traditional style. The main attraction of the park is its excellent provision for families, both in and out of doors.

Facilities

Two modern toilet blocks offer excellent facilities including large family showers. Facilities for disabled visitors and babies. Basic motorcaravan service point. Heated swimming pools (1/6-15/9). Club house and bar (Easter, 12.00-14.00 and from 19.00) with family room serving bar meals and takeaway in school holiday periods. Shop at petrol station at entrance. Entertainments room. One dog per unit. Off site: Beach, fishing and boat launching 1 mile.

Open: 1 March - 31 October.

Directions

Park is on northern outskirts of Aberaeron village with entrance on the right beside a petrol station. Brown signpost. GPS: 52.2445, -4.254917

Charges 2012

Per unit incl. 4 persons and electricity	£ 16.00 - £ 26.00
extra person (over 2 yrs)	£ 4.00
dog (max. 1)	£ 1.00

For latest campsite news visit
alanrogers.com

Abergavenny

Pont Kemys Caravan & Camping Park

Chainbridge, Abergavenny NP7 9DS (Monmouthshire) T: 01873 880688. E: info@pontkemys.com
alanrogers.com/UK5914

Pont Kemys is an attractive, peaceful touring park neatly arranged on the banks of the River Usk, only four miles from the town of the same name. There are 65 touring pitches, both on grass and with hardstanding, arranged around the perimeter of the park and within the central area. All have 16A electric hook-ups. An adult only area provides 21 fully serviced pitches. This is a quiet site without many amenities. The Chainbridge pub and a bar/restaurant at the local golf club are within walking distance. Entrance to the site is limited to units of less than 35 ft. due to access.

Facilities

The modern sanitary block is neat and clean. Baby room. Toilet/shower for disabled visitors. Laundry room. Kitchen area with microwave. Basic provisions and camping items from reception. Gas. TV lounge. Simple play area. Max. 2 dogs per pitch. Separate dog walking area. Free WiFi planned. Off site: Pub and golf club bar/restaurant within walking distance. Golf 400 m. Fishing 4 miles. Usk 4 miles. Many of South Wales' attractions such as the Millennium Stadium, Cardiff, the Big Pit Museum and the many castles are accessible by car.

Open: March - October.

Directions

From M4 exit 24 travel north on A449 and turn off into Usk. Take B4598 (Abergavenny) for 4 miles, cross Chainbridge and park is 300 yds on the right. From Abergavenny follow one-way system signed Monmouth, turn left on B4598 (do not join the A40 dual-carriageway). After 4 miles turn right for Usk at the Charthouse pub, then 2.5 miles to park. GPS: 51.746567, -2.946556

Charges guide

Per unit incl. 2 persons and electricity	£ 17.00 - £ 19.00
extra person	£ 2.00 - £ 3.00

Abergele

Plas Farm Caravan Park

Plas-yn-Betws, Betws-yn-Rhos, Abergele LL22 8AU (Conwy) T: 01492 680254.
E: info@plasfarmcaravanpark.co.uk **alanrogers.com/UK6685**

An attractive and welcoming site has been created as a series of terraces behind a working farm. Situated on the edge of the Snowdonia National Park, Plas Farm perfectly blends the campsite into the surrounding countryside. Sian and John Jones will give you a warm welcome and you get an immediate feel for the beautiful surroundings. The view is different from each of the terraces, and from the bottom terrace a woodland walk circles the site and is used as a dog walk. The 40 pitches all have electric hook-up (10/16A) and 31 are fully serviced. On a separate field there is provision for 30 tents, some with electric supply. Access could be difficult for large outfits, so telephoning in advance is recommended. The Conwy Valley is an ideal location for hill walking, golfing, rambling, tennis, sailing and watersports. You can visit the Welsh Mountain Zoo and narrow-gauge railways. Regular sea angling trips operate from the Conwy Quay and the Conwy River hosts an abundance of trout and salmon.

Facilities

Two brand new blocks were created in 2011, with a mixture of cubicles and open washbasins, showers and toilets for both sexes. For disabled visitors there is a shower, W.C. and washbasin. A family room has further disabled facilities and baby changing. Laundry with washing machine, tumble dryer and ironing facilities. Children's play area with low-level climbing frame. WiFi over site (charged). An area has been created above the site with benches to sit and admire the views. Off site: Pub within one mile of the site. Fishing and golf 2 miles. Riding 10 miles.

Open: 1 March - 31 October.

Directions

Heading towards North Wales, leave the A55 at junction 24, follow the A547 through Abergele town centre and continue straight over mini-roundabout at Tesco. Continue straight over the next mini-roundabout and then after approximately 0.5 miles, take next turning left signposted Rhyd-y-Foel/Dolwen. Travel approximately 3 miles until you reach a crossroads, turn left onto the B5381. Continue for 0.5 miles and take the first turning on your left signposted Abergele and Caravan Park. The farm is 200 yds. on the left. GPS: 53.252515, -3.651064

Charges guide

Per unit incl. 2 persons and electricity	£ 17.50 - £ 27.50
extra person	£ 5.00 - £ 6.00
child (3-16 yrs)	£ 2.00 - £ 3.00

For latest campsite news visit
alanrogers.com

Abergele
Hunters Hamlet Caravan Park

Sirior Goch Farm, Betws-yn-Rhos, Abergele LL22 8PL (Conwy) T: 01745 832237. E: huntershamlet@aol.com

alanrogers.com/UK6650

This small, family owned park is licensed for all units except tents (trailer tents are allowed). On a gently sloping hillside providing beautiful panoramic views, one area provides 15 well spaced pitches with hardstanding and 10A electricity, with access from a circular, hardcore road. A more recent area has been developed next to this of a similar design but with eight fully serviced super pitches (water, waste water, sewage, TV and 16A electricity). Shrubs and bushes at various stages of growth enhance both areas. A natural play area incorporating rustic adventure equipment set amongst mature beech trees with a small bubbling stream is a children's paradise. The site operates a no football policy. Milk and papers can be ordered and the Hunters will do their best to meet your needs. The park is well situated to tour Snowdonia and Anglesey and is within easy reach of Llandudno and Rhyl.

Facilities

The heated toilet block has fully tiled facilities including showers en-suite with toilets for both sexes. A sunroom to the rear houses laundry and dishwashing (hot and cold), washing machine and dryer, iron and board, freezer and fridge. Family bathroom (metered) and basic toilet and shower facilities for disabled visitors. Play area. WiFi over site (free). All year caravan storage. Max. 2 dogs per pitch. Off site: Fishing and golf 2 miles. Beach 3.5 miles. Sailing and boat launching 7 miles. Riding 10 miles.

Open: 21 March - 31 October.

Directions

From Abergele take A548 south for almost 3 miles; turn onto B5381 in direction of Betws-yn-Rhos and park is on left after 0.5 miles.
GPS: 53.248833, -3.6068

Charges guide

Per unit incl. 2 persons and electricity	£ 17.00 - £ 22.00
super pitch	£ 22.00 - £ 27.00
extra person	£ 4.00
child (at school)	£ 1.00
Less £5 on weekly bookings.	

Abergele
Ty Mawr Holiday Park

Towyn Road, Towyn, Abergele LL22 9HG (Conwy) T: 01745 832079.
E: holidaysales.tymawr@park-resorts.com **alanrogers.com/UK6655**

Ty Mawr Holiday Park is located close to the many attractions of the North Wales Coast and the Snowdonia National Park. The touring area has a refurbished toilet block. The pool complex has also been completely renovated during 2011 to provide an excellent indoor pool and flume. There is some traffic noise from the road adjacent to the meadow. Large outfits can be accommodated, but if they exceed 6 m. they are required to pay for two pitches. There is a large proportion of privately-owned and rental caravan holiday homes which are neatly sited on well manicured grass pitches.

Facilities

Two well maintained, functional blocks which can be heated serve the main touring area with Portacabin style units on the open meadows. They are regularly cleaned. Washbasins are open style, preset showers have curtains and hooks, but no seats. Baby rooms. Facilities for disabled visitors (key). Launderette. Ice pack service. Shop. Bar with meals, caféteria and takeaway. Indoor pool. Multisport courts. Excellent play areas and children's clubs. Evening family entertainment. WiFi (charged). Off site: Beach 0.25 miles. Bicycle hire 0.5 miles. Golf, riding and boat launching 3 miles. Fishing 6 miles. The island of Anglesey and the historic towns of Conwy and Caernarfon are within easy reach.

Open: Mid March - end October.

Directions

Take the A55 in a westerly direction into North Wales and take exit for Abergele. Follow signs for A548 Rhyl towards Towyn. Shortly after Towyn turn right into site. GPS: 53.29867, -3.55442

Charges guide

Per pitch	£ 5.00 - £ 33.00
incl. electricity	£ 8.00 - £ 36.00
dog	£ 1.00 - £ 3.00
Units over 6 metres in length are charged for 2 pitches.	

Aberystwyth

Glan-y-Mor Leisure Park

Clarach Bay, Aberystwyth SY23 3DT (Ceredigion) T: 01970 828900. E: glanymor@sunbourne.co.uk

alanrogers.com/UK6290

Follow the road to Clarach Bay and on the seafront is Glan-y-Mor, a busy, holiday style park with an enviable situation. On a wet day you may not wish to go far with the comprehensive leisure centre on site – it is open eight months of the year with reduced entry fee for campers. Although the balance of pitches is very much in favour of caravan holiday homes (3:1) which dominate the open park and bay, there are 50 touring pitches, 45 with electricity (10A) and four new super pitches. They are rather small and are pressed together in two small sections on the lower part of the park.

Facilities

The heated toilet block is on the lower touring area with a laundry room, plus a toilet for disabled visitors. A Portacabin type block (high season) is on the ridge ground. A suite including shower for disabled visitors is in a block in the upper static site, with further facilities at the leisure centre (Radar key). Motorcaravan service point. Supermarket. Play area. Sports field. Swimming pool. Licensed restaurant and takeaway (from Easter). WiFi (charge). Off site: Reduced rates at local golf courses.

Open: 1 March - 31 October.

Directions

Clarach is signed west from the A487 (Aberystwyth - Machynlleth) in village of Bow Street (take care at narrow bridge). Follow signs over crossroads to beach and park. Access for caravans from Aberystwyth on B4572 is difficult.
GPS: 52.43625, -4.08025

Charges guide

Per unit incl. up to 6 persons and electricity	£ 15.00 - £ 26.50

Amroth

Pantglas Farm Caravan Park

Tavernspite, Amroth SA34 0NS (Pembrokeshire) T: 01834 831618. E: pantglasfarm@btinternet.com

alanrogers.com/UK5974

A secluded, rural, family run park with a nice atmosphere, Pantglas Farm is four miles from the coast with extensive views over rolling countryside and down to the sea. Set in three gently sloping paddocks spread over 14 acres, there are 83 generously sized, fairly level pitches with electricity (10A), on gravel hardstanding. This is a popular and attractive site close to the main resorts but enjoying a more tranquil atmosphere. An on-site clubhouse also has a lounge with TV and a games room, with some simple entertainment activities arranged at Bank Holidays, some weekends and in high season.

Facilities

Two good toilet blocks (one can be heated) include large controllable showers and some washbasins in cubicles. Facilities for disabled visitors. Laundry facilities. Licensed clubhouse (evenings only every day for B.Hs and peak season, weekends only low season). Updated play area. Games field. Games room. TV lounge. Off site: Fishing 1 mile. Golf 4 miles. Supermarket at Whitland 3 miles. Beaches at Amroth and Pendine 4 miles.

Open: 23 March - 19 October.

Directions

Site is 3 miles southwest of Whitland. From the A477 Tenby-Pembroke road turn right at Red Roses crossroads to Tavernspite for 1.25 miles. At village pump take middle road. Site is 0.5 miles on left.
GPS: 51.778317, -4.645417

Charges guide

Per unit incl. 2 persons and electricity	£ 19.00 - £ 21.00
extra person	£ 3.00

Bala

Pen-y-Bont Touring & Camping Park

Llangynog Road, Bala LL23 7PH (Gwynedd) T: 01678 520549. E: penybont-bala@btconnect.co.uk

alanrogers.com/UK6340

This is a pretty little park with 59 touring pitches, 47 of which have hardstanding. Connected by circular gravel roads, they are intermingled with trees and tall trees edge the site. Electricity connections (16A) are available, including 11 for tents, and there are 28 serviced pitches with hardstanding, electricity, water and drainage. There are also pitches for 25 seasonal units. The park entrance, the stone building that houses reception and the well stocked shop provide quite a smart image. With views of the Berwyn mountains, Pen-y-bont has a peaceful and useful location being the closest park to Bala town.

Facilities

The toilet block includes washbasins in cubicles and spacious hot showers. Two new cubicles with washbasin and WC. Separate laundry room and an en-suite unit for disabled visitors, that doubles as a baby room, operated by key (£5 deposit). Motorcaravan service point. Shop. Bicycle hire. Caravan storage. WiFi (charged). Off site: Fishing 200 yds. Boat launching, golf and riding 2 miles. Mon. market in Bala.

Open: 1 March - 31 October.

Directions

Park is 0.5 miles southeast of Bala village on the B4391. Bala is between Dolgellau and Conwen on the A494. GPS: 52.901717, -3.590117

Charges guide

Per unit incl. 2 persons and electricity	£ 18.50 - £ 22.50
tent pitch incl. 2 persons	£ 15.00 - £ 20.00
extra person	£ 7.50

Bala

Glanllyn Lakeside Caravan & Camping Park

Llanuwchllyn, Bala LL23 7ST (Gwynedd) T: 01678 540227. E: info@glanllyn.com

alanrogers.com/UK6345

This 16-acre site lying alongside the southern end of Bala lake has 204 pitches. With around 40 seasonal units, this leaves 164 tourist pitches, 94 of which have electric hook-ups. In this location, virtually all the pitches have wonderful views of the lake or the surrounding mountain sides. The terrain is grassy, fairly open and level, but with natural terraces. There are around 19 individual hardstandings and a further hardstanding area by the beach is a favourite with motorcaravanners. The site is served by main tarmac access roads with speed bumps. An ideal base for some serious walking.

Facilities

Centrally located complex of three toilet blocks (one can be heated and is used in low season) with preset hot showers. Facilities for babies and suite for disabled visitors. Laundry room. Motorcaravan service point. Shop at reception (Easter-Oct). Adventure style playground. Only 2 dogs per unit. Breathable groundsheets only and only for min. 3-day stay. Off site: Bicycle hire, indoor swimming pool and golf in Bala 3 miles. Riding 18 miles.

Open: Easter - mid October.

Directions

From Bala take A494 southwest towards Dolgellau for 3 miles, entrance on left, on right hand bend. GPS: 52.877667, -3.64665

Charges guide

Per unit incl. 2 persons and electricity	£ 20.00 - £ 25.00
tent pitch incl. 2 persons	£ 14.00 - £ 20.00
extra person	£ 3.00 - £ 6.00

Barmouth

Hendre Mynach Touring Caravan & Camping Park

Llanaber, Barmouth LL42 1YR (Gwynedd) T: 01341 280262. E: mynach@lineone.net

alanrogers.com/UK6370

A neat and tidy family park, colourful flowers and top rate facilities make an instant impression on arrival down the steep entrance to this park (help is available to get out if you are worried). Of the 240 pitches, 60 are for touring guests and are allocated in various areas, with substantial tenting areas identified. All 60 touring pitches are fully serviced with electricity, water taps and waste water. The beach is only 100 yards away but is separated from the park by a railway line. It can be crossed by pedestrian operated gates, which could be a worry for those with young children.

Facilities

Two toilet blocks, one modern and one traditional, both offer excellent facilities including spacious showers and washbasins in cubicles. An extension to the traditional block has added a good unit for disabled visitors. Motorcaravan service point. Shop incorporating a snack bar and takeaway (Easter-1/11). WiFi. Off site: Beach 100 m. Fishing, boat launching and bicycle hire within 0.5 miles. Riding 5 miles. Golf 9 miles.

Open: All year excl. 10 January - 28 February.

Directions

Park is off the A496 road north of Barmouth in village of Llanaber with entrance down a steep drive. GPS: 52.73300, -4.06618

Charges guide

Per unit incl. 2 persons and electricity	£ 17.00 - £ 29.00
extra person	£ 4.00
child (2-14 yrs)	£ 2.00
Plus £2 per night for certain weekends.	

Barmouth

Trawsdir Touring Caravans & Camping Park

Llanaber, Barmouth LL42 1RR (Gwynedd) T: 01341 280999. E: enquiries@trawsdir.co.uk

alanrogers.com/UK6380

With sea views from almost every pitch and with a backdrop of hills, this campsite has something for everyone. Entrance and exit via the site barrier, and access to the facilities are by a key fob. A well equipped children's play area with safety surface is close to reception. Of the 142 touring pitches, 70 are for tents (48 with electricity) the remaining 72 touring pitches are fully serviced and can take RVs. The campsite has a large dog walking field and from the corner of the site is a lit walk to the Wayside Inn without the need to go on the main road. A member of the Best of British Group.

Facilities

Two toilet blocks are furnished to a very high standard, however one is kept in reserve for when cleaning is being done except for the busiest times. Facilities for disabled visitors with good access (Radar key). Baby changing facilities in both male and female toilets. Covered dishwashing area and fully equipped laundry. Shop. WiFi (charged). Off site: Sea fishing trips from Barmouth. Golf at Royal St Davids Golf Club is 20 minutes away in Harlech. Pony trekking is about 30 minutes drive away. A private beach is available at sister site across the road.

Open: 1 March - 6 January.

Directions

From Barmouth follow signs for Harlech (do not take beach road), pass through the town. Having passed through the town passing the church, up the hill and leave the 40 mph speed limit. Pass the Caerddaniel Holiday Home Park and the Wayside Pub. Trawsdir entrance is just beyond and is on the right hand side. GPS: 52.749871, -4.080361

Charges guide

Per unit incl. 4 persons and electricity	£ 16.00 - £ 30.00

Barmouth

Islawrffordd Caravan Park

Talybont, Barmouth LL43 2AQ (Gwynedd) T: 01341 247269. E: info@islawrffordd.co.uk

alanrogers.com/UK6385

If you like to park up and have all amenities within easy access, then this site is ideal. Family owned and run since being established in 1957, Islawrffordd Caravan Park offers the very best in quality, which is evident as you enter the park. There are 75 fully serviced touring pitches (some seasonal) and 30 tent pitches. The fully serviced pitches all have courtesy light, electricity, fresh and waste water points and chemical disposal. Facilities include a minimarket, a bar/restaurant, takeaway and indoor swimming pool with sauna, jacuzzi and tanning suite. The site has private access to a sandy beach.

Facilities

The immaculate, modern toilet facilities have underfloor heating and climate control, a toilet for disabled visitors (Radar key) and baby changing room. The launderette. The toilet block and the entrance and exit of the park are activated by a key fob (deposit required). WiFi throughout (charged). Off site: Sea fishing trips from Barmouth. Golf at Royal St Davids Golf Club (15 mins) in Harlech. Pony trekking (30 mins drive). Portmeirion, Harlech, Barmouth and Porthmadog are a short drive.

Open: All year.

Directions

Approximately four miles north of Barmouth, turn off the main A496 on to Fford Glan Mor Road, over a narrow railway bridge, past the Talybont Railway Halt and neighbouring campsites. The park is almost at the end and is signed to the left.
GPS: 52.772491, -4.100299

Charges guide

Per serviced pitch incl. 5 persons	£ 32.50
tent pitch incl. up to 5 persons	£ 27.50

Beddgelert

Forest Holidays Beddgelert

Caernarfon Road, Beddgelert LL55 4UU (Gwynedd) T: 01766 890288. E: info@forestholidays.co.uk

alanrogers.com/UK6590

Forest Holidays is a partnership between the Forestry Commission and The Camping and Caravanning Club. This well equipped site is in the heart of Snowdonia, set in a marvellous, natural, wooded environment on the slopes of Snowdon. Well equipped and well managed, the site provides 204 pitches – tents in a semi-wooded field area and caravans amongst the trees with numbered hardstandings, and 105 places with 10/16A electricity. Tents may pitch where they like in their areas leaving six metres between units or there are six new grass pitches with electrical hook-ups. Metal tent pegs may be best.

Facilities

Two modern toilet blocks provide large, free hot showers (with good dry areas). Laundry facilities. Toilet and washbasin for disabled visitors. Excellent drive-through motorcaravan service point. Shop (Easter-end Sept). Well equipped adventure playground. Log cabin common room. Off site: Pub within walking distance (under 1 mile) and other eating places nearby. Bicycle hire 1 mile.

Open: All year.

Directions

Site is clearly signed to the left 1 mile north of Beddgelert on the A4085 Caernarfon road.
GPS: 53.02075, -4.119767

Charges guide

Per unit incl. 2 persons	£ 8.00 - £ 20.50
extra person	£ 4.25 - £ 6.25
child (5-14 yrs)	£ 1.75 - £ 3.25

Benllech

Plas Uchaf Caravan & Camping Park

Benllech Bay, Benllech LL74 8NU (Isle of Anglesey) T: 01407 763012

alanrogers.com/UK6636

This spacious, family run, campsite is set in 16 acres of flat, well mown grass with 12 hardstandings. A separate area for 60 tents is available. Within the park there are woodland walks and a play route for children to explore, a play area and a dog walk. All in an open, rural setting this park offers a safe haven for young families to enjoy. The pitches are set around the perimeter of six individual areas, each with picnic tables for communal use and all 110 touring pitches offer electricity (10/16A) and a water supply. Motorcaravans over 26 ft. are not accepted. Large outfits are advised to phone in advance. A new reception/games room and walkers' accommodation will be ready for the 2012 season.

Facilities

Three clean, traditional style sanitary blocks have separate facilities for men and women, with hot showers (charge), open style washbasins, hairdryers and small baths. Baby areas. Facilities for disabled visitors are planned for the new building. Limited laundry. Large playing field, play equipment and dog walk. Freezer facilities. Off site: Shops, bars, restaurants, fishing, golf, sandy beach, riding and sailing all within 1 mile.

Open: 14 March - 14 October.

Directions

From the Britannia Bridge take the A5025. In Benllech turn left onto the B5108. After the fire station on left, turn first right and the park is signed.
GPS: 53.32676, -4.23956

Charges guide

Per unit incl. 2 persons and electricity	£ 14.00 - £ 18.00
extra person (over 3 yrs)	£ 2.00 - £ 3.00
No credit cards.	

Brecon

Pencelli Castle Caravan & Camping Park

Pencelli, Brecon LD3 7LX (Powys) T: 01874 665451. E: pencelli@tiscali.co.uk

alanrogers.com/UK6040

This high quality park is on the edge of Pencelli village. Set in the grounds of an old castle amidst the Brecon scenery, the park has both atmosphere and character. It offers excellent facilities in peaceful, rural tranquillity. The owners, Liz and Gerwyn Rees, have retained the country charm but have added an all embracing range of spacious, heated, luxury facilities. There are three touring fields. The Orchard has some fully serviced pitches with hardstanding, amongst shrubs, fruit trees and a stone cider mill. TheOaks taking a mix of motorcaravans, caravans and tents and The Meadow' for tents only are bordered by majestic trees and the Monmouthshire and Brecon Canal. All the fields are level with neatly mown grass. The historic manor house is adjacent to arched barns that house a collection of vintage farm machinery. For mountain bikers and walkers, a path leaves the village to reach the top of the Brecon Beacons or there is an easy towpath ramble to Tal-y-Bont where there are pubs and tea rooms.

Facilities

The toilet block is very well designed and includes some private cubicles, two large rooms for families and disabled visitors with double showers, baby changing and bath facilities. Laundry. Drying room with lockers. Information and planning room. Motorcaravan service point. Small shop. Playground and nature trail. Bicycle hire. WiFi throughout. Only assistance dogs are accepted. Off site: The Royal Oak Inn with meals 100 yds. Riding 2 miles. Golf and bicycle hire 5 miles.

Open: 30 December - 30 November.

Directions

From A40 south after Brecon bypass take B4558 at signs for Llanfrynach and later Pencelli (narrow bridge). If travelling north on A40, approach via Tal-y-Bont. Site at south end of Pencelli. GPS: 51.914783, -3.317867

Charges guide

Per unit incl. 2 persons and electricity	£ 21.10 - £ 26.20
extra person	£ 6.75 - £ 7.75

Brynsiencyn

Fron Caravan & Camping Park

Brynsiencyn, Anglesey LL61 6TX (Isle of Anglesey) T: 01248 430310. E: mail@froncaravanpark.co.uk

alanrogers.com/UK6635

A traditional, all touring campsite in a peaceful rural location, Fron has panoramic views over the surrounding countryside. From the entrance gate a tarmac drive passes through a two acre level grass paddock, which is reserved for 35 large sized tent and trailer tent pitches. The drive leads up to the old farmhouse which houses reception, behind which is another two acre sloping paddock with 40 caravan and motorcaravan pitches, five with hardstandings, and 57 electricity hook-ups (10A). By the farmhouse a heated swimming pool is well controlled by the owners and has a retractable roof.

Facilities

Toilet facilities are in three units of varying ages. These include a unit for ladies with some basins in cubicles, hot showers (20p), a baby area and a suite for disabled visitors. Laundry facilities. Motorcaravan service point. Heated swimming pool (30x14 ft; May-Sept). Max. 2 dogs per pitch. Torches useful. Off site: Brynsiencyn (0.5 miles) has a hotel and Spar shop. Fishing 1.5 miles. Riding 3 miles. Golf 4 miles. Nearby are Anglesey Sea Zoo, Foel Farm Park and the Menai Bridges.

Open: Easter/1 April - end September.

Directions

Cross the Britannia Bridge and take first slip road (Llanfairpwll A4080), then next left (Newborough and Brynsiencyn). Continue on A4080 for 5 miles, turning right in village at the Groeslon Hotel. Continue through Brynsiencyn for 1 mile to site at western end of village. The entrance requires a wide sweep for a car and caravan. GPS: 53.176217, -4.28785

Charges guide

Per unit incl. 2 persons and 2 children	£ 22.00
No credit cards.	

Builth Wells

Fforest Fields Caravan & Camping Park

Hundred House, Builth Wells LD1 5RT (Powys) T: 01982 570406. E: office@fforestfields.co.uk

alanrogers.com/UK6320

This secluded park is set on a family hill farm within seven acres in the heart of Radnorshire. This is simple country camping and caravanning at its best, with no clubhouse, swimming pool or games room. The facilities include 80 large pitches on level grass on a spacious and peaceful, carefully landscaped field by a stream. Electrical connections (mostly 16A) are available and there are 17 hardstanding pitches, also with electricity. Several additional areas without electricity are provided for tents. There are two new lakes, one for boating and fly fishing, the other for coarse fishing. George and Katie, the enthusiastic owners, have opened up much of the farm for woodland and moorland trails.

Facilities

The toilet facilities are acceptable with baby bath, dishwashing and laundry facilities including washing machines and a dryer. Milk, eggs, orange juice and gas are sold in reception, otherwise there are few other on-site facilities. Fishing. Torches are useful. WiFi throughout. Off site: Pub at Hundred House village 1 mile. Bicycle hire and golf 5 miles. Riding 10 miles.

Open: Easter - October.

Directions

Park is 4 miles east of Builth Wells near the village of Hundred House on A481. Follow brown signs. Do not use postcode on sat nav. GPS: 52.17121, -3.31621

Charges guide

extra person	£ 4.00
child (2-16 yrs)	£ 2.50
Per unit incl. 2 persons and electricity	£ 16.00
dog (max. 2)	free

Discounted low season rates for senior citizens. No credit cards.

Caernarfon

Bryn Gloch Caravan & Camping Park

Betws Garmon, Caernarfon LL54 7YY (Gwynedd) T: 01286 650216. E: eurig@bryngloch.co.uk

alanrogers.com/UK6600

Bryn Gloch is a well kept, family owned touring park in the impressive Snowdonia area – an unusual feature is the mountain railway which passes through the park. Neat and quiet, it takes some 160 units on five flat, wide meadows with some breathtaking views. With tarmac access roads and free areas allowed in the centre for play, of the 152 touring pitches, 80 have hardstanding, electricity (10A), water and drainage. In addition, there are 15 caravan holiday homes. Fishing is possible on the river bordering the park with a barbecue and picnic area, adventure play area and field for ball games. Tourist information is provided in the complex by the reception/shop and the park is very popular with walkers and cyclists. Caernarfon with its famous castle is five miles away.

Facilities

The two very clean and modern main toilet blocks include washbasins in cabins, large showers, a family bathroom (hot water £1), baby room and complete facilities for visitors with disabilities (coded access). The far field has a Portacabin style unit containing all facilities, for use in peak season. Well equipped laundry and separate drying room. Motorcaravan service point and car wash. Shop (1/3-31/10). TV and games rooms with computer, pool tables and amusement machines. Minigolf. Entrance barrier with coded access. WiFi. Off site: Pub 1 mile. Riding 2.5 miles. ATM at garage in Ceathro 3 miles. Bicycle hire and golf 5 miles.

Open: All year, limited facilities 1 November - 28 February.

Directions

From Caernarfon take A4085 signed Beddgelert. Park is just beyond Waunfawr, 5.6 miles southeast of Caernarfon. After crossing river bridge, entrance is immediately on right, opposite St Garmon church. GPS: 53.095183, -4.1884

Charges guide

Per unit incl. 2 persons and electricity	£ 18.00 - £ 28.00
extra person	£ 4.00
child (3-16 yrs)	£ 2.00
dog (max. 2)	£ 1.00

For latest campsite news visit
alanrogers.com

Caernarfon

Tafarn Snowdonia Parc Brewpub & Campsite

Waunfawr, Caernarfon LL55 4AQ (Gwynedd) T: 01286 650409. E: info@snowdonia-park.co.uk

alanrogers.com/UK6605

Set on the banks of the River Gwyrfai and amongst spectacular scenery, this no frills campsite is adjacent to the station for the Welsh Highland Railway. There are 32 grass pitches, (20 with 16A electricity) of variable size. They are set in an open field and serviced by two clean shower and toilet blocks (refurbished in 2010). Enjoy riverside walks and free fishing (licence required) before calling in at the adjoining pub with its own microbrewery (listed in the CAMRA Good Beer guide) and home cooked food. Children are well catered for with a family room in the pub, two gardens and a playground.

Facilities	Directions
One small toilet block in main camping field. A second block with separate showers and toilets for men and ladies, together with laundry facilities, is reached via a footbridge over the railway track. Both have been upgraded, but may become stretched when site is full. Full bar, restaurant and takeaway facilities. TV. Games room. Playground. Fishing (with licence). Off site: Riding 800 yds. Golf 3 miles. Beach and sailing 5 miles.	From Caernarfon take the A4085 for around 4 miles and campsite is on the left. The entrance is at the far end of pub/railway station car park. GPS: 53.10611, -4.20176

Charges guide	
Per unit incl. 2 persons and electricity	£ 22.00
children and dogs	free

Open: All year.

Caernarfon

Plas Gwyn Caravan & Camping Park

Llanrug, Caernarfon LL55 2AQ (Gwynedd) T: 01286 672619. E: info@plasgwyn.co.uk

alanrogers.com/UK6620

In a beautiful location, this traditional, family run touring site is within the grounds of a house that was built in 1785 in the Georgian style with a colonial style veranda. The 30 touring caravan pitches are set around the perimeter of a slightly sloping grass field, and there are eight hardstandings for motorcaravans. The separate tent field has ten pitches. There are 36 electric hook-ups (16A) of which 17 also provide water and waste water. In 2011, two 'timber tents' were added for a touch of luxury camping. There is minimal site lighting on the caravan field and none on the tent field. A member of the Countryside Discovery Group. Large units should telephone ahead to check availability.

Facilities	Directions
An older style building houses the toilet facilities with controllable hot showers (modern fittings and kept neat and tidy). Good laundry room. No dedicated facilities for babies and disabled visitors. Drive-over motorcaravan service point. Gas stocked. Reception stocks basic food items. Breakfast 'butties' made to order and delivered. WiFi. Off site: Golf 1 mile. Riding 2.5 miles. Bicycle hire 3 miles. Fishing 4 miles.	Site is on A4086, 3 miles from Caernarfon, and 2.5 miles from Llanberis, well signed with easy access. GPS: 53.146733, -4.212233

Charges guide	
Per unit incl. 2 persons and electricity	£ 16.00 - £ 19.50
extra person	£ 2.50
tent pitch	£ 4.00 - £ 12.50

Open: 1 March - 31 October.

Cardiff

Cardiff Caravan Park

Pontcanna Fields, via Sophia Close, Cardiff CF11 9XR (Cardiff) T: 029 2039 8362

alanrogers.com/UK5925

Run by the city council, this popular site is set within acres of parkland, one mile from the city centre, ideal for visiting the many attractions of the city of Cardiff. The campsite has 61 pitches which are on a fairly open area, with 43 on a grassed grid surface with electric hook-ups (16A), the remainder are on grass. There is a public right of way through the site. Security is good with an on-site warden 24 hours a day, and security cameras (infrared) constantly scanning the whole area. Large units should phone ahead to arrange for access.

Facilities	Directions
Two heated buildings each with key code entry systems, the one by reception has a laundry with washer and dryer, and facilities for disabled campers. Both have controllable hot showers. Baby facilities. Bicycle hire (the site specialises in cycles adapted for disabled visitors). Riding can be arranged. Off site: The Millennium Stadium, Glamorgan County Cricket Ground, Cardiff Bay. Local shops and services within easy walking distance. Fishing 0.25 mile. Golf 4 miles.	From the A48 turn south on A4119 (Cardiff Road). Pass church on left following signs for SWALEC Stadium and at next traffic lights turn into Sophia Close and Gardens. Turn left at Institute of Sport and pass County Cricket Ground on right. Continue along avenue to site on left. GPS: 51.49155, -3.20313

Charges guide	
Per unit incl. electricity	£ 20.00 - £ 22.50
tent	£ 9.00 - £ 21.00

Open: All year.

For latest campsite news visit

alanrogers.com

Colwyn Bay

Bron-Y-Wendon Touring Caravan Park

Wern Road, Llanddulas, Colwyn Bay LL22 8HG (Conwy) T: 01492 512903.
E: bron-y-wendon@northwales-holidays.co.uk **alanrogers.com/UK6690**

Bron-Y-Wendon is right by the sea between Abergele and Colwyn Bay on the beautiful North Wales coast road. This is a quiet park which, by its own admission, is not really geared up for families – there is no playground here, although there is a games room with table tennis and a TV room. The park is manicured to the highest standards and caters for a large number of seasonal caravans on pitches with gravel bases. There are a further 65 grass based, and 20 hardstanding touring pitches, all with electricity (16A) and tarmac access roads. All pitches have coastal views and the beach is just a short walk away. Trailer tents are accepted, but not other tents.

Facilities

Two toilet blocks, both with heating, provide excellent facilities including men's and women's shower rooms separate from the toilets and washbasins. Good facilities for disabled visitors. Laundry facilities. Mobile shop visits daily. Gas supplies. WiFi (charged). Off site: Llanddulas village with shops and several good pubs. Fishing 1 mile. Golf 4 miles. Riding 6 miles. Bicycle hire 15 miles.

Open: All year.

Directions

From A55 Chester - Conwy road turn at Llanddulas interchange (A547), junction 23. Turn right opposite Shell garage and park is 400 yds, signed on coast side of the road. GPS: 53.29185, -3.6445

Charges guide

Per unit incl. 2 persons and electricity	£ 20.00 - £ 23.00
extra person	£ 2.00 - £ 3.00

Conwy

Bron Derw Touring Park

Llanrwst, Conwy LL26 0YT (Conwy) T: 01492 640494. E: bronderw@aol.com
alanrogers.com/UK6644

Nestling between the mountains and the edge of the small village of Llanrwst, Bron Derw has two camping areas, one for adults only and one for families. The 43 pitches (all with 16A electric supply) are well spaced out on hardstandings around the edge of the site, giving a feeling of spaciousness which matches the surrounding countryside. It is a family run site and this shows in the level of service and welcome which is received. Larger outfits are advised to phone ahead to check pitch availability.

Facilities

Two very modern toilet blocks, one in each area. The adults only block (opened 2011) has high quality fittings. The other block was refurbished at the same time. Both have facilities for disabled visitors, and laundry facilities. Motorcaravan service point. Utility room. Public telephone. Off site: Within the Snowdonia National Park and only 20 minutes drive to the coastal resorts of North Wales. Fishing within 1 mile. Marin Trail mountain biking route 2 miles. Tree Top Adventure within 4 miles. Golf and bicycle hire 4 miles. Betws-y-Coed 5 miles.

Open: 1 March - 31 October.

Directions

From the coast follow the A55 on to the A470 for Betws-y-Coed and Llanrwst, in Llanrwst turn left into Parry Road then turn left again at T-junction. Take first farm entrance on the right signed 'Bron Derw' and continue up the drive to the campsite. GPS: 53.143639, -3.797126

Charges guide

Per unit incl. 2 persons and electricity	£ 17.00 - £ 19.00
extra person	£ 4.00

Criccieth

Llanystumdwy Camping & Caravanning Club Site

Tyddyn Sianel, Llanystumdwy, Criccieth LL52 0LS (Gwynedd) T: 01766 522855
alanrogers.com/UK6580

Overlooking mountains and sea, Llanystumdwy is one of the earliest Camping and Caravanning Club sites. It is an attractive, sloping site with well manicured grass areas surrounded by trees and with good facilities. The wardens are very helpful and know their site and can advise on the most suitable pitch and even have a supply of chocks. There are 70 pitches in total (20 ft. spacing), 45 with 10A electricity connections, spaced over two hedged fields with mainly caravans in the top field with four hardstandings for motorcaravans, tents are sited lower down. Some road noise may be experienced by those in tents on the lower field. A good base from which to explore Snowdonia National Park.

Facilities

A purpose-built toilet block to one side includes excellent, full facilities for disabled visitors including access ramp, one washbasin each in a cubicle for male and female and extra large sinks. Facilities for babies. Laundry (taps with fitting for disabled campers). Gas supplies. WiFi over site (charged). Off site: Riding and fishing 0.5 miles. Golf 2.5 miles. Beach 3 miles.

Open: March - October.

Directions

Follow A497 from Criccieth west and take second right to Llanystumdwy. Site is on the right. GPS: 52.920867, -4.27885

Charges guide

Per person	£ 5.53 - £ 8.17
child (6-18 yrs)	£ 2.65 - £ 2.85
non-member pitch fee	£ 7.10

For latest campsite news visit
alanrogers.com

Dulas

Tyddyn Isaf Caravan & Camping Park

Lligwy Bay, Dulas LL70 9PQ (Isle of Anglesey) T: 01248 410203

alanrogers.com/UK6637

This warm, welcoming family site cascades down the hillside from the bar/restaurant at the top of the site to the beach. The site has had the same owners for over 30 years. Lligwy Bay, with its sandy beach and sheltered waters, is ideal for children to play on and is accessible from the site. There are 80 touring pitches (of which 40 are seasonal) all with 16A electric hook-up. The tent pitches (some with 10A electricity) are on separate fields. The owners insist that all visitors are escorted to their pitch and, if required, helped with siting. Ireland is only a 90 minute ferry ride across the Irish Sea.

Facilities

Two toilet blocks with free electric showers (timed; activated by a key fob). The upper toilet block can be overstretched in peak times. A third toilet block is next to the bar. Laundry facilities. Shop selling basics. Bar serving snacks and main meals, takeaway food (mid May-mid Sept). WiFi. Off site: Golf is a short drive away. Sea and fresh water fishing. Numerous cycle paths and walks including the coastal walk to Moelfre. Anglesey has its own vineyard producing some excellent wines.

Open: Easter - 20 October.

Directions

From A55 drive over the Britannia bridge onto Anglesey. Look for turning (Benllech and Amlwch). Drive to roundabout, follow A5025 through Pentraeth, then through Benllech and left at second roundabout. Continue to Brynrefail, turn right opposite gift shop and follow site signs. GPS: 53.3625, -4.27545

Charges guide

Per unit incl. 2 adults, 2 children and electricity	£ 21.00 - £ 27.50
extra person	£ 3.00 - £ 5.00

No credit cards.

Harlech

Barcdy Caravan & Camping Park

Talsarnau, Harlech LL47 6YG (Gwynedd) T: 01766 770736. E: anwen@barcdy.co.uk

alanrogers.com/UK6350

Barcdy is partly in a sheltered vale, partly on a plateau top and partly in open fields edged by woods. There are fells to the rear and marvellous views across the Lleyn peninsula in one direction and towards the Snowdon range in another. The Roberts family opened to their first visitors over 60 years ago. The grass pitches are level or sloping, either secluded in the valley or enjoying the view from the plateau or lower field. There are 92 pitches, including 40 fully serviced for touring caravans and 40 for tents, with or without 10A electricity, plus 30 caravan holiday homes. Member of the Countryside Discovery group.

Facilities

Two toilet blocks, the one at the top of the valley opened in high season only, include large showers that open direct to the outside. Two family shower rooms at each block, one for each sex. WiFi throughout (charged). Dogs are not accepted. Off site: Fishing 0.5 miles. Riding 4 miles. Golf 4 and 6 miles.

Open: Easter/1 April - 30 September.

Directions

Park is just off A496 between Llandecwyn and Talsarnau, 4 miles north of Harlech. If coming from Porthmadog do not attempt to use toll road if towing or over 2 tonnes. GPS: 52.912983, -4.0524

Charges guide

Per unit incl. 2 persons	£ 20.00 - £ 26.00
extra person	£ 8.00

Harlech

Woodlands Caravan Park

Harlech LL46 2UE (Gwynedd) T: 01766 780419. E: info@woodlandsparkharlech.com

alanrogers.com/UK6355

This delightful little site is lovingly tended by its owners and has just 18 pitches for tourists, all with gravel hardstanding and electric hook-up (10A) for caravans and motorcaravans only. Tents are not accepted. There are also 22 privately owned holiday homes, and three holiday cottages. However, the location of this site certainly makes up for its diminutive size, nestling under the massive rock topped by Harlech Castle, now a designated World Heritage Site. The narrow lane running alongside the site up to the old town above, is the steepest hill in Britain.

Facilities

The modern stone built toilet facilities are heated, clean and tidy with controllable showers (50p), vanity style washbasins, a small laundry with a baby changing area, but with no dedicated facilities for disabled visitors. Chemical disposal point but no motorcaravan service point. WiFi. Off site: Golf 0.25 miles. Steam train pleasure trips (July/Aug). Harlech Castle. The town also has a theatre and cinema. Fishing and riding 3 miles. Portmeirion 8 miles. Barmouth 10 miles.

Open: 1 March - 31 October.

Directions

From Barmouth take A496 to Harlech and continue downhill past Royal St David's Golf Course. Fork right immediately before railway. Site is 200 yds. on right. DO NOT turn towards town centre on B4573 (narrow and congested). GPS: 52.86155, -4.107633

Charges guide

Per unit incl. 2 persons and electricity	£ 17.00 - £ 21.00
extra person	£ 2.50

No credit or debit cards.

Harlech

Min-y-Don Holiday Home & Touring Park

Beach Road, Harlech LL46 2UG (Gwynedd) T: 01766 780286. E: manager@minydonholidayhomepark.co.uk

alanrogers.com/UK6365

Set within the Snowdonia National Park, this super park was totally rebuilt for the 2009 season. It is a level site with first class facilities and providing 82 well drained grass touring pitches. These include 21 pitches with full services (seven with hardstanding for large motorcaravans). Tents are not accepted. In a separate area there are 112 caravan holiday homes. With three miles of golden sand beaches and the Snowdon mountain range as a backdrop, Min-y-Don overlooks the famous Royal St David's Golf Course. Harlech town, dominated by its 13th-century castle, is within walking distance.

Facilities

New toilet facilities are excellent with private cabins and underfloor heating. Large separate unit for disabled visitors. Baby room. Two private bathrooms for rent. Motorcaravan services. Laundry facilities. Play area. Football pitch. Bike track. Wildlife area. Putting green. WiFi. Off site: Supermarket and leisure centre 800 yds. Harlech with shops, pubs and restaurants within walking distance. Beach nearby. Coastal train. Bus service. Ffestiniog steam railway. Portmeirion. Snowdon.

Open: March - November.

Directions

From Barmouth go north on the A496 to Harlech. Go over level crossing and turn left into Beach Road. From the north on the A496 in Harlech, right into Beach Road before level crossing. Park is on the right in 400 yds. GPS: 52.862366, -4.11526

Charges guide

Per person	£ 5.50 - £ 7.00
child (5-15 yrs)	£ 2.00 - £ 3.50
pitch	£ 6.50 - £ 13.00

Haverfordwest

Creampots Touring Caravan & Camping Park

Broadway, Broad Haven, Haverfordwest SA62 3TU (Pembrokeshire) T: 01437 781776

alanrogers.com/UK5992

This peacefully located and beautifully manicured, garden-like park is ideal for couples and families, and is a convenient base within easy reach of beaches or for touring the local area. Creampots has 72 spacious, level pitches all with 10A electric hook-ups, including 21 with gravel hardstanding, and pitches for tents. There is a separate field and an overflow area taking 30 tents for the August peak holiday time. This is an ideal location for the local attractions.

Facilities

The single small white-washed sanitary unit is a modern building which can be heated. Two free hot showers per sex, open style washbasins. Washbasin and WC for disabled visitors. These facilities were clean and tidy but may come under pressure at peak times. Tiny laundry room (for one person at a time). Off site: Summer bus service (May-Sept) 500 yds. from site entrance. Shop and pub in Broad Haven 1 mile. Fishing 1 mile. Beach 1.5 miles. Riding 4 miles. Sailing 6 miles. Golf 7 miles.

Open: March - October.

Directions

Site is 5 miles west of Haverfordwest. From Haverfordwest take B4341 to Broad Haven, at Broadway follow brown tourist sign on left. GPS: 51.777333, -5.072283

Charges guide

Per unit incl. 2 persons and electricity	£ 18.95 - £ 23.75
dog	free

Haverfordwest

Redlands Touring Caravan & Camping Park

Hasguard Cross, Little Haven, Haverfordwest SA62 3SJ (Pembrokeshire) T: 01437 781300.

E: info@redlandscamping.co.uk **alanrogers.com/UK5994**

This peaceful, family run site is located in the heart of the Pembrokeshire countryside, close to many lovely sandy beaches. Redlands takes around 80 touring units in three areas divided by banks topped with pine trees, 32 hardstandings and 69 with 10A electricity. The first two areas take 60 caravans and motorcaravans and include 20 hardstandings; the third takes 19 tents on a level grassy meadow. There are fine views across rolling countryside to St Brides Bay. Breathable groundsheets must be used. American RVs – advance booking only.

Facilities

The traditional style toilet block is well kept and heated early and late season. It has all the usual requirements including two extra shower, basin and WC suites. Laundry facilities. Shop. Freezers. Wet suit washing area. Dogs are welcome but must be kept on lead. Off site: Summer bus service. Fishing and boat launching 1.5 miles. Shops and ATM in Broadhaven 2 miles. Riding and sailing 5 miles. Golf 6 miles.

Open: 1 March - mid December.

Directions

Site is 6.5 miles southwest of Haverfordwest. From Haverfordwest take B4327 road (Dale). Site is on the right at Hasguard Cross. N.B. Do not approach via Broad Haven. GPS: 51.755567, -5.112383

Charges guide

Per unit incl. 2 persons and electricity	£ 17.70 - £ 22.95
extra person	£ 4.50
No credit cards.	

For latest campsite news visit

alanrogers.com

Llandovery

Erwlon Caravan & Camping Park

Brecon Road, Llandovery SA20 0RD (Carmarthenshire) T: 01550 721021. E: peter@erwlon.co.uk

alanrogers.com/UK5955

Just outside Llandovery and on the edge of the Brecon Beacons National Park, Erwlon is an attractive and welcoming campsite. Of the 110 pitches, seven are used for privately-owned caravan holiday homes, 33 have seasonal caravans and 70 are for touring units. Most are on hardstanding with electricity connections and 12 have water and a drain as well. There is a flat field for tents at the bottom of the park with some electrical outlets, an open-sided, covered area for eating, food preparation and bicycle storage. The site has a relaxed atmosphere where consideration for others minimises the need for formal rules. It is ideal for young families, walkers, cyclists and fishermen. Gold mines and the National Showcaves Centre for Wales (including dinosaur park) are within an easy drive. A member of the Best of British Group.

Facilities

New heated toilet block with washbasins in cabins, 4 family rooms (basin, shower, toilet) and a room for families and disabled visitors which includes a baby unit. Combined, well equipped laundry and dishwashing room. Motorcaravan service point. Fridge freezer. Fishing. Bicycle hire. WiFi (charge). Off site: Supermarket 500 yds. Town amenities (shops, pubs, restaurants and indoor pool) within 1 mile. Golf 1 mile. Riding 8 miles. Beaches about 25 miles.

Open: All year.

Directions

Park is about half a mile outside the town boundary of Llandovery on the A40 to Brecon.
GPS: 51.99491, -3.78076

Charges guide

Per unit incl. 2 persons	£ 13.00 - £ 16.00
incl. services	£ 16.00 - £ 19.00
extra person	£ 1.50 - £ 2.00
dog	free

No credit cards.

Erwlon is a family run park with a warm welcome and excellent award winning facilities including a heated amenity block, family rooms, laundry, super pitches, a motor caravan service point and plenty of landscaped pitches available.

Erwlon
Caravan & Camping Park
Llandovery
Brecon Road | Llandovery
Carmarthenshire SA20 0RD
Phone: 01550 721021 / 720332
Email: peter@erwlon.co.uk

Llandovery

Rhandirmwyn Camping & Caravanning Club Site

Rhandirmwyn, Llandovery SA20 0NT (Carmarthenshire) T: 01550 760257

alanrogers.com/UK6070

This is a popular site with those who like a peaceful life with no on-site entertainment, just fresh air and beautiful countryside. The site is only a short drive from the magnificent Llyn Brianne reservoir and close to the Dinas RSPB nature reserve, where a two mile trail runs through oak and alder woodland alongside the River Tywi and the wildlife includes many species of birds including red kites. The site is in a sheltered valley with 90 pitches on level grass, 51 electric hook-ups (16A) and 17 hardstandings. The village is within walking distance although there is a fairly steep hill to negotiate and you can take a short cut through the woodland grove dedicated to John Lloyd, a former Chairman of the Club.

Facilities

The single heated sanitary block is kept very clean and tidy. Some washbasins in cubicles, dishwashing sinks and fully equipped laundry. Drive-over motorcaravan service point. Small playground with rubber base. Off site: The village has a Post Office and general store and the Royal Oak Inn serves good value meals. Farmers' market in Llandovery twice a month. Fishing 6 miles. Golf and bicycle hire 7 miles. Riding 11 miles.

Open: 29 March - 5 November.

Directions

From centre of Llandovery take A483 towards Builth Wells, after a short distance turn left by the fire station, signed Rhandirmwyn, continue for about 7 miles along country lanes.
GPS: 52.077017, -3.783833

Charges 2012

Per person	£ 5.95 - £ 9.35
child (6-18 yrs)	£ 2.70 - £ 2.95
non-member pitch fee	£ 7.10

For latest campsite news visit
alanrogers.com

Llandrindod Wells

Dolswydd Caravan Park

Dolswydd, Pen-y-Bont, Llandrindod Wells LD1 5UB (Powys) T: 01597 851267.
E: Hughes@dolswydd.freeserve.co.uk **alanrogers.com/UK6250**

Dolswydd is on the edge of a pretty, traditional working farm. A tranquil site with excellent views of the Welsh hills and surrounding area, it has modern facilities and 25 good spacious pitches mainly on hardstandings, all with electrical connections (16A). The Hughes family extends a warm and friendly welcome to their little park, surrounded by hills and wandering sheep, which is ideal as a touring base or for a one night stop, but booking is recommended, especially at peak times, Bank Holidays and during the Victorian Festival (last week in August). A footpath leads to the rear of the local pub.

Facilities

Modern facilities include plenty of hot water, laundry and a WC/washroom for disabled visitors. Fishing in the river alongside the site (free, but licence required). Off site: Within walking distance are the local pub and garage. Riding 1 mile. Golf and bicycle hire 5 miles.

Open: Easter - end October.

Directions

Pen-y-Bont is 2 miles east of the junction of the A44 and A483 roads at Crossgates. Take A44 (Kington). Go through Pen-y-Bont and immediately after crossing cattle grid, site is on right. On arrival drive across farm cattle grid and reception is at second farmhouse. GPS: 52.15857, -3.18773

Charges guide

Per unit incl. 2 persons
and electricity £ 12.00

Llandysul

Brynawelon Touring & Camping Park

Sarnau, Llandysul SA44 6RE (Ceredigion) T: 01239 654584. E: info@brynawelon.co.uk
alanrogers.com/UK6005

Paul and Liz Cowton have turned Brynawelon into a friendly, attractive and well appointed campsite. It is in a stunning rural location within two miles of the Ceredigion coast with its beaches, and close to the River Teifi with plenty of water based activities. All the 40 pitches have electricity hook-ups and of these, 25 are serviced hardstanding pitches (electricity, water and waste). A number of all-weather pitches for tents have been added recently. The remainder are on level grass. The park has ample room for children to play, an enclosed play area, an indoor games room with TV, and a sauna next to reception.

Facilities

Modern toilet block with toilets, showers, washbasins in cabins, two full suites in each side and a separate room for families and disabled visitors. Laundry/kitchen. Enclosed play area. Games room with electronic games, TV and library. Sauna (charged). Dog walking area. WiFi (charged). Off site: Shops and pub 1 mile. Links with local farm shop (pre-order delivery, voucher scheme). Beach 1 mile. Fishing 2 miles. Golf and riding 3 miles. Dolphin trips at Newquay 10 miles. White-water rafting 10 miles.

Open: March - 31 October.

Directions

Travelling north on the A487 from Cardigan turn right (southeast) at the crossroads in Sarnau village, signed Rhydlewis. Site is on the left after 650 yds. Note: the cross-country approach is not advised. GPS: 52.13001, -4.45401

Charges guide

Per unit incl. 2 persons and electricity	£ 25.00
incl. 4 persons, hardstanding and services	£ 12.50

No credit cards.

Llanelli

Pembrey Country Park Caravan Club Site

Pembrey, Llanelli SA16 0EJ (Carmarthenshire) T: 01554 834369
alanrogers.com/UK5940

Set on the edge of a 520 acre country park, this popular Caravan Club site enjoys a wonderful location with a vast range of outdoor activities, including the use of an eight mile stretch of safe, sandy beach a mile away. Well sheltered, the site is set in 12 acre grounds and provides 130 touring pitches, of which 68 are on hardstanding for caravans and motorcaravans. All are equipped with 16A electricity. Thoughtful landscaping has included the planting of many species of tree and a circular, one-way tarmac road provides easy access. Service points provide fresh water and waste disposal of all types.

Facilities

The toilet block is of an excellent standard including washbasins in cubicles, facilities for disabled visitors and a baby room. Laundry room. Motorcaravan service point. Gas available. Local tradesmen visit each morning selling milk, bread and newspapers. New play area. Late arrivals area (with electricity). Off site: Amenities of the country park. Shops 1 and 2.5 miles. Beach 1 mile (dogs are restricted on the beach May-Sept).

Open: March - January.

Directions

Leave M4 exit 48 onto A4138 (Llanelli). After 4 miles turn right onto A484 at roundabout (Carmarthen). Continue for 7 miles to Pembrey. Follow country park signs in preference to sat nav. Country park is signed off the A484 in Pembrey; entrance on right 100 yds. before gates. GPS: 51.681817, -4.297417

Charges guide

Per person	£ 5.40 - £ 7.60
pitch incl. electricity (non-member)	£ 13.20 - £ 17.50

Llangadog

Abermarlais Caravan Park

Llangadog SA19 9NG (Carmarthenshire) T: 01550 777868. E: aberma@tiscali.co.uk

alanrogers.com/UK5960

Apart from the attractions of south or mid Wales for a stay, this sheltered, family run park could also double as a useful transit stop close to the main holiday route for those travelling to Pembrokeshire. In a natural setting, up to 88 touring units are accommodated in one fairly flat, tapering five acre grass field edged by mature trees and a stream. Pitches are numbered and generously spaced around the perimeter and on either side of a central, hedged spine at the wider end, with 48 electrical hook-ups (10A) and some hardstanding. Backpackers have a small, separate area. A torch would be useful.

Facilities

The one small toilet block is older in style, but is clean and adequate with controllable showers. No laundry facilities (nearest about 5 miles). Motorcaravan service point. Shop doubles as reception. Gas supplies. Play area. Tennis and volleyball nets. Winter caravan storage. Off site: Pubs and shops at Llangadog. Restaurants nearby. Fishing 2 miles.

Open: 14 March - 14 November.

Directions

Park is on the A40, between the junctions with the A4069 and A482, between Llandovery and Llandeilo. GPS: 51.951583, -3.9003

Charges guide

Per person	£ 2.00
pitch incl. electricity	£ 9.00

Llangollen

Ty-Ucha Farm Caravan Park

Maesmawr Road, Llangollen LL20 7PP (Denbighshire) T: 01978 860677

alanrogers.com/UK6700

Only a mile from Llangollen, Ty Ucha has a rather dramatic setting, nestling under its own mountain and with views across the valley to craggy Dinas Bran castle. It is a neat, ordered park, carefully managed by the owner and providing 40 pitches (30 with 10A electrical hook-up) for caravans and motorcaravans only (tents are not accepted). They are well spaced around a large, grassy field with an open centre for play. One side slopes gently and is bounded by a stream and wood in which a nature trail has been made. Because of overhead cables, kite flying is forbidden; no bike riding either.

Facilities

The single toilet block, although of Portacabin style, is clean and well maintained and can be heated. It includes two metered showers for each sex (a little cramped). No laundry facilities but there is a launderette in Llangollen. Games room. Late arrivals area. Note: tents are not accepted. Off site: Golf and hotel with reasonably priced meals 0.5 miles. Fishing 1 mile.

Open: Easter - October.

Directions

Park is signed off A5 road, 1 mile east of Llangollen (250 yds). Do not approach from Birch Hill using sat nav but proceed to Maesmawr Road. GPS: 52.96546, -3.14569

Charges guide

Per unit incl. 2 persons and electricity	£ 15.00
extra person	£ 2.00
No credit cards.	

Llantwit Major

Acorn Camping & Caravanning

Ham Lane South, Llantwit Major CF61 1RP (Vale of Glamorgan) T: 01446 794024.
E: info@acorncamping.co.uk **alanrogers.com/UK5927**

A peaceful, family owned, rural site, Acorn is situated on the Heritage Coast, one mile from the beach and the historic town of Llantwit Major. The 105 pitches are mostly on grass, with a few private and rental mobile homes at the far end, leaving around 90 pitches for tourers, including 8 gravel hardstandings and 71 electric hook-ups (10A). There is a separate area for tents. Reception houses a very well stocked shop which includes groceries and essentials, souvenirs, children's toys, camping gear, a delicatessen, and takeaway meals cooked to order. There is occasional aircraft noise.

Facilities

A warm, modern building houses spacious shower cubicles with washbasins, ample WCs, a family/baby room, and a suite for disabled campers. Laundry facilities. Drinks machine. Shop. Gas. Snooker room. Games room (charged). Play area with free trampoline. WiFi (free). Off site: Glamorgan Heritage Coastal footpath. Llanerch Vineyard. Cosmeston Lakes Country Park at Penarth. Beach and sea fishing 1 mile. Riding 2 miles. Lake 4 miles. Golf and boat launching 9 miles.

Open: 5 February - 4 December.

Directions

From east from M4 exit 33 follow Cardiff airport, take B4265 for Llantwit Major. Left at lights, through Broverton and left (Ham Lane East), finally left (Ham Manor Park). Follow signs to site. GPS: 51.40409, -3.48181

Charges guide

Per unit incl. 2 persons and electricity	£ 15.15 - £ 16.50
extra person	£ 4.75

Llanwrda

Springwater Lakes

Harford, Llanwrda SA19 8DT (Carmarthenshire) T: 01558 650788. E: bookings@springwaterlakes.com

alanrogers.com/UK5880

Set in 20 acres of Welsh countryside, Springwater offers a selection of fishing lakes to keep even the keenest of anglers occupied. However, it is not just anglers who will enjoy this site – it is a lovely base to enjoy the peace and tranquillity of this part of Wales. Springwater offers 30 spacious, flat pitches either on grass or 20 gravel hardstanding, all with 16A electricity and 10 fully serviced pitches, plus 10 tent pitches. Malcolm and Shirley Bexon are very proud of their site and welcome all visitors with a smile. This is not a site for children unless they enjoy fishing (no play areas). If you want to learn about fishing Malcolm or Mark will be happy to help.

Facilities

The modern, heated, toilet block is very clean and includes facilities for disabled visitors (there is also wheelchair access to the lakes for fishing). Fishing. Tackle/bait shop. Off site: Spar shop and garage 500 yds. (other shops 5 miles). Riding 2 miles. Golf 4 miles.

Open: 1 March - 31 October.

Directions

From A40 at Llanwrda take A482 to Lampeter. After 6 miles go through village of Pumsaint and site is 2 miles further on the left, just before garage shop. GPS: 52.067417, -3.98225

Charges guide

Per unit incl. 2 persons and electricity	£ 20.00
extra person (over 2 yrs)	£ 5.00
dog	free - £ 2.00
No credit cards.	

Machynlleth

Morben Isaf Touring & Holiday Home Park

Derwenlas, Machynlleth SY20 8SR (Powys) T: 01654 781473. E: manager@morbenisaf.co.uk

alanrogers.com/UK6245

Morben Isaf provides 13 touring pitches with multi-services, all with electricity (16A), water tap, waste water drain and a satellite TV hook-up. There is further grassy space below the touring pitches, beyond the fishing lake which is normally used as a playing field and football pitch but can accommodate around ten tents which do not need any services. On a lower level, behind the site manager's bungalow, and barely visible from the touring site, are 87 privately owned caravan holiday homes. Also on the site is an unfenced coarse fishing lake which campers are free to use. Machynlleth is a market town, home of Owain Glyndwr's fifteenth century Welsh Parliament building and the Celtica Centre, and is also close to the Tal-y-Llyn Steam Railway, the Centre for Alternative Technology, Corris Craft Centre and King Arthur's Labyrinth. Adjacent to the site is the Dyfi Osprey Project visitor centre – for the first time in 2007, a nest platform was erected and was occupied by a pair of ospreys. This park is in a convenient location for an overnight halt, or a short stay whilst visiting all these attractions.

Facilities

Small but well equipped, heated modern toilet block includes spacious controllable showers, baby changing and child seats in both ladies' and men's. Facilities for disabled campers. Well equipped laundry. Internet access (free). Off site: Pub serving hot food 1.5 miles. Leisure Centre, shops and services in Machynlleth 3 miles (market on Wed). Dyfi Osprey Project visitor centre adjacent. Centre for Alternative Technology 6 miles.

Open: Mid March - 31 October.

Directions

Site is 3 miles southwest of Machynlleth beside A487. GPS: 52.570067, -3.91145

Charges guide

Per unit incl. 2 persons and electricity	£ 18.00
tent (2 persons)	£ 12.50

Moelfre

Home Farm Caravan Park

Marianglas, Anglesey LL73 8PH (Isle of Anglesey) T: 01248 410614. E: enq@homefarm-anglesey.co.uk

alanrogers.com/UK6640

A tarmac drive through open fields and a barrier/intercom system leads to this neatly laid out, quality park, with caravan holiday homes to one side. Nestling below what was once a Celtic hill fort, later decimated as a quarry, the park is edged with mature trees and farmland. A circular, tarmac access road leads to the 102 well spaced and numbered touring pitches. With five types available, there are pitches for everyone; ranging from grass with no electricity, to oversized, deluxe hardstandings with electricity, water tanks/taps, waste water drain and TV hook-ups. All electricity is 16A and there are separate well maintained grass fields/areas for tents. Some areas are slightly sloping. The 'pièce de résistance' must be the children's indoor play area, large super adventure play equipment, complete with tunnels and bridges on safe rubber matting, not to mention an outside fenced play area and fields available for sports, football, etc. and walking. Various beaches, sandy and rocky, are within a mile. A member of the Best of British Group.

Facilities

Two purpose built toilet blocks are of similar design, can be heated and are maintained to a high standard. En-suite provision for visitors with disabilities (with key). Small bathroom for children with baby bath and curtain. Family room (with key). Laundry room. Motorcaravan service point. Ice pack service. A new reception building with shop provides basic essentials, gas and some caravan accessories. Indoor and outdoor play areas. TV and pool table. Small library. Hard tennis (extra charge) with racquet hire. WiFi (charged). Off site: Beach 1 mile. Restaurants, shops and ATM at Benllech 2 miles. Fishing and golf 2 miles. Riding 8 miles.

Open: April - October.

Directions

From the Britannia Bridge take second exit left signed Benllech and Amlwch on the A5025. Two miles after Benllech keep left at roundabout and park entrance is 300 yds. on the left beyond the church. GPS: 53.34055, -4.256367

Charges guide

Per unit incl. 2 persons and electricity	£ 18.00 - £ 31.50
extra person	£ 3.50 - £ 6.00
child (3-15 yrs)	£ 2.00 - £ 4.00
dog (max. 2)	£ 1.00 - £ 2.00

Monmouth

Glen Trothy Caravan & Camping Park

Mitchel Troy, Monmouth NP25 4BD (Monmouthshire) T: 01600 712295. E: enquiries@glentrothy.co.uk

alanrogers.com/UK5890

Glen Trothy is a pretty park on the banks of the River Trothy and visitors are greeted by an array of colourful flowerbeds and tubs around the entrance and reception area. Three fields provide level touring and tent pitches. The first and largest field has a circular gravel road with seasonal pitches arranged on the outer side and touring pitches on the inner side. These have slabs for vehicle wheels and electricity hook-ups. The second field, just past the toilet block, has pitches for trailer tents and tents only (16 with electricity), whilst the camping field is for tents only (no cars are allowed on this area).

Facilities

Some improvements have been made to the sanitary block (possibly stretched at peak times). Facilities for disabled visitors. Laundry facilities. Tourist information in hut opposite reception. Small play area. Free fishing (from the camping field only). Dogs are not accepted. Off site: Golf, canoeing, shopping and supermarkets at the historic town of Monmouth 1.5 miles. The Wye Valley and the Forest of Dean are nearby for outings.

Open: 1 March - 31 October.

Directions

At Monmouth, take A40 east to Abergavenny. Exit at first junction and at T-junction, where site is signed, turn left onto B4284. Follow signs for Mitchel Troy. Site is on right just past village sign. GPS: 51.790967, -2.7341

Charges guide

Per unit incl. 2 persons and electricity	£ 12.00 - £ 18.00
extra person	£ 3.00
child under 4 yrs	free

Montgomery
Smithy Park

Abermule, Montgomery SY15 6ND (Powys) T: 01584 711280. E: info@smithypark.co.uk
alanrogers.com/UK6305

Smithy Park is set in four acres of landscaped ground bordered by the River Severn and the Shropshire Union Canal, in the tranquil rolling countryside of central Wales. It does have 60 privately owned caravan holiday homes, but beyond these is a separate touring area which has the benefit of being closest to the river with the best views and a small picnic and seating area on the bank. This area has 26 fully serviced hardstanding pitches (16A electricity, water, waste water and satellite TV hook-ups). A timber chalet provides all the sanitary facilities, and is located in one corner of the touring area.

Facilities

The timber clad chalet building provides two good sized showers per sex, washbasins in cubicles, a family room suitable for less able campers (there is a step up to the building). Additional toilet and washbasin in new building. Laundry room. Fishing in the river Severn. Fenced playground. Gas stocked. WiFi (charged). Off site: Bus stop in village. Supermarkets and all other services in Newtown 3 miles. Golf 3 miles. Riding 5 miles.

Open: 1 March - 31 October.

Directions

Site is 3 miles north of Newtown in the village of Abermule. Turn off the A483 into village, and turn down the lane beside the Waterloo Arms, opposite the village shop and Post Office. Site is at end of lane. GPS: 52.544217, -3.238717

Charges guide

Per unit incl. 2 persons and electricity	£ 18.00 - £ 25.00

Montgomery
Daisy Bank Touring Caravan Park

Snead, Montgomery SY15 6EB (Powys) T: 01588 620471. E: enquiries@daisy-bank.co.uk
alanrogers.com/UK6330

For adults only, this pretty, tranquil park in the Camlad Valley has panoramic views, and is an ideal base for walkers. Attractively landscaped with old English flower beds and many different trees and shrubs, this small park has been carefully developed. The Welsh hills to the north and the Shropshire hills to the south overlook the three fields which provide a total of 83 pitches. The field nearer to the road (perhaps a little noisy) is slightly sloping but there are hardstandings for motorcaravans, while the second field is more level. All pitches have 16A electricity, water and waste water drainage and TV hook up. Two camping pods were added in 2011 and more are planned for 2012.

Facilities

The well equipped, heated toilet block has modern, en-suite units and facilities for disabled visitors. A second block provides four en-suite units and two WCs. Dishwashing sinks under cover. Laundry facilities. Shop in reception (operates an honesty policy at certain times). Gas supplies. Brick built barbecues. Putting green (free loan of clubs and balls). Bicycle hire. Tourist information. Small library. WiFi. Off site: Supermarket 2 miles.

Open: All year.

Directions

Site is by A489 road 2 miles east of Churchstoke in the direction of Craven Arms. GPS: 52.529917, -3.0297

Charges guide

Per unit incl. 2 persons and all services	£ 18.00 - £ 26.00
extra person	£ 5.00
tent (per person)	£ 9.00 - £ 11.00

Narberth
Little Kings Park

Amroth Road, Ludchurch, Narberth SA67 8PG (Pembrokeshire) T: 01834 831330.
E: littlekingspark@btconnect.com **alanrogers.com/UK5975**

This superb family run park has a number of attributes to make your stay both comfortable and memorable. There are stunning views over Carmarthen Bay to the Gower and beyond to the coast of Somerset and North Devon. At night no fewer than seven lighthouses can be seen blinking out their warnings. A touring field provides 56 well spaced, large touring pitches all with 10A electricity, 21 with gravel hardstanding and fully serviced. An attractive playground is in the central open grass area. A further seven pitches are in a different area. There are 60 pitches for tents in an adjoining paddock with 31 electricity hook-ups. This is an ideal site for a family holiday or for touring the area.

Facilities

The two modern and well equipped toilet blocks include controllable hot showers, open style washbasins, a family shower room and a suite for disabled campers. Laundry rooms. Shop with bakery. Takeaway, bar and restaurant with conservatory (limited opening). Covered swimming pool. Games rooms. Playground. Ball games area. Gas supplies. Off site: Nearest supermarket and ATM at Kilgetty 2.5 miles. Fishing 1.5 miles.

Open: 1 March - 31 October.

Directions

From A477 Carmarthen to Pembroke road, 2 miles after Llanteg at petrol station, turn left towards Amroth, Wiseman's Bridge, Ludchurch. After 1 mile, at crossroads, turn right (Ludchurch, Narberth) and park is 800 yds. GPS: 51.751517, -4.6879

Charges guide

Per unit incl. 2 persons and electricity	£ 15.00 - £ 26.00
extra person (over 3 yrs)	£ 2.20

For latest campsite news visit
alanrogers.com

Newcastle Emlyn
Cenarth Falls Holiday Park

Cenarth, Newcastle Emlyn SA38 9JS (Ceredigion) T: 01239 710345. E: enquiries@cenarth-holipark.co.uk

alanrogers.com/UK6010

The Davies family has developed an attractively landscaped, part wooded holiday home park with 89 units (one for rent). A neat well cared for, sheltered area at the top of the park provides 30 touring pitches, accessed via a tarmac road. All are on shingle hardstanding with 16A electricity). A sunken, kidney shaped outdoor pool with landscaped surrounds and sunbeds is a focal point. The Coracles Health and Country Club provides an indoor pool, spa, sauna and steam rooms and fitness suite (reduced rates for campers). It also provides a bar with evening meals, an adult-only lounge and a large function room where live entertainment is organised during the main season. Everything is of a high quality. A member of the Best of British Group.

Facilities

The heated sanitary block has ramped (key) access. A 'P.I.R.' system controls heating, lighting, water and air freshener on entry. Provision for disabled visitors, spacious well equipped showers and one washbasin in a roomy private cabin. Laundry room. Gas supplies. Outdoor pool (late May-late Sept). Coracles Health and Country Club. Play area. Games room. No dogs on touring field in high season. Off site: Fishing 0.25 miles. Shop within 0.5 miles.

Open: 1 March - mid November.

Directions

Follow A484 Cardigan - Newcastle Emlyn road and park is signed before Cenarth village. GPS: 52.0499, -4.531717

Charges guide

Per unit incl. up to 4 people and electricity	£ 16.00 - £ 27.00
extra person	£ 2.00

Newport
Cwmcarn Forest Drive Campsite

Cwmcarn, Crosskeys, Newport NP11 7FA (Newport) T: 01495 272001. E: cwmcarn-vc@caerphilly.gov.uk

alanrogers.com/UK5930

This forest site, run by Caerphilly Council, is set in a narrow, sheltered valley with magnificent wooded slopes. The park is not only central for the many attractions of this part of Wales, but there is also much of the natural environment to enjoy, including a small fishing lake and the seven mile forest drive. The site has a slightly wild feel, but is well located and has 27 well spaced, flat pitches, most with 15A electricity (three with concrete hardstanding), spread over three small fields between the new Visitor Centre and the small lake. Three timber camping pods have been added with another three planned. Wardens are on hand daily. The climb up to the Twmbarlwm ancient hill fort is well worth making.

Facilities

The single, heated toilet block includes toilet facilities for disabled visitors, laundry facilities, small cooker and fridge. The Visitors' Centre has a coffee shop selling drinks and snacks. Guided walks and mountain bike trail. WiFi. Dogs accepted by prior arrangement. Large units (over 24 ft) not accepted due to access. Timber camping pods to rent. Off site: Shops, leisure centre and takeaway in village.

Open: All year excl. 23 December - 2 January.

Directions

Cwmcarn Forest Drive is well signed from exit 28 on the M4. From the Midlands and the 'Heads of the Valleys' road (A465), take A467 south to Cwmcarn. GPS: 51.63771, -3.11877

Charges guide

Per unit incl. 2 persons and electricity	£ 14.00 - £ 18.00
extra person	£ 4.00 - £ 6.00

Newport
Tredegar House Country Park Caravan Club Site

Coedkernen, Newport NP10 8TW (Newport) T: 01633 815600

alanrogers.com/UK6060

This immaculate Caravan Club site is ideally situated for breaking a journey or for longer stays. It can accommodate 79 units, all with 16A electricity hook-up and 68 with gravel hardstanding. A further grass area is allocated for 10 tents, with its use limited to families and couples – no single sex groups are accepted. The site itself is set within the gardens and park of Tredegar House, a 17th-century house and country park which is open to the public to discover what life was like 'above and below stairs'. The park entrance gates are locked at dusk so contact the site reception for details of latest arrival times. Some road noise may be expected at times, but otherwise this is an excellent site.

Facilities

The sanitary block is of an excellent standard with a digital lock. It includes washbasins in cubicles, facilities for disabled visitors, baby and toddler bathroom. Laundry. Motorcaravan service point. Visitors' centre (Easter-Sept). Adventure play area. WiFi (charged). Off site: Large supermarket 0.5 miles. Bus service 10 minutes walk.

Open: All year.

Directions

From M4 take exit 28 or from A48 junction with M4 follow brown signs for Tredegar House. The caravan park is indicated to the left at the house entrance. GPS: 51.56148, -3.03341

Charges guide

Per person	£ 4.30 - £ 6.20
pitch incl. electricity (non-member)	£ 12.90 - £ 16.00

For latest campsite news visit

alanrogers.com

Newtown

Cringoed Caravan Park

Cringoed, Llanbrynmair, Newtown SY19 7DR (Powys) T: 01650 521237. E: enquiries@cringoed.co.uk

alanrogers.com/UK6240

Cringoed is a pleasant, peaceful, small park with a river to one side, hills on the other and trees at either end. There are 30 spacious pitches available for touring and these are in a level open field, each with hardstanding and 16A electricity. About 36 caravan holiday homes are placed at either end of the site, some amongst trees and some in a newer, more open area. There are also ten tent pitches, some with electricity. This is a relaxing base where you can sit and listen to the river and watch the wildlife, but it is also within easy reach of some of mid-Wales' best scenery and not far from the coast. Paul and Sue Mathers continue landscaping the site and will make you very welcome.

Facilities

The single toilet block is neat, modern and quite adequate. Laundry and dishwashing. Adventure play area. Small tourist information room. WiFi (free). Off site: Shops 1 mile (ATM at Spar in Carno 6 miles). Bicycle hire 1 mile. Fishing 5 miles. Golf 8 miles. Riding 12 miles.

Open: 7 March - 30 November.

Directions

From A470 between Newton and Machynlleth in Llanbrynmair take B4518 (Staylittle). After 1 mile just before bridge turn right, go over site bridge and turn right into site. GPS: 52.598333, -3.644383

Charges guide

Per unit incl. 2 persons
and electricity   £ 14.00 - £ 17.00
No credit cards.

Pembroke

Freshwater East Caravan Club Site

Trewent Hill, Freshwater East, Pembroke SA71 5LJ (Pembrokeshire) T: 01646 672341.

alanrogers.com/UK5990

Located within the Pembrokeshire Coast National Park, this Caravan Club site is open to non-members (for all units). The park is flanked by trees on one side with a mix of grass and hardstanding tiered pitch areas to choose from. There is a total of 130 pitches, all with 16A electrical hook-ups. There are a few pitches for tents. The beach and the Pembroke Coastal Path are just a few minutes walk. This is an excellent area for walking with magnificent cliff views and bird watching. You will find St Davids, the smallest cathedral city, well worth a visit. Note: TV aerial connections are available, but you will need your own extension cable.

Facilities

The two heated toilet blocks are modern and clean with washbasins in cubicles, and free hairdryers or sockets for your own. Facilities for disabled visitors. Fully equipped laundry rooms. Waste point for motorcaravans. Gas supplies. Reception keeps basic food items. Information kiosk. Small play area. WiFi. Off site: Beach 400 yds. Shop 0.5 miles. Public transport 1 mile. Fishing 5 miles.

Open: 27 March - 26 October.

Directions

From east on A477, fork left 1.25 miles past Milton onto A4075 Pembroke road. After 2 miles in Pembroke (just after railway bridge) turn sharp left at roundabout on A4139 Tenby road. In 1.75 miles in Lamphey turn right onto B4584 (Freshwater East). In 1.75 miles turn right (Stackpole) and after 400 yds. right at Club sign. GPS: 51.645262, -4.872512

Charges guide

Per person   £ 4.60 - £ 6.20
pitch incl. electricity (non-member)   £ 13.50 - £ 16.00

Penmaenmawr

Tyddyn Du Touring Park

Conwy Old Road, Penmaenmawr LL34 6RE (Conwy) T: 01492 622300. E: stay@tyddyndutouringpark.co.uk

alanrogers.com/UK6695

This attractively landscaped adults only campsite is conveniently situated close to the A55 and positioned on a hillside with panoramic views across Conwy Bay to The Great Orme at Llandudno and Puffin Island. Offering peace and quiet in a superb location between mountains and the sea and being within easy reach of Conwy, Snowdonia National Park and many historic regions of North Wales, this is an ideal base for exploring the area. Tarmac roads connect the three levels which are tiered to maximise the views for everyone. There are 92 touring pitches on grass or hardstanding, all with 16A electricity.

Facilities

Two well maintained sanitary blocks provide showers, open style washbasins and hairdryers. En-suite facilities for disabled visitors (Radar key). Motorcaravan service point. Laundry room. Small library. £5 (cash only) refundable deposit for entry card. WiFi (charged). Off site: Golf 0.5 mile. Pub at entrance to park. Shops and restaurants within 1 mile. Sandy beach 10-15 minutes walk.

Open: 22 March - 31 October.

Directions

From A55 take exit 16, at roundabout (Penmaenmawr) turn sharp left into Ysguborwen Road. Entrance to park is about 300 yds. on the right. GPS: 53.27425, -3.90632

Charges guide

Per unit incl. 2 adults
and electricity   £ 20.00 - £ 22.00

For latest campsite news visit
alanrogers.com

Pontarddulais

River View Touring Park

The Dingle, Llanedi, Pontarddulais SA4 0FH (Carmarthenshire) T: 01269 844876.
E: info@riverviewtouringpark.com **alanrogers.com/UK5945**

Nestling in the valley of the River Gwili, River View is an attractive, quiet and friendly park made up of three fields: one by the river which is kept mainly for adults and two on a plateau up a steep slope on the opposite side of the lane. Particular care has been taken to protect the natural environment. There are 65 level, generously sized pitches of which 49 are touring pitches, the remainder seasonal. All have electricity (16A), 44 have hardstandings and 6 are fully serviced. This is a popular rural retreat for young families and older couples. The park is close to the end of the M4. This allows easy access and there is plenty to do or see in the near vicinity, including castles, gardens, beaches, wildfowl reserves and a water park. A Site of Special Scientific Interest is located immediately at the back of the park. The bird life visible from the site is varied and includes buzzards and red kites, and dippers on the river. The toilet block, including an en-suite family room with baby changing facilities and one for the disabled, is modern and equipped to a very high standard, including underfloor heating and automatic lighting.

Facilities

The modern, heated, toilet block is spotless with spacious showers, family room and suite for disabled visitors. Laundry with sinks, washing machine, tumble dryer, iron and ironing board. Small shop for basics and local fresh produce. Large grassy recreation area on main field. Fishing. Off site: Shop, bar and restaurant 1 mile. Bicycle hire and golf 5 miles. Beach 12 miles.

Open: 4 March - 20 November.

Directions

From M4 exit 49 take A483 signed Llandeilo. Take the first turn left (after layby) and park is on left after 300 yds. GPS: 51.75817, -4.06288

Charges guide

Per unit incl. 2 persons and electricity	£ 15.00 - £ 19.00
incl. services	£ 18.00 - £ 22.00
extra person	£ 3.50 - £ 4.50
child (under 4 yrs)	£ 1.00 - £ 2.00
dog	free - £ 2.00

No credit cards.

Environmentally friendly, award winning **4 star site** set in beautiful **Carmarthenshire countryside**. Modern toilet/shower block. Small shop and laundry on site. 40 all weather and 10 service pitches,16amp hook up.

The Dingle · Llanedi Pontarddulais · Swansea, Wales, SA4 0FH
www.riverviewtouringpark.com · info@riverviewtouringpark.com · Tel: 01269 844876

Prestatyn

Nant Mill Family Touring Caravan & Tenting Park

Gronant Road, Prestatyn LL19 9LY (Denbighshire) T: 01745 852360. E: nantmilltouring@aol.com
alanrogers.com/UK6660

This traditional style, family owned and run park of around five acres, takes some 150 units arranged over four fields. There are some distant sea views to be had from many pitches. These are carefully allocated to ensure that the largest, central, sloping field is reserved for families. A smaller more intimate field for tents only is to one side of this and two small paddocks on the other side are for couples who might prefer a quieter, more level location. There are 96 electrical connections (10/16A) but tents are not permitted on pitches with hook-ups. The pitches nearer the road may experience some noise.

Facilities

The main toilet block is older in style but very well kept, with showers, an ample number of open style washbasins and baby changing in both ladies' and men's rooms. Extra showers are in a small modern Portacabin style unit alongside. Showers are charged (50p), with a £1 deposit for the cubicle key (return after each shower). A separate Portacabin unit with ramp provides a full suite of services for disabled visitors. Large utility room with washing machines, dryers, spin dryer, ironing facilities, together with sinks for hand washing and dishes plus a hairdressing station. Playground and play field. Off site: Beach, sea fishing, golf, town with supermarkets, shops and gas supplies all 0.5 miles. Bicycle hire 4 miles.

Open: End March - mid October.

Directions

Site entrance is 0.5 mile east of Prestatyn on A548 coast road. GPS: 53.33765, -3.3932

Charges guide

Per unit incl. 2 persons and electricity	£ 17.75 - £ 20.75
extra person (over 3 yrs)	£ 1.50

No credit/debit cards.

For latest campsite news visit
alanrogers.com

Aberfoyle

Trossachs Holiday Park

Aberfoyle FK8 3SA (Stirling) T: 01877 382614. E: info@trossachsholidays.co.uk

alanrogers.com/UK7230

Nestling on the side of a hill, three miles south of Aberfoyle, this is an excellent base for touring this famously beautiful area. Lochs Lomond, Ard, Venachar and others are within easy reach, as are the Queen Elizabeth Forest Park and, of course, the Trossachs. Very neat and tidy, there are 45 well laid out and marked pitches arranged on terraces with hardstanding. All have electricity and most also have water, drainage and TV connections. There is also a large area for tents. There are trees between the terraces and lovely views across the valley. The adjoining oak and bluebell woods are a haven for wildlife, with wonderful walks. You will receive a warm welcome from the friendly staff at this well run, family park. A member of the Best of British Group.

Facilities

A timber building houses sanitary facilities providing a satisfactory supply of toilets, showers and washbasins, the ladies' area being rather larger, with two private cabins. Laundry room. Well stocked shop (all season). Games room with TV. Play equipment (on gravel). Off site: Golf, boat launching and fishing 3 miles. Sailing 6 miles. Discount scheme arranged with a local leisure centre provides facilities for swimming, sauna, solarium, badminton, tennis, windsurfing, etc.

Open: 1 March - 31 October.

Directions

Park is 3 miles south of Aberfoyle on the A81 road, well signed. GPS: 56.140133, -4.3555

Charges guide

Per unit incl. 2 persons and electricity	£ 15.00 - £ 19.00
incl. all services	£ 17.00 - £ 21.00
tent pitch incl. 2 persons	£ 14.50 - £ 18.50
extra person	£ 2.00

TROSSACHS HOLIDAY PARK - ABERFOYLE STIRLING FK8 3SA
www.trossachsholidays.co.uk **Tel:** 01877 382614 **(anytime)**

One of the finest Environmental parks on the edge of the National Park
40 Exclusive landscaped Touring Pitches - mostly fully serviced
Holiday Caravans and Lodges For Sale and Hire
• Practical Caravan Top 100 Parks Winner 2006 - 2008 Inclusive • Visit Scotland 5 Star Holiday Park
• 2004 Thistle Awards Customer Care • Park of the Year • Green Tourism Business Scheme Gold Award
• David Bellamy 10 Year Gold Award

Aberlour-on-Spey

Aberlour Gardens Caravan & Camping Park

Aberlour-on-Spey AB38 9LD (Moray) T: 01340 871586. E: Aberlourgardens@aol.com

alanrogers.com/UK7540

This pleasant park is within the large walled garden of the Aberlour Estate on Speyside. The owners have made many improvements to the sheltered, five-acre, family-run park which provides a very natural setting amidst spruce and Scots pine. Of the 73 level pitches, 35 are for touring units leaving the remainder for holiday homes (two for rent) and seasonal units. All the pitches have 10A electrical connections and 16 are all-weather pitches. This is an ideal area for walking, birdwatching, salmon fishing or pony trekking, or for following the only Malt Whisky Trail in the world, while Aberlour has a fascinating old village shop – a time capsule. A member of the Best of British Group.

Facilities

The toilet facilities are now a little dated (there are plans for refurbishment). Facilities for visitors with disabilities can also be used as family or baby changing room. Laundry facilities. Motorcaravan service point. Small licensed shop stocking basics and with an information area. Play area. WiFi throughout (charged). Caravan storage. Off site: Riding 0.5 miles. Swimming and bicycle hire 1 mile. Fishing 1 and 5 miles. Golf 4 miles.

Open: 1 March - 28 December.

Directions

Turn off the A95 midway between Aberlour and Craigellachie onto unclassified road. Site signed in 500 yds. Vehicles over 10'6" high should use the A941 Dufftown road (site signed). GPS: 57.47485, -3.1986

Charges guide

Per unit incl. 2 persons and electricity	£ 17.00 - £ 21.25
extra person (over 5 yrs)	£ 2.50
backpacker and tent (per person)	£ 7.70 - £ 9.00
dog	free

For latest campsite news visit
alanrogers.com

Acharacle

Resipole Farm Caravan & Camping Park

Loch Sunart, Acharacle PH36 4HX (Highland) T: 01967 431235. E: info@resipole.co.uk

alanrogers.com/UK7800

This quiet, open park is marvellously set on the shores of Loch Sunart, eight miles from Strontian, on the Ardnamurchan peninsula. It is a must for anyone seeking peace and tranquillity and really worth the journey. With wonderful views across the water and regularly visited by wild deer, Resipole Farm offers a good base for exploring the whole of this scenic area or, more locally, for fishing, boating (launching from the site's own slipway) and walking in the unspoilt countryside. There are 48 level and well drained touring pitches here, 40 with electricity (10/16A). Tents are sited by the hedges. This is a good location for day trips to Mull via the Lochaline ferry.

Facilities	Directions
The central, modern sanitary block can be heated and is kept very clean. Excellent provision for visitors with disabilities. Laundry facilities. Motorcaravan service point. Caravan storage. Art gallery and studios. Fishing. WiFi in some areas (free).	From A82 Fort William road, take Corran ferry, 8 miles south of Fort William. Leaving ferry, turn south along A861. Park is on north shore of Loch Sunart, 8 miles west of Strontian. Single track road for 8 miles approaching Resipole - care needed. GPS: 56.710933, -5.720217
Open: Easter/1 April - 31 October.	**Charges guide**

Per unit incl. 2 persons and electricity	£ 18.50
backpacker tent incl. 2 persons	£ 12.00

Arrochar

Forest Holidays Ardgartan

Ardgartan, Arrochar G83 7AR (Dunbartonshire) T: 01301 702293. E: fe.holidays@forestry.gsi.gov.uk

alanrogers.com/UK7260

Forest Holidays is a partnership between the Forestry Commission and The Camping and Caravanning Club. Ardgartan is a rugged site in the Argyll Forest Park. Splendidly situated with mountains all around and lovely views of Loch Long, there are lots of sightseeing and activity opportunities. The 175 pitches are in sections which are well divided by grass giving an uncrowded air. Most with hardstanding and marked by numbered posts, they are accessed from hard surfaced roads and 54 have electrical hook-ups. There are additional grass areas for tents. Midges can be a problem in this area of Scotland – go prepared. The site gate is locked 22.00-07.30.

Facilities	Directions
The main toilet block is opposite the reception and shop. Refurbished for 2009 it includes facilities for disabled visitors and babies. Launderette. Play equipment (bark surfaces). Raised barbecues are allowed. Bicycle hire. Fishing. Boat launching. Off site: Arrochar village with fuel, general stores and a restaurant 2 miles.	From A82 Glasgow - Crianlarich road take A83 at Tarbet signed Arrochar and Cambletown. Site is 2 miles past Arrochar, the entrance on a bend. GPS: 56.188783, -4.781667
	Charges guide
Open: All year.	Per unit incl. 2 persons £ 10.00 - £ 20.50
	Discounts for families, disabled guests and seniors.

Auchterarder

Grand Eagles Caravan Park

Nether Coul, Auchterarder PH3 1ET (Perth and Kinross) T: 01764 663119. E: info@grandeagles.co.uk

alanrogers.com/UK7270

This is a charming small park, purpose designed and landscaped. In a sheltered position, it is conveniently situated for exploring central Scotland and the Highlands with many leisure activities close at hand (particularly golf) and within walking distance of the village (one mile). The 21 original pitches, all with electricity (6A) and hardstanding, 12 with drainage, are well spaced around the edge of the elongated, level grass park. Marked pitches with grass frontage back on to raised banks which are planted with trees. Further pitches have been developed to one side of the site.

Facilities	Directions
Toilet facilities (with key system) include controllable, well equipped hot showers. A toilet for disabled visitors is provided in both the male and female units. Laundry room with sink and washing machine; an iron can be provided. Fishing. Caravan storage. Off site: Village and golf 1 mile. Bicycle hire and riding 4 miles. The historic cities of Perth and Stirling are less than half an hour's drive away.	Park is between the A9 and A824 roads east of Auchterarder village, only 2 miles from the main road. It is reached by turning on to the B8062 (Dunning) road from the A824. GPS: 56.304333, -3.676167
	Charges guide
Open: All year.	Per unit incl. up to 4 persons and electricity £ 14.50
	extra person (over 5 yrs) £ 1.00
	No credit cards.

For latest campsite news visit
alanrogers.com

Aviemore

Forest Holidays Glenmore

Aviemore PH22 1QU (Highland) T: 01479 861271. E: info@forestholidays.co.uk

alanrogers.com/UK7680

Forest Holidays is a partnership between the Forestry Commission and The Camping and Caravanning Club. This site is attractively laid out in a fairly informal style in several adjoining areas connected by narrow, part gravel, part tarmac roads, with access to the lochside. One of these areas, the Pinewood Area, is very popular and has 32 hardstandings (some distance from the toilet block). Of the 220 marked pitches on fairly level, firm grass, 122 have electricity (16A). This site, with something for everyone, would be great for family holidays. The Glenmore Forest Park lies close to the sandy shore of Loch Morlich amidst conifer woods and surrounded on three sides by the impressive Cairngorm mountains.

Facilities

New toilet and shower blocks. Next to the site, a range of amenities includes a well stocked shop (all year), a café serving meals and snacks, and a Forestry Commission visitor centre and souvenir shop. Barbecues are not permitted in dry weather. Bicycle hire. Fishing. Sandy beach (Blue Flag). Off site: The Aviemore centre with indoor and outdoor recreation activities including skiing 7 miles. Golf within 15 miles. Fishing and boat trips.

Open: All year.

Directions

Immediately south of Aviemore on B9152 (not A9 bypass) take B970 then follow sign for Cairngorm and Loch Morlich. Site entrance is on right past the loch. If travelling in winter, prepare for snow. GPS: 57.167033, -3.694717

Charges guide

Per unit incl. 2 persons
and electricity   £ 18.00 - £ 25.50

Balloch

Lomond Woods Holiday Park

Tullichewan, Old Luss Road, Balloch G83 8QP (West Dunbartonshire) T: 01389 755000.
E: lomondwoods@holiday-parks.co.uk **alanrogers.com/UK7240**

A series of improvements over the last few years has made this one of the top parks in Scotland. Almost, but not quite, on the banks of Loch Lomond, this landscaped, well planned park is suitable for both transit or longer stays. Formerly known as Tullichewan Holiday Park, it takes 110 touring units on well spaced, numbered pitches on flat or gently sloping grass. Most have hardstanding, all have electrical connections (10A) and 27 have water and waste water too. Watersport activities and boat trips are possible on Loch Lomond, with a visitor attraction, Lomond Shores, nearby. This is a well run park, open all year, with very helpful wardens and reception staff.

Facilities

The single large heated, well kept toilet block includes some showers with WCs, baths for ladies, a shower room for disabled visitors and two baby baths. Covered dishwashing sinks. Launderette. Motorcaravan service points. Games room with TV. Playground. Caravan storage. American motorhomes accepted with prior notice. WiFi (charged). Off site: Fishing and boat launching 400 yds. Riding 4 miles. Restaurants in Balloch (5 mins).

Open: All year.

Directions

Turn off A82 road 17 miles northwest of Glasgow on A811 Stirling road. Site is in Balloch at southern end of Loch Lomond and is well signed. GPS: 56.00155, -4.592233

Charges guide

Per unit incl. up to 2 persons
and electricity   £ 18.00 - £ 22.00
incl. mains services and awning   £ 22.00 - £ 26.00

Blairgowrie

Nethercraig Caravan Park

By Alyth, Blairgowrie PH11 8HN (Perth and Kinross) T: 01575 560204.
E: nethercraigholidaypark@btconnect.com **alanrogers.com/UK7280**

Nethercraig is a family run touring park, attractively designed and beautifully landscaped, with views across the Strathmore valley to the long range of the Sidlaw hills. The 40 large touring pitches are accessed from a circular, gravel road, all with 10A electrical connections and all but one with hardstanding (for awnings too). In addition, there are five large pitches for tents on flat grass. There is a personal welcome for all visitors at the attractive modern reception building and shop. A one mile circular woodland walk from the park has picnic benches and a leaflet guide is provided.

Facilities

The central, purpose built toilet block is well equipped and maintained, and can be heated. Unit for disabled visitors (entry by key). Separate sinks for dishwashing and clothes are in the laundry room (metered hot water), plus a washing machine, dryer and iron, and clothes line. Shop. Play area. Small football field. Fishing. Caravan storage. Off site: Fishing 2 miles. Golf within 4 miles.

Open: 15 February - 13 January.

Directions

From A926 Blairgowrie - Kirriemuir road, at roundabout south of Alyth join B954 (Glenisla). Follow caravan signs for 4 miles and turn right onto unclassified road (Nethercraig). Park is on left after 0.5 miles. GPS: 56.6614, -3.1998

Charges guide

Per unit incl. 2 persons
and electricity   £ 15.00 - £ 18.00

For latest campsite news visit
alanrogers.com

Callander

The Gart Caravan Park

Stirling Road, Callander FK17 8LE (Perth and Kinross) T: 01877 330002. E: enquiries@theholidaypark.co.uk

alanrogers.com/**UK7220**

Gart Caravan Park is situated within the Loch Lomond and Trossachs National Park, just a mile from the centre of Callander. Surrounded by mature trees, this attractive, family run park is peaceful and spacious. All is kept in a pristine condition and a very warm welcome awaits on arrival with a superb information pack given to all. The 128 all grass touring pitches are reasonably level, open plan and marked, with electricity (16A), water and drain. Tents and pup tents are not accepted, groundsheets are not permitted. Privately owned caravan holiday homes are located away from the touring section near the river which runs for 200 yards along the park boundary.

Facilities

Modern heated central facilities are immaculate, with toilets and showers, plus extra areas with showers, baby changing and hair washing basins. Separate facilities for disabled visitors. Fully equipped laundry. Drive-over motorcaravan service point. Gas sales. No shop on site but a breakfast car arrives at 09.00 with papers and basic provisions. Large adventure play area, part undercover. Separate field for ball games. Free fishing (not Sun). Max. 2 dogs. Off site: Bicycle hire 1 mile. Riding 6 miles.

Open: 1 April - 15 October.

Directions

From the south take M9. Near Stirling, leave at exit 10 and follow A84 through Doune. Park is on the left, 1 mile before Callander town centre. GPS: 56.2365, -4.1891

Charges guide

Per unit incl. services	£ 22.00
awning	£ 2.00

Castle Douglas

Mossyard Caravan Park

Gatehouse of Fleet, Castle Douglas DG7 2ET (Dumfries and Galloway) T: 01557 840226.

E: enquiry@mossyard.co.uk alanrogers.com/**UK6890**

Mossyard is a family run park set within a working farm right beside the sea in a sheltered bay. The park and farmhouse appear together suddenly over the horizon and in the distance as you approach, with some breathtaking views across the Solway where the Galloway Hills and the waters of Fleet Bay meet. There are 37 grass pitches, 12 for caravans and motorcaravans on an elevated area that slopes in parts. The remaining 25 pitches for any unit are on a level field which adjoins the beach but is a little way from the sanitary facilities. Electrical connections (16A) are available to all.

Facilities

Some of the farm buildings have been utilised for the toilet facilities. Showers are coin operated (20p). Spacious facilities for disabled visitors double as a family bathroom. Purpose built laundry, dishwashing area and information room with freezer and fridge for visitors' use. No shop. Off site: Gatehouse of Fleet with shops, pubs and restaurants 4 miles. Riding 1 mile. Bicycle hire and golf 5 miles.

Open: 30 March - 3 November.

Directions

Take A75 road from Dumfries towards Stranraer and park is signed to the left, 4 miles west of Gatehouse of Fleet, about 1 mile down a single track farm road. GPS: 54.840183, -4.26015

Charges guide

Per unit incl. 2 persons and electricity	£ 16.50 - £ 18.50

Castle Douglas

Loch Ken Holiday Park

Parton, Castle Douglas DG7 3NE (Dumfries and Galloway) T: 01644 470282.

E: office@lochkenholidaypark.co.uk alanrogers.com/**UK6940**

Loch Ken Holiday Park sits right on the shore of the loch, adjacent to the RSPB bird reserve and the Galloway Forest Park – it is a peaceful haven in an Area of Outstanding Natural Beauty. This is a family owned park with 40 touring pitches and 33 caravan holiday homes, ten of which are for rent. The touring pitches, all with 10A electricity, are quite separate and are arranged in a mostly open plan way on a large, neatly mown grass area beside the water. Some of this area is gently undulating. Mature trees border the park and provide an area for walking dogs. Site lighting is minimal so torches are advised.

Facilities

The toilet block has been refurbished to modern standards and was exceptionally clean when we visited. Separate facilities in a modern Portacabin unit are in the tent area. Facilities for disabled visitors. Gas supplies. Well stocked shop. Good play area. Bicycles, canoes and dinghies for hire. Boat launching (permit from reception). Fishing (permit). Off site: Limited buses stop at entrance, Skiing 0.5 miles. Golf and riding 7 miles. Bars and restaurants in Castle Douglas 9 miles. Kirkcudbright 15 miles.

Open: 1 March - 31 October.

Directions

From Castle Douglas take A713 north for 7 miles. Site entrance is on left in Parton. GPS: 55.0104, -4.05568

Charges guide

Per unit incl. 2 persons, 2 children under 10 yrs and electricity	£ 17.00 - £ 21.00
tent, no electricity	£ 12.00 - £ 17.00
extra person	£ 2.00
dog	£ 2.00

For latest campsite news visit

alanrogers.com

Castle Douglas

Barlochan Caravan Park

Palnackie, Castle Douglas DG7 1PF (Dumfries and Galloway) T: 01557 870267.
E: info@gillespie-leisure.co.uk **alanrogers.com/UK6945**

Barlochan Caravan Park is situated on a hillside overlooking the Urr Estuary on the Solway Coast close to Dalbeattie and Castle Douglas, with the small village of Palnackie being a short walk away. Set on terraces, level, marked and numbered, most of the touring and tent pitches are on grass with a limited number of hardstandings available. There are 21 with 16A electrical connections. In addition, 55 holiday homes (5 for hire) are positioned on terraces high above the touring areas and screened by mature shrubs and trees. Just to the left of the entrance there is a minigolf course and an adventure play area screened from the park with mature trees. The sheltered outdoor swimming pool is popular. Through the village, under a mile from the park, there is a coarse fishing lake which is free for visitors to the park. Dalbeattie Forest nearby provides miles of walking and mountain bike trails. Castle Douglas is just nine miles away and gardeners will enjoy an afternoon at the well known Threave Gardens.

Facilities

The refurbished sanitary facilities are kept spotlessly clean. Shower cubicles have recently been made larger, suitable for wheelchair entry, but if required there is also a separate unit with WC and basin. Fully equipped laundry with outside drying area. Reception and well stocked shop. Heated outdoor swimming pool and terrace. Large games room and TV room. Minigolf. Off site: Fishing 300 yds. Bicycle hire 3 miles. Golf 7 miles. Riding and beach 10 miles. Village pub nearby. Dalbeattie Forest for cycling and walking.

Open: Easter/1 April - 31 October.

Directions

From Dumfries take A711 west to Dalbeattie. Continue through Dalbeattie for 0.5 miles, bear left at T-junction (Auchencairn). Site is 2 miles on the right. GPS: 54.895023, -3.842564

Charges guide

Per unit incl. 2 persons and electricity	£ 16.95 - £ 22.45
extra person	£ 2.00
child (4-15 yrs)	£ 1.35
dog	£ 2.50

See advertisement on page 281

Comrie

Twenty Shilling Wood Caravan Park

Comrie PH6 2JY (Perth and Kinross) T: 01764 670411. E: alowe20@aol.com
alanrogers.com/UK7310

Everyone gets a warm welcome from the Lowe family when they arrive at Twenty Shilling Wood. Set amongst 10.5 acres of wooded hillside, this unusual park has a few touring pitches for caravans and motorcaravans (no tents), plus a number of owner occupied caravan holiday homes. However, with terracing and landscaping, not many of these are visible and flowering trees and shrubs help to hide them. The lowest level is the entrance where there is a late arrivals area and visitor car park. You will be escorted to your pitch. There are just ten level touring pitches on gravel with grass bays between them, all with electricity hook-ups (10A). Television reception is poor.

Facilities

Clean and spacious toilet blocks have some washbasins in cubicles for both men and women. Dishwashing area and laundry. No shop but rolls, milk and papers can be ordered at reception. Games room with pool table, table tennis (both free) and lounge area with comfortable seating and well stocked library. Fenced adventure playground for all ages. Entrance barrier (£10 deposit for card). Only two dogs per pitch are accepted. Off site: Buses pass the gate. Comrie is 1 mile where most things can be purchased. Golf and fishing within 1 mile. Auchingarrich Wildlife centre 2.5 miles. Riding and bicycle hire 6 miles. Glen Turret, Scotland's oldest distillery at Crieff 7 miles. Watersports at Loch Earn 11 miles.

Open: 17 March - 22 October.

Directions

Park is on north side of A85 Crieff - Lochearmead road, about 0.75 miles west of B827 junction, 0.5 miles west of Comrie. GPS: 56.375217, -4.0065

Charges guide

Per unit incl. 2 persons and electricity	£ 16.00
extra person (over 2 yrs)	£ 1.75
dog (max. 2)	free
awning (rock pegs required)	£ 1.50

Connel

Oban Camping & Caravanning Club Site

Barcaldine, By Connel PA37 1SG (Argyll and Bute) T: 01631 720348

alanrogers.com/UK7810

Owned by the Camping and Caravanning Club, this site at Barcaldine, 12 miles north of Oban, is a small, intimate site taking 75 units. Arranged within the old walled garden of Barcaldine House, the walls give it some protection from the wind and make it quite a sun trap. There are 23 level, fairly small pitches with hardstanding and 52 electrical hook-ups (16A). It can be wet underfoot in bad weather. Being a small site, it has a very cosy feel to it, due no doubt to the friendly welcome new arrivals receive.

Facilities	Directions
The central toilet block can be heated and is kept very clean with free hot showers, hairdryers and plenty of washbasins and WCs. Excellent unit for disabled visitors. Laundry. Motorcaravan service point. Small shop open a few hours each day for basic provisions and gas. Small play area with effective safety base. WiFi (charged). Off site: Sea Life Centre 2 miles. Bus every hour at gate.	Entrance is off the A828 road on south side of Loch Creran, 6 miles north of Connel Bridge. From the south, go past Barcaldine House and site is 300 yds. on right. GPS: 56.5265, -5.309933

Open: 29 March - 5 November.

Charges 2012

Per person	£ 5.95 - £ 9.35
child (6-18 yrs)	£ 2.70 - £ 2.95
non-member pitch fee	£ 7.10

Crail

Sauchope Links Park

Crail KY10 3XJ (Fife) T: 01333 450460. E: info@sauchope.co.uk

alanrogers.com/UK7285

Sauchope Links Park is a member of the Largo Leisure Parks group with a good range of facilities on offer, notably a heated swimming pool, an indoor recreation room and a play area for children. The site's location is very attractive with miles of rocky shore to be explored. Pitches here are grassy and of a good size. A number of fully serviced pitches are available and also hardstandings. Alternatively, a number of mobile homes and micro lodges (small wooden chalets) are available for rent.

Facilities	Directions
Small shop. Games room. Play areas. Tourist information. Mobile homes and other accommodation for rent. Off site: Top class golf (Crail golf club is the 7th oldest in the world and the Royal and Ancient club at St Andrews needs little introduction). Walking and cycle tracks. Fishing. Riding. Scone Palace. Craigtoun Country Park.	Approaching from St Andrews on A918, on entering Crail at a sharp right hand corner, turn left down an unclassified road. Site is signed 400 yds. on right. Follow signs to the site, which is down by the sea. GPS: 56.261606, -2.612724

Open: 21 March - 31 October.

Charges guide

Per unit incl. 2 persons and electricity	£ 16.00 - £ 22.00
extra person	£ 5.00

Crieff

Braidhaugh Holiday Park

South Bridgend, Crieff PH7 4DH (Perth and Kinross) T: 01764 652951. E: info@braidhaugh.co.uk

alanrogers.com/UK7275

Braidhaugh is a member of the Largo Leisure Parks group and is situated on the banks of the River Earn among the scenic surroundings of Perthshire. There are 39 touring pitches, all with electricity, water and drainage. The site is well located for exploring Central Scotland, as well as being within walking distance of shops, restaurants, places of interest and many sporting facilities. The Earn is renowned for its salmon and trout fishing and permits can be purchased from the reception. The small shop stocks the essentials and a larger supermarket is close at hand. Other on-site amenities include a games room with TV. For younger children, there is an outdoor play area and the public play ground next to the park provides a larger play area and space for ball games.

Facilities	Directions
Small shop. Games room. Play areas. Fishing. Tourist information. Mobile homes and other accommodation for rent. Off site: Top class golf (courses at Muthill, Crieff and Comrie). Walking and cycle tracks. Fishing. Riding. Leisure centre.	Approaching from Perth, drive through Crieff and turn left onto A822 (Stirling). At bottom of hill cross a bridge over River Earn. Turn right immediately after the bridge and take the first right to enter park. GPS: 56.366771, -3.853455

Open: All year.

Charges guide

Per unit incl. 2 persons and electricity	£ 20.00 - £ 23.00

For latest campsite news visit

alanrogers.com

Dalbeattie

Sandyhills Bay Leisure Park

Sandyhills, Dalbeattie DG5 4NY (Dumfries and Galloway) T: 01387 780257. E: info@gillespie-leisure.co.uk

alanrogers.com/UK6880

Sandyhills Bay is a small, quiet park beside a sheltered, sandy beach. Reception is on the left through a car park used by visitors either walking the hills or enjoying the beach. Beyond is a large flat camping area, above which, divided by a tree lined hedge, are 60 pitches, 36 taken by holiday homes situated around the perimeter. The 24 touring pitches, most with 16A electricity connections are in the centre of the flat grass area. Wooden wigwams with a terrace and picnic bench are available to rent. This is an excellent family park, with the beach and a children's play area on the park. Within walking distance, at Barend, is an approved riding centre suitable for all the family. There is a well stocked licensed shop and a takeaway with table and chairs outside from where you can enjoy the well kept garden and splendid views across the Solway.

Facilities

The sanitary facilities are of traditional design, situated in one central block to the side of the touring area. Laundry room (tokens from reception). Shop. Adventure play area by the beach. Visitors can also use the facilities at Brighouse Bay, the largest park in the Gillespie Group. Barrier at entrance and beach car park (returnable deposit). Off site: Clifftop walk from Sandyhills to Rockcliffe 10 miles. Pleasant drive to Rockcliffe and Kippford, a well known sailing centre. Golf and riding 500 yds. Bicycle hire 2 miles. Fishing 10 miles.

Open: Easter/1 April - 31 October.

Directions

From Dumfries take A710 Solway coast road (about 16 miles). Site is on left just after signs for Sandyhills. GPS: 54.879017, -3.731033

Charges guide

Per unit incl. 2 persons	
and electricity	£ 16.95 - £ 22.45
extra person	£ 2.10
child (4-15 yrs)	£ 1.35
dog	£ 2.50

See advertisement on page 281

Dalbeattie

Glenearly Caravan Park

Dalbeattie DG5 4NE (Dumfries and Galloway) T: 01556 611393. E: enquiries@glenearlycaravanpark.co.uk

alanrogers.com/UK6870

Glenearly is owned and managed by Mr and Mrs Jardine. Rurally located, it has been tastefully developed from farmland into a touring and mobile home, all year park. There are 39 marked, open pitches, all with 16A electrical connections and TV, most on hardstandings. Seasonal units use some pitches. Walls and shrubs divide the touring section from the caravan holiday homes (two for rent), with mature trees around the perimeter. There are attractive views over the hills and forest of Barhill and buzzards, yellow wagtails, woodpeckers and goldfinch are some of the birds that can be seen, along with the park's own donkeys and ponies. This is a very well kept, well designed park.

Facilities

Situated in the centre of the touring area, the toilets and showers are fitted out to a high standard. Unit for disabled visitors and families. Laundry room with washing machines and dryer and an outside drying area. Large games room. Play area. Max. 2 dogs accepted. Off site: Shops, pubs, restaurants, etc. at Dalbeattie. Golf 1 mile. Fishing and riding 5 miles. Beach 5 miles. Bicycle hire 10 miles.

Open: All year.

Directions

From Dumfries take A711 towards Dalbeattie. 6 miles beyond Beeswing, after passing sign for Edingham Farm, park is signed with entrance on right (beside a bungalow). GPS: 54.944867, -3.822283

Charges guide

Per unit incl. 2 persons	
and electricity	£ 16.50 - £ 18.50
extra person (over 5 yrs)	£ 2.00
dog (max. 2)	free

Dumfries

Southerness Holiday Village

Southerness, Dumfries DG2 8AZ (Dumfries and Galloway) T: 01387 880256.
E: enquiries@parkdeanholidays.co.uk **alanrogers.com/UK6875**

Set beside a two mile stretch of sandy beach, at the foot of the beautiful Galloway Hills, is Southerness Holiday Village. Part of the Parkdean Group, it is a large park with the main emphasis on caravan holiday homes. However, there are also 100 open plan pitches for caravans, motorcaravans and tents. Set away from the static units, these are divided into two areas, some on level hardstanding with water connection, others on grass and all with 16A electrical connections. The light and airy reception office displays local information including a weekly 'What's On' programme as the main leisure complex is located a short walk from the touring area. This park is well organised with lots going on for all the family.

Facilities	Directions
A modern toilet block provides en-suite facilities throughout (key entry). Well maintained, it is kept very clean by on-site wardens. Excellent unit for disabled visitors. Well equipped laundry. Shop. Bar with large TV. Bistro, takeaway and coffee shop. Indoor swimming pool. Indoor soft play area. Amusement arcade. Comprehensive evening entertainment programme in the Sunset Show bar. Outdoor adventure play area. Nature trails. Beach. Off site: Golf course adjacent. Fishing 2.5 miles. Bicycle hire 3 miles. Riding 9 miles. Coastal drive to Rockcliffe and Kippford, a well known sailing centre. Bus from outside gate (limited servce).	From Dumfries take A710 Solway Coast road for about 10 miles. Sign for Holiday Village is on the left. GPS: 54.87613, -3.60037

Charges guide

Per unit incl. 4 persons	£ 14.00 - £ 31.50
incl. services	£ 16.00 - £ 35.50
extra person	£ 2.50 - £ 3.50
dog	£ 2.00 - £ 3.00

Open: Before Easter - 31 October.

Dunbar

Belhaven Bay Caravan & Camping Park

Belhaven Bay, West Barns, Dunbar EH42 1TU (East Lothian) T: 01368 865956.
E: belhaven@meadowhead.co.uk **alanrogers.com/UK7065**

Located in the John Muir Country Park, Belhaven Bay Caravan Park is just one mile from the historic town of Dunbar, where the ancient castle ruin stands guard over the town's twin harbours. This is an excellent family park with easy access to the beach and to the clifftop trail which has spectacular views capturing the beauty of the countryside and seascapes. The park's 66 caravan holiday homes (five for rent) are located quite separately from the touring and tent areas. These are surrounded by mature trees and are arranged in large open bays. There is a new tent and touring area with electricity points, so now there are 60 reasonably level, mostly grass touring pitches, 48 with electricity (10A). There is much to see nearby with Dunbar's Lifeboat and underground museums, golf courses, a local smokery and the Belhaven Brewery. Attractions for children include the John Muir Country Park, Lauderdale Park and a tropical leisure pool. During daytime some train noise may be heard on the park.

Facilities	Directions
Facilities are central and include a unit for disabled visitors. Laundry room. Motorcaravan service point. Reception also has a small shop and tourist information. Cyber Café and WiFi Internet access. Play area and ball game area. Off site: Bus stop at entrance. Golf 1 mile. Riding and boat launching 2 miles.	From the A1 (north or south) exit at the Thistley Cross roundabout west of Dunbar. Park is about 1 mile down the A1087 towards Dunbar. GPS: 55.996767, -2.545117

Open: 13 March - 31 October.

See advertisement on page 275

Charges guide

Per unit incl. 2 persons and electricity	£ 17.50 - £ 26.50
extra person (over 5 yrs)	£ 5.00
tent, 2 persons with car	£ 9.00 - £ 15.00
dog	£ 3.00

Dunbar

Thurston Manor Leisure Park

Innerwick, Dunbar EH42 1SA (East Lothian) T: 01368 840643. E: info@thurstonmanor.co.uk

alanrogers.com/UK7075

In a rural setting and nestling at the foot of the Lammermuir hills, this holiday park offers either a restful or a lively stay. It is close to historic Dunbar with its beaches, harbour and ruined castle. The 129 touring pitches are set away from the 510 holiday homes. All have 10A electricity connections. Thirty of these are 'super pitches with electricity, water and drainage. The indoor heated swimming pool and leisure complex offer space to relax and work out. There are woodland walks, safe play areas for children and fishing in a well stocked pond.

Facilities

The clean, well equipped and fully heated sanitary block provides constant hot water for showering, dishwashing and family bathing. Mini market. Restaurant and sports bar. Leisure centre with heated swimming pool (10x6 m), sauna, steam room, fitness room and solarium. Children's play areas. Function room with live family entertainment. WiFi. Off site: Riding and beach 2 miles. Bicycle hire and sailing 4 miles. Golf 5 miles.

Open: 1 March - 7 January.

Directions

From the North or South on the A1 take the Innerwick turnoff (near Dunbar). Follow the road for half a mile. Thurston Leisure Park is on the right hand side. GPS: 55.959847, -2.46221

Charges guide

Per unit incl. 2 persons and electricity	£ 19.00 - £ 29.50
extra person	£ 2.00
dog	£ 3.00

Durness

Sango Sands Oasis Caravan & Camping Site

Durness via Lairg IV27 4PZ (Highland) T: 01971 511726. E: keith.durness@btinternet.com

alanrogers.com/UK7735

Sango Sands Oasis is a quiet, ten-acre site overlooking the beautiful Sango Bay, a Blue Flag beach. The site was established by the family in 1978 and they have worked hard improving the facilities over the years. There are 82 pitches for tents and touring caravans, 48 with electricity hook-ups (16A). The land is well drained and fairly level. It is possible to see whales, porpoise, dolphins and seals from the site plus a variety of sea birds which nest nearby. An ideal area for walkers, including the less adventurous, there are numerous marked paths and there is an excellent variety of angling, from rivers to the sea.

Facilities

Traditional toilet and shower blocks are lit at night but a torch may be useful. Free showers with curtains. Showers and toilets are separate. With the beach so close don't be surprised to find sand in the showers. En-suite facilities for disabled visitors. Laundry with sinks, washing machines, dryers, irons and boards. Campers' kitchen with cooking rings. Café, bar and licensed restaurant. TV. Games room with pool and darts. Off site: Two grocery stores, post office, ATM, petrol, diesel and gas supplies in the village. Visitor Centre with extensive information on the area. Golf 1.5 miles. Boat launching 2 miles.

Open: All year.

Directions

From Thurso take the North Coast road (A836 as far as Tongue, where it continues on as the A838 to Durness). Site is on the right as you go through the village. From Ullapool follow A835 north to Ledmore junction and turn left on the A837. After 8 miles turn right onto the A894 and continue to Laxford Bridge. Turn left on A838. Durness is 19 miles further on this road. Site is on the left going through the village. GPS: 58.56449, -4.74221

Charges guide

Per person	£ 6.20
child (5-15 yrs)	£ 2.20 - £ 3.80
electricity	£ 3.50

For latest campsite news visit

alanrogers.com

Edinburgh

Linwater Caravan Park

West Clifton, East Calder, Edinburgh EH53 0HT (Edinburgh) T: 01313 333326. E: linwater@supanet.com

alanrogers.com/UK7045

This delightful, small, family run park is set in the countryside but is still close to the city of Edinburgh. The park is level and the 60 large touring pitches are a mixture of grass and hardstanding; 49 have 16A electricity connections. Parts of the park are screened off by trees and fences. Two sides are sheltered by trees and shrubs and one side is open with views over fields. With just the occasional sound of aircraft from the airport, it is difficult to believe that you are so close to a major city. Linwater is a useful park for visiting Edinburgh and areas outside the city. The reception area has a wealth of information on places to visit. Just four miles down the road is a park and ride scheme and the purchase of a Day Saver ticket is a cheap way to get into Edinburgh and to explore the area. The Falkirk Wheel, houses, castles and gardens are all within easy reach.

Facilities

The modern and well maintained heated sanitary block has private cabins. Facilities for disabled visitors. Laundry. Gas supplies. Milk, bread and newspapers to order (by 21.00 for the next morning). Home produced free range eggs and bacon from reception (and strawberries in season). Sand pit. Three timber tents for hire. Off site: Fishing 1 mile.

Open: 13 March - 1 November.

Directions

From the A720 Edinburgh bypass, leave at sign for Wilkieston on the A7. In Wilkieston turn right at traffic lights (park signed). Continue to next sign indicating left and site 1 mile further on the right. GPS: 55.91104, -3.43588

Charges guide

Per unit incl. 2 persons	£ 14.00 - £ 20.00
tent incl. 2 persons	£ 12.00 - £ 18.00

A family-run touring park just west of Edinburgh with easy access to Edinburgh, Royal Highland Showground and Falkirk Wheel. Excellent amenities and lovely walks to Canal and Country Park. Call in on your way north or south, or stay awhile, you will be most welcome.

Linwater Caravan Park, West Clifton, East Calder, West Lothian, EH53 0HT Tel: 0131 333 3326 queries@linwater.co.uk www.linwater.co.uk

Edinburgh

Edinburgh Caravan Club Site

35-37 Marine Drive, Edinburgh EH4 5EN (Edinburgh) T: 01313 126874

alanrogers.com/UK7050

Situated as it is on the northern outskirts and within easy reach of the city of Edinburgh, this large, busy Caravan Club site (open to non members) provides an ideal base for touring. Enter the site through rather grand gates to find the visitors' car park and reception to the left. There are 147 large flat pitches (103 hardstandings, 12 with water tap and waste water disposal) with electric hook-ups (16A) and TV aerial, and provision for 50 tents in a separate field (hook-ups available) with a covered cooking shelter and bicycle stands close by.

Facilities

Two heated, well kept toilet blocks provide washbasins in cubicles, hair and hand dryers, an en-suite room for campers with disabilities, plus a baby and toddler room with child-size facilities. Each block houses a dishwashing and vegetable preparation area, and a laundry. Drying room. No shop, but milk, bread, and newspapers can be ordered, with ice creams and gas from reception. Fenced play area. Boules. Dog walk in the only natural wood in Edinburgh (part of the site). WiFi. Off site: Bicycle hire nearby. Health club (with Internet access) 400 yds. – ask at site for introduction card.

Open: All year.

Directions

Turn right off A720 at Gogar roundabout at end of bypass (signed City Centre, A8). Shortly turn left on to A902 (Forth Road Bridge), then right onto A90. At Blackhall junction traffic lights fork left into Telford Road (A902). At Crewe Toll roundabout turn left (B9085) and at T-junction (after bridge) turn right at traffic lights towards Leith, A901. Turn left at traffic lights (Silverknowes, Davidson's Mains). In half a mile at roundabout turn right into Marine Drive. Site is half a mile on the left. GPS: 55.97755, -3.2645

Charges guide

Per person	£ 5.10 - £ 6.90
child (5-16 yrs)	£ 1.55 - £ 2.55
pitch incl. electricity (non-member)	£ 13.10 - £ 16.60
Tent campers apply to site.	

Edinburgh

Mortonhall Caravan & Camping Park

38 Mortonhall Gate, Frogston Road East, Edinburgh EH16 6TJ (Edinburgh) T: 01316 641533.
E: mortonhall@meadowhead.co.uk **alanrogers.com/UK6990**

Mortonhall Park makes a good base to see the historic city of Edinburgh and buses to the city leave from the park entrance every ten minutes (parking in Edinburgh is not easy). Although only four miles from the city centre, Mortonhall is in quiet mature parkland, in the grounds of the Mortonhall estate, and easy to find with access off the bypass. There is room for 250 units, mostly on numbered pitches on a slight slope with nothing to separate them, but marked by jockey wheel points. Over 180 places have electricity (10/16A), several with hardstanding, water and drainage as well, and there are many places for tents. The park is very popular but only part is reserved and tourists arriving early may find space. An attractive courtyard development houses a lounge bar and restaurant, open all year and to all, with good value meals in pleasant surroundings. There are mobile homes (20) and wooden family camping cabins (wigwams) for rent.

Facilities

Two modern toilet blocks with outside, but covered dishwashing sinks, but the only cabins are in the third excellent facility at the top of the park, which has eight unisex units incorporating shower, washbasin and WC. The courtyard area provides further basic facilities and Portacabin type units are added for the high season to serve the large number of tents. Facilities for disabled visitors. Laundry room with washing machines and dryer. Motorcaravan services. Bar/restaurant. Self-service shop (all season). Games and TV rooms. Play area. Late arrivals area with hook-ups. Torches useful in early and late season. Security lockers. Internet access at reception (£1 per half an hour). WiFi Internet access (£5 per day). Off site: Bus from site gate. Riding, golf courses and driving range 2 miles. Bicycle hire 4 miles.

Open: 20 March - 4 January.

Directions

Park is well signed south of the city, 5 minutes from A720 city bypass. Take the Mortonhall exit from the Straiton junction and follow camping signs. Entrance road is alongside the Klondyke Garden Centre. GPS: 55.902889, -3.181705

Charges guide

Per unit incl. 2 persons and electricity	£ 16.50 - £ 29.00
tent pitch (4 persons)	£ 13.50 - £ 24.75
extra person (5 yrs and over)	£ 5.00
dog	£ 3.00

Fort William

Glen Nevis Caravan & Camping Park

Glen Nevis, Fort William PH33 6SX (Highland) T: 01397 702191. E: camping@glen-nevis.co.uk

alanrogers.com/UK7830

Just outside Fort William, in a most attractive and quiet situation with views of Ben Nevis, this spacious park is used by those on active pursuits as well as sightseeing tourists. It comprises eight quite large fields, divided between caravans, motorcaravans and tents (steel pegs required). It is licensed for 250 touring caravans but with no specific tent limits. The large touring pitches, many with hardstanding, are marked with wooden fence dividers, 174 with electricity (13A) and 100 also have water and drainage. The park becomes full in the peak months but there are vacancies each day. If reception is closed (possible in low season) you site yourself. There are regular security patrols at night in busy periods. The park's own modern restaurant and bar with good value bar meals is a short stroll from the park, open to all. A well managed park with bustling, but pleasing ambiance, watched over by Ben Nevis. Around 1,000 acres of the Glen Nevis estate are open to campers to see the wildlife and explore this lovely area.

Facilities

The four modern toilet blocks with showers (extra showers in two blocks); and units for visitors with disabilities. An excellent block in Nevis Park (one of the eight camping fields) has some washbasins in cubicles, showers, further facilities for disabled visitors, a second large laundry room and dishwashing sinks. Motorcaravan service point. Shop (Easter-mid Oct), barbecue area and snack bar (May-mid Sept). Play area on bark.
Off site: Pony trekking, golf and fishing nearby.

Open: 15 March - 31 October.

Directions

Turn off A82 to east at roundabout just north of Fort William following camp sign.
GPS: 56.804517, -5.073917

Charges guide

Per person	£ 1.80 - £ 3.00
child (5-15 yrs)	£ 1.00 - £ 1.60
pitch incl. awning	£ 8.30 - £ 11.40
serviced pitch plus	£ 3.50 - £ 4.00

Fort William

Linnhe Lochside Holidays

Corpach, Fort William PH33 7NL (Highland) T: 01397 772376. E: relax@linnhe-lochside-holidays.co.uk

alanrogers.com/UK7850

This quiet well run park has a very peaceful situation overlooking Loch Eil, and it is beautifully landscaped with wonderful views. There are individual pitches with hardstanding for 65 touring units (12 seasonal) on terraces leading down to the water's edge. They include 32 with electricity connection (16A), water and drainage, plus 30 with electricity only (10A). A separate area on the lochside takes 15 small tents (no reservation). There are also 60 caravan holiday homes and 14 centrally heated pine chalets for hire. Fishing is free on Loch Eil and you are welcome to fish from the park's private beach or bring your own boat and use the slipway and dinghy park. About five miles from Fort William on 'The Road to the Isles', the park is conveniently placed for touring the Western Highlands. Easily accessible are Ben Nevis and the Nevis range (cable car to 2,000 ft), geological, Jacobite and Commando museums, distillery visits, seal island trips, the Mallaig steam railway and the Caledonian Canal.

Facilities

Toilet facilities are excellent, heated in the cooler months and include baths (£1). Dishwashing room. First class laundry and separate outdoor clothing drying room (charged per night). Self-service, licensed shop (end May-end Sept). Gas supplies. Barbecue area. Toddlers' play room and two well equipped play areas on safe standing. Large motorcaravans are accepted but it is best to book first. Caravan storage. Up to two dogs per pitch are accepted. Off site: Bicycle hire 2.5 miles. Riding, golf and skiing 5 miles.

Open: 15 December - 31 October.

Directions

Park entrance is off A830 Fort William - Mallaig road, 1 mile west of Corpach. GPS: 56.847817, -5.16025

Charges guide

Per unit incl. 2 persons and electricity	£ 17.00 - £ 19.00
extra person	£ 3.00
child (3-15 yrs)	£ 1.75
dog	£ 1.00

Seasonal rates available.

Touring, camping, chalets and caravans.
Fantastic views.
Wildlife and free fishing.
Friendly 5 star park.

Linnhe LOCHSIDE HOLIDAYS

Corpach, Fort William Scotland PH33 7NL

Tel. 01397772376 ● www.linnhe-lochside-holidays.co.uk

Glencoe

Invercoe Caravan & Camping Park

Invercoe, Glencoe PH49 4HP (Argyll and Bute) T: 01855 811210. E: holidays@invercoe.co.uk

alanrogers.com/UK7790

On the edge of Loch Leven, surrounded by mountains and forest, Iain and Lynn Brown are continually developing this attractively located park in its magnificent historical setting. It provides 63 pitches for caravans, motorcaravans and tents on level grass (can be a bit wet in bad weather) with gravel access roads (some hardstandings). You choose your own numbered pitch, those at the loch side being very popular. The only rules imposed are necessary for safety because the owners prefer their guests to feel free and enjoy themselves. This is a park you will want to return to again and again. There is much to do for the active visitor with hill walking, climbing, boating, pony riding and sea loch or fresh water fishing in this Area of Outstanding Natural Beauty.

Facilities

The well refurbished toilet block can be heated. Dishwashing under cover, excellent laundry facilities with a drying room. New large under cover eating area. Motorcaravan service point comprising multi-drainage point, fresh water, dustbins, and chemical disposal point. Shop (Easter-end Oct). Play area with swings. Fishing. New fore-shore hardstanding with slipway. WiFi. Off site: The village with pub and restaurant is within walking distance. Visitors' Centre at Glencoe 2 miles. Bicycle hire 2 miles. Golf 3 miles.

Open: All year.

Directions

Follow A82 Crianlarich - Fort William road to Glencoe village and turn onto the B863; park is 0.5 miles along, well signed. GPS: 56.686567, -5.105983

Charges guide

Per unit incl. 2 persons and electricity	£ 20.00
extra person	£ 4.00
child (3-15 yrs)	£ 2.00

Senior citizens less £1 per person outside July/Aug.

Glendaruel

Glendaruel Caravan Park

Glendaruel PA22 3AB (Argyll and Bute) T: 01369 820267. E: mail@glendaruelcaravanpark.co.uk

alanrogers.com/UK7860

Glendaruel is in South Argyll, in the area of Scotland bounded by the Kyles of Bute and Loch Fyne, yet is less than two hours by road from Glasgow and serviced by ferries from Gourock and the Isle of Bute. There is also a service between Tarbert and Portavadie. Set in the peaceful wooded gardens of the former Glendaruel House in a secluded glen surrounded by the Cowal hills, it makes an ideal centre for touring this beautiful area. The park takes 35 units on numbered hardstandings with electricity (10A), plus 15 tents, on flat oval meadows bordered by over 50 different varieties of mature trees. In a separate area are 28 privately owned holiday homes plus two for rent.

Facilities

The toilet block is ageing but it is kept very neat and tidy and can be heated. Washing machine and dryer. A covered area has picnic tables for use in bad weather and dishwashing sinks. Shop (hours may be limited in low season). Gas available. Games room with pool table, table tennis and video games. Behind the laundry is a children's play centre for under 12s and additional play field. Fishing. Torches advised. Off site: Sea fishing and boat slipway 5 miles, adventure centre (assault courses, abseiling and rafting) and sailing school close by. Golf 12 miles.

Open: 28 March - 26 October.

Directions

Entrance is off A886 road 13 miles south of Strachur. Alternatively there are two ferry services from Gourock to Dunoon, then on B836 which joins the A886 about 4 miles south of the park - this route not recommended for touring caravans. Do not use sat nav as this takes you along a very narrow back road and there is no entrance from here. Note: the park has discount arrangements with Western Ferries so contact the park before making arrangements (allow 7 days for postage of tickets). GPS: 56.033967, -5.212833

Charges guide

Per unit incl. 2 persons and electricity	£ 18.00
child (3-15 yrs)	£ 1.75

Special weekly rates and senior citizen discount outside July/Aug.

Grantown-on-Spey

Grantown-on-Spey Caravan Park

Seafield Avenue, Grantown-on-Spey PH26 3JQ (Highland) T: 01479 872474.
E: warden@caravanscotland.com **alanrogers.com/UK7670**

John Fleming takes care of this excellent park. Peacefully situated on the outskirts of the town, with views of the mountains in the distance, the park consists of well-tended gravel and grass pitches. There are 125 pitches for caravans and motorcaravans, all with electricity (10/16A) and 69 offer fresh and waste water facilities. In addition to this, a number of super pitches also offer 16A electricity, WiFi Internet connection and individual Sky TV box. A further 12 pitches are used for seasonal occupation and there is space for 50 or more tents. The park is affiliated to the Caravan Club. Trees and flowers are a feature of this attractive, landscaped location.

Facilities

The modern toilet and shower block has a laundry and drying room. A further block provides good, clean toilet facilities, with new washing cabins for ladies. Facilities for disabled visitors. Motorcaravan service point. Gas, ice creams, cold drinks and camping accessories available at reception. Games room. WiFi throughout (charged). Caravan and motorcaravan storage. Off site: Fishing, golf and mountain bike hire within 1 mile. Riding 3 miles.

Open: All year excl. Christmas and New Year.

Directions

Go into the town. Turn north at Bank of Scotland. Park straight ahead half a mile. GPS: 57.3348, -3.618617

Charges guide

Per unit incl. 2 persons and 10A electricity	£ 18.30 - £ 25.00
small 2-man tent	£ 10.00 - £ 15.00
extra person	£ 2.00 - £ 4.00

Huntly

Huntly Castle Caravan Park

The Meadow, Huntly AB54 4UJ (Aberdeenshire) T: 01466 794999. E: enquiries@huntlycastle.co.uk
alanrogers.com/UK7550

Huntly Caravan Park was opened in '95 and its hardworking owners, the Ballantynes, are justly proud of their neat, well landscaped 15 acre site that is affiliated to the Caravan Club (non members welcome). The 10 level grass and 50 hardstanding touring pitches are separated and numbered, with everyone shown to their pitch. Arranged in three bays with banks of heathers and flowering shrubs separating them, most pitches have electric hook-ups (16A) and 15 are fully serviced with water and waste water. Two bays have central play areas and all three have easy access to a toilet block.

Facilities

The three heated toilet blocks are well maintained, with washbasins (in cubicles for ladies) and large showers. Each block has a family shower room, dishwashing sinks and a room for disabled visitors. Laundry room. Milk and papers to order at reception. Activity centre (charged; also open to public; open weekends and all local school holidays). WiFi (charged). Off site: Huntly 10 minutes walk. Fishing, golf and bicycle hire within 1 mile. Riding 5 miles.

Open: 26 March - 28 October.

Directions

Site is well signed from A96 Keith - Aberdeen road. GPS: 57.45205, -2.7916

Charges guide

Per unit incl. 2 persons and electricity	£ 17.30 - £ 22.75
extra person	£ 5.25 - £ 6.90
child (5-16 yrs)	£ 1.65 - £ 2.75

Kildonan

Seal Shore Camping & Touring Site

Kildonan, Isle of Arran KA27 8SE (North Ayrshire) T: 01770 820320. E: enquiries@campingarran.com
alanrogers.com/UK7025

A warm welcome awaits here on the island of Arran from the resident owner, Maurice Deighton and his daughter. Located on the southernmost point of the island, this is a quiet and peaceful park situated along its own private beach with wonderful sea views. The open, grassy area, sloping in parts, takes caravans, motorcaravans and tents with ten electricity connections (16A). The reception doubles as a shop selling basics with a TV room adjacent. There are communal picnic and barbecue areas. The Kildonan Hotel is next door serving restaurant and bar meals. Permits are available for loch fishing and charters available from the owner, a registered fisherman. Golfers can choose from seven courses.

Facilities

The good toilet block is clean and tidy and includes full facilities for disabled visitors that double as a baby room. Laundry room with washing machine, dryers and iron. Indoor dishwashing with fridge and freezer for campers' use. Shop. Camping gas. Beach. Fishing. Sailing. Covered barbecue area. Off site: Nearest golf course at Whiting 6 miles. Heritage Museum in Brodick.

Open: March - October.

Directions

From Brodick take A841 south for 12 miles to sign for Kildonan. Site is downhill, on seashore, next to Kildonan Hotel. GPS: 55.44100, -5.11397

Charges guide

Per unit incl. 2 persons and electricity	£ 16.50
extra person	£ 6.00
child (5-15 yrs)	£ 3.00
tent pitch	£ 1.00 - £ 4.00

For latest campsite news visit
alanrogers.com

Killin

Loch Tay Highland Lodges

Milton Morenish Estate, by Killin, Loch Tay FK21 8TY (Perth and Kinross) T: 01567 820323.
E: info@lochtay-vacations.co.uk **alanrogers.com/UK7315**

Loch Tay Highland Lodges is situated in the central highlands on the shores of Loch Tay. Arguably one of the most beautiful areas of Scotland surrounded by mountains, rivers and lochs and still within easy driving distance of Edinburgh, Stirling and Glasgow. Loch Tay Highland Lodges is just a short drive from the scenic village of Killin and the picturesque Falls of Dochart. Highland Perthshire is renowned for its wealth of historical sites, natural beauty and wildlife. Tent pitches are grassy and of a good size. Additionally, a good selection of chalets and lodges are available for rent. Fishing is understandably popular and the site offers salmon fishing packages. Motorcaravans are not accepted.

Facilities

Restaurant. Small shop. Games room. Play area. Equestrian centre. Marina. Sailing. Archery. Canoeing. Quad biking. Chalets, yurts, tepees and other accommodation for rent. No camp fires. Off site: Deer stalking. White-water rafting. Wildlife safaris. Golf (Pitlochry, Aberfeldy and Taymouth Castle). Walking and cycle tracks. Fishing. Whisky tours. Ben Lawers nature reserve.

Open: All year.

Directions

Loch Tay Highland Lodges is situated between Aberfeldy and Killin on the A827.
GPS: 56.494024, -4.250357

Charges guide

Per tent	£ 15.00 - £ 18.00

Kirkcudbright

Seaward Caravan Park

Dhoon Bay, Kirkcudbright DG6 4TJ (Dumfries and Galloway) T: 01557 870267. E: info@gillespie-leisure.co.uk
alanrogers.com/UK6900

Seaward Caravan Park is little sister to the much larger Brighouse Bay Holiday Park, 3.5 miles away. Set in an idyllic location overlooking the bay, this park is suitable for all units. The terrain is slightly undulating, but most of the numbered pitches are flat and of a good size. There are 35 pitches (21 hardstandings) designated for caravans and motorcaravans, a further 14 for tents, plus 43 caravan holiday homes (six for hire). All of the pitches for touring units have electricity connections and 12 are also serviced with water and drainage. This is a quiet park with excellent views over the sea, ideally suited for that relaxing holiday or for touring the region.

Facilities

The principal, fully equipped toilet block is to the rear of the touring area. Four rooms with en-suite facilities are also suitable for disabled campers. Well equipped baby room. Laundry facilities. No motorcaravan service point but the manager can lift a manhole cover to empty waste water tanks. The reception/shop stocks basic provisions, books, gifts, gas, and tourist information. Unsupervised heated outdoor swimming pool with sunbathing area (1/5-30/9). Central play area with bark surface, rocking horse, table tennis and picnic tables. Excellent games room. Pitch and putt (charged). Off site: Beach and sea angling adjacent. Kirkcudbright 2.5 miles. Riding or bicycle hire 3.5 miles.

Open: 1 March - 31 October.

Directions

In Kirkcudbright turn onto A755 signed Borgue. Go over river bridge and after 400 yds. turn left onto B727 at international camping sign. Proceed with caution when turning right into site entrance as the turn is tight. GPS: 54.819767, -4.082117

Charges guide

Per unit incl. 2 persons and electricity	£ 17.55 - £ 23.30
extra person	£ 2.10
child (4-15 yrs)	£ 1.65
dog	£ 2.50

See advertisement opposite

For latest campsite news visit
alanrogers.com

Kirkcudbright

Brighouse Bay Holiday Park

Brighouse Bay, Borgue, Kirkcudbright DG6 4TS (Dumfries and Galloway) T: 01557 870267.
E: info@gillespie-leisure.co.uk **alanrogers.com/UK6950**

Hidden away within 1,200 exclusive acres, on a quiet, unspoilt peninsula, this spacious family park is only some 200 yards through bluebell woods from an open, sandy bay. It has exceptional all weather facilities, as well as golf and pony trekking. Over 90 per cent of the 210 touring caravan pitches have electricity (10/16A), some with hardstanding and some with water, drainage and TV aerial. The three tent areas are on fairly flat, undulating ground and some pitches have electricity. There are 120 self-contained holiday caravans and lodges of which about 30 are let, the rest privately owned. On-site leisure facilities include a golf and leisure club with 16.5 m. pool, water features, jacuzzi, steam room, fitness room, games room (all on payment), golf driving range, bowling green and clubhouse bar and bistro. The 18-hole golf course extends onto the headland with superb views over the Irish Sea to the Isle of Man and Cumbria. A nine-hole family golf course is a popular attraction. Like the park, these facilities are open all year. The TRSS Approved Pony Trekking Centre, also open all year, offers treks for complete beginners and a range of hacks for the more experienced. Also available are, riding lessons and stable management sessions for adults and children. This is a well run park of high standards. Member of the Best of British Group.

Facilities

The large, well maintained main toilet block includes 10 unisex cabins with shower, basin and WC, and 12 with washbasin and WC. A second, excellent block next to the tent areas has en-suite shower rooms (one for disabled visitors) and bathroom, separate washing cubicles, showers and baby room. Laundry facilities. Motorcaravan service point. Gas supplies. Licensed shop. Bar, restaurant and takeaway (all year). Golf and Leisure Club with indoor pool (all year). Play area (incl. toddlers' area). Pony trekking. Quad bikes, boating pond, 10-pin bowling, playgrounds, putting. Nature trails. Coarse fishing ponds plus sea angling and an all-tide slipway for boating enthusiasts. Caravan storage. Purpose built chalet for tourist information and leisure facility bookings.

Open: All year.

Directions

In Kirkcudbright turn onto the A755 and cross river bridge. In 400 yds. turn left onto B727 at international camping sign. Or follow Brighouse Bay signs off A75 just east of Gatehouse of Fleet.
GPS: 54.7875, -4.1291

Charges guide

Per unit incl. 2 persons and electricity	£ 19.70 - £ 26.00
extra person	£ 2.65
child (4-15 yrs)	£ 1.80
dog	£ 2.50

Contact park for full charges.
Golf packages in low season.

For latest campsite news visit
alanrogers.com

Kyle of Lochalsh

Reraig Caravan Site

Balmacara, Kyle of Lochalsh IV40 8DH (Highland) T: 01599 566215. E: warden@reraig.com

alanrogers.com/UK7760

This is a small, level park close to Loch Alsh with a wooded hillside behind (criss-crossed with woodland walks). Set mainly on well cut grass, it is sheltered from the prevailing winds by the hill and provides just 45 numbered pitches. There are electrical connections (10A) and 35 hardstandings (two without electricity). Large tents and trailer tents are not accepted at all. Small tents are permitted at the discretion of the owner, so it would be advisable to telephone first if this affects you. Reservations are not taken so it may be best to arrive before late afternoon in July and August.

Facilities

The single sanitary block is kept immaculately clean. Children have their own low basins. Controllable hot showers are on payment (10p for 2 minutes). Sinks for laundry and dishwashing. A slope replaces the small step into the ladies and sink rooms. Motorcaravan drainage point. WiFi throughout (charged). Off site: Adjacent to the park is the Balmacara Hotel (with bar), shop (selling gas), sub-post office and off licence.

Open: 1 May - 30 September.

Directions

On A87, park is 2 miles west of the junction with the A890, beside the Balmacara hotel. GPS: 57.283133, -5.626517

Charges guide

Per unit incl. 2 persons and electricity	£ 14.90
extra person (13 yrs or over)	£ 3.00
awning (May, June, Sept only)	£ 3.00

Lairg

Woodend Camping & Caravan Park

Achnairn, Lairg IV27 4DN (Highland) T: 01549 402248

alanrogers.com/UK7720

Woodend is a delightful, small park overlooking Loch Shin and perfect for hill walkers and backpackers. Peaceful and simple, it is owned and run by Mrs Cathie Ross, who provides a wonderfully warm Scottish welcome to visitors. On a hill with open, panoramic views across the Loch to the hills beyond and all around, the large camping field is undulating and gently sloping with some reasonably flat areas. The park is licensed to take 55 units and most of the 30 electrical hook-ups (16A) are in a line near the top of the field, close to the large, fenced play area which has several items of equipment on grass. There are opportunities for fishing and hill walking.

Facilities

The sanitary facilities are of old design but kept very clean and are quite satisfactory. Laundry with two machines and a dryer. Kitchen with dishwashing sinks and eating room for tent campers. Reception is at the house, Sunday papers, daily milk and bread may be ordered. Fishing licences for the Loch (your catch will be frozen for you). Off site: Mountain bikes can be hired in Lairg 5 miles. Several scenic golf courses within 20-30 miles.

Open: 1 April - 30 September.

Directions

Achnairn is near the southern end of Loch Shin. Turn off the A838 single track road at signs for Woodend. From the A9 coming north take the A836 at Bonar Bridge, 11 miles northwest of Tain. GPS: 58.080267, -4.44705

Charges guide

Per unit incl. electricity	£ 10.00 - £ 12.00
tent	£ 8.00 - £ 10.00

No credit cards.

Lerwick

Clickimin Caravan & Camp Site

Clickimin Leisure Complex, Lochside, Lerwick ZE1 0PJ (Shetlands) T: 01595 741000. E: clickimin.centre@srt.org.uk **alanrogers.com/UK7980**

The caravan and camping site is in the grounds of the Clickimin leisure complex, but it is not dominated by the building with its swimming pool and restaurant, etc. The site is arranged in two tiers which are well laid out with a tarmac road in the centre of each tier. The lower grass tier is separated into areas by shrubs and provides a camping area for 30 tents. The upper tier has 50 touring pitches, each with a large gravel area and divided from its neighbour by a wide concrete section for sitting out. A small lamp post with electricity, water and waste disposal points is provided at each pitch.

Facilities

The modern toilet block is clean and includes a toilet and shower cubicle for disabled visitors. Large, warm and well equipped laundry and drying room with an area for food preparation. Bar (evenings). Café and takeaway. Heated indoor and outdoor swimming pools. Off site: Shop and bicycle hire within 1 mile. Golf 3 miles. Riding 12 miles.

Open: May - September.

Directions

Site is on the west side of Lerwick and is signed as you start to leave Lerwick. Take the A969 north or south. Just before leaving the town is the road North Lochside (turn south) or South Lochside (turn north). Clickimin Leisure Centre is on this road. GPS: 60.15348, -1.15934

Charges guide

Per unit incl. electricity	£ 11.10

Lockerbie

Hoddom Castle Caravan Park

Hoddom, Lockerbie DG11 1AS (Dumfries and Galloway) T: 01576 300251. E: hoddomcastle@aol.com

alanrogers.com/UK6910

The park around Hoddom Castle is landscaped, spacious and well laid out on mainly sloping ground with many mature and beautiful trees, originally part of an arboretum. The drive to the site is just under a mile long with a one way system. Many of the 120 numbered pitches have good views of the castle and have gravel hardstanding with grass for awnings. Most have electrical connections (16A). In front of the castle are flat fields used for tents and caravans with a limited number of electricity hook-ups. The oldest part of Hoddom Castle itself is a 16th-century Borders Pele Tower, or fortified Keep. This was extended to form a residence for a Lancashire cotton magnate, became a youth hostel and was then taken over by the army during WW2. Since then parts have been demolished but the original 'Border Keep' still survives, unfortunately in a semi-derelict state. The site's bar and restaurant have been developed in the courtyard area from the coach houses, and the main ladies' toilet block was the stables. Amenities include a comfortable bar lounge with a TV. The park's nine-hole golf course is in an attractive setting alongside the Annan river, where fishing is possible for salmon and trout (tickets available). Coarse fishing is also possible elsewhere on the estate. This is a peaceful base from which to explore historic southwest Scotland.

Facilities

The main toilet block can be heated and is very well appointed. Washbasins in cubicles, 3 en-suite cubicles with WC and basin (one with baby facilities) and an en-suite shower unit for disabled visitors. Two further tiled blocks, kept very clean, provide washbasins and WCs only. Well equipped laundry room at the castle. Motorcaravan service point. Licensed shop at reception (gas available). Bar, restaurant and takeaway (restricted opening outside high season). Games room. Large, grass play area. Crazy golf. Mountain bike trail. Fishing. Golf. Guided walks (high season). Caravan storage.
Off site: Tennis nearby.

Open: 1 April - 30 October.

Directions

Leave A74M at junction 19 (Ecclefechan) and follow signs to park. Leave A75 at Annan junction (west end of Annan bypass) and follow signs.
GPS: 55.041367, -3.311

Charges guide

Per unit incl. 2 persons	£ 11.50 - £ 18.50
incl. electricity	£ 14.50 - £ 21.50
extra person	£ 3.00
child (7-16 yrs)	£ 1.50

Maybole

Culzean Castle Camping & Caravanning Club Site

Maybole KA19 8JJ (South Ayrshire) T: 01655 760627

alanrogers.com/UK7010

With wonderful views of the Firth of Clyde and over to the Isle of Arran from some pitches, this quiet Camping and Caravanning Club site is next door to Culzean Castle (pronounced Kullayne). Visitors can buy tickets to walk in the grounds (when open) with their 17 miles of footpaths. The campsite has 90 pitches, some level others slightly sloping, and 60 have electrical hook-ups (10A). A few level pitches are suitable for motorcaravans and 20 pitches have hardstanding. American style motorhomes (more than 25 ft) must contact the site prior to arrival as large pitches are limited.

Facilities

The toilet blocks, kept very clean, can be heated and include some washbasins in cubicles. Unit for disabled visitors has a WC, washbasin and shower – an excellent facility. Dishwashing sinks. Well equipped laundry. Small shop for basics opens for short periods morning and evening. Adventure playground. WiFi in some areas (charged). Units over 25 ft. long only accepted by prior arrangement. Off site: Riding 2 miles. Beach 3 miles. Golf 4 miles. Fishing 8 miles. Buses pass the gate.

Open: Easter - 31 October.

Directions

From Maybole follow signs for Culzean Castle and Country Park, turning in the town on B7023 which runs into the A719. Country Park entrance is clearly signed on right after 3.75 miles; entrance to caravan park is on the right in Country Park drive.
GPS: 55.35345, -4.76945

Charges guide

Per person	£ 5.90 - £ 9.05
child (6-18 yrs)	£ 2.65 - £ 2.85
non-member pitch fee	£ 7.10
services	£ 3.55

For latest campsite news visit
alanrogers.com

Maybole

The Ranch Holiday Park

Culzean Road, Maybole KA19 8DU (South Ayrshire) T: 01655 882446

alanrogers.com/UK7015

This holiday park is situated in the Ayrshire countryside, a mile from the small town of Maybole. The Ranch, a Caravan Club affiliated site, is managed by the McAuley family. The park is beautifully set out with 65 spacious touring pitches, all with 16A electricity connections and on level hardstanding. There are also 100 caravan holiday homes with one for rent. The superb facilities include a private leisure centre with an indoor heated pool, sauna, solarium and well equipped gym. This is complete with changing room, toilets, shower and hairdryers. Adjacent is a small, fenced play park for toddlers and to the rear is an enclosed play area for older children.

Facilities

Modern sanitary facilities, recently rebuilt, are clean and well located. There are washbasins in cubicles and large showers. Facilities for disabled visitors. Well equipped laundry with dishwashing area. Small shop in reception with good information area. Indoor heated pool, sauna, solarium and well equipped gym. WiFi throughout (charged). Off site: Golf courses at Turnberry. Fishing at Mochram Loch 1.5 miles. Beach 2 miles. Riding 3 miles.

Open: All year.

Directions

From Maybole turn onto B7023 (signed Culzean Maidens) for 1 mile and site is signed on left. GPS: 55.3559, -4.7061

Charges guide

Per unit incl. 2 persons	
and electricity	£ 12.60 - £ 21.40
extra person	£ 4.10 - £ 6.20
child	£ 1.30 - £ 2.20

Melrose

Gibson Park Caravan Club Site

High Street, Melrose TD6 9RY (Borders) T: 01896 822969

alanrogers.com/UK7030

This is an ideal transit park, being so close to the A68, but is also a perfect base for exploring this Southern Scotland area or indeed a trip to Edinburgh, only 35 miles away, by car or one of the regular buses which run from the park entrance. This small, three acre park has only 60 touring pitches plus, unusually, an extra 12 tent pitches (summer only) next to the adjacent rugby pitch. All touring pitches have electricity (16A) and TV connections (otherwise it is a bad signal here), 57 have hardstanding and ten are serviced with water and drainage. A one-way system on the tarmac roads is in operation.

Facilities

First rate toilet facilities are in a new building with spacious showers, washbasins in cabins, centrally heated and all fitted out with purpose made faced boarding giving a very pleasing finish. Laundry facilities. Separate room with shower and WC for disabled visitors. Motorcaravan service point. Gas is available. WiFi. Security barrier (operated by card). Off site: Situated on the edge of the little town of Melrose, a five minute walk, shops, pubs and restaurants are all within easy reach. Play area.

Open: All year.

Directions

Turn left off A68 Jedburgh - Lauder road at roundabout, 2.5 miles past Newton St Boswell onto A6091 Galashiels road. In about 3.25 miles at roundabout turn right onto B6374 to Melrose. Site is on right at filling station opposite rugby club, just before town centre. GPS: 55.598017, -2.72413

Charges guide

Per person	£ 4.60 - £ 6.20
child (5-16 yrs)	£ 1.30 - £ 2.20
pitch incl. electricity (non-member)	£ 13.15 - £ 16.00

Mintlaw

Aden Country Park Caravan Park

Station Road, Mintlaw AB42 5FQ (Aberdeenshire) T: 01771 623460

alanrogers.com/UK7530

Aden Country Park is owned by the Aberdeenshire local authority and is open to the public. The caravan and camping site is on one side of the park. Beautifully landscaped and well laid out with trees, bushes and hedges, it is kept very neat and tidy. It provides 48 numbered pitches for touring units, with varying degrees of slope (some level) and all with electrical hook-ups (16A), plus an area for tents. There are also 12 caravan holiday homes. The council plan to lease the campsite to private owners from 2012. The park is in a most attractive area and one could spend plenty of time enjoying all it has to offer.

Facilities

The modern toilet block is clean, with good facilities for disabled visitors. It can be heated and provides free, preset hot showers, hairdryer for ladies, and a baby bath. Dishwashing and laundry facilities (metered). Gas supplies. Motorcaravan service point. Small shop in reception area. Restaurant in the Heritage Centre. Games areas. Play equipment. Dog exercise area. Off site: Shops in Mintlaw 0.5 miles. Fishing 1 mile. Riding 2 miles.

Open: Easter - 25 October.

Directions

Approaching Mintlaw from west on A950 road, park is shortly after sign for Mintlaw station. From east, go to the western outskirts of village and entrance is on left – Aden Country Park and Farm Heritage Centre. GPS: 57.52475, -2.026117

Charges guide

Per unit incl. electricity	£ 17.50 - £ 20.00
tent (2 persons)	£ 9.00 - £ 9.50

Monifieth

Riverview Holiday Park

Marine Drive, Monifieth DD5 4NN (Angus) T: 01382 535471. E: info@riverview.co.uk

alanrogers.com/UK7410

A quiet, family park, Riverview overlooks a long sandy beach and has magnificent views over the River Tay towards the Kingdom of Fife and yet is within walking distance of Monifieth town. The park is neatly set out with flowering shrubs and bushes dividing 40 numbered touring pitches. Some enjoying river views, they are grassy and level, each with 16A electricity and two also with water and drainage. Bordering the park are 46 privately owned caravan holiday homes and four to rent. At the entrance to the park is a small reception office and separate tourist information room and a leisure suite with sauna, steam baths and gym (charged). A member of the Best of British Group.

Facilities	Directions
The spotlessly clean toilet block (key entry) has open washbasins, one in a cabin with WC, and preset showers. Baby bath. Facilites for disabled visitors. Well equipped laundry. Leisure suite. Games room and play area. Adventure play area. Off site: Picnic areas and small boat slipway adjacent. Riverview recreation park opposite has football pitches, putting, crazy golf, tennis, bowling and a well equipped adventure play park. Golf 800 yds. Fishing 2 miles. Riding 3 miles. Dundee city 5 miles.	From Dundee follow signs for Monifieth on A930, after passing Tesco. Turn right at sign for golf course and right again under railway bridge. Park is signed on the left. GPS: 56.47995, -2.811533

Open: 1 April - 31 October.

Charges guide

Per unit incl. 2 adults	
and 2 children	£ 20.00 - £ 23.00
extra person	£ 2.00
awning	£ 3.00

Motherwell

Strathclyde Country Park Caravan Site

Strathclyde Country Park, 366 Hamilton Road, Motherwell ML1 3ED (North Lanarkshire) T: 01698 402060. E: strathclydepark@northlan.gov.uk **alanrogers.com/UK7000**

The 1,200 acre Country Park is a large green area less than 15 miles from the centre of Glasgow. Well kept and open to all, it provides many amenities and sports facilities. The touring site, part of the park, is suitable for both overnight or longer stays (max. 14 days) and has 80 numbered pitches for caravans and tents, 70 with electrical connections (10A). Arranged in semi-circular groups on flat grass they are served by made-up access roads and the site is well lit. As it is close to the motorway, there may be some traffic noise.

Facilities	Directions
Four solidly built toilet blocks make a good provision. Enclosed sinks for dishwashing and food preparation. Laundry in two blocks (irons from reception). Block 4 has facilities for visitors with disabilities, block 3 has a baby room. Motorcaravan services. Shop within reception sells basics. Play equipment. Bicycle hire. Barrier card and toilet block key £10 deposit. Off site: Bar and restaurant facilities (100 yds) in the Country Park. Fishing 400 yds.	Take exit 5 from the M74 and follow sign for Strathclyde Country Park. Turn first left for site. GPS: 55.803917, -4.046733

Open: Easter - 18 October.

Charges guide

Per caravan pitch incl. 2 persons	
and electricity	£ 14.75
tent pitch (4 persons)	£ 9.70
extra person	£ 1.45
No credit cards.	

Musselburgh

Drum Mohr Caravan Park

Levenhall, Musselburgh EH21 8JS (East Lothian) T: 01316 656867. E: bookings@drummohr.org

alanrogers.com/UK6980

This family owned, attractively laid out touring park is on the east side of Edinburgh. It is a secluded, well kept modern park, conveniently situated for visits to Edinburgh, the Lothian and Borders regions. It has been carefully landscaped and there are many attractive plants, flowers and hedging. There are 120 individual pitches, 40 with hardstanding, for touring units of any type, well spaced out on gently sloping grass in groups of 12 or more, marked with white posts. All have electric hook-ups and 13 are fully serviced with water and waste water connections. Free space is left for play and recreation.

Facilities	Directions
The two toilet blocks are clean, attractive, of ample size and can be heated. Free hot water to washbasins (one cabin for men, two for ladies in each block) and to four external dishwashing sinks, showers and laundry sinks. Laundry facilities in each block. Motorcaravan service point. Well stocked, shop (gas available, bread and papers to order). Playground on sand. WiFi (on payment).	From Edinburgh follow A1 signs for Berwick-upon-Tweed for 6-7 miles. Turn off for Wallyford and follow camp signs. From south follow A1 taking junction after Tranent village (A199 Musselburgh) and follow signs. GPS: 55.950033, -3.011667

Open: All year.

Charges guide

Per unit incl. 2 persons	
and electricity	£ 18.00 - £ 25.00

For latest campsite news visit

alanrogers.com

North Berwick

Tantallon Caravan & Camping Park

Tantallon Road, North Berwick EH39 5NJ (East Lothian) T: 01620 893348. E: tantallon@meadowhead.co.uk

alanrogers.com/UK7060

Tantallon is a large park with views over the Firth of Forth and the Bass Rock. The park has 147 quite large, grass touring pitches in two lower, more sheltered areas (Law Park), with the rest having good views at the top (Bass Park). Many have some degree of slope. There are 75 electrical connections (10A) and ten pitches also with water and waste water. Each area has its own sanitary facilities, the top block a little way from the end pitches. About 55 caravan holiday homes for sale or hire are in their own areas. Wooden wigwams are also available. This is a mature, well managed park with good facilities. This area is a popular venue for birdwatchers with its world famous gannet colony. Tantallon and Dirleton Castles are also nearby. Access to the beach is through the golf course and then down the road or via cliff paths.

Facilities

Bass Park has 8 unisex units with shower, washbasin and toilet. The other areas have open washbasins. Two heated units for disabled visitors. Good launderette with spin dryer and iron. Motorcaravan service point. Reception sells a few ices, chocolate, cold drinks and newspapers at weekends. Games room with pool table and TV. Good playground and better than average putting green. Internet access in reception and WiFi. Dogs are only accepted by prior arrangement. Off site: Tesco within walking distance. Golf next door. Sea fishing and safe sandy beaches within walking distance. Town (with footpath) and bicycle hire 1 mile. Riding 5 miles.

Open: 13 March - 31 October.

Directions

Park is beside the A198 just to the east of North Berwick, which lies between Edinburgh and Dunbar. It is easily accessible from the A1.
GPS: 56.05575, -2.690833

Charges guide

Per unit incl. 2 persons and electricity	£ 17.75 - £ 28.75
extra person (over 5 yrs)	£ 5.00
child	£ 3.00
dog (max. 2)	£ 3.50

See advertisement on page 275

Peebles

Crossburn Caravan Park

Edinburgh Road, Peebles EH45 8ED (Borders) T: 01721 720501. E: enquiries@crossburncaravans.co.uk

alanrogers.com/UK6960

A peaceful, friendly small park, suitable as a night stop, Crossburn is on the south side of the A703 road, half a mile north of the town centre. The entrance has a fairly steep slope down to reception and the shop which also sells a very large selection of caravan and camping accessories. Passing the caravans for sale and the holiday homes you might think that this is not the site for you, but persevere as the touring area is very pleasant, with attractive trees and bushes. Of the 40 pitches, all have electricity (16A), 20 have hardstanding and eight are fully serviced. There is also a sheltered area for tents.

Facilities

One toilet block, with washbasins in cubicles, free hairdryers and spacious, controllable free showers. Campers' kitchen (key at reception) with free use of an electric hot plate, kettle and fridge. Shop. Adjacent is a large games room with snooker table and games machines. Good play area on bark chippings. Riverside dog walk. Card operated barrier (£10 deposit).
Off site: Buses from site gate or in Peebles (a short walk).

Open: Easter/1 April - October.

Directions

Park is by the A703 road, about 0.5 miles north of Peebles. GPS: 55.662167, -3.193333

Charges 2012

Per pitch	£ 22.00 - £ 24.00
hiker or cyclist plus tent	£ 9.00

For latest campsite news visit
alanrogers.com

Perth

Noah's Ark Caravan Park

Newhouse Farm, Perth PH1 1QF (Perth and Kinross) T: 01738 580661. E: info@perthcaravanpark.co.uk
alanrogers.com/UK7265

Noah's Ark Caravan Park is situated on the outskirts of Perth and enjoys panoramic views over the surrounding Grampian mountains. This is a good base for a golfing break, with no less than five excellent courses within a short distance, including St Andrews and Gleneagles. There are 46 touring pitches here. These are grassy and of a good size. All have electrical connections. A further 8 tent pitches are available (some with electricity). The site also has a number of Microlodge Hobbit Houses. These are unique wooden chalets, fully equipped to a high standard (even including a TV). On-site amenities include a Play Barn for children, which also houses a restaurant, karting, bowling and a golf driving range.

Facilities

Two sanitary blocks, one of wood construction, the other Portacabin style. Family shower and bathrooms. Facilities for disabled visitors. Motorcaravan service point. Gas. Noah's Galley café. Children's Play Barn. Karting. Golf driving range. Bowling. Minigolf. Local takeaway meals are delivered. WiFi throughout (free). Microlodges for rent. Off site: Golf (5 courses including Gleneagles and St Andrews). Perth (bus service). Walking. Mountain biking.

Open: 1 March - 31 October.

Directions

Site is on outskirts of Perth. From Inverness on A9, turn right at Inveralmond roundabout and then, having passed St Johnstone football club, follow signs for Noah's Ark. N.B. Do not use postcode for sat nav. GPS: 56.397285, -3.49119

Charges guide

Per unit incl. 2 persons and electricity	£ 12.00 - £ 22.00
extra person	£ 1.50

Pitlochry

The River Tilt Park

Golf Course Road, Blair Atholl, Pitlochry PH18 5TB (Perth and Kinross) T: 01796 481467.
E: stuart@rivertilt.co.uk **alanrogers.com/UK7295**

This good quality, family owned park is set on the banks of the River Tilt, a short walk from the village of Blair Atholl, where the 16th-century Blair Castle stands proud. There are 54 privately owned caravan holiday homes. Two central areas have been set aside for touring caravans, motorcaravans and tents, with 31 pitches mostly with hardstanding. Divided by mature shrubs and hedges, all have 10A electricity connections, 18 have water and a drain. One of the areas is reserved for dog owners and their pets. The Steadings Spa provides an indoor pool, solarium, steam room, spa pool and multigym, plus hair salon.

Facilities

The purpose built toilet block provides en-suite toilet and washbasin cabins and individual large preset showers, one suitable for disabled visitors. Baby facilities. Laundry. Motorcaravan service point. Bar and restaurant. Leisure spa complex with indoor pool, etc. Hair salon. Tennis. WiFi (free). Max. 2 dogs per pitch. Off site: Private fishing and golf adjacent. Bicycle hire 0.5 miles. Riding 1.5 miles.

Open: Two weeks after Easter - 10 November.

Directions

From the A9 just north of Pitlochry, take B8079 into Blair Atholl and follow signs for River Tilt. GPS: 56.76538, -3.83962

Charges guide

Per unit incl. 2 persons and electricity	£ 16.00 - £ 20.00
extra person	£ 1.50
child	£ 1.00

Pitlochry

Blair Castle Caravan Park

Blair Atholl, Pitlochry PH18 5SR (Perth and Kinross) T: 01796 481263. E: mail@blaircastlecaravanpark.co.uk
alanrogers.com/UK7300

This attractive, well kept park is set in the grounds of Blair Castle, the traditional home of the Dukes of Atholl. It has a wonderful feeling of spaciousness with a large central area left free for children's play or for general use. There is space for 250 touring units, all with electricity connections (10/16A), 63 with hardstanding and 44 fully serviced pitches with water and waste water facilities. Caravan holiday homes, 85 privately owned and 25 for hire, are in separate areas. A quality park, quiet at night and well managed. The castle is open to the public, its 30 fully furnished rooms showing a picture of Scottish life from the 12th century to the present day, while the beautiful grounds and gardens are free if staying on site.

Facilities

The five good, clean toilet blocks can be heated. Large hot showers, some with WC and washbasin, further cubicles with WC and washbasin. Facilities for disabled visitors. Baby changing mats. Laundry. Motorcaravan service point. Shop. Games room (Wii games consoles for hire) and Internet gallery. Gas supplies. American motorhomes are accepted (max. 30 ft./5 tons). Off site: Mountain bike hire, riding, golf and fishing.

Open: 27 February - 26 November.

Directions

From A9 just north of Pitlochry take B8079 into Blair Atholl. Park is in grounds of Blair Castle, well signed. GPS: 56.767039, -3.845791

Charges guide

Per unit incl. 2 persons and electricity	£ 20.00 - £ 23.00
extra person	£ 2.00

For latest campsite news visit
alanrogers.com

Pitlochry

Tummel Valley Holiday Park

Tummel Bridge, Pitlochry PH16 5SA (Perth and Kinross) T: 01882 634221.
E: enquiries@parkdeanholidays.co.uk **alanrogers.com/UK7305**

Set in the Tay Forest Park on the banks of the River Tummel, this large family holiday park is part of the Parkdean Group. Divided into two areas by the roadway, the main emphasis is on chalets to let on the side that overlooks the river. Privately owned caravan holiday homes and touring pitches are on the other, quieter side. The 26 touring pitches, open plan with hardstanding, electricity hook-up and a shared water point, overlook a small fishing lake, which is an added attraction for all the family. On arrival, you should turn right and park, then cross back to book in.

Facilities

The very clean toilet block (recently refurbished) has vanity style washbasins, preset showers and a bathroom in each section. Good facilities for disabled visitors. Laundry. Entertainment complex with bar and terrace, restaurant and takeaway. Indoor heated pool and toddlers' splash pool. Solarium and sauna. Amusements. All weather sports court. Adventure play area. Crazy golf. Nature trails. Bicycle hire. Fishing. Max. 2 dogs.

Open: Late March/Easter - 31 October.

Directions

Travel through Pitlochry. After 2 miles turn left on B8019 to Tummel Bridge (10 miles). Park is on both the left and right. Tourers should turn right and park, then return to reception on the left.
GPS: 56.70742, -4.02002

Charges guide

Per unit incl. 4 persons and electricity	£ 13.00 - £ 32.00
dog	£ 2.00 - £ 3.00

Port William

Kings Green Caravan Park

South Street, Port William DG8 9SG (Dumfries and Galloway) T: 01988 700489. E: kingsgreencp@gmail.com
alanrogers.com/UK6885

Kings Green Caravan Park is now owned and run by the Port William Community Association. Kept very natural and situated beside the sea overlooking Luce Bay and the Mull of Galloway, it is within walking distance of Port William, well known for its harbour and fishing community. The all grass, open site provides 30 marked and numbered pitches for caravans, motorcaravans and tents (21 with 10A electricity). On arrival visitors are given a welcome pack which includes a guide on the history of the area and local information.

Facilities

The small toilet block (key entry) is kept very clean and has vanity style washbasins, free electric showers and hairdryers. Facilities for disabled visitors (Radar key). Small outdoor dishwashing. Laundry with washing machine and dryer. Large play area adjacent. Off site: Shops, restaurants and bars in Port William. Fishing 50 yds. Sailing and boat launching 600 yds. Golf 2 miles. Riding 3 miles.

Open: 30 March - 31 October.

Directions

From Dumfries, take A75 to Newton Stewart. Follow A714 to Wigtown, then B7085 to Port William.
GPS: 54.755967, -4.581533

Charges guide

Per unit incl. 2 persons and electricity	£ 12.00 - £ 13.00

Saint Andrews

Craigtoun Meadows Holiday Park

Mount Melville, Saint Andrews KY16 8PQ (Fife) T: 01334 475959. E: craigtoun@aol.com
alanrogers.com/UK7290

This attractively laid out, quality park has individual pitches and good facilities. Although outnumbered by caravan holiday homes, the touring section is an important subsidiary. Its facilities are both well designed and comprehensive. With 56 units taken on gently sloping land, caravans go on individual hardstandings with grass alongside for awnings on most pitches. All caravan pitches are large (130 sq.m) and are equipped with electricity (16A), water and drainage. There are 15 larger 'patio pitches' with summer house, barbecue patio, picnic table and chairs, partially screened. Tents are taken on a grassy meadow at one end, also with electricity available.

Facilities

A deluxe, centrally heated sanitary building has washbasins in cabins and each toilet has its own basin. Showers are unisex, as are two bathrooms, with hand- and hairdryers. Facilities for disabled visitors and babies. Dishwashing room. Launderette. Licensed restaurant (restricted hours in low seasons). Games room. Well equipped playground, play field and eight acres of woodland. Information room. Animals are not accepted. Off site: Golf and bicycle hire 1.5 miles. Fishing 5 miles. Riding 6 miles.

Open: 15 March - 31 October.

Directions

From M90 junction 8 take A91 to St Andrews. Just after sign for Guardbridge (to left, A919), turn right at site sign and sign for Strathkinness. Go through village, over crossroads at end of village, left at next crossroads, then 0.75 miles to park.
GPS: 56.324617, -2.83745

Charges guide

Per unit incl. 2 persons and electricity	£ 22.00 - £ 28.50
tent	£ 19.00

Scourie

Scourie Caravan & Camping Park

Harbour Road, Scourie IV27 4TG (Highland) T: 01971 502060

alanrogers.com/UK7730

Mr Mackenzie has carefully nurtured this park over many years, developing a number of firm terraces with 60 pitches which gives it an attractive layout – there is nothing regimented here. Perched on the edge of the bay in an elevated position, practically everyone has a view of the sea and a short walk along the shore footpath leads to a small sandy beach. The park has tarmac and gravel access roads, with well drained grass and hardstanding pitches, some with 10A electric hook-ups. A few are on an area which is unfenced from the rocks (young children would need to be supervised here).

Facilities

The toilet facilities can be heated. Showers have no divider or seat. Laundry. Motorcaravan service point. The Anchorage restaurant at the entrance to the park (used as reception at quiet times) serves meals at good prices, cooked to order (l/4-30/9). Boat launching. Fishing permits can be arranged. Off site: Village with shop and post office. Gas is available from petrol station. Mobile banks visit regularly.

Open: Easter/1 April - 30 September, but phone first.

Directions

Park is by Scourie village on A894 road in northwest Sutherland. GPS: 58.351417, -5.156767

Charges guide

Per unit incl. 2 persons	£ 12.00 - £ 16.00
electricity	£ 2.00
extra person	£ 2.50
child (3-16 yrs)	£ 1.50

No credit cards.

Staffin

Staffin Caravan & Camping Site

Staffin IV51 9JX (Isle of Skye) T: 01470 562213. E: staffincampsite@btinternet.com

alanrogers.com/UK7750

This small camping site is just outside Staffin, where the broad sweep of the bay is dotted with working crofts running down to the sea. With 50 pitches, 26 with electricity (16A), some slope but many are reasonably level, with improved hardstanding for caravans and motorcaravans. The entrance to the site from the main road is by a single track road. A marked walk from the site leads to the seashore and slipway (good for walking dogs). Skye has many activities to offer and for the truly dedicated walker the Cuillins are the big attraction and the hills above Staffin are demanding in places!

Facilities

The modern sanitary block has large, controllable showers. Some hot water dishwashing sinks and laundry. Large hardstanding area has a motorcaravan service point. Gas available. Bicycle hire. Off site: Staffin village with a large shop (open six days a week), and restaurant 400 yds. The Columbia centre in the village provides Internet access. Fishing and boat launching 1 mile.

Open: 1 April - 30 September.

Directions

Site is 15 miles north of Portree on A855 (2 miles of single track at the start), just before 40 mph. signs on the right. GPS: 57.622017, -6.196

Charges guide

Per unit incl. 2 persons and electricity	£ 11.50 - £ 13.50
extra person	£ 1.50

No credit cards.

Stirling

Witches Craig Caravan Park

Blairlogie, Stirling FK9 5PX (Stirling) T: 01786 474947. E: info@witchescraig.co.uk

alanrogers.com/UK7320

Witches Craig is a neat and tidy park, nestling under the Ochil Hills. All 60 pitches have 10A electricity and hardstanding, seven of these being large (taking American style motorhomes easily). Reasonably level, the park covers five well maintained acres with the grass beautifully manicured. Being by the A91, there is some daytime road noise. Trees have been planted to try to minimise this but the further back onto the park you go, the less the traffic is heard. The area has a wealth of historic attractions, starting with the Wallace Monument which practically overlooks the park. Its 220 ft. tower dominates the surrounding area and the climb up its 246 steps gives spectacular views. Stirling is known as the 'gateway to the Highlands' and its magnificent castle is world renowned.

Facilities

The modern, heated toilet block is well maintained, and includes one cubicle with washbasin and WC each for ladies and men. Free controllable showers. Baby bath and mat. Good unit for disabled campers. Laundry, with free fridge/freezer facilities. Bread, milk, drinks and papers are available daily (supermarket 2.5 miles). Large play area. WiFi. Off site: Golf 1 mile. Riding and bicycle hire 2 miles.

Open: 1 April - 31 October.

Directions

Park is on the A91, 3 miles northeast of Stirling. GPS: 56.148033, -3.898667

Charges guide

Per unit incl. 2 persons and electricity	£ 19.50 - £ 21.50
extra person	£ 2.00

£5 deposit for key to facilities.

For latest campsite news visit
alanrogers.com

Stornoway
Laxdale Holiday Park
6 Laxdale Lane, Stornoway HS2 0DR (Isle of Lewis) T: 01851 706966. E: info@laxdaleholidaypark.com
alanrogers.com/UK7920

Whilst not in the most scenic of locations, this good park is well placed for touring. Surrounded by trees, it is on the edge of Stornaway (ferry port) and is well laid out with a tarmac road running through the centre. A level hardstanding area for touring caravans has 14 electricity hook-ups plus two for tents and a grassy area for tents gently slopes away to the trees and boundary. There are five holiday caravans and a self catering holiday bungalow available for rent on the site, plus a bunkhouse. The site is centrally situated in an ideal spot for touring the Isle of Lewis with easy access to all parts of the island.

Facilities

The well maintained and modern toilet block is heated and raised above the hardstanding area. Access is via steps or a gravel path to the ramp. Good (but narrow) showers with dividing curtain (50p). Well equipped laundry. Telephone. WiFi area (charged). Off site: Bus stop 200 yds. A comprehensive range of shops and restaurants in Stornoway. New sports centre with swimming pool. Library with free Internet access.

Open: 1 April - 31 October.

Directions

From Stornoway take the A857 for 1 mile then take the second turning on the left past the hospital.
GPS: 58.22738, -6.39254

Charges guide

Per unit incl. 2 persons and electricity	£ 15.00 - £ 20.00
extra person	£ 2.50 - £ 3.50

Credit cards accepted (over £50).

Stranraer
Aird Donald Caravan Park
London Road, Stranraer DG9 8RN (Dumfries and Galloway) T: 01776 702025. E: enquiries@aird-donald.co.uk
alanrogers.com/UK7020

Aird Donald is a good stopping off point when travelling to and from the Irish ferries, but it is also useful for seeing the sights around Stranraer. This tidy park comprises 12 acres surrounded by conifers, flowering trees and shrubs and the 300 yard drive is lit and lined with well trimmed conifers. There are grass areas for caravans and tents and hardstandings with electricity hook-up (these are very handy for hardy winter tourers). A small play area caters for young children, but the local leisure centre is only a walk away and provides swimming, table tennis, gym, etc, and a theatre.

Facilities

Two toilet blocks, the new block is heated, kept very clean with excellent, tiled facilities (kept locked with a key deposit of £5). There are two types of shower, an electric one which is metered (50p) and two others which are free. Washbasins are in vanity units, ladies having one in a cubicle. Unit for visitors with disabilities has a washbasin and WC. The original block has been renovated but is more basic with free showers and open all the time. Small laundry. Motorcaravan services. Play area.

Open: All year.

Directions

Enter Stranraer on A75 road. Watch for narrow site entrance on left entering town, opposite school.
GPS: 54.90185, -5.006217

Charges guide

Per unit incl. 2 persons and electricity	£ 16.00 - £ 18.00

No credit cards.

Stromness
Point of Ness Caravan & Camping Site
Well Park, Ness Road, Stromness KW16 3DN (Orkney) T: 01856 873535. E: recreation@orkney.gov.uk
alanrogers.com/UK7950

This quiet site is in an idyllic position bounded by the sea on one side (an entrance to the harbour). It is sheltered by the land from the open sea and has views to the mountains and the island of Hoy. There is a rocky beach close by and walks from the site. It is a level, firm grassy site, protected from the small drop to the sea by a low fence. Access to the steps to the sea is gained by a gate in the fence. Whilst being located at one end of Orkney, it is still easy to visit the Churchill Barriers and the Italian Chapel as well as the closer Maes Howe and Skara Brae sites.

Facilities

The well maintained traditional style toilet block has good-sized showers (20p) with curtains separating the changing area. Well equipped laundry. Telephone and tourist information. Lounge for campers is at one end of the block. Off site: Fishing, golf and bicycle hire all nearby.

Open: 28 April - 30 September.

Directions

Site is just west of Stromness and signed from town. Campers can walk along the narrow high street to the site on the edge of the town. Caravans and motorcaravans are advised to take the road at the back of the town (about 2 miles) and clearly marked.
GPS: 58.95443, -3.30041

Charges guide

Per pitch	£ 8.30
tent	£ 4.40 - £ 7.95

No credit cards.

Tarbert

Muasdale Holiday Park

Muasdale, Tarbert PA29 6XD (Argyll and Bute) T: 01583 421207. E: enquiries@muasdaleholidays.com

alanrogers.com/UK7250

Muasdale Touring Park has a beachside location with fine views of the sea and islands, between Campbeltown and Tarbert on Kintyre's west coast. This is a small, friendly site of just 16 pitches with 10 for touring units, 5 for tents and one used for a caravan holiday home to rent. The pitches are situated on a level, grass field, all with unobstructed sea views. All have electrical connections. You are advised to anchor tents and awnings securely as the winds are sometimes strong and gusty. The beach is a magnificent expanse of white sand with rock pools and an abundance of wildlife. The sunsets are frequently breathtaking. Sea canoeing and sea fishing are both popular.

Facilities

The single Portacabin style toilet block is clean, heated and adequate. No specific facilities for disabled visitors or babies. Laundry facilities. Games room. Direct beach access. Sea swimming and fishing. Canoeing. WiFi (in the games room; charged). Accommodation to rent. Off site: Well stocked village shop 100 yds. Kintyre Way walking trail. Whisky distilleries. Golf.

Open: April - mid October.

Directions

Approaching from Glasgow (Erskine Bridge), take the A82 towards Crianlarich, past Loch Lomond. At Tarbet take the A83 towards Campbeltown, through Inveraray, Lochgilphead and Tarbert (Loch Fyne) and on to Muasdale Village, from where the site is well signed. GPS: 55.597307, -5.686058

Charges guide

Per unit incl. 2 persons and electricity	£ 16.00 - £ 18.00
extra person	£ 1.75
child (5-15 yrs)	£ 1.25
dog	£ 1.25

Ullapool

Ardmair Point Caravan Park

Ardmair Point, Ullapool IV26 2TN (Highland) T: 01854 612054. E: sales@ardmair.com

alanrogers.com/UK7710

This spectacularly situated park, overlooking the little Loch Kanaird, just round the corner from Loch Broom, has splendid views all round. The 68 touring pitches are arranged mainly on grass around the edge of the bay, in front of the shingle beach. Electrical hook-ups (10A) are available and some gravel hardstandings are on the other side of the access road, just past the second toilet block. Tent pitches, together with cheaper pitches for some tourers are in a large field behind the other sanitary facilities. Scuba diving is popular at Loch Kanaird because the water is so clear.

Facilities

Two toilet blocks, both with good facilities. One block has wonderful views from the large windows in the launderette and dishwashing rooms. En-suite rooms for disabled visitors. Motorcaravan service point. Shop. Play area. Fishing. Sailing and boating (with your own boat). Off site: Ullapool for shopping 3 miles. Golf and bicycle hire 3 miles.

Open: 1 April - late September, depending on weather.

Directions

Park is off the A835 road, 3 miles north of Ullapool. GPS: 57.933967, -5.197017

Charges guide

Per unit incl. 2 persons and electricity	£ 15.00 - £ 20.00

For latest campsite news visit

alanrogers.com

With a diversity of unspoilt landscapes, ranging from wild coastlines to green valleys, rugged mountains and shimmering lakes, to the natural phenomenon of the Giant's Causeway, Northern Ireland, though small, is crammed full of sights offering something for everyone.

NORTHERN IRELAND COMPRISES THE FOLLOWING COUNTIES: ANTRIM, ARMAGH, DOWN, FERMANAGH, LONDONDERRY AND TYRONE

The rugged coastline of the Causeway Coast and the nine Glens of Antrim in the north, is an Area of Outstanding Natural Beauty, with white sandy shores and little bays, tranquil forests and romantic ruins and castles, full of tales of the ancient Irish Giants and other myths and legends. At over 60 million years old, with a mass of 4,000 tightly-packed basalt columns, each a polygon shape, the Giant's Causeway is a popular attraction. One of the most beautiful regions is in the west around Londonderry, a delightful walled city set on a hill on the banks of the Foyle estuary. Further south is the beautiful region of Fermanagh, with glistening lakes and little islands all surrounded by lush green fields, hillsides and forests. The large lake of Lough Erne is to be found here: made up of two channels, the lower and upper Loughs, the meeting point of these channels is Enniskillen, a town steeped in history, boasting numerous preserved buildings including a castle. Across to the eastern shores lies the ancient Kingdom of Down, with its endless miles of spectacular coastline, little fishing villages, country parks and the Mountains of Mourne. And, ringed by hills, sea lough and river valley is Belfast, a bustling city full of theatres, concert halls, art galleries and restaurants.

Places of interest

Antrim: Antrim Lough Shore Park; Rathlin Island; Giant's Causeway; Dunluce Castle near Portrush.

Belfast & environs: Belfast zoo and castle; Irish Linen Centre in Lisburn; Carrickfergus Castle.

Armagh: Gosford Forest Park near Markethill; Lough Neagh Discovery Centre on Oxford Island.

Down: County Museum and Downpatrick Cathedral; Mourne Mountains; Castlewellan forest park; Ballycopeland Windmill near Millisle.

Fermanagh: Enniskillen Castle and Castle Coole; village of Belleek; Marble Arch Caves, near Lough Macnean; Devenish Island on Lough Erne.

Londonderry: St Columb's Cathedral, Harbour Museum, Foyle Valley Railway Centre in Derry.

Tyrone: Omagh; Beaghmore stone circles near Cookstown; Dungannon; Sperrin Mountains.

Did you know?

Northern Ireland measures 85 miles from north to south and is about 110 miles wide.

The world's most famous ship, the Titanic, was built in Belfast.

Legend has it that the rugged Giant's Causeway was built by Finn McCool, the legendary Irish Giant, when he travelled to Scotland to bring back his sweetheart.

At 2,240 yards, an Irish mile is 480 yards longer than a standard English mile.

Mountsandel near Coleraine is where Ireland's first known house was built 9,000 years ago.

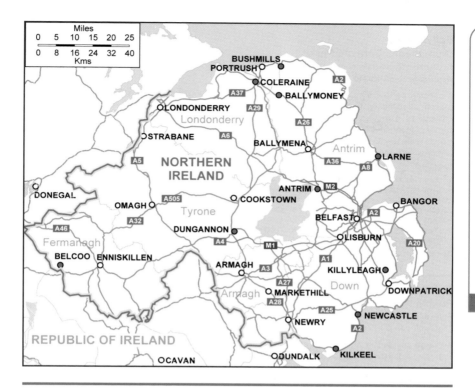

Antrim

Six Mile Water Caravan & Camping Park

Lough Road, Antrim BT41 4DG (Co. Antrim) T: 028 9446 4963. E: sixmilewater@antrim.gov.uk

alanrogers.com/UK8330

Six Mile Water is located at the Lough Shore Park and is adjacent to the Antrim Forum leisure complex, a major amenity area that includes swimming pools, a bowling green, an adventure playground for children, fitness and health gyms and sports fields. Managed by Antrim Borough Council, the park is easily accessible when travelling to and from the ports of Belfast and Larne, making it perfect for stopovers. There are 37 pitches with 13A electricity, arranged in a herringbone layout of hardstandings with grass for awnings, a grass area for eight tents to one side, plus picnic and barbecue areas. Advance booking is advisable. Six Mile Water is central for sightseeing in the area including the Antrim Castle Gardens and Clotworthy Arts Centre, and for shopping in Antrim town. The Lough Shore Park offers visitors boating and water activities and boat launching on the beautiful Lough Neagh, as well as walking and cycling the Lough Shore Trail which takes in 25 places of interest along its 128 mile cycle route. The nearby golf club also offers a 20-bay driving range.

Facilities

The small, modern toilet block has toilets, washbasins and showers. Facilities for disabled campers. Baby changing unit. Laundry room. TV lounge and games room. Fishing and boat launching. Off site: The facilities of Lough Shore Park, including a café, open all year round. Antrim Forum leisure centre. Bus service 1 mile. Shops, pubs and restaurants within 1.5 miles. Golf 1.5 miles. Riding 6 miles.

Open: March - October and weekends in Feb. and Nov.

Directions

Site is 1 mile south of the city centre. Follow signs for Antrim Forum and Lough Shore Park. On the Dublin road, turn off into Lough Road. Pass Antrim Forum and park is at the end of the road (with speed bumps). GPS: 54.71533, -6.23375

Charges guide

Per unit incl. electricity	£ 20.00 - £ 22.00
tent	£ 15.00 - £ 22.00

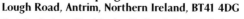

Ballymoney

Drumaheglis Caravan Park

36 Glenstall Road, Ballymoney BT53 7QN (Co. Antrim) T: 028 2766 0280. E: drumaheglis@ballymoney.gov.uk

alanrogers.com/UK8340

A caravan park which continually maintains high standards, Drumaheglis is popular throughout the season. Situated on the bank of the lower River Bann, approximately four miles from the town of Ballymoney, it appeals to watersports enthusiasts and makes a very good base for exploring this scenic corner of Northern Ireland. This attractive site is well laid out with trees, shrubs, flower beds and tarmac roads. There are 35 serviced pitches for touring units with hardstanding, electricity (5/16A), water points and drainage. The marina offers facilities for boat launching, waterskiing, cruising, canoeing and fishing.

Facilities

Modern toilet blocks are very clean and well maintained. Facilities for disabled visitors. Baby changing facilities and four en-suite shower rooms. Washing machine and dryer. Basic shop. Play area. Barbecue and picnic areas. Barrier with key system. Fishing. Boat launching. Off site: Marina. Bus service from park entrance. Bicycle hire and golf 4 miles. Riding 6 miles. Beach 10 miles.

Open: 17 March - end October.

Directions

From A26/B62 Portrush - Ballymoney roundabout continue for about 2 miles on the A26 towards Coleraine. Site is clearly signed - follow international camping signs. GPS: 55.07212, -6.59082

Charges 2012

Per unit incl. electricity	£ 24.00
tent pitch	£ 16.00

Belcoo

Rushin House Caravan Park

Holywell, Belcoo, Enniskillen BT93 5DU (Co. Fermanagh) T: 028 6638 6519.
E: enquiries@rushinhousecaravanpark.com **alanrogers.com/UK8515**

Although situated in Northern Ireland, this park, opened in 2007, is almost on the border with the Republic of Ireland. It has been carefully landscaped from farmland that sloped down to the tranquil Lough MacNean. There are 24 fully serviced pitches on hardstanding which form a friendly circle surrounding a fairy thorn tree. There is also a small camping area. The toilet block, boat jetty, picnic tables and play areas are only a short walk away from the pitches. The helpful owners live on site and are on call most of the time. This park provides a peaceful haven to relax after returning from days out in lovely Fermanagh. Nearby are the stark ruins of Templerushin Church and St Patrick's Holy Well.

Facilities

Heated toilet block, beautifully appointed, with laundry and adjoining kitchen area. Separate facilities for disabled campers. Payphone. Boat jetty. Play area. All-weather sports facility. Picnic area. Tourist information. Off site: Golf course nearby. Twin border towns of Belcoo and Blacklion with shops and restaurants. Within 25 miles are historic Enniskillen, Marble Arch caves, Belleek Pottery, two National Trust properties, and the dramatic countryside of Fermanagh, Donegal and Sligo.

Open: 11 March - 31 October.

Directions

From Enniskillen follow the A4 for 13 miles to Belcoo. Turn right on to the B52 towards Garrison and in about 1 mile you will see the signs for Rushin House. GPS: 54.306584, -7.89505

Charges guide

Per unit incl. services	£ 22.00
extra person	£ 3.00

Bushmills

Bush Caravan Park

97 Priestland Road, Bushmills BT57 8UJ (Co. Antrim) T: 028 2073 1678. E: bushcaravanpark@tiscali.co.uk

alanrogers.com/UK8350

A good base for touring the North Antrim Coast, this family run park is only minutes away from two renowned attractions: the Giant's Causeway and the Old Bushmills Distillery. Located just off the main Ballymoney - Portrush Road (B62), it is approached by a short drive. The park is partly surrounded by mature trees and hedging, but views across the countryside can still be appreciated. Tarmac roads lead to 47 well laid out and spacious pitches with hardstanding and 16A electricity or to a grass area for pup tents. The owners may organise occasional barbecues, tours to the distillery and coastal trips.

Facilities

The toilet block (opened by key pad) is modern, clean and equipped to a high standard. Facilities include controllable showers with excellent provision for campers with disabilities (can also be used by families). Washing machine and dryer. Central play area. Recreation room for all ages. Off site: Riding 2 miles. Golf, beach and fishing 3 miles. Bicycle hire and boat launching 4 miles.

Open: Easter - 31 October.

Directions

From the A26 turn onto the B62 for 7 miles. Turn onto the B17 Priestlands Road and site is immediately on the left. GPS: 55.17103, -6.57114

Charges guide

Per unit incl. 2 persons and electricity	£ 20.00
awning	£ 2.00

For latest campsite news visit

alanrogers.com

Bushmills

Ballyness Caravan Park

40 Castlecatt Road, Bushmills BT57 8TN (Co. Antrim) T: 028 2073 2393. E: info@ballynesscaravanpark.com
alanrogers.com/UK8360

Ballyness is immaculately cared for and is designed with conservation in mind. In keeping with the surrounding countryside, it is extensively planted with native trees and shrubs. A pathway encircles several ponds which attract local wildlife and birds. The overall appearance of this park, with its white stone pillared entrance gate and broad tarmac drive is attractive. There are 48 hardstanding pitches all with electricity, water and drainage. Privately-owned caravan holiday homes are placed away from the touring pitches. The village of Bushmills, with its famous whisky distillery, is within walking distance. The Giant's Causeway and the majestic Antrim coast are only a short drive.

Facilities

One spotlessly clean and well decorated, cottage style heated sanitary block (key coded). Facilities for disabled visitors (toilet and shower). Shop for basic food supplies, gas and campers' essentials. Family room with bath. Laundry room. Play area and play park. WiFi. Off site: Bus service 0.5 miles. Bicycle hire, beach and fishing 1 mile. Boat launching and championship golf courses 1.5 miles. Riding 5 miles.

Open: 16 March - 3 November.

Directions

From M2 follow A26. At Ballymoney turn right on B66 towards Dervock and turn left. Stay on B66 and site is 5.5 miles on right. GPS: 55.20121, -6.52096

Charges guide

Per unit incl. 2 persons, electricity, water and drainage	£ 22.00
extra person (over 6 yrs)	£ 1.00
awning or pup tent	£ 2.00

BALLYNESS CARAVAN PARK
BUSHMILLS, CO ANTRIM
NORTHERN IRELAND'S PREMIER 5 STAR PARK
MULTI-AWARD WINNING PARK IN A BEAUTIFUL RURAL LOCATION, FULLY SERVICED HARD STAND PITCHES, WIFI, PLAY AREA, FULL RANGE OF FACILITIES
028 2073 2393   www.ballynesscaravanpark.com

Coleraine

Tullans Farm Holiday Park

46 Newmills Road, Coleraine BT52 2JB (Co. Londonderry) T: 028 7034 2309. E: tullansfarm@hotmail.com
alanrogers.com/UK8590

A well run family park convenient for the Causeway coast, Tullans Farm has a quiet, heart of the country feel, yet the university town of Coleraine is within a mile, the seaside resorts of Portrush and Portstewart five miles and a shopping centre a five minute drive. The toilet block is clean and attractive flower displays add to the park's well cared for appearance. Around the park roads are gravel and the 36 pitches are on hardstanding; all with electric hook-ups (10A), water and drainage. In season the owners organise barbecues, barn dances and line dancing (raising funds for charity). A central building houses the reception, toilet block and TV room. Plans have been passed for an extension to provide caravan holiday home accommodation.

Facilities

The toilet and shower rooms, including a family shower unit, are spacious, modern and include facilities for disabled visitors. Laundry and washing up room with sinks, washing machine, dryers and fridge. Play areas. TV lounge. Games room. Barn used for indoor recreation. Snooker room for adults. Caravan storage. Off site: Public transport in Coleraine 1 mile. Fishing and riding 1.5 miles. Golf, beach and bicycle hire 5 miles.

Open: March - 30 September.

Directions

From the Lodge Road roundabout (south end of Coleraine) turn east onto A29 Portrush ring road and proceed for 0.5 miles. Turn right at sign for park and Windy Hall. Park is clearly signed on left. GPS: 55.12557, -6.63923

Charges guide

Per unit incl. all persons, electricity and awning	£ 20.00
tent	£ 10.00 - £ 18.00

Dungannon

Dungannon Park

Moy Road, Dungannon BT71 6DY (Co. Tyrone) T: 028 8772 8690. E: dpreception@dungannon.gov.uk
alanrogers.com/UK8550

This small touring park nestles in the midst of a 70 acre park with a multitude of tree varieties, brightly coloured flower beds and a charming 12 acre fishing lake. The 12 pitches, some with lake views, are on hardstanding each with dedicated water, waste and 16A electricity connections. Hedging provides some separation. There is also an unmarked grass area for tents. Run by Dungannon Council the park, which also incorporates tennis courts, football and cricket pitches, lies about a mile south of Dungannon town.

Facilities

Sanitary facilities are to the rear of the Amenity Centre and include showers (by token), washbasins, baby changing mat and spacious unit for disabled visitors. Laundry room with washing machine and dryer, dishwashing area and chemical disposal unit. Excellent play area. TV lounge. Tennis. Fishing. Walking. Orienteering. Off site: Bus stop and shop at main entrance to park. Restaurants, shops, leisure facilities in Dungannon. Interesting walking and cycling in Clogher Valley. Local markets.

Open: 1 March - 31 October.

Directions

Leave M1 motorway at junction 15 to join A29 towards Dungannon. Turn left at second traffic lights signed Dungannon Park. GPS: 54.390217, -6.757967

Charges guide

Per unit incl. services	£ 15.00

Kilkeel

Cranfield Caravan Park

123 Cranfield Road, Cranfield West, Kilkeel BT34 4LJ (Co. Down) T: 028 4176 2572.
E: jimchestnut@btconnect.com alanrogers.com/UK8405

On the shores of Carlingford Lough with direct access to a Blue Flag beach, this friendly, family-run park immediately impresses with its well cared for flower beds, neat hedging, cordyline palms and the elegant building which incorporates the family home and reception. Despite the many privately owned caravan holiday homes on site, touring pitches are kept separate and are situated towards the park entrance. Most pitches have a sea view, hardstanding and all have tower units providing an electricity hook-up (10A), water, waste water point and TV outlet. Tents are not accepted.

Facilities

A modern, heated toilet block (entrance by key) is well maintained with tiled walls/floors, preset showers (token) and open style washbasins. Excellent suite for disabled visitors doubles as a family room, also a night WC (by key). Dishwashing sinks and well equipped laundry in a separate building. Play area (outside park). Sea fishing, boat launching and beach (with lifeguard). WiFi (charged). Off site: Kilkeel town (3.5 miles). Golf, hill walking in the Mournes. Anglo Norman castle.

Open: 17 March - 30 September.

Directions

Travelling southeast on A2 Newry - Kilkeel Road turn right about 5.5 miles after passing through Rostrevor onto local road, signed Cranfield/Greencastle. If approaching from Kilkeel follow signs for Cranfield West. Site signed at end of road. GPS: 54.029933, -6.0683

Charges guide

Per unit incl. all persons and electricity	£ 20.00
awning	£ 2.00

Kilkeel

Sandilands Caravan Park

30 Cranfield Road, Cranfield East, Kilkeel BT34 4LJ (Co. Down) T: 028 4176 3634.
E: info@chestnuttholidayparks.com alanrogers.com/UK8407

In the very popular area of Cranfield, Sandilands is set slightly apart from its neighbours, looking south east over the Irish Sea rather than Carlingford Lough. The park largely comprises privately owned caravan holiday homes, but has an attractive and enclosed area for 30 touring units. It makes the most of its coastal plain situation to the immediate south of the Mourne Mountains. Kilkeel and the mountain foothills can be reached in a few minutes by car. Sandilands is pleasantly laid out with an inviting entrance and may be just the answer for those seeking a quieter location whilst visiting the area.

Facilities

Laundry and toilet block (entrance to all facilities by key) is well maintained. It has preset showers (token) and open style washbasins and a night WC. There are no dedicated facilities for disabled visitors. Play area and small football pitch. Off site: Sea fishing and boat launching nearby. Pretty village of Rostrevor, well known for its ceilidhs and Irish music 7 miles. Kilkeel and Annalong are interesting fishing towns.

Open: 17 March - 31 October.

Directions

From the north leave the A2 in the middle of Kilkeel and follow signs for Cranfield East until the sign for Sandilands appears on the left. From Newry pass through Rostrevor and after about 6 miles look for signs to Cranfield East. GPS: 54.029932, -6.058391

Charges guide

Per unit incl. services	£ 19.00
awning	£ 1.00

For latest campsite news visit
alanrogers.com

Kilkeel

Chestnutt HolidayPark

3 Grange Road, Kilkeel, Newry BT34 4LW (Co. Down) T: 028 4176 2653. E: info@chestnuttholidayparks.com

alanrogers.com/UK8410

Chestnutt Caravan Park is one of the best in the southernmost corner of Northern Ireland. There are two areas designated for touring units, one on each side of the entrance road and all pitches have electricity, light, water and waste. The park is surrounded by dramatic scenery and unspoilt countryside and is an attractive choice for a beach-based holiday. The adjacent beach, with lifeguard, tennis court, small football pitch and playpark will keep youngsters happy all day. The backdrop of the Mourne Mountains to the north give the area shelter.

Facilities

Each touring section has a toilet block with token-operated showers. The large well equipped laundry (also token operated), toilets and full facilities for disabled campers have been completely refurbished. Shop, restaurant and takeaway (all open Easter weekend, Jul/Aug). Tennis court. Play area. WiFi (charged). Off site: Mountain and coastal walks. Sea canoeing and other water sports, sea fishing and golf nearby.

Open: 17 March - 31 October.

Directions

From the north follow the A2 from Newcastle and at Kilkeel follow signs for Cranfield West and then Chestnutt Holiday Park. From Newry, pass through Rostrevor and about 6 miles further you will see signs for Cranfield West.
GPS: 54.030864, -6.068868

Charges guide

Per unit incl. awning and electricity	£ 20.00

Killyleagh

Delamont Country Park Camping & Caravanning Club Site

Delamont Country Park, Downpatrick Road, Killyleagh BT30 9TZ (Co. Down) T: 028 4482 1833.
E: delamont.site@thefriendlyclub.co.uk **alanrogers.com/UK8460**

This is Northern Ireland's first Camping and Caravanning Club site and is now one of the country's more popular sites. Facilities on the campsite itself are excellent and it has an orderly, neat and tidy appearance. Reception stands beside the entrance to the site and the sanitary block towards the rear. The 65 all weather pitches on level terrain all have electricity, plus water and waste hook-ups. The site is surrounded by trees and the rich vegetation of the country park, and the young shrubs and trees around the pitches are slowly maturing.

Facilities

The single modern toilet block, with heating, has wash cubicles and a baby bath. En-suite facilities for disabled visitors. Laundry sinks, washing machine and dryer. Small shop area. Adventure playground and miniature railway in country park. Free admittance to country park for campers. WiFi (charged). Off site: Fishing and riding 1 mile. Golf 4 miles. Tyrella beach 7 miles.

Open: 15 March - 12 November.

Directions

From Belfast follow A22 southeast to village of Killyleagh. Pass through village and site entrance is on left after 1 mile. GPS: 54.38656, -5.67657

Charges 2012

Per unit incl. 2 persons and electricity	£ 15.50 - £ 22.45
non-member pitch fee	£ 7.10

Larne

Carnfunnock Country Park Caravan Park & Campsite

Coast Road, Ballygally, Larne BT40 2QG (Co. Antrim) T: 028 2827 0541. E: carnfunnock@larne.gov.uk

alanrogers.com/UK8310

In a magnificent parkland setting overlooking the Irish Sea and Scotland, what makes this touring site popular are its scenic surroundings and convenient location. It is 3.5 miles north of the market town of Larne on the famed Antrim Coast Road and offers 31 level super pitches, including three extra long pitches, all with hardstanding, water, electricity (16A), drainage, individual pitch lighting and ample space for an awning. The site has a neat appearance with a tarmac road following through to the rear where a number of pitches are placed in a circular position with allocated space for tents. Run by the Borough Council and supervised by a manager, the surrounding Country Park is immaculately kept.

Facilities

A small building beside the entrance gates houses clean toilet facilities (entry by key) which have had a major refurbishment. There are shower units, a family bathroom and facilities for disabled visitors. Baby changing room. Off site: Facilities of the adjacent Country Park include: gift shop, restaurant and coffee shop, adventure playground, maze, putting green, 9-hole golf course, forest walks. Fishing and boat launching 400 yds. Larne with bus services 3.5 miles. Riding 7 miles.

Open: 16 March - 4 November.

Directions

From ferry terminal in Larne, follow signs for Coast Road and Carnfunnock Country Park; well signed 3.5 miles on A2 coast road.
GPS: 54.888193, -5.845231

Charges guide

Per caravan or motorcaravan incl. electricity and awning	£ 19.00 - £ 21.00
tent incl. 2 persons	£ 11.50 - £ 12.50
tent (per extra person)	£ 2.00

For latest campsite news visit
alanrogers.com

Larne

Curran Caravan Park

131 Curran Road, Larne BT40 1DD (Co. Antrim) T: 028 2827 3797. E: robinsonsservicestation@hotmail.co.uk

alanrogers.com/UK8320

Attractive garden areas add to the charm of this small, neat park which has recently been purchased by the owner of the garage/shop opposite. It is very conveniently situated for the ferry terminal and only a few minutes walk from the sea. The new owner has been making some upgrades and now provides four hardstanding pitches for motorcaravans. The 34 pitches, all with electricity connections (14A), give reasonable space off the tarmac road and there is a separate tent area of 1.5 acres. Larne market is on Wednesdays. You may consider using this site as a short term base for discovering the area as well as an ideal overnight stop, especially for early or late ferry crossings.

Facilities	Directions
The toilet block is clean and adequate without being luxurious but there are no facilities for disabled visitors. Laundry room with dishwashing facilities. Bowls and putting adjacent and also play areas with good equipment and safety surfaces. Late arrivals can call at the garage if open. Off site: Train station and bus stop within a few minutes walk. Many other amenities are very close by including a shop (100 yds), restaurants, tennis and a leisure centre with swimming pool (300 yds). Boat launching 500 yds. Bicycle hire 0.5 miles. Golf 2 miles.	Immediately after leaving the ferry terminal, turn right and follow camp signs. Site is 400 yds. on the left. GPS: 54.84995, -5.80818

Charges guide

Per caravan, motorcaravan or large tent incl. electricity and awning	£ 15.00
tent	£ 10.00

Open: Easter - 31 October.

Newcastle

Tollymore Forest Caravan Park

178 Tullybrannigan Road, Newcastle BT33 0PW (Co. Down) T: 028 4372 2428

alanrogers.com/UK8420

This popular park, for touring units only, is located within the parkland of Tollymore Forest which is noted for its scenic surroundings. The forest park is approached by a majestic avenue of Himalayan cedars and covers an area of almost 500 hectares. Situated two miles from the beaches and resort of Newcastle, it is backed impressively by the Mourne mountains. The open grassy site is attractively laid out with hardstanding pitches, 72 of which have electricity (6A). The Forestry Service Rangers are very helpful and ensure that the caravan site is efficiently run and quiet, even when full.

Facilities	Directions
The timbered toilet blocks have wash cubicles, showers, dishwashing and laundry area. Fishing (permit required). Off site: Confectionery shop and tea room nearby in high season. Small grocery shop a few yards from the exit gate of the park with gas available.	Approach Newcastle on the A24. Before entering the town, at roundabout, turn right on to A50 signed Castlewellan and follow signs for Tollymore Forest Park. GPS: 54.22630, -5.93449

Charges guide

Per unit incl. car and occupants	£ 10.50 - £ 15.50
electricity	£ 1.50

Open: All year.

For latest campsite news visit

alanrogers.com

Famed for its folklore, traditional music, and friendly, hospitable people, the Republic of Ireland offers spectacular scenery contained within a relatively compact area. With plenty of beautiful areas to discover, and a decidedly relaxed pace of life, it is an ideal place to unwind.

IRELAND IS MADE UP OF FOUR PROVINCES: CONNAUGHT, LEINSTER, MUNSTER AND ULSTER, COMPRISING 32 COUNTIES, 26 OF WHICH FALL IN THE REPUBLIC OF IRELAND

Ireland is the perfect place to indulge in a variety of outdoor pursuits while taking in the glorious scenery. There are plenty of way-marked footpaths, which lead through woodlands, across cliffs, past historical monuments and over rolling hills. The dramatic coastline, with its headlands, secluded coves and sandy beaches, is fantastic for watersports: from sailing to windsurfing, scuba diving and swimming; or for just simply relaxing and watching the variety of seabirds that nest on the shores. The Cliffs of Moher, in particular, is a prime location for birdwatching and Goat Island, just offshore, is where puffins make their nesting burrows. Fishing is another popular activity; the country is full of pretty streams, rivers, hidden lakes and canals, which can all be explored by hiring a boat. In the south, the beautiful Ring of Kerry is one of the most visited regions. This 110-mile route encircles the Inveragh Peninsula, and is surrounded by mountains and lakes. Other sights include the Aran Islands, home to some of the most ancient Christian and pre-Christian remains in Ireland, and the Rock of Cashel, with its spectacular group of medieval buildings; not to mention the bustling cities of Dublin, Galway and Cork.

Places of interest

Connaught: Boyle Abbey; Connemara National Park; Céide Fields at Ballycastle; Kylemore Abbey; Aran Islands; Galway city; Westport; Sligo Abbey; megalithic tombs of Carrowmore.

Leinster: Wicklow Mountains National Park; Rock of Cashel; Killkenny Castle; Guinness brewery, Trinity College and National Museum in Dublin; Dunmore Cave at Ballyfoyle; Wexford Wildfowl Reserve.

Munster: harbour towns of Kinsale and Clonakilty; Blarney Castle in Cork; historical city of Limerick with 13th-century castle fortress and old town; Ring of Kerry; Bunratty Castle; Cliffs of Moher; Killarney National Park.

Ulster: Glenveagh National Park; Slieve League, the highest sea cliffs in Europe; Donegal Castle; Newmills Corn and Flax Mills in Letterkenny.

Did you know?

The official currency of the Republic of Ireland is the Euro.

The international dialling code for the Republic of Ireland is 00 353 (then drop the first '0' of the number).

The Blarney Stone, reputedly cast with a spell by a witch to reward a king who saved her from drowning, is said to bestow the gift of eloquence on all those who kiss it.

The harp is a symbol of the Irish people's love of music: since Medieval times it has been the official emblem for Ireland.

Hurling is the oldest native sport.

On display in Trinity College, the Book of Kells is one of the oldest books in the world, written around the year 800 AD.

Athlone

Lough Ree (East) Caravan & Camping Park

Ballykeeran, Athlone (Co. Westmeath) T: 090 647 8561. E: athlonecamping@eircom.net

alanrogers.com/IR8960

This touring park is alongside the river, screened by trees but reaching the water's edge. Drive into the small village of Ballykeeran and the park is discreetly located behind the main street. The top half of the site is in a woodland situation and after the reception and sanitary block, Lough Ree comes into view and the remaining pitches run down to the shoreline. There are 60 pitches, 20 with hardstanding and 52 with electricity (6A). With fishing right on the doorstep there are boats for hire locally and the site has its own private mooring buoys, plus a dinghy slip and harbour. A restaurant and 'singing' pub are close.

Facilities

The toilet block is clean without being luxurious. Hot showers (€ 1). Dishwashing sinks outside. Laundry room (wash and dry € 8). A wooden chalet houses a pool room with open fire and campers' kitchen (no cooking facilities). Off site: Riding 4 km. Golf 8 km.

Open: 1 April - 30 September.

Directions

From Athlone take N55 towards Longford for 4.8 km. Park is in the village of Ballykeeran, clearly signed. GPS: 53.44815, -7.88992

Charges guide

Per unit incl. 2 persons and electricity	€ 23.00

No credit cards.

Athy

Forest Farm Caravan & Camping Park

Dublin Road, Athy (Co. Kildare) T: 059 863 1231. E: forestfarm@eircom.net

alanrogers.com/IR9080

This site makes an excellent stopover if travelling from Dublin to the southeast counties. It is also ideally placed to visit local places of interest including the Shackleton exhibition, the Japanese Gardens and the Irish National Stud. Part of a working farm, the campsite spreads to the right of the modern farmhouse, which also provides B&B and holiday apartments. The owners have cleverly utilised their land to create a site which offers 64 unmarked touring pitches on level ground. Of these, 32 are for caravans, all with electricity and ten with hardstanding, and 32 places are available for tents.

Facilities

The centrally located, red brick toilet block is heated and double glazed, providing quality amenities. Spacious shower unit for disabled visitors. Family room with shower and WC. Laundry room. Campers' kitchen with fridge/freezer, cooker, table and chairs. Comfortable, large lounge/games room (a TV can be provided). Sand pit and picnic tables. Off site: Shop, bar and restaurant 3 km. Golf courses nearby. Course and game fishing 4 km.

Open: All year.

Directions

Site is 4.8 km. northeast of Athy town off the main N78 Athy - Kilcullen road. GPS: 53.0139, -6.9256

Charges guide

Per person	€ 4.00
child	€ 2.00
pitch incl. electricity	€ 2.00
hiker, cyclist or motorcyclist incl. tent	€ 6.00

Ballaghaderreen

Willowbrook Camping & Caravan Park

Kiltybranks, Ballaghaderreen (Co. Roscommon) T: 094 986 1307. E: info@willowbrookpark.com

alanrogers.com/IR8815

This is a campsite with a difference. Willowbrook is a small family run caravan and camping park, which offers a unique holiday in an unspoiled part of Ireland. It has eight hardstanding pitches with electricity and a central level grass area without power, all with ample water points. An additional tenting area is available in the adjoining field. The main difference is that meditation, Tai Chi and other relaxation techniques, all adding to the tranquillity of the setting, are organised by Dave and Lin Whitefield whose aim is to ensure their guests relax and unwind in this idyllic hideaway. Archery, guided walks on the Suck Valley Way and in the Ox and Curlieu mountains, and coarse fishing for more active relaxation are also provided. It is ideal as a holiday base or as a stop over on the Dublin - Mayo route to the west of Ireland.

Facilities

The toilet block is immaculate and lit at night, with separate shower cubicles and facilities for disabled campers. Laundry room. Campers' kitchen with microwave, kettle and toaster. Library and reading room with TV. Fishing. Torches useful. Off site: Local sporting activities available include tennis, golf and fishing.

Open: All year.

Directions

Park is 6 km. from Ballaghaderreen. Take the R293 from Ballaghaderreen towards Castlerea and Ballyhaunis, then the R325 over the bridge. Bear left, still towards Castlerea and Ballyhaunis for 1.5 km. Turn right at sign to site in 500 m. GPS: 53.86672, -8.60214

Charges guide

Per unit incl. 2 persons and electricity	€ 23.50
family tent incl. 2 adults and 2 children	€ 23.00

No credit cards.

For latest campsite news visit

alanrogers.com

Bantry

Eagle Point Caravan & Camping Park

Ballylickey, Bantry (Co. Cork) T: 027 506 30. E: eaglepointcamping@eircom.net

alanrogers.com/IR9510

Midway between the towns of Bantry and Glengarriff, the spectacular peninsula of Eagle Point juts into Bantry Bay. The first impression is of a spacious country park rather than a campsite. As far as the eye can see this 20-acre, landscaped, part-terraced park, with its vast manicured grass areas separated by mature trees, shrubs and hedges, runs parallel with the shoreline providing lovely views. Suitable for all ages, this is a well run park mainly for touring units, with campers pitched mostly towards the shore. It provides 125 pitches with electricity (6A), although many are seasonally occupied.

Facilities

Three well maintained, well designed toilet blocks are of a high standard. Laundry. Motorcaravan services. Play area. Tennis. Football field, well away from the pitches. Fishing. Boat launching. Supermarket at park entrance. Dogs are not accepted. WiFi. Off site: Bicycle hire 6 km. Riding 10 km. Golf 2 km.

Open: 20 April - 24 September.

Directions

Take N71 to Bandon, then R586 Bandon to Bantry. From Bantry take N71 to Glengarriff. 6.4 km. from Bantry; or N22 Cork to Macroom, R584 to Ballylickey Bridge, N71 to Glengarriff. Entrance opposite Cronins petrol station.
GPS: 51.718333, -9.455278

Charges 2012

Per unit incl. 2 persons	
and electricity	€ 29.00 - € 32.00
extra person	€ 10.00
child	€ 3.00
motorcyclist, hiker or cyclist (per person)	€ 12.00

Belleek

Belleek Caravan & Camping Park

Belleek, Ballina (Co. Mayo) T: 096 715 33. E: lenahan@belleekpark.com

alanrogers.com/IR8750

Belleek has a quiet woodland setting, only minutes from Ballina, a famed salmon fishing centre. With excellent pitches and toilet block, the family owners are committed to ensuring that it is immaculate at all times. From the entrance gate, the park is approached by a drive that passes reception and leads to 58 well spaced pitches. With a very neat overall appearance, 32 pitches have hardstanding, 45 have electricity hook-ups, and you may choose your pitch. Sports facilities within a short distance of the park include a swimming pool, tennis and bicycle hire. There is a Blue Flag beach at Ross.

Facilities

Spotlessly clean, tastefully decorated toilet block providing showers (€ 1 token). Baby bath. Facilities for disabled campers. Laundry facilities. Reception includes a shop (June-Sept) and a tea room also serving breakfast. Campers' kitchen and emergency accommodation with beds provided. TV room. Games room. Play area. Ball game area. Tennis. Barbecue area. Off site: Fishing 1 km. Bicycle hire 2 km. Golf 3.5 km. Beach 10 km.

Open: 1 March - 1 November, by arrangement all year.

Directions

Take R314 Ballina - Killala road. Park is signed on right after about 3 km. GPS: 54.1345, -9.1585

Charges guide

Per unit incl. 2 persons and electricity	€ 23.00
extra person	€ 5.00
child	€ 2.50
hiker/cyclist and tent	€ 9.00
Low season discounts for stays of 3 or more nights when pre-paid.	

For latest campsite news visit

alanrogers.com

Bennettsbridge

Nore Valley Park

Annamult, Bennettsbridge (Co. Kilkenny) T: 056 772 7229. E: norevalleypark@eircom.net

alanrogers.com/IR9230

This lovely site is set on a grassy hill overlooking the valley of the River Nore, with a woodland setting behind. Situated on a working farm, it offers 70 touring pitches, 50 of which have 6A electricity. There is an additional area for tents and four mobile homes for rent. The owners, Samuel and Isobel, are proud of their park and her baking and jams must be sampled. An attractive courtyard houses several unusual facilities including a sand pit and a straw loft play area for wet weather. Animal park, outdoor chess, tractor rides and go-karts in the fields. There is easy access to Waterford city, famous for its crystal.

Facilities	Directions
The modern toilet block is kept clean and can be heated. Two units suitable for disabled visitors. Laundry room. Motorcaravan services. Shop (basic items such as milk, bread and camping gaz) and café (June-Aug). Lounge. Games room. Play area. Minigolf. Off site: Bennettsbridge 3 km. Outdoor pursuits nearby such as canoeing, walking and fishing 4 km. Riding 6 km. Golf 10 km. Open: 1 March - 31 October.	From Kilkenny take R700 to Bennettsbridge. Just before the bridge turn right at sign for Stoneyford and after about 3 km. site is signed Nore Valley Park. GPS: 52.56307, -7.19506

Charges 2012

Per unit incl. 2 persons and electricity	€ 22.00 - € 24.00
extra person	€ 4.00

Blarney

Blarney Caravan & Camping Park

Stone View, Blarney (Co. Cork) T: 021 451 6519. E: con.quill@camping-ireland.ie

alanrogers.com/IR9480

There is a heart of the country feel about this 'on the farm' site, yet the city of Cork is only an 8 km. drive. What makes this friendly, family run park so appealing is its secluded location and neatly laid out, open appearance. The terrain on the three-acre park is elevated and gently sloping, commanding views towards Blarney Castle and the surrounding mountainous countryside. The 80 pitches, 39 of which have hardstanding and 10A electrical connections, are with the caravans near the entrance, and tents are pitched slightly further away. There are gravel roads, well tended young shrubs and a screen of mature trees. Tidy hedging marks the park's perimeter.

Facilities	Directions
Excellent toilet facilities in converted farm buildings. Reception and small shop are now at entrance. Good facilities for disabled visitors. Laundry room. Campers' kitchen. Motorcaravan service point. Shop (1/6-31/8). TV lounge. Internet and WiFi (charged). Delightful 18-hole golf and pitch and putt course. Off site: Bar 100 m. Within easy reach of the ports of Cork and Rosslare. Open: 30 March - 29 October.	Site is 8 km. northwest of Cork, just off the N20. Take N20 from Cork for about 6 km. and then left on R617 to Blarney. Site clearly signed at Top petrol station in village, in 2 km. GPS: 51.94787, -8.54622

Charges guide

Per unit incl. 2 persons and electricity	€ 25.00 - € 27.00
extra person	€ 6.50
child (under 14 yrs)	€ 3.00 - € 3.50

Boyle

Lough Key Caravan & Camping Park

Lough Key Forest Park, Boyle (Co. Roscommon) T: 071 966 2212. E: info@loughkey.ie

alanrogers.com/IR8825

This caravan and camping park is set deep in the 320 hectares of the Lough Key Forest Park. Comprising mixed woodland including giant red cedar, beech, ash and oak trees, the forest is bounded by Lough Key and incorporates several of its islands. The rustic design of the main building on the park (which houses reception, a campers' kitchen, a TV room, and the sanitary and laundry facilities) blends well with the wooded environment. The well landscaped, five-hectare site provides space for 52 touring units with electricity connections and ample water points. There is a separate area for tents. The history of the parkland goes back to 1184.

Facilities	Directions
The main toilet block includes metered hot showers (€ 2). Facilities for disabled campers (key required). Campers' kitchen and sheltered eating area. Laundry. TV room. Play area in the centre of the park with adventure type play equipment in a hedged area, plus seating for parents. Forest walks and trails. Boat tours and boat hire. Security barrier closed at night. Off site: Restaurant at Rockingham harbour. Boyle 3 km. Bicycle hire and golf 5 km. Open: Easter - mid September.	Park is 4 km. east of Boyle on the N4 Dublin - Sligo Road. GPS: 53.98125, -8.235167

Charges guide

Per unit incl. 2 persons and electricity	€ 25.00
No credit cards.	

For latest campsite news visit

alanrogers.com

Caherdaniel

Wave Crest Caravan & Camping Park

Caherdaniel (Co. Kerry) T: 066 947 5188. E: wavecrest@eircom.net

alanrogers.com/IR9560

It would be difficult to imagine a more dramatic location than Wave Crest's on the Ring of Kerry coast. Huge boulders and rocky outcrops tumble from the park entrance on the N70 down to the seashore which forms the most southern promontory on the Ring of Kerry. There are spectacular southward views from the park across Kenmare Bay to the Beara peninsula. Sheltering on grass patches in small coves that nestle between the rocks and shrubbery, are 65 hardstanding pitches and 20 on grass offering seclusion. Electricity connections are available (13A). This park would suit older people looking for a quiet, relaxed atmosphere.

Facilities

Two blocks house the sanitary and laundry facilities and include hot showers on payment (€ 1). Small shop and takeaway service (June-Sept). Small play area. Fishing and boat launching. Off site: Riding 1 km. Bicycle hire and golf 10 km. Small beach near and Derrynane Hotel with bar and restaurant.

Open: All year.

Directions

On the N70 (Ring of Kerry), 1.5 km. east of Caherdaniel. GPS: 51.75881, -10.09112

Charges guide

Per unit incl. 2 persons and electricity	€ 27.00
extra person	€ 6.00
child	€ 2.00

Cahir

The Apple Camping & Caravan Park

Moorstown, Cahir (Co. Tipperary) T: 052 744 1459. E: con@theapplefarm.com

alanrogers.com/IR9410

This fruit farm and campsite combination offers an idyllic country holiday venue in one of the most delightful situations imaginable. For tourers only, it is located off the N24, midway between Clonmel and Cahir. The park has 32 pitches in a secluded situation behind the barns; they are mostly grass with 14 hardstandings and 25 electricity connections (13A, Europlug). Entrance is by way of a 300 m. drive flanked by the orchard fields and various non-fruit tree species, which are named and of interest to guests who are free to spend time walking the paths around the farm.

Facilities

Toilet facilities, kept very clean, quite modern in design and with heating, comprise showers, washbasins with mirrors, electric points, etc. in functional units occupying two corners of the large floor space. Facilities for disabled visitors. Also in the barn are dishwashing sinks, washing machine and a fridge/freezer for campers to use. Good drive-on motorcaravan service point. Good tennis court (free). Play area. Dogs accepted by prior arrangement. Off site: Fishing, golf, bicycle hire and riding within 6 km.

Open: 1 May - 30 September.

Directions

Park is 300 m. off main N24, 9.6 km. west of Clonmel, 6.4 km. east of Cahir. GPS: 52.37663, -7.84262

Charges guide

Per unit incl. 2 persons and electricity	€ 15.50
extra person	€ 6.50
child	€ 4.50
No charge per unit.	
Less 20% for groups of 4 or more.	

Cahirciveen

Mannix Point Camping & Caravan Park

Cahirciveen (Co. Kerry) T: 066 947 2806. E: mortimer@campinginkerry.com

alanrogers.com/IR9610

A tranquil, beautifully located seashore park, it is no exaggeration to describe Mannix Point as a nature lovers' paradise. Situated in one of the most spectacular parts of the Ring of Kerry, overlooking the bay and Valentia Island, the rustic seven-acre park commands splendid views in all directions. The park road meanders through the level site and offers 42 pitches of various sizes and shapes, many with shelter and seclusion. There are 42 electrical connections (10A) available. A charming, old flower bedecked fisherman's cottage has been converted to provide facilities including reception, excellent campers' kitchen and a cosy sitting room with turf fire. There is no television, but compensation comes in the form of a knowledgeable, hospitable owner who is a Bord Fáilte registered local tour guide. A keen gardener, Mortimer Moriarty laid out the site over 20 years ago and his intention to cause as little disruption to nature as possible has succeeded. The site opens directly onto marshland which teems with wildlife (a two-acre nature reserve) with direct access to the beach and seashore. A viewing platform allows observation of seals and birdlife and to consider the secrets of the park sculpture, 'the pinnacle'. This park retains a wonderful air of Irish charm aided by occasional impromptu musical evenings. This is also an ideal resting place for people walking the Kerry Way.

Facilities

Toilet and shower facilities were clean when we visited. Modern and well equipped campers' kitchen and dining area. Comfortable campers' sitting room. Laundry facilities with washing machines and dryer. Motorcaravan service point. Picnic and barbecue facilities. Fishing and boat launching from site. Off site: Bicycle hire 800 m. Riding 3 km. Golf 14 km. Pubs, restaurants and shops 15 mins. walk. Watersports, birdwatching, walking, photography. Local cruises to Skelligs Rock with free transport to and from the port for walkers and cyclists.

Open: 15 March - 15 October.

Directions

Park is 300 m. off the N70 Ring of Kerry road, 800 m. southwest of Cahirciveen (or Cahersiveen) on road towards Waterville. GPS: 51.941517, -10.24465

Charges guide

Per unit incl. 2 persons and electricity	€ 27.00
extra person	€ 6.00

Reductions for activity groups and rallies if pre-paid. No credit cards.

Castlebar

Carra Caravan & Camping Park

Belcarra, Castlebar (Co. Mayo) T: 094 903 2054. E: post@mayoholidays.com

alanrogers.com/IR8790

This is an ideal location for those seeking a real Irish village experience in a value-for-money park. Small, unpretentious and family run, it is located in Belcarra, a regular winner of the Tidiest Mayo Village award. Nestling at the foot of a wooded drumlin, it is surrounded by rolling hills and quiet roads which offer an away from it all feeling, yet Castlebar the county's largest town is only an 8 km. drive. On the pleasant 1.5-acre park, the 20 unmarked touring pitches, 15 with electric hook-up (13A Europlug), are on flat ground enclosed by ranch fencing and shaded in parts by trees.

Facilities

The new toilet block has well equipped showers (€ 1). Combined kitchen with dishwashing, laundry area with fridge/freezer, sink, table, chairs, washing machine and dryer. Comfortable lounge with TV, books and magazines located at reception. Off site: Village shops, a post office and 'Flukies' cosy bar with traditional Irish music most Friday nights. Leisure centre and tennis court. Free fishing area and special loop walkway by the river. Golf 8 km.

Open: 31 March - 10 November.

Directions

From Castlebar follow the N84 towards Ballinrobe. On the outskirts of Castlebar, 100 m. after the railway bridge turn left for Belcarra (Ballycarra) 8 km. GPS: 53.80205, -9.21622

Charges guide

Per unit incl. all persons and electricity	€ 16.00

No credit cards.

For latest campsite news visit

alanrogers.com

Castlebar

Lough Lannagh Caravan Park

Old Westport Road, Castlebar (Co. Mayo) T: 094 902 7111. E: info@loughlannagh.ie

alanrogers.com/IR8810

Lough Lannagh is an attractive holiday village on the lake shore, comprising quality accommodation, self catering cottages and a caravan park. It is within walking distance of Castlebar with its restaurants, pubs, theatres and shops. County Mayo's main attractions are also within a short drive. The caravan park has 20 touring pitches, well laid out in a separate dedicated corner of the village, all on hardstanding with electric connections. There is a separate grass area for tents. One reception area serves all and is situated to the right of the security barrier; check in prior to 18:00. When not out and about, there are many on-site activities for all the family.

Facilities

One modern heated sanitary block provides washbasins and well equipped, preset showers. En-suite unit for disabled visitors. Laundry room with sink, washing machines and dryers. Café (serving breakfast). Fitness suite (free entry and over 18s only admitted). Table tennis. Boules. Badminton. Tennis. Dogs are not accepted in July/Aug.

Open: 22 April - 30 September.

Directions

To get to Castlebar take the N5, N60 or N84. At Castlebar ring road follow directions for Westport. Site is signed on all approach roads to the Westport roundabout. GPS: 53.8491, -9.3119

Charges guide

Per unit incl. 2 persons, electricity and hardstanding	€ 21.00 - € 28.00
tent incl. 2 persons (no car)	€ 15.00 - € 18.00
child	€ 1.50

Castlegregory

Anchor Caravan Park

Castlegregory (Co. Kerry) T: 066 713 9157. E: anchorcaravanpark@eircom.net

alanrogers.com/IR9550

Of County Kerry's three long, finger like peninsulas which jut into the sea, Dingle is the most northerly. Anchor Caravan Park is 20 km. west of Tralee, the main town, and under 4 km. south of Castlegregory on Tralee Bay. Its situation, just 150 m. from a fine sandy beach, provides ideal opportunities for safe bathing, boating and shore fishing. A secluded and mature, five acre park, it is enclosed by shrubs and trees that give excellent shelter. There are 30 pitches, all with electric hook-ups and some also with drainage and water points. Although there are holiday homes for hire, these are well apart from the touring pitches. The approach roads to the park are narrow and may be difficult for larger units.

Facilities

Toilet facilities (entry by key) are kept very clean and provide showers on payment (€ 0,50), two private cabins, some low level basins and a toilet with handrail. No facilities for disabled campers. Laundry facilities (incl. drying room, clothes lines and ironing). Campers' kitchen with fridges, freezers and seating. Motorcaravan services. Two play areas. Games and TV rooms. Off site: Beautiful sandy beach 2 minutes. Fishing 2 km. Riding and bicycle hire 3 km. Golf 4 km.

Open: Easter - 30 September.

Directions

From Tralee follow the N86 Dingle coast road for 19 km. At Camp take the R560 towards Castlegregory. Park is signed from Camp junction. GPS: 52.24393, -9.98579

Charges guide

Per unit incl. 2 persons and electricity	€ 20.00 - € 22.00
extra person	€ 5.00
child	€ 2.00
No credit cards.	

Clondalkin

Camac Valley Tourist Caravan & Camping Park

Green Isle Road, Clondalkin Dublin 22 (Co. Dublin) T: 014 640 644. E: reservations@camacvalley.com

alanrogers.com/IR9100

Opened in 1996, this campsite is not only well placed for Dublin, but also offers a welcome stopover if travelling to the more southern counties from the north of the country, or vice versa. Despite its close proximity to the city, being located in the 300-acre Corkagh Park gives it a heart-of-the-country atmosphere. There are 163 pitches, 48 for tents placed to the fore and hardstandings for caravans laid out in bays and avenues with electrical connections, drainage and water points. Maturing trees and shrubs separate pitches and roads are of tarmac. Beyond the entrance gate and forecourt stands an attractive timber fronted building housing the site amenities.

Facilities

Heated sanitary facilities include good sized showers (token). Facilities for disabled visitors. Baby room. Laundry. Shop and coffee bar. Playground with wooden play frames and safety base. Fishing. Electronic gate controlled from reception and 24 hour security. Off site: Bicycle hire 1.5 km. Golf 6 km. Riding 9 km.

Open: All year.

Directions

From north follow signs for West Link and M50 motorway. Exit M50 at junction 9 onto N7 Cork road. Site is on right of dual-carriageway (beside Green Isle Hotel) after 2 km. At City West business park, cross bridge, return on dual-carriageway. Site is on left after 800 m. GPS: 53.30445, -6.41533

Charges guide

Per unit incl. 2 persons	€ 20.00 - € 24.00
up to 4 children	€ 21.00 - € 26.00

Cong

Cong Caravan & Camping Park

Lisloughrey, Quay Road, Cong (Co. Mayo) T: 094 954 6089. E: info@quietman-cong.com

alanrogers.com/IR8740

It would be difficult to find a more idyllic and famous spot for a caravan park than Cong. Situated close to the shores of Lough Corrib, Cong's scenic beauty was immortalised in the film, The Quiet Man. This well kept park is 1.6 km. from the village of Cong, near the grounds of the magnificent and renowned Ashford Castle. The owner's house that incorporates reception, shop and the hostel, stands to the fore of the site. Toilet facilities and the holiday hostel accommodation are entered from the courtyard area. The 40 grass pitches, 36 with electricity, are placed at a higher level to the rear, with the sheltered tent areas below and to the side. The park can be crowded and busy in high season.

Facilities

Toilet facilities are tastefully decorated, kept clean and are heated when necessary. Hot showers with curtains (€ 1 charge). Campers' kitchen. Launderette service. Shop. Catering is a feature – full Irish and continental breakfast, dinner and packed lunch may be ordered, and home baked bread and scones purchased in the shop. Barbecue, games room and extensive play area. TV lounge. Bicycle hire. Off site: Riding and golf within 2 km.

Open: All year.

Directions

Leave N84 road at Ballinrobe to join R334/345 signed Cong. Turn left at end of the R345 (opposite Ashford Castle), take next road on right (300 m) and the park is on right. GPS: 53.53945, -9.27263

Charges guide

Per unit incl. 2 persons and electricity	€ 20.00 - € 25.00
Camping Cheques accepted.	

Corofin

Corofin Village Camping & Caravan Park

Main Street, Corofin (Co. Clare) T: 065 683 7683. E: info@corofin.camping.com

alanrogers.com/IR9460

This compact green oasis in the centre of the village of Corofin occupies one acre and adjoins the family's hostel. The owners, Jude and Marie Neylon, live on the site and have a policy of always having a family member on hand at all times. They are very environmentally aware and have excellent recycling facilities. The 16 touring pitches all have electricity and there are ample water points. The site now includes a small separate tent area which is quite private and well sheltered. A campers' kitchen, laundry room and the TV and games room are separate to the hostel facilities. This little site is neat and well maintained and makes an ideal base for sightseeing throughout Clare.

Facilities

The sanitary block is bright and clean with free hot showers. Separate facilities for disabled campers. Laundry room with washing machine and dryer. Campers' kitchen. TV and games room. CCTV security. Free WiFi. Torches useful. Site is not suitable for large units. Off site: Fishing and boat launching 2 km. Riding 8 km. Bicycle hire 10 km.

Open: 1 April - 30 September.

Directions

Corofin village is 12 km. from Ennis, from where you take the N85 towards Ennistymon and after 2 km. (well signed) turn right onto R476. Site is in the centre of the village. GPS: 52.9407, -9.058933

Charges guide

Per unit incl. 2 persons and electricity	€ 25.00
No credit cards.	

For latest campsite news visit

alanrogers.com

Donard

Moat Farm Caravan & Camping Park

Donard (Co. Wicklow) T: 045 404 727. E: moatfarm@ireland.com

alanrogers.com/IR9160

Providing a true feel of the countryside, this park is part of a working sheep farm. It offers incredible vistas across a scenic landscape, yet is within driving distance of Dublin and Rosslare. Driving into the village of Donard you little suspect that alongside the main street lies a pleasant, well cared for and tranquil five acre campsite. The entrance is approached by way of a short road where the ruins of a Medieval church sit high overlooking the forecourt and reception. There are 40 pitches for caravans and tents. Spacious pitches with hardstanding line both sides of a broad avenue, incorporating ample space for awnings and all with electricity and drainage. A large field takes tents and further caravans.

Facilities

The toilet block is kept very clean and includes spacious showers. Facilities for visitors with disabilities. Well equipped laundry room. Good quality campers' kitchen. Large recreation/entertainment room with open fire. Three large barbecues and patio area. Caravan storage. Off site: Mountain climbing and sites of archaeological interest nearby. Fishing 3 km. Golf and riding 13 km. Bicycle hire 15 km.

Open: 15 March - 30 September.

Directions

Park is 16.5 km. south of Blessington. Leave M50 Dublin ring motorway at exit 10 to join N81 southwest for 19 km. to Blessington. Continue on N81 for a further 16.5 km. and turn left at Old Toll House pub onto local road and follow signs to park in Donard village (3.5 km). GPS: 53.0212, -6.61562

Charges guide

Per unit incl. 2 persons and electricity	€ 23.00
extra person	€ 5.00
child	€ 3.00
motorcyclist, cyclist or hiker incl. tent	€ 10.00

No credit cards.

Doolin

Nagle's Doolin Camping & Caravan Park

Doolin (Co. Clare) T: 065 707 4458. E: ken@doolincamping.com

alanrogers.com/IR9465

This neat and tidy seaside site is located just one kilometre from the cliffs of Moher, and a short ferry ride from the sparsely populated Aran Islands. The nearby village of Doolin, famed for its traditional music, has a good range of shops, restaurants and pubs. The four-hectare site, which enjoys spectacular views over the bay to Conemara, has 99 pitches, including 76 level hardstandings (with 10A electricity, water and drainage) and grass pitches for tents. They are not separated by hedges, but the site is divided into bays by limestone walls. There is excellent WiFi coverage over the whole site. Walkers and nature lovers will be in their element among the rare species of flowers and insects found in this limestone region known as the Burren. Doolin itself is home to a number of traditional pubs with lively, impromptu music sessions featuring musicians from Ireland and overseas. A complete contrast is offered by the many signposted coastal walks along the eight-kilometre headland, with its panoramic views towards the Aran Islands, just 20 minutes away by high speed ferry.

Facilities

One modern, well equipped toilet block is unheated but has good facilities including en-suite unit for disabled visitors. Laundry with 3 washers and 3 dryers (charged). Kitchen with cooking rings (charged), fridge/freezer and dishwashing sinks with hot water. Shop (June-Aug). Motorcaravan service point. Gas. WiFi throughout. Off site: Pitch and putt, boat launching and ferry to Aran Islands all 300 m. Fishing, riding, bicycle hire, shops, hot food and bars within 1-2 km. Golf 10 km.

Open: Open from St Patrick's weekend to mid/end October (check with site).

Directions

From Limerick take N85 round Ennis to Ennistymon, then N67 towards Lisdoonvarna. After 11 km. turn left for Doolin and then Doolin Pier. Site signed. From Galway take N18 and then in 20 km. N67 to Lisdoonvarna and follow signs as above. GPS: 53.01677, -9.402

Charges guide

Per unit incl. 2 persons and electricity	€ 21.00 - € 23.00
extra person	€ 7.00
child	€ 3.00

For latest campsite news visit

alanrogers.com

Dungarvan

Casey's Caravan & Camping Park

Clonea, Dungarvan (Co. Waterford) T: 058 419 19

alanrogers.com/IR9330

This is a very large park by Irish standards. Set on 20 acres of flat grass, edged by mature trees, this family run park is well managed and offers 284 pitches which include 110 touring pitches all with electrical hook-ups and 60 with hardstanding. There is even a large, open and flat field without services for high season overspill arrivals. The remainder are occupied by caravan holiday homes. There is direct access from the park to a sandy, Blue Flag beach with a resident lifeguard during July and August. A highly recommended leisure centre is adjacent should the weather be inclement. The park is 5.5 km. from Dungarvan, a popular town for deep sea angling, from where charter boats can be hired and three, 18-hole golf courses are within easy driving distance. Suggested drives include the scenic Vee, the Comeragh Mountain Drive and the coast road to Tramore – the last having a series of magical coves and the remains of old copper mines. The pretty 'English' village of Lismore and the picturesque and historic town of Youghal, once home to Sir Walter Raleigh, are each about 30 km. drive away.

Facilities

The central toilet block (key access), has good facilities kept spotlessly clean. Showers on payment (€ 1). Small laundry with washing machine and dryer. A further modern block provides an excellent campers' kitchen, laundry room and toilet for disabled visitors. Large adventure play area. Large, well equipped games room. TV lounge. Minigolf. Gas supplies. Full time security staff in high season. Play area (under 4 yrs). WiFi throughout (free). Off site: Two village stores near the beach. Hotel for food and drink. Golf 5 km. Fishing 4 km. Riding 20 km.

Open: 5 April - 9 September.

Directions

From Dungarvan centre follow R675 east for 3.5 km. Look for signs on the right to Clonea Bay and site. Site is about 1.5 km. GPS: 52.094767, -7.546167

Charges guide

Per unit incl. 2 persons and electricity	€ 29.00 - € 33.00
extra person	€ 7.00 - € 8.00
child	€ 3.00
hiker, biker, cyclist	€ 10.00 - € 10.50

No credit cards.

Fermoy

Blackwater Valley Caravan & Camping Park

Mallow-Killarney Road, Fermoy (Co. Cork) T: 025 321 47. E: blackwatervalleycaravanpark@gmail.com

alanrogers.com/IR9470

The location of this park provides the best of both worlds, as it backs onto green fields adjacent to the Blackwater river, yet is within 200 metres of Fermoy town. Pat and Nora Ryan live overlooking the park which ensures supervision and prompt attention. Well situated for touring, there are 25 pitches, all with hardstanding and electricity connections (13A). Water taps are convenient to all pitches. Considerable additional space for tents is available towards the rear of the park. There are five caravan holiday homes to rent. Fermoy provides many amenities, such as a cinema, restaurants and pubs, many providing traditional music. The town park has a leisure centre with pool.

Facilities

Modern, tiled toilet block provides the usual facilities including an en-suite shower room for disabled visitors. Laundry room with ironing facilities. Campers' kitchen with cooking facilities and dining area. TV and games room. Motorcaravan service point. Off site: Fishing adjacent. Internet access 100 m. Bicycle hire 1 km. Golf 3.5 km. Beach 35 km.

Open: 15 March - 31 October.

Directions

In Fermoy town take the N72 for Mallow. Park is 200 m. from the junction. GPS: 52.141498, -8.281873

Charges guide

Per unit incl. 2 persons and electricity	€ 24.00
extra person	€ 6.00
child	€ 3.00

No credit cards.

Galway

Salthill Caravan Park

Salthill (Co. Galway) T: 091 523 972. E: info@salthillcaravanpark.com

alanrogers.com/IR8870

Salthill Caravan Park was first opened in 1960, and has been run by the O'Malley family ever since. The park comprises 5 acres of mobile homes and a 3 acre campsite. The park has some superb views of Galway Bay, and has easy access to the beach, just 20 m. distant. Pitches are grassy and sunny, and most have electrical connections (10A). A number of hardstandings are available. Adjacent to the site, there is a pleasant coastal pathway which leads to Galway City. Off site, there is a friendly pub (200 m) and a well-stocked supermarket (600 m). Salthill beach is actually several sandy Blue Flag beaches separated by rocky outcrops. Windsurfing, kayaking and paddle boarding are all popular, and courses are available nearby. The Galway Atlantiquaria is Ireland's premier aquarium, and boasts more than 170 species of fresh water and marine life. Galway City is renowned for its important Arts festival in July, when the city welcomes over 100,000 visitors for a programme of visual art, music, theatre and dance.

Facilities

Beach adjacent. Play area. Games room. Tourist information. Fully equipped mobile homes for rent. Off site: Watersports. Fishing. Golf. Supermarket 600 m. Pub 200 m.

Open: April - 26 September.

Directions

From Galway City take R336 which leads through Salthill Village, along the ocean front and then to Salthill Caravan Park. GPS: 53.256798, -9.104914

Charges guide

Per unit incl. 2 persons and electricity	€ 24.00 - € 29.00
extra person	€ 5.00
child	free - € 3.00
dog	free

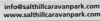

West of Ireland's only **3 star caravan park** on the shores of the famous Galway bay. Ideal for touring Connemara and the Burren. There is a bus service into Galway city every 35 mins from the park. Not to be missed is O'Connor's famous Irish pub.

Open from the 1st April till 29 September 2012

Tel. 00353 (0)91 523 972

info@salthillcaravanpark.com
www.salthillcaravanpark.com

Galway will be hosting the world renowned Volvo ocean race on the end of June 2012 the final leg not to be missed!

Glandore

The Meadow Camping Park

Glandore (Co. Cork) T: 028 332 80. E: meadowcamping@eircom.net

alanrogers.com/IR9500

The stretch of coast from Cork to Skibbereen reminds British visitors of Devon before the era of mass tourism. This is rich dairy country, the green of the meadows matching the emerald colours of the travel posters. Thanks to the warm and wet Gulf Stream climate, it is also a county of gardens and keen gardeners. The Meadow is best described not as a site but as a garden surrounded, appropriately, by lush meadows. The owners, who live on the park, have cunningly arranged accommodation for 19 pitches, 14 with 6A electric hook-ups (12 Europlugs), among the flower beds and shrubberies of their extended garden. There are 12 hardstandings. Among the homely features are a campers' kitchen and a dining area.

Facilities

Facilities are limited but well designed and maintained with brand new solar panels. Showers on payment. Washing machine and dryer. Larger units may be accepted depending on length and available space; contact park before arrival. Football and cycling are not permitted on the park. WiFi (charged). Off site: Riding 5 km. Fishing, swimming, boat launching and sailing at Glandore 2 km. Bicycle hire 10 km. Golf 19 km.

Open: Easter - 15 September.

Directions

Park is 1.5 km. east of Glandore, off N71 road, on R597 midway between Leap and Rosscarbery (coast road). Approach roads are very narrow. GPS: 51.56693, -9.09702

Charges 2012

Per unit incl. 2 persons and electricity	€ 23.00
extra person	€ 6.00
child (under 16 yrs)	€ 3.00

No credit cards.

For latest campsite news visit

alanrogers.com

Glenbeigh

Glenross Caravan & Camping Park

Ring of Kerry, Glenbeigh (Co. Kerry) T: 087 137 6865. E: glenross@eircom.net

alanrogers.com/IR9600

Its situation on the spectacular Ring of Kerry and the Kerry Way footpath gives Glenross an immediate advantage, and scenic grandeur around every bend of the road is guaranteed as Glenbeigh is approached. Quietly located before entering the village, the park commands stunning views of Rossbeigh Strand, (within walking distance) and the Dingle Peninsula. On arrival, a good impression is created with the park being well screened from the road and with a new stone entrance and gates. With 30 touring pitches, 26 with hardstanding and all with 10A electricity (Europlug), and six caravan holiday homes, the park is attractively laid out. There is a dedicated small tent area.

Facilities	Directions
Well maintained modern toilet block includes facilities for laundry and dishwashing. Motorcaravan service point. Games room. Bicycle hire. Shelter for campers and new dining area. Bar, restaurant and takeaway (all season). WiFi throughout (free). Off site: Playground at Blue Flag Rossbeigh beach (5 minutes). Watersports and tennis nearby. Riding and fishing 200 m.	Park is on the N70 Killorglin - Glenbeigh road, on the right just before entering the village. GPS: 52.05887, -9.93198

Open: 6 April - 24 September.

Charges guide

Per unit incl. 2 persons and electricity	€ 29.00 - € 30.00
extra person	€ 8.00

No credit cards.

Keel

Keel Sandybanks Caravan & Camping Park

Keel, Achill Island (Co. Mayo) T: 098 432 11. E: info@achillcamping.com

alanrogers.com/IR8730

This is a park offering a taste of island life and the opportunity to relax in dramatic, scenic surroundings. Achill, Ireland's largest island, is 24 km. long and 19 km. wide and is connected to the mainland by a bridge. The site is situated beside Keel village and approached by the R319 from the swivel bridge at Achill Sound. Although there are static holiday mobile homes on this site, the 42 pitches for caravans and 42 for tents are kept separate. Some with hardstanding are located at the perimeter fence overlooking the beach. Although sand based, the ground is firm and level. Roads are tarmac and there is direct access to the beach which is supervised by lifeguards.

Facilities	Directions
Two modern toilet blocks, one beside reception and the other in a central position. Heated facilities include WCs (one for disabled visitors), washbasins and hot showers (on payment). Hair- and hand dryers. Play area. TV room. Watersports enthusiasts can enjoy surfing, canoeing and board sailing on Keel Strand and Lough. Fishing trips can be arranged. WiFi throughout (charged). Off site: Bicycle hire and golf 200 m. Riding 6 km.	From Achill Sound follow the R319 for 16 km. Site is on the left before Keel village. GPS: 53.97535, -10.0779

Open: 22 April - 12 September.

Charges 2012

Per unit incl. 2 persons and electricity	€ 18.00 - € 21.00
child	€ 2.00
extra person	€ 3.00

Killarney

Fossa Caravan & Camping Park

Fossa, Killarney (Co. Kerry) T: 064 663 1497. E: fossaholidays@eircom.net

alanrogers.com/IR9590

This park is in the village of Fossa, ten minutes by car or bus (six per day) from Killarney town centre. Fossa Caravan Park has a distinctive reception building and hostel accommodation, a stimulating play area and shop. The park is divided in two – the touring caravan area lies to the right, tucked behind the main building and to the left is an open grass area mainly for campers. Touring pitches, with electricity (10/15A) and drainage, have hardstanding and are angled between shrubs and trees in a garden setting. To the rear at a higher level and discreetly placed are 30 caravan holiday homes, sheltered by the thick foliage of the wooded slopes which climb high behind the park.

Facilities	Directions
Modern toilet facilities include showers on payment. En-suite unit for campers with disabilities. Laundry room. Campers' kitchen. Shop. Takeaway (8/7-25/8). TV lounge. Tennis. Play area. Picnic area. Games room. Security patrol. Off site: Fishing and golf 2 km. Riding 3 km. Bicycle hire 5 km. Woodland walk into Killarney. A visit to Killarney National Park is highly recommended.	Approaching Killarney, follow signs for N72 Ring of Kerry/Killorglin. At last roundabout join R562/N72. Continue for 5.5 km. and Fossa is the second park to the right. GPS: 52.07071, -9.58573

Open: 1 April - 30 September.

Charges guide

Per unit incl. 2 persons	€ 22.00 - € 26.00
extra person	€ 6.00

For latest campsite news visit

alanrogers.com

Killarney
Fleming's White Bridge

Ballycasheen Road, Killarney (Co. Kerry) T: 064 663 1590. E: info@killarneycamping.com

alanrogers.com/IR9620

The main road from Cork to Killarney (N22) runs through the gentle valley of the Flesk river. Between the two sits Fleming's White Bridge Camping Park. Its ten-hectare site is within comfortable walking distance of Killarney centre. Surrounded by mature broad-leafed trees, the park is flat, landscaped and generously adorned with flowers and shrubs. It comprises 92 pitches, the majority for touring caravans on well-kept grass pitches with electricity hook-ups, although some have concrete handstanding and some pitches are reserved for tents.

Facilities

Three toilet blocks are of a high standard. Motorcaravan service point. Campers' drying room and two laundries. Small shop (1/6-1/9). Two TV rooms and a games room. Fishing (advice and permits provided). Canoeing (own canoes). Bicycle hire. Woodland walks. Off site: Riding 3 km. Golf 2 km.

Open: 15 March - 31 October.

Directions

From Cork and Mallow: at N72/N22 junction continue towards Killarney and take first turn left (signed Ballycasheen Road). Proceed for 300 m. to archway entrance on left. GPS: 52.05595, -9.47458

Charges guide

| Per unit incl. 2 persons and electricity | € 30.00 - € 31.00 |
| extra person | € 8.00 |

No credit cards.

Killarney
Donoghues White Villa Farm Caravan & Camping Park

Lissivigeen, Killarney - Cork Road N22, Killarney (Co. Kerry) T: 064 662 0671.
E: killarneycamping@eircom.net alanrogers.com/IR9630

This is a very pleasing small touring park in scenic surroundings off the N22 Cork - Killarney road. Set in the countryside surrounded by green fields, yet only five minutes away from Killarney town. There are many trees and shrubs around the park but dominant is a magnificent view of the MacGillicuddy's Reeks. There are 30 pitches for caravans and tents, 20 with hardstanding and a grass area for awnings, electricity (10A Europlug), water points and night lighting. One pitch is designated for disabled campers and there is an en-suite facility for their use. An unusual novelty is that old school desks are placed in pairs around the site as picnic tables, plus an antique green telephone box. One can also enjoy walking through the oak wood, fishing on the Flesk or visiting the site's own National Farm Museum.

Facilities

The toilet block, a sandstone coloured building, is kept spotlessly clean and houses showers on payment (€ 1), a good toilet/shower room for disabled visitors, laundry room and dishwashing sinks. Motorcaravan service area. Campers' kitchen with TV. Play area. Max. 2 dogs (not certain breeds). Daily coach tours from park. WiFi throughout (free). Off site: Riding, golf and bicycle hire 3 km. Pub/restaurant 1 km. Killarney town 5 minutes, the National Park is 10 minutes away.

Open: Easter - 1 October.

Directions

Park is 3 km. east from Killarney town on N22 Cork road. Park entrance is 300 m. east of N22/N72 roundabout. From Killarney follow N22 Cork road signs and White Villa Farm finger signs from Park Road roundabout. GPS: 52.04724, -9.45358

Charges 2012

| Per unit incl. 2 persons | € 22.00 - € 23.00 |
| extra person | € 6.00 |

No credit cards.

Killarney
Killarney Flesk Caravan & Camping Park

Muckross Road, Killarney (Co. Kerry) T: 064 663 1704. E: killarneylakes@eircom.net

alanrogers.com/IR9640

At the gateway to the National Park and Lakes, near Killarney town, this family run, seven-acre park has undergone extensive development and offers high quality standards. Pitches vary in size and spacing and have electricity (10A). Many pitches have a good grass area for awnings, and 11 also have dedicated electricity, water and drainage. The grounds are neat and tidy with a feeling of space. The toilet block is central to most pitches and camp security appears to be tight. This site would appeal to young people wanting to be close to the action in Killarney.

Facilities

Modern, clean toilet blocks are well designed and equipped. Baby room. En-suite facility for disabled campers (key operated). Laundry room. Campers' kitchen. Games room. Night time security checks. Winter caravan storage. Off site: Hotel (same ownership) with bar and restaurant. Fishing 300 m. Boat launching 2 km.

Open: 17 April - 30 September.

Directions

From Killarney follow the N71 and signs for Killarney National Park. Site is 1.5 km. on the left beside the Victoria House Hotel. GPS: 52.04304, -9.49954

Charges guide

| Per unit incl. 2 persons and electricity | € 29.00 - € 30.00 |
| extra person | € 8.50 |

For latest campsite news visit
alanrogers.com

Kilmacanogue

Valley Stopover & Caravan Park

Killough, Kilmacanogue (Co. Wicklow) T: 012 829 565. E: rowanbb@eircom.net

alanrogers.com/IR9140

In a quiet, idyllic setting in the picturesque Rocky Valley, this small, neat, family run park is convenient for the Dublin ferries. Situated in the grounds of the family home, covering under an acre, it can be used either as a transit site or for a longer stay. It will appeal to those who prefer the more basic 'CL' type site. There are four grassy pitches with electric hook-ups, nine hardstandings, a separate area for three tents, two water points, night lighting and a security gate. Staying here, you are only minutes from Enniskerry which lies in the glen of the Glencullen river.

Facilities	Directions
Toilet facilities, clean when we visited, are housed in one unit and consist of two WCs with washbasins, mirrors, etc. and a shower. Laundry sink, spin dryer. Campers' kitchen. Full cooked Irish breakfast in the family guest house. Off site: Riding 3 km. Golf 7 km. Fishing 16 km.	Turn off N11 Dublin - Wexford road at Kilmacanogue, following signs for Glendalough. Continue for 1.6 km. and take right fork signed 'Waterfall'. Park is second opening on the left in about 200 m. GPS: 53.1671, -6.1634
Open: Easter - 31 October.	**Charges guide**

Per unit incl. 2 persons and electricity	€ 20.00
extra person	€ 1.25

Knock

Knock Caravan & Camping Park

Claremorris Road, Knock (Co. Mayo) T: 094 938 8100. E: caravanpark@knock-shrine.ie

alanrogers.com/IR8780

This park is immediately south of the world famous shrine that receives many visitors. Comfortable and clean, the square shaped campsite is kept very neat with tarmac roads and surrounded by clipped trees. The pitches are of a decent size accommodating 50 caravans and motorcaravans, 20 tents and 18 caravan holiday homes (for rent). All pitches have hardstanding (five doubles) and there are 52 electrical connections (13A), with an adequate number of water points. There is also an overflow field. Because of the religious connections of the area, the site is very busy in August and indeed there are unlikely to be any vacancies at all for 14-16 August. Besides visiting the shrine and Knock Museum, it is also a good centre for exploring scenic County Mayo.

Facilities	Directions
Two heated toilet blocks have good facilities for disabled visitors and a nice sized rest room attached, hot showers (on payment) and adequate washing and toilet facilities. Laundry room. Gas supplies. Playground. Restaurant. WiFi. Off site: Fishing 4.5 km. Golf and riding 11 km.	Exit from the N17 at the Knock bypass and from the roundabout follow signs to the site which is just south of the village. GPS: 53.7877, -8.9194
Open: 1 March - 31 October.	**Charges guide**

Per unit incl. 2 persons and electricity	€ 23.50 - € 25.50
extra person	€ 2.00 - € 2.50
child	€ 1.00
No credit cards.	

Lauragh

Creveen Lodge Caravan & Camping Park

Healy Pass, Lauragh (Co. Kerry) T: 064 668 3131. E: info@creveenlodge.com

alanrogers.com/IR9570

The Healy Pass is the well known scenic summit of the R574 road that crosses the Beara Peninsula, shortening the original journey from Kenmare Bay in the north to Bantry Bay in the south by nearly 70 km. As this narrow coast road starts to climb steeply, on the mountain foothills you will arrive at Creveen Lodge, a working hill farm with a quiet, homely atmosphere. The park provides 20 attractive pitches, 16 with 10A electricity and an area of hardstanding for motorcaravans. To allow easy access, the steep farm track is divided into a simple one-way system. Creveen Lodge, commanding views across Kenmare Bay, is divided among three gently sloping fields separated by trees. The park is carefully tended with neat rubbish bins and rustic picnic tables informally placed. Although not so famed as the Iveragh Peninsula, around which runs the Ring of Kerry, the northern Beara is a scenically striking area of County Kerry. This is walking and climbing countryside, with Derreen Gardens nearby.

Facilities

Well appointed and maintained, the small toilet block provides token operated showers (€ 1). Communal room with cooking facilities, a fridge, freezer, TV, ironing board, fireplace, tables and chairs. Reception is in the farmhouse. Play area. Off site: Water sports, riding, 'Seafare' cruises, shops and a restaurant nearby. Fishing 2 km. Bicycle hire and boat launching 9 km.

Open: Easter - 31 October.

Directions

Park is on the Healy Pass road (R574) 1.5 km. southeast of Lauragh. GPS: 51.75562, -9.76193

Charges guide

Per unit incl. 2 persons and electricity	€ 22.00
extra person	€ 3.00
child	€ 1.00

No credit cards.

Mullingar

Lough Ennell Camping & Caravan Park

Tudenham Shore, Mullingar (Co. Westmeath) T: 044 934 8101. E: eamon@caravanparksireland.com

alanrogers.com/IR8965

Natural, rustic charm is the visitor's first impression on arrival at Lough Ennell Caravan Park. Set in 18 acres of mature woodland beside a Blue Flag lake, Eamon and Geraldine O'Malley run this sheltered and tranquil park with their family, who live on the site. They receive a blend of visitors – seasonal residents in camping holiday homes (private and to rent), caravanners and motorcaravanners and there are ample areas for tents. Pitches are varied, sheltered with trees and natural shrubbery, and spacious with gravel or gravel and grass combinations. There are 44 touring pitches with electricity (7A Europlug) available on 25 hardstanding and grass pitches, with water points on or nearby all pitches; there are also 80 tent pitches. The site is a paradise for fishermen, with brown trout, rainbow trout, pike, tench, roach, perch, rudd and bream available. There is also one lake stocked with carp. Just an hour from Dublin, it provides a good holiday base or a useful stopover en-route to the West of Ireland. The watersports permitted on the lake include canoeing, sailing, windsurfing, boating, fishing and safe swimming. The woodlands offer ample opportunities for walking and cycling. The site has several other lakes within a 10 to 15 minute drive. Some are coarse fishing only while others are stocked lakes with multiple varieties of fish. Other activities might include tennis, riding, golf, dog racing and, of course, forest walks. Belvedere House and Tullynally Castle are nearby and the large town of Mullingar, known as the capital of the lake lands, is just 6 km. away.

Facilities

The toilet block provides toilets, washbasins and hot showers (€1 coin). Additional dishwashing areas are around the park. Laundry. Small shop (all season). Café and coffee shop with takeaway. TV and games room. Play areas and area for ball games. Small lakeside beach. Fishing. Late arrivals area outside. Security including CCTV. Some breeds of dog are not accepted. Off site: Bus service 8 km. Golf 1.5 km. Riding 4 km. Bicycle hire 6 km. Boat hire on Lough Ennell and most other lakes.

Open: Easter/1 April - 30 September.

Directions

From N4 take the N52. Follow signs for Belvedere House and take turn 300 m. south of Belvedere House (signed for site). Continue to the shores of Lough Ennell and turn left. If in difficulty, telephone the site. GPS: 53.466111, -7.375278

Charges guide

Per unit incl. 2 persons	
and electricity	€ 23.00 - € 25.00
extra person	€ 5.00
child	€ 3.00

No credit cards.

Rathdrum

Hidden Valley Caravan & Camping Park

Rathdrum (Co. Wicklow) T: 086 727 2872. E: info@irelandholidaypark.com

alanrogers.com/IR9155

This pleasant, level park occupies over seven hectares on both banks of the pretty Avonmore River near the small town of Rathdrum. It has 100 pitches arranged around a boating pond. The pitches are mostly concrete hardstandings with a few on grass. All have safe 16A electricity hook-ups and close access to a water tap and waste drainage. Across a fine footbridge is a large, flat area for tents – most of them used by families at holiday time. Spring 2010 saw major landscaping work on what must now be regarded as one of the best camping park play areas in Ireland.

Facilities

Well equipped and very modern toilet block finished in local slate. Facilities for campers with disabilities. Motorcaravan service point. Laundry. Dishwashing and hobs for cooking. Small shop. Takeaway. Fishing in the river may be arranged. Impressive play park. Canoes and boats for hire on lake. Bicycle hire. Log cabins for rent. Off site: Golf and riding within 5 miles. Beach within 15 miles. The open moorland of the Wicklow Mountains.

Open: 1 April - 30 September.

Directions

Leave M11 at junction signed Rathnew. From village follow signs for Rathdrum (c.15 mins). Over the bridge approaching Rathdrum turn right immediately at large new apartment building. Take care over speed humps for 100 m. Park gate is on the right. GPS: 52.938693, -6.22898

Charges guide

Per unit incl. 2 persons	
and electricity	€ 25.00 - € 27.00
extra person	€ 6.00
child (2-15 yrs)	€ 4.00

For latest campsite news visit
alanrogers.com

Redcross Village

River Valley Caravan & Camping Park

Redcross Village (Co. Wicklow) T: 040 441 647. E: info@rivervalleypark.ie

alanrogers.com/IR9150

In the small country village of Redcross, in the heart of County Wicklow, you will find this popular, family run park. It is within easy reach of beauty spots such as the Vale of Avoca (Ballykissangel), Glendalough and Powerscourt, plus the safe beach of Brittas Bay. The 145 touring pitches at River Valley are mostly together in a dedicated area, all have electricity connections (6A) and offer a choice of hardstanding or grass – you select your pitch. There is a new, hardstanding area for adults only, with its own amenity block. A late arrivals area has electricity hook-ups, water and night lighting.

Facilities

A new sanitary block is modern and well designed. Excellent facilities for disabled visitors. Showers are charged (€ 1). Laundry area. Campers' kitchen. Motorcaravan service points. Gas supplies. Bar and restaurant. TV and games room. Tennis courts. Par 3 golf course. Beer garden with children's entertainment (July/Aug). Sports complex. Adventure and toddlers' playgrounds. Caravan storage. WiFi (free). Off site: Riding 2 km.

Open: 14 March - 4 November.

Directions

From Dublin follow N11 Wexford road south, bypassing Ashford and Rathnew. After passing The Beehive pub look out for Doyle's pub on the right. Turn right at the pub and continue for 5 km. to the park at the top of Redcross village. GPS: 52.8884, -6.14528

Charges 2012

| Per unit incl. 2 persons and electricity | € 25.00 - € 27.00 |
| extra person | € 6.00 |

Roscrea

Streamstown Caravan & Camping Park

Streamstown, Roscrea (Co. Tipperary) T: 050 521 519. E: streamstowncaravanpark@eircom.net

alanrogers.com/IR9420

This family run site, set on a dairy farm in the centre of Ireland, has been open for over 40 years. It is conveniently situated off the M7 Dublin - Limerick road and makes a good overnight halt or for a longer stay if you are seeking a quiet, restful location with little to disturb the peace. There are 27 touring pitches, ten with hardstanding and separated by low hedges. The remainder are on grass and more suitable for units with awnings. This is a working farm and the owners, who are friendly and welcoming, have made some attractive improvements.

Facilities

The sanitary facilities, very clean when we visited, are housed in a modern block. Showers (free), toilets and washbasins (two washbasins in cubicles). Facilities for disabled visitors in family shower room. Good laundry room. Good campers' kitchen with fridge/freezer, electric cooker and TV. Small play area. TV, pool table and games room. Caravan storage. Accommodation to rent. A torch would be useful. Off site: Fishing 1.5 km. Golf 5 km.

Open: Easter - 1 October, (other times by arrangement).

Directions

Leave M7 by Roscrea exit. From Roscrea follow signs for R491 Shinrone. Continue towards Shinrone following site signs for about 2.5 km. and site entrance is on left. GPS: 52.95720, -7.83937

Charges guide

Per unit incl. 2 persons and electricity	€ 24.00
extra person	€ 4.50
child (under 14 yrs)	€ 2.00

Rosses Point

Greenlands Caravan & Camping Park

Rosses Point (Co. Sligo) T: 071 917 7113. E: noelineha@eircom.net

alanrogers.com/IR8690

Just off the N15 road and 8 km. from Sligo town, this is a well run park at Rosses Point, in the sand hills adjoining a championship golf course. It is thoughtfully laid out with small tents placed to the front of reception and the hardstanding touring pitches separated from the trailer tent pitches which occupy the rear. Electric hook-ups (10A) are available for touring units. The ground is undulating and adds interest to the overall appearance. Your view depends on where you are pitched – look towards Coney Island and the Blackrock lighthouse which guards the bay, take in the sight of Benbulben Mountain or appreciate the seascape and the water lapping the resort's two bathing beaches.

Facilities

Modern toilet facilities, recently extended and refitted, are kept exceptionally clean, with hot showers (€ 1 token). Washing machine, dryer and iron. Motorcaravan service point. Campers' kitchen. Information point and TV room by reception. Play area. Off site: Shop, restaurant and evening entertainment in the village. Fishing and boat launching 100 m. Golf 50 m. Bicycle hire 8 km.

Open: 30 April - 14 September.

Directions

From Sligo city travel about 800 m. north on N15 road, turn left onto R291 signed Rosses Point. Continue for 6.5 km. and park is on right after village. GPS: 54.30628, -8.56889

Charges guide

Per unit incl. 2 persons	€ 19.00 - € 21.00
extra person	€ 5.00
electricity (10A)	€ 4.00

Rosslare

Saint Margaret's Beach Caravan & Camping Park

Lady's Island, Rosslare Harbour (Co. Wexford) T: 053 913 1169. E: info@campingstmargarets.ie

alanrogers.com/IR9170

'This park is loved', was how a Swedish visitor described this family-run, environmentally-friendly caravan and camping park, the first the visitor meets near the Rosslare ferry port. Landscaping with flowering containers and maze-like sheltered camping areas and a pretty sanitary block all demonstrate the Traynor family's attention to detail. Most pitches give shelter from the fresh sea breeze and ferries can be seen crossing the Irish sea. Just metres away, the safe, sandy beach (part of the Wexford coastal path) curves around in a horseshoe shape ending in a small pier and slipway. Tourist information on the area is provided in the well stocked shop.

Facilities

The toilet block is spotless. Laundry room. Campers' kitchen including toaster, microwave and TV. Shop (June-Aug). Fresh milk and bread daily. Mobile homes for rent. Sun/TV room. WiFi throughout (charged). Off site: Walking, beach and fishing. Pitch and putt 2 km. Boat slipway 2.5 km. Riding 6 km. Pubs and restaurants. The JFK Arboretum, Johnstown Castle and Gardens, the Irish National Heritage Park, Kilmore Quay and Marina, and Curracloe beach (featured in the film Saving Private Ryan).

Open: Mid March - 31 October.

Directions

From the N25 south of Wexford town, outside village of Tagoat, follow signs for Lady's Island and Carne. After 3 km. pass Butler's Bar and take next left and continue for 2.5 km. Site is well signed. GPS: 52.206433, -6.356417

Charges 2012

Per unit incl. 2 persons and electricity	€ 22.00 - € 24.00
extra person	€ 2.50
child (2-16 yrs)	€ 1.50

Roundwood

Roundwood Caravan & Camping Park

Roundwood (Co. Wicklow) T: 012 818 163. E: info@dublinwicklowcamping.com

alanrogers.com/IR9130

In the heart of the Wicklow mountains, the hospitable owner of this park maintains high standards. It is neatly laid out with rows of trees dividing the different areas and giving an attractive appearance. There are 44 hardstanding pitches for caravans and motorcaravans, all with electricity (6A), plus 33 pitches for tents, arranged off tarmac access roads. There are excellent walks around the Varty Lakes and a daily bus service to Dublin city. Close by are the Wicklow Mountains and the Sally Gap, Glendalough, Powerscourt Gardens, plus many other places of natural beauty. Apart from its scenic location, this site is well placed for the ferry ports.

Facilities

The renovated sanitary block is kept clean, with adequate washing and toilet facilities, plus spacious showers on payment (€ 1). Good laundry facilities, but ask at reception as machines are not self-service. Motorcaravan service point. Campers' kitchen and dining room. TV room. Adventure playground. WiFi (charged). Bicycle hire. Off site: Roundwood village has shops, pubs, restaurants, takeaway food, and a Sunday market. Fishing within 1 km. Riding, golf 3 km.

Open: 29 April - 31 August.

Directions

Turn off N11 Dublin - Wexford road at Kilmacanogue towards Glendalough and then 15 km. to Roundwood. Park is on the north side of the village. GPS: 53.06924, -6.22269

Charges guide

Per unit incl. 2 persons and electricity	€ 28.00 - € 30.00
extra person	€ 8.00 - € 9.00
child (under 14 yrs)	€ 4.00
dog	free

No credit cards.

Skibbereen

The Hideaway Camping & Caravan Park

Skibbereen (Co. Cork) T: 028 222 54. E: skibbereencamping@eircom.net

alanrogers.com/IR9505

A sister park to The Meadow at Glandore, the Hideaway is ideally situated as a touring base for the West Cork region. It is a well run site under the constant supervision of the owners and although it enjoys tranquil surroundings, including preserved marshland, it is only ten minutes walk from the busy market town of Skibbereen. The Hideaway is a two-hectare, touring only park with 60 pitches, including 50 with hardstanding and 6A electric hook-up. The remainder are for tents. Shrubs and low hedges divide the park giving an open feel overall and commanding views across the fields and hills. One long building houses reception, the toilet facilities and a games room.

Facilities	Directions
The modern toilet block has non-slip floors, well equipped showers (on payment). Baby room with bath. En-suite unit for disabled visitors. Laundry. Campers' dining room. Motorcaravan service point. Adventure play area. WiFi (charged). Football and cycling not permitted on the park. WiFi (charged). Off site: Fishing 1.6 km. Golf 2 km. Riding 4 km. Bicycle hire 1 km. Interesting towns of Skibbereen, Rosscarbery and Clonakilty.	From Skibbereen town centre take R596 (signed Casteltownsend). Site is on the left after 1 km. GPS: 51.54167, -9.26008

Charges 2012

Per unit incl. 2 persons and electricity	€ 23.00
extra person	€ 6.00
child (under 16 yrs)	€ 3.00

No credit cards.

Open: Easter - 15 September.

Strandhill

Strandhill Caravan & Camping Park

Strandhill (Co. Sligo) T: 071 916 8111. E: strandhillcvp@eircom.net

alanrogers.com/IR8695

This seaside park is located on 20 acres of undulating grass with a sandy base, with natural protection from the onshore breezes of the famous Strandhill beach. There are 55 hardstanding pitches for caravans and motorcaravans, with electricity and ample water points, and two camping areas for tents, one with views of the sea and the second more sheltered. Throughout the site many hollows provide ideal pitches for tents. Strandhill, world recognised as a surfing Mecca, also provides activities for all the family. There are miles of sandy beach and dunes, and the Knocknarea Mountain for walkers.

Facilities	Directions
The toilet block (keys provided on deposit) is clean and fresh with hot showers (token €1.50), electric hand dryers and hairdryer. New reception building, including tv room, games room, campers kitchen, laundry and full disabled facility. Automatic gate and door control. Off site: Public transport from village. Shops, restaurants, takeaway, pubs and ATM are just beyond the park's boundary in the village. Strandhill golf course 500 m. Riding 2 km. Swimming pool and sports centre in Sligo 8 km.	Strandhill is 8 km. west of Sligo city on the R292. Site is on the airport road. GPS: 54.27242, -8.60448

Charges guide

Per unit incl. 2 persons	€ 20.00
plus 2 children	€ 22.00
electricity (10A)	€ 4.00
extra person	€ 3.00 - € 5.00

Open: 4 April - 30 September.

Timoleague
Sextons Caravan and Camping Park
R600 Timoleague/Clonakility Road, Bandon (Co. Cork) T: 023 884 6347. E: info.sextons@gmail.com

alanrogers.com/IR9490

Sexton's is an unpretentious two-star site that has been in existence for over 40 years. At the time of writing, the owners were proud of their recently-completed reception, allowing the old shop area to be converted into a comfortable lounge area for campers. They also have plans to convert a part of the laundry into an en-suite facility for use by campers with disabilities. The 2.5-hectare park contains 50 pitches for touring vans and tents, 30 of these on gravel hardstanding and the remainder on well kept lawn grass.

Facilities
Two small toilet blocks with free showers are in old farm buildings. Small shop (1/5-30/9). Gas. Small but comfortable camp kitchen with local TV. Sitting room for campers. Laundry. Internet and WiFi (charged). Small playground, football field and games room. Bicycle hire can be arranged. Off site: Beaches, riding, boat launching, fishing and golf, all within 6 km.

Open: 15 March - 30 September.

Directions
N71 into Clonakilty, then follow R600 towards Timoleague for approx. 5 km. – site on right. Look for John Wayne statue guarding the entrance. GPS: 51.635006, -8.800821

Charges guide
Per unit incl. 2 persons and electricity	€ 23.00
extra person	€ 5.00
child	€ 3.00

No credit cards.

Tipperary
Ballinacourty House Caravan & Camping Park
Glen of Aherlow, Tipperary (Co. Tipperary) T: 062 565 59. E: info@camping.ie

alanrogers.com/IR9370

Ballinacourty House and its cobble-stoned courtyard form the centrepiece of this south-facing park with views of the Galtee Mountains. Accessed by a tree-lined lane, the reception area is in part of the renovated 18th-century building, as is the adjoining restaurant. The park is level with 26 touring pitches with 6A electricity and 19 grassy pitches for tents. Some areas are shaded and there are open spaces to accommodate rallies and larger groups. Self-catering cottages and B&B are also available. This tranquil site is very appealing to families with young children. It is a good base from which to tour the Rock of Cashel, the Mitchelstown Caves, Swiss Cottage and the towns of Tipperary, Cahir and Cashel.

Facilities
Sanitary facilities provide free hot water and showers. Baby room. Laundry with ironing facilities. Campers' kitchen. Ice pack freezing. Licensed restaurant (early booking advised). Motorcaravan services. Gas supplies. Frisbee golf. TV and games rooms. Picnic benches. Tennis. Play area. Off site: Riding, fishing, golf within 5 miles.

Open: Easter - last Sunday in September.

Directions
Follow the N24 from Tipperary or Cahir to Bansha. Turn on to R663 for about 7 miles, passing Glen Hotel after 6 miles. Follow signs for Ballinacourty House. GPS: 52.41614, -8.21047

Charges guide
Per unit incl. 2 persons and electricity	€ 24.00 - € 27.00
extra person	€ 5.00
child	€ 4.00

Tipperary
The Glen of Aherlow Caravan & Camping Park
Newtown, Glen of Aherlow (Co. Tipperary) T: 062 565 55. E: rdrew@eircom.net

alanrogers.com/IR9400

The owners of one of Ireland's newest parks, George and Rosaline Drew, are campers themselves and have set about creating an idyllic park in an idyllic location. This three-hectare park is set in one of Ireland's most picturesque valleys and is open all year. There are beautiful views of the wooded and hilly areas of Slievenamuck and the Galtee Mountains. There are 42 large and level touring pitches, with both hardstanding and grass places, each pair sharing a double hook-up 10A post and water point. The Drew family is happy to welcome large groups and rallies, and large units can be accommodated. The new stone-built reception, shop and coffee bar beside the gate should now be complete.

Facilities
The modern toilet block includes free showers and facilities for disabled visitors. Motorcaravan service point. Laundry room with ironing. Campers' kitchen. Recreation and TV rooms. Shop, bicycle hire and Internet café planned. Off site: Holiday homes to rent 300 m. Restaurant nearby. Outdoor activities. Fishing in Aherlow River. Golf and riding 7 km.

Open: All year.

Directions
From Tipperary town take N24 to Bansha, then R663 to Newtown. Continue through village and pass Coach Road Inn to park in 300 m. GPS: 52.4161, -8.2105

Charges guide
Per unit incl. 2 persons and electricity	€ 28.00
extra person	€ 6.00
child (2-18 yrs)	€ 2.00

For latest campsite news visit
alanrogers.com

Tralee

Woodlands Park Touring Caravan & Camping Park

Dan Spring Road, Tralee (Co. Kerry) T: 066 712 1235. E: wdlands@eircom.net

alanrogers.com/IR9650

This family-run park is located in the heart of Kerry, on the gateway to the Dingle peninsula and just north of the Ring of Kerry and Killarney. Woodlands is an ideal base, only ten minutes' walk from Tralee town centre via the town park and famous rose garden. Located on a 16-acre elevated site approached by a short road and a bridge that straddles the River Lee; once on site the town seems far removed with a countryside environment taking over. Hedging, trees, grazing fields and the distant Slieve Mish Mountain create the setting. There are 135 pitches including 85 super pitches with hardstanding, electricity, water and drainage and a grass area. The park has a landscaped entrance; tropical shrubs, cordyline palms and flower beds have been planted around the park. The owners of Woodlands have designed and equipped their park to a high standard including a clubhouse. The town park is home to the Kerry County Museum and the National folk theatre of Ireland with nightly performances. In addition to the river, there is a canal bank walk to Blennerville village and its famous windmill.

Facilities

Excellent, heated sanitary facilities include sizeable showers (€ 1 token) and provision for disabled guests. Campers' kitchen. Laundry room with washing machines and dryer. Gas for sale. Motorcaravan service point. Club house with café/snack bar. Shop. Games room. TV and adult only room. Internet and WiFi access. Fenced adventure play area. Public telephone on site.
Off site: The nearby Aqua Dome offers half price admission after 18.00. Golf 6 km. Riding 2 km. Blue Flag beaches on the Dingle Peninsula. Sailing 10 km.

Open: Easter - 30 September.

Directions

Site is 1 km. southwest of Tralee town centre. From N21/N69/N86 junction south of Tralee follow site signs for 2.4 km. to park, 200 m. off the N86 Tralee - Dingle road. Site is 300 m. east of the Aqua Dome GPS: 52.26157, -9.70338

Charges guide

Per unit incl. 2 persons and electricity	€ 21.00 - € 24.00
extra person	€ 6.00
child (under 16 yrs)	€ 3.00

Award Winning Touring Park perfect for family holiday's and an ideal base to explore beautiful Co. Kerry.
Enjoy the quiet Woodland Setting just a few minutes stroll to Tralee town centre.
Guests get discounted entrance to the Aqua Dome. **Voted Irelands best Inland Park 2010**

www.kingdomcamping.com

Tramore

Newtown Cove Camping & Caravan Park

Newtown Road, Tramore (Co. Waterford) T: 051 381 979. E: info@newtowncove.com

alanrogers.com/IR9340

Well run and friendly, this very attractive small park is only five minutes walk from the beautiful Newton Cove. It offers views of the famous and historic Metal Man and is 2.5 km. from Tramore beach and 11 km. from Waterford. Neatly set out on gently sloping grass are 40 pitches, with the abundance of shrubs and bushes reflecting the efforts of the owners. All pitches have electrical connections (10A), some with hardstanding also, and access is by well lit, tarmac roads. There are around 50 privately owned caravan holiday homes. A modern building at the entrance houses reception, the amenities and additional sanitary facilities.

Facilities

The main sanitary block at the bottom end of the site provides good, clean facilities including a bathroom. Showers on payment (token from reception). Excellent motorcaravan services. Campers' kitchen with cooking facilities, sheltered eating area, lounge and small laundry. Small shop (1/7-30/8). TV room. Games room. Small play area. Off site: Beach 400 m. Fishing 400 m. Golf 800 m. Riding 3 km.

Open: Easter - 25 September.

Directions

From Tramore on R675 coast road to Dungarvan. Turn left 2 km. from town centre, following signs. GPS: 52.14763, -7.17274

Charges guide

Per unit incl. 2 persons and electricity	€ 24.00 - € 29.00
extra person	€ 6.00
child (3-16 yrs)	€ 3.00
hiker, cyclist or motorcyclist	€ 8.00 - € 11.00

No single sex groups.

Tuosist

Beara Camping The Peacock

Coornagillagh, Tuosist (Co. Kerry) T: 064 668 4287. E: bearacamping@eircom.net

alanrogers.com/IR9580

Five minutes from Kenmare Bay, The Peacock is a unique location for campers who appreciate the natural world, where disturbance to nature is kept to a minimum. This five-acre site offers simple, clean and imaginative camping facilities. Located on the Ring of Beara, bordering the counties of Cork and Kerry, visitors will be treated with hospitality by a Dutch couple, Bert and Klaske van Bavel, almost more Irish than the Irish, who have made Ireland their home and run the site with their family. The variety of accommodation at Beara Camping includes a hostel, caravan holiday homes, secluded hardstanding pitches with electricity and level grass areas for tenting.

Facilities

Three small blocks, plus facilities at the restaurant provide toilets, washbasins and free hot showers. Laundry service (charged). Campers' kitchens and eating area. Restaurant and takeaway (May-Oct). Pets are not permitted in rental accommodation or tents. Off site: Public transport from the gate during the summer months. Pub and shop 900 m. Riding 6 km. Golf 12 km. Boating, fishing and sea angling 200 m. Beach (pebble) 500 m.

Open: 1 April - 31 December.

Directions

From the N22, 17 km. east of Killarney, take the R569 south to Kenmare. In Kenmare take R571, Castletownbere road and site is 12 km. GPS: 51.8279, -9.7356

Charges guide

Per unit incl. 2 persons and electricity	€ 22.50
extra person	€ 3.50
child (0-10 yrs)	€ 2.00

Westport

Westport House Caravan and Camping Park

Westport House Country Park, Westport (Co. Mayo) T: 098 277 66. E: camping@westporthouse.ie

alanrogers.com/IR8770

Located in the grounds of an elegant country estate, this is a popular park. From Westport Quay, you enter the grounds of the estate by way of a tree lined road that crosses the river and leads to the site. In an attractive, sheltered area of the parkland, set in the trees, are 95 pitches, all with hardstanding and electricity (5A). Early in the season the site may not be fully prepared, and only minimal facilities may be available. There is the choice of a pitch only booking, or a special deal (minimum stay three nights). This includes free admission to Westport House and many of the activities of the adjoining leisure park.

Facilities

Toilet facilities are provided at various points on the site, plus a 'super-loo' located in the farmyard buildings. Facilities for disabled visitors. Laundry facilities. Fifties style function room and bar with food and musical entertainment at weekends. Fishing. Tennis. Westport House and Country Park. Dogs are not accepted in July and August. WiFi. Off site: Within 5 km. are an 18-hole golf course and deep sea angling on Clew Bay.

Open: 1 April - 31 September.

Directions

Take R335 Westport - Louisburgh road and follow signs for Westport Quay, then turn in through gates of Westport House and continue through estate following signs for camping. GPS: 53.8053, -9.5395

Charges guide

Per unit incl. 2 persons and electricity	€ 26.00 - € 30.00
hiker or cyclist	€ 10.00 - € 20.00
Family weekend rates in June.	

For latest campsite news visit
alanrogers.com

A visit to the Channel Islands offers a holiday in part of the British Isles, yet in an area which has a definite continental flavour. All the islands have beautiful beaches and coves, pretty scenery and fascinating histories.

THE CHANNEL ISLANDS ARE MADE UP OF THE ISLANDS OF: JERSEY, GUERNSEY, SARK, HERM AND ALDERNEY

The largest of the Channel Islands is Jersey, which is also the most commercial with more entertainment on offer. It has long stretches of safe beaches for swimming and water-based activities such as windsurfing and banana rides. Caravans and motorcaravans are allowed on Jersey, but with a number of limitations (for example, length of stay, width and length of the unit). A permit is required, which is obtained as part of the booking procedure with the campsite of your choice. You must book in advance but the campsite owner will advise you on all aspects of your visit.

Guernsey will suit those who prefer a quieter, more peaceful holiday. Caravans and motorcaravans are not allowed here. Guernsey too has wide, sandy beaches plus sheltered coves. The historic, harbour town of St Peter Port has steep and winding cobbled streets, with plenty of shops, cafés and restaurants.

For those who want total relaxation, one of the smaller islands – Sark or Herm, would be ideal. No cars are permitted on either of these islands. Explore on foot, by bicycle or horse-drawn carriage.

Shopping on all the islands has the advantage of no VAT – particularly useful when buying cameras, watches or alcohol.

Places of interest

Jersey: St Helier; Jersey Zoo; Jersey war tunnels; Elizabeth Castle; German Underground Hospital in St Lawrence; Samarès Manor in St Clement; Shell Garden at St Aubin; Battle of Flowers Museum in St Ouen.

Guernsey: Castle Cornet at St Peter Port Harbour; Victor Hugo's House; Guernsey Folk Museum; German Occupation Museum; Fort Grey Shipwreck Museum; Saumarez Park.

Sark: La Coupée; La Seigneurie, with old dovecote and gardens; Gouliet and Boutique Caves; Le Pot on Little Sark; Venus Pool; Little Sark Village.

Herm: This tiny island has beautiful, quiet, golden beaches and a little harbour village and hotel. Arrive by ferry from Guernsey for a wonderful day out.

Did you know?

Jersey has been associated with knitting for nearly 400 years.

The Channel Islands were the only part of the British Isles to be occupied by the Germans during the Second World War.

Herm island is just one and a half miles long and only half a mile wide.

Le Jerriais is the native language of Jersey, a blend of Norse and Norman French.

Note: The reciprocal health services agreement between the British Government and the Channel Islands ended in April 2009. The EHIC card does not cover emergency health care as the Channel Islands are not part of the EU. Travel insurance is now essential.

Castel

Fauxquets Valley Campsite

Candie Road, Castel, Guernsey GY5 7QL T: 01481 255460. E: info@fauxquets.co.uk

alanrogers.com/UK9780

Situated in the rural centre of the island, Fauxquets is in a pretty sheltered valley, hidden down narrow lanes away from busy roads, and is run by the Guille family. It was once a dairy farm, but the valley side has now been developed into an attractive campsite, with the old farm buildings as its centre. Plenty of trees, bushes and flowers have been planted to separate pitches and to provide shelter around the various fields which are well terraced. The 86 touring pitches are of a good size, most marked, numbered and with electricity, and there is lots of open space. There are also 15 smaller places for backpackers. The site has 23 fully equipped tents for hire, but there are no tour operators.

Facilities

Good toilet facilities have controllable showers, some washbasins in private cabins with a shower, baby bath and changing unit. Dishwashing facilities under cover and a tap for free hot water. Laundry room with free irons, boards and hairdryers. Heated swimming pool (20x45 ft) with paddling pool. Restaurant and bar (25/6-7/9). Small shop with ice-pack hire and gas. TV room. Table football and table tennis. Small play area and play field. Bicycle hire. Torches useful. Off site: Riding and golf 2 miles. Fishing, sailing and boat launching 3 miles.

Open: April - 15 September.

Directions

From harbour take second exit from roundabout. At top of hill, turn left at 'filter in turn' into Queens Road, then right at next filter. Follow straight through traffic lights and down hill past hospital, through pedestrian lights and straight on at next lights at top of hill. Continue for 0.75 miles, then turn right opposite sign for German Hospital. Fourth left is pedestrian entrance, cars carry on for 400 yds. to gravel entrance on left. GPS: 49.46812, -2.58843

Charges guide

Per person	£ 8.00 - £ 10.50
child (4-14 yrs)	£ 5.50 - £ 7.50
electricity (6A)	£ 3.50

Herm Island

Seagull Campsite

The Administration Office, Herm Island GY1 3HR T: 01481 750000. E: reservations@herm.com

alanrogers.com/UK9830

This tiny site, and indeed the island of Herm, will appeal to those who are looking for complete tranquillity and calm. Reached by boat (20 minutes and approx. £10.50 return fare for adults, £5.50 for children) from Guernsey, the 300-acre island allows no cars, only tractors, on its narrow roads and paths (no bicycles either). The campsite is a 20 minute, uphill walk from the harbour, but your luggage will be transported for you by tractor. It consists of several terraced areas offering a total of 90 pitches, and 26 fully equipped tents for hire on flat grass areas. There are no electricity hook-ups. One may bring one's own tent and equipment or hire both (but not bedding, crockery and lighting) from the site.

Facilities

Small, modern, but open, toilet block. Hot showers (£1 payment – there is a shortage of water on Herm). Laundry facility and small kitchen. Freezer for ice-packs. No dogs or pets are allowed. Torches useful. Off site: The harbour village is about ten minutes walk for small shop, gas, a post office, pub, restaurants and café. Fishing on the island.

Open: May - first w/end in September.

Directions

Reached by boat from St Peter Port - report to Administration Office on arrival. Do not take your car as it is unlikely you will be able to park long term in St Peter Port. GPS: 49.46997, -2.445745

Charges guide

Per person	£ 7.00
child (under 14 yrs)	£ 3.50
transportation of luggage	£ 7.50

Equipped tents for hire.
Groups of single people not accepted.

For latest campsite news visit

alanrogers.com

Saint Martin

Rozel Camping Park

Rozel, Saint Martin, Jersey JE3 6AX (Jersey) T: 01534 855200. E: rozelcampingpark@jerseymail.co.uk

alanrogers.com/UK9710

This family owned park is within walking distance of the famous Jersey Zoo and the pretty harbour and fishing village of Rozel, where the north coast cliff path commences. There are two main camping areas providing 130 pitches of which 120 have electric hook ups (10/16A) and 16 are used for fully equipped tents to hire. Some pitches, mainly for smaller tents are arranged on terraced areas. The remainder are on a higher, flat field where pitches are arranged in bays with hedges growing to separate them into groups. The site has provided easy access for caravans and motorcaravans, plus chemical and grey waste disposal facilities.

Facilities

Two first rate, heated sanitary buildings include a bathroom for disabled visitors with a shower, toilet and washbasin. Family shower room with small heater for cooler weather. Fully equipped laundry. Shop. Takeaway (peak season). Swimming pool (June-Sept) with children's pool and sunbathing areas. Play area. Crazy golf. Games room, reading and TV room. Torches useful. Bicycles for hire can be delivered to each pitch. Off site: Fishing 1 mile. Beach 2 miles. Riding 3 miles. Golf 4 miles.

Open: 21 May - 9 September.

Directions

Leave harbour by Route du Port Elizabeth, take A1 east through the tunnel and the A17. At fourth set of lights turn left on A6. Keep in the middle lane. Continue to Five Oaks and on to St Martin's church. Turn right, then immediately left at The Royal pub on B38 to Rozel, continue to end of road, turn right and park is on the right. GPS: 49.23841, -2.05058

Charges guide

Per person	£ 8.60 - £ 9.00
child (4-11 yrs)	£ 5.00
electricity	£ 2.00

Tent hire and travel packages.

Saint Martin

Beuvelande Camp Site

Beuvelande, Saint Martin, Jersey JE3 6EZ (Jersey) T: 01534 853575. E: info@campingjersey.com

alanrogers.com/UK9720

What a pleasant surprise we had when we called here – the outstanding sanitary building gives campers facilities often associated with top class hotels. A licensed restaurant with a covered terrace area is also situated in this building, open morning and evening all season, but perhaps a few less hours at quiet times. There are 150 pitches, 60 with fully equipped tents for hire, but with plenty of space for those with their own. Cars may be parked next to your tent. One hundred pitches have electric hook ups (5/10A). Torches would be useful. Car and bicycle hire can be arranged. This family run park prides itself on quality, cleanliness and hospitality.

Facilities

The toilet block is tiled top to bottom and spotlessly clean, with controllable showers, two fully equipped bathrooms for disabled visitors, and a baby room. Plenty of dishwashing facilities and a laundry. Games room with arcade games and pool. TV room. Well stocked shop open 08.00-19.00 during peak times and stocks gas. Licensed restaurant. Ice pack and battery charging services for a small charge. Outdoor heated swimming pool (41x17 ft) with a sun terrace and small waterslide. Play area and large playing field. Evening entertainment. Off site: Beach and sailing 1.5 miles. Fishing, golf and riding within 2 miles.

Open: 1 April - 30 September.

Directions

On leaving the harbour by Route du Port Elizabeth, take A1 east through the tunnel and the A17. At the fourth set of traffic lights turn left on A6. Continue to Five Oaks and on to St Martin's RC church, then right into La Longue Rue, right again Rue de L'Orme then left to site. GPS: 49.21294, -2.05615

Charges guide

Per person	£ 7.00 - £ 9.00
child (2-14 yrs)	£ 6.00

Single sex groups not accepted.

For latest campsite news visit

alanrogers.com

UK1780 Freshwater Beach Holiday Park

▶ see report page 91

Burton Bradstock, Bridport DT6 4PT

AR1 – BUDGET – Mobile Home

Sleeping: 3 bedrooms, sleeps 6: 1 double, 4 singles, pillows and blankets provided

Living: living/kitchen area, heating, TV, shower, WC

Eating: fitted kitchen with hobs, oven, grill, fridge, freezer

Outside: table & chairs

Pets: not accepted

AR2 – SUPER DELUXE – Mobile Home

Sleeping: 3 bedrooms, sleeps 6: 1 double, 4 singles, pillows and blankets provided

Living: living/kitchen area, heating, TV, shower, WC

Eating: fitted kitchen with hobs, oven, microwave, grill, fridge, freezer

Outside: table & chairs

Pets: not accepted

Open: 18 March - 13 November

Weekly Charge	AR1	AR2
Low Season (from)	£ 210	£ 350
High Season (from)	£ 690	£ 980

UK2290 Sandy Balls Holiday Centre

▶ see report page 115

Godshill, Fordingbridge SP6 2JZ

AR1 – PINE LODGE ENSUITE – Chalet

Sleeping: 3 bedrooms, sleeps 6: 1 double, 4 singles, pillows and blankets provided

Living: living/kitchen area, heating, TV, shower, WC

Eating: fitted kitchen with hobs, oven, microwave, grill, fridge, freezer

Outside: barbecue

Pets: not accepted

AR2 – READY TENT – Tent

Sleeping: 2 bedrooms, sleeps 6: 6 singles

Living: living/kitchen area

Eating: fitted kitchen with hobs, fridge

Outside: table & chairs

Pets: not accepted

Other (AR1 and AR2): bed linen, cot, highchair to hire

Open: All year

Weekly Charge	AR1	AR2
Low Season (from)	£ 149	£ 165
High Season (from)	£ 1399	£ 599

UK2920 Bay View Park

▶ see report page 141

Old Martello Road, Pevensey Bay BN24 6DX

AR1 – FESTIVAL SUPER – Mobile Home

Sleeping: 2 bedrooms, sleeps 6: 1 double, 2 singles, sofa bed, pillows and blankets provided

Living: living/kitchen area, heating, TV, shower, seperate WC

Eating: fitted kitchen with grill, fridge

Outside: table & chairs

Pets: not accepted

AR2 – RICHMOND DELUXE – Mobile Home

Sleeping: 2 bedrooms, sleeps 6: 1 double, 2 singles, sofa bed, pillows and blankets provided

Living: living/kitchen area, heating, TV, shower, WC

Eating: fitted kitchen with grill, fridge

Outside: table & chairs

Pets: not accepted

Other (AR1 and AR2): bed linen, cot, highchair to hire

Open: 1 March - 31 October

Weekly Charge	AR1	AR2
Low Season *(from)*	£ 265	£ 299
High Season *(from)*	£ 573	£ 635

UK3850 Rivendale Caravan & Leisure Park

▶ see report page 171

Buxton Road, Alsop-en-le-Dale, Ashbourne DE6 1QU

AR1 – SENATOR – Mobile Home

Sleeping: 2 bedrooms, sleeps 6: 2 doubles, 1 single, pillows and blankets provided

Living: living/kitchen area, heating, TV, shower, WC

Eating: fitted kitchen with hobs, oven, microwave, grill, fridge, freezer

Outside: table & chairs, barbecue

Pets: accepted

AR2 – FAMILY POD – Pod

Sleeping: sleeps 4

Living: heating

Pets: accepted

Open: 29 January - 31 December

Weekly Charge	AR1	AR2
Low Season *(from)*	£ 336	£ 336
High Season *(from)*	£ 490	£ 339

UK4520 Flower of May Holiday Park

Lebberston Cliff, Scarborough YO11 3NU

● see report page 204

AR1 – 4 BERTH GOLD – Mobile home

Sleeping: 2 bedrooms, sleeps 4: 1 double, 2 singles, pillows and blankets provided

Living: living/kitchen area, heating, TV, shower, WC

Eating: fitted kitchen with hobs, oven, microwave, grill, fridge, freezer

Pets: not accepted

AR2 – 6 BERTH GOLD – Mobile home

Sleeping: 3 bedrooms, sleeps 6: 1 double, 4 singles, pillows and blankets provided

Living: living/kitchen area, heating, TV, shower, WC

Eating: fitted kitchen with hobs, oven, microwave, grill, fridge, freezer

Pets: not accepted

Other (AR1 and AR2): bed linen to hire

Open: 30 March - 4 November

Weekly Charge	AR1	AR2
Low Season *(from)*	£ 360	£ 410
High Season *(from)*	£ 610	£ 660

UK4640 Goose Wood Caravan Park

Carr Lane, Sutton-on-the-Forest, York YO61 1ET

● see report page 210

AR1 – ELM – Mobile home

Sleeping: 2 bedrooms, sleeps 4: 1 double, 2 singles, pillows and blankets provided

Living: living/kitchen area, heating, TV, shower, WC

Eating: fitted kitchen with hobs, oven, microwave, grill, dishwasher, fridge, freezer

Outside: table & chairs

Pets: accepted (with supplement)

AR2 – LAUREL/BIRCH – Mobile home

Sleeping: 3 bedrooms, sleeps 6: 1 double, 4 singles, pillows and blankets provided

Living: living/kitchen area, heating, TV, shower, WC

Eating: fitted kitchen with hobs, oven, microwave, grill, dishwasher, fridge, freezer

Outside: table & chairs

Pets: accepted (with supplement)

Other (AR1 and AR2): bed linen to hire

Open: 2 March - 31 December

Weekly Charge	AR1	AR2
Low Season *(from)*	£ 295	£ 295
High Season *(from)*	£ 645	£ 645

Low Cost Flights

An Inexpensive Way To Arrive At Your Campsite

Many campsites are conveniently served by a wide choice of low cost airlines. Cheap flights can be very easy to find and travellers increasingly find the regional airports often used to be smaller, quieter and generally a calmer, more pleasurable experience.

Low cost flights can make campsites in more distant regions a much more attractive option: quicker to reach, inexpensive flights, and simply more convenient.

Campsites are seeing increased numbers of visitors using the low cost flights and are adapting their services to suit this clientele. An airport shuttle service is not uncommon, meaning you can take advantage of that cheap flight knowing you will be met at the other end and whisked to your campsite. No taxi queues or multiple drop-offs.

Obviously, these low cost flights are impractical when taking all your own camping gear but they do make a holiday in campsite owned accommodation much more straightforward. The low cost airline option makes caravan holiday home holidays especially attractive: pack a suitcase and use bed linen and towels provided (which you will generally need to pre-book).

Open All Year

The following parks are understood to accept caravanners and campers all year round. It is always wise to phone the park to check as the facilities available, for example, may be reduced.

England

South West England
Cornwall

Bodmin	UK0270	Mena
Bodmin	UK0306	Ruthern Valley
Newquay	UK0165	Monkey Tree
Newquay	UK0215	Sun Haven Valley
Newquay	UK0540	Carvynick
Padstow	UK0430	Padstow
Redruth	UK0114	Globe Vale HP
Saint Ives	UK0030	Ayr
Saint Martins-Looe	UK0320	Polborder House
Saltash	UK0440	Dolbeare
Truro	UK0012	Killiwerris
Truro	UK0180	Carnon Downs
Truro	UK0185	Cosawes

South West England
Devon

Braunton	UK0710	Hidden Valley
Dawlish	UK0970	Cofton
Dawlish	UK1010	Lady's Mile
Drewsteignton	UK1250	Woodland Springs
Ilfracombe	UK0690	Stowford Farm
Modbury	UK0820	Moor View
Newton Abbot	UK0980	Lemonford
Paignton	UK0870	Beverley
Plymouth	UK0810	Riverside (Plymouth)
South Molton	UK0745	Riverside (S Molton)
Tavistock	UK0790	Harford Bridge

South West England
Somerset, Wiltshire, West Dorset

Bath	UK1460	Newton Mill
Bishop Sutton	UK1510	Chew Valley
Bridgwater	UK1306	Mill Farm
Bristol	UK1440	Baltic Wharf
Martock	UK1420	Southfork
Minehead	UK1301	Westermill Farm
Salisbury	UK1640	Greenhill Farm
Salisbury	UK1655	Church Farm
Sparkford	UK1500	Long Hazel
Taunton	UK1340	Cornish Farm
Taunton	UK1350	Quantock Orchard
Taunton	UK1520	Waterrow
Westbury	UK1630	Brokerswood
Weymouth	UK1820	Bagwell Farm

Southern England

Banbury	UK2600	Barnstones
Bere Regis	UK2050	Rowlands Wait
Bletchingdon	UK2590	Greenhill Farm
Cowes	UK2530	Waverley
Fordingbridge	UK2290	Sandy Balls
Oxford	UK2595	Diamond Farm
Wareham	UK2030	Wareham Forest

South East England

Ashford	UK3040	Broadhembury
Bexhill	UK2955	Kloofs
Brighton	UK2930	Sheepcote
Canterbury	UK3070	Canterbury
Chertsey	UK2810	Chertsey
Folkestone	UK3090	Black Horse
Horsham	UK2940	Honeybridge
Marden	UK3030	Tanner Farm
Redhill	UK2800	Alderstead Heath
Washington	UK2950	Washington

London

Abbey Wood	UK3260	Abbey Wood
Crystal Palace	UK3270	Crystal Palace

East of England

Bury Saint Edmunds	UK3345	The Dell
Great Yarmouth	UK3382	Rose Farm
Great Yarmouth	UK3485	Clippesby
Hunstanton	UK3520	Searles
Ipswich	UK3310	Low House
Norwich	UK3455	Deer's Glade
Peterborough	UK3580	Ferry Meadows
Pidley	UK3575	Stroud Hill
Swaffham	UK3470	Breckland
Woodbridge	UK3322	Run Cottage

Heart of England

Ashbourne	UK3854	Peak Gateway
Bridgnorth	UK4400	Stanmore Hall
Buxton	UK3845	Clover Fields
Coleford	UK4160	Christchurch
Coventry	UK4075	Hollyfast
Grantham	UK3765	Woodland Waters
Grantham	UK3775	Wagtail C.P.
Lutterworth	UK3890	Stanford Hall
Matlock	UK3815	Lickpenny
Meriden	UK4070	Somers Wood

Open All Year continued

Moreton-in-Marsh	UK4130	Moreton-in-Marsh
Newark	UK3940	Smeaton's Lakes
Newark	UK3945	Milestone
Nottingham	UK3935	Thornton's Holt
Oakham	UK3903	Rutland
Peterchurch	UK4300	Poston Mill
Ripley	UK3865	Golden Valley
Shrewsbury	UK4410	Beaconsfield
Shrewsbury	UK4430	Oxon Hall
Skegness	UK3730	Skegness Sands
Slimbridge	UK4170	Tudor
Stamford	UK3760	Tallington Lakes
Stourport-on-Severn	UK4210	Lickhill Manor
Woodhall Spa	UK3690	Bainland
Worksop	UK3920	Riverside (Worksop)

Yorkshire

Pickering	UK4570	Spiers House

North West England

Chester	UK5220	Manor Wood
Ormskirk	UK5280	Abbey Farm
Preston	UK5290	Royal Umpire

Cumbria

Appleby-in-Westmorland	UK5570	Wild Rose
Penrith	UK5560	Sykeside
Penrith	UK5630	The Quiet Site
Wigton	UK5505	Stanwix Park

Northumbria

Belford	UK5755	South Meadows
Berwick-upon-Tweed	UK5800	Ord House
Durham	UK5705	The Grange
Stockton-on-Tees	UK5740	White Water

Wales

Barmouth	UK6385	Islawrffordd
Beddgelert	UK6590	Beddgelert
Caernarfon	UK6600	Bryn Gloch
Caernarfon	UK6605	Tafarn Snowdonia
Cardiff	UK5925	Cardiff
Colwyn Bay	UK6690	Bron-Y-Wendon

Llandovery	UK5955	Erwlon
Montgomery	UK6330	Daisy Bank
Newport	UK6060	Tredegar House
Wrexham	UK6680	James'

Scotland

Arrochar	UK7260	Ardgartan
Auchterarder	UK7270	Grand Eagles
Aviemore	UK7680	Glenmore
Balloch	UK7240	Lomond Woods
Crieff	UK7275	Braidhaugh
Dalbeattie	UK6870	Glenearly
Durness	UK7735	Sango Sands
Edinburgh	UK7050	Edinburgh
Glencoe	UK7790	Invercoe
Killin	UK7315	Loch Tay Highland Lodges
Kirkcudbright	UK6950	Brighouse Bay
Maybole	UK7015	The Ranch
Melrose	UK7030	Gibson Park
Musselburgh	UK6980	Drum Mohr
Stranraer	UK7020	Aird Donald

Northern Ireland

Newcastle	UK8420	Tollymore
Athy	IR9080	Forest Farm

Republic of Ireland

Ballaghaderreen	IR8815	Willowbrook
Caherdaniel	IR9560	Wave Crest
Clondalkin	IR9100	Camac Valley
Cong	IR8740	Cong
Tipperary	IR9400	Glen of Aherlow

Channel Islands

Sark	UK9870	Pomme de Chien

Dogs

For the benefit of those who want to take their dogs with them or for people who do not like dogs at the parks they visit, we list here the parks that have indicated to us that they do not accept dogs. If you are planning to take your dog we do advise you to phone the park first to check – there may be limits on numbers, breeds, etc. or times of the year when they are excluded.

Never – these parks do not accept dogs at any time:

UK0065	Wayfarers	41	UK4100	Hoburne Cotswold	174
UK0115	Tehidy	43	UK4498	South Cliff	195
UK0250	Pentewan Sands	41	UK5890	Glen Trothy	254
UK0302	South Penquite	24	UK5980	Moreton Farm	259
UK0785	South Breazle	77	UK5985	Manorbier	261
UK0870	Beverley	78	UK6040	Pencelli Castle	244
UK0940	Holmans Wood	61	UK6350	Barcdy	248
UK1075	Golden Coast	86	UK7290	Craigtoun Meadows	288
UK1150	Ruda	62	UK9770	Vaugrat	325
UK1490	Greenacres	103	UK9830	Seagull	323
UK2130	Grove Farm	114	UK9870	Pomme de Chien	325
UK2300	Ashurst	110	IR9410	The Apple	304
UK3060	Yew Tree	137	IR9510	Eagle Point	302
UK3120	Gate House Wood	145			

Sometimes – these parks do not accept dogs at certain times of the year or have other restrictions, contact park:

UK0010	Chacewater	48	UK4770	Rosedale	202
UK0030	Ayr	46	UK5350	Silverdale	213
UK0215	Sun Haven Valley	40	UK5710	Doe Park	233
UK0485	Franchis H.P.	31	UK5750	Waren	233
UK0735	Woolacombe Sands	84	UK5930	Cwmcarn Forest	256
UK0850	Galmpton	60	UK5995	Caerfai Bay	260
UK0860	Whitehill	77	UK6010	Cenarth Falls	256
UK1540	Batcombe Vale	103	UK6280	Aeron Coast	238
UK2500	Heathfield Farm	116	UK6290	Glan-y-Mor	241
UK2510	Whitecliff Bay	111	UK6660	Nant Mill	258
UK2572	Swiss Farm	117	UK6990	Mortonhall	275
UK2590	Greenhill Farm	113	UK7060	Tantallon	286
UK3095	Little Satmar	142	IR8770	Westport House	321
UK3485	Clippesby	156	IR8810	Lough Lanagh	306
UK3520	Searles	159	UK9710	Rozel	324
UK4496	Skipsea Sands	207			
UK4520	Flower of May	204			

Fishing

We are pleased to include details of parks which provide facilities for fishing on site. Many other parks, particularly in Scotland and Ireland, are in popular fishing areas and have facilities within easy reach. Where we have been given details, we have included this information in the reports. It is always best to contact parks to check that they provide for your individual requirements.

England

UK5280	Abbey Farm	216
UK3680	Ashby Park	178
UK1540	Batcombe Vale	103
UK4410	Beaconsfield	187
UK2610	Bo Peep	110
UK2965	Brakes Coppice	135
UK4320	Broadmeadow	186
UK1410	Broadway House	96
UK1630	Brokerswood	106
UK4500	Burton Constable	199
UK1665	Burton Hill	99
UK3855	Callow Top	171
UK1545	Cheddar Bridge	96
UK2810	Chertsey	137
UK2875	Chichester Lakeside	139
UK3845	Clover Fields	173
UK0970	Cofton	65
UK4150	Croft Farm	192
UK3455	Deer's Glade	163
UK5710	Doe Park	233
UK1590	Exe Valley	98
UK2915	Fairfields Farm	140
UK3290	Fen Farm	154
UK4380	Fernwood	175
UK2221	Fishery Creek	116
UK3750	Foreman's Bridge	188
UK1780	Freshwater Beach	91
UK3970	Glencote	179
UK1740	Golden Cap	90
UK1075	Golden Coast	86
UK3865	Golden Valley	185
UK4640	Goose Wood	210
UK1640	Greenhill Farm	102
UK2590	Greenhill Farm	113
UK2130	Grove Farm	114
UK0790	Harford Bridge	82
UK2360	Hill Cottage	115
UK5615	Hill of Oaks	229
UK4100	Hoburne Cotswold	174
UK1480	Home Farm	93
UK3300	Homestead Lake	154
UK3055	Hop Farm	144
UK2900	Horam Manor	142
UK2820	Horsley	140
UK2700	Hurley	118
UK4090	Island Meadow	177
UK3430	Kelling Heath	164
UK4190	Kingsgreen	180
UK4720	Knight Stainforth	206
UK4210	Lickhill Manor	190
UK3480	Little Lakeland	158
UK5625	Lowther	226
UK4310	Luck's All	178
UK5220	Manor Wood	214
UK0415	Meadow Lakes	45
UK0270	Mena	23
UK3945	Milestone	183
UK0750	Minnows	84
UK0165	Monkey Tree	40
UK3320	Moon & Sixpence	166
UK4610	Moorside	209
UK5272	Moss Wood	215
UK0685	Newberry Valley	61
UK2465	Ninham	125
UK1570	Northam Farm	93
UK3400	Old Brick Kilns	156
UK1390	Old Oaks	99
UK5600	Pennine View	223
UK0250	Pentewan Sands	41
UK1090	Peppermint Park	66
UK0235	Porth Beach	38
UK4300	Poston Mill	185
UK3850	Rivendale	171
UK0950	River Dart	56
UK5285	Riverside HP	217
UK4715	Riverside Lancaster	198
UK4760	Riverside Meadows	203
UK0745	Riverside Sth Molton	81
UK4080	Riverside Stratford	190
UK1150	Ruda	62
UK0695	Sandaway	70
UK2290	Sandy Balls	115
UK3410	Sandy Gulls	162
UK3520	Searles	159
UK4588	Sleningford Watermill	202
UK3940	Smeaton's Lakes	183
UK0302	South Penquite	24
UK3575	Stroud Hill	165
UK2572	Swiss Farm	117
UK3760	Tallington Lakes	189
UK3030	Tanner Farm	143
UK3685	Tattershall Lakes CP	191
UK4510	Thorpe Hall	196
UK3655	Thorpe Park	174
UK4345	Townsend	179
UK0530	Trethiggey	39
UK0170	Trevella	32
UK0220	Trevornick	38
UK0500	Trewince Farm	53
UK4170	Tudor	189
UK1575	Unity	93
UK3775	Wagtail C.P.	177

Bicycle Hire

We understand that the following parks have bicycles to hire on site or can arrange for bicycles to be delivered. However, we would recommend that you contact the park to check as the situation can change.

England

UK1415	Alpine Grove	94
UK3855	Callow Top	171
UK3485	Clippesby	156
UK3455	Deer's Glade	163
UK4360	Doward Park	186
UK1590	Exe Valley	98
UK3750	Foreman's Bridge	188
UK4560	Golden Square	197
UK1490	Greenacres	103
UK3904	Greendale Farm	184
UK1640	Greenhill Farm	102
UK1725	Hawkchurch CP	57
UK0210	Hendra	33
UK3430	Kelling Heath	164
UK0475	Lower Polladras	30
UK0750	Minnows	84
UK3330	Moat Barn	167
UK2465	Ninham	125
UK1390	Old Oaks	99
UK0014	Porthtowan	49
UK1350	Quantock Orchard	104
UK3850	Rivendale	171
UK0950	River Dart	56
UK2315	Riverside (Hamble)	117
UK0025	Roselands	47
UK2050	Rowlands Wait	112
UK0306	Ruthern Valley	25
UK4540	Saint Helens	203
UK0695	Sandaway	70
UK2290	Sandy Balls	115
UK3520	Searles	159
UK2120	South Lytchett Manor	120
UK4570	Spiers House	201
UK5505	Stanwix Park	228
UK3685	Tattershall Lakes CP	191
UK3655	Thorpe Park	174
UK1575	Unity	93
UK4620	Upper Carr	201
UK3660	Walesby Woodlands	181
UK1580	Warren Farm	94
UK2510	Whitecliff Bay	111
UK5570	Wild Rose	221
UK5605	Woodclose	224

Wales

UK5925	Cardiff	246
UK6330	Daisy Bank	255
UK6345	Glanlynn	242
UK6040	Pencelli Castle	244
UK6340	Pen-y-Bont	241
UK6685	Plas Farm	239
UK6670	The Plassey	262

Scotland

UK7260	Ardgartan	266
UK6950	Brighouse Bay	281
UK7680	Glenmore	267
UK6940	Loch Ken	268
UK7315	Loch Tay Highland Lodges	280
UK7000	Strathclyde	285
UK7230	Trossachs	265

Republic of Ireland

IR8740	Cong	307
IR9620	Flemings	312
IR9400	Glen of Aherlow	319
IR9600	Glenross	311
IR9155	Hidden Valley HP	315
IR9640	Killarney Flesk	312
IR9130	Roundwood	317
IR9490	Sextons	319

Channel Islands

UK9780	Fauxquets	323

Golf

We understand that the following parks have facilities for playing golf on site. Where facilities are within easy reach and we have been given details, we have included this information in the individual reports. However, we recommend that you contact the park to check that they meet your requirements.

Horse Riding

We understand that the following parks have horse riding stables on site. Where facilities are within easy reach and we have been given details, we have included this information in the individual reports. However, we recommend that you contact the park to check that they meet your requirements.

UK1370	Burrowhayes	101	UK0690	Stowford Farm	70
UK1780	Freshwater Beach	91	UK1575	Unity	93
UK2900	Horam Manor	142	UK0735	Woolacombe Sands	84
UK0360	Lakefield	26	UK1060	Yeatheridge	62
UK1306	Mill Farm	90	UK6950	Brighouse Bay	281
UK2290	Sandy Balls	115			

Boat Launching

We understand that the following parks have boat slipways on site. Where facilities are within easy reach and we have been given details, we have included this information in the individual reports. However, we recommend that you contact the park to check that they meet your requirements.

UK4500	Burton Constable	199	UK6950	Brighouse Bay	281
UK2810	Chertsey	137	UK7850	Linnhe Lochside	277
UK4150	Croft Farm	192	UK6940	Loch Ken	268
UK3290	Fen Farm	154	UK7315	Loch Tay Highland Lodges	280
UK2221	Fishery Creek	116	UK6890	Mossyard	268
UK5615	Hill of Oaks	229	UK7250	Muasdale H P	291
UK3055	Hop Farm	144	UK7800	Resipole	266
UK2700	Hurley	118	UK7410	Riverview	285
UK4210	Lickhill Manor	190	UK7025	Seal Shore	279
UK4310	Luck's All	178	UK8405	Cranfield	296
UK0750	Minnows	84	UK8340	Drumaheglis	294
UK0250	Pentewan Sands	41	UK8515	Rushin House	294
UK4080	Riverside Stratford	190	UK8407	Sandilands	296
UK3760	Tallington Lakes	189	UK8330	Sixmilewater	293
UK3685	Tattershall Lakes CP	191	IR9510	Eagle Point	302
UK2520	Thorness Bay	114	IR8965	Lough Ennell	315
UK2510	Whitecliff Bay	111	IR8960	Lough Ree	301
UK6345	Glanlynn	242	IR9610	Mannix Point	305
UK6385	Islawrffordd	243	IR9560	Wave Crest	304
UK7260	Ardgartan	266			
UK7710	Ardmair Point	291			

Adults Only

We list here the parks that have indicated to us that they do not accept children at any time during the year, at certain times, or in certain areas of their park.

UK6330	Daisy Bank	UK4610	Moorside
UK4410	Beaconsfield	UK1390	Old Oaks
UK1770	Bingham Grange	UK4534	Overbrook
UK3470	Breckland	UK1680	Plough Lane
UK1545	Cheddar Bridge	UK5245	Royal Vale
UK3650	Cherry Tree	UK4070	Somers Wood
UK1510	Chew Valley	UK3575	Stroud Hill
UK1590	Exe Valley	UK5650	The Ashes
UK4580	Foxholme	UK5510	The Larches
UK3904	Greendale Farm	UK3420	Two Mills
UK0012	Killiwerris	UK1520	Waterrow
UK5240	Lamb Cottage	UK0065	Wayfarers
UK3450	Little Haven	UK0900	Widdicombe Farm
UK1500	Long Hazel	UK1250	Woodland Springs
UK1355	Lowtrow Cross	UK2620	Wysdom
UK0820	Moor View		

Been to any good campsites lately?
We have

You'll find them here...

The UK's market leading independent
guides to the best campsites

Also available on iPad alanrogers.com/digital

GO THERE NOW!

... also here...

101 great campsites, ideal for your specific
hobby, pastime or passion

Also available on iPad **alanrogers.com/digital**

GO THERE NOW!

Want independent campsite reviews at your fingertips?

You'll find them here...

Insurance Service

High quality, low cost insurance you can trust

Price Beater **GUARANTEE***

Caravan Insurance **SAVE** UP TO 60%

We've been entrusted with readers' campsite-based holidays since 1968, and they have asked us for good value, good quality insurance.

We have teamed up with Shield Total Insurance – one of the leading names in outdoor leisure insurances – to bring you peace of mind and huge savings. Call or visit our website for a no obligation quote – there's no reason not to – and trust us to cover your valued possessions for you.

* Price Beater GUARANTEE
Motorhomes and Static Caravans
We guarantee to beat any genuine 'like for like' insurance renewal quote by at least £25. Subject to terms & conditions.

- Caravans - **Discounts up to 60%**
- Park Homes - **Fantastic low rates**
- Tents - **Prices from only £30**

Instant quote

Call **0844 824 6314**

alanrogers.com/insurance

NEW digital iPad editions

FREE Alan Rogers bookstore app
- digital editions of all 2012 guides

alanrogers.com/digital

GO THERE NOW!

Getting the most from
off peak touring

£13.95/night
single tariff
2 people

There are many reasons to avoid high season, if you can. Queues are shorter, there's less traffic, a calmer atmosphere and prices are cheaper. And it's usually still nice and sunny!

And when you use Camping Cheques you'll find great quality facilities that are actually open and a welcoming conviviality.

Did you know?
Camping Cheques can be used right into mid-July and from late August on many sites. Over 90 campsites in France alone accept Camping Cheques from 20th August.

Save up to 60% with Camping Cheques

Camping Cheque is a fixed price scheme allowing you to go as you please, staying on over 600 campsites across Europe, always paying the same rate and saving you up to 60% on regular pitch fees. One Cheque gives you one night for 2 people + unit on a standard pitch, with electricity. It's as simple as that.

Special offers mean you can stay extra nights free (eg 7 nights for 6 Cheques) or even a month free for a month paid! Especially popular in Spain during the winter, these longer-term offers can effectively halve the nightly rate. See Site Directory for details.

Check out our amazing Ferry Deals!

Why should I use Camping Cheques?

- It's a proven system, recognised by all 600+ participating campsites
  - so no nasty surprises.

- It's flexible, allowing you to travel between campsites, and also countries, on a whim - so no need to pre-book. (It's low season, so campsites are rarely full, though advance bookings can be made).

- Stay as long as you like, where you like - so you travel in complete freedom.

- Camping Cheques are valid 2 years - so no pressure to use them up.
  (If you have a couple left over after your trip, simply keep them for the following year, or use them up in the UK).

Tell me more... (but keep it brief!)

Camping Cheques was started in 1999 and has since grown in popularity each year (nearly 2 million were used last year). That should speak for itself. There are 'copycat' schemes, but none has the same range of quality campsites that save you up to 60%.

Ask for your **FREE** continental road map, which explains how Camping Cheque works
01580 214002

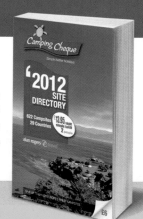

FREE

downloadable Site Directory
alanrogers.com/directory

campingcheque.co.uk

2012 warms up
at ExCeL ...

Scotland
page 263

Northern
Ireland
page 292

Northumbria
page 231

Cumbria
page 219

North West
England
page 211

Yorkshire
page 194

Republic of Ireland
page 299

Heart of England
page 168

East of England
page 150

Wales
page 237

Southern
England
page 108

South West England
page 22

South East
England
page 133

London
page 146

Channel Islands
page 322

Town & Village Index

Town & Village Index continued

Index by Campsite Number

England

Index by Campsite Number continued

Index by Campsite Number continued

Index - Campsite Number

357

Wales

Index by Campsite Number continued

Index by Campsite Region, County & Name

England

South West England

Index by Campsite Region, County & Name continued

North West England

Northumbria

Wales